THE FUTURE OF PRESS FREEDOM

This groundbreaking volume assembles an unparalleled roster of media experts and First Amendment luminaries to chart the future of press freedom in America's changing media landscape. Current and former deans of top US law schools, a Pulitzer Prize-winning journalist, former Supreme Court clerks, and renowned scholars of law and communications offer their collective wisdom on safeguarding journalism amidst unprecedented challenges. Their contributions provide an incisive analysis of emerging threats to press freedom, from technological and economic disruptions to eroding public trust, while proposing innovative legal and policy solutions. The volume tackles cutting-edge issues like artificial intelligence in news production and the evolving definition of "the press" in the digital age. Blending rigorous scholarship with practical insights, this essential resource equips journalists, press advocates, policymakers, and engaged citizens with expert knowledge to defend press freedom. This title is also available as Open Access on Cambridge Core.

RonNell Andersen Jones is a University Distinguished Professor and the Teitelbaum Chair in Law at the University of Utah S.J. Quinney College of Law. She is a regular press-freedom commentator for national media outlets, an Affiliated Fellow at the Yale Information Society Project, and an elected member of the American Law Institute.

Sonja R. West is the Brumby Distinguished Professor in First Amendment Law at the University of Georgia School of Law and Grady College of Journalism and Mass Communication. She is one of the nation's foremost experts on constitutional protections for the press.

The Future of Press Freedom

DEMOCRACY, LAW, AND THE NEWS IN CHANGING TIMES

Edited by

RONNELL ANDERSEN JONES
University of Utah

SONJA R. WEST
University of Georgia

CAMBRIDGE
UNIVERSITY PRESS

CAMBRIDGE
UNIVERSITY PRESS

Shaftesbury Road, Cambridge CB2 8EA, United Kingdom

One Liberty Plaza, 20th Floor, New York, NY 10006, USA

477 Williamstown Road, Port Melbourne, VIC 3207, Australia

314–321, 3rd Floor, Plot 3, Splendor Forum, Jasola District Centre, New Delhi – 110025, India

103 Penang Road, #05–06/07, Visioncrest Commercial, Singapore 238467

Cambridge University Press is part of Cambridge University Press & Assessment, a department of the University of Cambridge.

We share the University's mission to contribute to society through the pursuit of education, learning and research at the highest international levels of excellence.

www.cambridge.org
Information on this title: www.cambridge.org/9781009515535

DOI: 10.1017/9781009515511

First published 2025

A catalogue record for this publication is available from the British Library

A Cataloging-in-Publication data record for this book is available from the Library of Congress

ISBN 978-1-009-51553-5 Hardback
ISBN 978-1-009-51550-4 Paperback

To our families

Contents

Contributors

Mike Ananny is an Associate Professor at the Annenberg School for Communication and Journalism at the University of Southern California (USC), where he studies how people build the digital news infrastructures, algorithmic systems, and artificial intelligences that create public life. He codirects USC's interdisciplinary research collectives "MASTS" (Media as Socio Technical Systems) and "AIMS" (Artificial Intelligence in Media and Storytelling), and is the author of *Networked Press Freedom* (MIT Press) and coeditor of *Bauhaus Futures* (MIT Press).

RonNell Andersen Jones is a University Distinguished Professor and the Lee E. Teitelbaum Chair in Law at the University of Utah. She is an Affiliated Fellow at Yale Law School's Information Society Project. A former newspaper reporter and editor, Andersen Jones is a First Amendment scholar who researches and writes on legal issues affecting the press and on the intersection between media and the courts, with an emphasis on the U.S. Supreme Court. She previously served as a law clerk for U.S. Supreme Court Justice Sandra Day O'Connor.

Samantha Barbas is a Professor of Law and the Aliber Family Chair in Law at the University of Iowa College of Law. Her most recent book, *Actual Malice: Civil Rights and Freedom of the Press in* New York Times v. Sullivan (University of California Press, 2023), tracks the saga behind one of the most important First Amendment rulings in history, *New York Times v. Sullivan.*

Hannah Bloch-Wehba is an associate professor of law at Texas A&M University School of Law who teaches and writes on law and technology. She is also an affiliated fellow at Yale Law School's Information Society Project, an affiliated scholar at NYU School of Law's Policing Project, and a fellow at the Center for Democracy & Technology.

Joseph Blocher is the Lanty L. Smith '67 Distinguished Professor of Law and the senior associate dean of faculty at Duke University School of Law. He is the coauthor of *Free Speech Beyond Words: The Surprising Reach of the First Amendment* (NYU Press, 2017) and *The Positive Second Amendment: Rights, Regulation, and the Future of Heller* (Cambridge University Press, 2018) and serves as co-director of the Duke Center for Firearms Law.

Erin C. Carroll is a professor of law and legal practice at Georgetown University Law Center. Her teaching and research interests focus on legal analysis and communication, rhetoric, the free press, technology, and the intersection of these subjects. She serves as chair of the Association of American Law Schools' Section on Communication, Media and Information Law.

Erwin Chemerinsky became the thirteenth Dean of Berkeley Law on July 1, 2017, when he joined the faculty as the Jesse H. Choper Distinguished Professor of Law. Prior to assuming this position, from 2008 to 2017, he was the founding Dean and Distinguished Professor of Law, and Raymond Pryke Professor of First Amendment Law, at the University of California, Irvine School of Law.

Alan K. Chen is the Thompson G. Marsh Law Alumni Professor at the University of Denver Sturm College of Law, where he teaches and writes about free speech doctrine and theory. He is the coauthor of *Free Speech Beyond Words: The Surprising Reach of the First Amendment* (NYU Press, 2017) and has published numerous scholarly articles about the First Amendment in leading national law journals.

Meredith D. Clark is an associate professor of race and political communication in the Hussman School of Journalism & Media at the University of North Carolina at Chapel Hill. Her research focuses on the intersections of race, media, and power in digital, social, and news media, and is informed by the years she spent working in newsrooms as an editor, editorial writer, and columnist.

Amy Gajda is a journalist turned lawyer recognized internationally for her expertise in privacy and media law. Much of her scholarship explores the tensions between social regulation of access to information and First Amendment values, particularly the shifting boundaries of press freedoms and rising public anxieties about the erosion of privacy.

Katy Glenn Bass is the research director of the Knight First Amendment Institute at Columbia University. She is responsible for conceptualizing and executing all of the Institute's research initiatives, including the production of scholarship and research materials, the organization of conferences and symposia, and the Institute's Visiting Research Scholars program.

Richard L. Hasen is the Gary T. Schwartz Endowed Chair in Law and professor of political science at UCLA. He is an internationally recognized expert in election law, writing as well in the areas of legislation and statutory interpretation, remedies, and torts, and is the coauthor of leading casebooks in election law and remedies. Hasen served in 2020 as a CNN Election Law Analyst and as an NBC News/ MSNBC Election Law Analyst in 2022. He directs UCLA Law's Safeguarding Democracy Project.

Vicki C. Jackson, Laurence H. Tribe Professor of Constitutional Law (previously known as the Thurgood Marshall Professor of Constitutional Law), writes and teaches about U.S. constitutional law, federal courts, and comparative constitutional law. She is the author of *Constitutional Engagement in a Transnational Era* (2010), and coauthor, with Mark Tushnet, of *Comparative Constitutional Law* (3d ed. 2014), a course book in the field.

Jameel Jaffer is the executive director of the Knight First Amendment Institute at Columbia University. Until August 2016, Jaffer served as deputy legal director at the ACLU, where he oversaw the organization's work on free speech, privacy, technology, national security, and international human rights.

Heidi Kitrosser is William W. Gurley Professor of Law at Northwestern University. Kitrosser is an expert on the constitutional law of federal government secrecy and on separation of powers and free speech law more broadly. She has written, spoken, and consulted widely on these topics. Her book, *Reclaiming Accountability: Transparency, Executive Power, and the U.S. Constitution*, was published in 2015 by the University of Chicago Press. It was awarded the 2014 IIT Chicago-Kent College of Law/Roy C. Palmer Civil Liberties Prize.

Christina Koningisor is an associate professor of law at UC Law San Francisco (formerly UC Hastings). Her scholarship focuses on constitutional law, media law, and the law of information access and government transparency. Her articles have appeared or are forthcoming in the *Columbia Law Review*, *Northwestern University Law Review*, *University of Pennsylvania Law Review*, *Virginia Law Review*, and *Yale Law Journal*.

Margaret B. Kwoka is the Lawrence Herman Professor in Law at The Ohio State University Moritz College of Law, where she teaches courses on civil procedure, federal courts, and administrative law. Her articles on government transparency have appeared in leading law reviews and her book, *Saving the Freedom of Information Act*, was published by Cambridge in 2021. She has served on the federal FOIA Advisory Committee, as a consultant to the Administrative Conference of the United States and testified before the U.S. Congress on freedom of information laws.

Lili Levi is a Professor of Law at the University of Miami School of Law and a Life Member of the American Law Institute. Her substantial scholarship focuses on communications and media law from a law and society perspective.

Lyrissa Lidsky is the Raymond & Miriam Ehrlich Chair in U.S. Constitutional Law at the University of Florida Levin College of Law. She previously served as dean of the University of Missouri School of Law from 2017 to 2022. Lidsky is co-reporter on the Restatement of Defamation and Privacy, recently succeeded Judge Robert Sack as the author of Sack on Defamation, and has authored media law and First Amendment casebooks.

Wesley Lowery is one of the nation's leading reporters on issues of race and justice. His "Fatal Force" project, focused on people shot and killed by the police, won the Pulitzer Prize for National Reporting, the George Polk Award, and the Peabody Award. Lowery has worked for CBS News and the Washington Post.

Gregory P. Magarian is the Thomas and Karole Green Professor of Law at the Washington University School of Law in St. Louis. He teaches and writes about U.S. constitutional law, focusing on expressive freedom. His first book, *Managed Speech: The Roberts Court's First Amendment*, was published in 2017 by Oxford University Press. His writing also examines church and state, gun regulation, and regulations of the media and the political process. He received his B.A. from Yale and his law degree from the University of Michigan. He previously served as a law clerk for U.S. Supreme Court Justice John Paul Stevens.

Martha Minow has taught at Harvard Law School since 1981, where her courses include civil procedure, constitutional law, fairness and privacy, family law, international criminal justice, jurisprudence, law and education, nonprofit organizations, and the public law workshop. An expert in human rights and advocacy for members of racial and religious minorities and for women, children, and persons with disabilities, she also writes and teaches about digital communications, democracy, privatization, military justice, and ethnic and religious conflict. Her most recent book is *Saving the News: Why the Constitution Calls for Government Action to Preserve the Freedom of Speech* (2021).

Helen Norton is the University Distinguished Professor and Rothgerber Chair in Constitutional Law at the University of Colorado School of Law. Her work focuses on constitutional law and antidiscrimination law, and includes *The Government's Speech and the Constitution*, published by Cambridge University Press.

Jacob Noti-Victor is an associate professor at the Benjamin N. Cardozo School of Law. His research focuses on how the law impacts innovation, culture, and the deployment of new technologies. His most recent articles have appeared in the *Washington University Law Review*, the *Minnesota Law Review*, and the *Stanford Law Review*.

Victor Pickard is the C. Edwin Baker Professor of Media Policy and Political Economy at the Annenberg School for Communication, where he codirects the Media, Inequality & Change (MIC) Center. He has authored or edited six books, most recently, *Democracy Without Journalism? Confronting the Misinformation Society*.

Robert C. Post is Sterling Professor of Law at Yale Law School. He served as the school's sixteenth dean from 2009 until 2017. Post specializes in constitutional law, with a particular emphasis on the First Amendment.

Amanda Shanor is an Assistant Professor at the Wharton School of the University of Pennsylvania who teaches and writes about constitutional law, particularly the freedom of speech. Shanor's research explores the changing meaning of the First Amendment and the forces that affect it; democratic theory, illiberalism, and equality; and the intersection of constitutional law and economic life.

Nik Usher, Ph.D. (they/them) is an associate professor at the University of San Diego (USD) in the department of communication. Usher's research focuses on news in the changing digital environment, blending insights from media sociology and political communication. Usher is the author of three books: *Making News at The New York Times* (University of Michigan Press, 2014), *Interactive Journalism: Hackers, Data, and Code* (University of Illinois, 2016), and *News for the Rich, White, and Blue: How Place and Power Distort American Journalism* (Columbia, 2021), and coeditor of *Journalism Research That Matters* (Oxford, 2021), with Valerie Belair-Gagnon.

Sonja R. West holds the Otis Brumby Distinguished Professorship in First Amendment Law at the University of Georgia, a post shared by the School of Law and Grady College of Journalism and Mass Communication. A former journalist and media law attorney, West served as a law clerk for U.S. Supreme Court Justice John Paul Stevens. She now specializes in constitutional law, media law, and the U.S. Supreme Court.

Foreword

Jameel Jaffer and Katy Glenn Bass

The question this book explores – the future of press freedom – is one the United States has returned to again and again since its founding, when the framers saw fit to assign the press specific constitutional protection. What that protection means, how far it extends, the relationship between the press and the health of our democracy, and what press functions deserve the greatest degree of protection, are questions the courts and the public have debated ever since. These debates often grow most urgent at times of major upheavals in the technologies and structures of news-gathering and production, as we are now experiencing.

This book includes contributions from some of the nation's leading thinkers on the freedoms of speech and the press. It represents a monumental effort to assess the state of the press and press freedom in the United States, and to think critically about what the press does, who the press is, and how to ensure that the key roles played by the press continue to be protected at a moment of dramatic technological change, and of deep uncertainty about the future of our democracy.

The book is the result of a year-long collaboration between the Knight First Amendment Institute at Columbia University and Professors RonNell Andersen Jones and Sonja R. West, who served as Senior Visiting Research Scholars at the Institute during the 2023–24 academic year. The collaboration also encompassed a day-long academic symposium – held in New York City on World Press Freedom Day, May 3, 2024 – which tackled the same questions addressed in these pages: Why is the press specifically protected? What is the role of a free and protected press in preserving a healthy American democracy? How do the Supreme Court's evolving First Amendment frameworks view protections for newsgatherers and newsgathering? What are the benefits and disadvantages of being singled out in the First Amendment, and what are the benefits and disadvantages of building a more robust press function doctrine? Are new or better protections for newsgatherers and news-gathering needed for the digital age?

The many excellent contributions in this volume address these questions and illuminate promising paths forward for protecting press freedom. We are grateful to Professor Andersen Jones and Professor West for their leadership of this exciting and fruitful collaboration, to the many brilliant authors who contributed chapters to this book, and to Cambridge University Press for its work to shepherd the manuscript to publication. We feel confident that this book will galvanize support for press freedom and for reshaping legal protections to reflect the changing reality of news-gathering. That latter task could hardly be more important for our democracy.

PART I

Introduction

1

The Future of Press Freedom

RonNell Andersen Jones and Sonja R. West

The American press is facing a perilous moment. A confluence of economic, cultural, technological, and political shifts has abruptly upended our longstanding sense of how the news media operates. Suddenly, it seems, these sweeping changes have realigned the traditional relationships between and among democracy, newsgathering, and press freedom, prompting new questions about what it means to value and support a free press in the United States.

Throughout the twentieth century, judges and scholars routinely praised journalists for fulfilling key societal roles.[1] In our modern sociopolitical and media environments, however, journalism is undergoing rapid transformation. Government officials are increasingly targeting the news media directly in calculated attacks aimed at undercutting its legitimacy. At the same time, traditional news outlets are vanishing before our eyes, leaving an information vacuum that other communicators – like social media influencers, corporate agents, and purveyors of political propaganda – are rushing to fill. The rise of artificial intelligence introduces additional complexity, blurring the lines between human-created and machine-generated content. Alongside these current stressors, there is an emerging reckoning with the industry's past failures to represent many voices and perspectives of marginalized groups during the era once hailed as journalism's glory days, underscoring the need for a more inclusive press. This radically changing media ecosystem requires us to revisit first principles. It raises hard but vital questions about which functions of the press are essential to a healthy democracy, why these functions matter, who is fulfilling them, and, crucially, what legal and policy protections are necessary to safeguard them.

[1] RonNell Andersen Jones & Sonja West, *The Disappearing Freedom of the Press*, 79 WASH. & LEE L. REV. 1377 (2022); RonNell Andersen Jones, *The Dangers of Press Clause Dicta*, 48 GA. L. REV. 705 (2014); Sonja R. West, *The Stealth Press Clause*, 48 GA. L. REV. 729 (2014).

It is, to be sure, a tricky moment to be talking about "the press." At this time of radical change, as "the press" in its twentieth century form hemorrhages resources, credibility, and its once-ubiquitous reach, many feel tempted to abandon any effort to breathe meaning and substance into press-specific rights – to throw up our collective hands and announce that law and policy simply cannot protect this role.[2] Recent data show that the U.S. Supreme Court may be on its way to abandoning the concept of freedom of the press altogether.[3] Yet American democracy continues to need the press *functions* even as the media landscape in which they are performed evolves. Indeed, as both figurative and literal attacks on these roles intensify[4] and as reliable access to shared facts dwindles, we must work even more urgently to craft legal doctrine that will identify and protect these roles in enduring ways. Rather than fixating on who is the press, our focus should be on what can be done to ensure a future for the press function.

This volume unites nearly thirty of the nation's leading legal and media studies scholars to launch this crucial conversation. They bring to the discussion deep expertise in law, journalism, communications theory, education, technology, history, and political science. By examining the challenges to press freedom through these multidisciplinary lenses, they offer fresh insights into the obstacles and opportunities that lie ahead for this fundamental pillar of democracy.

2 *See, e.g.*, Citizens United v. FEC, 558 U.S. 310, 326 (2010) ("We must decline to draw, and then redraw, constitutional lines based on the particular media or technology used to disseminate political speech from a particular speaker."); First Nat'l Bank of Boston v. Bellotti, 435 U.S. 765, 80 (1978) (Burger, C.J., concurring) (arguing that "[t]he very task of including some entities within the 'institutional press' while excluding others, whether undertaken by legislature, court, or administrative agency, is reminiscent of the abhorred licensing system of Tudor and Stuart England – a system the First Amendment was intended to ban from this country."); *see also* Sonja R. West, *Awakening the Press Clause*, 58 UCLA L. Rev. 1025, 1026–29 (2011) (discussing the definitional problem).

3 *See generally* RonNell Andersen Jones & Sonja R. West, *The U.S. Supreme Court's Characterizations of the Press: An Empirical Study*, 100 N.C. L. Rev. 375 (2022).

4 *See generally Quick Facts*, U.S. Press Freedom Tracker, https://pressfreedomtracker.us/ (last visited July 9, 2024); RonNell Andersen Jones & Sonja R. West, *The Fragility of the Free American Press*, 112 Nw. U. L. Rev.567–72 (2017) (discussing former President Donald Trump's attacks on the press); *see, e.g.*, *Pulitzer Prize-Winning Photojournalist Shoved to the Ground by LAPD*, U.S. Press Freedom Tracker (May 31, 2020), https://pressfreedomtracker.us/all-incidents/pulitzer-prize-winning-photojournalist-shoved-ground-lapd/; Marc Tracy & Rachel Abrams, *Police Target Journalists as Trump Blames 'Lamestream Media' for Protests*, N.Y. Times (June 1, 2020), https://www.nytimes.com/2020/06/01/business/media/reporters-protests-george-floyd.html; Katie Shepherd, *This Portland Journalist Has Been Gassed and Shoved by Federal Officers. She's Only 17*, Wash. Post (July 23, 2020, 6:32 AM), https://www.washingtonpost.com/nation/2020/07/23/portland-protests-teenage-reporter/; Courtney Douglas, *Amid Black Lives Matter Protests, A Crushing Moment for Journalists Facing Record Attacks, Arrests at the Hands of Law Enforcement*, Reps. Comm. (Sept. 4, 2020), https://www.rcfp.org/black-lives-matter-press-freedom/; Clare Duffy, *Journalist Partially Blinded While Covering Protests: There's No Way They Could Have Mistaken Me for Anything but Press*, CNN (June 14, 2020), https://www.cnn.com/2020/06/14/media/linda-tirado-reliable/index.html.

From the collective insights of these scholars emerge five crucial themes. Each marks a significant step forward in a space that has not previously received sufficient attention, laying the foundation for a new era of press freedom scholarship.

1.1 DEMOCRACY AND THE PRESS FUNCTION

One thing is clear: We cannot effectively protect something we do not fully understand. Thus, we must more carefully theorize and articulate the role the press function plays in democratic society.

In recent years, political and governmental actors have launched an unprecedented wave of attacks on the press, dramatically reshaping the boundaries of acceptable discourse when it comes to the characterization and treatment of working journalists. By branding the press as "fake news,"[5] threatening governmental action against dissident outlets,[6] applauding the use of force against reporters,[7] and restricting the access the press has to important people and events,[8] these actors are shifting the public tone. Today's newsgatherers face harassment, threats, violence, and arrests. They increasingly struggle to do the work of bearing witness to our most urgent scenes. Perhaps unsurprisingly, the international press freedom ranking of the United States has plummeted over the past decade.[9]

5 *See, e.g.*, Roy S. Gutterman, Opinion, *After Four Damaging Years, Biden Must Restore Press Freedom*, SYRACUSE.COM (Dec. 10, 2020, 10:00 AM), https://www.syracuse.com/opinion/2020/12/after-4-damaging-years-biden-must-restore-press-freedom-roy-s-gutterman.html (cataloguing Donald Trump's use of this and other terms disparaging the press during his presidency).

6 *See, e.g.*, Jordan Weissmann, *Donald Trump Wants to Get Revenge on Jeff Bezos by Messing with Amazon's Taxes*, SLATE: MONEYBOX (Mar. 28, 2018, 3:04 PM), https://slate.com/business/2018/03/donald-trump-wants-to-get-revenge-on-jeff-bezos-by-messing-with-amazons-taxes.html; Mathew Yglesias, *Donald Trump Threatens Amazon as Payback for Washington Post Articles He Doesn't Like*, VOX (May 13, 2016), https://www.vox.com/2016/5/13/11669850/donald-trump-threatens-amazon; Alex Pfeiffer, *Source: Trump Doesn't Back the Time Warner and AT&T Merger If Zucker Still Heads CNN*, DAILY CALLER (July 6, 2017), http://dailycaller.com/2017/07/06/source-trump-doesnt-back-the-time-warner-and-att-merger-if-zucker-still-heads-cnn/; *see also* Sonja R. West, *Presidential Attacks on the Press*, 83 MO. L. REV. 915, 917 (2018) (detailing how President Trump used "the power of his presidency in an attempt to punish or silence press organizations that displease[d] him" during his first term.)

7 *See, e.g.*, Brett Samuels, *Trump Mocks Reporters Who Were Roughed Up by Police During Protests*, THE HILL (Sept. 22, 2020), https://thehill.com/homenews/media/517713-trump-mocks-reporters-who-were-roughed-up-by-police-during-protests (quoting President Donald Trump describing excessive police force against reporters as a "beautiful sight").

8 *See, e.g.*, *The Latest: EPA Bars AP, CNN from Summit on Contaminants*, ASSOCIATED PRESS (May 22, 2018), https://apnews.com/d799f4e096cc42cf99ae01b02d1e0688; Callum Borchers, *White House Blocks CNN, New York Times from Press Briefing Hours After Trump Slams Media*, WASH. POST (Feb. 24, 2017, 4:10 PM), https://www.washingtonpost.com/news/the-fix/wp/2017/02/24/white-house-blocks-cnn-new-york-times-from-press-briefing-hours-after-trump-slams-media.

9 *See World Press Freedom Index 2024*, REPS. WITHOUT BORDERS, https://rsf.org/en/index (last visited July 9, 2024) (showing the United States falling to 55th in the world, behind both Chile and Ivory Coast).

We must more carefully probe the relationship between a healthy press and a healthy democracy and think seriously about what these dynamics teach us about the most urgent components of our efforts to craft sustainable press-protective doctrines. The press fulfills several distinct and identifiable constitutional roles – including, as Robert Post explores, contributing to public discourse, distributing democracy-enhancing information, checking government and the powerful, and creating a public sphere.[10] Each of these roles illuminates a different aspect of the constitutional meaning of "the press" and points to a different array of rights that ought to accrue.[11] By scrutinizing these roles and identifying threats to them when they emerge, we can more effectively safeguard the future of press freedom.

This effort also requires us to recognize how the press provides an important link between the First Amendment's democratic values and its truth-seeking goals, enhancing the marketplace of ideas during a time of heightened dysfunction. As anti-democratic forces exploit our increasingly oversaturated and underinformed community dialogue, we need to take seriously the increasingly complicated relationship between press freedom, violence, and public discourse.[12] Because, as Joseph Blocher notes, "if a democracy cannot establish the boundaries of violence, then violence will end up establishing the boundaries of democracy – including the freedom of the press."[13]

Notably, this work will also demand that press advocates engage in a more rigorous examination of journalism's role in a pluralistic society and of our responsibilities as citizens in our communications ecosystem. Gregory Magarian cautions that we must tussle not only with the tensions between objectivity and subjectivity but also with the competing pressures of institutionalism and populism.[14] This process may require us to more fully reconceptualize citizenship in an era in which professional journalism plays a significantly diminished role in directly shaping our local news and information environment.[15] Nik Usher suggests that we identify the unique roles of professional journalism as a civic institution and then fill the gaps that remain in our public discourse by fostering the expectation that individual community members will more actively facilitate the circulation of reliable civic information within communities.[16]

[10] Robert Post, *The Press and American Democracy*, *in* THE FUTURE OF PRESS FREEDOM: DEMOCRACY, LAW, AND THE NEWS IN CHANGING TIMES 17 (RonNell Andersen Jones & Sonja R. West eds. 2025) [hereinafter THE FUTURE OF PRESS FREEDOM].

[11] *Id.*

[12] Joseph Blocher, *"Murder the Media": Press Freedom, Violence, and the Public Sphere*, *in* THE FUTURE OF PRESS FREEDOM, *supra* note 10, at 54.

[13] *Id.*

[14] Gregory P. Magarian, *Political Tensions and the Democratic Press*, *in* THE FUTURE OF PRESS FREEDOM, *supra* note 10, at 28.

[15] Nik Usher, *Post-Newspaper Democracy and the Rise of Communicative Citizenship: The Good Citizen as Communicator*, *in* THE FUTURE OF PRESS FREEDOM, *supra* note 10, at 38.

[16] *Id.*

Ultimately, our efforts to protect and nurture the press function must evolve alongside our understanding of its multifaceted role in democracy, including adapting to the challenges of our changing times while preserving the core values that make a free press indispensable to a thriving democratic society.

1.2 EVOLVING THREATS TO THE PRESS FUNCTION

The once relatively stable world of journalism now faces tectonic disruptions. Scholars are beginning to highlight the ways that we are reshaping not only how news is produced and consumed but also the very nature of the press's relationship with society. The new threats emerging from these shifts are unlike any experienced in the past. Charting their contours is essential to preserving the press's freedom and its role in democracy.

Journalism today faces a complex array of problems extending far beyond the traditional press freedom issue of government censorship. Primary among them, as Lyrissa Lidsky notes, may be an erosion of public trust in the news media, driven by the "declining cultural investment in the sustained and systematic gathering of high-quality news."[17] This unprecedented crisis of legitimacy for the press, she notes, is not easily fixable through any one doctrine but must be a centerpiece of all of our conversations about the press's future. Indeed, understanding what Lili Levi describes as an "evolving mosaic of threats"[18] – institutional, journalistic, legal, technological, and audience-based – requires complex and comprehensive thinking on the issue. Never before has the risk calculation for press freedom had so many moving parts, and never has it been so urgent to consider all of them in conjunction with each other.

More broadly, we face the very real threat that old jurisprudence simply has not kept pace with new communications realities. Traditional free speech and press doctrines are proving inadequate for addressing the challenges posed by the modern communications landscape. As Erwin Chemerinsky notes, the unprecedented speed of information dissemination, the blurred lines between publishers and platforms, and the amplification of both beneficial and harmful speech[19] all necessitate a reevaluation of our doctrinal frameworks to better meet the moment.

These issues will only intensify as artificial intelligence reshapes the very nature of journalism and information creation. The advent of Generative AI (GenAI), in particular, presents profound implications for traditional press freedom norms.

[17] Lyrissa Lidsky, *Defamation Law and the Crumbling Legitimacy of the Fourth Estate*, *in* The Future of Press Freedom, *supra* note 10, at 101.

[18] Lili Levi, *Countering the Mosaic of Threats to Press Functions*, *in* The Future of Press Freedom, *supra* note 10, at 79.

[19] Erwin Chemerinsky, *Fitting a Square Peg into a Round Hole: Why Traditional Free Press Doctrines Fail in Dealing with Newer Media*, *in* The Future of Press Freedom, *supra* note 10, at 67.

Mike Ananny explores this phenomenon through the lens of press self-correction, arguing that GenAI may compromise press autonomy.[20] He proposes a "recursive press freedom" model to ensure that technological advancements enhance rather than undermine the press.[21] Technological innovations are not just impacting the tools of journalism but fundamentally altering the press function itself, requiring us to acknowledge emerging dangers and explore new conceptual frameworks for combatting them.

Underlying these modern threats is the systemic danger that the public will underappreciate the unique value of the press. Our current discourse too often fails to adequately convey to both public and judicial audiences the full scope of what journalism contributes to a democracy and how vital it is that we sustain a free and independent press.[22] In response, Erin Carroll advocates for a strategic shift in rhetoric in which we employ more positive, benefit-oriented language when discussing the press.[23] We can no longer assume that the public understands and appreciates the work the press does; instead, we must actively cultivate this awareness through carefully considered communication that highlights journalism's indispensable worth.

Addressing these interrelated threats requires a holistic approach that recognizes press freedom's dynamic nature. Efforts to rebuild public trust and ensure recognition and support for the press's vital role must buttress any wider strategies to safeguard journalism's crucial work in democracy.

1.3 LEGAL PROTECTION FOR THE PRESS FUNCTION

Armed with this better understanding of the press function, and emerging threats to it, press-freedom advocates must work to ensure there is sufficient constitutional and statutory protection of it.

Courts and legislatures have struggled in the past with the question of whether speakers and publishers performing the press function need legal protections beyond those available to all speakers.[24] As local journalism fades and reporters increasingly come under attack, the need for these safeguards becomes clearer – as do the losses to accountability and transparency that come from doctrinal homogeneity without any press exceptionalism.[25] Establishing these safeguards requires work at both a broad level, erecting scaffolding to help us think about the place the press should

[20] Mike Ananny, *Recursive Press Freedom as the Capacity to Control and Learn from Mistakes*, *in* The Future of Press Freedom, *supra* note 10, at 128.

[21] *Id.*

[22] Erin Carroll, *Press Benefits and the Public Imagination*, *in* The Future of Press Freedom, *supra* note 10, at 116.

[23] *Id.*

[24] *See* West, *supra* note 2, at 1035–41.

[25] *See* Sonja R. West, *Press Exceptionalism*, 127 Harv. L. Rev. 2434, 2446–47 (2014).

occupy in rights-based frameworks,[26] and in narrower ways, honing in on specific legal sub-doctrines that must be fortified for the work of the press to continue.

One clear focus should be advocating for a reinvigorated Press Clause that can more reliably protect the press function. Helen Norton proposes that courts view Press Clause claims through the lens of "negative theory."[27] This approach is "rooted in distrust of the government's self-interested efforts to punish and thus silence the press" and "has long offered an important tool for understanding the Press Clause."[28] By adopting this perspective, courts could develop a more robust shield against government retaliation, informing both their choices of legal rules and the application of those rules.

Another useful step toward persuading the courts of press freedom's status as a fundamental right may be to look to the evolving jurisprudence surrounding religious freedom. There, the Court has increasingly recognized a heightened level of constitutional protection, often described by commentators as "Most Favored Nation" status. Amanda Shanor explores this concept, arguing that granting the press a similar status would ensure that journalists receive, at a minimum, the same exemptions from generally applicable laws that are afforded to any other entities.[29] This approach would safeguard the ability of press actors to serve as public proxies, allowing them to remain present at crucial events, protect confidential sources, and access government records – all essential components of their role in fostering transparency and accountability. In light of the Court's recent recognition of a special role for religious freedom, we should seize the opportunity to advocate for equal or greater protection of press freedom as part of this broader conversation of First Amendment expansionism.

State constitutions, which often contain provisions explicitly safeguarding the press's unique role, present an additional promising avenue for bolstering press protections. Christina Koningisor's research reveals that the text, drafting histories, and interpretive precedents of these state clauses offer press freedom advocates a wealth of resources.[30] These state-level provisions can also serve as compelling models for expanding federal protections under the First Amendment, potentially influencing the evolution of national press freedom jurisprudence. This dual-track approach – leveraging state constitutions while simultaneously informing federal

[26] *See* Sonja R. West, *The Majoritarian Press Clause*, 2020 U. CHI. LEGAL F. 311, 314 (2020) (suggesting the Press Clause be interpreted through the lens of "safeguarding our collective, majoritarian right to a republican form of government.").

[27] Helen Norton, *Reinvigorating the Press Clause Through Negative Theory*, *in* THE FUTURE OF PRESS FREEDOM, *supra* note 10, at 162.

[28] *Id.*

[29] Amanda Shanor, *The Constitutional Exceptionalism of Religion and the Press*, *in* THE FUTURE OF PRESS FREEDOM, *supra* note 10, at 170.

[30] Christina Koningisor, *The Other Press Clauses*, *in* THE FUTURE OF PRESS FREEDOM, *supra* note 10, at 182.

interpretation – could provide a more immediate and comprehensive framework for press protection.

Beyond these sweeping methodologies, the press freedom crisis further demands that we pay urgent attention to specific statutory and common law protections for performers of the press function. Critical areas include the law of access to government information, where Margaret Kwoka's work advocating for major structural reforms to the Freedom of Information Act will be foundational.[31] Similarly, we may need to reevaluate the legal doctrines that govern undercover investigations. Alan Chen's in-depth research into the *Food Lion* case illustrates how current laws potentially chill vital public-serving reporting.[32] And even long-established press protections, such as the doctrine emerging from *New York Times Co. v. Sullivan*, now need reinforcement and renewed justification. Samantha Barbas warns that if *Sullivan*'s current opponents succeed in weakening these protections, "it would become substantially riskier for speakers, including the press, to comment on public affairs."[33] To advance the press freedom agenda, we must highlight how these doctrines have enhanced newsgathering and how their erosion would impoverish public discourse.

1.4 IDENTIFYING PERFORMERS OF THE PRESS FUNCTION

Identifying performers of the press function in our new media landscape has become one of the most persistent challenges in safeguarding press freedom. This task, once relatively straightforward, has grown increasingly complex as the public now routinely consumes information from diverse sources – including social media influencers, bloggers, and citizen journalists – alongside traditional media outlets. Still, in many cases, we must identify those who are fulfilling the press function in order to protect them.

In the past, "the press" was generally recognizable in both public perception and legal contexts. It primarily consisted of established newspapers, magazines, radio stations, and television networks. The journalists who worked for these entities typically had formal training and credentials. Press outlets had clear organizational frameworks and a widely understood gatekeeping role. The digital revolution, however, has blurred these once-distinct boundaries.

Despite this diversification, it is worth remembering that identifying "the press" today is not as daunting as it is often portrayed. We are not starting from scratch. Richard Hasen's empirical study, for example, shows that many government

[31] Margaret Kwoka, *Returning FOIA to the Press*, *in* The Future of Press Freedom, *supra* note 10, at 257.

[32] Alan Chen, *The Long Shadow of* Food Lion, in The Future of Press Freedom, *supra* note 10, at 210.

[33] Samantha Barbas, *The Enduring Significance of* New York Times Co. v. Sullivan, in The Future of Press Freedom, *supra* note 10, at 256.

agencies continue to share a common working definition of the press function that emphasizes core features like a commitment to factual reporting, regular news production, and adherence to journalistic ethics.[34] Coming to understand the traditional press's role as what Vicki Jackson has termed a "knowledge institution"[35] – and contrasting it with other knowledge institutions, like universities, that are also now facing both intense pressure and intense change – may further hone our sense of who is performing this work in our new media ecosystem.

But that ecosystem is unquestionably changing at breakneck speed. Consequently, any approach we develop to identify who is doing the work of the press must be flexible enough to adapt alongside advances in communication technology. Scholars are also warning us about pitfalls we must avoid in this process lest we develop identification frameworks that are ineffective or inequitable. As Amy Gajda's analysis of the common-law and privacy-tort contexts cautions, an overly expansive definition may ultimately become an ineffective one because "backlash against the actions of fringe actors who are eager to justify their behaviors as newsworthy lead to scalebacks that remove constitutionally valuable protections from those who are actually performing the press function."[36] Importantly, our reimagining of the press function must address historical shortcomings and reflect the diversity of our society. Meredith Clark's concept of "reparative journalism"[37] maps a plan for using this moment to cultivate a more inclusive press function, striving to remedy past exclusions of marginalized voices and educate future journalists about the multifaceted nature of their profession.

It is also not the case that the best route to protecting press freedom is only through press-exceptionalist approaches. Rather, there may be times when broader legal reforms will yield greater benefits. While the press plays a unique and vital role in our democracy, crafting legal exceptions solely for members of "the press" might sometimes be ineffectual – and even counterproductive – to our overall goals. Even with nominal special protections for members of the press, for example, our expansive criminal laws still enable law enforcement to investigate, monitor, and potentially punish press actors.[38] Instead, as Hannah Bloch-Wehba explores, in certain circumstances it may be more helpful to provide more robust expressive freedom for

[34] Rick Hasen, *From Bloggers in Pajamas to* The Gateway Pundit: *How Government Entities Do and Should Identify Professional Journalists for Access and Protection*, *in* The Future of Press Freedom, *supra* note 10, at 271.

[35] Vicki C. Jackson, *Journalism and Academic: Knowledge Institutions Buttressing Constitutional Democracy*, *in* The Future of Press Freedom, *supra* note 10, at 325.

[36] Amy Gajda, A *Professional Wrestler, Privacy, and the Meaning of News*, *in* The Future of Press Freedom, *supra* note 10, at 308.

[37] Meredith Clark, *Reconstructing the First Amendment: Teaching Disenfranchised Perspectives on Press Freedom*, *in* The Future of Press Freedom, *supra* note 10, at 309.

[38] Hannah Bloch-Webha, *Policing Press Freedom*, *in* The Future of Press Freedom, *supra* note 10, at 346.

all individuals. By curbing law enforcement overreach, we may be able to offer more effective protection for everyone, including performers of the press function.[39]

Ultimately, our approach to identifying performers of the press function must be nimble enough to adapt to technological changes, inclusive enough to represent diverse voices, and nuanced enough to be effective. By crafting such a framework, we can better safeguard the press's crucial role in fostering an informed citizenry and holding power to account, even as the nature of journalism continues to evolve.

1.5 SUPPORTING THE PRESS FUNCTION

Finally, these discussions must grapple with the practical reality that the commercial model that long sustained the news industry has collapsed. Internet platforms have siphoned off the legacy media's readers, advertisers, and profits, leading to widespread newsroom closures and cutbacks. How Americans consume their news has also undergone a radical shift. Increasingly, it is computer algorithms – not news editors – that dictate which stories make their way to readers' eyes. In many communities, no one is left to perform shared, traditional press roles or to advocate for government transparency.

The future of press freedom, therefore, may require policies that actively support, rather than merely protect, the press function. While nonprofit, philanthropic, and public-subsidy models show promise, we must also explore more inventive approaches. Martha Minow emphasizes that saving the news in the digital age, especially at the local level, "require[s] innovation, persistence, and care."[40] Christina Koningisor and Jacob Noti-Victor propose leveraging creative combinations of intellectual property protections and other government incentives, mirroring "innovation policy pluralism" that has successfully spurred other socially valuable services.[41] This blend of government regulation and free-market forces could yield more effective options for sustaining public-serving journalism.

More ambitious proposals advocate for positive-rights approaches that guarantee news production and distribution, echoing practices in other modern democracies. Wesley Lowery proposes a federal trust modeled on the National Science Foundation to fund local media outlets,[42] while Victor Pickard calls for a "universal public service journalism" model.[43] Both are rooted in a belief that freedom of the press rings hollow if no one remains to adequately serve the public's right to know.

39 *Id.*

40 Martha Minow, *Are We Saving the News?*, *in* THE FUTURE OF PRESS FREEDOM, *supra* note 10, at 485.

41 Christina Koningisor & Jacob Noti-Victor, *Innovation Policy and the Press*, *in* THE FUTURE OF PRESS FREEDOM, *supra* note 10, at 437.

42 Wesley Lowery, *The Right to Know*, *in* THE FUTURE OF PRESS FREEDOM, *supra* note 10, at 373.

43 Victor Pickard, *Legal Foundations for Non-Reformist Media Reforms: A Positive-Rights Paradigm for Guaranteeing a Universal Press System*, *in* THE FUTURE OF PRESS FREEDOM, *supra* note 10, at 415.

These strategies, however, raise practical and constitutional challenges, including ensuring diverse coverage and maintaining editorial independence from government influence and partisan capture. Heidi Kitrosser's "anti-distortion" principle offers a promising framework for dealing with these challenges, drawing on existing jurisprudence to prevent conditions on subsidized speech that would compromise its integrity and independence.[44] Clearing such doctrinal barriers will be crucial in shaping the future of American press freedom.

Indeed, if constitutional obstacles are raised against these efforts, it may be the Constitution itself that provides the solution. In her book *Saving the News*, Martha Minow argued that the future of press freedom will require recognition that "government inaction can also jeopardize constitutional guarantees."[45] When news infrastructure crumbles in communities, when attention-grabbing distractions overwhelm readers, and when accountability mechanisms fail, we must revisit the Constitution's fundamental principles. Today, Minow argues, the duty to take action to safeguard the press remains strong.[46] The First Amendment, far from being a barrier to press-supporting interventions, might mandate them. This view of press freedom opens up rich new terrain for scholars and jurists to reimagine the government's role in preserving a vibrant free press.

Launching these conversations, which weigh competing values in a society desperately in need of high-quality news, is a core component of the effort to stave off authoritarianism and shore up healthy self-rule. There is a lot of work to be done. But important voices are now exploring both the role of news in safeguarding democracy and the role of the law in safeguarding the news. Now is the time to turn attention to the future of press freedom and to build doctrine that guarantees the press function continues to be performed in our rapidly changing political and media terrain.

[44] Heidi Kitrosser, *Distorting the Press*, *in* The Future of Press Freedom, *supra* note 10, at 391.

[45] Martha Minow, Saving the News: Why the Constitution Calls for Government Action to Preserve Freedom of Speech (2021).

[46] Minow, *supra* note 40, at 466; *see also* Pickard, *supra* note 43, at 415.

PART II

Democracy and the Press Function

2

The Press and American Democracy

Robert C. Post

The First Amendment provides that "Congress shall make no law ... abridging the freedom of speech, or of the press." The last three words pose something of a puzzle.

If the "freedom of speech" clause endows each and every speaker with the rights necessary to protect expression, what additional rights can or should be claimed by the press? It is an essential canon of legal interpretation that no word in a legal text should be regarded as mere surplusage.[1] But then, what do the words "or of the press" add to freedom of speech?

If the press can claim rights different from those guaranteed to every speaker, it must be because we understand the Press Clause to serve constitutional values that are different from those served by the "freedom of speech" clause and because these values require distinct forms of rights for their protection.

In this chapter, I shall explore four distinct constitutional values that at various times have been claimed to be uniquely served by the press: (1) the value of public discourse, (2) the Meiklejohnian value of distributing information, (3) the checking value, and (4) the value of the public sphere. Each of these values will yield a different constitutional definition of the "press," and each might imply a different array of rights that ought to accrue to the press. Although these values are distinct, the press may simultaneously serve one or more of them.

2.1 THE VALUE OF PUBLIC DISCOURSE

Our First Amendment jurisprudence of freedom of speech does not treat all expression equally. The First Amendment primarily protects speech that we deem constitutionally relevant to the formation of public opinion.[2] The object of ordinary First Amendment doctrine is to ensure, as the Court instructed us in *West Virginia State Board of Education v. Barnette*, that in the United States, "authority ... is to be

[1] Antonin Scalia & Bryan A. Garner, Reading Law: The interpretation of Legal Texts 174–79 (2012).

[2] Robert C. Post, Democracy, Expertise, Academic Freedom: A First Amendment Jurisprudence for the Modern State 3–25 (2012).

controlled by public opinion, not public opinion by authority."[3] Because democracy is a form of "government by public opinion,"[4] our First Amendment doctrine is designed to protect "the market of public opinion."[5] Following the Court's usage, I shall use the term "public discourse" to refer to the set of communications considered integral to the formation of public opinion.[6]

Public discourse encompasses all the various forms of expression necessary to produce "that public opinion which is the final source of government in a democratic state."[7] This modern concept of public opinion emerged in the eighteenth century with the creation of what we now call the "public sphere."[8] The public sphere facilitated the emergence of a "public,"[9] whose "public opinion" is the lifeblood of our democracy. The appearance of the public was made possible by "the circulation of texts among strangers who become, by virtue of their reflexively circulating discourse, a social entity."[10] In the words of Michael Schudson, the public is "the fiction that brings self-government to life."[11]

The public sphere was produced by the invention of printing, which enabled the widespread circulation of texts to strangers. The public sphere became entrenched in the eighteenth century when the circulation of newspapers became

3 319 U.S. 624, 641 (1943).

4 CARL SCHMITT, CONSTITUTIONAL THEORY 275 (Jeffrey Seizer ed., trans., 2008) (1928). Pioneering American social psychologist Charles Horton Cooley writes that democracy is "the organized sway of public opinion." CHARLES HORTON COOLEY, SOCIAL ORGANIZATION: A STUDY OF THE LARGER MIND 118 (1909).

5 Thornhill v. Alabama, 310 U.S. 88, 105 (1940).

6 *See, e.g.*, Snyder v. Phelps, 562 U.S. 443, 460 (2011); Citizens United v. FEC, 558 U.S. 310, 373 (2010) (Roberts, C.J., concurring); Metromedia, Inc. v. San Diego, 453 U.S. 490, 515 (1981).

7 Masses Publ'g Co. v. Patten, 244 F. 535, 540 (S.D.N.Y.) (L. Hand, J.), *rev'd*, 246 F.24 (2nd Cir. 1917).

8 On the public sphere, *see* JÜRGEN HABERMAS, THE STRUCTURAL TRANSFORMATION OF THE PUBLIC SPHERE: AN INQUIRY INTO A CATEGORY OF BOURGEOIS SOCIETY (Thomas Burger trans., 1989); CHARLES TAYLOR, PHILOSOPHICAL ARGUMENTS 257–87 (1995). "The central conceptual feature of the public sphere is its openness to strangers. As opposed to private communication, public communication emerges wherever a speaker cannot control the boundaries of his or her audience. Public communication is communication to an anonymous audience, potentially engaging everyone." Andreas Koller, *The Public Sphere and Comparative Historical Research: An Introduction*, 34 SOC. SC. HISTORY 261, 263 (2010). "While the adjective *public* has . . . a long trajectory, 'public opinion' as a political concept is an invention of the eighteenth century. Neither the term *Öffentlichkeit* nor the sphere it denotes existed before the eighteenth century." *Id.* at 267.

9 JOHN B. THOMPSON, THE MEDIA AND MODERNITY: A SOCIAL THEORY OF THE MEDIA 126 (1995). "The public consists of those people who act together with an understanding of their relationship to each other.... There can be no vital political life, no viable institutions of government, no sense of mastery over our shared fate, no effective common endeavors of any kind without there being a foundation of public awareness and spirit." David Matthews, *The Public in Practice and Theory*, 44 PUB. ADMIN. REV. 120, 123 (1984).

10 MICHAEL WARNER, PUBLICS AND COUNTERPUBLICS 11–12 (2002).

11 Michael Schudson, *Why Conservation Is Not the Soul of Democracy*, 14 CRITICAL STUD. MASS COMM. 297, 304–05 (1997).

commonplace. "The true advent … of the public"[12] occurred when newspapers began to offer a continual stream of information and opinion that united masses of people into a public that corresponded in scale to the newly entrenched nation-state.[13]

At its outset, the press was "the public sphere's preeminent institution."[14] The press provided the steady stream of communications that created and maintained the public sphere. That is why Thomas Jefferson could observe in 1787 that "the basis of our governments being the opinion of the people, the very first object should be to keep that right; and were it left to me to decide whether we should have a government without newspapers, or newspapers without a government, I should not hesitate a moment to prefer the latter."[15]

At the present time, however, there are many other "media for the communication of ideas"[16] – like film, radio, television, art, or theater – which also serve this same function. They all underwrite the health of the public sphere, and they all thereby facilitate robust processes of public opinion formation. Because all such media allow multitudes of strangers to join together in common conversation, they are in First Amendment jurisprudence all presumptively categorized as public discourse.[17] As the first and most prominent medium for the communication of ideas, the legacy newspapers and magazines that we now colloquially call the "press" also receive this special constitutional treatment.

The categorization of the press as public discourse is, of course, only a default definition. Newspapers can carry commercial speech;[18] magazines can be obscene.[19] But unless special conditions obtain, speech carried by the press, like speech carried by any of the other media for the communication of ideas, will be classified as public discourse and will therefore receive full First Amendment protection. Speech within a newspaper is presumptively "newsworthy."[20] This is not the case with many other

[12] Gabriel Tarde, On Communication and Social Influence 278–80 (Terry N. Clark ed., 1969).

[13] On the relationship between the development of printing and the creation of the nation-state, *see* Benedict R. O'G. Anderson, Imagined Communities: Reflections on the Origin and Spread of Nationalism (1991).

[14] Habermas, *supra* note 8, at 181.

[15] Thomas Jefferson to Edard Carrington, Jan. 16, 1787, in 11 Papers of Thomas Jefferson 48, 49 (Julian P. Boyd ed., 1955). *See* James Madison, *Public Opinion*, Nat'l Gazette, Dec. 19, 1791, at 59.

[16] Post, *supra* note 2, at 19–20.

[17] Robert Post, *Recuperating First Amendment Doctrine*, 47 Stan. L. Rev. 1249, 1251–60 (1995).

[18] On the distinction between commercial speech and public discourse, *see* Robert C. Post, *The Constitutional Status of Commercial Speech*, 48 UCLA L. Rev. 1 (2000).

[19] Miller v. California, 413 U.S. 15 (1973).

[20] On the relationship between speech being "newsworthy" and speech being about "a matter of public concern," and hence within public discourse, *see, e.g.*, Bartnicki v. Vopper, 532 U.S. 514, 525 (2001); Time, Inc. v. Hill, 385 U.S. 374 (1967).

forms of speech. It is not the case, for example, with commercial speech or expression about matters of private concern privately communicated.[21]

The press thus enjoys the special status of being classified as presumptively public discourse. But the press shares this special status with all media for the communication of ideas. In terms of the value of participating in public discourse, the press can claim only the right to be treated equally with every other participant in public discourse. The press earns this right by continuously seeking to reach out and communicate with strangers.[22]

2.2 THE MEIKLEJOHNIAN VALUE OF DISTRIBUTING INFORMATION

In the last third of the twentieth century, the Supreme Court seemed repeatedly to hold that the press was not entitled to claim special First Amendment rights that were not available to all other participants in public discourse.[23] One cause of this difficulty was that the press repeatedly chose to justify claims for special

[21] Snyder v. Phelps, 562 U.S. 443, 451–53 (2011); Dun & Bradstreet, Inc. v. Greenmoss Builders, Inc., 472 U.S. 749 (1985).

[22] A slightly more sophisticated analysis might introduce additional complexities into this analysis. First Amendment protections do not precisely extend to media for the communication of ideas, but instead to speakers who choose to express themselves through these media. Speakers who communicate in this way are constitutionally presumed to be seeking to influence public opinion. They are accorded full First Amendment protection – enjoying what the Court in other circumstances has called "ordinary First Amendment standards," Mahanoy Area Sch. Dist. v. B.L., 141 S.Ct. 2038, 2045 (2021) – so that they might experience the constitutional value of democratic legitimation. Post, *supra* note 2, at 1–25. Ordinary First Amendment standards ensure that speakers can aspire to render the state democratically accountable to their views. Commercial corporations, however, are not natural human beings. Because they therefore cannot experience the value of democratic legitimation, different kinds of constitutional protections are often accorded to their speech, even if it occurs through media for the communication of ideas. Robert C. Post, Citizens Divided: Campaign Finance Reform and the Constitution 66–76 (2014). Yet "ordinary First Amendment standards" were originally fashioned to protect the legacy press, despite the fact that most legacy press institutions were also for-profit corporations. This might be because these press corporations are what we would now classify as "expressive associations," Board of Directors of Rotary Intern. v. Rotary Club of Duarte, 481 U.S. 537, 545 (1987), which are entitled to full First Amendment protection even though they have assumed a corporate form. Or it might be because the Press Clause offers a special dispensation to press institutions to be constitutionally characterized as participants in public discourse, even though they are otherwise commercial entities out to earn a profit. Post, *supra*, at 71 note*.

[23] As even Justice Brennan was moved to observe: "We protect the press to ensure the vitality of First Amendment guarantees. This solicitude implies no endorsement of the principle that speakers other than the press deserve lesser First Amendment protection. 'In the realm of protected speech, the legislature is constitutionally disqualified from dictating ... the speakers who may address a public issue.' The free speech guarantee gives each citizen an equal right to self-expression and to participation in self-government ... Accordingly, at least six Members of this Court (the four who join this opinion and Justice WHITE and THE CHIEF JUSTICE) agree today that, in the context of defamation law, the rights of the institutional media are no greater and no less than those enjoyed by other individuals or organizations engaged in the

constitutional treatment in terms of a constitutional value that members of the Court did not find convincing.

For many years, press lawyers argued that the unique constitutional value served by the press was the distribution of information necessary for self-government. In *Branzburg v. Hayes*,[24] for example, the press argued that it should receive a special privilege shielding the identity of confidential sources from grand jury subpoenas. The press contended that if a reporter is "forced to reveal these confidences to a grand jury, the source so identified and other confidential sources of other reporters will be measurably deterred from furnishing publishable information, all to the detriment of the free flow of information protected by the First Amendment."[25]

This argument was rooted in Alexander Meiklejohn's account of the First Amendment. Meiklejohn famously asserted that the reason why speech should receive constitutional protection is to ensure that citizens receive the information necessary for them to perform their civic obligations, like voting on referenda and candidates. In case after case, the press argued that it had a special responsibility to distribute information to citizens, who would not otherwise be informed about public matters requiring decision.

The Court explicitly rejected this argument. The Court did not deny that the First Amendment protected the circulation of information to citizens, but it did deny that any such need justified awarding distinct constitutional privileges to the press:

> Freedom of the press is a "fundamental personal right" which "is not confined to newspapers and periodicals. It necessarily embraces pamphlets and leaflets . . . The press in its historic connotation comprehends every sort of publication which affords a vehicle of information and opinion." The informative function asserted by representatives of the organized press in the present cases is also performed by lecturers, political pollsters, novelists, academic researchers, and dramatists. Almost any author may quite accurately assert that he is contributing to the flow of information to the public, that he relies on confidential sources of information, and that these sources will be silenced if he is forced to make disclosures before a grand jury.[26]

The press's Meiklejohnian arguments, in other words, were met with the objection that all speakers circulate information to the public. Indeed, a Meiklejohnian conception of the First Amendment holds that the very meaning of freedom of speech is nothing other than the freedom to convey information.[27] The Court did

same activities." Dun & Bradstreet, Inc. v. Greenmoss Builders, Inc., 472 U.S. 749, 783–84 (1985) (Brennan, J., dissenting).

24 408 U.S. 665 (1972).

25 *Id.* at 680.

26 *Id.* at 704–05.

27 Alexander Meiklejohn, Political Freedom: The Constitutional Powers of the People 8–28 (1948).

not answer the press's claim that it was uniquely responsible for the effective circulation of information, but in truth it is difficult to quantify the difference in how much information the press distributes as distinct from authors of bestselling nonfiction books or producers of popular documentary movies.

The press's efforts to invoke a Meiklejohnian account of the First Amendment to justify special constitutional treatment were met with decisive judicial skepticism. The Court believed that the press was not all that different from other speakers when it came to the Meiklejohnian distribution of information.[28] This premise led the Burger Court to frequently demote the press to being "simply members of the public."[29]

2.3 THE CHECKING VALUE

The press has appeared differently to the Court, however, in the context of a distinct constitutional value. In *Minneapolis Star and Tribune Co. v. Minnesota Commissioner of Revenue*,[30] the Court considered a Minnesota statute imposing a special tax on the cost of paper and ink products used in the production of newspapers. The Court was offended that the tax "singled out the press for special treatment."[31] Such a tax, the Court concluded "cannot stand unless the burden is necessary to achieve an overriding governmental interest."[32] The Court's reasoning is instructive:

> When the State imposes a generally applicable tax, there is little cause for concern. We need not fear that a government will destroy a selected group of taxpayers by burdensome taxation if it must impose the same burden on the rest of its constituency. When the State singles out the press, though, the political constraints that prevent a legislature from passing crippling taxes of general applicability are weakened, and the threat of burdensome taxes becomes acute. That threat can operate as effectively as a censor to check critical comment by the press, undercutting the basic assumption of our political system that the press will often serve as an important restraint on government.[33]

The passage contains an entirely different constitutional image of the press than that contained in *Branzburg*. The Court invokes a "basic assumption of our political system that the press will often serve as an important restraint on government."[34] If in *Branzburg*, the press was simply one means among many to distribute information to

[28] *See supra* note 23.
[29] Christopher G. Blood, *Note: The Eroded Power of the Press and the Need to Apply Separation of Powers Principles*, 15 J.L. & POL. 781, 782 (1999).
[30] 460 U.S. 575 (1983).
[31] *Id.* at 582.
[32] *Id.* at 583.
[33] *Id.* at 585.
[34] *Id.*

voters, in *Minneapolis Star and Tribune* the press was a unique institution operating to restrain government misconduct through "critical comment."[35]

This image of the press had been fully elaborated six years before in Vincent Blasi's pathbreaking article, "The Checking Value in First Amendment Theory."[36] Blasi argued that the press should be conceived as a specific kind of institution whose purpose was to guard "against breaches of trust by public officials."[37] Blasi built on the insight of Alexander Bickel that "the press was a constitutionally recognized countervailing power to the official branches of government."[38]

On this account, constitutional red flags would not be raised if Minnesota were to impose a special tax on films. Although movies are a medium for the communication of ideas, and although filmmakers are entitled to receive all the First Amendment rights accruing to participants in public discourse,[39] cinema is not an institution characterized by an adversarial relationship with government. It is not a "basic assumption of our political system" that films will "serve as an important restraint on government."

Following Blasi, I shall designate this constitutional conception of the press as the "checking value." From this perspective, the press should enjoy a unique constitutional role. If the press had appealed to the checking value in *Branzburg* instead of pushing a Meiklejohnian position, it is possible that the Court might have reached a different conclusion. We cannot know. All we can say with certainty is that in a context like *Minneapolis Star and Tribune*, where the press sought to prohibit legislation singling out the press for disadvantageous treatment, as distinct from a context like *Branzburg*, in which the press sought to claim special First Amendment privileges unavailable to other participants in public discourse, the Court was receptive to the checking value and prepared to give it constitutional effect.

The checking value imagines the press as an institution continually engaged with the government. The press is figured as an institution that is constantly seeking to hold the state accountable. It is certainly no accident that this image of the press rose to prominence during the time of Watergate[40] and the furor over the Pentagon Papers.[41] But if the checking value can justify awarding the press constitutional

[35] *Id. See also* Mills v. Alabama, 384 U.S. 214, 219 (1966): "The Constitution specifically selected the press ... to play an important role in the discussion of public affairs. Thus the press serves and was designed to serve as a powerful antidote to any abuses of power by governmental officials as a constitutionally chosen means for keeping officials elected by the people responsible to all the people whom they were selected to serve. Suppression of the right of the press to praise or criticize governmental agents ... muzzles one of the very agencies the Framers of our Constitution thoughtfully and deliberately selected to improve our society and keep it free."

[36] 1977 AM. BAR FDN. RES. J. 521.

[37] *Id.* at 527.

[38] John E. Nowak, *Using the Press Clause to Limit Government Speech*, 30 ARIZ. L. REV. 1, 13 (1988). *See* Cass R. Sunstein, *Government Control of Information*, 74 CALIF. L. REV. 889 (1986).

[39] Joseph Burstyn, Inc. v. Wilson, 343 U.S. 495 (1952).

[40] United States v. Nixon, 418 U.S. 683 (1974).

[41] New York Times Co. v. United States, 403 U.S. 713 (1971).

rights unavailable to other speakers in public discourse, it is far from obvious exactly how to define the "press" so as to serve this value.

Obviously, legacy press like The New York Times or The Washington Post would qualify as the press under the checking value. So also would proto-legacy institutions like ProPublica. But what about commentators like Tucker Carlson or Mark Levin? What about internet sites like Gawker or BuzzFeed? What about individual unaffiliated bloggers? Exactly what kind of speakers in the contemporary world are fit to participate in what Alexander Bickel called "the adversary game between press and government"?[42]

Should candidates for this game qualify merely because they hold an antagonistic attitude toward government? Or should they qualify only if they also abide by the professional standards that, after the progressive era, we have come to expect of the legacy press? For purposes of the checking value, must the press be institutionalized, so that it contains the full paraphernalia of editors and reporters and fact-checkers, or can the press consist merely of individuals bursting with antagonism toward government action? Must the press be an institution that also reports facts, or can it consist of the continuous broadcast of opinion, however shrill?

Minneapolis Star and Tribune is clear that those who constitutionally qualify for the "adversary game" ought to be accorded constitutional privileges that are unavailable to other participants in public discourse. These privileges form the rules of the "adversary game" that is a fact of our national life. These rules restrain government dealings with the press. Exemplary are regulations promulgated by the Attorney General to specify the precise, limited set of conditions under which the Department of Justice can issue subpoenas to "members of the news media."[43]

2.4 THE VALUE OF THE PUBLIC SPHERE

If the checking value identifies members of the press by virtue of their potentially antagonistic relationship to the state, there is yet a fourth constitutional conception of the press, one that is compatible with almost the complete absence of a unique voice attributable to the press. This conception of the press flows from the public sphere itself. It can most clearly be seen in the decision of the Court of Justice of the European Union (CJEU) in *Google Spain SL v. Agencia Española de Protección de Datos*.[44]

42 Alexander M. Bickel, The Morality of Consent 80 (1975).

43 Memorandum of the Attorney General on the "Use of Compulsory Process to Obtain Information From, or Records of, Members of the News Media" (July 19, 2021), at DOJ Formally Adopts New Policy Restricting Use of Compulsory Process to Obtain Reporter Information: Attorney General Memo on Compulsory Process (justice.gov).

44 Case C-131/12, Google Spain SL v. Agencia Española de Protección de Datos, 2014 E.C.R. 317 [hereinafter *Google Spain*].

In *Google Spain*, the CJEU was required to interpret Directive 95/46/EC,[45] which protected data privacy throughout the EU. The Directive, which was at the time "probably the most influential data privacy text in the world,"[46] put stringent conditions on the processing of private data, creating what has been called the "right to be forgotten."[47]

In *Google Spain*, a Spanish lawyer argued that Google violated his right to be forgotten when its search engine produced references to an old newspaper article describing official attachment proceedings against him. Because the Directive exempted the processing of private data "solely for journalistic" use,[48] a major question in the case was whether the Google search engine could claim this journalistic exception. The CJEU denied that the exception applied to the Google search engine, holding that Google could set against the Spanish lawyer's right to data privacy only "the economic interest" of the company.[49]

The traditional public sphere was created in the seventeenth and eighteenth centuries when printed newspapers circulated among strangers and united them into a "public" capable of holding Europe's newly created centralized states to political account. These newspapers were private commercial enterprises with their own economic interests. Yet these enterprises created the "public" that made possible what we now call democracy. The "press" was able to perform this feat not merely because its voice was potentially antagonistic to states but also because it distributed common information to strangers who were thereby enabled to come together to form a public.

The twenty-first century has witnessed an immense transformation, from analog to digital information.[50] Digital information circulates on the internet with virtually zero marginal cost. This has facilitated the emergence of digital institutions like the

[45] Directive 95/46/EC of the European Parliament and of the Council of October 24, 1995, on the Protection of Individuals with Regard to the Processing of Personal Data and on the Free Movement of such Data, 1995 O.J. (L 281) 31 (EC) [hereinafter Directive].

[46] Stefan Kulk & Frederik Zuiderveen Borgesius, *Privacy, Freedom of Expression, and the Right to Be Forgotten in Europe*, *in* CAMBRIDGE HANDBOOK OF CONSUMER PRIVACY (Jules Polonetsky et al. eds., 2018).

[47] *Factsheet on the "Right to Be Forgotten" Ruling (C-131/12)*, EUR. COMMISSION 1–2, http://ec.europa.eu/justice/data-protection/files/factsheets/factsheet_data_protection_en.pdf [https://perma.cc/QSK7-57UD].

[48] Directive, *supra* note 45, at art. 9. *See* David Erdos, *European Union Data Protection Law and Media Expression: Fundamentally Off Balance*, 65 INT'L COMP. L.Q. 139 (2016); David Erdos, *Statutory Regulation of Professional Journalism Under European Data Protection: Down but Not Out?* 8 J. MEDIA L. 229 (2016); DAVID ERDOS, EUROPEAN REGULATORY INTERPRETATION OF THE INTERFACE BETWEEN DATA PROTECTION AND JOURNALISTIC FREEDOM: AN INCOMPLETE AND IMPERFECT BALANCING ACT (Cambridge Legal Stud. Res. Paper Series, Paper No. 61/2015, 2015).

[49] *Google Spain*, *supra* note 44, at para 81.

[50] On the implications of this transformation, *see* Robert Post, *The Internet, Democracy, and Misinformation*, in DISINFORMATION, MISINFORMATION AND DEMOCRACY (A. Koltay et al. eds., Cambridge University Press, forthcoming 2025).

Google search engine, which circulates far more information than any previous entity. Whereas in the eighteenth century, newspapers used their unique voice to attract readers and so expose them to common information, the Google search engine provides common information as requested by its users. It has no need to develop a distinctive voice to invite readers to use its services and partake in a common pool of "public" information.

The Google search engine is thus able to circulate common information to vast numbers of people and so to maintain a public, without any audible voice at all. Without in any way fulfilling the checking value or purporting to speak in its own voice about public affairs, it nevertheless performs the same sociological, public-sustaining function as does the legacy press. It is a purely public-maintaining institution.

This is, in my view, a central constitutional function of the press, one that deserves the kind of protection that the Directive in fact awarded to journalism. It is a function that is threatened by the current trend toward the protection of data privacy.[51] If the press could not publish common facts, we could not sustain the public conversation necessary for democratic self-government. That is why data privacy regulations typically exempt the press. Yet, the CJEU was not able to recognize the Google search engine as an enterprise that served this journalistic function, most likely because the engine lacked the voice we have always associated with the legacy press.

If the CJEU had instead focused on the constitutional value of sustaining the public sphere, it might have reached a different conclusion. The Google search engine performs the same public-maintaining function as did the traditional, analog press. The search engine sustains a digital public. This is a constitutional value that deserves its own distinct form of constitutional protection.

2.5 CONCLUSION

We have thus identified four distinct constitutional functions performed by the "press": The press participates in public discourse, it distributes information, it is a potentially antagonistic counterweight to government, and it maintains the public sphere. Each of these different functions leads to a different specification of what institutions should be included in the constitutional definition of the press. Each leads to a different form of constitutional protection. Although these functions are conceptually distinct, they need not be incompatible. A particular institution of "the press" can simultaneously serve one or more of them.

As a speaker, the press is presumptively a participant in public discourse, entitled to all the same First Amendment protections as other speakers in public discourse.

[51] For a detailed exposition of the argument in text, *see* Robert Post, *Data Privacy and Dignitary Privacy: Google Spain, the Right to Be Forgotten, and the Construction of the Public Sphere*, 67 Duke Law Journal 981 (2018).

As a distributor of information, however, the Court has repeatedly held that the press is not entitled to any privilege not held by all other distributors of information. Yet the Court is prepared to recognize the press as distinctive insofar as it is potentially locked into an "adversary game" with the state. Our history and tradition have not cast other media in this unique role. If we take this constitutional value seriously, as has the Court in a few decisions, the press should be entitled to special constitutional privileges. The government should be prevented from unduly oppressing the press or from freely appropriating its resources.

Finally, there have emerged during the twenty-first century wholly new kinds of institutions that are engaged in the pure distribution of information without any pretension to voice. Exemplary is the Google search engine. These institutions, made possible by the digitization of information, produce publics in a manner analogous to the newspapers of the eighteenth century. They continuously endow strangers with common sources of information that are of interest to them.

These new digital institutions can certainly make no claim to the special privileges implied by the checking value. It is not even clear whether they should be entitled to rights that protect speakers who contribute to public discourse. But with regard to data privacy regulations like the Directive that seek specifically to block the transmission of data to strangers,[52] they ought to be able to claim the same protections as we are willing to give to the press generally.

[52] The Directive has now been superseded by the powerful General Data Protection Regulation (GDPR). *See* Regulation (EU) 2016/679 of the European Parliament and of the Council of 27 April 2016 on the Protection of Natural Persons with Regard to the Processing of Personal Data and on the Free Movement of Such Data, 2016 O.J. (L 119) 1.

3

Political Tensions and the Democratic Press

Gregory P. Magarian

"The freedom of speech," wrote Owen Fiss, "is a social state of affairs."[1] So too is the freedom of the press. The familiar insight that a healthy democratic political culture requires a vibrant, independent press establishes a great deal while leaving a great deal more in question. What should the press do? Who is part of it? How can and should legal doctrines enable its work? This chapter, which draws on my two decades of scholarship about the press, contends that all those questions are fundamentally political. By "political," I refer not to electoral politics but rather to foundational, constitutional politics: contested questions about normatively desirable forms of governance and means of managing societal conflicts. More than twenty years ago, Ed Baker explained that, in a democratic society, the normatively appealing shape of the news media necessarily varies with the society's preferred model of democracy.[2] How we conceive the democratic press depends on what kind of political community we want to form and how that community needs the press to function.

Framing press freedom in political terms may seem fraught at a moment when journalists face public hostility, official repression, and even violence.[3] Much conventional rhetoric calls for the press to stand above politics, or at least beside politics. When journalists in the last century conceived of the press as "the fourth branch of government," they posited a role for the news media that impelled dispassionate, nonpartisan chronicling.[4] The ideal of press neutrality forms a rhetorically stable platform from which to advocate press freedom. The reality, however, is more complicated. The press performs functions that require politically contingent choices about institutional design and journalistic practice. Persistent corporate

[1] Owen Fiss, Liberalism Divided: Freedom of Speech and the Many Uses of State Power 15 (1996) (internal quotation marks omitted).

[2] *See* C. Edwin Baker, Media, Markets, and Democracy 129–53 (2002).

[3] For a thorough, ongoing catalog of governmental and private threats to press freedom, *see* The U.S. Press Freedom Tracker, https://pressfreedomtracker.us/.

[4] *See* Douglass Cater, The Fourth Branch of Government (1959); Herbert Brucker, Freedom of Information (1949).

domination of our mass media surely embodies a political condition, though not a political choice by the people.[5] Reckoning with political questions about the free press is a necessary step in preserving and strengthening it.

This chapter discusses two related political tensions with major implications for the shape of our democratic press: the tension between objectivity and subjectivity and the tension between institutionalism and populism. My book *Managed Speech: The Roberts Court's First Amendment* advocates a vision of free speech and public discourse that I call *dynamic diversity*. The basic notion is that free speech law should promote conditions of public discourse that maximize both the range of participants and the variety of available ideas.[6] In line with that notion, the book sharply criticizes the Supreme Court's abandonment of press freedom.[7] This chapter's observations about political tensions and the democratic press reflect the value of dynamic diversity.

3.1 OBJECTIVITY AND SUBJECTIVITY

The most fundamental political conundrum of a twenty-first-century democratic press tracks the familiar debate between Enlightenment rationalism and postmodernist critique. To vastly oversimplify that debate: Rationalism, epitomized by the scientific method, relies on our capacity to discern objective, verifiable truth through experiment and analysis. Objective truth may be complex, but in substantial measure, we can discover it.[8] Postmodernist thought criticizes scientific rationalism for presenting a false promise of objective truth. Postmodernism posits a radical subjectivity, in which anyone's understanding of truth depends on their distinctive, contingent perspective and position. Truth as such does not exist; rather, groups and cultures construct subjective truths.[9]

Anxiety about the rationalist-postmodernist tension permeates our elite political discourse, mainly because contempt for rationalism has found a strong foothold in our popular political discourse. Kellyanne Conway infamously characterized one of the Trump administration's early lies as a valid account of "alternative facts."[10] Donald Trump himself routinely dismisses criticisms of his presidency as "fake

5 *See* Ben H. Bagdikian, The New Media Monopoly (2004); C. Edwin Baker, Media Concentration and Democracy: Why Ownership Matters (2007); Robert W. McChesney & John Nichols, The Death and Life of American Journalism: The Media Revolution That Will Begin the World Again (2010).

6 *See* Gregory P. Magarian, Managed Speech: The Roberts Court's First Amendment xvi–xx (2017).

7 *See id.* at 245–47.

8 *See, e.g.*, René Descartes, Meditations on First Philosophy (1641).

9 *See, e.g.*, Peter L. Berger & Thomas Luckman, The Social Construction of Reality (1966).

10 *See* Eric Bradner, *Conway: Trump White House Offered "Alternative Facts" on Crowd Size*, CNN (Jan. 23, 2017), https://www.cnn.com/2017/01/22/politics/kellyanne-conway-alternative-facts/index.html.

news," transmuting a warning about misinformation into a cudgel of misinformation.[11] Anti-vaccine misinformation has gained a mass following and produced a horrifying body count.[12] Denial of climate science literally threatens the life of our planet.[13] These indulgences damage our lives and corrode our political culture. Without shared grounding, including factual stipulations, constructive political discourse becomes impossible.[14] In these pathological conditions, insistence on the certainty of objective facts, what we can call *truth anxiety*, makes great psychological and political sense.

A core function of news organizations for much of the twentieth century was to provide a baseline of truth that enabled constructive political discourse. Objectivity became a defining norm of journalism. Walter Lippmann, reacting against partisan journalism in the early twentieth century, argued that journalists should adapt the scientific method to newsgathering and analysis.[15] The American Society of Newspaper Editors' Statement of Principles declared: "News reports should be free from opinion or bias of any kind."[16] That embrace of objectivity corresponded with the nationalization of news. In the latter half of the twentieth century, the three national television networks came to dominate news reporting, with their local affiliates, radio stations, and a diminishing number of newspapers playing supporting roles. These news outlets, as I have discussed elsewhere, functioned as dominant intermediaries between the world of information and the mass public.[17] Funded by advertising and sustained by appealing to broad audiences, they had every incentive to operate within a widespread consensus about essential facts and truths.

That mediated consensus, however, yielded a stifling homogeneity, bogging down public political debate in bland majoritarian norms. Government responded ambiguously. While much government policy and expression reinforced the news media's narrow consensus, some regulation encouraged greater dynamism in public discourse. Congress imposed structural regulations that dispersed the ownership of

[11] *See* Callum Borchers, *Trump Falsely Claims (Again) That He Coined the Term "Fake News,"* Wash. Post (Oct. 26, 2017), https://www.washingtonpost.com/news/the-fix/wp/2017/10/26/trump-falsely-claims-again-that-he-coined-the-term-fake-news/.

[12] *See, e.g.*, Azhar Hussain et al., *The Anti-Vaccination Movement: A Regression in Modern Medicine*, Cureus (July 3, 2018), https://www.ncbi.nlm.nih.gov/pmc/articles/PMC6122668/.

[13] *See, e.g.*, David Runciman, *How Climate Scepticism Turned into Something More Dangerous*, The Guardian (July 7, 2017), https://www.theguardian.com/environment/2017/jul/07/climate-change-denial-scepticism-cynicism-politics.

[14] *See* Robert Post, Constitutional Domains: Democracy, Community, Management 140–44 (1995) (discussing the importance of shared norms and understandings for enabling public discourse).

[15] *See* Walter Lippmann et al., *A Test of the News*, New Republic (Aug. 4, 1920), https://archive.org/details/LippmannMerzATestoftheNews.

[16] *American Society of Newspaper Editors: Statement of Principles* (1923, revised 1975), reprinted at Accountable Journalism, Codes of Ethics, https://accountablejournalism.org/ethics-codes/american-society-of-newspaper-editors-statement-of-principles.

[17] *See* Gregory P. Magarian, *Forward into the Past: Speech Intermediaries in the Television and Internet Ages*, 71 Okla. L. Rev. 237 (2018).

media outlets.[18] It also empowered the Federal Communications Commission to mandate, through a cluster of regulations called the Fairness Doctrine, that radio and television broadcasters cover issues of public concern and present opposing viewpoints about those issues. I'm one of few legal academics in recent memory to write anything favorable about the Fairness Doctrine.[19] On the negative side of the ledger, the doctrine was elitist in distinguishing established print media from upstart broadcasters, dangerous in imposing government content policies, and facile in presuming that political debates have only two sides. On the positive side, the doctrine pushed back against news media homogeneity by insisting that broadcast licensees present opposing viewpoints. The best defense of the Fairness Doctrine is that exposing audiences to direct conflicts between contrary views on public issues can nourish the critical faculties that enable democratic self-governance.[20] Today, we find ourselves in a cul-de-sac of public discourse where people's and groups' customization of truth threatens collective self-governance.[21] The Fairness Doctrine modeled, however imperfectly, a way out of that trap through critical contestation rather than imposed consensus.

Mediated consensus becomes hazardous when the media propagates truths that turn out to be lies. Consider two spasms of government violence, one at the old media's peak and the other on the slope of its decline: the 1970 Kent State massacre and the 2003 invasion of Iraq. In earlier work, I have situated these two events as catastrophic failures of both First Amendment law and the institutional press.[22] Over the past half century, our country has committed few greater crimes and suffered few deeper shames than Kent State and the Iraq War. These are exactly the sorts of government abuses that a democratic press should probe, hector, and shout to prevent. But the news media, despite its increasing criticisms by 1970 of the illegal war that ignited the Kent State protests, parroted government lies that the protesters had provoked National Guard troops to slaughter four students and maim nine more.[23] Just over thirty years later, our leading news organizations endorsed the Bush administration's lies about Iraqi weapons of mass destruction,[24] smoothing the path to another indefensible war that caused 300,000 needless deaths.[25]

[18] *See* C. Edwin Baker, *Media Structure, Ownership Policy, and the First Amendment*, 78 S. Cal. L. Rev. 755 (2005).

[19] *See* Gregory P. Magarian, *Substantive Media Regulation in Three Dimensions*, 76 Geo. Wash. L. Rev. 845 (2008).

[20] *See id.* at 881–89.

[21] *See* Magarian, *supra* note 17, at 256.

[22] *See* Gregory P. Magarian, *Kent State and the Failure of First Amendment Law*, 65 Wash. U. J. L. & Poly. 41, 49–51 (2021); Gregory P. Magarian, *The First Amendment, The Public-Private Distinction, and Nongovernmental Suppression of Wartime Political Debate*, 73 Geo. Wash. L. Rev. 101, 117–21 (2004).

[23] *See* Magarian, *Kent State*, *supra* note 22, at 49–51.

[24] *See* Magarian, *Public-Private*, *supra* note 22, at 117–21.

[25] *See* Iraq Body Count, https://www.iraqbodycount.org/.

Truth anxiety fogs our critical understanding of free speech and the free press. We sometimes forget that the foundational text of our First Amendment canon, Justice Holmes' famous *Abrams* concurrence, extolled free speech for *pursuing* truth, not for presuming it.[26] Present journalistic ethical codes admirably show heightened nuance, favoring guidelines for journalistic practice over aspirations to perfect neutrality or objectivity.[27] Thinking about what kind of democracy and what kind of press we want requires us to confront the postmodern challenge to rationalism. We need to consider, with clear eyes, what truths our insights justify asserting and what avenues of inquiry our uncertainties compel holding open. For my own part, I have no doubt that vaccines save lives, that our planet is overheating, and that debating those truths wastes the time we should instead spend addressing them. I have great doubt, though, about the integrity of our electoral system, the beneficence of our military and intelligence services, and the justice of our economic order. The last century's dominant news media did or would have treated all those issues as essentially settled. Looking forward, we must engage critically with the dilemma of which objective truths our democratic press should propound and which subjective positions it should interrogate.

3.2 INSTITUTIONALISM AND POPULISM

A second political tension with high salience for the democratic press concerns not what news reporting says but who says it. Beginning after the Civil War and accelerating in the twentieth century, news organizations in the United States developed strong institutional structures. Those structures enabled the professionalization of the press. News reporting became much more than just a job to perform expediently. It became a vocation that required rigorous training, often through journalism schools. The institutional news media inculcated professional norms alongside skills of the trade. News organizations built elaborate hierarchies, flowing from publishers to layers of editors and legions of reporters, to maximize effectiveness and project credibility. Professionalization encouraged competition among news outlets to achieve publicly valuable outcomes.

The news media's institutionalization and professionalization helped to earn journalists a special constitutional status as public trustees. The Supreme Court at some important moments embraced the idea that the press serves the people by checking the government and powerful private actors. First Amendment case law insulated newspapers from liability for criticizing government officials,[28] let them

[26] *See* Abrams v. United States, 250 U.S. 616, 630 (Holmes, J., dissenting).

[27] *See, e.g.*, Society of Professional Journalists Code of Ethics, https://www.spj.org/pdf/spj-code-of-ethics.pdf.

[28] *See* New York Times Co. v. Sullivan, 376 U.S. 254 (1964); *see also* Florida Star v. B.J.F., 491 U.S. 524 (1989) (holding that the First Amendment barred an action for damages against a newspaper for publishing truthful information).

publish explosive national security documents,[29] and gave them a presumptive right to cover criminal proceedings.[30] Over time, doctrinal emphasis shifted from protecting the press *for* the public to protecting the press *from* the public, with holdings that the First Amendment shielded newspapers from right-of-reply statutes[31] and did not compel the mass electronic media to sell airtime to political speakers.[32] All these Court decisions extolled the institutional news media's editorial discretion.

Eventually, though, the Court shifted to viewing the press as an ordinary, profit-making industry. The justices rejected major First Amendment priorities of the institutional press, most notably a claim of the right to protect the identities of confidential sources from law enforcement.[33] Ultimately the Court declared, in a sideline of its infamous *Citizens United* decision, that the First Amendment does not even countenance treating newspaper editorial boards' electoral endorsements as distinctly valuable for democracy.[34]

My writing has lamented the decline of journalistic professionalism.[35] The related decline of media institutions presents a more complicated issue.[36] We're better off without the big three networks' hegemonic power. At the same time, economic forces have decimated the ranks of newspapers.[37] Most surviving papers have had to scale back their journalistic missions.[38] Filling the void of lost professional journalists are dizzying throngs of internet and social media content providers. These new "journalists" generally operate outside institutional structures. They tend not to identify with the journalistic profession, and most of them work independently or in smaller, looser organizations. They largely forgo professional training. Some adhere to ethical standards, but many do not. Even many conscientious online news providers don't think or behave like professional journalists. The shift from institutional to disaggregated journalism has caused concern that today's news

[29] *See* New York Times Co. v. United States (Pentagon Papers Case), 403 U.S. 713 (1971).

[30] *See* Richmond Newspapers, Inc. v. Virginia, 448 U.S. 555 (1980).

[31] *See* Miami Herald Pub. Co. v. Tornillo, 418 U.S. 241 (1974).

[32] *See* Columbia Broadcasting Sys., Inc. v. Democratic Nat'l Comm., 412 U.S. 94 (1973).

[33] *See* Branzburg v. Hayes, 408 U.S. 665 (1972); *see also* Cohen v. Cowles Media Co., 501 U.S. 663 (1991) (holding that the First Amendment did not bar a promissory estoppel suit against a newspaper for breaking a promise not to reveal a source's identity).

[34] *See* Citizens United v. FEC, 558 U.S. 310, 352–54 (2010). For a critical commentary, *see* Sonja R. West, *Favoring the Press*, 106 Cal. L. Rev. 91(2018).

[35] *See* Gregory P. Magarian, *How Cheap Speech Underserves and Overheats Democracy*, 54 U.C. Davis L. Rev. 2455, 2470–77 (2021).

[36] *See* Magarian, *supra* note 17, at 239–50.

[37] For an updated database of newspaper losses, *see* Penelope Muse Abernathy, *The Expanding News Desert*, University of North Carolina Hussman School of Journalism and Media, https://www.usnewsdeserts.com/reports/news-deserts-and-ghost-newspapers-will-local-news-survive/the-news-landscape-in-2020-transformed-and-diminished/vanishing-newspapers/.

[38] *See* Pew Res. Serv., *Fact Sheets: State of the News Media* (Jun. 29, 2021), https://www.pewresearch.org/journalism/fact-sheet/newspapers/.

media lacks the requisite integrity and rigor to help sustain democracy.[39] That concern has prompted calls for further restrictions on press freedom, including arguments from Supreme Court justices[40] for overruling the actual malice standard for defamation in *New York Times Co. v. Sullivan*.[41]

Anxiety about the institutional news media's decline parallels a prominent theme in our broader political discourse. One of the strongest terms of condemnation in the twenty-first century political lexicon, the equivalent of "Lochnerist" among jurists or "humanist" among religious conservatives, is "populist." The problem with Donald Trump, his Republican critics insist, is that he's an erratic populist, nothing like their conservative paragon Ronald Reagan.[42] Bernie Sanders, to some liberal commentators, is just Trump in a cheaper suit, another populist bomb thrower.[43] Populism, in many accounts, spawned the January 6, 2021, insurrection.[44]

Disinformation about vaccines stems from populist opposition to scientific expertise.[45] Populism fosters nativist opposition to immigration[46] and – much worse – to free trade.[47] Only stable, responsible institutions can save us from the populist hordes.[48] This moral panic about populism once again conjures Lippmann, whose mistrust of the people's capacity to participate meaningfully in collective self-governance famously led him to advocate an elite, technocratic version of democracy.[49]

Our history, however, offers a radically different exemplar of populism. In the late nineteenth century, the agrarian populist movement challenged the burgeoning

39 *See, e.g.*, Philipp Lorenz-Spreen et al., *A Systematic Review of Worldwide Causal and Correlational Evidence on Digital Media and Democracy*, 7 Nature Hum. Behav. 74 (2023).

40 *See* Berisha v. Lawson, 141 S.Ct. 2424, 2427–28 (2021) (Gorsuch, J., dissenting from denial of certiorari); *see also id.* at 2424–25 (Thomas, J., dissenting from denial of certiorari).

41 376 U.S. 254, 279–80 (1964).

42 *See, e.g.*, Jonathan Swan, *Pence Calls Trump's Populism a "Road to Ruin" for the G.O.P.*, N.Y. Times (Sep. 6, 2023), https://www.nytimes.com/2023/09/06/us/politics/pence-populism-speech.html.

43 *See, e.g.*, George Packer, *The Populists*, New Yorker (Sep. 7, 2015), https://www.newyorker.com/magazine/2015/09/07/the-populists.

44 *See, e.g.*, Yascha Mounk, *After Trump, Is American Democracy Doomed by Populism?*, Council on Foreign Relations (Jan. 14, 2021), https://www.cfr.org/in-brief/after-trump-american-democracy-doomed-populism.

45 *See, e.g.*, Sarah Kohler & Isabell Koinig, *The Effect of Science-Related Populism on Vaccination Attitudes and Decisions*, 46 J. Behav. Med. No. 1–2, at 229 (2023).

46 *See, e.g.*, Demetrios G. Papademetriou et al., *In Search of a New Equilibrium: Immigration Policymaking in the Newest Era of Nativist Populism*, Migration Policy Institute (Nov. 2018), https://www.migrationpolicy.org/research/immigration-policymaking-nativist-populism.

47 *See, e.g.*, Lindsay Lloyd, *The Four Horsemen of the Apocalypse: Populism, Nativism, Isolationism, and Protectionism*, George W. Bush Presidential Center (July 21, 2020), https://www.bushcenter.org/publications/the-four-horsemen-of-the-apocalypse-populism-nativism-isolationism-and-protectionism (interview with Condoleezza Rice).

48 *See, e.g.*, Lane Crothers, *The Institutionalist Anti-Populism of the January 6 Committee: A Commentary*, Brill (Feb. 13, 2023), https://brill.com/view/journals/popu/6/1/article-p80_4.xml.

49 *See* Walter Lippmann, Public Opinion (1922).

power of capital, advanced the cause of organized labor, and led battles for policy and political reforms like the graduated income tax and direct election of US senators.[50] Populism, in the sense of that movement, seeks to ground a political program in a credible understanding of what the diverse mass of ordinary human beings needs in order to survive and flourish. That history exposes today's pejorative simplification of "populism" as a shabby rhetorical hustle and a pernicious occlusion of substantive politics. Trump is no populist; he's a megalomaniac, a criminal, and – most politically salient – a model conservative, as servile a bagman for capital as Reagan and sundry Bushes before him. Sanders, in contrast, is indeed a populist, one who, like his nineteenth-century forebears, promotes a specifically left-wing policy program. January 6 wasn't populist; it was incipiently fascist. Anti-vaccine mania isn't populist; it's blinkered and paranoid. Nativism isn't populist; it's . . . well, nativist. Flattening political differences under the damning mantra of "populism" is neoliberal gaslighting. Populism is a mode of political organization, not a substantive political agenda.

On the alarmist account of populism, today's online rabble "does their own research" and then screams whatever they want at the biggest audience they can excite.[51] The fragmented cacophony of online news sources is populism's shrill chorus.[52] On the more historically informed account, today's noninstitutional journalists are "populist" only at their best and despite their limitations. An honest effort to speak of and to the broad US public – working people, communities robust and marginal, people of diverse identities – is something our society sorely needed but rarely got from the last century's institutional news media. Most VIPs at the broadcast networks and newspapers of record were middle-class, white, ideologically centrist men. Most of their audience wasn't. The rise of identity-based liberation movements buckled the institutional media's ramparts, yielding a commercially marginal but dynamic alternative press.[53] At the same time, the institutional media's persistent market power inspired calls for public access to media outlets. Professor Jerome Barron contended that First Amendment law should compel the institutional media to provide platforms for ordinary people with differing perspectives.[54]

[50] *See* Lawrence Goodwyn, The Populist Moment: A Short History of the Agrarian Revolt in America (1978).

[51] *See, e.g.*, Nathan Ballantyne & David Dunning, *Skeptics Say, "Do Your Own Research." It's Not That Simple*, N.Y. Times (Jan. 3, 2022), https://www.nytimes.com/2022/01/03/opinion/dyor-do-your-own-research.html.

[52] *See, e.g.*, Clara Hendrickson & William A. Galston, *Why Are Populists Winning Online? Social Media Reinforces Their Anti-Establishment Message*, Brookings (Apr. 28, 2017), https://www.brookings.edu/articles/why-are-populists-winning-online-social-media-reinforces-their-anti-establishment-message/.

[53] *See* John McMillian, Smoking Typewriters: The Sixties Underground Press and the Rise of Alternative Media in America (2011).

[54] *See* Jerome A. Barron, *An Emerging First Amendment Right of Access to the Media?*, 37 Geo. Wash. L. Rev. 487 (1969); Jerome A. Barron, *Access to the Press – A New First Amendment Right*, 80 Harv. L. Rev. 1641 (1967).

My scholarship has pressed a variation on Barron's argument in the context of twenty-first-century politics and media.[55] Online communication may seem to have obviated the problem of media access. Communication technology lets more speakers than ever before reach large audiences and gives audiences access to more information than anyone can process. As I have emphasized, however, online speech architecture perpetuates and exacerbates economic disparities in speakers' capacities to reach audiences.[56] Social media platforms, search engines, and internet service providers loom even larger over today's communication landscape than the big three networks loomed over the late twentieth century.[57] Rather than directly dictating content, these new intermediaries control the infrastructure through which content travels and commodify the scarce resource of human attention.[58] Accordingly, the struggle for media access has evolved from pursuing airtime to the more complicated task of pursuing a democratic communication architecture. The left pushes net neutrality,[59] the right assails social media platforms' restrictions on hate speech and misinformation,[60] and the new online intermediaries resist all forms of regulation just as doggedly as the last century's intermediaries fought access mandates.

Disaggregated, populist online journalism embodies a form of resistance to concentrated power. At the same time, the dissipation of professional journalistic norms and practices threatens to degrade the news media's democratic function. Working through this tension carries high stakes for our beleaguered democracy. Journalism is ultimately a practice, and that practice must inspire public trust.[61] The news media needs sufficient resources to sustain careers in journalism and fund democratically essential investigative reporting and "deep dives." The media also needs sufficient resilience to weather pressures from government and private power centers. Journalistic coverage needs to extend from the wide world to local neighborhoods. The local end of that coverage needs to transcend the suburbs, where advertisers pan for profit, to reach both neglected urban centers and the diffuse towns in our growing news deserts.[62] Journalism should function not as a system of

[55] *See* Gregory P. Magarian, *Market Triumphalism, Electoral Pathologies, and the Abiding Wisdom of First Amendment Access Rights*, 35 Hofstra L. Rev. 1373 (2007).

[56] *See* Magarian, *supra* note 35, at 2465–69.

[57] *See* Magarian, *supra* note 17, at 250–60.

[58] *See* Tim Wu, *Is the First Amendment Obsolete?*, 117 Mich. L. Rev. 547, 554–57 (2018).

[59] Net neutrality proposals continue to rise and fall with partisan changes in presidential administrations. *See Fact Sheet: FCC Chairwoman Rosenworcel Proposes to Restore Net Neutrality Rules*, FCC Office of the Chairwoman (Sep. 26, 2023), https://docs.fcc.gov/public/attachments/DOC-397235A1.pdf.

[60] *See* Moody v. Netchoice, LLC, No. 22-277 (U.S. July 1, 2024) (slip op.) (remanding First Amendment challenges to Florida and Texas laws that constrain social media platforms' content moderation practices).

[61] *See* Erin C. Carroll, *Promoting Journalism as Method*, 12 Drex. L. Rev. 691 (2020); Sonja R. West, *Press Exceptionalism*, 127 Harv. L. Rev. 2434 (2014).

[62] *See* Abernathy, *supra* note 37.

content delivery to consumers but rather as a source of information for the people. Figuring out how best to satisfy these criteria for journalism will require sustained, critical public attention to the political challenge of optimally balancing reliable institutions and populist energy.

3.3 CONCLUSION

The First Amendment manifests a political choice to promote collective, democratic self-governance through the mechanisms of free speech and a free press. The Constitution, however, leaves much to ponder about what democratic self-governance means and about how the free press can and should contribute to democracy. The twenty-first century has delivered an information tsunami that has shaped many of our present political conflicts. The overwhelming crush of available information offers new opportunities for governments and private oligarchs to exercise dominance. In these political conditions, we struggle to balance our need for objective truth with our awareness of subjective contingency, and we struggle to reconcile the stable certainty of institutionalism with the creative potential of populism. Both of these political struggles must inform our efforts to fortify and enhance the democratic press and to create legal regimes we can trust to protect it.

4

Post-Newspaper Democracy and the Rise of Communicative Citizenship

Good Citizen as Good Communicator

Nik Usher

The answer to the question "What is journalism for?" often turns into a catalog of aspirations. That list might include informing the public, connecting communities, holding power to account, providing guidance and expertise, recording and remembering events, amplifying the voices of the marginalized, serving as a forum for public debate, enlightening readers and viewers, interpreting the complexity of institutions and social life, reflecting on the impact of policies, entertaining audiences, inspiring action, and helping people understand the world beyond their immediate experiences.[1] In reality, of course, journalism often fails to meet these aspirations, just as our actual democracy falls short of our ideal. But even accepting that perfection is never possible, it has become increasingly challenging for journalists today to attempt to meet these democracy-enhancing ideals.

Economic, technological, political, and cultural changes have put at risk the kinds of newsgathering and reporting that feed our civic culture – public affairs and investigative journalism. In the past, the commercial market did not fully support this type of valuable journalism; it was instead subsidized by the larger "newspaper bundle" – the revenue generated by the combination of crosswords, obituaries, and crime, sports, and lifestyle reporting that drove people to subscribe to newspapers.[2] Local newspapers, which have suffered the biggest cuts in journalism, have long served as the keystone for their communities, providing the most significant portion of original news coverage about any one geographically specific place.[3] According to

[1] Jay Rosen used this question as the title for his book. *See* Jay Rosen, What Are Journalists For? (1999). His introduction offers an overview of these arguments. *Id.* at 2–5.

[2] *See* in particular James T. Hamilton, *News Audiences: How Strong Are the Public's Interests in the Public Interest?*, *in* All the News That's Fit to Sell: How the Market Transforms Information into News 71 (2004).

[3] Rasmus Kleis Nielsen, *Local Newspapers as Keystone Media: The Increased Importance of Diminished Newspapers for Local Political Information Environments*, *in* Local Journalism: The Decline of Newspapers and the Rise of Digital Media 51, 51–52 (Rasmus Kleis Nielsen ed., 2015); Matthew Weber et al., Local News on Facebook (2019); *Newspapers Still the Best Bet for Local News*, Sanford Sch. of Pub. Pol'y (Sept. 12, 2019), https://sanford.duke.edu/story/newspapers-still-best-bet-local-news/.

Medill's Local News Initiative, over the fifteen-year span between 2004 and 2019, about 1,800 communities have lost access to regular local news.[4] Pew Research Center estimates that newspaper employment fell 57 percent between 2008 and 2020, while employment in newsrooms dropped 26 percent overall.[5] These declines have real impacts on what news organizations can do to cover communities, with estimates suggesting the annual loss of 300–500 news stories about politics per major metropolitan news outlet.[6] As news organizations are gobbled up by hedge funds looking to sell off distressed assets, they further cut journalism jobs.[7] Newspapers that are still open for business often have little local news reporting at all; some call them "ghost newspapers"[8] because they are visages of their former selves, hanging on with no life to them.

This type of journalism, which might be called the "institutional news media"[9] (although it is often called "mainstream media" by its detractors), has a specific commitment to truth. It serves as a critical institution within civil society and comprises fact-based, truth-seeking journalists and news organizations who see themselves as a part of a profession committed to standards and ethics situated more broadly in democratic norms. As the United States faces the real threat of democratic backsliding,[10] it becomes increasingly clear that the current commercial news media simply lacks the power and capacity to facilitate the development of the "informed citizen" who is foundational to liberal democratic ideals.[11] But if the informed citizen model implodes – thanks to factionalism, decaying trust in institutions, and digital platforms that further undermine media economics – what, then, is left?

This chapter argues for the need to reconceptualize citizenship in an era when professional journalism plays a significantly diminished role in directly shaping our

4 *See* Penelope Muse Abernathy, *News Deserts and Ghost Newspapers: Will Local News Survive?*, Hussman Sch. of Journalism and Media (2020), https://www.usnewsdeserts.com/reports/news-deserts-and-ghost-newspapers-will-local-news-survive/the-news-landscape-in-2020-transformed-and-diminished/.

5 Mason Walker, *U.S. Newsroom Employment Has Fallen 26% Since 2008*, Pew Rsch. Ctr. (July 13, 2021), https://www.pewresearch.org/short-reads/2021/07/13/u-s-newsroom-employment-has-fallen-26-since-2008/.

6 Erik Peterson, *Paper Cuts: How Reporting Resources Affect Political News Coverage*, 65 Am. J. Pol. Sci. 443 (2021) (*see* the abstract for an overview).

7 Erik Peterson & Johanna Dunaway, *The New News Barons: Investment Ownership Reduces Newspaper Reporting Capacity*, 707 Annals Am. Acad. Pol. & Soc. Sci. 1, 74–89 (2023).

8 *See* Margaret Sullivan, *News Deserts, Ghost Papers, and Beacons of Hope*, *in* Ghosting the News: Local Journalism and the Crisis of American Democracy (2020); *see also* Abernathy, *supra* note 4.

9 Stephen D. Reese, *The Crisis of the Institutional Press*, in The Crisis of the Institutional Press 1 (2020).

10 Steven Levitsky & Daniel Ziblatt, *Gatekeeping in America*, *in* How Democracies Die 33 (2018).

11 Michael Schudson, *Reluctant Stewards: Journalism in a Democratic Society*, 142 Daedalus 159 (2013). *See also* Barbie Zelizer, *On the Shelf Life of Democracy in Journalism Scholarship*, 14 Journalism 459 (2013).

news and information environment, especially at the local level. First, I make the case that we must consider what it means to live in a post-newspaper democracy. In a time of market failure for local news, both journalists and the public need to identify which functions are unique to professional journalism as a civic institution.[12] Second, I join others who have argued that we need to move away from the concept of the "good citizen"[13] as only a consumer of information/voter as their form of civic participation. Instead, I call for reimagining citizenship with communication at its center. Within this theory of "communicative citizenship," a good citizen plays the civic role of communicator, not as a replacement for journalists, but instead as a facilitator of the flow of reliable civic information from institutions to their fellow community members. If we accept that newspapers and for-profit, digital-first news outlets face an uphill battle to survive, yet we believe that their function is essential to democratic life, then perhaps it is possible to shift some of the responsibility for fulfilling these functions from newspapers to the people themselves.

4.1 THE POST-NEWSPAPER DEMOCRACY

The post-newspaper democracy is not a democracy without newspapers; rather, it is a democracy wherein newspapers can no longer take on all the roles we might hope. Still, newspaper journalism is inspirational: At its best, it is a benchmark to measure the expertise, ethics, and impact that professional journalism can have on society. If we think about the *best* that newspapers promise, we can also identify what is special about professional journalism itself, demarcating the expertise that ordinary people are unlikely to replicate in their own efforts in gathering and sharing news and information. As I have discussed in previous work, especially my book, *News for the Rich, White, and Blue: How Place and Power Distort American Journalism*,[14] a post-newspaper democracy takes seriously the reality that the model of civic life in which people are united together in an imagined community via what Benedict Anderson calls "print capitalism" is now over.[15] While we may lament the decline of newspapers and what that means for democracy, we may actually be mourning the loss of the *role* that newspaper journalism plays in civic life. Just because the local newspaper as we know it may be over in its functional form does not mean we have to give up on what newspapers bring to the civic imagination. Rather, we should focus on identifying the unique values that journalism, and no other social

[12] Nikki Usher, News for the Rich, White, and Blue: How Place and Power Distort American Journalism 237 (2021).

[13] *See* Michael Schudson, The Good Citizen: A History of American Civic Life 309–12 (2011).

[14] Usher, *supra* note 12.

[15] Benedict Anderson, Imagined Communities: Reflections on the Origin and Spread of Nationalism (2016) (*see* especially pages 22–36).

institution, provides and then on supporting those special attributes of journalistic professionalism and authority. This, in turn, helps us reimagine civic life with communication at the center, including how we practice citizenship and social organizing.

What unique roles do journalists, supported by news organizations, fulfill that make them different from other professions? Professions are defined as specialized jurisdictions over particular forms of work and are bounded by the unique tasks they perform that other professions cannot. They are then granted legal, institutional, and cultural license to do this work.[16] Because journalism is their full-time job, professional journalists are able to be physically present in places and at events that we cannot personally experience. They then share with the rest of us what they deem important for us to know in order to live our daily lives and make informed decisions. Journalists also get to be expert translators, interpreting complicated information that demands subject-matter expertise into insights for ordinary people.[17] While journalists do not always do this perfectly, most of us do not have time to comb through legislation, read scientific articles, and talk to experts about topics of public import. Journalists do this labor for the rest of us. With the concept of professional jurisdiction in mind, I see two roles of professional journalism that need to remain separate from what ordinary people might do in their roles as citizen communicators:

(1) investigative work/monitoring of powerful institutions, and
(2) voicing or centering the concerns of the most marginalized in public discourse.

First, journalists are best positioned to do the work of covering the powerful via routine inquiry and investigative projects. This work requires journalists to be in places that ordinary people cannot: at press conferences, in statehouses outside the reach of anyone without an ID badge, and even past airport security without having to fly anywhere. A press pass permits journalists entry into places where the powerful do their work, giving them a deep understanding of these inner workings.[18] Sharing this knowledge with the public requires skills that most people, even the best citizen communicators, may not have. Industry experts may have knowledge and even independence from the institutions and industries they are a part of, but making these insights understandable requires translation skills, converting complex ideas into words, pictures, sounds, and graphics to make them more understandable for

[16] *See* Andrew Abbott, The System of Professions: An Essay on the Division of Expert Labor 59–60, 86–90 (1988).

[17] Nicole Gesualdo et al., *Journalists as Knowledge Brokers*, 21 Journalism Stud. 127 (2020) (*see* the abstract for a most concise overview).

[18] Nikki Usher, *Using Unexpected Data to Study Up: Washington Political Journalism (and the Case of the Missing Press Pass)*, *in* Research Exposed: How Empirical Social Science Gets Done in the Digital Age 123 (Eszter Hargittai ed., 2021).

ordinary people. At their best, journalists have these translation skills to explain how people, power, and money can impact institutions and, ultimately, the public. In short, journalists tell stories about complicated issues and organizations that generally would not welcome an outsider's regular scrutiny.

Journalists, in turn, benefit from heightened legal protections for their activities.[19] When they are employed at news organizations, journalists (and we, as news consumers) also benefit from layers of editing, verification, fact-checking,[20] and, most importantly, independence. At least in theory, journalists will not get fired for holding institutions accountable when they are not beholden to them for employment. Despite critiques about journalists being embedded in power structures, they at least do not have to raise money from special interest groups to support an election campaign or to depend on a corrupt city government for their next paycheck.

This independence gives journalists a second critical role in civic life: the capacity to direct the public gaze by revealing injustice and holding truth to power. As "custodians of conscience," journalists can draw our attention to shared normative concerns that appeal to human dignity rather than partisan identity.[21] They remind us that children should not be abused, businesses should not knowingly harm employees or customers, politicians should not steal money, and, fundamentally, that the American democratic project, despite its imperfections, is worth supporting. Journalists, then, serve the role of connected amplifier and public conscience for human dignity. By turning systemic injustice into digestible narratives for public consumption, journalists can help amplify marginalized voices.

Unfortunately, the market failure of journalism jeopardizes the ability of journalists to draw attention to those most hurt by the excesses of institutional power.[22] As I argue in *News for the Rich, White, and Blue*, people from marginalized communities are even less likely to become journalists as jobs in the industry become ever more unstable.[23] Those with fewer resources lack a safety net if they lose their journalism jobs, and newsrooms have failed to make meaningful gains in diversity and equity over the past twenty years.[24] Moreover, marginalized groups

[19] RonNell Andersen Jones, *Media Subpoenas: Impact, Perception, and Legal Protection in the Changing World of American Journalism*, 84 Wash. L. Rev. 317, 348 (2009).

[20] Marju Himma-Kadakas & Indrek Ojamets, *Debunking False Information: Investigating Journalists' Fact-Checking Skills*, 10 Digit. Journalism 866, 848 (2022), https://www.tandfonline.com/doi/pdf/10.1080/21670811.2022.2043173.

[21] James S. Ettema & Theodore L. Glasser, Custodians of Conscience: Investigative Journalism and Public Virtue 3–4 (1998).

[22] Victor Pickard, America's Battle for Media Democracy: The Triumph of Corporate Libertarianism and the Future of Media Reform 212–31 (2014).

[23] As per Pew Research Center: "In 2020 alone, a third of large newspapers in the U.S. experienced layoffs, and as of August 2020, nearly 2,800 newspaper companies had received federal aid through the Paycheck Protection Program," Walker, *supra* note 5.

[24] Sakshi Venkatraman, *How the Journalism Industry Obstructs Lower Income People*, Wash. Square News (Sept. 3, 2019), https://nyunews.com/opinion/2019/09/02/journalism-obstacles-

are considered an audience that is unlikely to pay for news or support it philanthropically,[25] making it more difficult to tell these stories and maintain fidelity to the experiences of people in marginalized communities.

The specific professional jurisdiction of journalism is not so much that it informs people of important happenings in the community or knits communities together in a shared sense of place and purpose.[26] The best use of journalists' special expertise is to speak truth to power through investigative journalism and as custodians of conscience. Particularly in a time of scarce resources, journalists might forego chronicling the day-to-day and attempting to centralize the distribution of community knowledge – for example, spreading word that an event is taking place or a new municipal rule is being considered – because many other organizations can step in to fill basic information needs, from schools to churches to local government.[27] In fact, the ability of civic institutions other than journalism to inform the public has grown, and these institutions now have the ability to create and share stories about particular places and their present and past in ways that create identity, belonging, a shared sense of purpose, and cultural memories for communities. But thus far, we have overlooked another group who can also contribute to their local news environment and help mitigate the declines in local journalism – individual citizens.

4.2 DEMOCRACY AND THE EVERYDAY STORYTELLER

Most democratic theory tends to imagine journalism as a critical institution for transmitting the information people need to live their daily lives and make informed choices. But this transmission view of communication – the view that messages travel from point A to point B and, in turn, lead to attitude or behavioral changes – is a simplistic understanding that fails to capture the role of communication and citizenship as integral parts of community life. Scholar James Carey juxtaposed this transmission view, which roots communication in message transference, with the

low-income-inaccessibility/; Amanda Dejesus, *Despite Big Commitments to Improve Diversity, Newsrooms' Progress Remains Slow*, Latino Rep. (Aug. 4, 2022), http://latinoreporter.org/2022/big-commitments-improve-diversity-newsrooms-progress-remains-slow/.

25 Meredith D. Clark & Tracie M. Powell, *Architects of Necessity: BIPOC News Startups' Critique of Philanthropic Interventions*, 13 ISOJ J. 115 (2023), https://isoj.org/research/architects-of-necessity/.

26 Although I've argued elsewhere that this might *be* the most important role of journalists, I'm increasingly not sure that it is the best use of journalists' limited resources, as public holders of memory can extend beyond newsrooms. *See* Usher, *supra* note 18, at 234; *see also* Nikki Usher, *Putting "Place" in the Center of Journalism Research: A Way Forward to Understand Challenges to Trust and Knowledge in News*, 21 Journalism & Commc'n Monographs 84 (2019) (especially page 86 for an overview).

27 *See* Nikki Usher, *The Real Problems with the Problem of News Deserts: Toward Rooting Place, Precision, and Positionality in Scholarship on Local News and Democracy*, 40 Pol. Commc'n 238 (2023).

ritual view of communication.[28] Under the ritual view, communication, which shares a philological root with community, can also bring people together in a shared experience of the world around them. Ritual communication is part and parcel of the cultural practice of living in a community and sharing stories about who we are and what we value. While information is being transferred and messages are being communicated, the process is embedded in forms that are shared across individuals within a community rather than being atomized into units of individual consumption.

Different forms of democracy center on different communication regimes. Scholar C. Edwin Baker theorized that in elite democracy, journalism functions as a watchdog for the powerful and focuses on the actions and sanctions of other empowered actors while being less focused on informing ordinary people.[29] In contrast, liberal democracy centers on the atomized individual as a rights-bearing, informed citizen, with journalism serving as the primary definer of discourse in the public sphere. In this model, the good citizen is an informed citizen who turns to journalism for guidance about their civic participation. But this is not a model of citizenship that makes sense when there are decreasing sources of professional local news and information and when many Americans simply do not trust professional journalism.[30] Moreover, this form of democracy centers the individual as the ultimate authority for sensemaking, displacing the role of community as the setting and context through which people make sense of the world.

However, Baker's theory of representative democracy moves beyond the individual citizen and conceives of pluralism and communitarian beneficence as central goals of democratic life. In this mode, journalism is but one of many ways for people to communicate. Art, poetry, movies, entertainment, public forums, and interpersonal communication are all forms of communication that knit together people across differences into a shared cultural project of representative pluralist democracy.[31] Taken together, Carey and Baker support the idea that the news a representative democracy needs goes beyond just information; it also requires ritual communication grounded in community, with shared knowledge coming from journalism as well as other social institutions and interpersonal communication. This communitarian ethos is also pragmatic. If democracy is instantiated in discourse, the public sphere cannot maintain its dependency on journalism to facilitate the public's broader conversation,[32] especially given journalism's precarious financial model and public distrust in its legitimacy.

[28] James W. Carey, *A Cultural Approach to Communication*, 2 Commc'n 1 (1975), *reprinted in* James W. Carey, Communication as Culture 13 (1989).

[29] C. Edwin Baker, Media Concentration and Democracy: Why Ownership Matters (2006).

[30] Sara Fischer, *Americans' Trust in Media Plummets to Historic Low: Poll*, Axios (Oct. 24, 2023), https://www.axios.com/2023/10/24/americans-trust-in-media-plummets-to-historic-low-poll.

[31] Baker, *supra* note 29, at 129–53. Baker calls this "complex democracy."

[32] *See* journalism as not conversation: Michael Schudson, *Why Conversation Is Not the Soul of Democracy*, 14 Critical Stud. in Media Commc'n 297 (1997) (Carey in support on page 300).

4.3 COMMUNICATIVE CITIZENSHIP

To address the challenges facing democratic life as professional journalism faces market failure, I want to introduce the concepts of "communicative citizenship" and the "citizen communicator." This is a new approach that I have begun, theorizing about what ordinary people can do to more actively participate in creating an informed public sphere through and by communication. In the US context, the term "citizenship" can be problematic because it has too often been used as a gatekeeping mechanism for entry and access to participation and representation in government.[33] But given the association between citizenship as a word and its connotation of a shared responsibility in political life, the word remains a powerful way to describe buy-in to a common set of normative assumptions and values about democratic life.[34] Embracing my framing of "communicative citizenship" enables a more affective understanding of citizenship. Communicative citizenship is also a feeling – in the sense that people who do not know each other but share some defining characteristic, such as where they are physically located, can develop a sense of belonging beyond a mere legalistic relationship.[35] Communicative citizenship retains some of the fundamental premises of the informed citizen model of democracy, namely that good information is necessary to make informed decisions. However, it shifts some of the burden to ordinary people instead of depending on local newspapers to do the job in our communities. The good citizen centers on communication, not just information transfer, as an essential element of performing citizenship.

Communicative citizenship, embodied by citizen communicators, invokes the capacity of ordinary people to use "talk" to help strengthen their local information environments. This is achieved through a more intentional approach to their day-to-day engagement with their communities via both digital and physical spaces; civic institutions, friends, family, and geographically proximate strangers; and the built environment. Certainly not everyone has the same ability or desire to talk about shared concerns, especially with unfamiliar people and given entrenched power inequalities.[36] The realization of communicative citizenship is thus limited by the inequalities that plague democratic life more generally. Nonetheless, in their ideal form, the communicative citizen brings with them a willingness to talk about issues and concerns that matter to the community-level public sphere. They strive to be as

[33] Erika Lee, *A Nation of Immigrants and a Gatekeeping Nation: American Immigration Law and Policy*, *in* A Companion to American Immigration 3 (Reed Ueda ed., 2006) (*see* especially page 13).

[34] Carrie Hyde, Civic Longing: The Speculative Origins of US Citizenship 7 (2018).

[35] Cara Wong, *Community & Special Obligations*, *in* Boundaries of Obligation: Geographic, Racial, and National Communities 1 (2010).

[36] Nancy Fraser, *Rethinking the Public Sphere: A Contribution to the Critique of Actually Existing Democracy*, *in* 25/26 Social Text 56, 56–80 (1990).

informed as possible to effectively engage in dialogue with others about how to understand and solve community problems.

Citizen communicators are critical agents in helping others around them fulfill their critical information needs, or "those forms of information that are necessary for citizens and community members to live safe and healthy lives; have full access to educational, employment, and business opportunities; and to fully participate in the civic and democratic lives of their communities should they choose."[37] Communicative citizenship has three central pillars: the multifaceted role of the communicative citizen, the utilization of digital technology, and the purposeful use of communication. The communicative citizen serves as the sender, receiver, node, and infrastructure in the communication process, leveraging digital technology to amplify their efforts and employing communication to foster solidarity and a shared commitment to a hopeful vision for a better future.

4.3.1 *The Good Citizen as Sender and Receiver for Community Information Needs*

As both senders and receivers of news and information, ordinary people can take on a more deliberate and intentional role by actively surveilling local institutions, businesses, and localized spaces of civil society and passing on this knowledge to others. Communication theory has long recognized that certain individuals, often the heavy media consumers, become "opinion leaders" for their friends and family.[38] Information overload – from digital entertainment content, ads, peak TV, digital news content, social media messaging, search results, and more – is real.[39] Through their voracious and omnivorous news consumption, opinion leaders help their friends and family by filtering out irrelevant content and sharing the information they believe is essential. Opinion leaders are the people in your life who write long Facebook posts before elections about local candidates, send you reminders about various school deadlines, tell you when it is restaurant week, let you know when local politicians are in town, and so forth. Perhaps you are this person. As local newspapers are less able to comprehensively cover communities, this role becomes critically important because, without it, people will simply have to work even harder on their own to seek out the information they need.

Communicative citizenship goes one step beyond the news. For instance, when a new school board issue arises, journalists can help direct attention to the issue and explain where to find more information about the concern. But even if the journalist

37 Lewis Friedland et al., Review of the Literature Regarding Critical Information Needs of the American Public 5 (2012).

38 Elihu Katz, *True Stories*, 608 Annals Am. Acad. Pol. & Soc. Sci. 301, 301 (2006).

39 David Bawden & Lyn Robinson, *Information Overload: An Overview*, *in* Oxford Encyclopedia of Political Decision Making 4 (David P. Redlawsk ed., 2020), https://openaccess.city.ac.uk/id/eprint/23544/1/information%20overload%20-%20an%20overview.pdf.

has not been able to fully interrogate the news story and the issue at hand, the community does not have to step back and suffer from a deficit in news. Rather, people who have the capacity to learn more, interrogate further, and share this information play a critical role in filling the gaps that journalists cannot address. For instance, a community member with legal or accounting expertise can spend some extra time reviewing documents to assess various concerns about problematic expenditures or conflicts of interest. Not everyone will be able to be a citizen communicator, and even those who can be citizen communicators are unlikely to be generalists. Most will likely be subject-matter experts on issues they follow; one person might know the intricacies of park permitting while another may know the best way to deal with local utility companies, among many, many examples. Regardless, the good citizen of today has shifting opportunities to focus their energy on gathering, analyzing, filtering, and sharing information that is valuable to their community.

4.3.2 *The Communicative Citizen as Node and Infrastructure*

As node and infrastructure for community information needs, the citizen communicator is the interpersonal glue that connects people to other individuals, sources of professional news and information, organizations, and civic institutions or associations. Sandra Ball-Rokeach and her colleagues at the University of Southern California developed the "communication infrastructure theory," which conceives of these connections as a "storytelling network" embodied in "communication action contexts."[40] In other words, the spaces of communication are materially instantiated by people and places – not just as text, images, or sounds transferred, most often, via electronic or digital media. In this theory of community-distributed information and service sharing, physical experiences of place and space are critical, specifically third spaces like public libraries,[41] schools, coffee shops, post offices, hospitals, and other "structural infrastructure" of civil society. Empirical evidence supports the notion that stronger storytelling networks are connected to more robust measures of civic efficacy, better resilience among historically marginalized groups, and a stronger sense of community belonging, even across racial and ethnic differences.[42]

Communities that prioritize communication among people and places, across a variety of social institutions, and as a natural outgrowth of day-to-day experience can help bolster democratic culture. A key entry point for citizen communicators is to

[40] Yong-Chan Kim & Sandra J. Ball-Rokeach, *Civic Engagement from a Communication Infrastructure Perspective*, 16 Commc'n Theory 173 (2006); Yong-Chan Kim et al., *"Geo-ethnicity" and Neighborhood Engagement: A Communication Infrastructure Perspective*, Pol. Commc'n 421, 422 (2006).

[41] Eric Klinenberg, Palaces for the People: How Social Infrastructure Can Help Fight Polarization, and the Decline of Civic Life 16 (2018).

[42] Kim & Ball-Rokeach, *supra* note 40; Sandra J. Ball-Rokeach, *Storytelling Neighborhood: Paths to Belonging in Diverse Urban Environments*, 28 Commc'n Rsch. 392, 410 (2001).

consider how to reintroduce temporality, materiality, and common concerns into conversations that take place between people who live and work in geographically bounded communities. Citizen communicators can connect other people to storytelling networks and the stories that matter to them, as well as to the organizations that can help them find out more. Indeed, we can conceive of democratic life as the outgrowth of storytelling networks, where individuals, organizations, and media together serve as nodes of connection between people, places, and the resources individuals need to navigate everyday life.[43] As a result, information transfer does not need to be entirely professionalized but can be embedded in the fabric of everyday interactions as people engage in their daily lives, existing in shared spaces outside their individual dwellings and experiencing the serendipity of accidental encounters with new people and experiences. While we may not all be journalists, as homo narrans,[44] we are all storytellers. The capacity to share stories with others about experiences and perspectives they have not yet encountered is the starting point for thinking of communication as a central aspect of citizenship.

As nodes in a storytelling network, ordinary people bring together a diverse set of connections through their unique daily experiences. When these connections are activated to link and inform others who lack these same ties and domain-specific knowledge, ordinary people can also help bolster the infrastructure of the communication context in which they live. This infrastructure support comes through simple acts like sharing an email address or phone number or mentioning the name of a relevant organization to help another person meet a critical information need and, in turn, better navigate daily life. While our casual accumulated knowledge from the industries we work in or the places where we spend our leisure time is rarely thought of as useful in the service of citizenship, this folk expertise is the "node" – the knowledge hub that the citizen communicator can leverage. This is where the citizen communicator can shine: Our everyday engagement in politics is not so much political as it is civic.[45] Those who have leisure time and work in knowledge sector positions may need to be more intentional and confident about both their community knowledge and their efficacy in being the first stop for connecting not only friends and family but also acquaintances or even strangers.

4.3.3 *Citizen Communicators Mobilize Technology to Serve People, Not Profits*

When it comes to community life, communicative citizenship recenters the exchange of ideas and information away from the atomized digital ecosystem and

[43] Nikki Usher et al., *Media Policy for an Informed Citizenry: Revisiting the Information Needs of Communities for Democracy in Crisis*, 707 Annals Am. Acad. Pol. & Soc. Sci. 8, 13 (2023).

[44] Walter R. Fisher, *Narration, Reason, and Community*, *in* Writing the Social Text 199 (Richard Brown ed., 2017).

[45] Nancy L. Rosenblum, Good Neighbors: The Democracy of Everyday Life in America 234–36 (2016).

returns it to a space of collective sensemaking. The attention economy monetizes individualized acts of information consumption – one click, one user.[46] This mass individual content consumption – a "for you" that also appears in feeds of another one million people or more – is a false promise of collective experience. The targeted audience is imagined as an individual alone but at scale, with individuals making (forced) choices about information consumption and distribution as atomized units. Finding more individualized and customized ways to keep users on a site[47] requires fine-tuning algorithmic weights from an individual user's historical data matched with real-time preferences to be more precisely targeted to goose the dopamine of one person.

Communicative citizenship shifts the burden of citizenship from the individual to the collective and uses digital and physical spaces to counter platform power. The citizen communicator can augment community information ecologies by being physically present in places journalists can no longer go to because of resource constraints, such as school board meetings or high school football games. Ordinary people can use digital platforms like Facebook and WhatsApp to provide essential follow-ups, including posting conversations in community forums, sharing information among their friends and family, or using their spare time to ask new questions or connect people to additional resources. Collective sensemaking can happen through various channels, such as Facebook community pages, Nextdoor forums, community listservs, WhatsApp groups, and, most importantly, physical spaces for meeting and speaking about problems, concerns, and opportunities within communities or for celebrating the wins.

Digital platforms help the citizen communicator do the work of communication at scale. But one major challenge is that platform companies do not care about informed citizens; they care about maximizing their profits. The more time we spend on their sites (and thus the more data we share), the more money these companies can reap from the digital attention economy. Platform companies like Meta have de-emphasized local news, and local news about politics is often the least engaged content on Facebook.[48]

But demand still drives algorithmic discovery. As people search for content and reward the activities and posts of citizen communicators on digital platforms, our hunger for more information can help tilt the algorithmic black box to work *for* us. Here arises yet another critical role for the citizen communicator: educating others about algorithmic inequality and the power imbalances on platforms, which are often perceived as neutral brokers when they are not. Indeed, citizen communicators can help others establish greater knowledge and agency over how they use

[46] Siva Vaidhyanathan, *The Attention Machine, in* Antisocial Media: How Facebook Disconnects Us and Undermines Democracy 79 (2018).

[47] Nitasha Tiku, *The WIRED Guide to Internet Addiction*, WIRED (Apr. 18, 2018), https://www.wired.com/story/wired-guide-to-internet-addiction/.

[48] Weber et al., *supra* note 3.

digital platforms, directing others about how to be more deliberate in how they search for and engage with digital content.

There are modest movements afoot to reimagine digital infrastructure as public, such as alternative channels of publicly funded platforms.[49] While I do not see this effort as likely to catch on outside of the already existing platform infrastructure (in part due to network effects and the fact that people are already on commercial platforms), I do see another window to facilitate communicative citizenship. One regulatory option may be to create on these corporate platforms more algorithmically optimized, community-driven sites, many of which already exist in our communities. I can imagine how the town Facebook group can be institutionalized within legal frameworks through similar regulatory reasoning that the Federal Communications Commission (FCC) uses for licensing radio and television: A station should support "public interest, convenience and necessity."[50] Platform companies might similarly be required to work within this ethic for the public, facilitating civic information discovery through some sort of favorable algorithmic weighting.

Intentionally claiming these digitally mediated public spaces as places of dialogue helps to dislodge the responsibility put on individuals to do all the work alone, with the scales tilted against them as they are uniquely targeted for their preferences. Thus, a major reorientation from individual acts of content consumption to recognizing the collective power of communities sharing and engaging with media content, whether about civic life or something else, is a critical part of this new imagined citizenship.

4.4 CITIZEN COMMUNICATORS AND SOLIDARITY

Citizenship is often understood primarily through the lens of politics and political institutions[51] rather than the relationships that we have with each other and the communities around us. Because the state grants citizenship, it is also often framed as conditional, implying that citizens "owe" something to the state in exchange for being given the autonomy to help chart its direction.[52] This may include voting, being informed, and engaging with the community.[53] But the concept of the informed citizen has always been more of an ideal than a reality, particularly because being informed requires time, access, and the capacity to comprehend

[49] Ethan Zuckerman, *The Case for Digital Public Infrastructure*, 20-01 Knight First Amend. Inst. (Jan. 17, 2020), https://knightcolumbia.org/content/the-case-for-digital-public-infrastructure.

[50] Federal Communications Commission, *The Public and Broadcasting* 4 (Sept. 2021), https://www.fcc.gov/sites/default/files/public_and_broadcasting_0.pdf.

[51] *See generally* Hyde, *supra* note 34.

[52] Richard Haass, The Bill of Obligations: The Ten Habits of Good Citizens 14–15 (2023).

[53] *Id.*

and discern key insights for civic action amid a cacophony of strategic actors trying to influence the information available.

When good citizenship centers the role of communication, and the aim of that communication is to help connect others to navigate civic life and to engage more fully in their communities, the focus of democratic life shifts from cause-to-cause interactions to strengthening person-to-person community ties. Unfortunately, performing citizenship is a privilege accorded to those who have the time and the capacity to think beyond immediate survival needs. The reality of citizenship in a capitalist society is that not all citizens are able to participate equally due to structural inequalities such as racism, poverty, limited access to civic institutions, and other barriers. But talk is cheap, and people do have expertise about their own lives. The most marginalized members of our polity have valuable insights that those of us with more privilege need to hear. While the ability to communicate in a normative way also creates barriers, conversation may be the most direct way of connecting people with nothing in common. In this regard, citizenship that centers communication and refocuses our attention on people's agency to engage in the transfer of interpersonal knowledge becomes a building block for realizing a representative democracy that fosters pluralism, tolerance, and a shared commitment to hope for a better future.

5

"Murder the Media"

Press Freedom, Violence, and the Public Sphere

Joseph Blocher

The U.S. Justice Department recently estimated that the January 6 riot inflicted roughly $2.7 million in damages to the Capitol building and Capitol police.[1] Presumably, only a minuscule amount of those damages – perhaps a few dollars' worth of strong solvent or paint – are attributed to addressing the words "MURDER THE MEDIA" that were scrawled in permanent marker on the Capitol's Memorial Door. "Elders" of the far-right group the Proud Boys had left the ominous message in homage to their social media channel by the same name.[2] Yet the actual damages of this threat to the press and, by extension, the public, are surely much more significant. How, though, does one fully account for the damage that threats and violence against the media inflict, or for its causes?

On January 6, at least eighteen journalists were assaulted;[3] some later shared harrowing accounts of their experiences.[4] Outside the building, tens of thousands of dollars of press equipment was destroyed by a mob that posed for pictures with its handiwork.[5] Threats or harm to journalists are hardly limited to that day and place. A few years earlier and less than an hour's drive away in Maryland, five employees of the Annapolis Capital Gazette were murdered by a man who had unsuccessfully

[1] *Twenty-four Months Since the January 6 Attack on the Capitol*, U.S. Att'y's Office D.C. (Jan. 4, 2023), https://www.justice.gov/usao-dc/18-months-jan-6-attack-capitol.

[2] Spencer S. Hsu & Rachel Weiner, *Proud Boys Who Scrawled 'Murder the Media' at Capitol Plead Guilty*, Wash. Post (Sept. 9, 2022), https://www.washingtonpost.com/dc-md-va/2022/09/09/proud-boys-murder-media-capitol-jan6/. The Memorial Door is dedicated to two officers who died defending the Capitol against an armed intruder in 1988. *Id.*

[3] *Charges – and Punishments – for J6 Rioters Who Hurt Journalists, Damaged News Equipment*, U.S. Press Freedom Tracker, https://pressfreedomtracker.us/blog/charges-and-punishments-for-j6-rioters-who-hurt-journalists-damaged-news-equipment/ (last visited Dec. 8, 2023).

[4] Nicholas Fandos et al., *'Senate Being Locked Down': Inside a Harrowing Day at the Capitol*, N.Y. Times (Jan. 7, 2021), https://www.nytimes.com/2021/01/07/us/politics/capitol-lockdown.html.

[5] *'Murder the Media': What the Jan. 6 Attack on the Capitol Meant for US Journalists*, Committee to Protect Journalists (Jan. 6, 2023), https://cpj.org/2023/01/murder-the-media-what-the-jan-6-attack-on-the-capitol-meant-for-u-s-journalists/.

sued the paper after it reported on his alleged harassment of a former classmate.[6] Fifteen journalists have been killed in the United States in recent decades,[7] and one recent report counted 142 assaults on journalists in the United States in 2021 alone.[8] Highlighting the nation's failure to protect journalists, Reporters Without Borders recently declared that the United States is "no longer a champion of press freedom, either at home or abroad."[9]

Against that broad backdrop, this chapter has two aims. The first is to argue that the press as an institution is entitled to special solicitude under the First Amendment, not only because it is textually specified in the Constitution[10] or because it serves important roles, such as checking public and private power,[11] but because it can contribute to the marketplace of ideas in ways that a healthy democracy needs. In other words, the press as an institution can provide an important link between the First Amendment's epistemic and democratic values.

The chapter's second goal is to provide a rough and preliminary sketch of the relationship between press freedom, violence, and public discourse. Some elements seem straightforward enough. Violence and harassment obstruct the press's function,[12] including its traditional role in constituting and shaping public discourse.[13] But other elements of the relationship are more complex. Distrust, disinformation, violence, and press degradation exist in a mutually reinforcing ecosystem. And even as violence shapes the media, the media shapes the social conditions,

6 Lynh Bui et al., *Jarrod Ramos Admits Killing Five in Capital Gazette Newsroom Attack*, Wash. Post (Oct. 28, 2019), https://www.washingtonpost.com/local/public-safety/jarrod-ramos-admits-guilt-in-capital-gazette-shooting-that-killed-5/2019/10/28/39bcd226-f990-11e9-ac8c-8eced29ca6ef_story.html.

7 Margaux Ewen & Lara Shane, *Crimes against Journalists Are on the Rise and Are Seldom Punished*, Freedom House (Nov. 2, 2022), https://freedomhouse.org/article/crimes-against-journalists-are-rise-and-are-seldom-punished; *The Free Flow of Ideas: Freedom of the Press, the Journalists on the Frontline*, UNESCO (May 11, 2023), https://www.unesco.org/en/threats-freedom-press-violence-disinformation-censorship.

8 Kirstin McCudden, *Another Record Year for Press-Freedom Violations in the U.S.*, Colum. Journalism Rev. (Jan. 12, 2022), https://www.cjr.org/analysis/2021-press-freedom-prior-restraint-arrests.php.

9 Megan Specia, *In Turnabout, Global Leaders Urge U.S. to Protect Reporters amid Unrest*, N.Y. Times (Aug. 10, 2020), https://www.nytimes.com/2020/06/04/world/attacks-press-george-floyd.html.

10 Potter Stewart, *'Or of the Press'*, 26 Hastings L.J. 631, 633 (1975) (calling the press "the only organized private business that is given explicit constitutional protection").

11 Mills v. Alabama, 384 U.S. 214, 219 (1966) ("The Constitution specifically selected the press ... to play an important role in the discussion of public affairs. Thus, the press serves and was designed to serve as a powerful antidote to any abuses of power by governmental officials and as a constitutionally chosen means for keeping officials elected by the people responsible to all the people whom they were selected to serve.").

12 Erin C. Carroll, *Obstruction of Journalism*, 99 Denver L. Rev. 407 (2022) (detailing "how violence obstructs journalism ... on at least three levels: the story, the beat, and the pipeline").

13 *Cf.* Robert C. Post, Democracy, Expertise, and Academic Freedom: A First Amendment Jurisprudence for the Modern State 18 (2012); Robert Post, *Participatory Democracy and Free Speech*, 97 Va. L. Rev. 477, 482, 486 (2011).

understanding, and practice of violence in return. Journalism, albeit in different ways than legal interpretation,[14] "takes place on a field of pain and death," to repurpose Robert Cover's famous phrase – not only in describing it but in making it real. This, it should go without saying, is no excuse for violence *against* media members. The point is, rather, that a healthy press can be a bulwark not only for knowledge and democracy but against the kinds of private and public violence that threaten both.

The First Amendment, and constitutional law more broadly,[15] must grapple with violence – not merely its rhetorical reliance on violent metaphors,[16] but the ways in which interpersonal violence shapes democratic institutions and the public sphere. As Erin Carroll observes: "Violence against journalists is a means of controlling the boundaries of legitimate public discourse."[17] And as Reva Siegel and I have argued elsewhere,[18] if a democracy cannot establish the boundaries of violence, then violence will end up establishing the boundaries of democracy – including the freedom of the press.

5.1 KNOWLEDGE, DEMOCRACY, AND THE PRESS

Many of the First Amendment's paradigmatic scenes involve a lone speaker[19] – sometimes wise and eloquent, sometimes horrible and profane – and the freedom of speech is of course an individual right, exercised to a variety of autonomous ends. But free speech is ultimately embedded in social practices and can only be understood and analyzed in terms of the social values it serves. As for what those values are, some point to the role of speech in protecting or enabling democracy, others to

[14] *Cf.* Robert M. Cover, *Violence and the Word*, 96 YALE L.J. 1601 (1986) ("Legal interpretation takes place in a field of pain and death.").

[15] *See, e.g.*, Farah Peterson, *Our Constitutionalism of Force*, 122 COLUM. L. REV. 1539, 1549–50 (2022) ("[I]t is nonetheless impossible to fully account for the ordering of our society or for the interpretation of the textual Constitution without also understanding that violence has at times fueled the Constitution's evolution and defined the limits of constitutional amendment by more formal means.").

[16] Erin C. Carroll, *The Violence of Free Speech and Press Metaphors*, WASH & LEE L. REV. (forthcoming 2024) (identifying and exploring the use of violence metaphors in free speech law and scholarship).

[17] Carroll, *supra* note 12, at 419. *See also* Erin Carroll, *Obstruction of Journalism: A New Way to Combat Violence Against Journalists*, COLUM. JOURNALISM REV. (Jan. 13, 2022) ("The impact of violence against journalists radiates. It can alter the scope of news and information in our public sphere. That is, in fact, its goal. It is meant to frighten, shame, intimidate and, ultimately, to silence.").

[18] Joseph Blocher & Reva Siegel, *Guns Are a Threat to the Body Politic*, THE ATLANTIC (March 8, 2021).

[19] Kathleen M. Sullivan, *First Amendment Intermediaries in the Age of Cyberspace*, 45 UCLA L. REV. 1653, 1653 (1998) (noting the First Amendment's "frequent individualist rhetoric – including depictions of lone speakers on soapboxes and of buyers and sellers in a marketplace of ideas").

epistemic goals like the pursuit of truth in the marketplace of ideas, and others to speaker autonomy or other principles.[20]

In the context of press freedom, democracy seems to be the value most often invoked by judges, scholars, and for that matter journalists themselves – consider "Democracy Dies in Darkness," which The Washington Post adopted in 2017 as the first official motto in its 140-year history.[21] And the socially embedded nature of speech is probably also easiest to recognize in the context of democracy, which is itself a collective exercise. It thus seems perfectly natural – whether or not one considers the Fourth Estate to be the fourth branch of government – that many people accept that the press has an important institutional role to play in a well-functioning democracy by, among other things, holding government actors to public account.

Can the same be said for the institutional press under an *epistemic* account of the First Amendment – one that emphasizes the pursuit of truth and other cognitive values instead of the participatory and political stakes of democracy as such? Given the enormous influence of the marketplace of ideas metaphor,[22] it would be a significant loss for advocates of press freedom if the answer were no. Considering the significant anxiety that many people feel about our current "post truth" era[23] and the collapse in trust of knowledge institutions,[24] it seems especially urgent to articulate a role for the press in combatting disinformation and providing reliable expertise.[25]

My argument here, drawing on prior work, is that epistemic theories of the First Amendment can indeed provide a strong case for the recognition and protection of press freedom. And the role of the institutional press in the pursuit of truth, knowledge, and other epistemic values can in turn be connected back to the value of democracy itself.

[20] Though I have often written about epistemic theories of the First Amendment and will discuss them here, I count myself among those who think there is no single free speech value.

[21] Paul Farhi, *The Washington Post's New Slogan Turns Out to be an Old Saying*, WASH. POST (Feb. 24, 2017), https://www.washingtonpost.com/lifestyle/style/the-washington-posts-new-slogan-turns-out-to-be-an-old-saying/2017/02/23/cb199cda-fa02-11e6-be05-1a3817ac21a5_story.html.

[22] William P. Marshall, *In Defense of the Search for Truth as a First Amendment Justification*, 30 GA. L. REV. 1, 1 (1995) ("The most influential argument supporting the constitutional commitment to freedom of speech is the contention that speech is valuable because it leads to the discovery of truth."); *see also* Kent Greenawalt, *Free Speech Justifications*, 89 COLUM. L. REV. 119, 130 (1989) ("The most familiar argument for freedom of speech is that speech promotes the discovery of truth.").

[23] Amy B. Wang, *"Post-Truth" Named 2016 Word of the Year by Oxford Dictionaries*, WASH. POST (Nov. 16, 2016), https://www.washingtonpost.com/news/the-fix/wp/2016/11/16/post-truth-named-2016-word-of-the-year-by-oxford-dictionaries/ ("It's official: Truth is dead. Facts are passe.").

[24] TOM NICHOLS, THE DEATH OF EXPERTISE: THE CAMPAIGN AGAINST ESTABLISHED KNOWLEDGE AND WHY IT MATTERS (2017).

[25] *See* RonNell Andersen Jones & Lisa Grow Sun, *Freedom of the Press in Post-Truthism America*, 98 WASH. U. L. REV. 419 (2020).

To get there as a matter of First Amendment theory, it is helpful first to reject or at least modify the individualistic, atomistic conception of the marketplace of ideas that many accounts of free speech seem to adopt and, to be fair, that Justice Holmes might have had in mind when he helped launch the metaphor with his dissent in *Abrams*.[26] It is important instead to understand the marketplace of ideas and any production of truth it encourages as a set of social practices, governed by norms and rules that go beyond individualized and idealized transactions of thought.

Though there may be other good reasons to reject the market metaphor entirely, this particular conceptualization is entirely in keeping with economic theory. Economists, at least since Ronald Coase, have emphasized that the market is populated and constructed not only by individuals but by *institutions*, which Douglass North (one of the architects of New Institutional Economics, or NIE) described in his Nobel Prize lecture as "the humanly devised constraints that structure human interaction. They are made up of formal constraints (e.g., rules, laws, constitutions), informal constraints (e.g., norms of behavior, conventions, self-imposed codes of conduct), and their enforcement characteristics."[27] As fellow Nobel laureate Oliver Williamson explained:

> Students of the NIE eschew hypothetical ideals – which work off of omniscience, benevolence, zero transaction costs, full credibility, and the like – and deal instead with feasible organizational alternatives, all of which are flawed.[28]

A rich literature chronicles some ways in which these institutions can facilitate property rights and markets.[29]

The recognition of institutions and their role in economic exchange has a rough parallel in accounts of free speech that center the importance not only of broad speech values and discrete speech acts but of the social practices[30] and non-state actors[31] that enable and shape them. This is especially evident in "institutional"

[26] *See* Abrams v. United States, 250 U.S. 616, 624–31 (1919) (Holmes, J., dissenting); Pnina Lahav, *Holmes and Brandeis: Libertarian and Republican Justification for Free Speech*, 4 J.L. & POL. 451, 455 (1988).

[27] Douglass C. North, *Economic Performance Through Time*, 84 AM. ECON. REV. 359, 360 (1994) (reprinting North's 1993 Nobel Prize acceptance speech)

[28] Oliver E. Williamson, *The New Institutional Economics: Taking Stock, Looking Ahead*, 38 J. ECON. LIT. 595, 601 (2000).

[29] *See, e.g.*, JAMES M. ACHESON, THE LOBSTER GANGS OF MAINE (1988); ROBERT C. ELLICKSON, ORDER WITHOUT LAW (1991); BARAK D. RICHMAN, STATELESS COMMERCE: THE DIAMOND NETWORK AND THE PERSISTENCE OF RELATIONAL EXCHANGE (2017).

[30] Robert Post, *Recuperating First Amendment Doctrine*, 47 STAN. L. REV. 1249, 1278–79 (1995).

[31] Jack M. Balkin, *The Future of Free Expression in a Digital Age*, 36 PEPP. L. REV. 427, 432 (2009) ("A system of free speech depends ... on an infrastructure of free expression ... [which] includes the kinds of media and institutions for knowledge, creation, and dissemination that are available at any point in time.").

approaches of the First Amendment.[32] In the words of Fred Schauer, who penned some of the most influential articles in that vein,[33] "An institutional understanding of the First Amendment is structured around the principle that certain institutions play special roles in serving the kinds of values that the First Amendment is most plausibly understood to protect."[34] The list of institutions that play such "special roles" is commonly thought to include universities and, of course, the press.

In *Institutions in the Marketplace of Ideas*,[35] I attempted to pull together these two threads: the NIE on the one hand and the institutional First Amendment on the other. What NIE scholars advocated was attention to the social practices (i.e., institutions) that constitute an economy, rather than assuming away the messiness and focusing on an idealized process of exchange. Trust and social norms, for example, can facilitate trade even in the absence of formal law. Free speech theory can do the same, since "if the marketplace of ideas is the animating purpose of the First Amendment, it can be served by institutions as well as by individuals."[36] In other words, there are institutions that facilitate the marketplace of ideas through the equivalent of lowering transaction costs and should receive some special solicitude as a result.

Of course, there is deep disagreement about which institutions serve First Amendment values and how. In *Free Speech and Justified True Belief*, I focused more directly on that problem, suggesting that the underlying epistemic value of the First Amendment could be understood not as "truth" but as "knowledge" – roughly defined, in keeping with basic epistemology, as justified true belief.[37] Doing so could help clarify the underlying debate in the era of "fake news" and "alternative facts," which is not really about the importance of truth but about where it is to be found. Indeed, one of the central perversities of disinformation is that people in its grip firmly believe in the importance of truth and that they are in possession of it. The challenge, then, is to re-center the question of *justification*: the institutions and habits of mind that are valuable in forming true beliefs.

32 *See, e.g.*, Paul Horwitz, First Amendment Institutions (2013); Randall P. Bezanson, *Institutional Speech*, 80 Iowa L. Rev. 735 (1995) (arguing that only useful institutional speech should receive First Amendment protection); Frederick Schauer, *Towards an Institutional First Amendment*, 89 Minn. L. Rev. 1256, 1278 n.97 (2005); Symposium, *Constitutional "Niches": The Role of Institutional Context in Constitutional Law*, 54 UCLA L. Rev. 1463 (2007). For contemporary cautions and critiques, *see* Dale Carpenter, Response, *The Value of Institutions and the Values of Free Speech*, 89 Minn. L. Rev. 1407 (2005); Scott A. Moss, *Prisoners and Students and Workers – Oh, My! A Cautionary Note About Excessive Institutional Tailoring of First Amendment Doctrine*, 54 UCLA L. Rev. 1635, 1639 (2007).

33 *See, e.g.*, Frederick Schauer, *Principles, Institutions, and the First Amendment*, 112 Harv. L. Rev. 84, 85–86 (1998); Schauer, *supra* note 32.

34 Frederick Schauer, *Is There a Right to Academic Freedom?*, 77 U. Colo. L. Rev. 907, 925 (2006).

35 Joseph Blocher, *Institutions in the Marketplace of Ideas*, 57 Duke L.J. 821 (2008).

36 *Id.* at 887.

37 Joseph Blocher, *Free Speech and Justified True Belief*, 133 Harv. L. Rev. 439 (2019).

This is a question of epistemology, to be sure, but one focused on social practices and institutions, including the press:

> The institutional press improves the marketplace of ideas by serving as a clearinghouse for information. This, too, lowers search costs and makes ideas more easily accessible for consumption or rejection by individual idea consumers. The American press has played a particularly important role in explaining and distributing information about other institutions whose functioning would otherwise be impossible for the average citizen to follow. Without active and critical reporting about government, for example, it would be impossible for citizens to cast informed votes, and the politicians they elect could hardly claim to be triumphant in the marketplace of ideas.[38]

The point is that the press as an institution can play an important role in advancing the search for truth (or knowledge), and that doing so is – along with other press functions – important to the preservation of a healthy democracy. It can, along with other speech institutions, like universities, help bridge the gap between democratic and epistemological approaches to free speech.[39] As Robert Post notes, the First Amendment relies on "democratic competence," which is the "cognitive empowerment of persons within public discourse, which in part depends on their access to disciplinary knowledge."[40] And as Justice Powell recognized:

> No individual can obtain for himself the information needed for intelligent discharge of his political responsibilities . . . [The press] is the means by which the people receive that free flow of information and ideas essential to intelligent self-government.[41]

There are, of course, complications with any self-consciously institutionalist account, but those complications do not seem different in difficulty – nor perhaps even kind – from those that one finds elsewhere in free speech law.[42] There is admittedly no simple or objective way to identify the kinds of social practices that contribute to knowledge. But neither is there a way to identify which acts count as "speech" in the first place. It might also be difficult to separate the "press" from other speakers – a challenge that seems to have deterred many from the attempt.[43] But the question should presumably be one of activity (i.e., when is one engaged in

[38] Blocher, *supra* note 35, at 857 (internal citation omitted).

[39] Joseph Blocher, *Public Discourse, Expert Knowledge, and the Press*, 87 WASH. L. REV. 409, 413 (2012).

[40] POST, *supra* note 13, at 34; *see also* NICHOLS, *supra* note 24, at 216 ("[T]he collapse of the relationship between experts and citizens is a dysfunction of democracy itself.").

[41] Saxbe v. Washington Post Co., 417 U.S. 843, 863 (1974) (Powell, J., dissenting).

[42] Carpenter, *supra* note 32, at 1408 (critiquing institutional approach on various grounds noting that "the possible line-drawing difficulties do not seem that much more difficult than other line-drawing problems in the First Amendment").

[43] *See* First Nat'l Bank v. Bellotti, 435 U.S. 765, 801 (1978) (Burger, C.J., concurring) ("[A] fundamental difficulty with interpreting the Press Clause as conferring special status on a limited group is one of definition.").

journalism) rather than identity (i.e., is one a journalist),[44] which is on par with other challenging-but-foundational First Amendment inquiries, like whether one is speaking as a professional or as a public employee on a matter of public concern.

In any event, it is worth noting that those who *attack* the press – physically and otherwise – seem to have little difficulty separating traditional media from others. Those who scrawled "MURDER THE MEDIA" were not fazed by definitional difficulties and line-drawing, even if scholars and judges are. It is like a twist on a horror movie trope: Instead of the bad guys being invisible to all but the protagonists, the protagonists are invisible to all but the bad guys.

5.2 THE SURPRISINGLY COMPLICATED RELATIONSHIP BETWEEN THE PRESS AND VIOLENCE

Threats to press freedom come in many forms. Some are subtle or structural: judicial disregard,[45] changes in the media market,[46] or the proliferation of disinformation and misinformation online,[47] for example. The threat of violence, by contrast, is the proverbial wolf that comes as a wolf:[48] the apparent opposite of reasoned speech or, for that matter, democratic self-government. But the fact that its incidents are so visceral does not make it any less complex. Violence is not only a threat to journalism – though it certainly is that – but is shaped by it in return. Only by considering the relationship holistically can we understand how it shapes the boundaries of public discourse.

Though violence against the press has not been the subject of much extended scholarship,[49] it is nothing new in the United States.[50] The 1837 murder of abolitionist newspaper editor Elijah Lovejoy is one prominent example,[51] as is the attack

[44] *Cf.* Floyd Abrams, *The Press Is Different: Reflections on Justice Stewart and the Autonomous Press*, 7 Hofstra L. Rev. 563, 580 (1979) ("In the great preponderance of cases, a court has little difficulty knowing a journalist when it sees one."); Robert D. Sack, *Reflections on the Wrong Question: Special Constitutional Privilege for the Institutional Press*, 7 Hofstra L. Rev. 629, 629 (1979) ("[A]ll citizens exercising the press function, including, but not limited to, journalists employed by the 'institutional press,' warrant … protection.").

[45] RonNell Andersen Jones & Sonja R. West, *The U.S. Supreme Court's Characterizations of the Press: An Empirical Study*, 100 N.C. L. Rev. 375 (2022).

[46] *See, e.g.*, Martha Minow, Saving the News: Why the Constitution Calls for Government Action to Preserve Freedom of Speech (2021); Luke Morgan, *The Broken Branch: Capitalism, the Constitution, and the Press*, 125 Penn St. L. Rev. 1 (2020).

[47] Yochai Benkler et al., Network Propaganda: Manipulation, Disinformation, and Radicalization in American Politics (2018).

[48] *Cf.* Morrison v. Olson, 487 U.S. 654, 699 (1988) (Scalia, J., dissenting).

[49] John Nerone, *Violence Against Journalists*, Oxford Bibliographies (Sept. 22, 2021), https://www.oxfordbibliographies.com/display/document/obo-9780199756841/obo-9780199756841-0266.xml (noting that despite current coverage and monitoring, "general works on violence against journalists are relatively rare") (collecting sources).

[50] *See generally* John Nerone, Violence against the Press: Policing the Public Sphere in US History (1994).

[51] *Id.* at 107.

on Ida B. Wells-Barnett, whose printing press was destroyed by a white mob in Memphis in 1892.[52] As John Nerone notes in his excellent historical account of anti-press violence in the United States, "Violence was common when minorities claimed the press as a voice of their own."[53]

Broadly speaking, anti-press violence subsided for much of the twentieth century, coinciding with – and perhaps facilitated by – the rise of a less explicitly partisan, more homogenized, and more commercialized mass media.[54] But recently, there has been a disturbing resurgence in anti-press violence around the world, with more than 2,000 journalists killed in the past 30 years alone, 15 of them in the United States.[55] Killings are only one particularly horrific part of the story. The U.S. Press Freedom Tracker reports that in 2020 (which saw a spike in anti-press violence by private and public actors), more than 100 journalists were arrested or criminally charged in relation to their reporting, and roughly 300 were assaulted.[56] At least fifty journalists have sued law enforcement officers or other officials for violence and other mistreatment during coverage of protests following the murder of George Floyd.[57] Violence and threats against the press disproportionately target women and minorities,[58] and they are facilitated by the rhetoric of people like the former president, who regularly decries the "fake news," calls journalists "enemies of the people,"[59] and says the media should "pay a big price."[60]

52 Brent Staples, *How the White Press Wrote Off Black America*, N.Y. Times (July 10, 2021).

53 Nerone, *supra* note 50, at 15.

54 *Cf.* Jennifer E. Moore & Michael J. Socolow, *Violence against the Media Isn't New – History Shows Why It Largely Disappeared and Has Now Returned*, The Conversation (Sept. 10, 2018), https://theconversation.com/violence-against-the-media-isnt-new-history-shows-why-it-largely-disappeared-and-has-now-returned-102756 ("Does the end of the depoliticized mass audience era of journalism directly correlate to what seems to be a return of violence against the media?").

55 Ewen & Shane, *supra* note 7.

56 Kimberly Harris, *Journalists under Attack While Reporting on Protests*, UOregon School of Journalism and Communication (Dec. 11, 2022), https://journalism.uoregon.edu/journalists-under-attack-while-reporting-protests (reporting that more than 350 journalists reported arrests, assaults, or preventions from documenting protests between May and December, 2020); Katherine Jacobsen, *In 2020, U.S. Journalists Faced Unprecedented Attacks*, Comm. to Protect Journalists (Dec. 14, 2020) https://cpj.org/2020/12/in-2020-u-s-journalists-faced-unprecedented-attacks/.

57 Stephanie Sugars, *Supreme Court Ruling Limits Paths for Journalists to Hold Federal Officers Accountable*, U.S. Press Freedom Tracker (June 23, 2022), https://pressfreedomtracker.us/blog/supreme-court-ruling-limits-paths-for-journalists-to-hold-federal-officers-accountable/.

58 Silvio Waisbord, *Mob Censorship: Online Harassment of US Journalists in Times of Digital Hate and Populism*, 8 Digit. Journalism 1030, 1032–34 (2020). *See Also Threats that Silence: Trends in the Safety of Journalists*, UNESCO, https://www.unesco.org/reports/world-media-trends/2021/en/safety-journalists (last visited Dec. 18, 2023) ("Numerous reports and studies confirm that threats inordinately affect women journalists and those who represent minority groups.").

59 Michael Safi et al., *"I'm Getting Shot": Attacks on Journalists Surge in US Protests*, The Guardian (June 5, 2020), https://www.theguardian.com/media/2020/jun/05/im-getting-shot-attacks-on-journalists-surge-in-us-protests.

60 Matt Novak, *Trump Accuses Media of 'Treason' in Escalation of Social Media Threats*, Forbes (Sept. 24, 2023) https://www.forbes.com/sites/mattnovak/2023/09/24/trump-accuses-media-of-treason-in-escalation-of-social-media-threats/.

Violence *against* the press is a threat both to journalists and to democracy itself, and like other such threats, addressing it is both difficult and urgent. But it would be a mistake to see the connection in only one direction. When it comes to identifying and protecting the press function, as the organizers of this convening have challenged us to do, some of the most difficult phenomena to address are those that are simultaneously symptoms and causes. Distrust, misinformation, and the like are reasons for the press's current predicament and are also *results* of it. Violence must be understood in the same way.

Violence has its own ecosystem, of which the press is not just a victim but also a constitutive part. The ways in which the press reports on violence generally – or violent incidents specifically – shape how society understands, responds to, and practices that violence. For example, whether people perceive violent crime to be an increasing problem, and whether they see law enforcement as the appropriate response, will naturally be informed by what they learn from media sources. The same is true of police violence and other phenomena.

One area where the press's role has been especially prominent is in the coverage of firearm violence, as some experts have suggested that reporting "does more harm than good,"[61] especially when it comes to coverage of mass shootings, which "tests the skill of reporters and the judgment of news organizations."[62] In the words of one report, "media coverage tends to follow a clear pattern, peaking around mass shootings and fading with the next breaking news event."[63] This can undermine public support for regulatory approaches that address the full range of gun violence,[64] given that mass shootings account for just a tiny proportion of the nation's nearly 50,000 gun deaths per year. One researcher notes that while mass shootings account for about 1 percent of US gun deaths, they "soak up about 95 percent of the oxygen in terms of the national conversation of gun violence."[65]

[61] Jessica Beard, *How Media Reporting on Firearm Violence Does More Harm than Good*, It's All Reporting, https://itsalljournalism.com/579-how-media-reporting-on-firearm-violence-does-more-harm-than-good/ (last visited Dec. 18, 2023).

[62] Frank Ochberg & Bruce Shapiro, *Covering Mass Killings*, Dart Center for Journalism & Trauma (Jan. 9, 2011), https://dartcenter.org/content/covering-mass-killings.

[63] Jessica Weiss, *How the Trace Changed Reporting on Guns in America, Arnold Ventures*, Arnold Ventures (Apr. 14, 2022), https://www.arnoldventures.org/stories/how-the-trace-changed-reporting-on-guns-in-america.

[64] Afea Tucker, *These Philadelphia Researchers Want Journalists to Tell Better Stories about Gun Violence*, The Trace (Feb. 23, 2023), https://www.thetrace.org/2023/02/crime-news-reporting-harm-victims/.

[65] Shealeigh Voitl, *Not Shooting Straight: Corporate Media Gives Mass Shootings Blanket Coverage, While Missing Community-Level Gun Violence*, Project Uncensored (April 20, 2023), https://www.projectcensored.org/not-shooting-straight-corporate-media-gives-mass-shootings-blanket-coverage-while-missing-community-level-gun-violence/; Cydney Hargis, *The Media's Guide to Covering Gun Violence*, Media Matters for America (June 9, 2022), https://www.mediamatters.org/cnn/medias-guide-covering-gun-violence ("Outlets repeatedly choose to focus on the least common type of gun violence and on the small minority of people

Perhaps even more troubling, some research has found that mass shooters are significantly incentivized by the prominence of such events[66] – suggesting perhaps that media coverage is both a symptom and a cause. The same might well be true of gun use and gun displays more broadly. Charles Homans describes recent media coverage of armed militiamen in Richmond, Virginia, noting that journalists appeared to outnumber their subjects and that the latter were "waiting with transparent eagerness for reporters to swarm around them and feigning reluctance when they did."[67]

To be clear, the point is not to blame the press for the nation's gun violence problem. The point, rather, is to recognize and emphasize the importance of a well-functioning press in addressing it. That is entirely consistent with – indeed, provides supportive evidence of – the institutional account in Section 5.1. A press that develops and respects internal norms and best practices about reporting on gun violence is precisely the kind of norm-governed institution whose norms deserve deference, just like scholarly disciplinarity helps justify special First Amendment solicitude for universities.

It would require far more detailed work to know whether and how journalists follow desirable professional practices when reporting on gun violence, but it is evident that the profession is trying to develop such practices.[68] *A Journalist's Guide to Reporting on Mass Shootings*, for example, draws attention to the "Columbine Rule," which one journalist summarizes as, "a lot of what you find out in the first 48 hours turns out to be bullshit."[69] Other practices include focusing on gun violence beyond mass shootings, as well as not naming shooters. (The Buffalo and Uvalde shooters remain largely anonymous as compared to those from earlier shootings at Parkland and Charleston.)[70]

who don't support any regulation while mostly ignoring stories of states that have successfully implemented gun violence prevention laws, giving viewers an upside-down view of the crisis.").

66 Sherry Towers et al., *Contagion in Mass Killings and School Shootings*, PLOS One (July 2, 2015), https://doi.org/10.1371/journal.pone.0117259 (finding "significant evidence that mass killings involving firearms are incented by similar events in the immediate past").

67 Charles Homans, *Out of the Barrel of a Gun*, N.Y. Times (Jan. 26, 2021), https://www.nytimes.com/interactive/2021/01/26/magazine/armed-militia-movement-gun-laws.html.

68 *See, e.g.*, The Initiative for Better Gun Reporting, https://ibgvr.org/ (last visited Dec. 18, 2023) (reporting on "Better Gun Violence Reporting Summit" in Philadelphia); Kyle Pope, *It's Time to Rethink How Journalism Covers Guns and Mass Shootings*, Colum. Journalism Rev. (March 29, 2021) (partnership between Columbia Journalism Review and Dart Center for Journalism and Trauma).

69 Laura Wides-Muñoz, *A Journalist's Guide to Reporting on Mass Shootings*, NBCU Academy (Aug. 3, 2023), https://nbcuacademy.com/mass-shootings-media/.

70 Lucy Wescott, *'Trauma Makes Its Way Back to You': Four US Journalists on Covering Mass Shootings*, Comm. to Protect Journalists (May 21, 2023), https://cpj.org/2021/05/trauma-makes-its-way-back-to-you-four-us-journalists-on-covering-mass-shootings/ ("The challenge I've had reporting on gun violence is doing it in a way that, when you're talking to people and you're crafting questions and interviewing them, making sure you're not retraumatizing them.").

Of course, to do so well also requires significant time and resources, which only some newsrooms or organizations are able to commit. The Trace was founded in 2015 as the "only American newsroom dedicated to full-time coverage of gun violence"[71] and has contributed extraordinary journalism to a range of gun-related issues, including the NRA investigation that ultimately led to the organization being sued for violation of nonprofit laws.[72] Other newspapers have launched "projects" focused on state and local gun violence.[73] These developments should be celebrated and supported, just as violence against journalists must be condemned and prevented.

It is far beyond the scope of this brief chapter to fully map the ways in which violence and the press are intertwined or how the boundaries of public discourse are shaped in part by their relationship. But the discussion has hopefully illuminated two major concepts essential to that broader project. First, the press can play an important and overlapping role in furthering the First Amendment's epistemological and democratic values. Second, as violence against the press becomes more rhetorically and viscerally prominent, it is all the more urgent that we grapple with the complicated relationship between the two.

[71] Team Trace, *The Most Memorable Gun Violence Journalism of 2021*, The Trace (Dec. 23, 2021), https://www.thetrace.org/2021/12/best-gun-violence-journalism-2021/.

[72] Weiss, *supra* note 63.

[73] *See, e.g.*, *The Missouri Gun Violence Project*, Missouri Independent, https://missouriindependent.com/tag/missouri-gun-violence-project/ (last visited Dec. 18, 2023) (two-year project focusing on gun death in Missouri, including suicides); *Dispatch Reporters Unraveled the Plague of Gun Violence in Columbus: Here's How They Did It*, Columbus Dispatch (Oct. 5, 2023), https://www.dispatch.com/story/news/local/2023/10/05/heres-how-reporters-traced-a-weekend-of-gun-violence-in-columbus/70867114007/ (describing Under Fire, a yearlong project examining gun violence in Columbus, Ohio, including the deployment of twenty-eight journalists to cover gun violence over an 80-hour period).

PART III

Evolving Threats to the Press Function

6

Fitting a Square Peg into a Round Hole

Why Traditional Free Press Doctrines Fail in Dealing with Newer Media

Erwin Chemerinsky

The common law method is to try to apply existing precedents to new situations. It is therefore to be expected that lawyers and judges would apply well-established legal principles to the relatively new internet and social media. Although some basic principles apply to these media, as they do to all others, there are ways in which this approach fails because the internet and social media are different in kind from other methods of communication. Scholars and legal experts have given insufficient attention to the areas in which traditional First Amendment principles are inadequate for dealing with the internet and social media.

In this chapter, I begin by describing how the internet and social media are inherently different from other media. I then discuss traditional First Amendment doctrines that should apply to these newer media. With this as context, I then focus on three areas where current doctrine is inadequate for dealing with the internet and social media: These are false speech, how the internet and social media undermine the traditional press, and the issue of foreign influence in elections. My goal is not to offer solutions but to identify these areas where applying existing approaches is likely to fail because of the unique nature of the internet and social media as places for communication.

6.1 HOW THE INTERNET AND SOCIAL MEDIA ARE DIFFERENT FROM OTHER FORMS OF COMMUNICATION

How do the internet and social media differ from other forms of communication? First, the internet has democratized the ability to reach a mass audience. It used to be that to reach a large audience, a person had to be rich enough to own a newspaper or obtain a broadcast license. Now, though, anyone with a smartphone – or even just access to a library with a modem – can reach a huge audience instantaneously. No longer are people dependent on a relatively small number of news sources.

Scarcity of media outlets was a core characteristic of media until now. There are only so many broadcast channels,[1] and there are only so many newspapers that the economy will support, with each having only so many physical pages. But the internet and social media provide the opportunity for infinite speech. Scarcity is no longer an issue.

Further, the internet and social media empower individuals who would otherwise be voiceless to express their opinions and provide them a place to do so.[2] The internet provides a platform for those who cannot physically gather and organize.[3] Previously silenced or marginalized individuals now have an accessible method for disseminating their political ideas.[4]

But these characteristics of the internet and social media also mean that false information can be quickly spread by an almost infinite number of sources. Information that is true but confidential can be quickly disseminated.[5] There is even a name for such action: "doxing," which refers to publishing private information about a person on the internet, often with the malicious intent to harm the individual.[6] The internet and social media can be used to harass.[7] A study by the Pew Research Center "found [that] 40 percent of adult Internet users have experienced harassment online, with young women enduring particularly severe forms of it."[8]

Traditionally, newspapers have acted as an important filter by excluding false and other types of harmful information. They have an editorial process and, if not journalistic ethics, at least a fear of liability. Certainly, at times, the filters have failed and newspapers have done harm. But at least there *are* filters, while none exist for the internet and social media. Anyone can post anything for the world to see.

Second, the internet has dramatically increased the dissemination and permanence of information, or to phrase this differently, it has enormously increased the ability to access information. Lawyers and law students can do all of their research online, reading statutes, cases, and treatises – previously, this would have required a trip to the law library. We can visit the great museums of the world online anywhere,

1 *See* Red Lion Broadcasting v. F.C.C., 395 U.S. 367 (1969) (upholding the Fairness Doctrine on the grounds of the scarcity of the broadcast spectrum).

2 David M. Howard, *Can Democracy Withstand the Cyber Age: 1984 in the Twenty-first Century*, 69 Hastings L.J. 1355, 1373 (2018).

3 *Id.* at 1373; David M. Thompson, *Is the Internet a Viable Threat to Representative Democracy?*, 6 Duke L. & Tech. Rev. 1, 13 (2007–08).

4 Howard, *supra* note 2, at 1373.

5 *See* Lori Andrews, I Know Who You Are and I Saw What You Did: Social Networks and the Death of Privacy 121–35 (2011).

6 Danielle Keats Citron, Hate Crimes in Cyberspace 53 (2014).

7 *Id.* at 35–55.

8 Marlisse Silver Sweeney, *What the Law Can (and Can't) Do About Online Harassment*, Atlantic (Nov. 12, 2014), https://www.theatlantic.com/technology/archive/2014/11/what-the-law-can-and-cant-do-about-online-harassment/382638/.

anytime. We have access to virtually unlimited information from nearly infinite sources.

But there is a downside to this easy access and permanence. Take defamation as an example. Imagine, before the internet, that a local newspaper published false information about a person that harmed their reputation. The falsity would be known by readers of the paper and could be circulated by other media and by word of mouth. Eventually, however, the impact of the defamatory article would fade, and the false information would live on only in remote places like a library's microfiche archives. Now, though, the defamatory story can be quickly spread across the internet, accessed from anywhere, and is likely to remain there forever. It is enormously difficult, if not impossible, to erase something from the internet.

Finally, the internet does not respect national boundaries. Again, there are great benefits to this – for instance, totalitarian governments cannot easily cut off information to their citizens. When the revolution began in Egypt, the government tried to halt internet access, but people with satellite phones maintained access and disseminated what they learned.[9] Yet, there are also drawbacks. The Supreme Court has estimated that 40 percent of pornography on the internet comes from foreign countries, making any attempt to control it within a country impossible.[10] As occurred in the 2016 presidential election and evidenced by Special Counsel Robert Mueller's report, the lack of borders on the internet also gives foreign countries and foreign actors a vehicle for trying to influence the outcome of United States elections.[11]

6.2 BASIC FIRST AMENDMENT PRINCIPLES SHOULD APPLY TO THESE MEDIA

I do not want to overstate the First Amendment problems in dealing with newer media. The same basic First Amendment principles should apply to these media as to all other aspects of the press. Central to free speech analysis is whether a government regulation is content-based or content-neutral, with content-based regulations having to meet strict scrutiny and content-neutral laws needing to satisfy intermediate scrutiny. As the Court observed in *Police Department of Chicago v. Mosley*, "[A]bove all else, the First Amendment means that government has no power to restrict expression because of its message, its ideas, its subject matter or its content."[12] Hence, the Court endorsed a two-tier system of review. The Court

9 *When Egypt Turned Off the Internet*, Al Jazeera (Jan. 28, 2011), https://www.aljazeera.com/news/middleeast/2011/01/2011128796164380.html.

10 Ashcroft v. ACLU, 542 U.S. 656, 667 (2004).

11 Robert S. Mueller, III, *Report on the Investigation Into Russian Interference in the 2016 Presidential Election*, U.S. Department of Justice (March 2019), https://www.justice.gov/d9/report.pdf.

12 408 U.S. 92, 95–96 (1972).

applies “the most exacting scrutiny to regulations that suppress, disadvantage, or impose differential burdens upon speech because of its content.”[13] But, “[i]n contrast, regulations that are unrelated to the content of speech are subject to an intermediate level of scrutiny.”[14]

This should apply to government regulation of the internet and social media as it does to all other government regulation of speech. Likewise, the same categories of unprotected speech – incitement, true threats, defamation, false and deceptive advertisements – are applicable to expression made over the internet and social media.

A core aspect of freedom of the press is that the government cannot control the content of what is published. This should apply with equal force to the internet and social media. In *Miami Herald v. Tornillo*, the Court unanimously declared a right-of-reply law unconstitutional as applied to newspapers.[15] A Florida law required that a newspaper print a reply from any candidate for office whose character or official record had been attacked in its pages. The newspaper had to print the reply free of charge and in as conspicuous a place as the initial story was presented. The Court, in an opinion by Chief Justice Burger, stated the following:

> [T]he Florida statute exacts a penalty on the basis of the content of a newspaper. The first phase of the penalty . . . is exacted in terms of the cost in printing and . . . in taking up space that could be devoted to other material the newspaper may have preferred to print . . . Faced with [such a penalty], editors might well conclude that the safe course is to avoid controversy.[16]

The Court stressed that forcing newspapers to publish a reply intrudes on editorial discretion that is protected by the First Amendment. Likewise, regulating what social media companies do or don’t “publish” should be deemed to violate the First Amendment.[17]

6.3 THE INTERNET AND SOCIAL MEDIA RAISE UNIQUE ISSUES

Although the fundamental principles of the First Amendment apply to the internet and social media, it cannot be ignored that these newer media pose unique issues for which existing doctrine does not provide an adequate answer. First, there is the problem of false speech. False information can cause great harm, and social media facilitates the rapid dissemination of such information.[18] The unprecedented speed

[13] Turner Broadcasting v. FCC, 512 U.S. 622, 641 (1994).
[14] *Id.*
[15] 418 U.S. 241 (1974).
[16] *Id.* at 257.
[17] Alex Chemerinsky & Erwin Chemerinsky, *Misguided Federalism: State Regulation of the Internet and Social Media*, 102 N.C. L. REV. 1 (2023).
[18] *See generally* American Psychological Association, *Misinformation and Disinformation*, https://www.apa.org/topics/journalism-facts/misinformation-disinformation (misinformation is “false

and scale of digital communication have simplified the dissemination of false information like never before, frequently outpacing efforts to debunk it.[19] Social media algorithms can prioritize content more likely to generate user engagement regardless of its veracity.[20] Facebook and other social media are sending their users specific content based on the platform's assessment of their interests but with little regard to whether the information is true. In the political realm, this can change the outcome of elections, especially if the falsehoods are spread soon before election day when there is little time to refute them. The spread of disinformation and misinformation can prevent voters from accessing essential information required to make well-informed decisions regarding candidates for office and laws.[21] False accusations can be quickly and widely circulated, making all the difference between who wins and who loses. False speech has enormous implications for politics, public health, elections, and other domains where the availability of accurate information is vital. Additionally, and quite importantly, false information can undermine trust in reliable sources and credible news.[22]

Researchers at the Massachusetts Institute of Technology "found that false news spreads faster and to more people than true stories, reaching more people than any other type of information."[23] The First Amendment is predicated on the romantic notion – articulated by John Stuart Mill and Oliver Wendell Holmes – that there is a marketplace of ideas and that allowing all speech will lead to truth triumphing over falsehoods. But many studies have demonstrated that people are unlikely to change false beliefs when confronted with true information.[24] False information has a permanent effect. When 70 percent of Republican voters believe that Trump was cheated out of the presidency in 2020, how can there be faith in the notion that truth will triumph over falsity in the world of the internet and social media?

This problem will grow as technology becomes more sophisticated. It is all too easy to imagine how, in the days before an election, unscrupulous actors could circulate a deepfake of an opposing candidate saying something repulsive. What we see and hear for ourselves seems true, even if it is created by bots or artificial

or inaccurate information – getting the facts wrong," whereas disinformation is "false information which is deliberately intended to mislead – intentionally misstating the facts") (last visited June 27, 2024); *see* Bharat Dhiman, *Key Issues and New Challenges in New Media Technology in 2023: A Critical Review*, 5 J. of Media & Mgmt. 1, 3 (2023).

19 Dhiman, *supra* note 18, at 3; Andrea Butler, *Protecting the Democratic Role of the Press: A Legal Solution to Fake News*, 96 Wash. U. L. Rev. 419 (2018).

20 Dhiman, *supra* note 18, at 2.

21 *Id.*

22 *Id.*

23 William M. Brooks, *Democracy on the Edge: Use the First Amendment to Stop False Speech by Government Officials*, 53 Memphis L. Rev. 255, 270 (2023), citing Soroush Vosoughi et al., *The Spread of True and False News Online*, 359 Science 1146–51 (Mar. 2018), https://science.sciencemag.org/content/.359/6380/1146.

24 Brooks, *supra* note 23.

intelligence. A deepfake depicting a politician taking a bribe would create lingering doubts for many, and be believed by some, even after it is revealed to be fictitious.

In fact, one place where the law has changed is in the area of injunctions in defamation cases. Traditionally, the only remedy in defamation cases was money damages, in accord with the maxim that equity would not enjoin defamation.[25] But because of the internet and social media, the law in this area has changed, and injunctions in defamation cases have now become commonplace.[26]

A solution to false speech over the internet and social media is likely elusive under existing First Amendment doctrine. The Supreme Court has rightly and emphatically declared the importance of protecting false speech. The most important case in this regard – and one of the most important free speech decisions of all time – is *New York Times Co. v. Sullivan*.[27] The Court reversed a defamation judgment against the newspaper and stated that the fact that some of the statements were false was not sufficient to deny the speech First Amendment protection.[28] The Court explained that a false "statement is inevitable in free debate and [it] must be protected if the freedoms of expression are to have the 'breathing space' that they 'need ... to survive.'"[29] This surely is correct. If any false statement about a government official, no matter how minor, would be a basis for liability, speech about our government would be chilled and lost.

Subsequently, in a very different context, the Court again recognized the importance of judicial protection of false speech in *United States v. Alvarez*.[30] A federal law made it a crime for a person to falsely claim to have received military honors or decorations.[31] Writing for a plurality of the Court, Justice Kennedy expressly rejected the government's argument that false speech is inherently outside the scope of the First Amendment.[32] He declared that there is not "any general exception to the First Amendment for false statements" and stressed that "some false statements are inevitable if there is to be an open and vigorous expression of views in public and private conversation, expression the First Amendment seeks to guarantee."[33] Justice Kennedy further explained that "the Court has been careful to instruct that falsity alone may not suffice to bring ... speech outside the First Amendment."[34]

[25] David Ardia, *Freedom of Speech, Defamation, and Injunctions*, 55 Wm. & Mary L. Rev. 1, 4 (2013) ("It has long been a fixture of Anglo-American law that libel plaintiffs are not entitled to injunctive relief; their remedies are solely monetary. Indeed, it has been repeated as a truism: 'equity will not enjoin a libel.'")

[26] Jim Stewart & Len Niehoff, *Zombies Among Us: Injunctions in Defamation Cases Come Back from the Dead*, 30 Fall Comm. Law 28 (2014).

[27] New York Times Co. v. Sullivan, 376 U.S. 254 (1964).

[28] *Id.* at 271.

[29] *Id.* at 271–72.

[30] United States v. Alvarez, 567 U.S. 709 (2012).

[31] *Id.* at 715–16.

[32] *Id.* at 725–26.

[33] *Id.* at 718.

[34] *Id.* at 719.

Given its harms, why is there First Amendment protection for false speech? In large part, it is because of the danger of giving anyone, including (or maybe especially) the government, the power to decide what is true and what is false. Allowing the government to prohibit false speech grants it the role of arbiter of truth. As Justice Kennedy explained: "Our constitutional tradition stands against the idea that we need Oceania's Ministry of Truth."[35] Would Democrats want the Trump administration, or would Republicans want the Biden administration, to have the power to create an agency that could scour the internet and social media and remove what it deems false? It is so much easier to put faith in the marketplace of ideas to refute falsehoods, even when we know that it is likely to fail in many instances.

But it is wrong to think that the First Amendment never allows restrictions of false speech. There are contexts in which the Supreme Court has refused to protect false speech and has allowed it to be prohibited and punished. For example, it is clearly established that the First Amendment does not protect false and deceptive advertisements.[36] The government, of course, can constitutionally prohibit making false statements under oath (perjury) or to law enforcement officials. But these are limited areas where false speech can be punished. The Court generally has treated commercial speech as being of lower value than political speech, which may make it easier to say that false advertising is entitled to no constitutional protection. As for perjury, there must be proof of a knowing and intentional falsehood.

The Court's inconsistent statements about false speech can be understood as reflecting the competing interests inherent in First Amendment analysis. On the one hand, false speech can create harm, great harm even. Speech is protected particularly because of its importance for the democratic process, but false speech can distort that process. Speech is safeguarded, too, because of the belief that the marketplace of ideas is the best way for truth to emerge. But false speech can infect that marketplace, and there is no reason to believe that truth will triumph. The Supreme Court has recognized this and declared that "[f]alse statements of fact are particularly valueless [because] they interfere with the truth-seeking function of the marketplace of ideas."[37]

A great deal of the problem is simply the amount of speech transmitted over social media and how difficult that makes content moderation. The quantity of information posted daily is staggering, and social media companies already conduct an enormous amount of content moderation. For example, Facebook reported that between October and December 2021, it took action against terrorism content 7.7 million times, bullying and harassment 8.2 million times, and child sexual

[35] Alvarez, 567 U.S. at 723.

[36] *See, e.g.*, Cent. Hudson Gas & Elec. Corp. v. Pub. Serv. Comm'n of N.Y., 447 U.S. 557, 566 (1980).

[37] Hustler Magazine, Inc. v. Falwell, 485 U.S. 46, 52 (1988).

exploitation material 19.8 million times.[38] In the last quarter of 2020, Facebook took action on over 1.1 million pieces of content *per day*.[39] Designing a system to exclude false speech – even if it could be decided what is false and even if mandating this would not violate the First Amendment – seems an insurmountable task.

But one should have no illusions. There will be elections decided because of false speech circulated over social media, especially in the days before voting. The threat to democracy is real and will grow. We need new First Amendment doctrines to deal with false speech over the internet and social media.

In addition, we must acknowledge how the internet and social media endanger traditional media and thus undermine the crucial newsgathering functions of the press. Much of the country is now facing a crisis of news deserts, which refers to places where local newspapers no longer exist.[40]

A recent study by the Medill School of Journalism found that since 2005, the country has lost more than one-fourth of its newspapers and is on track to lose one-third by 2025. Between late 2019 and May 2022, more than 360 newspapers closed. The report concluded:

> [M]ost of the communities that have lost newspapers do not get a print or digital replacement, leaving 70 million residents – or a fifth of the country's population – either living in an area with no local news organizations, or one at risk, with only one local news outlet and very limited access to critical news and information that can inform their everyday decisions and sustain grassroots democracy.[41]

Most newspapers that have survived have had to cut their staffs. From 2008 to 2017, total newspaper newsroom staffing almost halved, dropping from 71,000 employees to 39,000.[42]

[38] Guy Rosen, *Community Standards Enforcement Report Q4 2021*, META (Mar. 1, 2022), https://about.fb.com/news/2022/03/community-standards-enforcement-report-q4–2021/. Much of this moderation is either performed by algorithms or aided by algorithms. In the second and third quarters of 2022, alone, Facebook acted against 24.1 million posts containing hate speech: Guy Rosen, *Integrity and Transparency Reports, Third Quarter 2022*, META (Nov. 22, 2022), https://about.fb.com/news/2022/11/integrity-and-transparency-reports-q3–2022/ (It attributed its moderation actions in part to improved "proactive detection technology."). For discussion of algorithmic moderation, *see, e.g.*, Hannah Bloch-Wehba, *Automation in Moderation*, 53 CORNELL INT'L L. J. 41 (2020); Evelyn Douek, *Governing Online Speech: From "Posts-as-Trumps" to Proportionality and Probability*, 121 COLUM. L. REV. 759, 791 (2021); Tim Wu, *Will Artificial Intelligence Eat the Law? The Rise of Hybrid Social-Ordering Systems*, 119 COLUM. L. REV. 2001 (2019); Aziz Z. Huq, *A Right to a Human Decision*, 106 VA. L. REV. 611 (2020).

[39] Douek, *supra* note 38, at 791.

[40] *See* MARTHA MINOW, SAVING THE NEWS: WHY THE CONSTITUTION CALLS FOR GOVERNMENT ACTION TO PRESERVE FREEDOM OF SPEECH (2021).

[41] *More Than Half of U.S. Counties Have No Access or Very Limited Access to Local News*, NORTHWESTERN UNIVERSITY, MEDILL SCHOOL OF JOURNALISM (Nov. 16, 2023), https://www.medill.northwestern.edu/news/2023/more-than-half-of-us-counties-have-no-access-or-very-limited-access-to-local-news.html

[42] *Id.*

Many studies have shown that when a community does not have a strong print or digital news organization, corruption increases and voter participation decreases. One study of eleven California cities found that when there are fewer reporters covering an area, fewer people run for mayor and fewer people vote.[43]

The internet and social media have contributed to this because they allow people to get their news for free, and thus, they do not need to purchase newspapers. Few newspapers have successfully found a way to monetize their online presence. Google, Facebook, Instagram, and others link to news stories and reap the advertising revenue, with none of the money going to the news organizations that did the actual reporting. The tech platforms are swallowing the profits that otherwise would go to the newspapers that are covering events, conducting investigations, and writing stories.

When news organizations vanish, there is no one to go to the city council meetings or do the investigative reporting to uncover corruption or report on local elections. Google and Facebook and Instagram do not have newsrooms to do this work, and they are not going to create them.

There is a bill pending in the California legislature – the California Journalism Preservation Act – that would help solve this problem. Assembly Bill 886 would require platforms to pay a fee for the news on their platforms, which would allow journalism providers to recoup their fair share of revenue for the news stories they produce. The law would require that these internet and social media platforms pay a "journalism usage fee" to news outlets for news content appearing on their sites. The law would create an arbitration process with newsrooms and establish a fee that the companies would pay to carry news articles.

The experience of other countries suggests that this type of legislation works. In 2021, Australia passed a law requiring social media companies to share a portion of the profits they make from news content with news companies. The law generated almost $150 million in revenue in its first year.[44] Canada adopted a similar law last year.

Yet, it is unclear whether such targeted financial assessments would survive First Amendment scrutiny. In *Arkansas Writers' Project, Inc. v. Ragland*, the Court ruled that the government cannot discriminate among types of publications.[45] A state exempted from its sales tax special interest publications, such as religious, professional, trade, and sports journals, but did not exempt general interest magazines. The Court emphasized that any differential taxation of the press – either of the press

43 Michael Hiltzik, *How the Decline of Local News Exposes the Public to Lies and Corruption*, L.A. Times (August 29, 2022), https://www.latimes.com/business/story/2022-08-29/decline-of-local-news.

44 Bill Grueskin, *Australia Pressured Google and Facebook to Pay for Journalism. Is America Next?*, Colum. Journalism Rev. (Mar. 9, 2022), https://www.cjr.org/business_of_news/australia-pressured-google-and-facebook-to-pay-for-journalism-is-america-next.php.

45 481 U.S. 221 (1987).

as opposed to others in society or of particular parts of the press – risked chilling reporting. Yet there is a key distinction: The current proposal would not impose a tax on social media but would rather require that they pay for what they use.

The point is that the internet and social media endanger the press, and protecting freedom of the press requires deliberate action. First Amendment doctrines will need to be adapted to accomplish this.

Finally, another way the internet and social media threaten democracy is when foreign nations and foreign entities use them to influence the outcome of elections. As mentioned earlier, there is now incontrovertible evidence that Russia engaged in a concerted effort to use speech, including false speech, to influence the outcome of the 2016 presidential election.[46] This was suspected during the campaign, and American intelligence agencies confirmed it soon after the election.[47] In February 2018, Special Counsel Robert Mueller issued a 37-page indictment charging thirteen Russians and three companies with executing a scheme to subvert the 2016 election and help to elect Donald Trump as president.[48] Mueller's indictment details "how the Russians repeatedly turned to Facebook and Instagram, often using stolen identities to pose as Americans, to sow discord among the electorate by creating Facebook groups, distributing divisive ads and posting inflammatory images."[49]

Although condemning Russia's meddling in the American election is easy, solving the underlying First Amendment issue is difficult. Certainly, illegal conduct, such as hacking into the Democratic National Committee headquarters and subsequently disseminating unlawfully gained information,[50] is not constitutionally protected. But what about foreign speech that is legal and that expresses an opinion – or even false speech?

The Supreme Court has repeatedly stated that the source of information does not matter for First Amendment purposes. In *First National Bank of Boston v. Bellotti*, in 1978, the Supreme Court declared unconstitutional a Massachusetts law that prohibited banks or businesses from making contributions or expenditures in connection with ballot initiatives and referenda.[51] Justice Powell, writing for the Court, concluded that the value of speech is in informing the audience. Any restriction on speech, regardless of its source, therefore undermines the First Amendment. Justice Powell explained: "The inherent worth of the speech in terms of its capacity for

46 *See, e.g.*, Mueller, *supra* note 11.

47 *Id.*

48 Indictment, United States v. Internet Research Agency, LLC, No. 1:18-cr-00032-DLC (D.D.C. Feb. 16, 2018), 2018 WL 914777.

49 Sheera Frenkel & Katie Benner, *To Stir Discord in 2016, Russians Turned Most Often to Facebook*, N.Y. Times (Feb. 17, 2018), http://www.nytimes.com/2018/02/17/technology/indictment-russians-tech-facebook.html.

50 Raphael Satter, *Inside Story: How Russians Hacked the Democrats' Emails*, AP (Nov. 4, 2017), https://www.apnews.com/dea73efc01594839957c3c9a6c962b8a.

51 First Nat. Bank of Bos. v. Bellotti, 435 U.S. 765, 767–68 (1978).

informing the public does not depend upon the identity of its source, whether corporation, association, union, or individual."[52]

The Court relied heavily on this in *Citizens United v. Federal Election Commission* to hold that corporations have the constitutional right to spend unlimited amounts of money directly from their treasuries to elect or defeat candidates for political office.[53] The Court stressed that the value of the speech does not depend on the speaker's identity and held that corporate speech is protected not because of the inherent rights of corporations but because all expression contributes to the marketplace of ideas. The Court wrote that "the First Amendment bars regulatory distinctions based on a speaker's identity."[54] On other occasions, too, the Court has declared that "[t]he identity of the speaker is not decisive in determining whether speech is protected."[55]

But if this is so, why should it matter that a speaker is a foreign government or a foreign individual? Federal law prohibits foreign governments, individuals, and corporations from contributing money to candidates for federal office.[56] A federal court upheld this restriction on foreign speech, declaring, "It is fundamental to the definition of our national political community that foreign citizens do not have a constitutional right to participate in, and thus may be excluded from, activities of democratic self-government." As a result, it asserted that "the United States has a compelling interest for purposes of First Amendment analysis in limiting the participation of foreign citizens in activities of American democratic self-government, and in thereby preventing foreign influence over the US political process."[57] But can this be reconciled with the Supreme Court's declaration that the speaker's identity should not matter in First Amendment analysis? Although it is not a comfortable answer, I do not see a way to exclude foreign speakers that would be consistent with the Court's premise that the speaker's identity cannot be the basis for regulation. The First Amendment assumes that more speech is better, whether the speaker is foreign or domestic.

At the very least, however, it would be desirable to disclose speakers' identities so that people can know when speech is coming from a foreign government or other foreign source. But this, too, raises First Amendment issues, as the Supreme Court has held that there is a First Amendment right to speak anonymously. In *McIntyre v. Ohio Elections Commission*, the Court declared unconstitutional a law prohibiting the distribution of anonymous campaign literature.[58] Justice Stevens, writing for the Court, stated that "an author's decision to remain anonymous, like other

[52] *Id.* at 776–77 (emphasis added).
[53] Citizens United v. Fed. Election Comm'n, 558 U.S. 310, 319 (2010).
[54] *Id.* at 350, 394.
[55] Pac. Gas & Elec. Co. v. Pub. Utils. Comm'n of Cal., 475 U.S. 1, 8 (1986) (plurality opinion).
[56] Blauman v. FCC, 800 F. Supp. 2d 281, 284 (D.D.C. 2011), *aff'd*, 565 U.S. 1104 (2012).
[57] *Id.* at 288.
[58] McIntyre v. Ohio Elections Comm'n, 514 U.S. 334, 357 (1995).

decisions concerning omissions or additions to the content of a publication, is an aspect of the freedom of speech protected by the First Amendment."[59] Further, Justice Stevens contended that anonymity also provides a way for a speaker "who may be personally unpopular to ensure that readers will not prejudge her message simply because they do not like its proponent."[60]

All that said, there is a compelling interest in stopping speakers from masking their identity and deceiving voters. It is one thing to speak anonymously but another to falsely present oneself, especially to deceive and manipulate voters. Whether the speaker is domestic or foreign, that should be regarded as a form of fraud that is unprotected by the First Amendment. At the very least, we should implement laws that prohibit this, along with stronger disclosure laws, especially for foreign speakers. The Supreme Court has consistently upheld the constitutionality of laws that require disclosure of the identity of those spending money in election campaigns. These requirements must be significantly strengthened.

The transnational nature of the internet makes exercising control over speech elusive, even if it were to be constitutional. As the 2016 presidential election demonstrated, foreign governments can use the internet and social media to influence elections without their officials and agents ever physically entering the United States. It is unclear how American law could be successfully applied to them. The internet thus enables them to engage in false speech (and all other kinds of expression) with relatively little fear of legal sanctions, and whether there could be meaningful international sanctions is uncertain at best.

6.4 CONCLUSION

It is crucial to recognize that the internet and social media are different from the modes of communication that preceded them and that they will require new doctrines for First Amendment analysis because of the inadequacy of the doctrines applied to traditional media. The internet and social media provide great benefits in terms of speech, but they also pose unprecedented harms as well.

[59] *Id.* at 341–42.
[60] *Id.* at 342.

7

Countering the Mosaic of Threats to Press Functions

Lili Levi

The idealized press, which generated effusive praise from the Supreme Court during the golden age of media law in the late twentieth century, was a mature, economically robust, and politically powerful industry. As an industry, the press in that era fulfilled a number of key functions, such as setting the agenda of public issues, swaying the conduct of political campaigns and elections, informing the public of current events, and curating a common understanding of newsworthy developments. The news media had a comfortable relationship of give-and-take with the government but also acted as the Fourth Estate by uncovering, publishing, and amplifying information about government malfeasance[1] and political disinformation.[2] Against this backdrop, courts praised newspapers for their multiple functions as public proxies, audience educators, and watchdogs tasked with keeping government abuse in check. In turn, surveys indicated that the public had faith in the press.[3]

But over the last several decades, a confluence of economic, technological, and sociopolitical change has upended both the news industry and the public's view of it. While it is unrealistic to hope for a return to the old days of the press, the

[1] In the most high-profile example, The Washington Post's reporting on the Watergate break-in helped end Richard Nixon's presidency. For the reporters' account, *see* CARL BERNSTEIN & BOB WOODWARD, ALL THE PRESIDENT'S MEN (1974). Under threat of impeachment and with his claim of executive privilege rejected by the Supreme Court, President Nixon resigned from office on August 9, 1974. *See* United States v. Nixon, 418 U.S. 683 (1974).

[2] In publishing excerpts from the "Pentagon Papers," The New York Times and Washington Post were combating government lies about the conduct and progress of the Vietnam war (as well as testing the boundaries of prior restraint doctrine under the First Amendment). *See* New York Times Co. v. United States, 403 U.S. 713 (1971).

[3] *See, e.g.*, Jeffrey M. Jones, *Confidence in U.S. Institutions Down; Average at New Low*, GALLUP (July 5, 2022), https://news.gallup.com/poll/394283/confidence-institutions-down-average-new-low.aspx. Public approval varied over the years. *See* Erin C. Carroll, *Beyond the Watchdog: Using Law to Build Trust in the Press*, 3 J. FREE SPEECH L. 57, 60 (2023) and sources cited therein.

functions the press has historically played remain essential to democracy. Indeed, one can imagine the press playing an even more robust role today in combating disinformation disseminated by a variety of sources. Yet the news industry today is no longer economically powerful: Newspapers are in peril, television and cable viewership are in decline, news deserts dot the landscape, and jaw-dropping numbers of journalistic staff cuts have drained expertise from newsrooms.[4] Social media have cannibalized content and replaced a scarcity of frequencies with a scarcity of attention, the news industry has far less political power, cell phones have allowed everyone to claim citizen journalist status, both the right and the left have complaints about the asserted bias of press organs, and a common understanding of public issues is a pipe dream in a highly polarized political landscape.

Under these circumstances, the fate of the press's functions is an existential question both for the news media as we know it and for contemporary American democracy. Managing the complexity of this kind of information environment[5] calls for independent and principled engagement with issues of public concern by those who hew to journalistic values, such as truth, verification, completeness, investigation, and context. It also calls for appropriate legal protections.

In this chapter, I seek to explore the evolving mosaic of threats facing the American press and consider what, if any, legal rights the wielders of the press function need in response. I begin by identifying a set of key threats facing the press – economic, legal, technological, and audience-based developments. I then propose some initial responses to these threats along five dimensions – funding conditions, a mixed legal strategy, artificial intelligence (AI) policy, industry restructuring, and trust enhancement. I also call for a commitment to press self-examination from the vantage point of fundamental journalistic values in a democracy.

7.1 EVOLVING THREATS TO PRESS FUNCTIONS

Challenges to press functions today can be grouped into four categories – institutional/journalistic, legal, technological, and audience-based. In combination, they

4 Pew Research Center, *State of the Media*, https://www.pewresearch.org/topic/news-habits-media/news-media-trends/state-of-the-news-media-project/; Michael Lipka & Elisa Shearer, *Audiences Are Declining for Traditional News Media in the U.S. – With Some Exceptions*, Pew Rsch. Ctr. (Nov. 28, 2023), https://www.pewresearch.org/short-reads/2023/11/28/audiences-are-declining-for-traditional-news-media-in-the-us-with-some-exceptions/.

5 For example, the tech platforms from which many Americans now get their news do not – and do not seek to – perform the press's traditional functions. Falsity and conspiracy theories travel virally online. At the same time, the business models and technological limitations of these information intermediaries inhibit effective content moderation and increase the circulation of polluted information.

undermine journalistic norms and routines, erode the perceived legitimacy of the press, and hamper its democracy-promoting work.

7.1.1 *Economic Instability and Its Institutional/Journalistic Consequences*

The combination of declining advertising revenue and increased profit-maximizing public company ownership has led to a financial crisis for the news sector. Many Americans now rely on social media for their news, rather than on local or national news outlets.[6] The social media sector has not shouldered the cost of lost traffic to news sites or adequately compensated the press for the use of its content. The economic decline of the news industry has led to compromised journalistic norms, a disaster for journalistic personnel, and, with few exceptions, a practical abandonment of the press's watchdog role.[7]

Traditional editorial judgments have been unduly compromised by the desire to retain audiences, including via story selection designed to produce clicks.[8] Pressures on journalists have increased their reliance on social media to generate stories. Insufficiently mindful of the questionable information environment, reporters have participated in normalizing bias and information skews bred online by reporting on, and thereby amplifying, unreliable material originating online. Established news outlets have served as megaphones for conspiracy theories. The rise in the use of native advertising in the news section has joined newsworthiness decisions driven by audience analytics to blur the traditionally sacrosanct line between advertising and the news.[9] The failure of press institutions to resist commercial pressures as they chase partisan audiences has also resulted in bleed-through between opinion and news programming – as evidenced by Fox News' role in amplifying the "stolen" election trope regarding the 2020 presidential election. More generally, claims of political and ideological partisanship by media outlets have been made by both

6 *See, e.g.*, Jacob Liedke & Jeffrey Gottfried, *U.S. Adults Under 30 Now Trust Information from Social Media Almost as Much as from National News Outlets*, Pew Rsch. Ctr. (Oct. 27, 2022), https://www.pewresearch.org/short-reads/2022/10/27/u-s-adults-under-30-now-trust-information-from-social-media-almost-as-much-as-from-national-news-outlets/. Recently, only 2 percent of the people offered free newspaper subscriptions to their local newspapers in Philadelphia in an academic experiment accepted the offer. Kevin Lind, *They Gave Local News Away for Free. Virtually Nobody Wanted It*, Colum. Journalism Rev. (Feb. 8, 2024), https://www.cjr.org/business_of_news/they-gave-local-news-away-for-free-virtually-nobody-wanted-it.php.

7 For example, investigative journalism is a victim of lack of funding and reduced reporter resources and expertise. At a minimum, expense limits the number of investigative pieces published and decisions about choice of investigative targets.

8 The strategy of using technology to increase revenue in the digital space through subscriptions and paywalls appears to have worked well only for a few of the powerhouse national outlets (such as *The New York Times*).

9 *See, e.g.*, Lili Levi, *A "Faustian Pact"? Native Advertising and the Future of the Press*, 57 Ariz. L. Rev. 647 (2015); Ellen P. Goodman, *Stealth Marketing and Editorial Integrity*, 85 Tex. L. Rev. 83 (2006).

conservatives and progressives for some time. An NPR editor's claim of liberal bias in NPR programming has brought the matter to the forefront of public discussion again recently.[10]

Financial problems have also led to the closure of many local and regional news outlets. News deserts and the failure to cover local news, politics, and the state house have had significant negative effects – both on underserved local communities and on efforts to check local and regional corruption.[11] The financial strictures have also led publishers to outsource reporting functions to nonemployee journalists, with all the instability for the workers and additional oversight responsibilities that hiring freelancers entails. And with fewer professionally trained news staff, the risk that shoddy reporting practices will affect the quality of the final product rises. Meanwhile, news organizations have been forced increasingly to rely on packaged news and information provided by public relations companies and entities whose partisanship is disguised (sometimes referred to as "pink slime" journalism[12]), which further undermines the independence of the press function.[13]

7.1.2 *The Chilling Effects of Increasing Legal Ambivalence and Uncertainty*

The evolving legal hurdles for the press are both substantive and procedural, including questions about the judicial recognition of constitutional privileges for the press. For example, media law scholars have highlighted the risk to press function from recent attacks on the press-protective The New York Times Co.

[10] *See, e.g.*, Benjamin Mullin & Katie Robertson, *NPR in Turmoil After It Is Accused of Liberal Bias*, N.Y. Times (Apr. 11, 2024), https://www.nytimes.com/2024/04/11/business/media/npr-criticism-liberal-bias.html; Benjamin Mullin, *NPR Suspends Editor Whose Essay Criticized the Broadcaster*, N.Y. Times (Apr. 11, 2024), https://www.nytimes.com/2024/04/16/business/media/npr-suspends-business-editor.html; Oliver Darcy, *NPR Faces Right-Wing Revolt and Calls for Defunding After Editor Claims Left-Wing Bias*, CNN (Apr. 11, 2024), https://www.cnn.com/2024/04/11/media/npr-uri-berliner-left-bias-right-wing-media/index.html.

[11] *See, e.g.*, Richard L. Hasen, *Cheap Speech and What It Has Done (To American Democracy)*, 16 First Amend. L. Rev. 200, 209 (2017).

[12] On "pink slime" journalism, *see, e.g.*, Priyanjana Bengani et al., *"Pink Slime": Partisan Journalism and the Future of Local News*, Tow Ctr. for Digital Journ., https://towcenter.columbia.edu/sites/default/files/content/%E2%80%9CPink%20Slime%E2%80%9D_%20Partisan%20journalism%20and%20the%20future%20of%20local%20news.pdf (describing it as a subset of partisan news – mimicking the appearance of local news but "whose primary original contribution is partisan content or reputation laundering that lacks transparency around intent, authorship, ownership, and funding.")

[13] Much "news" is produced today by entities with propagandistic goals distinct from journalistic values. *See, e.g.*, *id.* Think tanks funded by ideological groups, new outfits such as Project Veritas that seek the mantle of the press when convenient but that practice "gotcha" journalism and editorial manipulation in order to achieve particular political purposes, untrained individuals who take to YouTube channels to disseminate their conspiracy-inflected take on current events are all dangerous to the goal of a free press working to shore up democracy in the public interest.

v. Sullivan doctrine.[14] On the Supreme Court itself, Justices Gorsuch and Thomas have called for reconsideration of the doctrine.[15]

In lower courts, some judges appear less disposed than previously to dismiss actual malice-grounded defamation cases despite the heightened pleading requirements of *Bell Atlantic Corp. v. Twombly* and *Ashcroft v. Iqbal*.[16] In turn, juries have granted multi-million-dollar damage awards, which include massive punitive components.[17] Settlements are also more likely in such circumstances, at least in part because of concerns about revelations in discovery.[18] The possibility of fee-shifting can also be expected to have a chilling effect.[19] Moreover, procedural hurdles under state law, such as supersedeas bonds, have also made it difficult for news organizations to attempt to challenge extensive damages assessed against them.[20]

14 *See, e.g.*, Lili Levi, *Disinformation and the Defamation Renaissance: A Misleading Promise of "Truth,"* 57 Richmond L. Rev. 1235 (2023). Although the Court has not yet granted *certiorari* in numerous cases that have purported to raise the question (and has recently cited *Sullivan*'s actual malice standard in a non-defamation, true threats context in Counterman v. Colorado, 143 S.Ct. 2106 (2024)), political plaintiffs – such as Sarah Palin – continue to advance claims seeking to undermine the line of cases establishing the boundaries of the actual malice doctrine. *See, e.g.*, Josh Gerstein, *Appeals Court Mulls Reviving Sarah Palin's Suit Against New York Times – Again*, Politico (Nov. 6, 2023), https://www.politico.com/news/2023/11/06/sarah-palin-libel-lawsuit-appeal-00125595; Blankenship v. NBCUniversal, 60 F.4th 744 (4th Cir. 2023), 144 S.Ct. 5 (2023); Coral Ridge Ministries Media Inc. v. Southern Poverty Law Center, 6 F.4th 1247, 1251–53 (11th Cir. 2021), *cert. denied*, 142 S.Ct. 2453 (2022). The Court could grant *cert* in the "right" case or a majority could revise the press-protective doctrines adopted in what are typically styled *Sullivan*'s "progeny."

15 *See, e.g.*, McKee v. Cosby, 139 S.Ct. 675 (Thomas, J. concurring in the denial of *certiorari*); Berisha v. Lawson, 141 S.Ct. 2424 (Gorsuch, J. & Thomas, J. dissent from denial of *certiorari*).

16 *See, e.g.*, Levi, *supra* note 14, at n. 176 and accompanying text.

17 *See, e.g.*, *id.*; Jeremy W. Peters & Katie Robertson, *Fox Will Pay $787.5 Million to Settle Defamation Suit*, N.Y. Times (Apr. 18, 2023), https://www.nytimes.com/2023/04/18/business/media/fox-dominion-defamation-settle.html. *See also* Gabriel Tynes, *Oklahoma Jury Reaches $25 Million Verdict Against Newspaper in Defamation Case*, CNS (Feb. 5, 2024), https://www.courthousenews.com/oklahoma-jury-reaches-25-million-verdict-against-newspaper-in-defamation-case/ (reporting on jury award of $5 million in compensatory and $20 million in punitive damages on an Oklahoma newspaper for misidentifying an announcer who uttered racist comments into a hot mike during coverage of a high school athletic event.)

18 *See, e.g.*, Quinta Jurecic, *Dominion v. Fox Is Just the Beginning*, Lawfare (Apr. 19, 2023), https://www.lawfaremedia.org/article/dominion-v.-fox-is-just-the-beginning ("the pretrial discovery process allowed Dominion to make public an extraordinary amount of damaging information about Fox's operations and the mechanics of the Big Lie of 2020 election fraud.")

19 Recently, for example, a federal judge ordered a plaintiff in a defamation suit to pay the defendants' legal fees when his case was dismissed. *See* Jack Baer, *Patrick Reed Ordered to Pay Legal Fees for Defendants in Dismissed $1 Billion Lawsuit*, Yahoo Sports (Jan. 7, 2024), https://sports.yahoo.com/patrick-reed-ordered-to-pay-legal-fees-for-defendants-in-dismissed-1-billion-lawsuit-054407072.html. Although this was press-protective in this case, in which a golfer had sued eighteen news organizations for defamation, the possibility of fee shifting could well threaten press defendants in an atmosphere of growing judicial ambivalence about the press.

20 *See, e.g.*, Lili Levi, *The Weaponized Lawsuit Against the Media: Litigation Funding as a New Threat to Journalism*, 66 Amer. U. L. Rev. 761, 772–73, 815–13 (2017).

State legislatures have entered the arena as well. Although some have enacted laws to protect the press – such as New York's amendment to its anti-SLAPP law to adopt actual malice as a state requirement[21] – others, such as Florida, have been considering legislation under which publishing a story only supported by an anonymous source would be considered reckless disregard of falsity, regardless of context.[22]

There also appears to be a new willingness to prosecute, enforce, or litigate claims against the press over its coverage. The recent rise of a powerful plaintiff's defamation bar has already had a notable impact.[23] Many of the pro-press rulings by courts – including the Supreme Court – between the 1960s and the 1980s were litigated by a sophisticated media defense bar on behalf of well-heeled newspapers. Now the press and the media defense bar are hard-pressed to afford rights-expanding litigation. By contrast, Peter Thiel's funding of Hulk Hogan's privacy lawsuit against Gawker led to a $140 million mega-verdict that resulted in the magazine's bankruptcy.[24] The *Gawker* case also indicates the use of doctrines other than defamation law to impose liability on the press for publication.[25]

[21] N.Y. Civ. Rights Law § 79-a(1)(a)(1)–(2) (2020).

[22] *See, e.g.*, Emily Hockett & Joe Wolf, *For Second Straight Year, Florida Lawmakers Consider Bills Targeting Defamation Law*, Reporters Comm. for Freedom of the Press (Feb. 28, 2024), https://www.rcfp.org/fla-defamation-analysis-2024/.

[23] *See* Levi, *supra* note 14, at 1279–84.

[24] *See* Levi, *supra* note 20. (To be sure, the sensationalist Gawker may not have been the best example of responsible journalism on which to base an argument for increased press rights, but the publication *did* sometimes engage in "real" journalism, and many important constitutional rights have been litigated on behalf of problematic defendants.) Analogously, the open offer of litigation funding by Elon Musk to employees "unfairly treated" by their employers due to their posts on X (formerly Twitter) is another example of increased incentives for the plaintiff's bar to engage in censorious suits even if the outcome is not a sure bet for the plaintiff. *See, e.g.*, Michael Sin & Vlad Savov, *Musk Promises to Fund Legal Fights of Discriminated X Users*, Bloomberg (Aug. 6, 2023), https://www.bloomberg.com/news/articles/2023-08-06/musk-says-discriminated-x-users-will-get-help-with-legal-bills. Litigation funding by third parties does not seem to be limited to conservative funders. *See* Jose Pagliery, *E. Jean Carroll Moves to Keep Who's Bankrolling Her Trump Rape Lawsuit a Secret*, Daily Beast (Apr. 21, 2023), https://news.yahoo.com/e-jean-carroll-moves-keep-190419292.html?guccounter=1&guce_referrer=aHRocHM6Ly93d3cuYmluZy5jb20v&guce_referrer_sig=AQAAABbOzZoquBF7d1yN36b5So7wotrnw09x6TfA7VUZLQJPbiFPsFq3b-9CiUORnh2_3S0G-r3_N5J0vdq8GNe1bOfuuKvtTGhYroJGIXcSCzjJdtvLL0JmkGa04iFHKYplO6xD3RfrIIIbU3ltPv9TZndX5RYU5gPSmcFpu0UDJhMN.

[25] For example, business torts such as interference with contractual relations appear increasingly to be drafted into service against press coverage. Privacy law presents a particularly attractive avenue as well. Clever plaintiff's lawyers are also bringing suits under corporate law against news organizations. In a recent action against Fox Corp., for example, the plaintiffs have argued in the Chancery Court of Delaware that the board of Fox News's parent company breached its fiduciary duties of oversight under Delaware corporate law by allowing Fox News to propagate false programming that put the company at risk of catastrophic legal liability for defamation. Schwartz v. Murdoch & Fox Corp., https://www.dandodiary.com/wp-content/uploads/sites/893/2023/04/Fox-Derivative-Lawsuit-Complaint.pdf.

The plaintiff's defamation bar has also used the demand letter requesting pre-publication review – with extensive document retention demands – as a tool to attempt to deter

In addition to publication, there are also evolving hurdles to the press's newsgathering functions.[26] For example, on the criminal side, there has been an increase since the Obama administration in the number of instances in which the government has threatened reporters with liability under the Espionage Act for refusing to reveal their sources. Concerns with freedom of the press and worries about the criminalization of the normal practices of national security reporters led many to object to the Department of Justice's (DOJ) request for Julian Assange's extradition to the United States to face trial on Espionage Act charges.[27] The Computer Fraud and Abuse Act (CFAA) has recently been used to justify the indictment of journalist Tim Burke.[28] The government's ability to get access to a reporter's notes and information via subpoenas to third-party platforms (such as email or social media services) has been a practical problem. Outside the criminal context, access to information has also been cut significantly – and certainly since the COVID-19 pandemic.[29] In addition, newsgathering is indirectly impeded by the popularity of nondisclosure agreements (NDAs) signed by sources.[30]

To be sure, the press can still count on significant legal protection – particularly for publication – under current constitutional, statutory, and common law. But the trends described here suggest an increasingly skeptical attitude by courts, legislatures, and government actors toward the press in the legal sphere. This mixed legal picture presents its own complex type of threats to the press, including the particular incentive effects of uncertainty and the need for a variety of responsive legal and policy strategies.

publication. *See* Lachlan Cartwright, *New York Times, NBC, and '60 Minutes' Bigwigs Hired These Media Assassins to Fight #MeToo Stories*, Daily Beast (Jul. 20, 2018), https://www.thedailybeast.com/60-minutes-boss-hired-law-firm-over-metoo-story.

26 For a superb account of shifts in the "First Amendment equilibrium" between the press and the executive, *see generally* Christina Koningisor & Lyrissa Lidsky, *First Amendment Disequilibrium*, 110 Va. L. Rev. 1 (2024) (discussing, *inter alia*, the law governing access to national security materials, confidential source protection, and informational access rights).

27 *See, e.g.*, Mathew Ingram, *Can Julian Assange Appeal His Extradition to the US? A British Court Will Decide*, Colum. Journalism Rev. (Feb. 22, 2024), https://www.cjr.org/the_media_today/assange_appeal_extradition_wikileaks_press_freedom.php. Assange agreed to a plea deal in June 2024; the impact of this plea deal on the work of national security journalism is not yet clear.

28 *See, e.g.*, Sarah Jeong, *When Does a Journalist Become a Hacker?*, The Verge (Feb. 23, 2024), https://www.theverge.com/2024/2/23/24081656/tim-burke-journalism-hacking-cfaa.

29 *See, e.g.*, GAO, *Freedom of Information Act: Selected Agencies Adapted to the COVID-19 Pandemic but Face Ongoing Challenges and Backlogs* (Jan. 26, 2022), https://www.gao.gov/products/gao-22-105040.

30 Michelle Dean, *Contracts of Silence*, Colum. Journalism Rev. (Feb. 14, 2018), https://www.cjr.org/special_report/nda-agreement.php; Gabriel Arana, *Journalists Aren't as Tied by NDAs as They Think*, Colum. Journalism Rev. (Dec. 11, 2017), https://www.cjr.org/watchdog/journalists-nda-nondisclosure-harassment-metoo-newsrooms.php.

7.1.3 *The Dual Effects of Technological Change, Including Generative AI*

Many functional problems for the press – from newsgathering to story generation and topic selection – are bound up with technology.[31] For example, due to the availability of spyware like Pegasus, surveillance cameras in the streets and on commercial buildings, Ring cameras on people's houses, and the ubiquitous cell phone camera, Bob Woodward and Carl Bernstein's meeting with Deep Throat could never remain secret today. Technological advances have also brought danger to the journalistic enterprise and to press workers, including through online harassment, particularly of reporters of color, women reporters, and non-Christian reporters.[32]

The evolving technological challenges for the press function are likely to metastasize in the age of generative AI. Many newsrooms are already using generative AI to accomplish a variety of tasks.[33] The current rhetoric about generative AI is largely binary and hyperbolic. On the one end of spectrum, optimistic media observers identify potentially powerful benefits that generative AI could bring to journalism, particularly in saving time and effort in routinizing a variety of tasks and helping small newsrooms.[34] Other observers, however, have a more dystopian vision of generative AI's effects on journalism – including concerns about the possibility of training bias and the unequal distribution of access to the tools of generative AI around the world.[35]

One major concern is the prospect of the "daily me" on steroids.[36] The CEO of OpenAI opined to Axios that large language models would provide hyper-personalized

[31] This is not only with respect to the technological tools reporters can use for their newsgathering functions, but also with respect to the challenges posed for their work by the imperatives of developing technology. With respect to newsgathering as such, for example, journalists are now faced with increasing technological surveillance by government and private users and challenges to source anonymity and access to their preparatory materials. Just as the availability of technology to allow the mining of large datasets of information can enable the discovery of sophisticated stories about systemic problems, technological advances and the structure of technological tools can affect the types of stories that the press covers and news organizations' values.

[32] *See* Lili Levi, *Racialized, Judaized, Feminized: Identity-Based Attacks on the Press*, 20 First Am. L. Rev. 35 (2022) and sources cited therein. Such harassment occurs constantly online for at least some journalists, and sometimes even crosses over IRL. *Id.* It stands to reason that campaigns of harassment have chilling impacts, especially over time.

[33] Publishers argue that relying on generative AI for routine journalistic tasks will leave room for professional journalists to engage in deeper and better work in the public interest. While this is theoretically possible, the reality of the cost-cutting at news organizations in the recent past casts some doubt on whether news organizations – particularly corporate-owned businesses – will consistently be willing to expend money saved by AI on reporters and expensive deep-dive journalism. For a critique of the trend toward "digital piecework," *see* Bengani et al., *supra* note 12 (citing Nicole Cohen). These are issues that deserve to be taken up at a minimum in contract negotiations and union talks.

[34] *See, e.g.*, Charlie Beckett & Mira Yaseen, *Generating Change: A Global Survey of What News Organisations Are Doing with AI*, JournalismAI (2023).

[35] *See id.* (describing some journalist responses).

[36] Cass R. Sunstein, Republic.com 2.0 (2007) (elaborating on the "daily me," a notion introduced by Nicholas Negroponte).

content.[37] If the American public continues to be politically polarized, then won't this degree of hyper-personalization lead to an even more fractured polity? In a related vein, some worry that the efficiency-based logic of AI tools could potentially transform the nature of news in ways inconsistent with traditional journalism.[38] The answer may depend on AI design[39] and the sophistication of news organizations' generative AI use policies and negotiation tactics in their dealings with AI companies.

Another concern for news purveyors is the likelihood of increased claims of copyright infringement, defamation, invasion of privacy, breach of rights of publicity, and other such allegations.[40] Much attention must be paid to the mix of AI production and human review in order to reduce potential liability.[41]

Finally, the increased use of AI in newsrooms carries obvious concerns about the impact on public trust in journalism – which, as I describe below, is reportedly at a troubling low already.

7.1.4 *The Politicization of the Press and Loss of Faith*

An undergirding problematic development is the politicization of the press and the public's loss of faith in the media. Both anecdotal evidence and public surveys have shown a marked decline in institutional trust, including of the press, in the past decade in the United States.[42] President Donald Trump's unending attacks on the

[37] *See, e.g.*, Jim Love, *Sam Altman: The Future of AI Could Be "Troubling,"* Axios (Jan. 17, 2024), https://www.itworldcanada.com/post/sam-altman-the-future-of-ai-could-be-troubling.

[38] Felix M. Simon, *Artificial Intelligence in the News: How AI Retools, Rationalizes, and Reshapes Journalism and the Public Arena*, Tow Ctr. for Digital Journ., Dec. 2023, at 3–5, https://academiccommons.columbia.edu/doi/10.7916/ncm5-3v06.

[39] In Finland, for example, the personal "news assistant" Voitto offers subscribers article summaries relating to subjects of their interest but also ensures that a variety of viewpoints are reflected. *See* Barbara Gruber, *Facts, Fakes and Figures: How AI is Influencing Journalism*, Kulturtechniken 4.0, Goethe-Institut, https://www.goethe.de/prj/k40/en/lan/aij.html. Particularly if hyper-personalization could lead to financial security for those engaging in the press's functions, perhaps attention to design could reduce concerns about echo chamber effects. To be sure, however, the failure of personalized news app Artifact, brainchild of Instagram's co-founders, demonstrates that these types of tools have not yet achieved financial sustainability. So the hype of personalization has not yet borne fruit in practice, though it will likely do so in the future.

[40] Outside the press context, training-focused copyright litigation is currently ongoing. For recent discussions of AI liability, *see*, e.g., Peter Henderson et al., *Where's the Liability in Harmful AI Speech?*, 3 J. Free Speech L. 589 (2023); Eugene Volokh, *Large Libel Models? Liability for AI Output*, 3 J. Free Speech L. 489 (2023). In addition, query how courts will apply the *Sullivan* doctrine to articles based on false information produced by generative AI. At least one defamation claim is currently being litigated against OpenAI. *See* Ashley Belanger, *OpenAI Faces Defamation Suit After ChatGPT Completely Fabricated Another Lawsuit*, Ars Technica (June 9, 2023), https://arstechnica.com/tech-policy/2023/06/openai-sued-for-defamation-after-chatgpt-fabricated-yet-another-lawsuit/.

[41] There have been many reports of "hallucinations" by generative AI tools. The likelihood of error and bias in the work of generative AI services is exacerbated by the fact that over time, the training data for the large language models will include AI LLMs themselves, including their hallucinations.

[42] *See* Lili Levi, *Real "Fake News" and Fake "Fake News,"* 16 First Amend. L. Rev. 232 (2018).

mainstream press as purveyors of "fake news" and "enemies of the American people" doubtless served as a factor in reinforcing that sense of public distrust.[43] One of the most harmful effects of such delegitimizing tactics is the politicization of the press, which results in generalized and partisan doubt about everything produced by a particular outlet, rather than simply skepticism about any specific news story.[44] If the audience does not believe what the press reports, what is gained even with journalistic or legal reform?[45] As noted above, these effects seem likely to become even more dismal if, as is likely, the use of generative AI optimizes the dissemination of false information via increasingly convincing deepfakes.

7.2 THE MULTIPLICITY OF RESPONSES NEEDED

These various challenges to the functions of the press cannot be solved by interventions in any one area alone. The particular sorts of threats identified should influence the particular responses, and this should be an iterative and evolutionary process.

43 The news media in general no longer constitute the kind of powerful industry of the past, and former President Trump's attacks on the media prove that politicians feel far less at risk if they criticize the press.

44 Whether audiences don't believe anything because they don't know what to believe, or are particularly credulous when they hear political conspiracy theories, or simply respond according to their subconscious biases and heuristics (*e.g.*, confirmation bias), or deploy different degrees of skepticism depending on the party affiliation of the speaker, the widespread distrust of the American people in the press – or at least in the press whose politics do not align with theirs – is a major stumbling block in ensuring the effectiveness of the press in its various functions.

45 The audience's lack of faith in the press is paralleled by rising objections within the journalism profession itself to the twentieth-century consensus on objectivity and neutrality as journalistic aspirations. *See, e.g.*, Levi, *supra* note 32; Levi, *supra* note 42. While many journalists and news organizations still articulate norms of neutrality and impartiality, some reporters have been challenging the false equivalencies of "he said-she said" reporting and calling for press outlets to take substantive positions on controverted social issues and events. Journalists who see reporting primarily as a tool to advance social justice and those who suggest that a commitment to anti-racism may require distancing from journalistic objectivity have been leading the charge to expand journalistic norms. *See* sources cited in Levi, *supra* note 32. Some news organizations, such as The Intercept, are explicit in their commitments to partisan journalism and replace what they consider false objectivity with ideological transparency. At the same time, this challenge to traditional journalistic norms of neutrality has led to conflict within major mainstream news organizations. *See, e.g.*, Alexandra Bruell, *New York Times Bosses Seek to Quash Rebellion in the Newsroom*, Wall St. J. (Apr. 12, 2024) https://www.wsj.com/business/media/new-york-times-reporters-rebellion-a6951d91. *See also* A. G. Sulzberger, *Journalism's Essential Value*, Colum. Journalism Rev. (May 15, 2023), https://www.cjr.org/special_report/ag-sulzberger-new-york-times-journalisms-essential-value-objectivity-independence.php (arguing for continuing benefits of journalistic independence and distinguishing between independent and advocacy journalism.)

In a parallel institutional move, the press ecosystem now reflects more explicit ideological divergence on political issues than heretofore, even among mainstream news outlets, and greater political polarization and openness to disinformation. *See* Yochai Benkler et al., Network Propaganda: Manipulation, Disinformation, and Radicalization in American Politics (2018).

7.2.1 *Funding to Reverse Consequences of Economic Decline*

Everyone agrees that the question of funding is existential for today's hollowed-out press, although there is variation in the recommendations for achieving stable funding.[46] While enhanced funding for journalism is critical, I argue that evaluating funding recommendations should require testing vis-à-vis public trust and comparative evaluations of viability.

Attention to funding does not mean that we should blindly shore up the existing institutional press simply because it has traditionally performed press functions. The history of the American press reveals a variety of different funding strands – an approach that could, in principle, provide helpful checks and balances. We should not discount the commercial press as some have suggested. There is much to be gained for public discourse from the systematic exploration of events and institutions by well-trained reporters hewing to shared professional standards – and such journalists inhabit commercial as well as nonprofit spaces. While many have expressed concern about philanthropic funding of the press by billionaires, a more granular look at alternative philanthropic scenarios raises different issues (and perhaps less

[46] It is beyond the scope of this chapter to address the details of the numerous proposals for financial sustainability being explored by scholars and media activists. *See* Damian Radcliffe & Nick Mathews, *Building a Stronger Local Media Ecosystem: The Role of Media Policy*, COLUM. JOURNALISM REV (April 20, 2023), https://www.cjr.org/tow_center_reports/building-a-stronger-local-media-ecosystem-the-role-of-media-policy.php (providing an overview of some proposals); Koningisor & Lidsky, *supra* note 26, at 67–69; Cameron Joseph, *Can Legislation Save Journalism in California?*, COLUM. JOURNALISM REV. (Feb. 16, 2024), https://www.cjr.org/the_media_today/california_news_bill_buffy_wicks.php. Some focus on ways for news organizations to obtain payments from social media platforms and generative AI companies for the use of their content (some through antitrust law and others through new regulatory models). Others explore philanthropic and not-for-profit approaches. *See, e.g.*, Cameron Joseph, *This Nonprofit Has Newsrooms in All 50 State Capitals. Is It the Future of State Journalism?*, COLUM. JOURNALISM REV. (April 5, 2024), https://www.cjr.org/the_media_today/states-newsroom-local-politics-policy-model.php. Still other suggestions look to direct or soft government subsidies and taxation options. Some suggest expansion of the collaborative project Report for America. https://www.reportforamerica.org/. There are many possibilities and little clear consensus. *See, e.g.*, Jeff Jarvis, *The California Journalism Preservation Act Would Do More Harm Than Good. Here's How the State Might Better Help News*, NIEMANLAB (Apr. 10, 2024), https://www.niemanlab.org/2024/04/the-california-journalism-preservation-act-would-do-more-harm-than-good-heres-how-the-state-might-better-help-news/ and sources cited therein.

Financial problems have been an important driver fueling at least some criticisms of the American press – for sensationalism, carelessness, and engagement-focused bias – and must therefore be a prime focus in stabilizing press functions going forward. And no single funding avenue will be able to replace the rich profits of newspapers in the mid to late twentieth century. The problem may be enhanced when generative AI tools summarize the content of many news stories in response to user prompts. The financial threats can be intensified if such generative AI summaries remove or minimize story branding and provenance and obviate the need to link to publishers' sites – factors that could help support the press economically in performing its democratic functions. *See* Simon, *supra* note 38, at 35.

ideological ones).[47] And while public funding is attractive in principle and likely necessary, a pragmatic approach must focus on the specific design of the initiatives, including its realism and legal viability. This is particularly true when the explicit political partisanship of today seems to lead people to accept politically motivated censorship so long as it is consistent with their political views. Media scholarship should further engage in close comparative evaluation of funding proposals – particularly from the pragmatic point of view of practicability today.[48]

Furthermore, it is important to recognize that journalism funding questions and issues of public trust should be deeply tied. Unlike the media landscape of the late twentieth century, even a well-funded news ecosystem today will consist of a diversity of outlets, voices, and ideological vantage points – some explicitly partisan and some not. We cannot assume that declining public trust in the press will be reversed simply by better and more stable funding of the entire sector. The public's trust in the bona fides and accuracy of the press will require more – including, perhaps, more transparency about funding and point of view.[49] Perhaps more and better watchdog journalism or even different forms of journalism, such as community journalism, could improve the public perception of the press's work.[50] Considering the issue of public trust in evaluating press funding can optimize the inquiry for public interest reporting.

7.2.2 *Countering Legal Ambivalence*

Almost 60 percent of American journalists, regardless of the political leanings of their outlet's audiences, report being very or extremely concerned about possible

47 *See, e.g.*, David Folkenflik, *Philanthropies Pledge $500 Million to Address 'Crisis in Local News'*, NPR (Sept. 7, 2023), https://www.npr.org/2023/09/07/1198029284/macarthur-knight-journalism-news-press-forward; Jennifer Preston et al., *Journalism and Philanthropy: Growth, Diversity, and Potential Conflicts of Interest*, Media Impact Funders (Oct. 2023), https://mediaimpactfunders.org/wp-content/uploads/2023/08/MIF-report-updated-.pdf.

48 One pragmatic warning: economic sustainability recommendations should be realistic when proposed, albeit with full recognition that what is realistic can change. Right now, for example, Congress is unlikely to increase its spending on public media although critics who point to the United States's abysmal comparative position on such funding are surely right as a matter of principle. Radcliffe & Mathews, *supra* note 46 (discussing stalled Congressional initiatives to bolster local journalism); Naomi Forman-Katz & Sarah Naseer, *Most U.S. Journalists Are Concerned About Press Freedoms*, Pew Rsch. Ctr. (May 2, 2023), https://www.pewresearch.org/short-reads/2023/05/02/most-u-s-journalists-are-concerned-about-press-freedoms/. The slow-and-steady approach, focusing on achievable goals, is not definitionally inconsistent with commitments to broader and more radical change over time.

49 It is at least possible that increased transparency about the funding, training, precommitments, political viewpoints, and ideological inclinations of the providers of news could help consumers assess the reliability of the information they receive.

50 *See, e.g.*, Carroll, *supra* note 3. While Professor Carroll suggests that watchdog journalism, with its adversarial character, may not be the right model to respond to public distrust today, I do not see public distrust as a singular phenomenon. Exposure to reliable examples of a diversity of types of journalism – including the watchdog reporting for which I believe there is an increasing need in both the government and private corporate contexts – can mitigate the distrust of a variety of publics with different reasons for lack of institutional faith.

restrictions on press freedoms.[51] Regarding the legal challenges facing the press function, press advocates call for new affirmative rights to assist journalists in doing their work as watchdogs. For the past decade, they have been unsuccessful in persuading Congress to pass federal newsgathering protections in the form of a federal shield law. In 2024, however, the House passed, and there was bipartisan support in the Senate for, the PRESS Act – a very broad set of protections against journalists having to identify their sources and governments having easy access to journalistic records from third-party providers.[52] Such support seemed to indicate a governmental recognition of the benefits of broad newsgathering access for those who engage in the press function.

Even a broadly protective shield law does not eliminate the need for additional assistance for newsgathering efforts, however.[53] More work needs to be done to obtain legal support to boost the now-fragile press's watchdog functions – including, for example, to combat state law anti-press initiatives; to seek clarifications of the Espionage Act and other press-affecting statutes such as the CFAA; and to enhance waning documentary access under FOIA and state sunshine rules.

Still, the attempt to enact new press protections should not distract from the need to conduct a defensive campaign addressing the erosion of existing rights and agreed-upon practices regarding publication. For example, close attention must be paid to resisting the call to reverse *Sullivan*; addressing changes to existing appeal bond statutes and other procedural hurdles for press defendants; reinforcing state-level protections; and arguing against the strategic and chilling deployment of non-media legal doctrines against the press.

One of the difficulties for this reclamation project is the recent reframing of defamation law as a weapon to combat disinformation.[54] Press advocates, however,

[51] Forman-Katz & Naseer, *supra* note 48.

[52] *See* Protect Reporters from Exploitative State Spying Act, H.R. 4250, 118th Cong. (2d Sess. 2024); Protect Reporters from Exploitative State Spying Act, S. 2074, 118th Cong. (1st Sess. 2023), https://www.congress.gov/bill/118th-congress/house-bill/4250. *See also* Clayton Weimers & Seth Stern, Opinion, *Why Political Rivals Can and Should Come Together for Press Freedom*, The Hill (Feb. 1, 2024), https://thehill.com/opinion/congress-blog/4442351-why-political-rivals-can-and-should-come-together-for-press-freedom/. Because of President Trump's well-known attacks on the mainstream press, it would have been useful if the Act had been passed before the start of the second Trump Administration. But the bipartisan measure – which had been brought to the Senate floor in mid-December 2024 for passage by unanimous consent – did not advance at that time due to objection by Senator Tom Cotton.

[53] Some examples worth considering include improved informational access rights, state and federal sunshine act reforms, press-protective amendments to the Espionage Act and statutes like the CFAA, protections for reporters covering protests etc. *See also* Koningisor & Lidsky, *supra* note 26, at 60–67 (evaluating judicial and legislative fixes).

[54] Both the plaintiff's defamation bar and scholars such as David Logan have made this argument, which seems to have influenced the views at least of Justice Gorsuch. *See* Berisha v. Lawson, 594 U.S. ___ (2021) (Gorsuch, J. dissenting from denial of *certiorari*) (citing to David Logan, *Rescuing Our Democracy by Rethinking* New York Times Co. v. Sullivan, 81 Ohio St. L. J. 759, 794 (2020)).

will need to remind the courts (including the Supreme Court) that individual defamation suits are not particularly effective tools to suppress political disinformation in most cases[55] and that most journalism today is not in fact "fake news" or disinformation as charged. Likewise, they should warn the courts against generalizing on the basis of the most high-profile examples of journalistic failure. It will be necessary to attack developing anti-press presumptions by demonstrating the value of free-press-first principles to tackling democratic challenges today.

All this will involve litigation, as well as lobbying, activism, and scholarly work. One of the more hopeful developments in effective resistance to the "fake news" trope is the increase in the number of media law clinics in American law schools.[56] A revival of pro bono work by the First Amendment defense bar through outside funding would also further reinforce the project of protecting the existing protections for press functions in legal doctrine and policy.

Because today's legal approach to press functions reflects both press protections and retrenching trends,[57] this chapter recommends a mixed legal strategy focusing on both new press-protective legislation to boost accountability journalism and a set of reframed arguments to support traditional protections under federal, state, and common law.[58] Although legal uncertainty may invite activism by the plaintiff's bar at the same moment that a fragile and risk-averse press has incentives to overinterpret doctrinal ambivalence as prohibition,[59] uncertainty also leaves room for revision, and the press's modern legal status is not yet fixed. A two-pronged legal strategy arguing for new newsgathering protections while showing the benefits of existing press rights and their history might bear some fruit before rollbacks of press rights become set in stone.

7.2.3 *Technological Impacts and the Special Case of Generative AI*

Now is the moment for news organizations to address issues of design and boundaries for use of generative AI tools in newsrooms without succumbing to the

55 *See* Levi, *supra* note 14; RonNell Andersen Jones, *Defamation, Disinformation, and the Press Function*, 3 J. FREE SPEECH L. 103 (2023) (accord).

56 Karen Sloan, *Hear Ye, Hear Ye! First Amendment Clinics Trending at Law Schools*, LAW.COM (Sept. 24, 2019), https://www.law.com/2019/09/24/hear-ye-hear-ye-first-amendment-clinics-trending-at-law-schools/.

57 *See* Koningisor & Lidsky, *supra* note 26, at 34–48 (demonstrating that there has been a reduction in press protections accompanied by an increase in government's ability to keep secrets).

58 A granular exploration of existing press protections under state and common law, for example, might provide supporting precedent. For example, freedom of the press is enshrined in the constitution of Florida. Constitution of the State of Florida, Art. 1, § 4. *Cf.* Genevieve Lakier, *The Non-First Amendment Law of Speech*, 134 HARV. L. REV. 2299 (2021) (exploring the history of free speech protections beyond the First Amendment). To be sure, such an exploration must look not only at the law on the books but in application as well. As mentioned above, recent legislative initiatives in Florida seem inconsistent with the constitutional commitment but have taken a lot of lobbying to head off and keep being reintroduced.

59 Further complicating the matter is that some press organs, for a variety of reasons, may respond in a more risk-averse fashion than others to legal change.

binary – utopian and dystopian – hype about AI.[60] News organizations should adopt AI standards after a realistic and granular analysis of where the benefits of AI tools for press functions will outweigh the risks and costs.[61] Who is invited to the table in standard-setting is critical as well.[62]

Another fundamental issue concerns building journalistic values into AI tools to be used by the press. Observers suspect that it would not be cost-effective for most news media to build their own, journalism-focused generative AI tools.[63] As many have already done, press organizations could rely on off-the-rack products created by commercial AI companies.[64] Query then how to ensure the centrality of journalistic values.

Moreover, relying on tech company products exposes news organizations to the dangers of lock-in – such as changes in pricing, availability, design decisions, access, and utility.[65] Without specifically negotiated contract terms, these decisions would

60 This standard-setting process has already begun. *See, e.g.*, *Paris Charter on AI and Journalism*, Nov. 10, 2023 (convened by Reporters Without Borders), https://rsf.org/sites/default/files/medias/file/2023/11/Paris%20Charter%20on%20AI%20and%20Journalism.pdf; WAN-IFRA, *Charter for AI and Journalism*, https://wan-ifra.org/2023/11/wan-ifra-steps-back-from-endorsing-new-charter-for-ai-and-journalism/#:~:text=AI%20systems%20used%20in%20journalism,ensure%20content%20origin%20and%20traceability; Associated Press, *AP, Other News Organizations Develop Standards for Use of Artificial Intelligence in Newsrooms*, Associated Press (Aug. 16, 2023), https://www.ap.org/media-center/ap-in-the-news/2023/ap-other-news-organizations-develop-standards-for-use-of-artificial-intelligence-in-newsrooms/. *See also* Kim Bjorn Becker et al., *Policies in Parallel? A Comparative Study of Journalistic AI Policies in 52 Global News Organisations* (Sept. 6, 2023), https://ora.ox.ac.uk/objects/uuid:b527b298-a12b-4f0d-bf77-543e3375cdf7/files/sp2676x005 (unpublished paper) (finding similarities but variations as well).

61 For example, AI can continue to be useful to news organizations on the business and distribution side, and there are certainly a range of newsroom tasks that gen AI tools will make speedier, more efficient, and – over time – increasingly accurate. However, many aspects of journalism cannot – and should not – be accomplished or made more efficient with AI tools. *See, e.g.*, Simon, *supra* note 38, at 11–22. *See generally* Nicholas Diakopoulos, Automating the News: How Algorithms are Rewriting the Media (2019) (addressing AI in journalism and discussing the human influence in automation); David Caswell, *AI and Journalism: What's Next?*, Reuters Inst. (Sept. 19, 2023), https://reutersinstitute.politics.ox.ac.uk/news/ai-and-journalism-whats-next (describing variety of uses of AI in journalism).

62 Journalism societies should collaborate in presumptive standard-setting and journalists should be at the forefront of boundary-setting for particular publishers. The interests of news executives, publishers, and corporate management are not necessarily congruent with those of journalists and editors. While the economic realities central to news executives are certainly relevant to tech-related decisions, a focus on journalistic values in the AI context is important for the future of news.

63 Simon, *supra* note 38, at 4, 22–31. It is the case, though, that Reuters has developed a significant number of AI tools in-house and the BBC has been reported to be considering creating its own in-house large language model trained on its archives. However, producing and keeping up at least some journalistic AI tools would be prohibitively expensive for smaller and resource-poorer press outfits.

64 Even if customized to some degree, the genesis of these tools is not journalism and they are not developed and trained specifically for the press's functions and values.

65 *See* Simon, *supra* note 38, at 4, 28–31 (elaborating on this point).

all be made by the technology companies and platforms.[66] Realistically, then, the decisions of tech companies will impact journalistic work both methodologically and substantively.

Another issue to be addressed in negotiations between news organizations that rely on commercial AI products and the AI companies should be the question of access to information regarding how their products and services work, including training data and error rates for generative AI applications.[67]

Journalists who worry about the ways in which nontransparent editorial decisions by an oligopoly of powerful first movers in the generative AI space could constrain reportorial functions and editorial discretion might consider collaboration with universities and other nonprofit partners engaged in the development of alternatives to commercial AI company products.[68] Government funding and access to resources for such research and partnerships could help advance such collaborations.

[66] As of now, there are few such companies, most of which already have relationships with the major tech enterprises.

At this point, the power relationships and associated negotiation possibilities between the platforms and news organizations in the future are unclear, which will affect both the press and the public arena. *See* Simon, *supra* note 38, at 34 ("the public arena will also be reshaped in accordance with how the balance of control shakes out between platforms and publishers.") Given that platforms have taken over much of news outlets' access to audiences, the visibility of news content on platform and search companies and the extent to which they send traffic to publishers' sites "will depend on strategic choices made by a set of powerful actors over whom the news industry has little control . . ." *Id.* at 35. Such choices could affect the news organizations' bargaining power in their AI-related negotiations. Nevertheless, the platforms and AI companies are both under the regulatory microscope, both at home and in Europe. This too affects bargaining power. In addition, and if we are to take them at their word, at least some of the tech companies have made public commitments to journalism and the responsible use of AI. *See, e.g.*, Noreen Gillespie, *Here's How We're Working with Journalists to Create the Newsrooms of the Future with AI*, Microsoft Blog (Feb. 5, 2024), https://blogs.microsoft.com/on-the-issues/2024/02/05/journalism-news-generative-ai-democracy-forward/#:~:text=Microsoft%20365-,Here's%20how%20we're%20working%20with%20journalists%20to%20create%20the,of%20the%20future%20with%20AI&text=What%20will%20the%20newsroom%20of,organizations%20to%20adopt%20generative%20AI. *See also* Francesco Marconi, *AI and Journalism Need Each Other*, Wall St. J., Dec. 28, 2023.

[67] Principle 3 of the *Paris Charter on AI and Journalism* provides that AI systems used by media "undergo an independent, comprehensive, and thorough evaluation involving journalism support groups" and "demonstrate adherence to the core values of journalistic ethics." I am not persuaded that this broad a requirement (and particularly one that does not identify the "journalism support groups" to be charged with this evaluation) is realistic.

[68] Although the initiative includes several commercial AI firm partners, help might also come in part from the National Science Foundation's recent announcement of a national AI research resource pilot program in order to promote a "shared research infrastructure that will strengthen and democratize access to critical resources necessary to power responsible AI discovery and innovation." NSF News, *Democratizing the Future of AI R&D: NSF to Launch National AI Research Resource Pilot*, U.S. Natn'l Science Found. (Jan. 24, 2024), https://new.nsf.gov/news/democratizing-future-ai-rd-nsf-launch-national-ai.

7.2.4 *Rethinking Industry Structure and the Distribution of the Press's Multiple Functions*

Under today's precarious circumstances, it is also worth considering the extent to which structural, organizational, and process-focused changes could advance press functions today. The current picture of the news industry should make us question whether traditional notions of outlet generalism, news organization competition, institutional-structure type, and homogeneity of journalistic standards continue to be either realistic or beneficial for the public.[69]

For example, at a time of decreasing economic resources for journalism, it would be unreasonable to expect that each news outlet or self-defined TikTok journalist could serve all these functions particularly well.[70] Not every news organization can seek to undertake all the press functions that courts have heretofore celebrated. Nor, perhaps, should they. Perhaps press conditions now require us to explore questions about the order of primacy of possible functions and about which entities are best positioned to perform them. Perhaps audiences do not need blanket coverage of the same events by every outlet. Perhaps funding and attention should focus on areas in which news failures have already demonstrated public harm. Perhaps different outlets should offer the public different forms of journalism.[71]

Competition norms too are worth challenging, both as to reporting and as to developing journalism-native generative AI models. There have already been examples of important reporting via collaboration rather than the traditional attitude

[69] Admittedly, there are significant differences among the various persons and entities performing press functions – even within the professional press cohort. Moreover, some – and especially the reputable national outlets – have adapted to the new environment better than others financially and in continuing their investigative work.

[70] Moreover, if an increasing use of video and AI transcript access in public proceedings will make them available to anyone at no or low cost, then one might argue that the press's role as the public's proxy in attending such proceedings on behalf of the public has been adequately fulfilled. Reporters could then emphasize interviewing, investigating, explaining, contextualizing, and historicizing. If the availability of data and processing capacity enable broader and richer types of data journalism looking at systemic problems, then perhaps some who currently perform the full gamut of press functions could focus first on data journalism. One thing such an approach could require is granular attention to the particular socio-political, historical, economic, informational, and technological context and which news and information providers are best placed to address the most critical issues of the time. For example, if the apparent worldwide turn to populism and authoritarianism continues, then perhaps a principal role for the national press should be the watchdog function – the role that traditionally promotes accountability with respect to government power, but now also with respect to private and corporate power as well. Of course, on the legal front, such a role requires attention to specific protections for investigative reporting and newsgathering. But, in addition, this kind of work seems most clearly fit for professional, well-trained, well-sourced, and well-funded journalists and news organizations – although counterexamples can also easily be imagined.

[71] *See, e.g.*, Carroll, *supra* note 3 (arguing that community journalism might at this moment be more effective at boosting public trust in the media than the adversarial and hierarchical watchdog journalism of the Watergate decade).

of commercial press competition. A shift from a competitive to a collaborative mindset could well enable greater impact for the resulting journalistic output. Collaborations with journalism schools and student reporters could also help.

7.2.5 *Enhancing Public Trust*

Ultimately, the robustness of the press function depends on public trust – so ensuring its viability involves sustained inquiry into reversing public distrust of the press. This requires extensive empirical and interdisciplinary study – including by political scientists, social psychologists, media scholars, and cognitive scientists – of the bases for press distrust and of how people change their minds.[72] While existing studies have already documented confirmation bias with respect to particular issues as to which there is no consensus, what about the possibility of enhancing trust in less controverted and politicized contexts? Trust does not have to be an all-or-nothing matter.

Moreover, since empirical research thus far indicates that distrust in the press has been asymmetrical between Democrats and Republicans, with conservatives having significantly more distrust in the mainstream press,[73] further granular exploration of the particular barriers to trust on the conservative side could be helpful in increasing the effectiveness of trust-promoting interventions. Additional work on the spread and debunking of conspiracy theories is also called for in the research mix.

Journalists and news organizations themselves are far from free of blame. Self-examination and diagnostic attention to their own practices and methods are necessary.[74] The press could study and advance effective types of fact-checking. Just as there was value – at least aspirationally – to the demarcation between "hard news" and "opinion" or "op-ed pages" in the traditional newspaper, the failures of

[72] Lili Levi, *"Media Literacy" Beyond the National Security Frame*, 2020 UTAH L. REV. 941 (2020). *See also* Bengani et al., *supra* note 12, at 140–41 (on journalists' failures to explain what happens in the newsroom adequately, especially in light of new technology and the opportunity for media literacy efforts now); Stephanie Craft et al., *News Media Literacy and Conspiracy Theory Endorsement*, 2:4 COMMC'N & PUB. 388 (Dec. 2017), https://doi.org/10.1177/2057047317725539 (finding that media literacy can decrease the endorsement of conspiracy theories).

[73] *See, e.g.*, Jeffrey Gottfried & Jacob Liedke, *Partisan Divides in Media Trust Widen, Driven By a Decline Among Republicans*, PEW RSCH. CTR. (Aug. 30 2021), https://www.pewresearch.org/short-reads/2021/08/30/partisan-divides-in-media-trust-widen-driven-by-a-decline-among-republicans/.

[74] Professional journals such as the Columbia Journalism Review engage in such assessments of journalistic practices. *See, e.g.*, Derek Kravitz, *Opinion, Failures Like Rolling Stone's Do Not Happen in Every Newsroom*, COLUM. JOURNALISM REV. (Sept. 26, 2023), https://www.cjr.org/opinion/wenner-uva-rolling-stone-scandal.php (discussing failures in Rolling Stone's "A Rape on Campus" reporting). *Cf.* Michael M. Grynbaum, *NBC News Faces Rebellion over Hiring of Former Republican Party Chair*, N.Y. TIMES (Mar. 25, 2024), https://www.nytimes.com/2024/03/25/business/media/nbc-ronna-mcdaniel-rebellion.html (describing "escalating revolt" among NBC anchors over the network's hiring of former RNC chair as political analyst on grounds of her prior support of election denial claims).

Fox News teach us that today's news purveyors should work to distinguish opinion to the extent possible.[75] As for partisan complaints of press bias, failure to disclose the reporter's slant, the nature of the newsgathering and reporting process, and the information on which an article's conclusions rest could reasonably undermine audience trust and be addressed consistent with professional norms.[76] Journalists could build reputations vis-à-vis expertise, ideological vantage point, reliability, and type of journalistic focus. In light of the likelihood of increased disinformation via increasingly believable deepfakes, journalists should focus on combatting "manipulation of large-scale public opinion trends" by the spread of false information.[77]

It would also be worthwhile for researchers and journalists to inquire further into what functions today's various audiences think are properly those of the press. Although this does not mean that the press should simply respond to what audiences assertedly want, or that there is no room today for traditional watchdog journalism, it does suggest the benefits to news professionals of better understanding the range of public expectations. A recent Pew Research Center report indicates that although many Americans rely on social media for news, there has been a material increase in the number of people who are concerned about inaccuracy.[78] So even if Americans

[75] To be sure, Fox is not the only outlet airing news-focused opinion shows. Such programming is doubtless far less expensive to produce than factual, investigative reporting. *See* Cameron Joseph, *The Ronna McDaniel Incident Reveals a Deeper Dilemma for Journalism*, Colum. Journalism Rev. (Mar. 29, 2024), https://www.cjr.org/the_media_today/ronna-mcdaniel-nbc-trump-journalism-dilemma.php. Far less than fact-focused programming, opinion talk shows also raise the risk of partisan bias and/or difficulty controlling and containing guest responses.

[76] To be sure, some are transparency skeptics, arguing that transparency as to errors may increase public distrust. *See, e.g.*, Dan Gillmor, *The Corrections Dilemma: Admitting Your Mistakes Increases Accuracy but Reduces Audience Trust, A New Study Finds*, NiemanLab (Mar. 27, 2023), https://www.niemanlab.org/2023/03/the-corrections-dilemma-admitting-your-mistakes-increases-accuracy-but-reduces-audience-trust-a-new-study-finds/; Bengani et al., *supra* note 12, at 141–43. Even if that is true in the short term, query whether it holds for the long term. Moreover, error-correction is not the transparency issue discussed in text.

[77] *See* Steven Waldman, Opinion, *How AI Could Sap – or Save – Local News*, Poynter (Jan. 25, 2024), https://www.poynter.org/commentary/2024/how-ai-could-sap-or-save-local-news/ (citing article).

[78] Luxuan Wang & Naomi Forman-Katz, *Many Americans Find Value in Getting News on Social Media, but Concerns About Inaccuracy Have Risen*, Pew Rsch. Ctr. (Feb. 7, 2024), https://www.pewresearch.org/short-reads/2024/02/07/many-americans-find-value-in-getting-news-on-social-media-but-concerns-about-inaccuracy-have-risen/. Admittedly, however, there has also been a documented decline in how closely Americans follow the news. Naomi Forman-Katz, *Americans Are Following the News Less Closely Than They Used To*, Pew Rsch. Ctr. (Oct. 24, 2023), https://www.pewresearch.org/short-reads/2023/10/24/americans-are-following-the-news-less-closely-than-they-used-to/. Still, a recent study showing that Americans find fact-checking labels created by professional fact checkers to be more effective than labels by algorithms or crowd-sourcing, and similarly that news media-created labels are ranked as second-most effective, suggests that "people put more faith in institutions especially equipped with journalistic professionalism and expertise than algorithms or peer users in terms of verifying facts." Chenyan Jia & Taeyoung Lee, *Journalistic Interventions Matter: Understanding How Americans Perceive Fact-Checking Labels*, Mis/information Rev. (Apr. 11, 2024), https://misinforeview.hks.harvard.edu/article/journalistic-interventions-matter-understanding-how-

report increased distrust in the press, many also express a desire for accurate news and information – which leaves room to shift at least some assumptions about the reliability of the press.[79]

A well-thought-out and evidence-based approach to media literacy would also be beneficial. This could be particularly constructive when joined by community engagement on the press side when research reveals disconnects between press and public expectations.[80]

Structural and policy changes responsive to shifts in press practices as discussed above could also address public concerns. For example, reports suggest that the crisis of trust in national journalism is not yet accompanied by an equivalent distrust of local news.[81] Therefore, a focus on increasing the sustainability of local news might also help chip away at the media distrust problem.

Finally, we should not forget that distrust in the press is only one aspect of declining public faith in institutions generally. It is worth exploring whether press

americans-perceive-fact-checking-labels/. The authors also found that "the positive relationships between news media trust and the efficacy of labels by both news media and fact checkers became stronger for those who were exposed to such labels more frequently. These findings suggest that raising the visibility of fact-checking labels can help increase their effectiveness, especially among those who trust news media." *Id.* Given the asymmetry between the views of Republicans and Democrats on the effectiveness of fact-checking, the study also calls on "professional fact checkers ... to be transparent and objective in their selection of claims to verify" in order to promote conservative users' trust in fact-checking. *Id.*

79 To the extent that the impression of unbridgeable polarization in America reflects partisan clashes among comparatively small but highly engaged publics, the quieter and more disengaged citizens may be interested in accurate and appropriately presented information and amenable to finding middle ground. *Cf.* David French, *America's Most Overlooked Political Divide Is Also Its Most Revealing*, N.Y. Times (Mar. 22, 2024), https://www.nytimes.com/2024/03/22/opinion/christian-nationalists-polling-divide.html. Journalists may be well positioned to serve that need, which could in turn improve their public perception.

80 For example, a recent Pew Research Center study reports that 76 percent of Americans "say journalists should always strive to give all sides equal coverage," while 55 percent of journalists surveyed report that "every side does not always deserve equal coverage in the news." Naomi Forman-Katz & Mark Jurkowitz, *U.S. Journalists Differ from the Public in Their Views of 'Bothsidesism' in Journalism*, Pew Rsch. Ctr. (July 13, 2022), https://www.pewresearch.org/short-reads/2022/07/13/u-s-journalists-differ-from-the-public-in-their-views-of-bothsidesism-in-journalism/; Bengani et al., *supra* note 12, at 132 ("[b]othsideism remains a heated debate.") Of course, this does not mean that journalists should simply make false claims of objectivity or disguise their partisan content with neutral editorial tones. The Pew report results could also mean that they have different understandings of "equal coverage" rather than a more fundamental divide. In any event, the different expectations could be bridged by more transparent disclosure of a reporter's journalistic stance and a clear explanation of why she believes a "both sides" story does not tell enough of the truth, clear understandings on both sides of what equal coverage means, and whether different communities view the issue differently and as to what kinds of coverage questions.

81 *See* Bengani et al., *supra* note 12, at 151–54. Admittedly, as the Tow Center report points out, an increase in partisan "pink slime" reporting designed to achieve particular results (such as swinging tight elections) could undermine trust in local news more broadly. But for now, local news outlets fare better than the concentrated national press.

reporting on and explaining the work of other contested institutions – such as, for example, the administrative state – could indirectly serve to enhance the perceived legitimacy of both.[82]

7.3 CONCLUSION

An effective press sector consisting of a variety of actors committed to journalistic values can support democracy. It can know, inform, and educate its many publics. It can discover what the powerful do not want discovered, act as a watchdog, dispel disinformation, and help sustain local and underrepresented communities. Shoring up these functions for the press is a worthwhile enterprise in the public interest. But today's economic, technological, legal, professional, and consumer contexts are a far cry from those of the press's golden age. Still, the press and its allies should continue to proselytize the value of journalism's ideal functions – while acknowledging the instances in which the modern press fails to meet the mark. They should pressure-test reform proposals for viability; develop responsible technology policies; revisit antiquated functions and industry expectations; and use the lessons of interdisciplinary research to explore effective ways to counter public distrust. They should also call for normalizing self-examination across the entire sector to enhance compliance with fundamental journalistic norms. Such targeted steps can help rehabilitate journalism's public role and allow society to reap the benefits of an independent press. We ought not surrender this promise.

[82] *See* Gabriel Scheffler & Daniel E. Walters, *The Submerged Administrative State*, 3 Wis. L. Rev. 789 (2024) (arguing that the public's faith in government is undermined *inter alia* because administrative agencies are constrained in their communications with the public and frequently engage in opaque actions).

8

Defamation Law and the Crumbling Legitimacy of the Fourth Estate

Lyrissa Lidsky

Just a half-century ago, "the news media were one of America's most trusted institutions."[1] Today, however, almost half of Americans say they have little or no trust in newspapers, and more than half say the same about television news.[2] Although some degree of public distrust of the media is healthy, distrust of this magnitude represents a crisis of legitimacy.

The role of the press in safeguarding democracy is enshrined in the U.S. Constitution. The Constitution protects press freedom not as an end in itself and "not as a favor to a particular industry"[3] but as a means of making our system of government possible. The framers recognized that the republic's fate depends on citizens having access to reliable and timely information about their world. Trustworthy news enables us to participate in informed public discussion, forge consensus, and hold democratically elected leaders accountable.[4] If we lack access to (or cannot agree upon) the most basic facts about global, national, and local events or the myriad issues that affect our lives, it is impossible to understand and

1 Jonathan M. Ladd, Why Americans Hate the Media and How It Matters 1 (2012) (providing results of American National Election Study). In 1974, a Gallup poll found that 69 percent of Americans had a "great deal" or "fair amount" of trust in the media to report "the news fully, accurately and fairly." *Media Use and Evaluation*, Gallup, https://news.gallup.com/poll/1663/media-use-evaluation.aspx (last visited Apr. 22, 2024). The same poll conducted in 2022 found that only 16 percent of Americans had a "great deal" or "quite a lot" of confidence in newspapers, and television news fared even worse, with only 11 percent expressing those levels of confidence. Megan Brenan, *Media Confidence Ratings at Record Lows*, Gallup (July 18, 2022), https://news.gallup.com/poll/394817/media-confidence-ratings-record-lows.aspx; Jeffrey M. Jones, *Confidence in U.S. Institutions Down; Average at New Low*, Gallup (July 5, 2022), https://news.gallup.com/poll/394283/confidence-institutions-down-average-new-low.aspx.

2 Brenan, *supra* note 1. Forty-six percent of Americans say that they have little or no trust in newspapers, and 53 percent say they have little or no trust in television news. *Id.*

3 Berisha v. Lawson, 141 S. Ct. 2424, 2425 (2021) (Gorsuch, J., dissenting from denial of certiorari).

4 For further discussion of the views of the framers concerning the role of the press, *see* Christina Koningisor & Lyrissa Barnett Lidsky, *First Amendment Disequilibrium*, 110 Va. L. Rev. 1, 10–11 (2024).

respond to the challenges facing us and our country. Without shared facts about the world, the stability of our communal life is in jeopardy.[5]

It may seem quixotic to lament the public's loss of faith in traditional media actors at a time when we have – on demand – an unprecedented level of access to information.[6] Social media enables more people than ever before to share content and commentary with mass audiences. Yet this very informational abundance – soon to be magnified by generative artificial intelligence – can make it increasingly difficult to know which information to trust. And even though some types of information are superabundant, other types are becoming scarcer. Case in point: Historically, local newsgatherers played a key, democracy-enhancing role by keeping their communities informed about local events and holding local elected officials to account. Now, however, the market for local news has evaporated, turning more and more cities into "news deserts." Meanwhile, fewer national legacy news providers can afford to invest in the processes and expertise needed to produce high-quality news about our increasingly complex world.[7] As such, the true crisis of press legitimacy is the declining cultural investment in the systematic gathering of high-quality news produced by independent, transparent, and trustworthy sources.

What caused the Fourth Estate to crumble? Although scholars usually point to a handful of cultural and economic factors as undermining news quality and press credibility, various critics now identify a more covert culprit: the U.S. Supreme Court. The Court is partly to blame for the press's declining credibility, these critics claim, because the Court's First Amendment decisions hinder the ability of state defamation law to hold the press accountable for defamatory falsehoods. The implication is that the press would regain much of its credibility if the Court were to remove these constitutional barriers – especially the requirement that public officials and public figures demonstrate "actual malice" on the part of the press for a defamation claim to prevail. As this chapter explains, the current landscape of high-profile defamation cases, and the public reaction to them, casts doubt on whether restoring public trust in the press could be so easy.

5 Richard L. Hasen, Cheap Speech: How Disinformation Poisons Our Politics – and How to Cure It 24 (2022) (describing the threat to democracy posed by "a public that cannot determine truth or make voting decisions that are based on accurate information, and a public susceptible to political manipulation through repeatedly amplified, data-targeted, election-related content, some of it false and misleading").

6 Jack M. Balkin, *Free Speech v. the First Amendment*, 70 UCLA L. Rev. 1206, 1264 (2023) ("Digital media can make more valuable information about public issues available to more people than ever before in human history.").

7 For discussion of the Fourth Estate ideal, *see*, for example, Erin C. Carroll, Platforms and the Fall of the Fourth Estate: Looking beyond the First Amendment 529–31 (2020); Leonard Levy, Emergence of a Free Press xii (1985) (describing the conception of press freedom during the framing era: "[a] free press meant the press as the Fourth Estate, or, rather, in the American scheme, an informal or extraconstitutional fourth branch that functioned as part of the intricate system of checks and balances that exposed public mismanagement and kept power fragmented, manageable, and accountable").

8.1 THE USUAL SUSPECTS

Scholars and commentators have identified a number of potential contributors to the deterioration of public trust in the press. For example, many observers suggest that the growing distrust in the news media is simply a facet of the public's declining trust in all types of public and private institutions.[8] A recent Gallup poll found historically low levels of public trust in the justice system, the medical system, the presidency, public schools, Congress, and many other institutions.[9] However, even in the context of this overall decline of institutional trust, the growing skepticism toward news media is exceptional: Journalists are less trusted than most other professionals, and only 11 percent of those polled expressed a great deal or quite a lot of confidence in television news; newspapers fared slightly better, but only 16 percent of those polled expressed confidence in them.[10]

A primary contributor to public distrust in traditional news media providers is the collapse of the economic model supporting news production. Over the past quarter of a century, the Internet has gobbled up advertising revenues that were once used to finance news production, while simultaneously subjecting traditional news providers to increased competition from low-quality "cheap news." The rise of generative artificial intelligence threatens to accelerate these competitive forces,[11] which fuel public distrust in the press by making fact-based news both less profitable to produce and harder to distinguish from misinformation. These forces also change

[8] Ideally, identification of the factors contributing to the crisis of legitimacy facing the press would be provided by polling a representative sample of Americans and recording their answers. In fact, Pew research provides tantalizing clues about why Americans distrust the media. Jeffrey Gottfried et al., *Americans Are Largely Skeptical of the News Media, But Say There Is Room for Confidence to Improve*, PEW RESEARCH CENTER (Aug. 31, 2020), https://www.pewresearch.org/journalism/2020/08/31/americans-are-largely-skeptical-of-the-news-media-but-say-there-is-room-for-confidence-to-improve/. Other researchers are conducting qualitative research to uncover the explanation. *Assessing the News Media: Trust, Coverage, and Threats to a Free Press*, AP-NORC, https://apnorc.org/projects/assessing-the-news-media-trust-coverage-and-threats-to-a-free-press/ (last visited Apr. 22, 2024). One problem, however, is that people are not always aware of why they feel the way they do, and the reasons they give for their distrust are not always the reasons that motivate them.

[9] Jones, *supra* note 1. Journalists are less trusted than most other professionals as well. Megan Brenan & Jeremy M. Jones, *Ethics Ratings of Nearly All Professions Down in U.S.*, GALLUP (Jan. 22, 2024), https://news.gallup.com/poll/608903/ethics-ratings-nearly-professions-down.aspx. Public distrust in news media also extends beyond the United States. Nic Newman, *Overview and Key Findings of the 2023 Digital News Report*, REUTERS (June 23, 2023), https://reutersinstitute.politics.ox.ac.uk/digital-news-report/2023/dnr-executive-summary; Nic Newman & Richard Fletcher, *Bias, Bullshit and Lies: Audience Perspectives on Low Trust in the Media*, REUTERS (Dec. 1, 2017), https://reutersinstitute.politics.ox.ac.uk/our-research/bias-bullshit-and-lies-audience-perspectives-low-trust-media.

[10] Brenan & Jones, *supra* note 9.

[11] Mark Jamison, *Journalism's Creative Destruction Opportunity*, AMERICAN ENTERPRISE INSTITUTE (Mar. 7, 2024), https://www.aei.org/technology-and-innovation/journalisms-creative-destruction-opportunity/.

both the style and substance of news content in ways that can undermine press credibility.

Instead of relying on traditional media to set their news agenda, many Americans now rely on social media connections, algorithms, and influencers to curate their (mostly free) news content.[12] Although some of this free content is produced by news entities that once would have reaped advertising revenue from providing it, the vast bulk of that revenue is now rechanneled to online classified advertising sites[13] or to platforms that offer the kind of micro-targeted advertising precision that even digital news providers simply cannot match.[14] This flight of advertising revenue has disrupted various legacy news producers,[15] but newspapers – long the bedrock of news production and resource-intensive investigative journalism[16] – have experienced the most dramatic impact.[17]

It is not just advertisers who have fled to the tech platforms – so, too, have audiences.[18] Between roughly 2000 and 2022, daily newspapers lost two-thirds of their readers,[19] with total revenues falling by over 80 percent.[20] While The New York Times and The Wall Street Journal have been able to offset lost advertising revenue

[12] Newman, *supra* note 9.

[13] Eero Korhonen, *Research: What Really Happened to Newspaper Revenue*, Google in Europe (June 3, 2021), https://blog.google/around-the-globe/google-europe/research-what-really-happened-newspaper-revenue/.

[14] Emily J. Bell et al., *The Platform Press: How Silicon Valley Reengineered Journalism*, Tow Center for Digital Journalism (May 26, 2017), https://academiccommons.columbia.edu/doi/10.7916/D8R216ZZ.

[15] An excellent recent article by Dr. Laurie Thomas Lee (*How Local TV News Is Surviving Disruption as Newspapers Fail: Lessons Learned*, 3 J. Free Speech L. 241 (2023)) describes how federal regulation and oversight, along with other competitive strategies and advantages, have been key to the financial survival of local news. It is not clear whether television news reporters make up for the loss of local newspaper reporters, which one writer has described as "the backbone of every local journalism ecosystem." Frank Racioppi, *Can Podcasting Replace the Death of Local Journalism*, Ear Worthy (Nov. 4, 2022), https://medium.com/ear-worthy/can-podcasting-replace-the-death-of-local-journalism-ee486f9d2e74.

[16] *How News Happens*, Pew Research Center (Jan. 11, 2010), https://www.pewresearch.org/journalism/2010/01/11/how-news-happens/.

[17] The cable news picture is mixed. Cable news today is more profitable in 2022 than it was a decade ago, but audiences are shifting. Fox News experienced primetime news audience growth of 10 percent between 2021 and 2022, but CNN's primetime audience fell by 25 percent, and MSNBC's by 10 percent. *Trends and Facts on Cable News: State of the News Media*, Pew Research Center (Sep. 14, 2023), https://www.pewresearch.org/journalism/fact-sheet/cable-news/.

[18] Heather Kelly, *From TV to TikTok, How We Get the News Is Changing Fast*, Wash. Post (Nov. 23, 2023), https://www.washingtonpost.com/technology/2023/11/15/news-trends-social/.

[19] *Trends and Facts on Cable News*, *supra* note 17.

[20] Dana A. Sherer & Clare Y. Cho, *Stop the Presses? Newspapers in the Digital Age*, Cong. Rsch. Serv., R47018 (2022), https://crsreports.congress.gov/product/pdf/R/R47018. *See also* Accenture, USA News Media Landscape Trends 5 (2021), https://newsmediaanalysis.com/wpcontent/uploads/2021/06/accenture_analysis_USAnewsmedia.pdf [https://perma.cc/Z3YY-QRHG] ("Between 2004 and 2018 total newspaper revenues fell by $30 billion, to $27.4 billion. This amounted to a 52% fall.").

with subscription dollars,[21] they are the rare exceptions. Between 2004 and 2020, more than 2,100 papers closed,[22] and some of the survivors dwindled to become what the NewsGuild has labeled "ghost newspapers" – downsized shells of their former selves.[23]

The declining financial fortunes of newspapers have affected overall news quality across the media landscape. How could they not? The brain drain in journalism over the last two decades has been cataclysmic. Between 2008 and 2020, newspapers cut newsroom employees by 57 percent.[24] In 2023, newsrooms experienced the "worst job cuts" in years, and 2024 began with reports of storied newspapers – including, for example, the Los Angeles Times and the Washington Post – delivering more bad news about newsroom staffing.[25] However, it is not only the evisceration of expertise that hurts news quality. It is also that resources have been disproportionately withdrawn from the production of local news and investigative journalism; these are the very kinds of journalism that help citizens participate meaningfully in shaping their communities and holding officials to account. Without journalistic watchdogs, corruption flourishes and communities suffer.

In the meantime, the need to compete for attention in a crowded marketplace has shaped news content in ways that magnify public distrust. To survive, legacy media have been forced to compete to break news faster than their online competitors, to hijack readers' attention with sensational content, and, in many cases, to cultivate niche audiences by appealing to partisan loyalties.[26] This competition forces the

[21] Adam Grundy, *Internet Crushes Traditional Media: From Print to Digital*, U.S. CENSUS BUREAU (June 7, 2022), https://www.census.gov/library/stories/2022/06/internet-crushes-traditional-media.html.

[22] PENELOPE MUSE ABERNATHY, NEWS DESERTS AND GHOST NEWSPAPERS: WILL LOCAL NEWS SURVIVE? 9, 15 (2020). *See also id.* at 12 ("[A]bout 1,800 of the communities that have lost a paper since 2004 do not have easy access to any local news – such as a local online news site or a local radio station." Some of the surviving papers and chains have been bought by hedge funds, who have been accused of "selling everything not bolted down, cutting every possible cost, and taking every penny of cash flow home with them."). Jeff Jarvis, *Is It Time to Give Up on Old News?* WHITHER NEWS (Jan. 24, 2024), https://medium.com/whither-news/is-it-time-to-give-up-on-old-news-488194f359ba.

[23] *The 'Ghost Newspapers' Are Here*, THE NEWSGUILD (Mar. 28, 2018), https://newsguild.org/the-ghost-newspapers-are-here/

[24] *U.S. Newsroom Employment Has Fallen 26% Since 2008*, PEW RESEARCH CENTER (July 13, 2021), https://www.pewresearch.org/short-reads/2021/07/13/u-s-newsroom-employment-has-fallen-26-since-2008/. *See also* Sasha Lekach, *Fewer Than Half of Newspaper Jobs from 15 Years ago Still Exist*, MASHABLE (Apr. 4, 2017), https://mashable.com/article/newspaper-publishers-jobs-decline-bls.

[25] Oliver Darcy & Jon Passantino, *News Industry off to Brutal 2024 Start as Mass Layoffs Devastate Publishers, Raising Questions About the Future of Journalism*, CNN BUSINESS (Jan. 25, 2024), https://www.cnn.com/2024/01/25/media/news-industry-future/index.html; Michael M. Grynbaum et al., *The News About the News Business Is Getting Grimmer*, N.Y. TIMES (Jan 1, 2024), https://www.nytimes.com/2024/01/24/business/media/media-industry-layoffs-decline.html.

[26] It is well known at this point that social media platforms prioritize "engagement." *See* Cortelyou C. Kenney, *Defamation 2.0*, 56 LOY. L. REV. 1, 18–19 (2023) (discussing the effect

legacy press to try to give audiences what they want, which paradoxically causes those same audiences to disrespect the press for pandering.

Of course, it does not help that the term "news" is frequently applied not only to fact-based reporting on newsworthy events but also to commentary, infotainment, and clickbait. Nor does it help that the purveyors of all of these forms of content often adopt the label of "journalists." Even legacy media themselves have contributed to blurring the lines between these categories, making it unsurprising that the public mistrusts their motives. They have also contributed to the problem by, at times, constructing their own "filter bubbles," hobbling their ability to connect with those they cover. In the meantime, demagogues stoke the public's disdain for the press for their own political gain, portraying the press as biased and untrustworthy and encouraging partisans to brand any news with which they disagree as "fake."[27]

8.2 IS LIBEL LAW TO BLAME?

These factors have contributed to media distrust, but certain prominent voices point to an unexpected contributor to the eroding public trust in US media: American libel law exceptionalism.

8.2.1 *Does US Libel Law Incentivize Press Irresponsibility?*

Libel law in the United States provides broader protections for media errors than its common law counterparts. This is by design. Until 1964, in both the United States and the United Kingdom, a plaintiff could succeed in a libel action by proving the publication of a defamatory communication concerning the plaintiff. Fault was presumed, falsity was presumed, and damages were presumed, though defendants could escape liability by proving privilege or truth.

of engagement strategy in the exacerbation of polarization). Newspapers respond to the economic incentives by gearing their content to online audiences. *See* Richard Posner, *Bad News*, N.Y. TIMES (July 31, 2005) (discussing the economic incentives propelling media toward sensationalism and partisanship) and Balkin, *supra* note 6, at 1265 ("In the attention economy, what often works best is repetition, attention seeking, and the generation of conflict and spectacle.").

[27] *See generally* Sonja R. West, *Presidential Attacks on the Press*, 83 MO. L. REV. 915 (2018) (discussing what makes some of President Donald Trump's attacks on the press different than those of his predecessors); Lili Levi, *Real "Fake News" and Fake "Fake News,"* 16 FIRST AM. L. REV. 232 (2017) (discussing President Donald Trump's successful deployment of the term "fake news" to influence public beliefs about the press); RonNell Andersen Jones & Lisa Grow Sun, *Enemy Construction and the Press*, 49 ARIZ. L.J. 1301 (2017) (discussing President Donald Trump's description of the press as "the enemy" and the risks such construction poses); HASEN, *supra* note 5, at 21 ("Rather than improving our politics, cheap speech makes political parties increasingly irrelevant by allowing demagogues to appeal directly and repeatedly at virtually no cost to voters for financial and electoral support, with incendiary appeals and often with lies.").

US law began to diverge markedly from UK law starting with the U.S. Supreme Court's 1964 decision in *New York Times Co. v. Sullivan*.[28] In *Sullivan*, the Court, for the first time, held that the First Amendment imposes limits on the common law of defamation.[29] Most famously, the Court held that states could not allow public officials to recover compensation for defamation unless they proved actual malice using clear and convincing evidence.[30] In other words, defendants would face liability for defamatory statements about public officials only if they knew the statements to be false or recklessly disregarded the truth or falsity.[31] A defendant's negligence in ascertaining truth was insufficient. The Court reasoned that negligent errors are "inevitable" in public debate[32] and thus held that imposing liability for them would dampen the vigor of the press in its coverage of public officials.[33]

Sullivan was only the beginning. The Court soon extended the actual-malice rules to criminal defamation cases and to cases brought by "public figures" – people we might today call influencers. Lower courts embraced a broad view of this category, burdening a wide swath of plaintiffs with proving that media defamation defendants "in fact entertained serious doubts as to the truth"[34] of what they published about them before they could recover compensation for damage to their reputations. The Court subsequently established a different set of rules for private figures involved in newsworthy events or "matters of public concern." These plaintiffs cannot recover compensation without proving falsity and some degree of fault: If they choose to prove negligence, they must also prove actual injury; if they choose to prove actual malice, presumed damages are available.[35] In addition, all categories of plaintiffs described above can only sue for defamation based on assertions of objective fact.[36] This last move rendered the Supreme Court's First Amendment overhaul of the common law almost total, with practically no element left

[28] 376 U.S. 254 (1964).

[29] *Id.* at 264–65.

[30] *Id.* at 279–80.

[31] *Id.*

[32] Restatement (Second) of Torts §613 cmt. j (Am. L. Inst. 1977) (stating that requiring proof of fault as to falsity "has, as a practical matter, made it necessary for the plaintiff to allege and prove the falsity of the communication, and from a realistic standpoint, has placed the burden of proving falsity on the plaintiff").

[33] The Court also held that a government official cannot construe "an otherwise impersonal attack on governmental operations [as] a libel of an official responsible for those operations." Sullivan, 376 U.S. at 292. The effect was to set limits on states' application of the common law element of identification in defamation actions.

[34] St. Amant v. Thompson, 390 U.S. 727, 731 (1968).

[35] Philadelphia Newspaper v. Hepps, 475 U.S. 767, 777 (1986) ("the common-law presumption that defamatory speech is false cannot stand when a plaintiff seeks damages against a media defendant for speech of public concern.")

[36] Although the Court indicated in *Dun & Bradstreet* that states may be free to impose strict liability for defamation in cases involving private figures and matters of purely private concern, such cases are but a sliver of all defamation cases, and rarely do such cases involve media defendants. *See* Dun & Bradstreet, Inc. v. Greenmoss Builders, Inc., 472 U.S. 749, 759 (1985).

untouched. However, probably the most consequential change was overturning the common law's presumptions of fault and falsity and imposing an actual-malice requirement in the vast bulk of cases involving the media.

Together, these changes meant that US plaintiffs – especially public officials and public figures – face a higher barrier to holding the media accountable for defamatory falsehoods than plaintiffs in other common law countries do. Unlike the United States, these countries do not require proof of actual malice. Under UK law, for instance, courts will presume fault if plaintiffs can demonstrate "serious harm." Falsity is also presumed, although UK law continues to make truth a defense.[37] Defendants may also avoid liability if they can show that they acted reasonably in publishing a matter in the public interest.[38] This defense is the codified version of what was once called a privilege for "responsible journalism."[39] When invoked, it has the effect of applying a fault requirement to the media defendant that is akin to a negligence standard. Australia, Canada, and South Africa follow similar approaches.

8.2.2 *Defamation Law and Public Trust in the Press*

So how might American libel law exceptionalism affect public trust? According to critics, libel laws can incentivize the press to get things right by holding them responsible for getting things wrong. By absolving the press of responsibility for getting things wrong about public officials or public figures unless they "in fact entertained serious doubts"[40] as to the information's truth or falsity, the United States' actual-malice rule has removed this incentive for accuracy. For these observers, the extent to which ordinary people in the United States understand how difficult it is for those in the public eye to hold the press (or any other speaker) responsible for falsehoods about public matters is inversely related to the likelihood of those ordinary people believing what they read or hear and trusting those who write or speak.

Defamation scholar David Anderson made essentially this argument thirty years ago,[41] although in a more extended and sophisticated form. Anderson argued that

[37] Defamation Act 2013, c. 26, § 2(1) (UK) (providing that truth is a defense to a defamation action).

[38] Defamation Act of 2013, sec. 4. Dario Milo, Defamation and Freedom of Speech 72–73 (2008).

[39] *Id.* at 85, 93. The UK passed anti-SLAPP legislation in 2023. This legislation, which was passed in the form of amendments to the Economic Crime and Corporate Transparency Act 2023, only applies to allegations of economic crime. The new law places the burden on the claimant to show likelihood of success at trial. *See* Juliette Garside, *"Designed to Distress and Deter": The Impact of SLAPP Lawsuits on Journalists and Free Speech*, The Guardian (Nov. 23, 2023), available at https://www.theguardian.com/media/2023/nov/03/designed-to-distress-and-deter-the-impact-of-slapp-lawsuits-on-journalists-and-free-speech.

[40] *St Amant*, 390 U.S. at 731.

[41] David A. Anderson, *Is Libel Law Worth Reforming?*, 140 U. Pa. L. Rev. 487, 490 (1991). Anderson also argued that "[w]ithout libel law, [the] credibility of the press would be at the

the actual-malice rule degrades news quality: "[B]y eliminating most of the risks associated with the journalism of scandal, at least when it is directed at public officials or public figures,"[42] the actual-malice rule makes it easier for the press to give in to the ever-present "market pressures to serve the public appetite for scandal."[43] Roughly contemporaneously, Anderson's argument was echoed by then-scholar (now-Supreme Court Justice) Elena Kagan, who asked, "Is it possible that *Sullivan* bears some responsibility for a change in the way the press views itself and its conduct – a change that the general public might describe as increased press arrogance?"[44] Like Anderson, Kagan decried the actual-malice rule's contribution to "the 'tabloidization' of the mainstream press"[45] and questioned whether a different standard might, "in the long term[,] benefit journalism" and improve the quality of public discourse.[46]

The social media revolution has lent these arguments renewed resonance. Supreme Court Justices Clarence Thomas and Neil Gorsuch have criticized *Sullivan*'s legacy in nonprecedential opinions dissenting from the Court's denial of certiorari. For Thomas, beyond being the product of "policy-driven decision masquerading as constitutional law," constitutionalizing libel law was bad policy. According to his account, the actual-malice rule enables "media organizations and interest groups 'to cast false aspersion on public figures with near impunity.'" Gorsuch amplified the "bad policy" aspect of Thomas's position by focusing on how the actual-malice rule, together with changes in the communications environment since 1964, undermines high-quality, fact-based, democracy-enhancing journalism.[47]

mercy of the least scrupulous among us, and public discourse would have no necessary anchor in truth." *Id.* Yonathan A. Arbel has constructed lab experiments that confirm the existence of the "credibility effect" of defamation law. *See generally The Credibility Effect: Defamation Law and its Audiences*, 52 J. Legal Stud. 417 (2023) (finding defamation law makes people more trusting of reports from various media sources).

[42] *Id.* at 534.

[43] *Id.* at 533.

[44] Elena Kagan, A *Libel Story: Sullivan Then and Now*, 18 Law and Social Inquiry 197, 208 (1993) (reviewing Anthony Lewis, Make No Law: The Sullivan Case and the First Amendment (1991)).

[45] *Id.* at 207.

[46] *Id.*

[47] U.S. Supreme Court Associate Justice Clarence Thomas called for reconsideration of *New York Times Co. v. Sullivan* in 2019 in three opinions: McKee v. Cosby, 139 S. Ct. 675, 675 (2019) (Thomas, J., concurring in denial of certiorari); Berisha v. Lawson, 141 S. Ct. 2424, 2424 (2021) (Thomas, J., dissenting from denial of certiorari); Coral Ridge Ministries Media v. S. Poverty L. Ctr., 142 S. Ct. 2453, 2454 (2022) (Thomas, J., dissenting from denial of certiorari). Justice Thomas's critique of *Sullivan* is largely grounded in originalism concerns. He asserts that the Court should inquire "whether either the First or Fourteenth Amendment, as originally understood, encompasses an actual malice standard for public figures or otherwise displaces vast swaths of state defamation law." McKee, 139 S. Ct. at 680 (Thomas, J., concurring). Federal appeals court judge Lawrence Silberman subsequently echoed Justice Thomas's criticisms in Tah v. Glob. Witness Publ'g, Inc., 991 F.3d 231, 251 (D.C. Cir. 2021) (Silberman,

In his dissent in *Berisha v. Lawson*, Gorsuch postulated that the framers understood the importance of press freedom for the healthy functioning of democracy.[48] However, he also suggested that press freedom comes with a duty "to try to get the facts right," implying that the press no longer make this effort, even if they once did.[49]

Gorsuch lays a portion of the blame on the social media revolution, acknowledging that economic and technological changes have not been kind to "our [n]ation's media."[50] Citing scholars David Logan and Richard Epstein, Gorsuch first explains how changes to the economic model supporting traditional media undermined their incentives and ability to invest in the reporters, editors, and fact-checkers necessary to get the facts right.[51] Before the social media revolution, "many major media outlets" invested the time and resources necessary "to report true stories" because they could reap the economic benefits of the public's "confidence that what they read [wa]s true."[52] However, in this "new media environment," false information "costs almost nothing to generate," spreads more effectively than real news, and is more lucrative to generate than real news.[53]

Despite acknowledging these contributors to declining press credibility, Gorsuch also blames the Supreme Court's interpretation of the First Amendment for undermining journalistic incentives for accuracy. He specifically targets the actual-malice rule and its expansion beyond public officials to the growing category of those in the public eye.[54] For Gorsuch, even if the actual-malice rule might have made sense in an environment in which media actors had professional and economic incentives not to publish "defamatory falsehoods and misinformation," the rule's rationale has evaporated along with those "other safeguards"[55] for accuracy. Today, he claims, the combination of the actual-malice rule "with the business incentives fostered by our new media world" works "against those with traditional (and expensive) journalistic

J., dissenting). Recently, Justice Alito weighed in, also in a dissent from the denial of certiorari in a defamation case concerning whether the existence of a false factual assertion is a question for the judge or the jury. Nat'l Rev., Inc. v. Mann, 140 S. Ct. 344, 344 (Alito, J., dissenting from denial of certiorari). However, Justice Alito did not focus on actual malice but instead expressed concern about whether existing standards provide sufficient protection for opinion on important public policy issues. *Id.* at 346–48. For further analysis of the arguments of Justices Thomas and Gorsuch, *see* generally RonNell Andersen Jones, *Defamation, Disinformation, and the Press Function*, 3 J. FREE SP. LAW 103 (2023); Lili Levi, *Disinformation and the Defamation Renaissance: A Misleading Promise of "Truth,"* 57 U. RICH. L. REV. 1235 (2023); Lyrissa Lidsky, *Cheap Speech and the Gordian Knot of Defamation Reform*, 3 J. FREE SP. LAW 79 (2023); Lyrissa Lidsky, *Untangling Defamation Law: Guideposts for Reform*, 88 MO. L. REV. 663 (2023).

48 Berisha, 141 S. Ct. at 2425 (Gorsuch, J., dissenting from denial of certiorari).

49 *Id.* at 2426.

50 *Id.* at 2427.

51 *Id.* at 2427–28.

52 *Id.* at 2428.

53 *Id.* at 2427.

54 *Id.* at 2428–30.

55 *Id.* at 2427.

standards – and in favor of those who can disseminate the most sensational information as efficiently as possible without any particular concern for truth."[56] Gorsuch even argues that the actual-malice rule incentivizes the media to publish reputation-damaging falsehoods "without investigation, fact-checking, or editing." This argument ignores the mechanics of the actual-malice rule: Defendants' efforts to confirm the truth tend to negate the fact that they entertained serious doubts as to falsity and to absolve them of liability.[57] Regardless, the argument that the actual-malice rule acts as "an ironclad subsidy for the publication of falsehoods by means and on a scale previously unimaginable"[58] rather pointedly raises the question of whether reforming that rule might produce more of the kinds of news that democracy can use.

It is intuitively persuasive that replacing the actual-malice rule with a negligence standard might enhance news quality. But Gorsuch's argument contains many assumptions that do not hold up under scrutiny, particularly considering the spate of recent defamation victories that plaintiffs have won against the press and other high-profile defendants – with no noticeable improvement to our information ecosystem.

Gorsuch's argument ignores the fact that the scope of defamation law is limited and contributors to misinformation are many. Defamation law exists to protect reputations by vindicating victims of reputational injury and compensating them for dignitary, relational, and economic harms. While defamation law plays a role in setting the boundaries of civilized discourse – and thus, indirectly anchoring that discourse in truth – it can only do so in cases involving an individual plaintiff whose reputation has been harmed. However, most falsehoods that pollute public discourse are not aimed at individuals but instead involve complex public policy issues. Many of these falsehoods emanate not from legacy media but from sources unlikely to be deterred by defamation lawsuits, such as state actors, politicians peddling lies for political ends, delusional conspiracy theorists, and fervent partisans who believe what they want to believe. Journalists who fail to investigate, edit, or verify the information they publish – sometimes because of bias – undoubtedly contribute to the problem, but the only cases that defamation law can address are those involving reputational harm.

Gorsuch also overstates the difficulties plaintiffs face in proving actual malice. Actual malice is difficult to prove, but it is not "effective immunity from liability,"[59] as evidenced by the success of plaintiffs in achieving large jury verdicts in recent cases involving proof of actual malice.[60] In the two defamation cases brought by

56 *Id.* at 2428.

57 *Id.*

58 *Id.*

59 Berisha, 141 S. Ct. at 2428 (Gorsuch, J., dissenting from denial of certiorari).

60 Another notable recent victory by a private figure was Gibson Bros., Inc. v. Oberlin College, 187 N.W.3d 629 (Ct. App. Oh. 2022) (affirming a judgment of $22.8 million for bakery owners against a private college and its dean of students).

writer E. Jean Carroll against President Donald Trump,[61] one jury awarded Carroll $10 million, and another jury awarded her $83.3 million. Elsewhere, an appeals court affirmed an award of over $10 million to actor Johnny Depp in a case against his ex-wife, Amber Heard,[62] and a jury awarded a climate scientist, Michael Mann, over $1 million in damages.[63]

Aside from jury verdicts demonstrating that actual malice is not an insurmountable barrier to plaintiff recovery, Gorsuch ignored that many defamation cases – including those involving media misconduct – lead to settlements. A case in point is the jaw-dropping $787.5 million settlement in *Dominion Voting Systems v. Fox News*.[64] While many lessons can be drawn from the case – as discussed below – the size of the settlement surely indicates that Fox did not believe that the actual-malice rule provided "effective immunity"[65] from defamation liability.

Another flaw in this argument is that it focuses solely on the actual-malice rule in isolation, overlooking the incentive structure of US defamation law as a whole. Under current defamation law, media organizations face the ever-present threats of enormous litigation costs and stratospherically large damages awards, which surely affect their incentives at least as much as the actual-malice rule. For smaller news organizations, the cost of defending a defamation action can be ruinous, even if the organization is likely to win. Furthermore, even a small prospect of being held liable for enormous damages is an incentive to get the facts right – at least for most rational

[61] E. Jean Carroll brought two defamation cases against former President Donald Trump, before his reelection, and won both. Carroll successfully proved actual malice in the first trial, which ended in a $5 million verdict in May 2023. Carroll v. Trump, No. 20-CV-7311 (LAK), 2024 WL 97359 (S.D.N.Y. Jan. 9, 2024). The first jury's finding had an issue-preclusive effect in the second trial. Carroll v. Trump, No. 20-CV-7311 (LAK), 2023 WL 5731152 (S.D.N.Y. Sept. 6, 2023) (holding that jury's finding of actual malice in prior defamation action against the former President was entitled to issue-preclusive effect). In 2024, the second trial resulted in a verdict of $83.3 million for the plaintiff.

[62] Depp, II v. Heard, No. CL-2019-0002911, 2022 WL 2342058 (Va. Cir. June 24, 2022) (trial order) (reducing jury award of $5 million in punitive damages to actor Johnny Depp to $350,000 but leaving standing the jury's verdict of $10 million in compensatory damages).

[63] Plaintiff Michael Mann was a university professor who sued the National Review, Competitive Enterprise Institute, Rich Lowry, and writers Rand Simberg (for CEI) and Mark Steyn (for National Review). For a description of the litigation, *see* Nat'l Rev. v. Mann, 140 S. Ct. 344 (mem.) (Alito, J., dissenting from denial of certiorari) (2019). The original caption of the case was Mann v. National Review, but National Review and Lowry were dropped from the case before trial. The Editors, *Michael Mann Owes Us $1 Million*, NATIONAL REV. (Mar. 13, 2024, 2:11 PM), https://www.nationalreview.com/2024/03/michael-mann-owes-us-1-million/. Mann prevailed against Simberg and Steyn. For a description of the jury verdict, *see* Suman Naishadham, *Jury Awards Climate Scientist Michael Mann $1 Million in Defamation Lawsuit*, ASSOCIATED PRESS (Feb. 8, 2024, 9:36 PM), https://apnews.com/article/climate-change-defamation-michael-mann-penn-state-61289ee2d8d2143768d28995c83899ef.

[64] David Folkenflik & Mary Yang, *Fox News Settles Blockbuster Defamation Lawsuit with Dominion Voting Systems*, NPR (Apr. 18, 2023, 4:35 PM), https://www.npr.org/2023/04/18/1170339114/fox-news-settles-blockbuster-defamation-lawsuit-with-dominion-voting-systems.

[65] Berisha, 141 S. Ct. at 2428 (Gorsuch, J., dissenting from denial of certiorari).

actors with something to lose. Defamation law might not offer the solution to improving news quality if these incentives are failing, as they appear to be.

Moreover, a set of recent high-profile defamation cases indicate that some defendants are almost impervious to the supposed accountability incentives of defamation law. These cases suggest that if defamation law should re-anchor public discourse in truth, it simply is not happening. One such case involves the legacy media defendant Fox News. In 2021, Dominion Voting Systems sued Fox News for defamation in the course of the network's coverage of the 2020 election.[66] In the wake of the election, then-President Trump and some of his partisans began to insist that election fraud deprived Trump of victory.[67] Among those they blamed for fraud was Dominion Voting Systems, the producer of the electronic voting machines used in some states.[68] Although Fox News had initially declared that former Vice President Joe Biden won the election, it hosted and sometimes seemed to endorse various Trump partisans presenting spurious "evidence" that Dominion rigged its voting machines to deliver the election to Biden.[69] Dominion sued Fox for $1.6 billion.[70]

Discovery in the case unveiled considerable evidence that many of Fox's executives and hosts doubted the veracity of the "evidence" against Dominion. Emails and texts between them suggested that they knew the falsehoods about Dominion were untrue, with some even referring to the allegations and those peddling them as "nuts" and "crazy."[71] Nonetheless, Fox continued to air lies about Dominion, making the calculated gamble that its audience would desert it if it stopped publicizing "the Big Lie," a gamble that appeared to pay off.[72] Despite entering into the largest libel settlement in history, Fox News overcame what should have been a serious reputational setback for a news purveyor to remain the most-watched

66 *See generally* Complaint, U.S. Dominion, Inc. v. Fox New Network, 2021 WL 1153152 (Del. Super. Ct. 2021).

67 Jemima McEvoy, *These Are the Voter Fraud Claims Trump Tried (and Failed) to Overturn the Election With*, Forbes (Dec. 17, 2020, 3:35 PM), https://www.forbes.com/sites/jemimamcevoy/2020/12/17/these-are-the-voter-fraud-claims-trump-tried-and-failed-to-overturn-the-election-with/?sh = f05dcdf58c5a.

68 *Id.*

69 Brian Stelter, *'Tons of Crazy': The Inside Story of How Fox Fell for the 'Big Lie'*, Politico (Nov. 15, 2023, 5:00 AM), https://www.politico.com/news/magazine/2023/11/15/big-lie-fox-news-brian-stelter-book-00127133.

70 Jonah E. Bromwich & Ben Smith, *Fox News Is Sued by Election Technology Company for over $2.7 Billion*, N.Y. Times (Feb. 4, 2021), https://www.nytimes.com/2021/02/04/business/media/smartmatic-fox-news-lawsuit.html.

71 Alison Durkee, *'Mind Blowingly Nuts': Fox News Hosts and Execs Repeatedly Denounced 2020 Election Fraud Off-Air – Here Are Their Most Scathing Comments*, Forbes (Feb. 17, 2023, 8:04 AM), https://www.forbes.com/sites/alisondurkee/2023/02/17/mind-blowingly-nuts-fox-news-hosts-and-execs-repeatedly-denounced-2020-election-fraud-off-air-here-are-their-most-scathing-comments/?sh = 2800063318f3.

72 *See supra* note 64.

cable news network in the United States.[73] In fact, a year on from the settlement, it attracts more viewers to its prime-time news than its two top cable competitors combined.[74] Although it is impossible to know whether the settlement has increased Fox's commitment to providing its viewers with fact-based news, one observer noted that they "don't see any reason why the lawsuit changes the way that Fox does business because the way it does business makes it money."[75]

Scholar RonNell Andersen Jones made this point in an opinion piece in *The New York Times*, and she has documented further failures of libel law to produce accountability.[76] President Trump has promised to continue to repeat his defamatory accusations about Carroll "a thousand times," even after juries found him liable for almost $90 million for accusing her of lying about him sexually assaulting her.[77] Likewise, Trump's former attorney, Rudy Giuliani, has continued to accuse two Georgia poll workers of election fraud despite a jury's deliberation leading to their being awarded $148 million.[78] Elsewhere, internet radio personality Alex Jones has continued to tell lies about the families of children killed at Sandy Hook despite a jury verdict of almost $1 billion against him. In these cases, court judgments ostensibly provided the plaintiffs with authoritative declarations of truth, and yet large segments of the court of public opinion remained unconvinced. Consider, for example, that mere months after Carroll won her second verdict,[79] Trump secured the Republican nomination for president.[80] Carroll's

[73] Dominick Mastrangelo, *Fox News Takes the Hits, but Its Audience Looks Resilient*, The Hill (Mar. 12, 2023, 12:00 PM), https://thehill.com/homenews/media/3894411-fox-news-takes-the-hits-but-its-audience-looks-resilient/.

[74] Business Wire, *FOX News Channel Crushes CNN and MSNBC Combined in Total Day and Primetime Viewers for the First Quarter of 2023*, Yahoo Finance (Apr. 2, 2024), https://finance.yahoo.com/news/fox-news-channel-crushes-cnn-194000383.html?.

[75] *The Dominion Lawsuit Showed the Limits of Fox's Influence over Its Audience*, The Economist (Apr. 17, 2023), https://www.economist.com/united-states/2023/04/17/the-dominion-lawsuit-showed-the-limits-of-foxs-influence-over-its-audience (quoting A. J. Bauer, Assistant Professor in the Department of Journalism and Creative Media at the University of Alabama).

[76] RonNell Andersen Jones, *The E. Jean Carroll Verdict Exposes the Limits of Libel Law*, N.Y. Times (Jan. 28, 2024), https://www.nytimes.com/2024/01/28/opinion/donald-trump-e-jean-carroll-libel-damages.html.

[77] *Id.*

[78] Lindsay Whitehurst & Alanna Durkin Richer, *Jury Awards $148 Billion in Damages to Georgia Election Workers over Rudy Guliani's 2020 Vote Lies*, AP News (Dec. 15, 2023, 7:13 PM), https://apnews.com/article/giuliani-2020-election-georgia-defamation-moss-freeman-6f6446c4f5224f521db8ff7763fb12d1#.

[79] *New Polling Shows Female Support for Trump Has Dropped*, NBC News (Mar. 11, 2024), https://www.nbcnews.com/now/video/new-polling-shows-female-support-for-trump-has-dropped-206210117618 (discussing Quinnipiac University poll).

[80] Stephen Fowler, *Trump and Biden Clinch 2024 Presidential Nominations*, NPR (Mar. 12, 2024, 11:56 PM), https://www.npr.org/2024/03/12/1238033721/donald-trump-joe-biden-nomination-delegates.

defamation victory provided only partial vindication and no deterrence, for reasons having nothing to do with defamation law exceptionalism and everything to do with political polarization and demagogic populism.

Although defendants like Trump, Jones, and Giuliani seem undaunted by enormous libel verdicts, libel lawsuits continue to force other defendants to err substantially on the side of caution. Only the largest, most well-resourced members of the legacy media can easily combat even a meritless libel action, and the rich and powerful can inflict significant penalties on their critics just by suing them.[81] High litigation costs and the inability to predict whether an action will result in a multimillion-dollar verdict also mean that few media defendants can afford to blithely publish falsehoods about individuals on the assumption that the actual-malice rule will protect them.

If one needed confirmation of this thesis, the evidence from the UK is instructive. Despite its more reputation-protective and press-punishing defamation laws, the British public does not appear to trust the British press significantly more than the American public trusts the American press.[82] Moreover, distrust in institutions, including the press, is a worldwide phenomenon. Distrust in the press is merely a symptom of what United Nations Secretary-General António Guterres has called a worldwide "Trust Deficit Disorder."[83] This disorder is fueled by a complex set of factors, including "inequality . . . undermining faith in the social contract,"[84] which do not lend themselves to simple solutions. The depressing upshot of this analysis seems to be that defamation law is too small a piece of the distrust puzzle to make defamation reform the answer.

However, even if defamation reform is not the answer, defamation does need reform. As I have written elsewhere, defamation must introduce remedies that vindicate individual reputations and surface the truth more readily. Lower courts have already expanded the use of injunctions in libel cases, and further broadening the repertoire of remedies to include declaratory judgments might re-anchor the law's role in vindicating plaintiffs' truths. But such reforms should not be conducted in isolation. While expanding plaintiffs' opportunities for vindication, defamation law reforms should also consider restricting remedies (such as presumed and

[81] Katie Balevic, A *Judge Dismissed a Wisconsin Politician's Defamation Suit Against a Newspaper, but the Legal Fees May Still Shutter the Paper*, BUSINESS INSIDER (Aug. 20, 2023, 4:23 PM), https://www.businessinsider.com/dismissed-defamation-suit-wi-politician-may-shutter-local-newspaper-2023-8; *Little Saigon News Files for Bankruptcy Following Defamation Dispute*, AMERICAN BANKRUPTCY INSTITUTE, https://www.abi.org/feed-item/little-saigon-news-files-for-bankruptcy-following-defamation-dispute (last visited Apr. 22, 2024).

[82] Amy Watson, *Trustworthiness of News Media Worldwide*, STATISTA (Sept. 25, 2023), https://www.statista.com/statistics/308468/importance-brand-journalist-creating-trust-news/.

[83] António Guterres, *Secretary-General's Address to the General Assembly* (Sept. 25, 2018), https://www.un.org/sg/en/content/sg/statement/2018-09-25/secretary-generals-address

[84] *Id.*

punitive damages) that allow the rich and powerful to sue their critics into silence. Procedural mechanisms designed to reduce the cost of litigation should also be at the forefront of reform efforts. In one sense, Gorsuch and other critics of *Sullivan*'s regime are right: Defamation *should* be recalibrated to reward journalists who adhere to professionally developed standards for getting the facts right. But eliminating actual malice? If only it were that simple.

9

Press Benefits and the Public Imagination

Erin C. Carroll

In an era when the press faces unprecedented challenges, from financial instability to declining public trust, those who believe in the importance of a free press find themselves playing defense. Press advocates have been forced to articulate, with renewed clarity and urgency, why the press is not merely important but vital to an effective democracy and why it needs to be saved from what has been described as a "death spiral"[1] and an "extinction-level event."[2] These arguments often focus on the crucial role the press plays – the "press function," as lawyers call it – in informing the public, holding power to account, and facilitating democratic discourse. Advocating for the press's value has become an essential task because the survival of this indispensable institution depends on the public understanding and appreciating its necessity.

Scholars and commentators generally discuss the press function through one of two lenses. Legal scholars tend to describe the press function through existing Supreme Court doctrine in which the Court has told us that the press serves as a watchdog, an educator, and a proxy for the public. Political theorists, meanwhile, will situate the press within our overall democratic structure, explaining that a free press is integral to democracy because it maintains the public sphere and facilitates discourse.

These explanations are fundamental. But they are also insufficient, especially in an age when delegitimizing the press is a political tactic. To deliver the press from extinction, the public needs not only to *know* what the press does, it needs to *care*.

Many thanks to RonNell Andersen Jones and Sonja R. West for organizing this project, for their longtime commitment to ensuring a free and vibrant press, and for their insightful feedback. Thanks, too, to Katy Glenn Bass and Joseph Blocher, for their extremely helpful feedback. All errors are mine.

[1] Pete Vernon, *Cuts at the Daily News Highlight a Local News Crisis*, Colum. Journalism Rev. (July 24, 2018), https://www.cjr.org/the_media_today/daily-news-cuts.php.

[2] Clare Malone, *Is the Media Prepared for an Extinction-Level Event?*, New Yorker (Feb. 10, 2024), https://www.newyorker.com/news/the-weekend-essay/is-the-media-prepared-for-an-extinction-level-event.

This means that beyond conceptualizing the press function as a matter of doctrine and theory, press advocates must conceptualize it as a matter of rhetoric. Advocates should be rethinking how to describe what the press does when they are speaking to judges, legislators, and other citizens. These audiences can ensure – through enhanced First Amendment rights, public subsidies, public-media models, statutory protections, or subscription dollars – that the free press survives and flourishes instead of succumbs.

The act of naming is not a small thing. New language can persuade and motivate. Rethinking how we talk about the press – and press functions, in particular – could prompt Americans to care about the press and to find common ground regarding the reasons for this caring. Talking about the press in newly positive ways is also how the public might begin to envision a reinvigorated and dynamic institution. As communication scholar Mike Ananny writes, "[P]ress freedom is a normative and institutional product of any given era: it is what people think press freedom should mean and how people have arranged people and power to achieve that vision."[3] What the "people think press freedom should mean" is shaped by the language they use. As of now, that language often does not account for the true value of the press's work. This needs to change.

This chapter outlines how press advocates can think rhetorically about press functions in the service of a reinvigorated press and democracy. First, it proposes a shift in terminology from the dry "press function" to a descriptor that is not just more inspirational but more apt: "press benefits." Second, it goes a level deeper and examines two time-honored press benefits – the watchdog and proxy roles – and suggests how these benefits might be renamed and reconceptualized. Third, it describes how we might use rhetoric as a framework for naming other press functions, even aspirational ones, that the courts have not previously recognized. This framework can be a means of both supporting the existing press and transforming it into one that is ever closer to best supporting the collective flourishing of citizens. Finally, the chapter ends by sketching out methods for both dispersing updated press-benefits rhetoric around the world and continuing to generate that rhetoric.

9.1 FROM PRESS FUNCTIONS TO PRESS BENEFITS

In naming what the press does, the Supreme Court has settled on the word "function."[4] Sometimes the justices have made the reference a bit more grandiose by rendering it plural: "functions."[5] Academics (including me) have followed suit

[3] Mike Ananny, Networked Press Freedom: Creating Infrastructures for a Public Right to Hear 3 (2018) (emphasis omitted).

[4] *See, e.g.*, Houchins v. KQED, Inc., 438 U.S. 1, 8 (1978); Pell v. Procunier, 417 U.S. 817, 835 (1974) (Powell, J., concurring).

[5] *See, e.g.*, Branzburg v. Hayes, 408 U.S. 665, 725 (1972) (Stewart, J., dissenting); Time, Inc. v. Hill, 385 U.S. 374, 420 (1967) (Fortas, J., dissenting).

and adopted the term.[6] The noun is accurate but uninspired. "Functions" are roles or purposes.[7] They are not inherently good or bad. They have no moral valence. Functions are anodyne, workmanlike, serviceable.

The press requires better. The work of the American press is not a mere collection of humdrum or trivial tasks. The press provides us with feats, public goods, and achievements, like documenting catastrophic flooding, revealing the scope of migrant child labor, explaining how dementia progresses and impacts families, and humanizing prisoners.[8]

In doing this work, the press performs more than a function. It provides a *benefit*. A benefit is an "advantage, profit, good," which, in the case of the press, redounds widely.[9] "Benefit" seems an especially fitting word given that journalism's calling is to assist with the perpetuation of democracy. As Bill Kovach and Tom Rosenstiel write in *The Elements of Journalism*, "The primary purpose of journalism is to provide citizens with the information they need to be free and self-governing."[10]

This is not institutional self-aggrandizement. Countless political scientists, philosophers, and judges have described the tight tie between the press and government.[11] The Supreme Court, in bygone eras, understood this link and the press's vital role in sustaining democracy well. Take Justice Felix Frankfurter, who wrote: "Without a free press there can be no free society."[12] Or Justice Hugo Black's Pentagon Papers concurrence that stated: "In the First Amendment, the Founding Fathers gave the free press the protection it must have to fulfill its essential role in our democracy."[13] Given this acknowledged importance of the press to democracy, it seems right to refer to its role as a benefit.[14]

By embracing the term "benefit," press advocates would be using rhetoric in all three of the forms that law and literature scholar James Boyd White described as

[6] *See, e.g.*, Erin C. Carroll, *Platforms and the Fall of the Fourth Estate: Looking Beyond the First Amendment to Protect Watchdog Journalism*, 79 Md. L. Rev. 529, 534 (2020).

[7] *Function*, Oxford English Dictionary, https://www.oed.com/dictionary/function_n?tab=meaning_and_use#3559828.

[8] These examples were taken from the winners of the 2024 Pulitzer Prizes. *See 2024 Pulitzer Prizes: Journalism*, The Pulitzer Prizes, https://www.pulitzer.org/prize-winners-by-year.

[9] *See Benefit*, Oxford English Dictionary, https://www.oed.com/dictionary/benefit_n?tab=meaning_and_use#23477071.

[10] Bill Kovach & Tom Rosenstiel, The Elements of Journalism: What Newspeople Should Know and the Public Should Expect 7 (2021).

[11] *See* Garrett Epps, The First Amendment: Freedom of the Press 74 (2008); Robert A. Dahl, *What Political Institutions Does Large-Scale Democracy Require?*, 120 Pol. Sci. Q. 187, 188–89 (2005).

[12] Pennekamp v. Florida, 328 U.S. 331, 354 (1946) (Frankfurter, J., concurring).

[13] New York Times Co. v. United States, 403 U.S. 713, 717 (1971) (Black, J., concurring).

[14] With this said, press advocates may find that in making certain arguments, "function" remains the more useful and accurate term. This could happen, for example, when arguing specifically about what journalists *do*. For this reason, I don't intend for "benefit" to supplant "function," but to complement it.

comprising "constitutive rhetoric."[15] These include speaking the language of the audience, modifying and rearranging the language of the law, and creating a community around legal language.[16] In using rhetoric in all of these forms, advocates can spark doctrinal and cultural change.

With respect to speaking the language of the audience and rearranging the language of the law, "benefit" has an emotional appeal that "function" lacks. This emotional resonance is fundamental to convincing Americans to care. Though lawyers often resist acknowledging the salience of emotion in advocacy, it is the appeal to pathos that rhetoricians from Aristotle forward have recognized as a key to persuasion.[17] As one former New York Times op-ed page editor put it: When it comes to persuasion, "[f]eelings are crucial, much more important than facts."[18] "Benefit" appeals to humans' deep-seated desire for that which is good. Making this change is a way of appealing to the language of the audience.

Using "benefit" is also an example of constitutive rhetoric's creation of community. The idea that the press provides benefits in service of democracy could help establish common ground among Americans who might otherwise remain polarized.[19] It is what legal scholar Joseph W. Singer calls a "public reason."[20] In the context of persuasion, public reasons are those ideas "that could or should be accepted by people with differing perspectives, religious traditions, moral frameworks, and experiences."[21] If Americans can agree that the press is an engine of democracy, there is a basis for the "shared factual assumptions" and "shared values" that White describes as drivers of a rhetorical community.[22] If we can assemble this community, we have exponentially improved the chances of protecting and promoting the press.

15 *See* James Boyd White, *Law as Rhetoric, Rhetoric as Law: The Arts of Cultural and Communal Life*, 52 Univ. of Chicago L. Rev. 684, 688 (1985).

16 *See id.* at 688–90.

17 *See* Kristen Konrad Tiscione, *Feelthinking Like a Lawyer: The Role of Emotion in Legal Reasoning and Decision-Making*, 54 Wake Forest L. Rev. 1159. 1168–69 (2019) (describing Aristotle's belief that rhetoric was based "in the invention, arrangement, style, and delivery of artistic appeals to *logos* (reason), *pathos* (emotion), and *ethos* (credibility)").

18 Trish Hall, Writing to Persuade: How to Bring People Over to Your Side xii (2019); Joseph Blocher, *"The Road I Can't Help Travelling": Holmes on Truth and Persuadability*, 51 Seton Hall L. Rev. 105, 116 (2020) ("Scholars writing on cultural cognition and motivated reasoning have powerfully – heartbreakingly – argued that people are not moved by facts and 'ideas' in the sense that most marketplace of ideas theorists probably conceptualize them.").

19 This creation of community through press-benefits rhetoric could complement the ways in which the press, as an institution, already creates community with its audience. *See* RonNell Andersen Jones, *Press Speakers and the First Amendment Rights of Listeners*, 90 Univ. of Colorado L. Rev. 499, 548 (2019) ("The press is not a mere conduit between other speakers and listeners. It is a unique institutional speaker itself, with a uniquely symbiotic relationship with listeners."); David A. Anderson, *The Press and Democratic Dialogue*, 127 Harvard L. Rev. F. 331, 333 (2014) ("News outlets sift, select, and package the news, and in so doing create a community.").

20 *See* Joseph William Singer, Persuasion: Getting to the Other Side 9 (2020).

21 *Id.*

22 *See* White, *supra* note 15, at 694.

It is this degree of sentiment and synergy that could help push through the inertia surrounding legislative efforts and legal strategies to protect the press. In Congress, press advocates have repeatedly fallen short of passing press-protective legislation.[23] Meanwhile, in the Supreme Court, this inertia is manifest in a sort of Press Clause paralysis – a refusal by the Court to read any meaning into the First Amendment's explicit reference to the press – and a more recent failure by the justices to speak positively about the press at all.[24]

At its root, the idea is that language evokes caring – a creation and realization of shared ground and community and ultimately an action in service of the thing (here, the press) about which the community cares. This action should plow back into improving the press, making it that much easier to care about. A shift in language can jumpstart this cycle and then fuel it.

9.2 RENAMING AND RETHINKING THE WATCHDOG AND PROXY BENEFITS

Beyond the adoption of "benefits," a relabeling and rethinking of some of those benefits themselves is in order. This effort is vital not simply so that we can describe the press more inspirationally but because it is long overdue. The Supreme Court opinions that set out the key press benefits are now about a half-century old – penned at a time when newsmen pounded out stories on typewriters in newsrooms ripe with the smell of stale cigarette smoke.

We can start with the watchdog. If there is a press function that has been most lauded by the Court and journalists themselves, it is the watchdog.[25] It is the concept that the press's primary purpose is a structural one – it exists as a check on the other three branches of government[26] as well as a check on private power.[27] Its primary role is to expose and attack government actors for bad behavior.[28]

[23] *See, e.g.*, Jim Magill, *Congress May Soon Pass Federal Shield Law. It's Been a Long Time Coming*, QUILL (Mar. 14, 2024), https://www.quillmag.com/2024/03/14/congress-may-soon-pass-federal-shield-law-its-been-a-long-time-coming/ (describing how press advocates have been trying to get reporter's shield bills passed since the 1970s).

[24] *See* RonNell Andersen Jones & Sonja R. West, *The U.S. Supreme Court's Characterizations of the Press: An Empirical Study*, 100 N.C. L. REV. 375, 428–29 (2022) ("Our large-scale empirical study shows an especially stark abandonment of positive judicial depictions of the press in the last fifty years.").

[25] *See* RonNell Andersen Jones, *What the Supreme Court Thinks of the Press and Why It Matters*, 66 ALA. L. REV. 253, 258 (2014) (noting that, of the positive roles the Supreme Court assigns to the press, the Court "overwhelmingly" characterizes the press "as a watchdog").

[26] *See* Vincent Blasi, *The Checking Value in First Amendment Theory*, 1977 AM. BAR FOUND. RSCH. J. 521, 527 (1977); Potter Stewart, *"Or of the Press,"* 26 HASTINGS L.J. 631, 634 (1975).

[27] *See* Sonja R. West, *The Stealth Press Clause*, 48 GA. L. REV. 729, 754 (2014) (noting that the Supreme Court has recognized that the press checks private power and not just government power).

[28] Erin C. Carroll, *The Violence of Free Speech and Press Metaphors*, 81 WASHINGTON & LEE L. REV. 87, 133–34 (2024).

This structural role is important, even necessary. But the watchdog label is flawed, and the prevalent belief that to be a watchdog is the press's raison d'être is also problematic. The watchdog metaphor is an unnecessarily violent one, especially for an entity providing a public good and service.[29] Watchdogs exist to sniff out wrongdoing and to pounce.[30]

The violent overtones of the metaphor are also evident in the way journalists routinely describe their role as hard-hitting and aggressive.[31] Watchdog reporting has been dubbed by some scholars as the "journalism of outrage" – designed to "prick[]" and "provoke."[32] Without it, these scholars argue, journalism would be "sterile" and "bloodless."[33] Given the way that metaphor functions, there is a chance that clinging to this violent metaphor is actually preventing journalists and citizens from conceiving of the press in ways that are not so pugilistic.

Instead of describing the benefit that the press provides when it checks government wrongdoing as "watchdogging," an alternative is to describe it as "independence." This word eliminates the violent overtones of the watchdog yet preserves the idea that the press is acting, as New York Times publisher Adolph S. Ochs wrote in 1896, "without fear or favor."[34] An independent press can be both a monitor and a collaborator as situations demand. With its patriotic overtones, "independence" also aligns well with a reconceptualizing of press functions as benefits in service of democracy.

A relabeling of the watchdog function might also help lead to deeper, and overdue, thinking about the parameters of this particular press benefit. For example, as it stands, journalists conceive of the watchdog role in much the same way that First Amendment theory has traditionally thought about free speech – that more is better and that its virtues are almost without bounds. But just as recent changes in our political and speech environments have demonstrated that sometimes too much speech may have costs (see, for example, the damage done by "troll armies," "'flooding' tactics that distort or drown out other speech," or the "deployment of propaganda robots"),[35] it is also worth examining whether there should be limits on the press's watchdog role. For example, one recent study conducted by researchers from the American Press Institute and the University of Chicago found that conservatives may be less likely to embrace the press's watchdog role.[36] If this is right, the

29 *Id.* at 133–41.

30 *Id.*; *see* KOVACH & ROSENSTIEL, *supra* note 10, at 218 (describing the "prosecution" function of watchdog journalism).

31 *Id.* at 138–39.

32 DAVID L. PROTESS ET AL., JOURNALISM OF OUTRAGE v, 5 (1991).

33 *Id.* at vi.

34 David W. Dunlap, *Looking Back: 1896 – 'Without Fear or Favor'*, N.Y. TIMES (Aug. 14, 2015), https://www.nytimes.com/2015/09/12/insider/1896-without-fear-or-favor.html.

35 *See* Tim Wu, *Is the First Amendment Obsolete?*, 117 MICH. L. REV. 547, 548 (2018).

36 In a study examining the relationship between people's "moral values" and the "core values" of journalism, researchers found that those "who most value loyalty and authority are much less

press's emphasis on it may contribute to the public feeling alienated by the press and, as a result, failing to support it.[37]

Framing this inquiry in terms of "independence" suggests that there may be times and ways in which press independence may need to vary depending on the circumstances.[38] For example, historically, journalists have staunchly opposed any sort of public funding precisely because of its potential to erode the press's independence. Yet, at a moment like the present, when the press's very existence might depend on public funding, press advocates are examining ways to publicly fund the press while ensuring that journalists retain editorial independence. In other words, "independence" can be nuanced. It is not all or nothing.

In addition to the watchdog role, another press benefit that could be relabeled and, in the process, rethought is the role of the press as a proxy. The term "proxy" has been used to refer to the press's role as a literal stand-in for the public, for example, when journalists witness newsworthy events and then report on them.[39] As the Supreme Court has written, "[I]n a society in which each individual has but limited time and resources with which to observe at first hand the operations of his government, he relies necessarily upon the press to bring to him in convenient form the facts of those operations."[40] Journalists have also long indicated that their proxy role involves gathering information from far-flung locales and bringing it to the public's doorstep. As journalist Walter Lippmann wrote in 1922, "[T]he real environment is altogether too big, too complex, and too fleeting for direct acquaintance."[41] Instead, he wrote, we "must have maps."[42] The press, in its proxy role, creates those maps.

But, like "function," the "proxy" label is uninspiring. Plus, it is perhaps not as accurate as it once was. Although there are still situations in which physical access to spaces is limited, the public now often has virtual access to newsworthy events. Meanwhile, today, serving as a proxy for the public on the world stage is an increasingly impossible feat given the rate of global information generation and sharing. Thus, what the public needs from today's press is to act not so much as a proxy than as a "curator."

likely than others to endorse the idea that there should be a watchdog over those in power," and about 86 percent of those in the study who valued loyalty and authority identified as conservative or moderate. *See* Associated Press-NORC Ctr. for Pub. Affs. Resch. & Am. Press Inst., A New Way of Looking at Trust in Media: Do Americans Share Journalism's Core Values 1, 4 (Apr. 2021), https://www.americanpressinstitute.org/wp-content/uploads/2021/04/Media-Insight-Project-Study-Report.pdf.

37 The same report concluded that "[t]o woo subscribers, the media will need to vary its messaging beyond traditional appeals about journalism being a watchdog." *Id.* at 4.

38 *See* Lorraine Daston & Peter Galison, Objectivity 42–50 (2007) (tracing the shifting meaning of "objectivity" in the sciences).

39 *See Houchins*, 438 U.S. at 8 (describing how the press acts "as the 'eyes and ears' of the public").

40 Cox Broad. Corp. v. Cohn, 420 U.S. 469, 491 (1975).

41 Walter Lippmann, Public Opinion 8 (Courier Corp. 2012) (1922).

42 *Id.*

By being a curator, the press surveys, selects, distills, prioritizes, and contextualizes.[43] It does this work by adhering to the evolving tenets of journalism. This process stands in stark contrast – and its value becomes especially clear – when compared to the most dominant method by which the information that so many of us ingest today is sifted and presented: content moderation by social media platform algorithms.

To be clear, I am not suggesting that the watchdog or proxy roles are unimportant. But when we rely on these metaphors to describe the press's work, we limit the public's conception of that work, at times in unproductive ways.[44] Using new language to describe the press's benefits could broaden our understanding of the press's potential and, in time, even transform the institution to fulfill that potential.

9.3 PRESS RHETORIC AND THE PUBLIC IMAGINATION

So far, this chapter has discussed renaming press functions – that is, finding new ways to label press functions that the law has already recognized with different descriptors. But there may be additional, and even more powerful, ways to use rhetoric to bolster the press. We could employ rhetoric as a framework for generating language to describe press benefits that the law has failed to recognize or has not yet even imagined. In fact, this type of communal envisioning may be the very essence of conceptualizing law as a branch of rhetoric.[45] As James Boyd White wrote, "It is the true nature of law to constitute a 'we' and to establish a conversation by which that 'we' can determine what our 'wants' are and should be."[46]

Now is the right moment to be engaged in this process. Along with institutions generally, the press is neck-deep in crisis. It lacks the public's trust and support.[47] This may be for good reason. Communication scholars Barbie Zelizer, Pablo Boczkowski, and C. W. Anderson have critiqued today's press as elitist, entrenched, and self-congratulatory.[48] They write, "Journalism finds itself less socially, politically and culturally relevant than it ought to be, and certainly less relevant than it thinks it is."[49]

But this crisis could be reframed as an opportunity for reimagining the press, starting with press benefits. Yes, as discussed, the press is a bulwark of democracy,

[43] *See* RonNell Andersen Jones & Lisa Grow Sun, *Freedom of the Press in Post-Truthism America*, 98 Washington Univ. L. Rev. 419, 464 (2020) (describing the press's role prioritizing and curating information); Andersen Jones, *supra* note 19, at 536 (discussing the importance of the press's role as a curator); Anderson, *supra* note 19, at 333 (discussing how journalists "sift, select, and package the news").

[44] *See* George Lakoff & Mark Johnson, Metaphors We Live By 12–13 (1980).

[45] *See* White, *supra* note 15, at 684 (conceptualizing law as a "branch of rhetoric").

[46] *Id.* at 698.

[47] *See* Megan Brenan, *Media Confidence in U.S. Matches 2016 Record Low*, Gallup (Oct. 19, 2023), https://news.gallup.com/poll/512861/media-confidence-matches-2016-record-low.aspx.

[48] Barbie Zelizer et al., The Journalism Manifesto 36–37, 46, 113 (2022).

[49] *Id.* at 113.

but in what ways? How does the press inform, create communities, and empower? To borrow Mike Ananny's wording, are the press's "institutional arrangements" such that they will "produce expansive, dynamic, diverse publics"?[50] If not, how might we change them? What publics do we want, and how do they differ from what we have? How might the press better help with solving collective problems? How might the press better connect with and serve various communities? Is the press promoting communal flourishing? What type of democracy is our press a bulwark for? Is this the type of democracy we want and need?

In trying to answer these questions, we might both discover and imagine all sorts of ways that the press is benefiting citizens or, conversely, is not benefiting them and needs to be. For example, we could focus on the role of the press as a facilitator and convener of the public square. In this role, the press creates the shared epistemic foundations that are necessary for democracy.[51] We might also recognize the press's role as a historian, creating vital records through which future generations will be able to study and build upon our generation's thoughts, advances, and missteps. We could imagine the press as a community storyteller, a preserver of traditions. We could envision the press as a sentinel and observer whose very presence improves outcomes. Perhaps we see the press as creating a kind of poetry – language grounded in fact but allowing us to see possibility.[52] We might aspire to a press that tends to communities through care-based practices.[53] Or we might decide these roles are too big or too many for the press, and we might think about how to distribute them or what other institutions or organizations or arrangements might fulfill them.

Even in the short term, this use of rhetoric and these conversations could help to create the kind of dynamic institution that some press thinkers argue is a productive path forward. Harnessing the public imagination is key. According to communication scholar Stephen D. Reese, "institutions are worth defending to the extent they contribute to a moral purpose and bind together historically the aspirational values they embody, connecting members to their society – past, present, and future."[54] As part of creating that worthy entity, Reese argues that we should think about the press as a "hybrid institution" – an entity that blends old and new and is constantly engaging, evolving, and emerging.[55]

50 Ananny, *supra* note 3, at 4.

51 *See* Erin C. Carroll, *Beyond the Watchdog: Using Law to Build Trust in the Press*, 3 J. of Free Speech L. 57, 65 (2023).

52 *See* Pico Iyer, The Half-Known Life: In Search of Paradise 21 (2023) ("[P]oetry is the form that shimmers between fact and fiction, a world of suggestions that does not allow one to settle into certainties").

53 *See* Sue Robinson & Patrick Johnson, *Rectifying Harm Through Care-Based Practices: How Journalists Might Tend to Disengaged Communities*, 25 Journalism Stud. 99, 100 (2024), https://www.tandfonline.com/doi/full/10.1080/1461670X.2023.2289889.

54 Stephen D. Reese, The Crisis of the Institutional Press 58 (2021).

55 *See id.* at 17–19.

The key to Reese's hybrid institution and to employing rhetoric more generally is not doing so with the goal of arriving at definitive answers to the questions posed. More important is the dialogue – the community it creates and the changing institution that the community can sustain. This is, at its core, the messy work of democracy. As philosopher Jason Stanley writes, democratic citizenship "demands a great deal of all of us. There are easier ways to live."[56] It may be that these conversations about the press prompt citizens to think about democracy in new ways. Our current press is a product of our particular American brand of liberal democracy, but different types of democratic government might demand other press benefits, roles, and forms.[57] And regardless of what shape our future democracy takes and what the needs of that democracy might be, building rhetorical frameworks to support the press both normatively and practically is a crucial task.

9.4 WHERE TO USE PRO-PRESS RHETORIC

As a new language around press functions is generated, the beauty of this rhetoric is that it can be deployed without cost and in abundance. It can take numerous forms and be directed at a variety of audiences.

Let's start with the judiciary. Given the judiciary's ability to shape the parameters of the press and invest it with power, it is critical that judges understand the value of the press's work. One direct way to demonstrate this value is through briefing. Press advocates can advance their cause by adopting updated language about the press in their merits briefs and in the numerous amicus briefs they file. As constitutional law scholars Eric Ruben and Joseph Blocher write, rhetoric is at the heart of legally instigated change: "Constitutional doctrine is shaped by the rhetorical moves that litigants, commentators, scholars, and judges make. Such rhetoric can become embedded in popular and legal understandings of constitutional rights."[58]

Advocates might also speak this language to legislators. Both at the federal and state levels, legislators convene hearings on the state of the press as well as draft and debate press-related legislation. Pro-press rhetoric in testimony and advocacy can find its way into law and policy.

Journalists, as public figures, must also become more accustomed to using their megaphones to bring attention to press benefits. Institutionally, the press has a bias against itself being at the center of the news.[59] Other than having a byline, some

[56] Jason Stanley, How Fascism Works: The Politics of Us and Them 184 (2020).

[57] *See* C. Edwin Baker, *The Media That Citizens Need*, 147 Univ. of Penn. L. Rev. 317, 320–40 (1998) (describing various democratic theories and their corresponding media).

[58] Eric Ruben & Joseph Blocher, *"Second-Class" Rhetoric, Ideology, and Doctrinal Change*, 110 Georgetown L.J. 613, 623 (2022) (examining the role of rhetoric in shaping Second Amendment rights).

[59] *See* Kevin Smith & Karen Grabowski, *SPJ Cautions Journalists: Report the Story, Don't Become Part of It*, Soc'y of Pro. Journalists (Jan. 22, 2010), https://www.spj.org/news.asp?ref=948

journalists want to disappear behind their stories. Traditionally, this is part of the feint of "objectivity" – or the so-called "view from nowhere."[60] But as the premise of objectivity has come under fire, perhaps, too, should the norm among journalists to keep relatively mum about the fate of their profession. As one journalism professor recently wrote in the *Columbia Journalism Review* about convincing conservative audiences of the press's value, "If local journalism is really to be revived, those who hope to revive it will need to try something more ambitious: they'll need to interject in the conversations about journalism within conservative networks, and offer a compelling new explanation of who local journalists are and why conservatives might want to listen to them."[61]

Employing pro-press rhetoric in these public ways and spaces is crucial both as a means of dispersing it and of continuing to germinate conversation about the press. In addition, it can perhaps blunt the effects of the rabidly anti-press rhetoric that has become a hallmark of numerous conservative politicians. To date, no one has effectively countered the populist rhetorical tirade against the press. To do so, we need both a reinvigorated language around the press and people willing to speak it.

9.5 CONCLUSION

In many ways, the American public has forsaken the press. This is obvious from vitriol – like the January 6 rioter who wrote "MURDER THE MEDIA" on a door of the U.S. Capitol.[62] But the more pernicious acts have been banal acts of omission, such as failing to provide financial support to the thousands of local news outlets that have gone dark in the past two decades.[63]

This unintentional forsaking is perhaps understandable. The press survived, and profited, for most of America's history without significant public intervention.

(cautioning that "injecting oneself into the story or creating news events for coverage is not objective reporting").

60 *See* Candis Callison & Mary Lynn Young, Reckoning: Journalism's Limits and Possibilities 4 (2020) (critiquing the "view from nowhere" and the notion of journalistic objectivity).

61 Doron Taussig, *The 'Fake News'-ification of Local News – and What to Do About It*, Colum. Journalism Rev. (Apr. 16, 2024), https://www.cjr.org/tow_center/the-fake-news-ification-of-local-news-and-what-to-do-about-it.php.

62 *See* Angela Fu, *Reporters Covering the Capitol Attack Were Used to Harassment and Heckling. But Wednesday Was Different*, POYNTER (Jan. 13, 2021), https://www.poynter.org/reporting-editing/2021/reporters-covering-the-capitol-attack-were-used-to-harassment-and-heckling-but-wednesday-was-different/.

63 *See* Elisa Shearer et al., *Americans' Changing Relationship with Local News*, Pew Rsch. Ctr. (May 7, 2024), https://www.pewresearch.org/journalism/2024/05/07/americans-changing-relationship-with-local-news/ (noting that only 15 percent of people surveyed had paid or given money to any local news source in the past year); Penelope Muse Abernathy, *The State of Local News: The 2023 Report*, Northwestern Medill Local News Initiative (Nov. 16, 2023), https://localnewsinitiative.northwestern.edu/projects/state-of-local-news/2023/report/ (indicating that about 2,900 American newspapers have closed since 2005).

It amassed power through the wealth it reaped from advertising. For the most part, it has not demanded much of citizens. But that heyday has passed. If Americans want a functioning press (which is to say, if Americans want a functioning democracy), we have to learn to do the work of supporting it.

One way we can all contribute is with rhetoric. As philosopher and novelist Iris Murdoch wrote, "[L]anguage itself is a moral medium, almost all uses of language convey value."[64] Ensuring we have a free press has significant moral stakes; how we talk about the press needs to convey its value. If we can conjure the language that describes the press we need and want, we come closer to bringing that press into being.

[64] Iris Murdoch, Existentialists and Mystics: Writings on Philosophy and Literature 27 (1999).

10

Recursive Press Freedom as the Capacity to Control and Learn from Mistakes

Mike Ananny

When you invent the ship, you also invent the shipwreck; when you invent the plane, you also invent the plane crash; and when you invent electricity, you invent electrocution … Every technology carries its own negativity, which is invented at the same time as technical progress.

Paul Virilio, *Politics of the Very Worst* (1999)

As I write this in May 2024, there is, yet again, anxiety about the power that an emerging technology, namely generative artificial intelligence (or GenAI), has to shape journalism, news, and the viability of a robust, economically healthy, and free press. While earlier panics focused on the influence of the internet and digital data on journalistic practice,[1] social media's control of attention and advertising,[2] and the power of complex and proprietary algorithms to create "echo chambers" and "filter bubbles"[3] that undermine journalism's role in democracy, the contemporary moment features a potentially more existentially destabilizing force.

Depending on which technologist, activist, scholar, or pundit you read,[4] the prediction of how GenAI is likely to influence journalism varies. It may free journalists from mundane tasks and empower them to pursue more complex reporting, or it may further shrink an already atrophying labor force struggling for stable work. It may infuse internet search results with high-quality news that has previously been scraped or licensed from publishers, or it may sequester news into opaque datasets and probabilistic language models that deliver neither reliably true results nor traffic to news advertisers. GenAI's propensity to haphazardly extract, combine, and hallucinate data may even further erode online public spheres, or it

1 Pablo Boczkowski, *Technology, Monitoring, and Imitation in Contemporary News Work*, 2 Commc'n, Culture & Critique 39 (2009).

2 Robert H. Giles, *New Economic Models for U.S. Journalism*, 139 Daedalus 26 (2010).

3 E. Pariser, The Filter Bubble (2011).

4 Jessica Lessin, *News Organizations Rushing to Absolve AI Companies of Theft Are Acting Against Their Own Interests*, Atl. Monthly (May 24, 2024), https://www.theatlantic.com/technology/archive/2024/05/fatal-flaw-publishers-making-openai-deals/678477/; Jennifer Cobbe, *The Politics of Artificial Intelligence: Rhetoric vs Reality*, 15 Pol. Insight 20 (June 2024), https://journals.sagepub.com/doi/10.1177/20419058241260785.

may privilege publishers as producers of high-quality news created in the public interest over the generic "big data" that technology companies greedily need for general computational models and advertising markets.

In many ways, GenAI is not a new threat to skilled workers like journalists. In his 1978 study of how workers responded to automatically controlled machine tools, David Noble identified three ways that technological innovations challenge workforces,[5] all of which apply to journalists in this moment of GenAI. First, workforces must "transcend the ideology of technological determinism by demystifying the technology itself."[6] Journalists often critique and attempt to undercut the fantastical claims that some technologists – and some fellow journalists – make about GenAI's power to produce believable, useful, and democratically forceful language.[7] Second, the workforce must "regain its confidence by preparing itself" and articulating "its own choices in its own . . . interest."[8] Journalists might differentiate what they do – reporting, writing, and editing with sophistication and in the public interest – from what GenAI, which is inscrutable and incapable of sentience, professionalism, or reflection, does, namely mimicking the statistical patterns of datasets and models that produce media. Finally, workers must "struggle, on the shop floor and politically, to get into the position to make these choices and thereby steer the course of 'progress.'"[9] That is, journalists must not only debunk the fantastical claims of GenAI proponents and differentiate their work from GenAI's outputs but must also be able to act in their *own* interests and know what those interests mean in different technological contexts. They must be able to practice their craft in ways that reflect what *they* think their profession and public obligations demand. This capacity to act with knowledge and intent requires, as a preliminary condition, knowing well enough how a technology works to appreciate how it matters to professional practices. Only then can professionals appreciate what they should *do* with a

5 David F. Noble, Forces of Production: A Social History of Industrial Automation (1986); David F. Noble, *Social Choice in Machine Design: The Case of Automatically Controlled Machine Tools, and a Challenge for Labor*, 8 Pol. & Soc'y 313 (1978).

6 Noble, Forces of Production, *supra* note 5, at 314.

7 For studies of how media organizations cover GenAI, including its promises, errors, and moral panics, *see* Veronica Barassi et al., *From ChatGPT to Crime: How Journalists Are Shaping the Debate Around AI Errors*, European Journalism Observatory (Apr. 25, 2023), https://en.ejo.ch/specialist-journalism/from-chatgpt-to-crime-how-journalists-are-shaping-the-debate-around-ai-errors; Jem Bartholomew & Dhrumil Mehta, *How the Media Is Covering ChatGPT*, Colum. Journalism Rev. (May 26, 2023), https://www.cjr.org/tow_center/media-coverage-chatgpt.php; Saba Rebecca Brause et al., *Media Representations of Artificial Intelligence: Surveying the Field*, *in* Handbook of Critical Stud. of A.I. 277 (Simon Lindgren ed., 2023); J. Scott Brennen et al., *What to Expect When You're Expecting Robots: Futures, Expectations, and Pseudo-Artificial General Intelligence in UK News*, 23 Journalism 22 (2022), https://journals.sagepub.com/doi/full/10.1177/1464884920947535.

8 Noble, Forces of Production, *supra* note 5, at 314.

9 *Id.* at 314–15.

technology and make informed and intentional choices about resisting or reshaping it and/or their professional standards.

This capacity to act with knowledge and purpose is a kind of press freedom. An autonomous press knows its systems well enough to reshape them in its own professional image, or to refuse them, and also understands its public obligation. A press that is beholden to a technology's fantastical claims or moral panics, or that cannot separate its own vision from that of the technologists, will be unable to structure and change itself, a hallmark of any profession's autonomy. By "autonomy," then, I mean the profession's capacity to make its *own* decisions about its practices – for example, what to cover, how to write, who to interview, when to publish, or which ledes to foreground. An autonomous press can see its own actions, reflect on them, and change them when *it* chooses to.

To explore how well the press can change itself, I focus here on how the press responds to mistakes by examining moments when the press has investigated, corrected, suffered, or tolerated some failed or broken-down aspect of either its own journalistic work or the larger information environment it operates within. My contention is that a strong, autonomous, self-empowered, and self-corrective press has the capacity to report and publish on mistakes – its own and others' – and that GenAI poses a particular threat to this capacity because so many aspects of synthetic media and its use in journalistic work are currently unknown.

Taking seriously the idea that an autonomous press self-monitors and self-corrects, we might question whether the institution has recursive press freedom – a capacity to create *for itself* the structures that enable journalism and serve the public interest. A *recursively* free press would confidently trace and shape the social, cultural, political, and technological forces that structure journalism and create news without needing to rely on outsiders for knowledge, permission, or capacity. Such recursive freedom would be especially critical in the context of the *synthetic* press, which refers to the journalistic practices, forms, and institutional conditions that are intertwined with GenAI and often unknowable and unchangeable within proprietary datasets, machine learning models, and private corporations. Recursive, synthetic press freedom would be the press's *own* capacity to shape GenAI according to its own journalistic mission and its own sense of public service.

This chapter investigates what this recursive, synthetic press freedom could look like in three parts. First, it briefly frames the current GenAI challenge to press freedom in terms of long-standing scholarship on journalism's relationship to technological change. Second, it presents a case study to illustrate this issue, focusing on how the free press pursues and self-corrects its own mission and how it deals with "error" in a variety of ways. Third, the chapter uses instances of recent GenAI errors to demonstrate how this new technology hampers the press's ability to know and change itself, thus damaging its autonomy. And, finally, inspired by Noble's study of how workers might regain autonomy in the face of outside technological change, the chapter sketches a model of "recursive press freedom" that all defenders of journalistic autonomy might adopt to understand and reshape this GenAI moment.

I hope that different scholarly audiences will find this chapter useful in multiple ways. Journalism scholars, for example, are rapidly endeavoring to understand the relevance and usefulness of GenAI to news production and its impact on normative ideals of the press.[10] Examining instances when GenAI *has failed* gives us a way to think about what a *successful* press is presumed to do and what good or proper uses of GenAI in journalism might be. When scholars or practitioners foreground journalistic errors and call for remedies, they reveal their capacity to monitor, correct, and envision a better press. The press's power to self-correct – to define, prioritize, and fix its own errors – is a key aspect of press freedom, and one that is increasingly critical as many aspects of reporting, editing, and publishing become intertwined with technological infrastructures existing beyond the control of newsrooms.

This is an important moment to develop a precise understanding of how technologies influence journalism because there are ramifications for understanding the scope and meaning of press rights. As Frederick Schauer cautioned, failing to appreciate the "sociological messiness of institutional demarcation"[11] – for example, how blogging, investigative journalism, pornography, sports broadcasting, or recommendation algorithms all pose different speech challenges – may cause a First Amendment "institutional 'compression'"[12] that leaves everyone with fewer rights than they might have had if journalists, technologists, and courts alike had better understood the significance of drawing the press's boundaries and of defining "the press" narrowly as what journalists do or more broadly as what technologies, technologists, and online audiences also do. Focusing on journalism's disposition toward errors and mistakes is one way of achieving empirical precision and of understanding how different institutions and forces constituting the press collide. This is a challenge ideally suited for scholars of science and technology studies, critical internet studies, and platforms studies who have long traced how technological practices, actors, values, and politics intersect to create newsrooms,

[10] For example, *see* Sachita Nishal & Nicholas Diakopoulos, *Envisioning the Applications and Implications of Generative AI for News Media, in* Ass'n for Computing Mach., CHI '23 Workshop on Generative AI and HCI, April 23–28, 2023, Hamburg, Germany (2023), https://arxiv.org/pdf/2402.18835; Felix M. Simon, *Escape Me If You Can: How AI Reshapes News Organisations' Dependency on Platform Companies*, 12 Digit. Journalism 149 (2023), https://www.tandfonline.com/doi/full/10.1080/21670811.2023.2287464; Chenyan Jia et al., *Promises and Perils of Automated Journalism: Algorithms, Experimentation, and "Teachers of Machines" in China and the United States*, 25 Journalism Stud. 38 (2024), https://www.tandfonline.com/doi/full/10.1080/1461670X.2023.2289881; T. J. Thomson et al., *Generative Visual AI in News Organizations: Challenges, Opportunities, Perceptions, and Policies*, Digit. Journalism (Apr. 8, 2024), https://www.tandfonline.com/doi/citedby/10.1080/21670811.2024.2331769?scroll=top&needAccess=true.

[11] Frederick Schauer, *Towards an Institutional First Amendment*, 89 Minn. L. Rev. 1273 (2005).

[12] *Id.* at 1272.

professional journalism, audience cultures, and news economics.[13] A focus on journalistic errors and GenAI may reveal how different social and technological actors define mistakes, debate causes, classify harms, anticipate risks, assign responsibility, and apply remedies. If press freedom emerges not only from intersections between journalism and jurisprudence but also among messy collisions – of people, professions, norms, institutions, data, and computation – then analyzing *mistaken* meetings and *failed* alignments should illustrate what press freedom could be if the power and politics of digital media were otherwise.

10.1 PRESS FREEDOM AS AN INSTITUTIONAL, INFRASTRUCTURAL ACHIEVEMENT

To better understand what press freedom means in this era of GenAI, it is essential to first understand how the "the press" is always a product of an era's institutional and technological forces and how the concept of "press freedom" always depends on ideals relating to its public power and obligations.

Though it is beyond the scope of this chapter to review the large, long-standing, and interdisciplinary research tracing the various forces that have constituted "the press," it is worth highlighting how three dimensions of the press – news forms, journalistic practices, and institutional relationships – have emerged from the collisions of social and technological forces, with this providing an expansive and flexible view of the press that may help stave off the compression of rights that Schauer cautioned against.

First, *news forms* – text, image, sound, video, virtual reality, games, and participatory forums – have always been intertwined with advances in media representations and publishing technologies. Advances in printing, layout, and graphics transmission enabled newspapers to develop brand-specific visual designs, direct readers' attention, sustain audience engagement across a newspaper, and use high-quality imagery to signal both journalists' authority to report and the authenticity of their accounts.[14] Subsequent advances in synchronized audio and visual content, chyron overlays, animated graphics, and data visualizations allowed news organizations to create immersive, layered news experiences that could display and interweave different information streams simultaneously.[15] Developments in transportation infrastructure, satellite networks, and lightweight cellular technologies enabled "live news" to emerge as a unique genre. And the popularization of communication

[13] For example, *see* Pablo J. Boczkowski, Digitizing the News: Innovation in Online Newspapers (2004); Henrik Bødker, *Journalism as Cultures of Circulation*, 3 Digit. Journalism 101 (2014); Tarleton Gillespie, *The Politics of 'Platforms'*, 12 New Media & Soc. 347 (2010); Jose van Dijck et al., The Platform Society (2018); Candis Callison & Mary Lynn Young, Reckoning: Journalism's Limits and Possibilities (2020).

[14] Kevin G. Barnhurst & John Nerone, The Form of News: A History (2001).

[15] John Nerone, *Genres of Journalism History*, 13 Commc'n Rev. 15 (2010).

technologies amongst readers – encompassing everything from cheap and reliable postal service and home telephones to online bulletin boards and social media platforms – spurred the creation of letters to the editor, call-in shows, and comment threads that blurred the distinction between the journalistic voice and public participation.

Every new technological advancement has prompted the question of what it means for news stories to be authoritative, authentic, timely, persuasive, and professionally produced. Put differently, to the extent that press freedom depends upon and enables journalists' ability to create stories that are defensible as *forms* of information – for example, that are factual, free of mistakes, and not manipulative – that freedom is always inseparable from an era's communication technologies and media representations.

Second, *journalistic practices* – fact-finding, interviewing, witnessing, writing, editing, and publishing – have always reflected how an era's communication technologies influence epistemological standards, modes of working, and professional norms. Publishers in the colonial era invested in boat-building techniques to produce small ships that could quickly reach ships arriving from England with news, mail, and commodity prices, ensuring that their newspapers had the timeliest information and feeding early anxieties about being scooped by competitors.[16] Advances in literacy, printing, distribution, industrial advertising, and market segmentation all fed the emergence of journalistic objectivity, not as an ideal of impartiality and public service but as an economic practice that let publishers avoid offending any one set of readers and, most importantly, advertisers.[17]

As technology has continued to advance, so too have modern debates about these new journalistic practices. Computer-assisted reporting and data-focused journalism have allowed investigative reporters to portray themselves as disinterested scientists reliably and defensibly discovering patterns of injustice[18] consistent with the moral standards of their times.[19] And now that online publishers can track how well their stories are performing in search engine results, digital advertising markets, and on social media platforms, newsrooms must grapple with how to do journalism that is aware of, but not beholden to, internet traffic patterns.[20] Similarly, journalists are

16 Michael Schudson, Discovering the News: A Social History of American Newspapers (1978).

17 Dan Schiller, *An Historical Approach to Objectivity and Professionalism in American News Reporting*, 29 J. of Commc'n 46 (1979); Michael Schudson, *The Objectivity Norm in American Journalism*, 2 Journalism 149 (2001).

18 Mark Coddington, *Clarifying Journalism's Quantitative Turn*, 3 Digit. Journalism 331 (2014); C. W. Anderson, Apostles of Certainty: Data Journalism and the Politics of Doubt (2018).

19 James S. Ettema & Theodore L. Glasser, Custodians of Conscience (1998).

20 Caitlin Petre, All the News That's Fit to Click (2021); Angele Christin, Metrics at Work: How Web Journalists Make Sense of Their Algorithmic Publics in the United States and France (2020).

wrestling with whether social media platforms like X[21] are places to seek out stories, find sources, speculate, publish independently, develop personal followings, or some combination thereof.[22] Advances in drone technologies, meanwhile, have opened new events and regions for journalists to observe, but they have also invited skepticism about the value of such high-altitude witnessing versus grounded reporting.[23] Encrypted tools like Signal, PGP keys, and the Tor network allow journalists to connect securely with potential sources and whistleblowers, and while the process is still cumbersome,[24] increasing efficiencies in Freedom of Information Act (FOIA) requests give journalists more access to public information more quickly, enabling new forms of public oversight reporting.[25]

Fast boats, mail service, computer databases, search engine analytics, social media platforms, drones, and encryption are just a few of the myriad technological advancements that have influenced journalistic practice, and it would be a mistake to see them as separate from how journalists make judgments about newsworthiness, facticity, audience engagement, public service, or source ethics. If press freedom is, in part, a journalist's ability to decide the workflows, norms, and practices that they believe align with *their* professional judgment, then it is impossible to separate these decisions from the communication systems that suggest actions, encode standards, enable practices, and generally structure information work. Is it a mistake or an infringement of press freedom if a journalist subconsciously trusts a source with a PGP key, a Twitter user with a blue checkmark, or an organization highly ranked by a search engine? These seemingly trivial examples point to a messy and implicitly structured space of journalistic practice that is inseparable from communication technologies.

Finally, *institutional relationships* – the press's connections to governments, markets, industries, and audiences – have always influenced how the press has understood its mission and scoped its autonomy. Defining institutions as "social patterns of behavior identifiable across the organizations that are generally seen within a society to preside over a particular social sphere,"[26] Cook showed how "the

[21] Formerly known as Twitter.

[22] Shannon C. McGregor & Logan Molyneux, *Twitter's Influence on News Judgment: An Experiment Among Journalists,* 21 JOURNALISM 597 (2018); Shannon C. McGregor, *Social Media as Public Opinion: How Journalists Use Social Media to Represent Public Opinion*, 20 JOURNALISM 1070 (2019).

[23] CATE DOWD, DIGITAL JOURNALISM, DRONES, AND AUTOMATION: THE LANGUAGE AND ABSTRACTIONS BEHIND THE NEWS (2020).

[24] Margaret Kwoka, *Returning FOIA to the Press*, *in* THE FUTURE OF PRESS FREEDOM: DEMOCRACY, LAW, AND THE NEWS IN CHANGING TIMES 257 (RonNell Andersen Jones & Sonja R. West eds., 2025) [hereinafter THE FUTURE OF PRESS FREEDOM].

[25] Karin Assmann, *Whistleblowers and Their Faith in Journalism*, JOURNALISM PRAC. 1 (Dec. 26, 2022), https://www.tandfonline.com/doi/full/10.1080/17512786.2022.2161067; Vera Slavtcheva-Petkova et al., *Conceptualizing Journalists' Safety Around the Globe*, 11 DIGIT. JOURNALISM 1210 (2023).

[26] TIMOTHY E. COOK, GOVERNING WITH THE NEWS 70 (1998).

press" is actually a set of relationships among not only news organizations but also government officials, public relations professionals, civil society actors, political parties, and other communicators interested in structuring communicative self-governance. These relationships, according to Cook, need and sustain the institutional practices of mimicry, isomorphism, and labor division to *distribute* the work and power of the press across largely invisible backstage processes.[27] Instead of seeing the press as an autonomous institution living within news organizations, professional bodies, and public ideals, we might more correctly see it as a pattern of distributed, intertwined communication practices that seem coherent to the extent that they resemble what a given era socially, culturally, economically, and technologically expects "the press" to be. This coherence is stabilized when, for example:

- a government spokesperson frames events and gives quotes in ways that resonate with a journalist's expectations and a publisher's conception of its audience;[28]
- public relations representatives position press releases and product launches to fit not only with their clients' goals but also with journalists' understanding of industry novelty and technological innovation;[29]
- news organizations perennially realign their judgments of newsworthiness and public service with social media platforms' own assessments of audience engagement and advertiser value (as seen in publishers' "pivot to video" to meet Facebook's expectations and contemporary investment in short videos that perform well on TikTok and YouTube);[30]
- fact-checking organizations structure their rhythms and standards of verification to align with the goals of the social media platforms that spread disinformation, creating a symbiotic service arrangement in which fact-checkers are essentially platform partners;[31] and

[27] For more in-depth discussion of these institutional dynamics, *see* Jeannette A. Colyvas & Spiro Maroulis, *Moving from an Exception to a Rule: Analyzing Mechanisms in Emergence-Based Institutionalization*, 26 Org. Sci. 311 (2015); P. J. DiMaggio & W. W. Powell, *Introduction*, *in* The New Institutionalism in Organizational Analysis (W. W. Powell & P. J. DiMaggio eds., 1991); W. W. Powell, *Neither Market Nor Hierarchy: Network Forms of Organization*, 12 Rsch. in Organizational Behav. 295 (1990).

[28] Timothy E. Cook, Making Laws and Making News (1989).

[29] Melissa Aronczyk & Maria I. Espinoza, A Strategic Nature: Public Relations and the Politics of American Environmentalism (2022).

[30] Nic Newman, *How Publishers Are Learning to Create and Distribute News on TikTok*, Reuters Inst. (Dec. 8, 2022), https://reutersinstitute.politics.ox.ac.uk/how-publishers-are-learning-create-and-distribute-news-tiktok.

[31] Mike Ananny, *The Partnership Press: Lessons for Platform-Publisher Collaborations as Facebook and News Outlets Team to Fight Misinformation*, Colum. Journalism Rev. (Apr. 4, 2018), https://www.cjr.org/tow_center_reports/partnership-press-facebook-news-outlets-team-fight-misinformation.php/.

- publishers like the Associated Press and NewsCorp license their content to OpenAI, ensuring that future ChatGPT results will somehow include or account for the journalism produced by those companies.[32]

These examples of the institutional perspective on press freedom may seem like reasonable arrangements that simply ensure journalism's survival and relevance in rapidly changing media systems. Without such alignments, patterns, and partnerships, the press might simply disappear. But they also suggest that a common-sense understanding of "the press" as comprising what journalists do and what publishers distribute is simply incorrect. The press is actually a set of largely invisible, strategic relationships with their own logics of alignment, their own standards of quality, and their own senses of what it means to tell factual stories in the public interest.

This image of "the press" as a powerful and messy interplay of social and technological arrangements has gained traction in recent years. Early digital newsrooms were shaped by mixes of journalistic and technological mindsets and practices.[33] Digital algorithms quickly influenced reporting and publishing practices.[34] As social media rose in prominence, a hybrid media system of seemingly disparate communicators emerged, which journalists both participated in and reported on.[35] Histories of the press show how its last fifty years have been inseparable from the datasets and computational epistemologies that journalists use to know their world.[36]

My own work has examined how the press's digital infrastructures enable the public to hear the perspectives of others and receive information that they would likely not seek out for themselves,[37] and Kate Crawford and I have suggested that the press is a "liminal" achievement somewhere between journalistic judgment and technological design.[38] Emily Bell and Taylor Owen have identified a "platform press" that has emerged from publishers' seemingly endless responses to new technologies and policies.[39] Matt Carlson and Seth Lewis have traced the

[32] Pete Brown, *Licensing Deals, Litigation Raise Raft of Familiar Questions in Fraught World of Platforms and Publishers*, Colum. Journalism Rev. (May 22, 2024), https://www.cjr.org/tow_center/licensing-deals-litigation-raise-raft-of-familiar-questions-in-fraught-world-of-platforms-and-publishers.php; Lessin, *supra* note 4.

[33] Boczkowski, *supra* note 13.

[34] C. W. Anderson, *Towards a Sociology of Computational and Algorithmic Journalism*, 15 New Media & Soc. 1005 (2013); C. W. Anderson, Rebuilding the News: Metropolitan Journalism in the Digital Age (2013).

[35] Andrew Chadwick, The Hybrid Media System: Politics and Power (2nd ed. 2017).

[36] Sylvain Parasie, Computing the News (2022).

[37] Mike Ananny, Networked Press Freedom: Creating Infrastructures for a Public Right to Hear (2018).

[38] Mike Ananny & Kate Crawford, *A Liminal Press: Situating News App Designers Within a Field of Networked News Production*, 3 Digit. Journalism 1 (2015).

[39] Emily Bell & Taylor Owen, *The Platform Press: How Silicon Valley Reengineered Journalism*, Colum. Journalism Rev. (Mar. 29, 2017), https://www.cjr.org/tow_center_reports/platform-press-how-silicon-valley-reengineered-journalism.php.

contemporary press through the complex boundary work of diverse laborers,[40] which Adrienne Russell has shown also includes digitally savvy activists, environmentalists, and solution-oriented journalists.[41] Stephen Reese has demonstrated how the crisis of the institutional press is a problem not only of journalism and publishing but also of information economics and political culture.[42] Newer work centered on artificial intelligence is revisiting these questions, with a focus on how computation, technologists, datasets, and experimental methods are currently structuring the press, its language, and its own understanding of its public service role.[43]

It is impossible in this chapter to fully capture the extent of this literature, but there is ample scholarship indicating that "the press" is and always has been a messy and historically situated mix of colliding social and technological forces. The idea, then, that "press freedom" is only, or even mostly, a matter of journalism and jurisprudence is incorrect. It is more accurately understood as an ongoing achievement of multiple, intertwined actors, existing in historical-technological moments, which create separations and dependencies that are continually judged against normative ideals of what journalistic autonomy is supposed to be and what journalism's public mission should be in any era.[44]

If these conceptions of the press and its freedom form a plausible framework, then the challenge becomes not only how to empirically observe these collisions of forces – these separations and dependencies – but also how to judge whether they move us closer to or further from any particular ideal of press freedom.

I want to bracket the discussion of *which* version of "press freedom" is worth pursuing amidst this mix of forces – much excellent scholarship has analyzed the term and the significance of various definitions[45] – and instead argue for a *way* of

[40] Matt Carlson, *The Many Boundaries of Journalism*, *in* BOUNDARIES OF JOURNALISM: PROFESSIONALISM, PRACTICES AND PARTICIPATION (Matt Carlson & Seth C. Lewis eds., 2015).

[41] ADRIENNE RUSSELL, NETWORKED: A CONTEMPORARY HISTORY OF NEWS IN TRANSITION (2011); ADRIENNE RUSSELL, THE MEDIATED CLIMATE: HOW JOURNALISTS, BIG TECH, AND ACTIVISTS ARE VYING FOR OUR FUTURE (2023).

[42] STEPHEN D. REESE, THE CRISIS OF THE INSTITUTIONAL PRESS (2021).

[43] Simon, *supra* note 10; Felix M. Simon, *Uneasy Bedfellows: AI in the News, Platform Companies and the Issue of Journalistic Autonomy*, 10 DIGIT. JOURNALISM 1832 (2022); MEREDITH BROUSSARD, MORE THAN A GLITCH: CONFRONTING RACE, GENDER, AND ABILITY BIAS IN TECH (2023); Mike Ananny & Jake Karr, *Press Freedom Means Controlling the Language of AI*, NIEMANLAB (Sept. 27, 2023), https://www.niemanlab.org/2023/09/press-freedom-means-controlling-the-language-of-ai/.

[44] I develop this idea further in ANANNY, *supra* note 37.

[45] For example, *see* Jack M. Balkin, *Free Speech Is a Triangle*, 118 COLUM. L. REV. 2011 (2018); Randall P. Bezanson, *Whither Freedom of the Press?*, 97 IOWA L. REV. 1259 (2012); LEE C. BOLLINGER, IMAGES OF A FREE PRESS (1991); LEE C. BOLLINGER, UNINHIBITED, ROBUST AND WIDE-OPEN: A FREE PRESS FOR A NEW CENTURY (2010); Erin C. Carroll, *A Free Press Without Democracy*, 56 U.C. DAVIS L. REV. 289 (2022); Theodore L. Glasser & Mark Gunther, *The Legacy of Autonomy in American Journalism*, *in* THE INSTITUTIONS OF AMERICAN DEMOCRACY: THE PRESS (Geneva Overholser & Kathleen Hall Jamieson eds., 2005); RonNell Andersen Jones & Sonja R. West, *The Fragility of the Free American Press*, 112 NW. U. L. REV. 567 (2017); RonNell Andersen Jones & Sonja R. West, *The Disappearing Freedom of*

seeing press freedom, namely, as the press's capacity to self-monitor and self-correct and to *learn* from its mistakes. Taking inspiration from Samuelson's call for a "freedom to tinker,"[46] scholarship on how "broken world thinking" offers new ways to see system maintenance and repair,[47] studies of institutional learning,[48] and organizational technologies,[49] I wish to suggest that a largely ignored aspect of press freedom is the press's ability to learn from mistakes. While some works have encouraged journalists to experiment with GenAI, learn how it can be useful for news work, and avoid making mistakes while using it,[50] I want to invoke a larger, more generative sense of experimentation to ask how the press might learn about itself by critically engaging with how GenAI mistakes happen, why they matter, and what they might mean for press freedom in our contemporary era of synthetic media. If an autonomous press can self-monitor and self-correct – knowing its own forces and reshaping them when they fail – then the autonomy of the *synthetic* press (the journalistic practices, forms, and institutional conditions intertwined with GenAI) depends upon how well it knows, learns from, and changes in response to its mistaken engagements with GenAI.

The remainder of the chapter argues that the press has always defined itself through relationships with "mistakes" (broadly construed), that the contemporary

the Press, 79 WASH. & LEE L. REV. 1377 (2022); Michael Schudson, *Autonomy From What?*, *in* BOURDIEU AND THE JOURNALISTIC FIELD (R. Benson & E. Neveu eds., 2005); Eugene Volokh, *Freedom for the Press as an Industry, or for the Press as a Technology? From the Framing to Today*, 160 U. PA. L. REV. 459 (2012).

46 Pamela Samuelson, *Freedom to Tinker*, 17 THEORETICAL INQUIRIES IN LAW 562 (2016).

47 Steven J. Jackson, *Rethinking Repair*, *in* MEDIA TECHNOLOGIES: ESSAYS ON COMMUNICATION, MATERIALITY, AND SOCIETY (Tarleton Gillespie et al. eds., 2013).

48 John Seely Brown & Paul Duguid, *Organizational Learning and Communities-of-Practice: Toward a Unified View of Work, Learning, and Innovation*, 2 ORGANIZATIONAL SCI. 40 (1991); JEAN LAVE & ETIENNE WENGER, SITUATED LEARNING: LEGITIMATE PERIPHERAL PARTICIPATION (1991); Roy D. Pea, *The Social and Technological Dimensions of Scaffolding and Related Theoretical Concepts for Learning, Education, and Human Activity*, 13 J. OF LEARNING SCIENCES 423 (2004); ETIENNE WENGER, COMMUNITIES OF PRACTICE: LEARNING, MEANING, AND IDENTITY (1998); Pamela Haunschild & David Chandler, *Institutional-Level Learning: Learning as a Source of Institutional Change*, *in* THE SAGE HANDBOOK OF ORGANIZATIONAL INSTITUTIONALISM (Royston Greenwood et al. eds., 2008).

49 P. Dourish & M. Mazmanian, *Media as Material: Information Representations as Material Foundations for Organizational Practice*, *in* HOW MATTER MATTERS: OBJECTS, ARTIFACTS, AND MATERIALITY IN ORGANIZATION STUDIES (Paul R. Carlile et al. eds., 2013); P. M. Leonardi, *When Flexible Routines Meet Flexible Technologies: Affordance, Constraint, and the Imbrication of Human and Material Agencies*, 35 MIS Q. 147 (2011); Wanda Orlikowski, *Technology and Organization: Contingency All the Way Down*, 29 RSCH. IN SOCIO. OF ORGANIZATIONS 239 (2010).

50 Nishal & Diakopoulos, *supra* note 10; Savvas Petridis et al., *Angle Kindling: Supporting Journalistic Angle Ideation with Large Language Models*, in ASS'N FOR COMPUTING MACH., CHI '23: PROCEEDINGS OF THE 2023 CHI CONFERENCE ON HUMAN FACTORS IN COMPUTING SYSTEMS (April 19, 2023), https://dl.acm.org/doi/10.1145/3544548.3580907; Mark Deuze & Charlie Beckett, *Imagination, Algorithms and News: Developing AI Literacy for Journalism*, 10 DIGIT. JOURNALISM 1913 (2022).

synthetic press is struggling to understand itself through GenAI failure, and that a press that can learn from its mistakes has a kind of "recursive press freedom" that will be essential for defining its own normative vision amidst continued technological turmoil.

10.2 THE PRESS AND MISTAKES: ITS OWN AND OTHERS'

In many ways, the press feeds on mistakes. Mistakes can be targets for correction, triggers for outrage, focuses of investigations, opportunities to teach audiences how knowledge develops, chances to develop and defend the profession, indicators of mistaken institutional relationships, and even matters to strategically ignore. While a complete review of how the press deals with mistakes, errors, and failures is beyond the scope of this chapter,[51] as context for understanding GenAI journalism mistakes, I offer five ways to understand the press's relationship to error: as (1) misinformation to correct, (2) transgressions spurring outrage, (3) professional malpractice and self-regulation, (4) misconfigured publishing systems, and (5) tolerated ambiguities.

(A note on terminology: I use the word "mistake" somewhat loosely and interchangeably with "error" or "failure" or "breakdown." This is not because I see these terms as synonymous – indeed, an extensive body of interdisciplinary literature differentiates these words more precisely[52] – but because I mean for this chapter

[51] For good recent general overviews of journalism and errors, *see* Joseph W. Campbell, Getting It Wrong: Debunking the Greatest Myths in American Journalism (2nd ed. 2016); Craig Silverman, Regret the Error: How Media Mistakes Pollute the Press and Imperil Free Speech (2007); Dominic L. Lasorsa & Jia Dai, *Newsroom's Normal Accident?*, 1 Journalism Prac. 159 (2007); Scott R. Maier, *Setting the Record Straight*, 1 Journalism Prac. 33 (2007); Tamar Wilner et al., *The Tragedy of Errors: Political Ideology, Perceived Journalistic Quality, and Media Trust*, 16 Journalism Prac. 1 (2021); Jakob Henke et al., *Forgiving the News: The Effects of Error Corrections on News Users' Reactions and the Influence of Individual Characteristics and Perceptions*, 23 Journalism Stud. 840 (2022); Erica Salkin & Kevin Grieves, *The "Major Mea Culpa": Journalistic Discursive Techniques When Professional Norms Are Broken*, 23 Journalism Stud. 1096 (2022); D. L. Eason, *On Journalistic Authority: The Janet Cooke Scandal*, 3 Critical Stud. in Mass Commc'n 429 (1986).

[52] Works distinguishing terms like "accident," "glitch," "mistake," "failure," "error," and "breakdown" include the following: Arjun Appadurai & Neta Alexander, Failure (2019); Campbell, *supra* note 51; Dietrich Dorner, The Logic of Failure: Recognizing and Avoiding Error in Complex Situations (1989); John Downer, Rational Accidents: Reckoning with Catastrophic Technologies (2024); Jack Halberstam, The Queer Art of Failure (2011); Charles Perrow, Normal Accidents: Living with High Risk Technologies (1984); Jessie Singer, There Are No Accidents (2022); Diane Vaughan, The Challenger Launch Decision: Risky Technology, Culture, and Deviance at NASA (1996); Sasanka Sekhar Chanda & Debarag Narayan Banerjee, *Omission and Commission Errors Underlying AI Failures*, 39 A.I. & Soc.937 (2022); Paolo Magaudda & Gabriele Balbi, *Theorizing Failure in Digital Media. Four Eclectic Theses*, Annals of Int'l Commc'n Ass'n 1 (2024), https://www.tandfonline.com/doi/full/10.1080/23808985.2024.2326056; Lauren E. Bridges, *Digital Failure: Unbecoming the "Good" Data Subject Through*

to broadly assert that the press's freedom requires a capacity to self-correct and to structure and change itself in relation to things that it sees as somehow wrong, failing, broken, or misaligned with its vision of ideal professional journalism or healthy, democratic, communicative self-governance.)

10.2.1 *Mistakes as Misinformation to Correct*

Part of what professional journalism does is create a framework of facts for understanding and governing social life, and it also fights mis- and disinformation that harms this framework. As Tucher argued in her history of "fake news" in American journalism, one of the profession's early motivations was to ferret out and correct misinformation.[53] Sometimes those errors came from "actors who [were] distorting, manipulating, misunderstanding, or faking the prevailing journalistic conventions in order to present 'truths' of their own for motives or reasons of their own"[54] and sometimes they result from a "clash *within* journalism between practitioners of the real seeking to defend their profession and perpetrators of the fake working to exploit it."[55] That is, sometimes fakery, errors, falsity, and failures come from outside journalism, and sometimes they exist as struggles among journalists with different visions of their roles. Most recently, this friction has played out in fact-checking communities populated with information producers, professional journalists, information activists, and platform content moderators. These actors attempt to define, find, correct, and prevent the circulation of information – some of it resembling

Entropic, Fugitive, and Queer Data, 8 BIG DATA & SOC. (2021), https://doi.org/10.1177/20539517209778882; Jill Walker Rettberg, *Algorithmic Failure as a Humanities Methodology: Machine Learning's Mispredictions Identify Rich Cases for Qualitative Analysis*, 9 BIG DATA & SOC. (2022), https://doi.org/10.1177/20539517221131290; Madeleine Clare Elish, *Moral Crumple Zones: Cautionary Tales in Human-Robot Interaction*, 5 ENGAGING SCI., TECH., & SOC. 40 (2019); Nassim Parvin & Anne Pollock, *Unintended by Design: On the Political Uses of "Unintended Consequences,"* 6 ENGAGING SCI., TECH., & SOC. 320 (2020); Kenneth Haynes, *Error*, *in* INFORMATION: A HISTORICAL COMPANION (Ann Blair et al. eds., 2021); S. Mo Jones-Jang & Yong Jin Park, *How Do People React to AI Failure? Automation Bias, Algorithmic Aversion, and Perceived Controllability*, 28 J. OF COMPUT.-MEDIATED COMMC'N 1 (2022); Mike Ananny, *Making Mistakes: Constructing Algorithmic Errors to Understand Sociotechnical Power*, 38 OSIRIS 223 (2023); Cindy Kaiying Lin & Steven J. Jackson, *From Bias to Repair: Error as a Site of Collaboration and Negotiation in Applied Data Science Work*, 7 PROC. ACM HUM.-COMPUT. INTERACT. 1 (2023); Rebecca Schneider, *Glitch*, *in* UNCERTAIN ARCHIVES: CRITICAL KEYWORDS FOR BIG DATA (Nanna Bonde Thylstrup et al. eds., 2021); Nanna Bonde Thylstrup, *Error*, *in* UNCERTAIN ARCHIVES: CRITICAL KEYWORDS FOR BIG DATA (Nanna Bonde Thylstrup et al. eds., 2021); Peter Galison, *Author of Error*, 72 SOC. RSCH. 63 (2005); Lorraine Daston, *Scientific Error and the Ethos of Belief*, 72 SOC. RSCH. 1 (2005); Neil J. Smelser, *The Questionable Logic of "Mistakes" in the Dynamics of Knowledge Growth in the Social Sciences*, 72 SOC. RSCH. 237 (2005).

[53] ANDIE TUCHER, NOT EXACTLY LYING: FAKE NEWS AND FAKE JOURNALISM IN AMERICAN HISTORY (2022).

[54] *Id.* at 2.

[55] *Id.* at 6.

news – seen as harmful to healthy democratic communication. As Graves chronicled,[56] the field of contemporary fact-checking works by identifying the forces that produce mistaken or erroneous information (within and outside of news organizations), intervening to correct particularly harmful or exemplary misinformation, and trying to structurally change media systems in ways that might curb the future production, circulation, and power of misinformation. Intentionally produced or not, misinformation is evidence of a broken media system that journalists must try to correct and fix.

10.2.2 *Mistakes as Transgressions Spurring Outrage*

Mistakes also play a role in shaping the press as a key institution of public investigation, monitoring, and oversight. This model of the press conceives of its role as going beyond simply providing information and uncovering facts; rather, the press does so selectively and with a keen sense that it is meant to be a bulwark against social injustice and transgressions by those in power. In some cases, investigative reporters, who see themselves as "custodians of conscience,"[57] uncover these transgressions by researching and building stories that reveal how a powerful figure or system has failed so egregiously that it defies common sense, with audiences expected to share the journalist's outrage.[58] In other instances, whistleblowers, leakers, and self-appointed watchdog sources bring transgressions to the attention of journalists, teaching reporters how to understand their worlds and recognize when a powerful industry, technology, or organization has grievously failed and why that failure is publicly significant. While the motivations and interests of whistleblowers and journalists alike are complex and often go unstated, many of the most notable examples of transgression-driven reporting – such as coverage of governmental failures, state surveillance, and tech industry corruption[59] – emerge from sources and journalists coming together around a shared sense that something has gone wrong and that investigative journalism may have a role to play

[56] Lucas Graves, Deciding What's True: The Rise of Political Fact-Checking in American Journalism (2016); Lucas Graves & C. W. Anderson, *Discipline and Promote: Building Infrastructure and Managing Algorithms in a 'Structured Journalism' Project by Professional Fact-Checking Groups*, 22 New Media & Soc. 342 (2020); Lucas Graves & Laurens Lauer, *From Movement to Institution: The "Global Fact" Summit as a Field-Configuring Event*, 14 Sociologica 157 (2020).

[57] Ettema & Glasser, *supra* note 19.

[58] Richard Stupart, *Anger and the Investigative Journalist*, 24 Journalism 2341 (2023).

[59] For discussions of whistleblowing from sources and the journalists they worked with, *see* Jeff Horwitz, Broken Code: Inside Facebook and the Fight to Expose Its Harmful Secrets (2023); Frances Haugen, The Power of One: How I Found the Strength to Tell the Truth and Why I Blew the Whistle on Facebook (2023); Glen Greenwald, No Place to Hide (2014); Miles Taylor, Blowback: A Warning to Save Democracy from the Next Trump (2023).

in fixing it.[60] The press's ability to decide which transgressions *it* thinks are worthy of investigation and publication is part of its freedom[61] – it has *autonomy from* whistleblowers' outrages and *autonomy to* choose mistakes, failures, and breakdowns that it sees as mattering to the public.

10.2.3 *Mistakes as Malpractice and Self-regulation*

Journalists care not only about mistakes that appear as misinformation, drive investigative reporting, or motivate sources' outrage. They are also concerned with errors that they themselves make in the course of their work. Sometimes these mistakes become infamous cases of misconduct. Notable examples include the instances of professional malpractice by Janet Cooke, Stephen Glass, Jayson Blair, Jack Kelley, Judith Miller, and Dan Rather, which all demonstrated how reporting judgment is often precarious, idiosyncratic, and susceptible to both individual deviation and organizational weaknesses.[62] Drawing on engineers' acceptance that their complex systems will fail with a regularity that enables risks to be anticipated and expected – what Perrow calls "normal accidents"[63] – media scholars[64] suggest that journalistic practices and newsroom cultures are *designed* to make mistakes. Newsroom leaders often inadvertently and systematically foster an environment conducive to errors by fostering weak internal communication, tolerating poor reporting habits, trusting journalists with bad track records, enabling substandard fact-checking, resisting regular performance reviews, failing to scrutinize source expertise, and "isolat[ing]

60 Assmann, *supra* note 25; Justin Hendrix, *Facebook Whistleblower Frances Haugen and WSJ Reporter Jeff Horwitz Reflect One Year On*, Tech Pol'y (Dec. 2, 2022), https://techpolicy.press/facebook-whistleblower-frances-haugen-and-wsj-reporter-jeff-horwitz-reflect-one-year-on/; K. Wahl-Jorgensen & J. Hunt, *Journalism, Accountability and the Possibilities for Structural Critique: A Case Study of Coverage of Whistleblowing*, 13 Journalism 399 (2012); Hannah Bloch-Wehba, *The Promise and Perils of Tech Whistleblowing*, 118 Nw. U. L. Rev. 1503 (2024); Thomas Olesen, *Whistleblowing and the Press: Complicating the Standard Account*, 24 Journalism 2418 (2023); Thomas Olesen, *The Politics of Whistleblowing in Digitalized Societies*, 47 Pol. & Soc. 277 (2019).

61 For a provocative argument that democratic autonomy, not just press freedom, relies upon negotiations between journalists and whistleblowers and media depictions of whistleblowers' own judgments of democratic transgression, *see* Thomas Olesen, *Democracy's Autonomy Dilemma: Whistleblowing and the Politics of Disclosure*, 39 Socio. Theory 245 (2021); Thomas Olesen, *The Democratic Drama of Whistleblowing*, 21 European J. of Soc. Theory 508 (2018).

62 For an excellent discussion of how journalists remember and invoke these instances of malpractice, *see* Matt Carlson, *Gone, but Not Forgotten: Memories of Journalistic Deviance as Metajournalistic Discourse*, 15 Journalism Stud. 33 (2013). And for an analysis of how different news beats make sense of ethical transgressions, *see* Mark Blach-Ørsten et al., *Ethics on the Beat: An Analysis of Ethical Breaches Across News Beats from 1999 to 2019*, 15 Journalism Prac. 3083 (2021).

63 Perrow, *supra* note 52.

64 Lasorsa & Dai, *supra* note 51; Paige L. Sweet & Danielle Giffort, *The Bad Expert*, 51 Soc. Stud. of Sci. 313 (2021).

deviance as individual misconduct in order to stave off systematic criticism."[65] By trusting journalists with too much independence and failing to implement strong management practices, newsrooms harm the public's freedom not to be deceived or misinformed.

Journalists sometimes call out their own mistakes explicitly, with many news organizations having explicit policies about when and why it issues corrections, clarifications, and, in rare cases, retractions. A long line of research, however, indicates that these policies are applied unevenly, with only a small fraction of errors ever receiving official corrections.[66] Many publications are rife with mistakes concerning objectively verifiable facts and offer interpretations that experts agree are mistaken. Most errors are never fixed and, if they are, it is often because a reporter has some personal connection to the topic or source. Fixes often fail to repair the original misunderstanding and echo through subsequent stories years after publication. Publications that fail to self-monitor and self-correct stories miss the opportunity to build trust with readers through apologies, to teach them about the challenges of journalism, and to educate readers on the positive aspects of learning from mistakes and building knowledge by grappling with error.[67] Indeed, when news organizations *do* acknowledge their mistakes, they often strategically contain them, their causes, and their harms. They explain away mistakes as rare and unavoidable missteps that are of little significance to journalism's entrenched habits and structures, or they address them with vague promises to do better and study internal processes.[68] Finally, newer work confirms that online publishers *are* constantly updating their stories, but the reasons for these updates are unclear. Sometimes events change and new reporting emerges, but sometimes earlier errors are corrected without comment or explanation. It may be that there is a subtle, error-correcting process at work among digital publishers, but the patterns and motivations of such practices are unclear.[69]

65 Carlson, *supra* note 62, at 4.

66 Scott R. Maier, *Accuracy Matters: A Cross-Market Assessment of Newspaper Error and Credibility*, 82 JOURNALISM & MASS COMMC'N Q. 533 (2005); Maier, *supra* note 51.

67 Marlis Stubenvoll & Jörg Matthes, *Why Retractions of Numerical Misinformation Fail: The Anchoring Effect of Inaccurate Numbers in the News*, 99 JOURNALISM & MASS COMMC'N Q. 368 (2022); Fred C. Berry, *A Study of Accuracy in Local News Stories of Three Dailies*, 44 JOURNALISM Q. 482 (1967); William B. Blankenburg, *News Accuracy: Some Findings on the Meaning of Errors*, 20 JOURNAL OF COMMC'N 375 (1970); Henke et al., *supra* note 51; Maier, *supra* note 66; Steve M. Barkin & Mark R. Levy, *All the News That's Fit to Correct: Corrections in the Times and the Post*, 60 JOURNALISM Q. 218 (1983); Yotam Ophir & Kathleen Hall Jamieson, *The Effects of Media Narratives About Failures and Discoveries in Science on Beliefs About and Support for Science*, 30 PUB. UNDERSTANDING OF SCI. 1008 (2021).

68 Salkin & Grieves, *supra* note 51; Lance W. Bennett et al., *Repairing the News: A Case Study of the News Paradigm*, 35 J. OF COMMC'N 50 (2006); Gabriel Snyder, *The Times Corrects Factual Errors. What About Bigger Controversies?*, COLUM. JOURNALISM REV. (June 22, 2020), https://www.cjr.org/public_editor/nyt-correction-factual-errors-editors-note.php.

69 For example, *see* Alexander Spangher et al., *NewsEdits: A News Article Revision Dataset and a Novel Document-Level Reasoning Challenge*, *in* PROCEEDINGS OF THE 2022 CONFERENCE OF

Across these scenes of journalistic mistakes – infamous malpractice, newsroom mismanagement, and rituals of correction – press freedom is about journalists strategically narrating, containing, and addressing their mistakes in ways that preserve their power to decide when and how news stories change. These choices leave largely intact the idea that published news is factual and that errors are rare and benign.

10.2.4 *Mistakes as Misconfigured Publishing Systems*

Another class of journalistic mistake involves publishers' relationships to technology company products and services. Though the details point to a variety of forces at work, examples abound of moments when platforms interfered with or mismanaged news stories that publishers intended to share through social media.

For example, Facebook removed from its platform a story that The Vindicator (a small Texas newspaper) had published as part of its reprinting of the U.S. Declaration of Independence because the story included the Declaration's phrase "merciless Indian Savages," which Facebook judged to violate its prohibition against hate speech.[70] Facebook similarly clashed with a publisher's editorial judgment when it attempted to censor a post by Aftenposten (Norway's largest newspaper) that included Nick Ut's Pulitzer-Prize-winning photo "Napalm Girl" because the platform's policies prohibit nudity.[71] Facebook reversed both decisions. In another instance, the company had to backtrack and apologize after it added to a DailyMail.com post "an AI-generated label of 'primates' to a news video ... that featured black men" being harassed by a white man.[72] Facebook also had to apologize after deleting from its site all stories by the Kansas Reflector; here, the company had labeled a Reflector series critiquing the climate policies of Facebook's

THE NORTH AMERICAN CHAPTER OF THE ASSOCIATION FOR COMPUTATIONAL LINGUISTICS: HUMAN LANGUAGE TECHNOLOGIES (Marine Carpuat et al. eds., 2022), https://aclanthology.org/2022.naacl-main.10.pdf. For a computational study of patterns in online news edits, and for a project trying to show readers how often news stories are changing without explanation, *see* John Fass & Angus Main, *Revealing the News: How Online News Changes Without You Noticing*, 2 DIGIT. JOURNALISM 366 (2014).

70 Eli Rosenberg, *Facebook Censored a Post for 'Hate Speech.' It Was the Declaration of Independence*, WASH. POST (July 5, 2018), https://www.washingtonpost.com/news/the-intersect/wp/2018/07/05/facebook-censored-a-post-for-hate-speech-it-was-the-declaration-of-independence/.

71 Sam Levin et al., *Facebook Backs Down from 'Napalm Girl' Censorship and Reinstates Photo*, THE GUARDIAN (Sept. 9, 2016), https://www.theguardian.com/technology/2016/sep/09/facebook-reinstates-napalm-girl-photo.

72 Keith Griffith, *DailyMail.com Wins Apology from Facebook for Ai Fail That Labelled Website's News Video of Black Men Being Harassed and Arrested as 'Primates'*, DAILY MAIL (Sept. 4, 2021), https://www.dailymail.co.uk/news/article-9957831/DailyMail-com-wins-apology-Facebook.html.

parent company Meta as a "cybersecurity threat."[73] The chain of events leading to this censorship was similar to the platform's deletion of stories by The Winchester Star mentioning sexual assault, which Facebook flagged as violating its community standards.[74] Scientists criticized the platform for labeling a scientific article by the British Medical Journal as "partly false" and "needing context," after one of Facebook's fact-checking partners wrongly concluded that the peer-reviewed scientific publication "could mislead people."[75]

These mistakes all occurred in slightly different contexts. Some involved platforms failing to understand the editorial context and journalistic value of words and images, others involved the algorithmic additions of metadata that overrode journalistic framings, and still others involved human judgments by platforms that failed to acknowledge and defer to subject-matter experts. All these errors indicate how publishing systems – content moderation guidelines, algorithmic labeling, fact-checking partnerships – can interfere not only with journalists' freedom to publish on their individual websites (channels they control) but also with their practical freedom to reach the large, algorithmically curated, and economically lucrative audiences that convene on social media platforms. It is noteworthy that three of the victims of these errors – the Vindicator, the Reflector, and the Star – were small publications with limited readerships and limited organizational capacity to anticipate or contest such errors, suggesting that the harms of platform mistakes may be unevenly distributed among publishers and have the most impact on small news organizations.

10.2.5 *Mistakes as Tolerated Ambiguities*

Finally, though far less common than some of the more observable examples of journalistic mistakes, communication and journalism scholars identify a more subtle type of error that complicates the assumption that journalists are committed to creating a clear factual record for the public. Three examples illustrate how the press creates and tolerates subtle and ambiguous forms of language that strict definitions of writing might call mistaken but that preserve journalism's power to create the stories that *it* thinks should be told – a kind of press freedom.

The first example falls under the umbrella of what Basil Bernstein referred to as "elaborated codes," or language that is shared and readily understood by a particular

[73] Allison Morrow, *Meta Is Accused of Censoring a Non-Profit Newspaper and an Independent Journalist Who Criticized the Company*, CNN (Apr. 5, 2024), https://www.cnn.com/2024/04/05/tech/meta-nonprofit-newspaper-independent-journalist-alleged-censorship/index.html.

[74] Louise Matsakis, *What Happens When Facebook Mistakenly Blocks Local News Stories*, WIRED (Aug. 30, 2018), https://www.wired.com/story/what-happens-when-facebook-mistakenly-blocks-local-news-stories/.

[75] Rebecca Coombes & Madlen Davies, *Facebook Versus the BMJ: When Fact Checking Goes Wrong*, 376 BMJ 095 (2022), https://www.bmj.com/content/376/bmj.095.

demographic group, social class, or community of interpretation.[76] While outsiders may find such language confusing or simply fail to appreciate its depth, insiders "get" it and signal their identity and social position by correctly reading the language's subtleties. News language is rife with such language. For example, throughout the AIDS epidemic, The New York Times and many other newspapers used the phrase "longtime companion" to euphemistically refer to a deceased person's gay partner, lover, or boyfriend. This phrase suggested a relationship that some readers would fail to notice but that others would understand and identify with. Journalists could thus steganographically signal a meaning of "longtime companion" that might have challenged the era's mores, tolerating stories with indirect language when strict adherence to principles of clear news writing would have required clarity. Though such language is not really "mistaken," it suggests that publishers sometimes take license to strategically use ambiguity and opacity if doing so serves their aims.

The second example of tolerated ambiguity is irony. Journalists can use ironic language to "direct readers, viewers, or listeners to a preferred or intended understanding"[77] of a story that may literally contradict a writer's words and that may subtly and winkingly invite the audience to share the journalist's *own* interpretation in a manner that would otherwise fail traditional tests of journalistic objectivity. For example, when veteran reporter Lou Cannon faced the conundrum of covering President Ronald Reagan's factually incorrect 1985 claim that South Africa had "eliminated" segregation (it had not), instead of juxtaposing Reagan's statement against experts who could debunk or contextualize it, Cannon used irony, highly selective quotations, and interpretive verbs like "contended" to simultaneously report on and discredit the president's words.[78]

Journalists also employ "stance verbs" to "reflect a speaker's attitude or stance toward the content of his or her speech" as a way to signal their own interpretation of statements or events. This practice involves appending words like "obviously," "clearly," "apparently," and "presumably" when they are not required by the reported facts.[79] While such words can seem like innocuous narrative devices when used in the context of reporting on official speech (for example, "the President clearly stated that . . ."), they subtly embed a journalist's own judgment. The use of interpretive words continues to be common. For example, a Washington Post story about the families of Sandy Hook Elementary School victims offering Alex Jones a settlement described the offer as "*only* about 6 percent of what he owes" (emphasis

[76] Basil Bernstein, *Social Class, Linguistic Codes and Grammatical Elements*, 5 Language and Speech 221 (1962).

[77] Theodore L. Glasser & James S. Ettema, *When the Facts Don't Speak for Themselves: A Study of the Use of Irony in Daily Journalism*, 10 Critical Stud. in Mass Commc'n 323 (1993).

[78] *Id.*

[79] Lisbeth Lipari, *Journalistic Authority: Textual Strategies of Legitimation*, 73 Journalism & Mass Commc'n Q. 823 (1996).

added).[80] When journalists use irony and stance words, they are not making "mistakes" of the kind that might be caught and corrected by editors and fact-checkers, but they are nonetheless straying from publishing strictly factual accounts. They are exercising autonomy over *language* and enjoying a freedom to embed subtle interpretations and leave ambiguities unresolved.

The third example concerns the profession's power; in his exhaustive historical study of misreported stories in American journalism, Joseph W. Campbell suggested that journalists often let mistakes stand when they align with how journalists would like the public to perceive their profession's power. Campbell illustrated this point by using Nick Ut's "Napalm Girl" photo as an example. When discussing the power of this photo, journalists persist in using phrases like "American napalm" and "American plane," thus perpetuating the trope that it played a major role in ending the Vietnam War. Per Campbell, however, while the napalm was indeed American-made, it was not dropped by American pilots; similarly, the plane that carried out the attack was American-made but not owned or operated by the American Air Force. While such details and distinctions may seem trivial in the context of the war's overall brutality, that seeming triviality is exactly what Campbell sought to highlight in arguing that some facts have been allowed to stand as ambiguous when they served what he called "misleading 'consensus narratives' . . . anecdotes and legends that are found at the heart of a profession's culture and are readily recalled."[81] These are the facts and stories that journalists *want* to be true about itself and its power to shape the world. Adopting Shelby Steel's phrase, Campbell asserted that such facts are "poetic truths" serving a "larger essential truth" that journalists sometimes prioritize over the facticity that their profession usually unyieldingly demands.[82]

* * *

Across these scenes of error – misinformation, transgressions of justice, professional malpractice, platform censorship, and ambiguous language – a distinct image of the press and its freedom emerges. This image depends upon seeing the press as a site of unfettered reporting, editorial judgment, and publishing; as a set of social and technological dependencies and separations; and *also* as a communication system with the power to diagnose, prioritize, fix, and tolerate mistakes. This press sees some errors as grievous mistakes demanding correction, others as social ills deserving its attention, others as unfortunate but understandable missteps, and still others as circumstances that it wants to have the power to contextualize, strategically contain, or altogether ignore.

80 Timothy Bella, *Sandy Hook Families Offer Alex Jones a Deal to Settle $1.5 Billion Debt*, WASH. POST (Nov. 28, 2023), https://www.washingtonpost.com/nation/2023/11/28/alex-jones-bankruptcy-sandy-hook-settlement/.

81 CAMPBELL, *supra* note 51.

82 *Id.* at 149.

In turning now to GenAI and its relationship to press freedom, it is worth keeping in mind these complex views of the press, press freedom, and journalism's relationship to mistakes. In doing so, we can more effectively consider what, exactly, is "wrong" with the "synthetic press" and ask which forces cause which failures and how contemporary efforts to diagnose and correct the synthetic press's failings reveal different understandings of the press and its freedoms.

10.3 THE SYNTHETIC PRESS AND ITS MISTAKES

The synthetic press, which encompasses journalistic practices, news forms, institutional relationships, economic models, and regulatory frictions prompted by GenAI datasets, large language models, and commercial products, presents a new space of mistakes, errors, and failures for thinking about press freedom.

A considerable body of recent scholarship has traced how journalists report on GenAI,[83] how newsrooms adopt and experiment with GenAI,[84] how media organizations establish GenAI guidelines,[85] how media guilds bargain around GenAI,[86] and how GenAI poses new normative and regulatory challenges.[87] But there has been little work so far framing GenAI as a press freedom problem.[88] Thus, the focus

[83] Brause et al., *supra* note 7; Brennen et al., *supra* note 7; Sukyoung Choi, *Temporal Framing in Balanced News Coverage of Artificial Intelligence and Public Attitudes*, 27 Mass Commc'n & Soc. 384 (2024).

[84] Hannes Cools et al., *Where Exactly Between Utopia and Dystopia? A Framing Analysis of AI and Automation in US Newspapers*, 25 Journalism 3 (2024); Hannes Cools et al., *Newsroom Engineering Teams as "Survival Entities" for Journalism? Mapping the Process of Institutionalization at The Washington Post*, 12 Digit. Journalism 1 (2023); M. Fridman, R. Krøvel & F. Palumbo, *How (Not to) Run an AI Project in Investigative Journalism*, 2023 Journalism Prac. 1; Jia et al., *supra* note 10; Marisela Gutierrez Lopez et al., *A Question of Design: Strategies for Embedding AI-Driven Tools into Journalistic Work Routines*, 11 Digit. Journalism 484 (2023); Rachel E. Moran & Sonia Jawaid Shaikh, *Robots in the News and Newsrooms: Unpacking Meta-Journalistic Discourse on the Use of Artificial Intelligence in Journalism*, 10 Digit. Journalism 1756 (2022); Bartosz Wilczek et al., *Transforming the Value Chain of Local Journalism with Artificial Intelligence*, 45 AI Mag. 200 (2024).

[85] Hannes Cools & Nicholas Diakopoulos, *Writing Guidelines for the Role of AI in Your Newsroom? Here Are Some, er, Guidelines for That*, Nieman Lab (July 11, 2023), https://www.niemanlab.org/2023/07/writing-guidelines-for-the-role-of-ai-in-your-newsroom-here-are-some-er-guidelines-for-that/; Kim Björn Becker et al., *Policies in Parallel? A Comparative Study of Journalistic AI Policies in 52 Global News Organisations*, SocArXiv Papers (Sept. 6, 2023), https://osf.io/preprints/socarxiv/c4af9.

[86] Errol Salamon, *Supporting Digital Job Satisfaction in Online Media Unions' Contracts*, *in* Happiness in Journalism (Valérie Bélair-Gagnon et al. eds., 2023); Errol Salamon, *Negotiating Technological Change: How Media Unions Navigate Artificial Intelligence in Journalism*, 26 Journalism & Commc'n Monographs 159 (2024).

[87] Natali Helberger et al., *Towards a Normative Perspective on Journalistic AI: Embracing the Messy Reality of Normative Ideals*, 10 Digit. Journalism 1605 (2022); Sarah K. Wiley, *The Grey Area: How Regulations Impact Autonomy in Computational Journalism*, 11 Digit. Journalism 889 (2021).

[88] *But see* Ananny & Karr, *supra* note 43; Simon, *supra* note 43; Simon, *supra* note 10.

of the present work is to understand how the press's mistaken or failed uses of GenAI might repeat or break its historical patterns of contextualizing, containing, tolerating, or ignoring mistakes.

Beginning around the fall of 2022, GenAI began appearing in new, popularly available systems like ChatGPT, Midjourney, Copilot, DALL-E, Meta AI, Claude, and Sora. It was already at work in familiar tools like Google Search, Microsoft Office, and Google Docs and in countless, largely invisible, back-end integrations with existing organizational information systems. Journalists were quick to use and misuse the technology.

Indeed, examples of mistaken or failed GenAI journalism already abound. The German magazine Die Aktuelle fired its editor-in-chief after he published a synthetically generated "interview" with race car driver Michael Schumacher, which gave audiences no indication that it was a fabricated story.[89] The Guardian discovered that ChatGPT was delivering plausible, but entirely fictional, news stories that the technology claimed the news organization had published.[90] USA Today apologized and corrected countless sports stories after discovering that many of them were synthetically generated and contained errors.[91] CNET paused using GenAI after it published a series of stories offering readers financial guidance that contained myriad mistaken formulas and calculations.[92] Gizmodo found itself running afoul of Star Wars fan communities after it used GenAI to publish several stories with errors about the franchise's characters and plots.[93] Microsoft was harshly criticized after its GenAI news platform placed a poll next to a Guardian story, inviting readers to speculate whether the subject of the story died by murder, accident, or suicide.[94] Sports Illustrated backtracked on its use of GenAI after an investigation found that it had published an undisclosed number of entirely fabricated stories under the bylines of synthetically generated journalist personas. The magazine blamed a third-party

[89] Amanda Holpuch, *German Magazine Editor Is Fired over A.I. Michael Schumacher Interview*, N.Y. Times (Apr. 24, 2023), https://www.nytimes.com/2023/04/24/business/media/michael-schumacher-ai-fake-interview.html.

[90] Chris Moran, *ChatGPT Is Making Up Fake Guardian Articles. Here's How We're Responding*, The Guardian (Apr. 6, 2023), https://www.theguardian.com/commentisfree/2023/apr/06/ai-chatgpt-guardian-technology-risks-fake-article.

[91] Benjamin Mullin & Katie Robertson, *USA Today to Remove 23 Articles After Investigation into Fabricated Sources*, N.Y. Times (June 16, 2022), https://www.nytimes.com/2022/06/16/business/media/usa-today-fabricated-sources.html.

[92] Mia Sato & Emma Roth, *CNET Found Errors in More Than Half of Its AI-Written Stories*, Verge (Jan. 25, 2023), https://www.theverge.com/2023/1/25/23571082/cnet-ai-written-stories-errors-corrections-red-ventures.

[93] Maggie Harrison Dupre, *Gizmodo's AI-Generated Star Wars Article Still Has Errors, and Now It's Ranking on Google*, Futurism (July 13, 2023), https://futurism.com/gizmodo-ai-star-wars-article-google.

[94] Dan Milmo, *Microsoft Accused of Damaging Guardian's Reputation with AI-Generated Poll*, The Guardian (Oct. 31, 2023), https://www.theguardian.com/media/2023/oct/31/microsoft-accused-of-damaging-guardians-reputation-with-ai-generated-poll.

content provider for the mistake.[95] Gannett paused its use of GenAI after it published several synthetically generated articles that contained information placeholders in place of story details (for example, running the lede "The Worthington Christian [[WINNING_TEAM_MASCOT]] defeated the Westerville North [[LOSING_TEAM_MASCOT]] 2-1 in an Ohio boys soccer game on Saturday.").[96] And MSN.com recently mistakenly featured a story falsely accusing an Irish broadcaster of sexual misconduct, a story that had been synthetically generated by a third-party chatbot that paraphrased real news stories.[97]

While some individual errors are amusing and idiosyncratic growing pains of technological experimentation, together they suggest that the *synthetic* press's inclusion of GenAI yields new types of journalistic mistakes and thus new ways to think about press freedom through GenAI mistakes. Note, for example, how these mistakes span questions of editorial judgment, failed third-party relationships, factual errors, journalistic taste or decorum, specialized knowledge, reporter identity, and system design. These instances of mistaken GenAI journalism all deserve deeper theorization and case studies, but taken together, they suggest a framework for thinking about synthetic press freedom. In the following, I briefly sketch three sites of GenAI journalistic mistakes, suggesting each site as a place to consider how press autonomy might appear in synthetic media systems.

10.4 JOURNALISTIC GENAI MISTAKES AS SYNTHETIC PRESS FREEDOM DYNAMICS

10.4.1 *Uncritically Using Tools and Infrastructure*

GenAI uses datasets and computational language models to produce media that its designers judge as producing statistically acceptable results. It does not "know" anything about the data it uses, the meaning of its patterns, or the nuances of the language it produces, and it is little more than a "stochastic parrot."[98] As scholarship on journalistic errors shows, reporters and editors have considerable freedom to choose sources, frame ledes, analyze data, phrase and juxtapose claims, and signal interpretations, with few errors or mistakes ever being corrected.[99] This individual

95 Maggie Harrison Dupre, *Sports Illustrated Published Articles by Fake, AI-Generated Writers*, Futurism (Nov. 27, 2023), https://futurism.com/sports-illustrated-ai-generated-writers.

96 Tyler Buchanan, *Dispatch Pauses AI Sports Writing Program*, Axios (Aug. 28, 2023), https://www.axios.com/local/columbus/2023/08/28/dispatch-gannett-ai-newsroom-tool.

97 Kashmir Hill & Tiffany Hsu, *It Looked Like a Reliable News Site. It Was an A.I. Chop Shop*, N.Y. Times (June 6, 2024), https://www.nytimes.com/2024/06/06/technology/bnn-breaking-ai-generated-news.html.

98 Emily M. Bender et al., *On the Dangers of Stochastic Parrots: Can Language Models Be Too Big?*, *in* 2021 FAccT '21: Proceedings of the 2021 ACM Conference on Fairness, Accountability, and Transparency 610, https://dl.acm.org/doi/10.1145/3442188.3445922.

99 Maier, *supra* note 66; Maier, *supra* note 51.

autonomy is a hallmark of the profession and a key element of seeing press freedom in terms of intrepid journalists pursuing truth at all costs.[100] Style guides and newsroom policies can go a long way toward setting standards and expectations for how, if at all, journalists should use GenAI (for example, catching factual errors and noncompliant language). However, more subtle forms of error can appear if journalists too quickly and uncritically accept as "good enough" the default results of synthetically generated source suggestions, story ledes, document analyses, research summaries, interview translations, transcripts, and a myriad other seemingly innocuous aspects of journalistic work.[101] In many news organizations, the pressures to produce many stories in a short timeframe that are deemed good enough may create uncritical reliance on tools and habits that are unlikely to ever rise to the level of an error demanding correction but that nonetheless erode the quality of the work.

News organizations with the money, data, engineering expertise, and editorial oversight to create their own GenAI tools and infrastructure (like The New York Times[102] and The Washington Post[103]) will have arguably more freedom to avoid the risks and errors that come with uncritically using publicly available synthetic media technologies. Being able to know what datasets a model includes, how it was trained, which tests it passed before release, and who is responsible for fixing errors is arguably a much stronger position from which to critically judge GenAI outputs. To the extent that the privilege of avoiding or controlling synthetic media mistakes is unevenly distributed – few small newsrooms can afford homegrown AI systems – the synthetic press is a field with uneven freedom.[104]

[100] Matthew C. Ehrlich & Joe Saltzman, Heroes and Scoundrels: The Image of the Journalist in Popular Culture (2015).

[101] For research on the power of default settings, suggested actions, and ranked results in software, *see* Jay P. Kesan & Rajiv C. Shah, *Setting Software Defaults: Perspectives from Law, Computer Science and Behavioral Economics*, 82 Notre Dame L. Rev. 583 (2006); Rajiv C. Shah & Jay P. Kesan, *Setting Online Policy with Software Defaults*, 11 Info., Commc'n & Soc. 989 (2008).

[102] Emilia David, *The New York Times Is Building a Team to Explore AI in the Newsroom*, Verge (Jan. 30, 2024), https://www.theverge.com/2024/1/30/24055718/new-york-times-generative-ai-machine-learning.

[103] Andrew Deck, *The Washington Post's First AI Strategy Editor Talks LLMs in the Newsroom*, NiemanLab (Mar. 28, 2024), https://www.niemanlab.org/2024/03/the-washington-posts-first-ai-strategy-editor-talks-llms-in-the-newsroom/.

[104] Note that the Associated Press, the Partnership on AI consortium, and Microsoft have all developed or announced tools, guides, trainings, and partnerships designed to help smaller, local news organizations create and use GenAI. For more details, *see AI Adoption for Newsrooms: A 10-Step Guide*, Partnership on AI, https://partnershiponai.org/ai-for-newsrooms/ (last visited June 29, 2024); Sophie Culpepper, *The AP Announces Five AI Tools to Help Local Newsrooms with Tasks Like Transcription and Sorting Pitches*, NiemanLab (Oct. 12, 2023), https://www.niemanlab.org/2023/10/the-ap-announces-five-ai-tools-to-help-local-newsrooms-with-tasks-like-transcription-and-sorting-pitches/; Laura Hazard Owen, *Microsoft, Pushing Generative AI in Newsrooms, Partners with Semafor, CUNY, the Online News Association, and Others*, NiemanLab (Feb. 5, 2024), https://www.niemanlab.org/2024/02/microsoft-pushing-generative-ai-in-newsrooms-partners-with-semafor-cuny-the-online-news-association-and-others/.

Little harm is likely to result from an individual journalist on a single beat or story uncritically accepting GenAI outputs as "good enough," but if many journalists too quickly accept the statistically generated outputs of similar tools across workflows and newsrooms, GenAI begins to look like a subtle, distributed, largely invisible, and hard-to-track curb on the autonomy of individual journalists. If the ideal of professional journalistic autonomy is that reporters and editors have the power to use their expertise to decide *for themselves* whether a story is publishable, then the gradual incursion of GenAI into those judgments – to suggest phrasings, speed up work, recommend sources, reorder text, summarize research, analyze interview transcripts, and more – has the real potential to displace the feeling or fact of professional independence. To be sure, tools have always structured human practices – journalists were not free from technological influences before GenAI[105] – but even if journalists seek out and approve of GenAI in their work, there is still an impact on work that they might have done without GenAI's help. And to the extent that journalists mistake commonly used GenAI tools as neutral, objective, innocuous, or even sentient,[106] they run the risk of implicitly surrendering some of their *own* freedom, and obligation, to scrutinize sources, research, facts, framings, language, and interpretations in the public interest.

10.4.2 *Echoing Past Errors*

Although it is difficult to quantify, research suggests that many published stories contain errors that have never been corrected. In a study of 2,700 stories containing factual errors or serious inaccuracies, published in 22 small and midmarket newspapers, Scott Maier found that a correction was issued only 11 percent of the time.[107] In another survey of 4,800 human sources cited in news stories and interviews, 61 percent of sources said the stories contained errors.[108] An internationally comparative study of news accuracy found errors in 48 percent of US stories, 60 percent of Swiss stories, and 52 percent of Italian stories.[109] Though the sources opined that the errors seriously damaged the value of the stories, they saw such errors as inevitable, correction processes as futile, and journalists as largely resistant to talking about a

[105] For example, research indicates that newsrooms are keenly aware of the data analytics showing how their stores fare on the web and in online markets; *see* Angèle Christin & Caitlin Petre, *Making Peace with Metrics: Relational Work in Online News Production*, 14 SOCIOLOGICA 133 (2020).

[106] For research on the power of GenAI's prompt-based conversational interfaces to seem autonomous and sentient, *see* Sarah Burkhardt & Bernhard Rieder, *Foundation Models Are Platform Models: Prompting and the Political Economy of AI*, 11 BIG DATA & SOC. (2024), https://journals.sagepub.com/doi/10.1177/20539517241247839.

[107] Maier, *supra* note 51.

[108] Maier, *supra* note 66.

[109] Colin Porlezza et al., *News Accuracy in Switzerland and Italy*, 6 JOURNALISM PRAC. 530 (2012).

story's accuracy after it has been published.[110] A meta-review of news accuracy studies from 1936 to 2005 revealed that newspapers have always been rife with errors, with between 41 and 61 percent of all published articles over that time period containing mistakes of some kind.[111]

Though often celebrated as exactly the kind of high-quality information that GenAI datasets should include, it seems that many news stories contain errors or inaccuracies. As makers of GenAI systems buttress their large language models with datasets of news stories, with the aim of increasing the veracity and reliability of synthetic outputs, they are potentially reproducing decades of errors contained in published news stories. It is highly unlikely that mistakes in any single news story will be reproduced in a GenAI output, and this is because GenAI datasets include multiple sources, machine learning outputs are probabilistic, and training methods like human-centered reinforcement learning try to reduce GenAI errors. Nevertheless, GenAI systems that include or prioritize news data may be reproducing past journalistic mistakes. As a matter of press freedom, this means that news errors that were created years ago, in part by individual journalists acting with autonomy, newsrooms with poor oversight, and publishers' reluctance to make corrections, all feed a contemporary situation in which journalists and general users alike find themselves using GenAI systems informed by mistake-riddled news. To be sure, all of these actors were exercising professional autonomy and choosing to practice in ways they saw fit, but the result of that autonomy is a news record with errors – a record that is now driving the datasets and machine learning models being used to generate synthetic news. Without auditing GenAI datasets for news, extracting erroneous news data, and updating large language models, it is practically impossible for anyone using or subject to GenAI to be free from the mistakes created by a profession that has historically protected its autonomy to define, find, correct, and ignore its errors.[112]

10.4.3 *Politics of Reproducing Datasets*

Beyond the risk of error-ridden news datasets creating ripples of mistakes and inaccuracies in GenAI systems, there is a more subtle danger, namely, that GenAI

[110] Maier, *supra* note 51.

[111] Maier, *supra* note 66.

[112] For research on the challenge of extracting problematic data (like news stories with mistakes) from large language models, *see* Alexandra Sasha Luccioni et al., *A Framework for Deprecating Datasets: Standardizing Documentation, Identification, and Communication*, *in* 2022 FAccT '22: Proceedings of the 2022 ACM Conference on Fairness, Accountability, and Transparency 199, https://dl.acm.org/doi/10.1145/3531146.3533086; Nanna Bonde Thylstrup, *The Ethics and Politics of Data Sets in the Age of Machine Learning: Deleting Traces and Encountering Remains*, 44 Media, Culture & Soc. 655 (2022); Antonio A. Ginart et al., *Making AI Forget You: Data Deletion in Machine Learning*, *in* Proc. of 33rd Int'l Conf. on Neural Info. Processing Sys. (2019), https://arxiv.org/pdf/1907.05012.

journalism reproduces the politics of the datasets underpinning synthetic media systems. As historians, cultural critics, and auditors of datasets have demonstrated, machine learning datasets often contain information that was unethically collected; excludes large swaths of people; organizes individuals into racist, gendered, homophobic, and xenophobic categories; and prioritizes English language and Western-centric descriptions of the world.[113]

These dataset politics have the potential to reappear if GenAI systems uncritically incorporate corpora of news stories without evaluating them for problematic histories or patterns. Because there is no such thing as data free from the influence of politics or history – historian Lisa Gitelman has referred to "raw data" as an oxymoron[114] – corpora of news stories reflect the traditions, languages, epistemologies, and ethics of the people and eras that created the narratives. As histories of the AP Stylebook, a powerful authority of language in many newsrooms, show, journalistic language is constantly changing. It was once editorially acceptable to use terms like "illegal immigrant," "transexual," or "addict." The New York Times had a long history of referring to women as only "Miss" or "Mrs." (calling "Ms." a linguistic fad[115]), and The Washington Post recently started capitalizing the word "Black" to "identify the many groups that make up the African diaspora in America and elsewhere."[116] While adherence to stylebooks can prevent replication of problematic individual words or phrases in contemporary stories, to the extent that GenAI datasets include these news stories, they are rife with claims, assumptions, and

[113] This is a large body of literature that cannot be fully captured in this chapter, but key citations include Louise Amoore et al., *A World Model: On the Political Logics of Generative AI*, 113 Pol. Geography 103134 (2024); Joy Buolamwini & Timnit Gebru, *Gender Shades: Intersectional Accuracy Disparities in Commercial Gender Classification* 81 Proc. of Mach. Learning Rsch. 77 (2018); Burkhardt & Rieder, *supra* note 106; Kate Crawford, *Archeologies of Datasets*, 128 Am. Hist. Rev. 1368 (2023); Kate Crawford & Trevor Paglen, *Excavating AI: The Politics of Training Sets for Machine Learning*, https://excavating.ai (last visited June 29, 2024); Emily Denton et al., *Bringing the People Back In: Contesting Benchmark Machine Learning Datasets*, arXiv (July 14, 2020), https://arxiv.org/abs/2007.07399; Emily Denton et al., *On the Genealogy of Machine Learning Datasets: A Critical History of ImageNet*, 8 Big Data & Soc. (2021), https://journals.sagepub.com/doi/10.1177/20539517211035955; Benjamin N. Jacobsen, *Machine Learning and the Politics of Synthetic Data*, 10 Big Data & Soc. (2023), https://journals.sagepub.com/doi/full/10.1177/20539517221145372; Tarleton Gillespie, *Generative AI and the Politics of Visibility*, 11 Big Data & Soc. (2024), https://journals.sagepub.com/doi/10.1177/20539517241252131; Lindsay Poirier, *Reading Datasets: Strategies for Interpreting the Politics of Data Signification*, 8 Big Data & Soc. (2021), https://journals.sagepub.com/doi/full/10.1177/20539517211029322.

[114] L. Gitelman, "Raw Data" Is an Oxymoron (2013).

[115] Fred Vultee, *A Paleontology of Style*, 6 Journalism Prac. 450 (2012); Steve Bien-Aimé, *AP Stylebook Normalizes Sports as a Male Space*, 37 Newspaper Rsch. J. 44 (2016); Lily G. Bessette et al., *The Associated Press Stylebook Changes and the Use of Addiction-Related Stigmatizing Terms in News Media*, 43 Substance Abuse 127 (2022).

[116] *The Washington Post Announces Writing Style Changes for Racial and Ethnic Identifiers*, Wash. Post (July 29, 2020), https://www.washingtonpost.com/pr/2020/07/29/washington-post-announces-writing-style-changes-racial-ethnic-identifiers/.

language politics that were once common and acceptable but that are now considered mistaken and unacceptable.[117]

The power of dataset politics also appears in the dominance of The New York Times "Annotated Corpus," a dataset of 1.8 million documents consisting of nearly every article published by The Times between January 1987 and June 2007 that is organized by topic, individuals, locations, and other elements within The Times' metadata system.[118] It has quickly become the de facto standard of news language for machine learning technologists and is regularly used as a benchmark dataset for teaching AI systems how to generate high-quality story summaries, recognize news events, and standardize language. The power of The New York Times and its "Annotated Corpus" dataset to computationally standardize news and signal acceptable news language (to both journalists and outsiders alike) is nothing new. It echoes an earlier "arterial process" that media sociologists determined could explain why so many of the nation's newsrooms tried to mimic The Times in terms of reporting techniques, editorial judgment, language choices, topic selection, audience relations, and publication timing.[119] The New York Times has long held a central position in American journalism, and it continues to do so through the leverage of its powerful datasets and indexes – information and power that it is currently suing Microsoft and OpenAI to protect.[120]

These dataset politics, which potentially include problematic collection practices, unethical categorizations, stylebook changes, and powerful indexes, mean that much of the language that informs synthetically produced journalism emerges from unexamined assumptions about who or what is newsworthy, how stories are told, and which organizations dominate. While individual journalists may feel a sense of independence as they report and write, whenever they use GenAI tools they are automatically and often unknowingly embedded in a system of datasets, categories, models, and organizations with uneven power and complex histories.

[117] Expanding on this point is beyond the scope of this chapter, but for a recent trenchant discussion of how the politics of language exist in larger structures of meaning beyond individual words or phrases, *see* David Beaver & Jason Stanley, The Politics of Language (2023).

[118] Evan Sandhaus, *The New York Times Annotated Corpus*, Academic Torrents, https://academictorrents.com/details/a48d52cbb929b7e2a601dcc1e48a30d0f16284ca (last visited June 29, 2024); Evan Sandhaus & Rob Larson, *A Century of Semantic Technology: Semantics at the New York Times*, N.Y. Times, https://graphics8.nytimes.com/packages/images/rd/final.pdf (last visited June 29, 2024).

[119] W. Breed, *Newspaper Opinion Leaders and the Process of Standardization*, 32 Journalism Q. 277 (1955). For a recent article finding that this phenomenon persists on social media platforms, *see* Qin Li et al., *Journalists' Networks: Homophily and Peering over the Shoulder of Other Journalists*, 18 PLOS One e0291544 (2023) (finding that "journalists at larger media outlets are more likely to be central in journalists' Twitter networks, providing evidence that journalists look to other journalists at larger outlets for direction in news coverage.").

[120] Michael M. Grynbaum & Ryan Mac, *The Times Sues OpenAI and Microsoft over A.I. Use of Copyrighted Work*, N.Y. Times (Dec. 27, 2023), https://www.nytimes.com/2023/12/27/business/media/new-york-times-open-ai-microsoft-lawsuit.html.

10.5 CONCLUSION: RECURSIVE PRESS FREEDOM FOR THE SYNTHETIC PRESS

Through this chapter, I have developed three lines of argument. First, I suggested that "the press" is most correctly understood as a set of intertwined social, cultural, political, and technological forces. Although often primarily associated with the work of journalists and the production of news, the press is, in reality, an entity shaped by the actions and influences of multiple actors.

Second, I argued that a key element of press freedom is the press's capacity to define, uncover, explain, control, fix, or ignore mistakes. Broadly understood, mistakes are a key means by which the press knows and regulates itself, as well as a lens through which it observes and endeavors to change society. Mistakes are an important and largely understudied way of understanding the press and its power.

Finally, I have tried to argue that, today, the press is a *synthetic* press to the extent that GenAI, through its datasets, models, and products, structures journalistic practices, news forms, institutional relationships, economic models, and regulatory frictions. And just as past eras of the press had their own types of errors, the synthetic press has its own emerging set of mistakes that manifest themselves in how journalists engage GenAI tools, how past errors echo in GenAI infrastructures, and how dataset politics structure journalism and news.

This conception of press freedom as the capacity to know, control, make, and learn from mistakes is not a stand-alone model of press freedom but is deeply connected to more general ideas about how institutions achieve their autonomy and how the public can govern themselves through communication technologies.

As Schauer argued,[121] institutions discover and demonstrate their independence, in part, through the capacity to create and control exceptions. When institutions reject default rules, carve out special cases, reverse precedents, and use their *own* judgment to evaluate the significance of their circumstances, they distinguish themselves from other institutions and demonstrate their ability to act with self-awareness, purpose, and confidence. A free press should see mistakes as exceptional opportunities to know itself better, to judge whether an error illustrates a pattern to tolerate or change, and sometimes to argue that a mistake is not its own but someone else's failure to treat it differently. A free *synthetic* press, for example, would make its own GenAI infrastructure that fixes, prevents, or tolerates errors as it sees fit, and a free synthetic press would reject or work to change GenAI infrastructure that causes errors that GenAI may tolerate but journalism cannot. In practice, and aligned with calls for institutional exceptions to data-driven rules,[122] synthetic press autonomy would demand *freedom from* unauthorized data scraping, unethical datasets,

[121] Frederick Schauer, *Exceptions*, 58 U. Chi. L. Rev. 871 (1991).

[122] Sarah H. Cen & Manish Raghavan, *The Right to Be an Exception to a Data-Driven Rule*, MIT Case Studies in Soc. & Ethical Resp. of Computing (2023), https://mit-serc.pubpub.org/pub/right-to-be-exception/release/2.

deceptive interfaces, and anachronistic language models and *freedom to* create its own GenAI systems. A free synthetic press would create exceptions for itself from general-purpose GenAI because the mistakes that would otherwise result would be unacceptable.

As Chris Kelty contended, publics become "recursive publics," when they have the "discursive and technical"[123] means of creating and recreating themselves. Put differently, they can talk about who they are and why they are structured as they are, and they have the expertise and material power to sustain and change themselves without relying on outsiders. A simple example of a recursive public is an online forum composed of people who have the communicative capacity to talk about why and how they convene and who have the engineering expertise to maintain or redesign the forum, all without the need to consult or rely upon external actors.

A recursively free press, then, is a press that knows and can confidently discuss the social, cultural, political, and technological relationships that structure its journalism and produce its news *and* that has the power to change those relationships with intention and without needing outsiders. A recursively free press, for example, would not try to emulate Mark Zuckerberg's model of community and would not need Google's funding. A recursive *synthetic* press would deeply understand GenAI's datasets, models, and products; would understand and be able to discuss their significance to journalism and news; and would be able to reject, change, or invent a GenAI infrastructure that it desires, without relying on outsiders. Such a press would have command of its future and be able to, as Erin Carroll has argued, "conjure the language that describes the press we need and want."[124]

Artificial intelligence pioneer and ultimate critic Joseph Weizenbaum wrote that "the computer scientist has a heavy responsibility to make the fallibility and limitations of the systems he is capable of designing brilliantly clear."[125] The same might be said for the GenAI journalist, who should know how and why the synthetic press fails, which failures matter, and how it might be fixed. Such a journalist would hold an image of journalism, debate it with others, and trace it across datasets, models, interfaces, economics, politics, ideals of the public, and imaginings of what the synthetic press could be if it were autonomous.

[123] Chris M. Kelty, *Geeks, Social Imaginaries, and Recursive Publics*, 20 CULTURAL ANTHROPOLOGY 185 (2005).

[124] Erin C. Carroll, *Press Benefits and the Public Imagination*, *in* THE FUTURE OF PRESS FREEDOM, *supra* note 24, at 127.

[125] Cited in Jack Stilgoe, *We Need a Weizenbaum Test for AI*, 381 SCI. EADK0176 (2023).

PART IV

Legal Protection for the Press Function

11

Reinvigorating the Press Clause Through Negative Theory

Helen Norton

Courts have been reluctant to interpret the First Amendment's Press Clause as providing the press with significant protections distinct from those provided to all of us by the Speech Clause. But courts could choose to do so, and litigants and scholars can help illuminate those choices. What work could an independent Press Clause do apart from the work already done by the Speech Clause? This question requires us to think about why and how the press is different from other speakers for First Amendment purposes – more specifically, what distinct functions does the press perform and what distinct vulnerabilities does the press possess?

In terms of distinct press functions, the press serves the public through its watchdog, educator, and proxy roles. The press performs a critically important checking function by reporting on the government's performance, including its misconduct.[1] The press informs the public about current affairs, science, health, the environment, art, entertainment, and much more. The press also serves as a proxy for the public by observing and reporting on events of importance to the public where the public does not have the time or other resources to observe those events directly.[2]

These functions, in turn, explain the press's distinct vulnerabilities to government retaliation: Because the press's primary purpose is to scrutinize the government for the public's benefit, the government has long perceived the press as inherently threatening to its political self-interest. Moreover, changes in the political environment (along with "the affordances of online social media platforms – anonymity, accessibility speed, and scale"[3]) have aggravated threats to journalists' physical safety, intensifying their vulnerability still further. As legal scholar Erin Carroll has detailed, "physical assaults against journalists in the United States increased nearly 1,400% in

[1] *See* Vince Blasi, *The Checking Value in First Amendment Theory*, 2 AM. B. FOUND. RES. J. 521, 538–39 (1977) ("The central value of the checking function is that the abuse of official power is an especially serious evil . . .").

[2] *See* RonNell Andersen Jones, *Press Speakers and Listener Rights*, 90 U. COLO. L. REV. 499, 537–43 (2019).

[3] Erin Carroll, *Obstruction of Journalism*, 99 DENV. L. REV. 407, 412 (2022).

2020" and "a 2018 study found that one in ten journalists surveyed had been threatened with death in the past year because of the work they do."[4] So too have contemporary changes in technology exacerbated these vulnerabilities by posing existential challenges to the press's financial survival.[5]

"Negative" First Amendment theory, as I've written previously, "is about a negative value: distrust of government. And because the government gives us plenty of reason to distrust it, negative theory packs substantial power."[6] Rooted in distrust of the government's self-interested efforts to punish and thus silence the press, negative theory has long offered an important tool for understanding the Press Clause. And negative theory is now more valuable as an interpretive tool than ever, as press organizations and individual journalists are increasingly vulnerable to the government's retaliation.

Among other things, negative theory can help us understand the Press Clause as providing an especially robust shield from the government's retaliation – a shield different from that offered the public more generally by the Speech Clause precisely because of the press's distinct functions and vulnerabilities. More specifically, directing judicial attention to the reasons to distrust the government's adverse treatment of the press can reinvigorate Press Clause doctrine by informing courts' choices of legal rules and their application of those rules once chosen.

A Press Clause doctrine informed by negative theory thus asks whether the government's action gives us reason to worry that its choices have the intent and potential effect of muzzling the press as a watchdog.[7] "Affirmative" theories, in contrast, focus less on the government's potential for regulatory abuse and more on the positive benefits of the press: Such theories urge that we interpret the Press Clause to provide the press with affirmative rights to newsgathering, like a right to receive information or access places not available to the public more generally.[8] Note, however, that applying negative theory to understand the Press Clause as providing a mighty shield against the government's retaliation does not preclude us from also understanding the clause to afford the press with such affirmative rights.

Indeed, courts and commentators often rely on multiple theories when considering specific First Amendment problems.[9] For instance, the Speech Clause's

4 *Id.* at 409, 415.

5 *See generally* MARGARET SULLIVAN, GHOSTING THE NEWS: LOCAL JOURNALISM AND THE CRISIS OF AMERICAN DEMOCRACY (2020).

6 Helen Norton, *Distrust, Negative First Amendment Theory, and the Regulation of Lies*, 22-07 KNIGHT FIRST AMEND. INST. 3 (Oct. 19, 2022), https://knightcolumbia.org/content/distrust-negative-first-amendment-theory-and-the-regulation-of-lies [https://perma.cc/L3LZ-CAMA].

7 *See* Ronald A. Cass, *The Perils of Positive Thinking: Constitutional Interpretation and Negative First Amendment Theory*, 34 UCLA L. REV. 1405, 1438–39 (1987).

8 *See* Pell v. Procunier, 417 U.S. 817 (1974) (rejecting such a theory to deny the press's assertion of a Press Clause right to conduct face-to-face interviews of those in prison).

9 *See* Toni M. Massaro & Helen Norton, *Free Speech and Democracy: A Pragmatic Primer for Twenty-first Century Reformers*, 54 U.C. DAVIS L. REV. 1631, 1658–62 (2021) (discussing pluralistic approaches to free speech theory).

protection of political dissent from the government's regulation can be explained in both negative terms (to guard against the government's self-interested efforts to silence its critics) and affirmative terms (because political dissent valuably contributes to democratic self-governance, enlightenment, and autonomy).[10] In other words, "negative" and "affirmative" Press Clause theories are not mutually exclusive, and the different theories can cash out with different doctrinal yields.

11.1 THE GOVERNMENT'S RETALIATION AGAINST THE PRESS, PAST AND PRESENT

We distrust the government's regulation in settings where experience leads us to conclude that the government's motives are self-interested or that its bias or competence is otherwise suspect. The framers of the Press Clause drew from exactly such experience, as they were all too aware of the government's history of interfering with press freedom through press licensing and seditious libel.[11] As Floyd Abrams has explained, "the Press Clause was, at the very least, a deeply felt response to the deprivations of press liberty that the colonists had witnessed and to which they had been subjected."[12]

One need not be an originalist, however, to interpret the Press Clause through the lens of negative theory. A structural understanding of the press's key functions explains the government's incentives for punishing and silencing the press: As Justice Potter Stewart explained, by providing the public with "organized, expert scrutiny of the government," a "free press" provides a "formidable check on official power."[13]

Examples abound – both old and new – of the government's propensity to stifle the press's scrutiny. Recall, for instance, the calculated efforts by Alabama government officials in the 1960s to drive journalists covering the Civil Rights Movement out of the state;[14] their tactics included weaponized defamation claims like those made in *The New York Times Co. v. Sullivan.*[15]

Consider, too, governments' punishment of local papers' critical scrutiny by pulling advertising from those papers or terminating contracts with them for printing legally required notices of tax sales, public meetings, and more. To be sure,

[10] Note that affirmative and negative free speech *theories* are different answers to the question of *why* the First Amendment protects certain rights while positive and negative *rights* instead reflect different answers to the question of *how* the First Amendment protects such rights.

[11] *See* Cass, *supra* note 7, at 1439 ("The framers were not intent on promoting some well-defined conception of the good, whether individual or societal. They were responding to problems that already had arisen and that they feared might recur.").

[12] Floyd Abrams, *The Press Is Different: Reflections on Justice Stewart and the Autonomous Press*, 7 HOFSTRA L. REV. 563, 579 (1979).

[13] Potter Stewart, *Or of the Press*, 26 HASTINGS L.J. 631, 634 (1975).

[14] GENE ROBERTS & HANK KLIBANOFF, THE RACE BEAT: THE PRESS, THE CIVIL RIGHTS STRUGGLE, AND THE AWAKENING OF A NATION 229–55 (2006).

[15] 376 U.S. 254 (1964).

governments have long engaged in such retaliation,[16] but newspapers' contemporary financial instability leaves them especially vulnerable to such actions, which threaten a considerable chunk of their revenue.[17]

As yet another illustration, think of the government's not-so-unusual practice of punishing journalists or press outlets critical of its performance by banning them from attending press conferences or communicating with government officials. Recall, for instance, former President Donald Trump's practice of revoking, or threatening to revoke, the White House press credentials of journalists whose questions or reporting criticized his administration's performance.[18]

So, we can find examples aplenty of the government's retaliatory tendencies with respect to the press. What to do about it?

11.2 HOW NEGATIVE THEORY COULD REINVIGORATE PRESS CLAUSE DOCTRINE

The contemporary Supreme Court leans heavily on negative theory when developing and applying its Speech Clause doctrine. Consider, for instance, *United States v. Alvarez*,[19] where the Court struck down a federal law that criminalized intentional falsehoods about receiving military honors, a law that neither punished nor chilled any valuable speech.[20] There, the Court relied on negative theory, focusing entirely on its distrust of the government's potential for regulatory mischief: "Permitting the government to decree this speech to be a criminal offense, whether shouted from the rooftops or made in a barely audible whisper, would endorse government authority to compile a list of subjects about which false statements are punishable. That governmental power has no clear limiting principle."[21]

Other examples of the Court's reliance on negative theory for Speech Clause purposes include *Heffernan v. City of Paterson*.[22] There, the Court upheld a First

[16] *See* El Dia, Inc. v. Governor Rossello, 165 F.3d 106, 109 (1st Cir. 1999) ("It would seem obvious that using government funds to punish political speech by members of the press and to attempt to coerce commentary favorable to the government would run afoul of the First Amendment."); *see also* CULVER SMITH, THE PRESS, POLITICS, AND PATRONAGE: THE AMERICAN GOVERNMENT'S USE OF NEWSPAPERS 1789–1875 4 (1977) ("Colonial newspapers, like those in England, had been subject to censorship by the government through privilege licenses that could be revoked.").

[17] *See How Local Officials Seek Revenge on Their Hometown Newspapers*, https://www.nytimes.com/2023/06/18/business/newspapers-public-notices.html; *In a Small Rhode Island Town, A Big Issue About the First Amendment*, https://www.bostonglobe.com/2023/08/29/metro/small-rhode-island-town-big-issue-about-first-amendment/.

[18] *See* Pen Am. Ctr., Inc. v. Trump, 448 F. Supp. 3d 309, 316–17 (2020).

[19] United States v. Alvarez, 567 U.S. 709 (2012).

[20] *See* Transcript of Oral Argument, *Alvarez*, 567 U.S. at 27, 35–36 (where the challenger's lawyer conceded that the law neither punished nor chilled valuable speech).

[21] *Alvarez*, 567 U.S. at 723.

[22] 578 U.S. 266 (2016).

Amendment challenge to government officials' demotion of an employee whom they mistakenly believed to have supported an opposition candidate. That the employee did not actually support – and thus had not engaged in protected political speech supporting – the candidate did not matter to the Court's analysis. Instead, the government's effort to suppress speech it perceived as threatening its political self-interest, by itself, violated the Speech Clause.

Yet the Court only occasionally invokes negative theory in its Press Clause cases. The rare exception – now four decades old – illustrates the rule: In *Minneapolis Star & Tribune Co. v. Minnesota Commissioner of Revenue*, the Court invoked a hefty dose of negative theory to strike down a state's taxing scheme that applied only to the press (a tax on paper and ink used in the production of periodicals like newspapers) and only to certain members of the press (those that annually spent more than $100,000 on ink and paper).[23] The Court's opinion reflected its deep distrust of the government's motives and its censorial potential. Consider this, for example:

> When the State singles out the press, though, the political constraints that prevent a legislature from passing crippling taxes of general applicability are weakened, and the threat of burdensome taxes becomes acute. That threat can operate as effectively as a censor to check critical comment by the press, undercutting the basic assumption of our political system that the press will often serve as an important restraint on government.[24]

And this (where the majority explained the danger of enabling the state to single out the press for a different method of taxation even if the press's tax burden were lighter than other businesses'):

> The very selection of the press for special treatment threatens the press not only with the current *differential* treatment, but with the possibility of subsequent differentially *more burdensome* treatment. Thus, even without actually imposing an extra burden on the press, the government might be able to achieve censorial effects, for "the threat of sanctions may deter [the] exercise of [First Amendment] rights almost as potently as the actual application of sanctions."[25]

Recognizing the law's "potential for abuse,"[26] the Court applied a version of strict scrutiny to strike it down.[27]

That negative theory is now so often absent from courts' Press Clause jurisprudence explains much of their failure to understand the Press Clause as doing work independent of the Speech Clause. Consider now two ways in which the robust infusion of negative theory could reinvigorate Press Clause doctrine.

[23] 460 U.S. 575 (1983).

[24] *Id.* at 585.

[25] *Id.* at 588 (quoting NAACP v. Button, 371 U.S. 415, 433 (1963)).

[26] *Id.* at 592.

[27] *Id.* at 585 ("[W]e cannot countenance such treatment unless the State asserts a counterbalancing interest of compelling importance that it cannot achieve without differential taxation.").

11.3 INFORMING COURTS' CHOICES OF PRESS-SPECIFIC RULES

First, reliance on negative theory – that is, concern for the government's capacity for, and the press's vulnerability to, retaliation – could in certain settings generate very different Press Clause rules. Think, for instance, how the Court's decision in *Branzburg v. Hayes*[28] might have turned out differently had it been informed by negative theory.

The *Branzburg* majority rejected the press's argument that the Press Clause should be interpreted to provide journalists with a shield from law enforcement subpoenas requiring them to disclose their confidential sources. The Court instead concluded that the Press Clause confers the press with no distinct rights of its own, such that members of the press must comply with subpoenas along with everyone else. In so holding, the majority downplayed negative theory concerns, discounting reasons for distrusting the government's exercise of its subpoena power specifically with respect to journalists:

> It is said that currently press subpoenas have multiplied, that mutual distrust and tension between press and officialdom have increased, that reporting styles have changed, and that there is now more need for confidential sources, particularly where the press seeks news about minority cultural and political groups or dissident organizations suspicious of the law and public officials. These developments, even if true, are treacherous grounds for a far-reaching interpretation of the First Amendment fastening a nationwide rule on courts, grand juries, and prosecuting officials everywhere.[29]

The dissent, in contrast, credited reasons to fear the government's potential to abuse its power to retaliate against the press – particularly in the grand jury setting, where "the judiciary has traditionally imposed virtually no limitations on the grand jury's broad investigatory powers."[30] The dissent's distrust of the government in this context thus led it to advocate a rule considerably less deferential to the government than the majority's rule. Under the dissent's preferred approach, the government would have been required to show probable cause to believe that a journalist has information "clearly relevant to a specific probable violation of law," "that the information sought cannot be obtained by alternative means less destructive of First Amendment rights," and that the government has a compelling need for the information.[31]

[28] 408 U.S. 665 (1972). To be sure, *Branzburg* is often described, and understandably so, as the majority's rejection of the press's claim to an affirmative right to newsgathering. My point here is that the majority also rejected the negative theory concerns raised by the challengers and by the dissent.

[29] *Id.* at 699.

[30] *Id.* 731 (Stewart, J., dissenting).

[31] *Id.* at 740.

As we can see, judicial awareness of the government's incentives and capacity to retaliate against the press can support courts' choice to apply Press Clause rules considerably more suspicious of the government.

11.4 INFORMING COURTS' APPLICATION OF EXISTING RULES IN PRESS CLAUSE CASES

Second, negative theory can valuably inform courts' application of rules already chosen. Under doctrine developed primarily for Speech Clause claims, an individual proves the government's retaliation in violation of the First Amendment if they can show that (1) they engaged in speech or other activity protected by the First Amendment, (2) the government took action that would chill a person of "ordinary firmness" from continuing to engage in such speech or protected activity, and (3) the government's action was substantially motivated by their speech or other protected activity.[32] Courts routinely apply this rule to retaliation claims brought by the press, just like any other speaker. Among the biggest barriers to the press's success under this framework is its difficulty in convincing courts that the government's action had the requisite potential to chill a person of "ordinary firmness." Attending to the government's self-interest in silencing critical coverage along with the press's vulnerabilities to such retaliation, however, can lead to different results.

Consider, for instance, the difference that negative theory could have made in *Baltimore Sun v. Ehrlich*.[33] There, the Fourth Circuit rejected a newspaper's challenge to Maryland Governor Robert Ehrlich's decision to bar state employees from speaking with two Baltimore Sun reporters because he was unhappy with those journalists' coverage of his administration.

The Sun's challenge emphasized negative theory concerns, taking pains to explain the burden of such actions on "small news organizations [that u]nlike *The Sun* ... do not have sufficient resources to attempt to withstand such a blatant attempt to influence their coverage."[34] Along the same lines, the amicus brief filed by The Washington Post described in detail how the governor's actions interfered with the press's checking functions in ways that ultimately harmed the public: "All [who report on the Maryland state government] have effectively been warned that if they are critical of the Governor or his administration, they too can be denied access to information that they need to do their job."[35] This brief also underscored the vulnerability of smaller news organizations to actions like the governor's, observing that "the problem is particularly acute for those newspapers covering state

32 *E.g.*, Revels v. Vincenz, 382 F.3d 870, 876 (8th Cir. 2004).

33 437 F.3d 410 (4th Cir. 2006).

34 Reply Brief of Appellants at *7, Baltimore Sun v. Ehrlich, 437 F.3d 410 (4th Cir. 2006).

35 Brief of Amicus Curiae Washington Post at *20–21, Baltimore Sun v. Ehrlich, 437 F.3d 410 (4th Cir. 2006).

government with small staffs [who] can ill afford to have the Governor blackball anyone they assign to the State House."[36]

Yet the Fourth Circuit rejected The Sun's claim, concluding that the governor's action would not have had a chilling effect on journalists of ordinary firmness. The panel held that "a reporter endures only *de minimis* inconvenience when a government official denies the reporter access to discretionary information or refuses to answer the reporter's questions because the official disagrees with the substance or manner of the reporter's previous expression in reporting."[37]

But an opinion attentive to negative theory concerns – in other words, an opinion attentive to the reasons to distrust the government's adverse treatment of the press or specific members of the press – would have supported a different result. More specifically, an opinion informed by negative theory would have recognized the threat posed to the press's checking function in general (and to the work of smaller news outlets in particular) when punitively denied access to the information that makes quality reporting possible. Today, nearly twenty years later, the precarious financial state of most media organizations means that nearly all press outlets – not just smaller outlets – are acutely vulnerable to such restrictions. In other words, a decision informed by negative theory could apply the traditional three-part anti-retaliation rule to conclude that the governor's action did indeed chill journalists of "ordinary firmness."

Note too that negative theory could also support a court's choice of an entirely different, more government-suspicious rule for evaluating such claims, as discussed above.[38] In other words, courts could choose to apply strict scrutiny – thus requiring the government to bear a heavy burden in justifying its action – when the government singles out specific press speakers for disadvantageous treatment due to the critical content of their coverage.[39] Indeed, this is the approach the contemporary Court purports to take for Speech Clause purposes whenever the government singles out specific messages for disadvantageous treatment.[40]

Relatedly, negative theory can inform courts' capacious understanding of the ways in which the government can retaliate against the press. For instance, negative theory can help us understand how, under some circumstances, the government's retaliatory lies, threats, or other speech can violate the Press Clause when they have the intent and effect of chilling journalists' and press outlets' critical coverage. Although the government's speech is generally exempt from First Amendment

36 *Id.* at *20.

37 *Baltimore Sun*, 437 F.3d at 420.

38 *See supra* notes 28–31 and accompanying text.

39 Reed v. Gilbert, 576 U.S. 155, 165 (2015) (announcing that, for Speech Clause purposes, the Court would apply strict scrutiny to all content- and speaker-based distinctions).

40 For an example, *see* Borreca v. Fasi, 369 F. Supp. 906, 910 (D. Haw. 1974) (applying strict scrutiny to, and preliminarily enjoining, a mayor's decision to deny a reporter access to news conferences based on the mayor's unhappiness with the reporter's coverage).

review, the government's speech can violate the Constitution when it interferes with its targets' constitutionally protected choices or opportunities in ways that would violate a constitutional right if the government's interference took the form of traditional lawmaking or regulation.[41]

More specifically, the government's speech can retaliate against press targets in violation of the First Amendment by changing the behavior of either of two sets of audiences: The government's speech may cause third parties to retaliate against the government's targets because of their protected activity, and the government's speech may directly silence their targets.[42] Examples of the former, for Speech Clause purposes, include the Mississippi State Sovereignty Commission's lies in the 1950s and 1960s to the employers, friends, families, and neighbors of civil rights activists – falsely asserting those activists' sexual misconduct, financial improprieties, or illegal drug use – to silence their speech advocating desegregation.[43] Examples of the latter include the government's threats of criminal or economic punishment directly against its targets.[44]

A Press Clause doctrine informed by negative theory would look for evidence of the government's retaliatory motives and chilling effects in its speech involving the press. For this reason, under some circumstances, the government's expressive attacks rise to the level of retaliation prohibited by the Press Clause not only if they directly threaten their targets but also if they have the intent and effect of causing third parties to retaliate – physically or economically – against the press.[45]

***

In short, a Press Clause doctrine illuminated by negative theory would reflect awareness of the government's incentives to retaliate against the press to disrupt the press's scrutiny of the government. And a Press Clause doctrine illuminated by negative theory would recognize the press's vulnerability to the government's retaliatory efforts to undermine its checking function. In this way, attention to negative theory can reinvigorate Press Clause doctrine by informing courts' choices of legal rules and by informing their application of rules once chosen.

[41] *See* Helen Norton, The Government's Speech and the Constitution 6–9 (2019).

[42] *See id.* at 106–12, 159–69 (discussing examples).

[43] *See* Helen Norton, *A Framework for Thinking about the Government's Speech and the Constitution*, 2022 U. Ill. L. Rev. 1669, 1683.

[44] Norton, *supra* note 41, at 159–62; *see also* David L. Bazelon, *FCC Regulation of the Telecommunications Press*, 1975 Duke L.J. 213, 214, 244–51 (1975) (detailing the negative theory concerns created "by a comprehensive system for the licensing of speakers" where those "who must obtain permission to engage in activity protected by the First Amendment are vulnerable to the various sub silentio pressures that prior approval permits" and documenting the Nixon administration's efforts to apply such pressure to the Washington Post and other critics).

[45] *See* Carroll, *supra* note 3 at 422–23 (discussing the ways in which government leaders sometimes urge their followers' violent reprisals against the press).

12

The Constitutional Exceptionalism of Religion and the Press

Amanda Shanor

Congress shall make no law respecting an establishment of religion, or prohibiting the free exercise thereof; or abridging the freedom of speech, or of the press; or the right of the people peaceably to assemble, and to petition the Government for a redress of grievances.[1]

The text of the First Amendment explicitly protects two foundational social institutions: religion and the press.[2] Since 2021, however, the Supreme Court has increasingly granted one of these two institutions – religion – a status of heightened constitutional privilege. In a series of cases, the justices have extended what commentators have dubbed "most favored nation" status to religious organizations and activities.[3] As a practical matter, this means that in any given circumstance, the government may not treat religious groups and activities less favorably than it treats the best-treated secular group or activity. For example, if a COVID-era regulation prohibited indoor gatherings of more than ten people but exempted grocery stores, under this line of reasoning the government must give the same exemption to houses of worship. The Court has, moreover, required this privileged treatment of religion regardless of whether the government's justification for the exemption applies or is relevant to the religious actor or activity.

I am grateful to Jack Balkin for the rich conversations that spurred this chapter and to Sandy Baron for organizing the forum that brought us together to discuss the future of the Press Clause. I am extraordinarily grateful, too, for the superb edits and suggestions provided by Sonja West and RonNell Andersen Jones and for the opportunity to be a part of this series.

1 U.S. Const. amend. I.

2 Civic groups that provide institutional organization of assemblies and petitions might be understood as an implied third.

3 Douglas Laycock is credited with inventing the most-favored-nation idea, though he opposes some of its later instantiations. Andrew Koppelman, *The Increasingly Dangerous Variants of the 'Most-Favored-Nation' Theory of Religious Liberty*, 108 Iowa L. Rev. 2237, 2242 (2023) ("MFN was invented by Professor Douglas Laycock"); Douglas Laycock, *The Remnants of Free Exercise*, 1990 Sup. Ct. Rev. 1, 49 (1990) (arguing "that religion [should] get something analogous to most-favored nation status. Religious speech should be treated as well as political speech, religious land uses should be treated as well as any other land use of comparable intensity, and so forth.")

This approach has been a sea change in religion law. Under late twentieth- and early twenty-first-century precedents, religion was deliberately treated as *un*exceptional, largely due to countervailing Establishment Clause concerns.[4] These cases dictated that the government was not only prohibited from favoring one religion over another but also could not favor religion over secular institutions or interest. Indeed, to avoid the entanglement of government and religion, the Court often permitted the government to treat religion *less* favorably – say, by providing government funding to pursue secular but not religious education.[5] That presumption has now flipped. Today, religion enjoys exceptional status.

In contrast, current law treats the other First Amendment institution – the press – as wholly unexceptional. However the press is defined – from newspapers to television to bloggers in pajamas to professional journalists[6] – it receives no greater constitutional protections than any other speaker. The Court has essentially read the Press Clause out of the Constitution, voiding its specific textual commitment, despite the absence of any countervailing constitutional provision parallel to the Establishment Clause. Until religion law's recent exceptional turn, the law's treatment of religion and the press were in some sense parallel. Recently, they have diverged, as press law has not kept pace with changes in religion law.

In this chapter, I argue that the press should be treated at least as constitutionally exceptional as religion, and I explore what such press exceptionalism might mean in practice.

In addition to both being named in the constitutional text, the press and religion share important sociological similarities. Both promote core components of the freedom of belief through *institutional* organization – religion protects self-determination of faith, while the press safeguards democratic self-determination. History also supports interpreting protections for religion and the press in parallel, as do the text of the First Amendment and Bill of Rights when read as a whole. Like much of the Bill of Rights, the First Amendment aims to protect forms of *organized* action, belief, and dissent – in religion, in the press, and in assembly – that could counter the power of the newly established federal government. In light of the Court's recent changes to religion law, courts and scholars should embrace a reading of the First Amendment that treats the press as the constitutionally exceptional institution that it is.[7]

4 Locke v. Davey, 540 U.S. 712, 718–19 (2004); *id.* at 718–19 ("[T]he Establishment Clause and the Free Exercise Clause[] are frequently in tension.… [T]here are some state actions permitted by the Establishment Clause but not required by the Free Exercise Clause.").

5 540 U.S. 712.

6 *See* Richard L. Hasen, *From Bloggers in Pajamas to The Gateway Pundit: How Government Entities Do and Should Identify Professional Journalists for Access and Protection in* The Future of Press Freedom: Democracy, Law, and the News in Changing Times 271 (RonNell Andersen Jones & Sonja R. West eds., 2025).

7 As discussed below, there are good reasons to treat the press at least as constitutionally exceptional as religion, if not more so, because there is no countervailing clause with respect

To identify how press exceptionalism should be organized, it is important to bear in mind that while the First Amendment's protections for religion and the press are structurally and functionally similar, they protect related but distinct values and institutions. The religion clauses ensure the institutional prerequisites of freedom of faith; the Press Clause protects the institutional prerequisites of democracy. For this reason, courts should shape press laws' exceptionalism around the role of the press as a democratic institution, focusing on how it uniquely supports and focuses informed public discourse, government accountability, and the robust exchange of ideas essential to self-governance.

12.1 THE GAP BETWEEN THE EXCEPTIONAL TREATMENT OF RELIGION AND THE PRESS

12.1.1 *The Advent of Religious Exceptionalism*

In the 1990 case of *Employment Division v. Smith*, the Supreme Court held that the Constitution does not require exemptions to generally applicable laws for religious actors. The Court explained that because of the wide diversity of religious beliefs in the country, "we cannot afford the luxury of deeming *presumptively invalid*, as applied to the religious objector, every regulation of conduct that does not protect an interest of the highest order."[8] Under *Smith*, courts should apply only rational basis review (which is highly deferential to the government) to generally applicable laws that incidentally burden religion. Shortly thereafter, the Court clarified that *Smith* applies only to neutral, generally applicable laws, not laws that "discriminate[] against some or all religious beliefs or regulate[] or prohibit[] conduct because it is undertaken for religious reasons."[9]

to the press as there is with respect to religion in the Establishment Clause. I bracket the question of whether recent religion law exemptions are correct. For reasons I articulate elsewhere, I do not believe that the freedoms of speech or association generally support exemptions from public accommodations or employment antidiscrimination laws. *See, e.g.*, Amanda Shanor & Sarah E. Light, *Greenwashing and the First Amendment*, 122 COLUM. L. REV. 2033 (2022); Amanda Shanor, *LGBTQ+ Need Not Apply*, REG. REV. (June 21, 2021), https://www.theregreview.org/2021/06/21/shanor-lgbtq-need-not-apply/; Amanda Shanor & Sarah E. Light, *Anti-Woke Capitalism, the First Amendment, and the Decline of Libertarianism*, 118 NW. UNIV. L. REV. 347 (2023); Br. for First Amendment Scholars as *Amici Curiae*, 303 Creative LLC v. Elenis, 600 U.S. 570 (2023), https://www.supremecourt.gov/DocketPDF/21/21-476/234114/20220819171031826_Creative_Amicus_Brief_SCOTUS.pdf.

8 Emp. Div., Dept. of Hum. Res. of Or. v. Smith, 494 U.S. 882, 888 (1990); *id.* at 879 ("[T]he right of free exercise does not relieve an individual of the obligation to comply with a 'valid and neutral law of general applicability on the ground that the law proscribes (or prescribes) conduct that his religion prescribes (or proscribes).'"); *see also generally* Gillette v. United States, *supra*, 401 U.S. at 461 ("Our cases do not at their farthest reach support the proposition that a stance of conscientious opposition relieves an objector from any colliding duty fixed by a democratic government.").

9 Church of the Lukumi Babalu Aye v. Hialeah, 508 U.S. 520, 532 (1993); *see also* Boerne (*Lukumi* applies to laws with "the object of stifling or punishing free exercise").

Both religious conservatives and liberals concerned about the disparate impact on minority religions have long criticized the Court's decision in *Smith*.[10] The recent turnover of the Court's membership, which established a solid 6-3 conservative supermajority that includes several members holding deep religious commitments, led many to speculate that *Smith*'s days were numbered.[11] Although the Court has not (yet) overruled *Smith*, in a series of cases it has adopted increasingly low thresholds for triggering religious exemptions. Collectively, these latest decisions have so dramatically expanded protections for religious actors that they have, in practical terms, nearly flipped *Smith*'s holding without formally overturning the precedent.

In the 2021 case *Tandon v. Newsom*, which Jim Oleske calls "the most important free exercise decision since [*Smith*],"[12] a majority of the Court formally adopted, for the first time, the most-favored-nation theory of religious exemptions.[13] Decided on the "shadow docket"[14] by summary order without briefing or argument, *Tandon* blocked California's COVID-related restrictions on in-home gatherings. The Court held that because the state permitted some secular businesses, such as grocery stores, to bring together more than three families, a three-family limit on in-home gatherings for any purpose, including religious ones, violated the Free Exercise Clause. The Court stated that "government regulations are not neutral and generally applicable, and therefore trigger strict scrutiny under the Free Exercise Clause, whenever they treat *any* comparable secular activity more favorably than religious exercise."[15]

Several months later, the Court extended and elaborated on *Tandon's* most-favored-nation approach in *Fulton v. City of Philadelphia*.[16] *Fulton* involved a challenge brought by Catholic Social Services to Philadelphia's requirement that

[10] *See, e.g.*, Laycock, *supra* note 3, at, 4, 50 (arguing that "oppressive laws may be enacted through hostility, sheer indifference, or ignorance of minority faiths" and that "[e]xemptions for secular interests without exemptions for religious practice reflect a hostile indifference to religion.").

[11] Thomas Berg & Douglas Laycock, *Protecting Free Exercise Under* Smith *and After* Smith, SCOTUSBLOG (Jun. 19, 2021), https://www.scotusblog.com/2021/06/protecting-free-exercise-under-smith-and-after-smith/ (observing that as of June, 2021, "five justices [have] said that *Smith* was mistaken, and there may be more."); Fulton v. City of Philadelphia, 593 U.S. 522, 545 (2021) (Alito, J., joined by Thomas & Gorsuch, JJ., concurring) (calling for the Court to revisit *Smith*); *id.* at 543 (Barrett, J., joined by Kavanaugh, J., concurring) (finding "textual and structural arguments against *Smith* . . . more compelling").

[12] Jim Oleske, *Tandon Steals Fulton's Thunder: The Most Important Free Exercise Decision Since 1990*, SCOTUSBLOG (April 15, 2021), https://www.scotusblog.com/2021/04/tandon-steals-fultons-thunder-the-most-important-free-exercise-decision-since-1990/.

[13] Tandon v. Newsom, 593 U.S. 61 (2021); Oleske, *supra* note 12.

[14] William Baude, *Forward: The Supreme Court's Shadow Docket*, 9 N.Y.U. J. L. & LIBERTY 1 (2015); Stephen I. Vladeck, *The Supreme Court Is Making New Law in the Shadows*, N.Y. TIMES (Apr. 15, 2021), https://www.nytimes.com/2021/04/15/opinion/supreme-court-religion-orders.html.

[15] *Tandon*, *supra* note 13, at 62.

[16] Fulton v. City of Philadelphia, 593 U.S. 522 (2021).

those who contract with the city to provide foster care placement services commit not to discriminate against certain classes, including LGBTQ+ couples. While explicitly declining to overturn *Smith*,[17] the Court held that because Philadelphia's foster care contracts included a "system of individual exemptions" available "at the sole discretion of the Commissioner," the city's antidiscrimination rule was not generally applicable. For that reason, strict scrutiny, rather than *Smith's* rational basis review, applied, and in the Court's view, Philadelphia had not sufficiently justified its refusal to grant Catholic Social Services an accommodation allowing it to refuse to serve LGBTQ+ couples.[18]

Many commentators have argued that the Court's adoption of the most-favored-nation theory of religious exemptions marks a radical change in religion law – and one with far-reaching consequences.[19] Douglas Laycock, the originator of the theory, has observed that "if a law with even a few secular exceptions isn't neutral

[17] Citing the need for a "more nuanced" approach, Justice Barrett filed a concurrence joined in full by Justice Kavanaugh and in part by Justice Breyer, in which all three disputed the "prevailing assumption" that, if *Smith* were overruled, strict scrutiny would apply to all generally applicable laws burdening religion. *Id.* at 543.

[18] *Fulton*, *supra* note 16.

[19] Note, *Pandora's Box of Religious Exemptions*, 136 Harv. L. Rev. 1178 (2023); Koppelman, *supra* note 3, 108 Iowa L. Rev. 2237 (2023); Stephen I. Vladeck, *The Most-Favored Right: COVID, the Supreme Court, and the (New) Free Exercise Clause*, 15 N.Y.U. J.L. & LIBERTY 699, 734 (2022); Oleske, *supra* note 12; Cary Coglianese & Daniel E. Walters, A *Trojan Horse from the Court's Conservatives?*, Reg. Rev. (June 21, 2021), https://www.theregreview.org/2021/06/21/coglianese-walters-trojan-horse-from-courts-conservatives/; Shanor, *supra* note 7. There is a broader literature on the most-favored-nation theory of religious exemptions. *See* Zalman Rothschild, *Individualized Exemptions, Vaccine Mandates, and the New Free Exercise Clause*, 131 Yale L.J.F. 1106 (2022); Mark Storslee, *The COVID-19 Church-Closure Cases and the Free Exercise of Religion*, 37 J.L. & Religion 72 (2022); Nelson Tebbe, *The Principle and Politics of Equal Value*, 121 Colum. L. Rev. 2397 (2021); Josh Blackman, *The "Essential" Free Exercise Clause*, 4 Harv. J.L. & Pub. Pol'y 637 (2021); Ira C. Lupu & Robert W. Tuttle, *The Radical Uncertainty of Free Exercise Principles: A Comment on Fulton v. City of Philadelphia*, 5 Am. Const. Soc'y Sup. Ct. Rev. 221 (2021); Zalman Rothschild, *Free Exercise's Lingering Ambiguity*, 11 Calif. L. Rev. Online 282 (2020); James M. Oleske, *Free Exerciee (Dis)Honesty*, 2019 Wisc. L. Rev. 689 (2019); Douglas Laycock & Steven T. Collis, *Generally Applicable Law & the Free Exercise of Religion*, 95 Neb. L. Rev. 1 (2016); James M. Oleske, Jr., *Lukumi at Twenty: A Legacy of Uncertainty for Religious Liberty and Animal Welfare Laws*, 19 Animal L. 295 (2013); Christopher C. Lund, A *Matter of Constitutional Luck: The General Applicability Requirement in Free Exercise Jurisprudence*, 26 Harv. J.L. & Pub. Pol'y 627 (2003); Alan Brownstein, *Protecting Religious Liberty: The False Messiahs of Free Speech Doctrine and Formal Neutrality*, 18 J.L. & Pol. 119 (2002); Vikram David Amar & Alan E. Brownstein, *"Most Favored-Nation" ("MFN") Style Reasoning in Free Exercise Viewed Through the Lens of Constitutional Equality*, Justia (May 21, 2021), https://verdict.justia.com/2021/05/21/most-favored-nation-mfn-style-reasoning-in-free-exercise-viewed-through-the-lens-of-constitutional-equality; Vikram David Amar & Alan E. Brownstein, *Exploring the Meaning of and Problems with the Supreme Court's (Apparent) Adoption of a "Most Favored Nation" Approach To Protecting Religious Liberty Under the Free Exercise Clause*, Justia (Apr. 30, 2021), https://verdict.justia.com/2021/04/30/exploring-the-meaning-of-and-problems-with-the-supreme-courts-apparent-adoption-of-a-most-favored-nation-approach-to-protecting-religious-liberty-under-the-free-exercise-c.

and generally applicable, then not many laws are."[20] And Cary Coglianese and Daniel Walters have argued that *Fulton* "opened the barn door for anyone with religious objections to escape from their duty to obey vast swaths of the law," because "provisions explicitly authorizing exceptions to otherwise seemingly general rules" are "rife throughout the law."[21] Without overruling *Smith*, *Fulton* and *Tandon* dramatically limited the contexts in which it applies.

The Roberts Court has expanded religious exceptionalism in other ways as well. It recently made it easier for employees to obtain religious accommodations at work under Title VII of the Civil Rights Act of 1964.[22] It broadened the contexts in which religious employers no longer need to follow workplace antidiscrimination laws.[23] It interpreted the Free Exercise Clause as requiring states to fund sectarian schools and programs if they fund nonsectarian ones.[24] And it protected a public school football coach from discipline for praying at midfield after games.[25]

Taken together, these shifts represent a revolution in religion law. In the eyes of the current Supreme Court, Derek Black has argued, religious rights are assuming "something of a superstatus"[26] in which the Court "seems to treat religious activity as preferred over all other activities, including the exercise of other fundamental rights." The Court has placed "free exercise rights at the top of a hierarchy of protected rights; free exercise can never be treated worse, but can be treated better, than other fundamentally protected activities."[27] Religion, in other words, has become constitutionally exceptional.

12.1.2 *The Currently Unexceptional Press*

By contrast, under current law, the press is constitutionally unexceptional. In *Citizens United v. Federal Election Commission*, the Court asserted that it has "consistently rejected the proposition that the institutional press has any constitutional privilege beyond that of other speakers,"[28] that "there is no precedent supporting laws that attempt to distinguish between corporations which are deemed

[20] Douglas Laycock, *The Broader Implications of Masterpiece Cakeshop*, 2019 BYU L. Rev. 167 (2019).

[21] Coglianese & Walters, *supra* note 19.

[22] Groff v. DeJoy, 600 U.S. 447 (2023). *See also* Bostock v. Clayton County, 590 U.S. 644 (2020) (suggesting a religious exemption might apply to religious employers who object to employing LGBTQ+ employees).

[23] Hosanna-Tabor Evangelical Lutheran Church and School v. EEOC, 565 U.S. 171 (2012); Our Lady of Guadalupe School v. Morrissey-Berru, 140 S.Ct. 2049 (2020).

[24] Carson v. Makin, 596 U.S. 767 (2022); Trinity Lutheran v. Comer, 582 U.S. 449 (2017).

[25] Kennedy v. Bremerton School District, 597 U.S. 507 (2022).

[26] Derek W. Black, *When Religion and Public-Education Mission Collide*, 132 Yale L.J.F. 559, 593, 596 (2022), https://www.yalelawjournal.org/pdf/F7.BlackFinalDraftWEB_gstabjb1.pdf.

[27] Amar & Brownstein, *"Most Favored-Nation" ("MFN") Style Reasoning*, *supra* note 19.

[28] 558 U.S. 310, 352 (2010) (quoting Austin v. Mich. Chamber of Commerce, 494 U.S. 652, 691 (1990) (Scalia, J. dissenting)).

to be exempt as media corporations and those which are not," and that such a distinction would raise constitutional concern as speaker-based discrimination.[29] As Sonja West describes,

> Under th[is] nondiscrimination view, the Press Clause does not function as an active protector of the press, allowing (and perhaps demanding) government efforts that enable the news media to do their job. Rather, proponents of this view see the Press Clause as an obstacle to government regulations that grant special privileges to select speakers including the news media. The right it secures, they argue, is simply the right of all speakers to be treated equally in their ability to publish speech.[30]

Eugene Volokh is a proponent of this nondiscrimination view. He construes the Constitution's mention of "the press" as "protect[ing] everyone's use of the printing *press* (and its modern equivalents) *as a technology*," rather than as a specialized industry or a social institution.[31]

12.2 THE PRESS AS A SOCIAL INSTITUTION ANALOGOUS TO RELIGION

The press should be understood as analogous not to other speakers but to religion. Just as religion is not just any type of belief system through which we can acquire values, morals, or ideas of right and wrong, the press is not just any speaker.[32] Both the press and religion fill fundamental societal roles as institutions that organize people into communities of common interests, beliefs, and purposes. These

[29] *Id.* at 352–53 ("[E]ven assuming the most doubtful proposition that a news organization has a right to speak when others do not, the exemption would allow a conglomerate that owns both a media business and an unrelated business to influence or control the media in order to advance its overall business interest. At the same time, some other corporation, with an identical business interest but no media outlet in its ownership structure, would be forbidden to speak or inform the public about the same issue. This differential treatment cannot be squared with the First Amendment.").

[30] Sonja West, *Favoring the Press*, 106 CALIF L. REV. 91, 93–94 (2018).

[31] Eugene Volokh, *Freedom for the Press as an Industry, or for the Press as a Technology? From the Framing to Today*, 160 U. PA. L. REV. 459, 462 (2012).

[32] Prominent constitutional thinkers, including Justice Potter Stewart, Floyd Abrams, Vince Blasi, and Sonja West, have argued that "the press is 'different' from 'everyone'; that it is, in a variety of circumstances, entitled to constitutional treatment distinct from that generally afforded those who exercise their freedom of expression." Floyd Abrams, *The Press Is Different: Reflections on Justice Stewart and the Autonomous Press*, 7 HOFSTRA L. REV. 563, 564 (1979); Vincent Blasi, *The Checking Value in First Amendment Theory*, 1977 AM. BAR FOUND. RSCH. J. 521 (1977); Sonja R. West, *Press Exceptionalism*, 127 HARV. L. REV. 2434 (2014); Potter Stewart, *"Or of the Press,"*26 HASTINGS L.J. 631 (1975); *Citizens United* at 431 n.57 (Stevens, J., concurring in part and dissenting in part); West, *supra* note 30, at 100 ("In other words, whether or not the Speech Clause allows for identity-based distinctions, the Press Clause is a clear endorsement of speaker categorization when it comes to the press. The Press Clause tells us that the government historically has, can, and sometimes must treat the press differently than other types of speakers.").

institutions not only structure and communicate ideas and values but also guide the attention and action of their followers. The press and religion are institutions that allow individuals to unite into groups with similar purposes, where they can accomplish common goals, meet challenges, and create meaning and community. Critically, both institutions provide essential platforms through which people can organize to oppose ideas, laws, or values with which they disagree.

It is important to recall that when the Bill of Rights was adopted, its rights applied only against the federal government, not the states.[33] As a result, the Bill of Rights juxtaposed the people and the states with the federal government, a contrast most explicitly seen in the Ninth and Tenth Amendments. The Bill of Rights protected the self-determination and resistance of the people as organized into self-determining bodies, including states and religious orders. This served a dual purpose: It protected the autonomy of subnational communities while also providing bulwarks against excessive federal power. The First Amendment protected both subnationally established religions and subnational republican governance.

As a whole, the First Amendment can be understood as privileging the protection of various forms of *organized* self-determination and dissent: in religion, in the press, and in assembly.[34] At the time of the founding, prior to the emergence of major political parties, the press and religion stood out as two of the most vital social institutions through which the people could stand up to more powerful actors. (Notably, the Second Amendment's protection of organized militias served a similar purpose.[35]) Seen through this lens, the First Amendment's parallel textual protection for "religion" and "the press" is a reflection of their similar social roles in fostering self-organization, self-determination, and self-protection.[36]

If religion is to be treated exceptionally, the press should be as well. In fact, there is justification for treating the press *more* exceptionally than religion. According to the constitutional text, the right to freely exercise one's religion must be balanced against the countervailing concerns of the Establishment Clause, which safeguards

[33] Most state constitutions protected the freedom of the press. David A. Anderson, *The Origins of the Press Clause*, 30 U.C.L.A. L. Rev. 455, 487 (1983). James Madison proposed another press clause that provided that "No State Shall violate the equal rights of conscience, or the freedom of the press, or the trial by jury in criminal cases," but it was not adopted. *Id.* at 483–84. Cf. Jud Campbell, *Natural Rights and the First Amendment*, 127 Yale L. J. 246 (2017) (discussing founding-era natural law conceptions of the freedoms of speech and the press). It was not until the first half of the twentieth century the freedoms of speech and religion were incorporated against the states. Gitlow v. New York, 268 U.S. 652 (1925); Cantwell v. Connecticut, 310 U.S. 296 (1940).

[34] *See generally* Burt Neuborne, Madison's Music (2015).

[35] Prior to District of Columbia v. Heller, 554 U.S. 570 (2008), the Second Amendment was widely viewed as extending only that far as well.

[36] This argument resonates with but is distinct from David Anderson's argument that the "case for constitutional protection of the press rests on its role as an organizer of democratic dialogue." David Anderson, *The Press and Democratic Dialogue*, 127 Harv. L. Rev. F. 8 (2014), https://harvardlawreview.org/forum/vol-127/the-press-and-democratic-dialogue/.

against governmental support for, favoritism of, or entanglement with religion. Yet the First Amendment's guarantee of a free press does not include a similar competing interest. At the very least, the exceptionalism of the press should be elevated to that of current religion law.

While the societal roles of religion and the press are similar, their specific purposes are not.[37] The Constitution protects the press as a *democratic* institution. Democracies depend on forms of discourse and shared reality. They require elements of a shared world – shared facts, shared concern, and shared focus – which form the basis and the possibility of collective action through governance.[38] It is for this reason that the First Amendment is "the guardian of our democracy."[39] The history of the origins of the Press Clause excavated by David Anderson supports this view.[40] As he points out, on the eve of the Revolutionary War, the Continental Congress explained the need for "the freedom of the press":

> The importance of this consists, besides the advancement of truth, science, morality, and arts in general, in its diffusion of liberal sentiments on the administration of Government, in its ready communication of thoughts between subjects, and its consequential promotion of union among them, whereby oppressive officers are shamed or intimidated, into more honourable and just modes of conducting affairs.[41]

Anderson elaborates that while the continental charters did not protect press freedoms, by the founding, most state constitutions did – explicitly as protectors of self-government:

> The first press clauses were written in response to a resolution of the Second Continental Congress, calling upon the states to repudiate the authority of the crown and establish their own governments. These press clauses were produced not merely as salutary additions to an existing order, but as part of the urgent process of establishing "such government as shall, in the opinion of the representatives of the people, best conduce to the happiness and safety of their constituents in particular, and America in general."[42]

The advent of press clauses during the Revolution and their adoption both in the federal and most early state constitutions demonstrates the perceived importance of the press to self-government.

[37] *See* Sonja R. West, *First Amendment Neighbors*, 66 ALA. L. REV. 357, 372–73 (2014).

[38] Prior to the rise of politically polarized media, a handful of mainline broadcast news channels created a relatively shared space of belief about facts in the world.

[39] Brown v. Hartlage, 456 U.S. 45, 60 (1982).

[40] Anderson, *supra* note 33, at 464.

[41] *Id.* at 463–64 (quoting *Address to the Inhabitants of Quebec* (1774), in BERNARD SCHWARTZ, THE BILL OF RIGHTS: A DOCUMENTARY HISTORY 223 (1971)).

[42] *Id.* at 489 (quoting SCHWARTZ, *supra*, at 229); *see id.* at 490 ("Throughout the formative period, the focus of discussion was on the role of the press in relation to the government.").

While religion and the press were adopted as parallel institutional bulwarks both of freedom and self-determination and against tyranny, the press serves a distinctly democratic purpose. For this reason, though the press and religion should be treated as institutional analogs for constitutional purposes, the doctrine should treat the press as exceptional in ways that reflect its organizing purpose to facilitate self-governance.

12.3 THE PRESS AS AN EXCEPTIONAL DEMOCRATIC INSTITUTION

What would be the practical result if the press was treated as exceptional in ways oriented around its constitutional purpose? What would "most-favored-nation status" mean for the press – that is, for the press to receive equivalently favorable treatment as religion does under current law?

At a conceptual level, most-favored-nation status for the press could mean a number of things.[43] It could mean (1) that if a law makes an exception for another speaker, the press must also receive that exception. That is, if any speaker receives a privilege, the press must as well. Or it could mean (2) that the press can, and sometimes must, receive rights or privileges that others do not. Courts and scholars should embrace both principles to harmonize press and religion law.

Practically, most-favored-nation status for the press could, for example, require that representatives of the press, however defined,[44] have privileged access to governmental information – at least, as in the religion context, where access to that information is provided to any non-press private actor. This could include access to governmental institutions, such as jails, prisons, and other governmental buildings, as well as government documents, such as Office of Legal Counsel memos or records of closed-door legislative deliberations. The Press Clause could function as a sort of constitutionally grounded sunshine law, allowing the press to access, disseminate, and provide a basis for public action on governmental actions.[45] A First Amendment doctrine that embraced the exceptional role of the press might likewise protect a reporter's privilege not to disclose confidential sources or exempt the press from surveillance or searches in some contexts – at least as long as any non-press actor also had the same privilege, as, for example, an attorney might in the context of attorney-client privilege.

43 *See* Koppelman, *supra* note 3 (analyzing different variants of MFN treatment in religion law and theory).

44 A question that has vexed press law, and for some augurs in favor of its unexceptional treatment, is the difficulty in defining "the press." *See* Hasen, *supra* note 6 at 1 ("One of the potential impediments to having the government grant special access or protection to 'the press' is identifying who counts as a journalist."). Defining religion faces similar difficulties, but this fact has not so far been understood to justify denying it exceptional treatment.

45 This might somewhat ameliorate the tendency of transparency laws to entrench economic interests, as David Pozen has found. David E. Pozen, *Transparency's Ideological Drift*, 128 Yale L.J. 100 (2018).

Most-favored-nation treatment for the press would also require the rejection of the current nondiscrimination theory of the press, which, as Sonja West has analyzed, prompted the Court in *Citizens United* to categorically extend First Amendment campaign expenditure rights to all corporations. Importantly, this could affect *other* areas of First Amendment law that currently depend on the equivalence of the press with all other speakers. Doctrine that recognized the exceptional status of the press could mean, for example, that campaign finance laws could limit non-press political expenditures more than press expenditures.

But press exceptionalism need not be constituted solely by negative rights against governmental action; it could require positive support for the press. Most importantly, it could mean constitutionally required funding for local news and public media. If a core purpose of the Press Clause is to disseminate shared facts and foster shared focus and concern – or, as the Continental Congress opined, "the advancement of truth, science, morality, and arts in general," the "diffusion of liberal sentiments on the administration of Government," "communication of thoughts" between citizens, and the "promotion of union among them, whereby" public officials can be embarrassed into "more honourable and just modes of conducting affairs"[46] – public funding of local journalism and public media could vitally advance that goal, particularly given the economic headwinds now facing the press.

First Amendment doctrine that embraced a most-favored-nation theory of the press might permit, or even require, market-structuring laws – such as antitrust, bankruptcy, or property rules – that facilitate and advance a flourishing press able to accomplish its constitutional purposes.[47] For example, press law might permit laws that require social media to pay news outlets. Or it might allow or require copyright rules that promote journalism, for example, by requiring artificial intelligence (AI) companies that rely on large language models trained on press creations to contribute to the support of local or public media as much or more than they are required to compensate non-press authors of training data.

***

The First Amendment's Press Clause provides explicit constitutional protection for the press as a fundamental democracy-enabling institution, just as the religion clauses distinctively protect religion as a central institutional protector of self-determination in the realm of faith and conscience. Given the current Court's recent embrace of religious exceptionalism – providing religious actors most-favored-nation status – there should be a parallel recognition of press

[46] *Id.* at 463–64 (quoting *Address to the Inhabitants of Quebec* (1774), in BERNARD SCHWARTZ, THE BILL OF RIGHTS: A DOCUMENTARY HISTORY 223 (1971)).

[47] *See* MARTHA MINOW, SAVING THE NEWS: WHY THE CONSTITUTION CALLS FOR GOVERNMENT ACTION TO PRESERVE FREEDOM OF SPEECH (2021).

exceptionalism. The text and history of the First Amendment, along with the structural role of the press in our constitutional system, support recognizing a special status for the press that is tailored to its democratic purpose. This press exceptionalism should permit, and may require, government action to promote a free and vibrant press that can foster the forms of discourse, shared knowledge, shared concern, and shared focus necessary for democratic self-governance.

13

The Other Press Clauses

Christina Koningisor

The Constitution's free expression clauses are famously bare-bones: "Congress shall make no law ... abridging the freedom of speech, or of the press."[1] The historical drafting record is likewise thin – the constitutional framers spent little time debating press protections at the Constitutional Convention.[2] Yet post-ratification, the paths of these two provisions have diverged. The Supreme Court has devoted substantial attention to the Speech Clause, interpreting it broadly to cover an array of activities. In contrast, it has largely ignored the Press Clause, reading it mostly as ancillary to the ever-expanding set of speech protections.[3] The Press Clause has little independent meaning today.[4]

Yet imagine a different text, with a different drafting history. What if the Constitution provided that "the liberty of the press shall forever remain inviolate,"[5] or that freedom of the press is "one of the invaluable rights of man?"[6] What if the Press Clause were a stand-alone provision, or the discussion of the meaning and scope of speech and press provisions had figured largely into the constitutional drafting debates?[7] Would protections for the press look different today?

1 U.S. CONST. amend. I.

2 *See* David A. Anderson, *The Origins of the Press Clause*, 30 UCLA L. REV. 455, 467 (1983) (noting that press clause protections were briefly debated, and speech rights were never proposed). *See also* Jud Campbell, *Natural Rights and the First Amendment*, 127 YALE L.J. 246, 250 (2017) (noting that "debates among the Founders" about the First Amendment "would seem to belie any broadly shared original understanding of speech and press freedoms").

3 *See, e.g.*, Branzburg v. Hayes, 408 U.S. 665, 704 (1972); Zurcher v. Stanford Daily, 436 U.S. 547, 565 (1978); Houchins v. KQED, Inc., 438 U.S. 1, 13 (1978). *See also* Sonja R. West, *Awakening the Press Clause*, 58 UCLA L. REV. 1025, 1027 (2011) (reviewing these cases and observing that "a majority of the Court has, in essence, dismissed the clause as a constitutional redundancy").

4 West, *supra* note 3, at 1027. This cuts against Chief Justice John Marshall's assertion in *Marbury v. Madison* that "[i]t cannot be presumed that any clause in the constitution is intended to be without effect." 5 U.S. 137, 174 (1803).

5 *See, e.g.*, Ark. CONST. art. II, § 6. *See also* Kan. CONST. § 11; Minn. CONST. art. I, § 3.

6 *See, e.g.*, Ark. CONST. art. II, § 6; Tenn. CONST. § 19.

7 *See, e.g.*, R.I. CONST. art. I, § 20 (providing stand-alone protections for the press).

Such language and history do exist – in state constitutions. All fifty states have adopted constitutions that explicitly shield freedom of speech and the press.[8] And nearly all of them contain language that is substantially different from the language of the First Amendment.[9] These state constitutions contain fifty separate speech and press provisions, each with different drafting processes and different histories of judicial interpretation.[10] Moreover, state constitutions contain myriad additional constitutional provisions – many without federal analogs – that both privilege and protect the press.[11]

Since the 1970s, members of the press have advocated for increased constitutional protections under the First Amendment.[12] Some of these efforts have been successful. Yet these rights have generally been extended to the public as a whole.[13] The Supreme Court has mostly rejected calls to read the First Amendment to extend exclusive constitutional protections for the press.[14] This has left the press without particularized constitutional shields for many newsgathering activities, like accessing prisons or shielding confidential sources.[15]

There are reasons to revisit these precedents today. The economic and political power of the institutional media has diminished in recent years, with local press institutions disappearing at alarming rates.[16] At the same time, attacks on journalists have increased.[17] In response to these growing pressures on the institutional media, scholars have turned their attention back to the First Amendment, asking, for example, whether the Press Clause could be "revitalized" or "awakened" to offer a more abundant set of rights and privileges for the press.[18]

8 *See* App'x A, State Constitutional Free Expression Provisions, https://knightcolumbia.org/documents/2nb16t1vb4.

9 The two exceptions are Hawaii and South Carolina. *See* Haw. Const. art. I, § 4; S.C. Const. art. I, § 2.

10 *See* App'x A, State Constitutional Free Expression Provisions, *supra* note 8.

11 *See, e.g.*, Cal. Const. art. I, § 2 (extending constitutional protection to journalists' confidential sources and information).

12 *See* discussion *infra* Section 13.1.3.

13 *See, e.g.*, Richmond Newspapers, Inc. v. Virginia, 448 U.S. 555, 580 (1980).

14 *See, e.g.*, Branzburg v. Hayes, 408 U.S. 665, 690 (1972); Houchins v. KQED, Inc., 438 U.S. 1, 13 (1978). *See also* Citizens United v. Fed. Election Comm'n, 130 S.Ct. 876, 928 n.6 (2010) (Scalia, J., concurring) (arguing that "freedom of the press" means "everyone's right to … publish").

15 *See Branzburg*, *supra* note 14, at 690; *Houchins*, *supra* note 14, at 13.

16 *See* Penelope Muse Abernathy & Tim Franklin, The State of Local News 5 (2022) ("Since 2005, the country has lost more than a fourth of its newspapers (2,500) and is on track to lose a third by 2025.").

17 *See* Kirstin McCudden, *Another Record Year for Press-Freedom Violations in the US*, Colum. Journalism Rev. (Jan. 12, 2022), https://www.cjr.org/analysis/2021-press-freedom-prior-restraint-arrests.php.

18 *See, e.g.*, West, *supra* note 3, at 1032, 1045. *See also* Christina Koningisor, *The De Facto Reporter's Privilege*, 127 Yale L.J. 1176, 1265 (2018) (presenting arguments in favor of revisiting *Branzburg* and recognizing a First Amendment-based reporter's privilege).

Earlier press law scholarship of this type focused on the meaning and scope of the Press Clause, including whether its drafters intended only to protect against prior restraints.[19] Professor David Anderson's landmark article from 1983 argued that the drafters intended the First Amendment to sweep more broadly. He contended that they envisioned constitutional press protections to operate as a structural check against governmental abuse.[20] More recent Press Clause scholarship has built upon this work, taking up related questions, such as how to define "the press" for constitutional purposes[21] and how the Supreme Court's perceptions of the press have changed over time.[22]

This work is rich and thoughtful, yet it focuses almost exclusively on the federal Constitution.[23] This chapter, in contrast, turns attention to the "other" press clauses, along with state constitutional speech protections and various other state constitutional provisions implicating the press. It asks how these various state-level protections might be utilized to protect the institutional press in new or better ways.[24] And it asks how the lessons of these state experiences might be applied back to the federal context.[25] In this way, the chapter plugs into two separate strands of scholarship.

The first is the small but expanding literature exploring the scope and meaning of the federal Press Clause.[26] The second is a larger body of work examining how state constitutional liberties offer expanded rights protection beyond what the federal Constitution guarantees.[27] This movement to expand state constitutional rights is

[19] *Cf., e.g.*, LEONARD W. LEVY, INTRODUCTION TO FREEDOM OF THE PRESS FROM ZENGER TO JEFFERSON xix, lvii (Leonard Levy ed., 1966) (arguing that the framers only intended the Press Clause to protect against prior restraints), *with* Anderson, *supra* note 2, at 455 (arguing that the drafters intended the press to operate as a meaningful check on government power and therefore sweep more broadly than a mere prohibition against prior restraint).

[20] Anderson, *supra* note 2, at 491.

[21] *See, e.g.*, Sonja R. West, *Press Exceptionalism*, 127 HARV. L. REV. 2434, 2453–62 (2014) (proposing a definition for who qualifies as the "press"); RonNell Andersen Jones & Lisa Grow Sun, *Freedom of the Press in Post-Truthism America*, 98 WASH. U.L. REV. 419, 460–72 (2020).

[22] *See, e.g.*, RonNell Andersen Jones & Sonja R. West, *The U.S. Supreme Court's Characterizations of the Press: An Empirical Study*, 100 N.C.L. REV. 375, 379 (2022); RonNell Andersen Jones & Sonja R. West, *Presuming Trustworthiness*, 75 FLA. L. REV. 799, 800 (2023).

[23] There are important exceptions. *See, e.g.*, Anderson, *supra* note 2, at 506–08 (chronicling the passage of state constitutional press protections); Sonja R. West, *The "Press," Then & Now*, 77 OHIO ST. L.J. 49, 65–71 (2016) (pointing to state constitutional press provisions for evidence of the "dual functions" of the Press Clause). For works examining specific state constitutional free expression provisions, *see infra* note 45.

[24] For a discussion of previous scholarship addressing various aspects of state constitutional free expression protections, *see infra* note 45.

[25] *See, e.g.*, West, *supra* note 3, at 1063–68 (applying lessons of state legislative definitions of the press back to the federal context).

[26] *See supra* notes 19–22 and accompanying text.

[27] A possible third strand of scholarship that is relevant here explores how the lessons of state laboratories of democracy are relevant to federal constitutional debates. *See, e.g.*, Joseph Blocher, *What State Constitutional Law Can Tell Us About the Federal Constitution*, 115

often described as "new judicial federalism." Supreme Court Justice William Brennan is widely credited as its founder, at least in the movement's modern form.[28] In his landmark 1977 Harvard Law Review article, State Constitutions and the Protection of Individual Rights, Brennan warned that the steady expansion of federal individual liberties' protections during the Warren Court had come to an end.[29] In the face of this federal rights retrenchment, he argued, state courts must take up the mantle of the progressive cause and construe state constitutional rights provisions to fill in these federal constitutional gaps. He urged state supreme courts to break with federal judges, even when interpreting analogous state constitutional provisions.[30]

Many did so. If the promise of state constitutional rights protection was overlooked at the time of Brennan's call to action, that is no longer true today. State courts have spent decades untangling the relationship between state and federal constitutional rights provisions.[31] They have developed a rich body of case law cataloging when and how state courts have interpreted state constitutional individual liberties provisions more expansively than their federal counterparts, as well as when they should.[32] Scholars have also developed typologies of different methodological approaches to state constitutional rights interpretation.[33] A wide variety of methods have been adopted, from "lockstep" interpretations adopting federal court constructions wholesale to "primacy" approaches that emphasize independent state

Penn St. L. Rev. 1035, 1036 (2011) (arguing that federal courts should look more often to the lessons of state constitutional law); Benjamin Silver, *Nondelegation in the States*, 75 Vand. L. Rev. 1211, 1215 (2022) (applying the "lessons of state nondelegation for the federal doctrine").

[28] *See* Stewart G. Pollock, *Address, State Constitutions as Separate Sources of Fundamental Rights*, 35 Rutgers L. Rev. 707, 716 (1983) (referring to the article as the "Magna Carta of state constitutional law"). Of course, there was ample previous state court precedent on this point, as well as previous scholarly exploration of independent state constitutional rights' protections. *See* Randall T. Shepard, *The Maturing Nature of State Constitution Jurisprudence*, 30 Val. U.L. Rev. 421, 422 n.5 (1996) (describing this earlier work).

[29] William J. Brennan, Jr., *State Constitutions and the Protection of Individual Rights*, 90 Harv. L. Rev. 489, 495–98 (1977).

[30] *Id.* at 502.

[31] *See* Fred R. Shapiro & Michelle Pearse, *The Most-Cited Law Review Articles of All Time*, 110 Mich. L. Rev. 1483, 1489 (2012) (showing that Brennan's article is among the most cited).

[32] *See, e.g.*, West v. Thomson Newspapers, 872 P.2d 999, 1006 (Utah 1994) (outlining the leading methodological approaches). *See also* Jeffrey S. Sutton, 51 Imperfect Solutions: States and the Making of American Constitutional Law 174–90 (2018) (describing the various methodological approaches employed to interpret state constitutions).

[33] There are many works addressing this topic. For some of the most prominent approaches, *see, e.g.*, James A. Gardner, Interpreting State Constitutions: A Jurisprudence of Function in a Federal System 180–275 (2005); Sutton, *supra* note 32, at 174–90; G. Alan Tarr, Understanding State Constitutions (2005); Robert F. Williams, The Law of American State Constitutions 135–232 (2009). *See also* Goodwin Liu, *State Constitutions and the Protection of Individual Rights: A Reappraisal*, 92 N.Y.U.L. Rev. 1307, 1310 n.15 (2017) (describing this literature); Jonathan L. Marshfield, *America's Misunderstood Constitutional Rights*, 170 U. Pa. L. Rev. 853, 873–74 (2022) (delineating between state constitutional "positivists," "pragmatists," and "constitutional universalists").

construction and give little weight to federal interpretations of equivalent provisions.[34]

This chapter mostly sidesteps these methodological debates.[35] It focuses instead on the specific context of state constitutional press protections.[36] Much of the "new judicial federalism" scholarship is subject specific. The courts' early jurisprudence in this area largely focused on the scope of criminal law protections, for example.[37] The Warren Court steadily expanded constitutional protections for criminal defendants, and in the face of the U.S. Supreme Court's retreat from this project, state supreme court judges asked whether state constitutions might fill the gap.[38] The legal scholarship followed suit.[39]

Since then, different substantive state constitutional provisions have captured judicial and scholarly attention at different moments. Today, for example, many advocates and scholars have turned to state constitutional privacy provisions as a potential source of reproductive rights protection in the wake of the Supreme Court's elimination of federal abortion protections in *Dobbs v. Jackson Women's Health Organization*.[40] And in the face of the growing climate crisis, advocates have

[34] *See Thompson Newspapers*, 872 P.2d at 1006 (describing these approaches).

[35] Such debates take different forms. Some scholars have argued in favor of lockstep interpretation only in the context of specific constitutional protections. *See, e.g.*, Michael E. Keasler, *The Texas Experience: A Case for the Lockstep Approach*, 77 Miss. L.J. 345, 367 (2007) (arguing in favor of lockstep interpretation for federal and state search and seizure protections). Others have argued in favor of lockstep interpretation only when state constitutional language closely tracks the federal text. *See, e.g.*, Gardner, *supra* note 33, at 6–7 (critiquing courts for "often appropriat[ing] and adopt[ing] federal constitutional doctrine as the rule of decision for state constitutional provisions not only when the state constitutional text is identical to its federal counterpart, but even when it differs in potentially significant ways"). Still others have argued that lockstep interpretation is especially problematic in the context of interpreting state constitutional structure. *See, e.g.*, Jonathan L. Marshfield, *America's Other Separation of Powers Tradition*, 73 Duke L.J. 545, 549–51 (2023) (arguing against a Madisonian inter-branch competition separation of powers justification for state constitutions, and in favor of a "public accountability" rationale that is more faithful to state constitutional history, text, and design). And so on.

[36] This chapter assumes that state court judges can and should construe state constitutional rights provisions independently, based on their own interpretive methods and precedents, and that there are a variety of acceptable methods of doing so. *See* Robert F. Williams, *Why State Constitutions Matter*, 45 New England L. Rev. 901, 905 (2011). Arguments against lockstep interpretation are especially strong where – as here – the federal and state constitutional texts diverge. *See* Gardner, *supra* note 33, at 6–7. In this context, forty-eight out of the fifty state constitutional press and speech provisions substantially diverge from the text of the First Amendment. App'x A, State Constitutional Free Expression Provisions (showing that Hawaii and South Carolina are the two exceptions).

[37] *See* Williams, *supra* note 36, at 905.

[38] *See* Liu, *supra* note 33, at 1308–09.

[39] *See supra* note 33 and accompanying text.

[40] *See, e.g.*, Robert L. Bentlyewski, *Abortion Rights Under State Constitutions: A Fifty-State Survey*, 90 Fordham L. Rev. Online 201, 203 (2022) (finding that as of 2022, all but one of the state supreme courts to address the issue had recognized a state constitutional right to an abortion).

looked to state constitutional provisions addressing public health rights or the right to a healthy environment as a promising source of new legal protection.[41] As the Supreme Court moves further to the right,[42] progressive scholars and advocates will most likely continue to look to state constitutions as an alternative source of rights protection.[43]

In the decades since Brennan's article, scholars and judges have also looked to state constitutional speech and press provisions.[44] They have asked whether these protections sweep more broadly than the First Amendment Speech and Press Clauses, as well as whether they should.[45] State courts have also explored the meaning of state free expression protections when construing state constitutional

[41] *See, e.g.*, Hari M. Osofsky, *Litigating Climate Change Infrastructure Impacts*, 118 Nw. U.L. Rev. Online 149, 163 (2023); Quinn Yeargain, *Decarbonizing Constitutions*, 41 Yale L. & Pol'y Rev. 1, 6 (2023).

[42] *See* Nina Totenberg, *The Supreme Court Is the Most Conservative in 90 Years*, NPR (July 5, 2022), https://www.npr.org/2022/07/05/1109444617/the-supreme-court-conservative.

[43] *See, e.g.*, Matthew Segal & Julie Murray, *State Supreme Courts Offer the Best Chance to Advance Rights*, Am. Civ. Liberties Union (May 2, 2023), https://www.aclu.org/news/civil-liberties/state-supreme-courts-offer-the-best-chance-to-advance-rights#:~:text=Each%20state%20has%20its%20own,or%20preserved%20under%20federal%20law. The Roberts Court has expanded First Amendment protections for certain speakers, especially corporate and religious speakers. *See* Citizens United v. Fed. Election Comm'n, 558 U.S. 310 (2010); 303 Creative LLC v. Elenis, 600 U.S. 570 (2023). In this sense, the First Amendment context is distinct from contexts like reproductive rights or climate change, where the Court has actively contracted federal constitutional protection. *See* Dobbs v. Jackson Women's Health Org., 597 U.S. 215 (2022); West Virginia v. Environmental Protection Agency, 597 U.S. 697 (2022). But the Roberts Court has not expanded First Amendment protection for all speakers, and it has not expanded protections for the press. To the contrary, some of the strongest voices for expanded religious and corporate speech protections have argued in favor of contracting First Amendment protections for press speakers. *See, e.g.*, Berisha v. Lawson, 141 S.Ct. 2424 (2021) (Thomas, J., dissenting from denial of cert.); *id.* at 2425 (Gorsuch, J., dissenting from denial of cert.).

[44] For articles comparing free expression provisions across multiple states, *see, e.g.*, Peter P. Miller, *Freedom of Expression Under State Constitutions*, 20 Stan. L. Rev. 318, 325–31 (1968); Todd F. Simon, *Independent but Inadequate: State Constitutions and Protection of Freedom of Expression*, 33 U. Kan. L. Rev. 305, 308 (1985); Kathryn Dix Sowle, *A Matter of Opinion: Milkovich Four Years Later*, 3 Wm. & Mary Bill Rts. J. 467, 519 (1994); Brady C. Williamson & James A. Friedman, *State Constitutions: The Shopping Mall Cases*, 1998 Wis. L. Rev. 883 (1998). For articles examining the meaning of state free expression provisions in a single state, *see, e.g.*, Jeremy J. Bethel, *Freedom of Expression in New York State: What Remains of People Ex Rel. Arcara v. Cloud Books, Inc.?*, 28 Fordham Urb. L.J. 1797 (2001); Michael A. Giudicessi, *Independent State Grounds for Freedom of Speech and of the Press: Article 1, Section 7 of the Iowa Constitution*, 38 Drake L. Rev. 9, 26–28 (1988); Joseph H. Hart, *Free Speech on Private Property – When Fundamental Rights Collide*, 68 Tex. L. Rev. 1469, 1470 (1990); Anthony W. Kraus, *Beyond the First Amendment: What the Evolution of Maryland's Constitutional Free-Speech Guarantee Shows About Its Intended Breadth*, 47 U. Balt. L.F. 83, 84 (2017); Seth F. Kreimer, *The Pennsylvania Constitution's Protection of Free Expression*, 5 U. Pa. J. Const. L. 12, 13 (2002).

[45] *See, e.g.*, Kraus, *supra* note 44, at 97–98 (arguing in favor of construing Maryland's free expression provisions more broadly than the First Amendment).

speech and press provisions.[46] But more could be done. Press advocates haven't always utilized these press and other state constitutional provisions effectively.[47] And state courts have often construed state constitutional free expression provisions in lockstep with the First Amendment, despite significant textual and historical distinctions.[48]

Further, legal scholars have largely overlooked state constitutional protections for the press. Some have compared the development of free expression rights in the state versus federal constitutional contexts for specific states.[49] Yet the scholarship examining state constitutional protections for the press is more limited.[50] This is true even though these state constitutional press protections offer crucial benefits. State constitutions can provide protection where the U.S. Constitution has failed. Many state constitutional press and speech provisions already sweep more broadly than the First Amendment under current state precedent. And many more could be reasonably construed this way.[51] Moreover, state constitutions are more easily amended in response to new or changing threats to the press.[52]

The lessons of state constitutional law can also be useful for advocates of expanded federal press protections. Many of the policy arguments advanced by the U.S. Supreme Court in the course of rejecting particularized rights for the press can be challenged by the experience of the states. The state constitutional experience offers alternative law and policy choices, distinct from the path the U.S. Supreme Court has chosen under the First Amendment. Mining these state law histories can be helpful for refuting the Court's policy-oriented claims and imagining alternative futures for federal constitutional press protections.[53]

This chapter proceeds in two sections. Section 13.1 outlines the text, drafting history, and interpretive precedents of federal and state press and speech clause protections, focusing attention where state courts have interpreted state constitutional press protections to sweep more broadly than the First Amendment. Section 13.2 examines the future of federal and state press and speech clauses. It identifies state constitutional provisions and precedents that could be seized upon by advocates to expand protections for the press. And it provides examples of ways that the experiences of the states can be used to bolster arguments for broader press protections under federal law.

[46] *See* discussion *supra* note 32 and accompanying text.

[47] *See* Sutton, *supra* note 32, at 8 (noting that most litigants fail to raise state constitutional claims when available and arguing that this is a mistake).

[48] *See, e.g.*, Howard Cnty. Citizens for Open Gov't v. Howard Cnty. Bd. of Elections, 201 Md. App. 605, 623 (2011); In re Letellier, 578 A.2d 722, 726, 17 Media L. Rep. 2169 (Me. 1990); State v. Turner, 550 N.W.2d 622, 628 (Minn. 1999).

[49] *See supra* note 45 and accompanying text.

[50] *Id.*

[51] *See infra* Section 13.1.3.

[52] *See infra* Section 13.2.1.

[53] *See infra* Section 13.2.2.

13.1 CONSTITUTIONAL PROTECTIONS FOR THE PRESS

Federal and state constitutions articulate very different textual protections for the press. This is true in terms of both press and speech clauses and more ancillary provisions like rights of information access. These state constitutions also have vastly different histories of drafting and judicial interpretation. This part maps out these distinctions across the federal and state contexts, focusing attention on the substantive areas where the states have extended press protections beyond what the First Amendment allows.

13.1.1 *Constitutional Text*

The Press Clause of the First Amendment provides that "Congress shall make no law . . . abridging the freedom . . . of the press."[54] It is paired with the Speech Clause, set off by semi-colons from both the religious clauses and the assembly and petition clauses that follow.[55] The U.S. Supreme Court has extended few, if any, substantive rights protections under the Press Clause alone.[56] Rather, press-related protections have been extended through some combination of speech and press rights. The Court has also repeatedly declined to extend exclusive constitutional protections enjoyed by press speakers alone.

In contrast, the states have taken a different approach. All fifty state constitutions extend protections for freedom of speech and the press.[57] But only two states – Hawaii and South Carolina – have adopted free expression provisions that track the language of the First Amendment.[58] The other forty-eight state constitutions depart from the federal model.[59] Many do so in ways that suggest strong protections for the press.

For example, many of these state free expression provisions protect a broader set of substantive rights than those contained in the First Amendment. Forty states protect the right to "speak, write, and publish" as three distinct components of freedom of expression.[60] A few state constitutions also make explicit the democratic role of free press provisions, specifying that the printing press must be free to those who wish to "examine" the work of "any branch of government."[61] Still others protect "the free

54 U.S. CONST. amend. I.

55 *Id. See also* West, *supra* note 3, at 1033–34 (arguing that the two semicolons suggest that the Speech and Press Clauses "were seen as sharing a commonality").

56 West, *supra* note 3, at 1028.

57 *See* App'x A, State Constitutional Free Expression Provisions, *supra* note 8.

58 Haw. CONST. art. I, § 4; S.C. CONST. art. I, § 2.

59 *See* App'x A, State Constitutional Free Expression Provisions, *supra* note 8.

60 *See* App'x A, State Constitutional Free Expression Provisions, *supra* note 8.

61 *See, e.g.*, Ky. CONST. § 8; Pa. CONST. art. I, § 7; Tenn. CONST. art. I, § 19.

communication of thought and opinion," which may encompass a broader set of activities than speech and press protections alone.[62]

Protections for the press are also articulated in stronger terms in some state constitutions. For example, Kansas' speech and press clause provides that "the liberty of the press shall be inviolate."[63] Virginia's stipulates that "freedoms of speech and of the press are among the great bulwarks of liberty and can never be restrained except by despotic governments."[64] And Mississippi's provides that "freedom of speech and of the press shall be held sacred,"[65] elevating free expression provisions to those "worthy of religious veneration."[66]

There are notable structural distinctions as well. Most state constitutions protect speech and press in a single stand-alone provision. Only two pair free expression with religious rights.[67] And one state, Rhode Island, protects the rights of speech and of the press in separate constitutional sections.[68] Such structural separation further supports construing press and speech protections separately rather than as coextensive rights.

Most state constitutions also articulate press and speech rights in positive terms. Only a handful contain an exclusively negative expression of these rights, analogous to the First Amendment's prohibition that "Congress shall make no law" abridging the freedom of speech or the press.[69] The rest articulate protection at least in part in positive terms. Around three-quarters of state constitutions provide that "every person" has an affirmative right to speak and publish freely.[70] And about half contain both negative and affirmative articulations. They provide that "every person shall be at liberty to speak, write or publish his opinions on any subject." And they provide that "no law shall ever be passed curtailing the liberty of speech or of the press."[71]

State courts have often found this negative/positive rights distinction salient when interpreting the scope of state constitutional press shields.[72] They have pointed to these affirmative constructions of state constitutional provisions as evidence of an

62 *See, e.g.*, De. Const. art. 1, § 5; Ind. Const. art. I, § 9; Tenn. Const. art. I, § 19. *See also* Utah Const. art. 1, § 1 (providing that all persons have the right "to communicate freely their thoughts and opinions").

63 Kan. Const. Bill of Rts. § 11.

64 Va. Const. art. I, § 12.

65 Miss. Const. art. III, § 13.

66 *See* Gulf Pub. Co. v. Lee, 434 So.2d 687, 696 (Miss. 1983).

67 Haw. Const. art. I, § 4; S.C. Const. art. I, § 2. *See also* R.I. Const. art. I, § 21 (combining speech, assembly, and petition protections).

68 R.I. Const. art. I, § 20 (freedom of the press); R.I. Const. art. I, § 21 (freedom of speech).

69 Haw. Const. art. I, § 4; Ind. Const. art. I, § 9; Or. Const. art. I, § 8; S.C. Const. art. I, § 2; Utah Const. art. I, § 15; W. Va. Const. art. III, § 7.

70 *See* App'x A, State Constitutional Free Expression Provisions, *supra* note 8.

71 *See id.*

72 *See, e.g.*, Davenport v. Garcia, 834 S.W.2d 4, 7–8 (Tex. 1992) (contrasting the affirmative expression of state constitutional rights with negative prohibitions contained in the First Amendment); Robert v. City of Norfolk, 188 Va. 413, 420, 49 S.E.2d 697, 700 (1948) (same); Immuno AG. v. Moor-Jankowski, 77 N.Y.2d 235, 249, 567 N.E.2d 1270 (1991) (same).

intentional decision by state constitutional drafters to provide broader free expression protections than those provided by the First Amendment. For example, New York's highest court has interpreted the state's constitution to offer stronger defamation protections for statements of opinion than the U.S. Constitution provides.[73] In doing so, it reasoned that these state speech and press provisions "reflect the deliberate choice of the New York State Constitutional Convention not to follow the language of the First Amendment, ratified 30 years earlier, but instead to set forth our basic democratic ideal of liberty of the press in strong affirmative terms."[74]

This is not to say that all state constitutional textual distinctions trend in this same direction, toward broader protection. Some contain more watered-down articulations of free expression rights. For example, a handful provide that the liberty of the press "ought" not be violated, in contrast with the more forceful prohibition contained in the First Amendment.[75] Many state constitutions also spell out the limits of these protections more explicitly than the First Amendment. For instance, forty state constitutions include language specifying that those who exercise speech and press rights are "responsible for their abuse."[76] And around half of state constitutional free expression provisions stipulate that truth must be accepted as a defense to libel, which some courts have read to be rights-contracting.[77] Yet overall, many of these textual distinctions and departures in state constitutions suggest expanded state-level protections for the press in comparison to the First Amendment.

13.1.2 *Constitutional Histories*

The First Amendment drafting history is thin. The drafters spent little time debating proposed press protections at the Constitutional Convention.[78] And the debates of the state ratifying conventions often yielded conflicting conclusions.[79] The drafters

[73] Immuno AG. v. Moor-Jankowski, 77 N.Y.2d 235, 255 (1991).

[74] *Id.* at 249.

[75] Md. Const. Decl. of Rts. art. 40; Mass. Const. Pt. 1, art. XVI; N.H. Const. Pt. 1, art. 22; Vt. Const. CH I, art. XIII.

[76] *See* App'x A, State Constitutional Free Expression Provisions, *supra* note 8.

[77] *See id.* Some courts have held these provisions are rights-contracting. *See, e.g.*, Ex Parte Tucci, 859 S.W.2d 1, 24 (Tex. 1993) (Philips, C.J., concurring) (arguing that the inclusion of such libel provisions "reflected the framers' rejection of a broad commitment to a vigorous, untrammeled press"); Commonwealth v. Blanding, 20 Mass. 304, 304 (1825) (emphasizing that the state constitutional provision protects only against prior restraints on speech). Others have interpreted these provisions to be rights-expanding because they broadened the common law rule in force at the time that truth was not a defense to libel. *See, e.g.*, People v. Croswell, 1804 WL 874, 391–92 (N.Y. Sup. Ct. 1804) (citing these truth-as-defense provisions as evidence of the drafters' commitment to freedom of the press).

[78] *See* Anderson, *supra* note 2, at 466–67 (describing two brief discussions on proposed press protections at the Constitutional Convention).

[79] *Id.* at 467–75 (describing press and speech clause discussions during the state ratifying conventions). *See also* Leonard Williams Levy, Legacy of Suppression 4 (1960) ("[W]e know very little ... about the original understanding of the First Amendment).

almost certainly intended to restrict prior restraints against speech.[80] But consensus has splintered from there over the original meaning of the First Amendment.[81] There is a vast literature plumbing these drafting histories for evidence of the federal constitutional drafters' original intent when enacting these constitutional press and speech protections.[82] Ultimately, much of the confusion likely stems from the drafters' own differing visions of speech and press protections.[83]

When it comes to the drafting histories of the fifty state free expression provisions, however, the interpretive task becomes even more difficult. There are fifty state press clauses contained in fifty separate state constitutions. Collectively, these state constitutions have been amended more than 7,000 times.[84] It is impossible to provide a detailed accounting of each of these histories. They are too varied, too long, and too complex. Yet even a cursory review yields some insights.

The earliest state constitutional press clauses were drafted during the revolutionary period, and these state constitutional provisions reflect the drafters' preoccupation with checking government abuse.[85] The colonists chafed at British control over the press, and revolutionary leaders seized upon the issue of press freedom both to shore up support for the cause and to distinguish themselves from British rule.[86] They declared freedom of the press to be "a great bulwark of liberty,"[87] necessary for the "ready communication of thoughts" among citizens.[88] And nine of the eleven state constitutions adopted during the Revolutionary War contained a press clause.[89] These state constitutions were "revolutionary manifestos."[90]

The state constitutional texts embody this revolutionary history. Pennsylvania's 1776 Declaration of Rights, for example, provides that "the printing presses shall be free to every person who undertakes to examine the proceedings of the legislature, or any part of government."[91] Virginia's 1776 Declaration of Rights declares that

80 *See* Erwin Chemerinsky, Constitutional Law 1177 (2020) ("It is widely accepted that the First Amendment was meant, at the very least, to abolish such prior restraints on publication").

81 *See* Campbell, *supra* note 2, at 250–51 (2017) ("After a century of academic debate, however, the meanings of speech and press freedoms at the Founding remain remarkably hazy.")

82 *Id.* at 250–51 (describing these scholarly debates).

83 *Id.* at 254 ("Debates about expressive freedom also were wide ranging because the Founders often vehemently disagreed about which regulations of speech promoted the public good.").

84 *See* John Dinan, *Constitutional Amendment Processes in the 50 States*, State Court Report (July 24, 2023), https://statecourtreport.org/our-work/analysis-opinion/constitutional-amendment-processes-50-states.

85 *See* Anderson, *supra* note 2, at 488–94.

86 *See* Bridges v. State of Cal., 314 U.S. 252, 264–65 (1941) (describing this history).

87 Levy, *supra* note 79, at 69 (quoting the Resolution of the Massachusetts House (1768).

88 Bernard Schwartz, The Bill of Rights 223 (1971) (reproducing *Address to the Inhabitants of Quebec* (1774)).

89 Anderson, *supra* note 2, at 464. Only two contained a speech clause. *Id.* at 508–09.

90 *Id.* at 489.

91 Schwartz, *supra* note 88, at 273 (reproducing the Pennsylvania Declaration of Rights, 1776). *See also* West, *supra* note 23, at 66–67 (noting that two press protections were contained in Pennsylvania's Declaration of Rights, one in the "rights" section, and another in the "structure"

"freedom of the press is one of the great bulwarks of liberty, and can never be restrained but by despotic governments."[92] And New Hampshire's 1783 Bill of Rights provides that "the liberty of the press is essential to the security of freedom in a state; it ought, therefore, to be inviolably preserved."[93] As Professor Anderson has argued, these early press clause provisions suggested that press freedom operated as a structural democratic check against governmental abuse.[94]

State constitutional drafting documents provide further support for this proposition. For example, William Cushing, the chief justice of the Massachusetts Supreme Court and one of the drafters of the Massachusetts Constitution, exchanged a series of letters with John Adams in 1789 about Massachusetts' press clause.[95] They asked whether truthful criticism of government could be punished under this provision. Both men concluded it could not, and they rooted their decisions in structural democratic concerns.[96] "The liberty of publishing truth can never effectually injure a good government," Cushing argued, but it might restrain a despotic one.[97] Adams agreed. Otherwise, "how are the characters and conduct" of elected representatives "to be known by their constituents, but by the press?"[98]

This is not to say that the drafters and ratifiers of these state constitutional press provisions envisioned a wholly expansive set of rights. To the contrary, they tolerated substantial punishment of printers who supported the British cause.[99] John Adams signed the Sedition Act, and William Cushing enforced it.[100] These drafting histories are voluminous and contain many contradictions.[101] Yet the authors of these state press clauses were expressly concerned with the implications of a free press for a functioning democracy. As Professor Anderson put it, the drafters "may not have been sophisticated enough to realize that true freedom of expression must include freedom for even the most dangerous ideas, but they had seen the connection between press criticism and political change."[102]

In contrast, the language of the First Amendment became abstracted away from these revolutionary era claims over the course of its drafting process. The initial "bulwark of liberty" language was dropped from the First Amendment text. The speech and press protections were then joined with other expressive and religious

section, and that these dual provisions support "two distinct purposes emanating out of a single concept of press freedom – protection of an expressive function and also a structural function").

92 *Id.* at 235 (reproducing Virginia Declaration of Rights, 1776).

93 *Id.* at 378 (reproducing the New Hampshire Bill of Rights, 1783).

94 Anderson, *supra* note 2, at 460.

95 *See* Levy, *supra* note 79, at 192–97.

96 *Id.*

97 *Id.* at 194.

98 *Id.* at 195.

99 Anderson, *supra* note 2, at 535.

100 Levy, *supra* note 79, at 198–99.

101 *See* Anderson, *supra* note 2, at 505 ("[T]he evidence is contradictory, and we cannot know whether the Framers intended to limit the courts and the executive.").

102 *Id.* at 535.

liberties.[103] Yet many state constitutions still contain these original declarations explicitly tying freedom of the press to the preservation of democratic self-governance and the prevention of governmental abuse.[104] The text and histories of these early press clauses suggest that these state constitutional drafters viewed the press as a key check against the threat of an oppressive government.[105]

Another key theme to emerge from these fifty distinct drafting histories is that state constitutions have been repeatedly altered and replaced over the course of 200 years. They have been amended at a much higher rate than the federal Constitution – an average of 115 times, versus the 27 amendments of the U.S. Constitution.[106] Of the original thirteen colonial constitutions, only Massachusetts' survives today. The rest have been replaced one or more times.[107]

This makes the task of ferreting out original intent difficult. Should a judge consider only the statements of the original drafters? What if other parts of the constitution were changed but the free expression clause remained intact? What does such legislative silence tell us? Such questions not only make it more complicated to identify original meaning but also make it more difficult to offer a coherent story about the drafting histories of these fifty state constitutions. Each state's constitutional drafting history merits its own book-length treatment. This chapter does not attempt to offer a comprehensive account, nor does it provide a cohesive or overarching story of free expression in the states.[108] Instead, it focuses attention on a handful of substantive areas where press privileges and freedoms have been most strongly implicated.

13.1.3 *Constitutional Interpretations*

State courts have diverged in their interpretations of state constitutional press protections. This part surveys these precedents, focusing attention on the substantive areas where state constitutional texts have yielded more expansive protections for the press than the First Amendment. These include protections for confidential sources,

[103] *See* U.S. Const. amend. I.

[104] Four still ensure that the printing press will be available to those who wish to examine government, for example. *See* De. Const. art. 1, § 5; Ky. Const. § 8; Pa. Const. art. I, § 7; Tenn. Const. art. I, § 19. Two refer to the press as a "great bulwark of liberty." N.C. Const. art. I, § 14; Va. Const. art. I, § 12. And one makes explicit that freedom of the press "can never be restrained except by despotic governments." Va. Const. art. I, § 12.

[105] *See* Anderson, *supra* note 2, at 490–92.

[106] *See* U.S. Const. amends. I–XXVII; Alicia Bannon, *Learning from State Constitutional Amendments*, NYU J. of L & Pub. Pol. (Apr. 18, 2023), https://nyujlpp.org/quorum/bannon-learning-from-state-constitutional-amendments/#:~:text=State%20constitutions%20are%20also%20far,contain%20more%20than%207%2C000%20amendments.

[107] *See* Bannon, *supra* note 106.

[108] *See, e.g.*, Gardner, *supra* note 33, at 1–22 (2005) (reviewing methodological questions that arise in the context of state constitutional interpretation).

recognition of constitutional rights of access, prohibitions against prior restraint, and protections against liability for defamation.[109]

Not all of these protections are press specific. Some, like protections against prior restraints and defamation liability, extend to all speakers. Yet in practice, they tend to have an outsized effect on the press. Courts have long assumed that press speakers are uniquely at risk when it comes to both defamation lawsuits and the effects of a prior restraint on publication.[110]

13.1.3.1 Reporter's Privilege

The U.S. Supreme Court has repeatedly rejected the press's claims to First Amendment-based protections for newsgathering processes, including protection for reporters' confidential sources and information. In its landmark 1972 decision *Branzburg v. Hayes*, the Court addressed the claims of three reporters who refused to comply with a grand jury subpoena to reveal confidential information and sources.[111] The journalists argued that such disclosures would imperil the journalist-source relationship and impede the free flow of information to the public. They appealed to the Court to recognize a constitutionally based evidentiary privilege for journalists' confidential sources and other confidential information.[112]

The Supreme Court declined to do so, at least in the grand jury subpoena context. It reasoned that such a privilege does not appear in the text of the Constitution.[113] Nor had the courts recognized such a privilege at common law.[114] For more than 200 years, the Court wrote, the press had "flourished" without a First Amendment-based evidentiary shield.[115] The press was "far from helpless to protect

[109] This is not an exclusive list. For example, state courts have extended broader speech protections on private property. *See* Williamson & Friedman, *supra* note 44, at 887–93 (1998). They have also protected obscene speech more broadly. *See, e.g.*, City of Portland v. Jacobsky, 496 A.2d 646, 653 (Me. 1985). This chapter focuses on the areas that have the greatest impact on protections for the press specifically.

[110] *See, e.g.*, New York Times Co. v. Sullivan, 376 U.S. 254, 294 (1964) (Black, J., concurring) ("The half-million-dollar verdict does give dramatic proof, however, that state libel laws threaten the very existence of an American press virile enough to publish unpopular views on public affairs and bold enough to criticize the conduct of public officials."); New York Times Co. v. United States, 403 U.S. 713, 717 (1971) ("In my view, far from deserving condemnation for their courageous reporting, the New York Times, the Washington Post, and other newspapers should be commended for serving the purpose that the Founding Fathers saw so clearly. In revealing the workings of government that led to the Vietnam war, the newspapers nobly did precisely that which the Founders hoped and trusted they would do.").

[111] Branzburg v. Hayes, 408 U.S. 665 (1972), at 667–80.

[112] *Id.*

[113] *Id.* at 689–90.

[114] *Id.* at 685–86.

[115] *Id.* at 698–99.

itself" and didn't require further constitutional protection.[116] "We are asked to create another [constitutional privilege] by interpreting the First Amendment to grant newsmen a testimonial privilege that other citizens do not enjoy," the Court wrote. But "this we decline to do."[117]

In the decades since, many federal circuits have recognized a First Amendment-based privilege in other contexts. They have narrowed the holding in *Branzburg* to grand jury subpoenas, recognizing a qualified constitutional or common-law privilege in other judicial proceedings.[118] But they have splintered widely in their interpretations of this privilege, leading to a patchwork and inconsistent set of case law from one circuit to another.[119] For example, five circuits have recognized a qualified First Amendment privilege in some criminal cases. Two have extended the qualified shield only in some civil contexts. And one – the U.S. Court of Appeals for the Seventh Circuit – has held there is no reporter's privilege for nonconfidential material.[120]

The states have pursued a different approach. Some have extended greater state constitutional protections for reporters' confidential information and sources. California, for example, has enshrined the privilege directly into its state constitutional text. Article I, § 2 of the state constitution provides that members of the press may not be held in contempt for refusing to disclose either their confidential sources or their unpublished information gathered in the course of the reporting process.[121]

The history of this provision is instructive. The California legislature enacted a statutory shield law in 1935.[122] But the courts began to push back, arguing that the law interfered with the judiciary's inherent constitutional authority to execute its judicial duties.[123] Judges began to hold reporters in contempt, in spite of the requirements of the shield law.[124] The public responded by passing a ballot initiative in 1980 constitutionalizing the privilege.[125] The pamphlet accompanying the ballot explained to voters that the Supreme Court had declined to recognize a First

[116] *Id.* at 706.

[117] *Id.* at 690. *See also* Zurcher v. Stanford Daily, 436 U.S. 547, 550–53 (1978) (declining to extend special protections against searches of newsrooms by police).

[118] *See Introduction to the Reporter's Privilege Compendium*, Rep. Comm. for Freedom of the Press (2021), https://www.rcfp.org/introduction-to-the-reporters-privilege-compendium/ (describing these precedents).

[119] *See* Koningisor, *supra* note 18, at 1197–98.

[120] *See* Mayze Teitler & Samuel Aber, *The Law of the Reporter's Privilege Is a Mess. A Federal Shield Law Could Help Fix It*, Knight Inst. (Aug. 13, 2021), https://knightcolumbia.org/blog/the-law-of-the-reporters-privilege-is-a-mess-a-federal-shield-law-could-help-fix-it (summarizing this case law).

[121] Cal. Const. art. I, § 2.

[122] *See* Cal. Evid. Code § 1070; initially codified as Cal. Civ. Proc. Code § 1881 (1935).

[123] Voter Information Guide, *Primary Election*, at 18 (June 3, 1980), https://repository.uclawsf.edu/cgi/viewcontent.cgi?article=1884&context=ca_ballot_props.

[124] *Id.*

[125] Playboy Enterprises, Inc. v. Superior Ct., 154 Cal. App. 3d 14, 20 (Ct. App. 1984) ("By constitutional amendment in 1980, provisions virtually identical to section 1070 were added to article

Amendment-based privilege in *Branzburg* and therefore enhanced state constitutional protection was needed. "If our democratic form of government – of the people, by the people – is to survive, citizens must be informed," the pamphlet stated. "A free press protects our basic liberties by serving as the watchdogs of our nation."[126]

While California is the only state to extend an explicit constitutional privilege for journalists, other state supreme courts have recognized an implicit privilege that derives from state speech and press protections.[127] Many others have enacted statutory shields, recognized a common law privilege, or extended protection through the rules of evidence.[128] These state privileges are often roughly equivalent to the scope of the qualified First Amendment privileges extended by the federal appellate courts.[129] But their boundaries can be distinct.[130] Moreover, these state provisions operate as an independent source of protection. This is significant, because the federal courts have been more reluctant in recent years to read *Branzburg* as extending constitutional protections for the press.[131] If the federal courts do roll back the scope of federal constitutional protections, such state-level shields will assume greater importance.[132]

13.1.3.2 Rights of Access

Throughout the 1970s, journalists petitioned the Supreme Court to recognize First Amendment rights to access government information. The Court repeatedly

I, section 2 of the California Constitution, elevating the newsperson's protection to the constitutional level.").

126 Voter Information Guide, *supra* note 123, at 19.

127 *See, e.g.*, In re Grand Jury Proc. (Ridenhour), 520 So.2d 372, 374 (La. 1988); O'Neill v. Oakgrove Const., Inc., 71 N.Y.2d 521, 524 (1988); Scott v. News-Herald, 25 Ohio St.3d 243, 245 (1986); Matter of Contempt of Wright, 108 Idaho 418, 419 (1985); Zelenka v. State, 83 Wis.2d 601, 617, 266 N.W.2d 279, 286 (1978); Winegard v. Oxberger, 258 N.W.2d 847, 852 (Iowa 1977); Opinion of the Justs., 117 N.H. 386, 389 (1977).

128 *See* Rep. Comm. for Freedom of the Press, Shield Law Statute, Comparison, https://www.rcfp.org/privilege-sections/a-shield-law-statute/ (listing these laws). For protection extended through the rules of evidence, *see, e.g.*, N.M. R. Evid. 11-514; Utah R. Evid. 509.

129 *See, e.g.*, Vaughn v. State, 259 Ga. 325, 326 (1989); In re Letellier, 578 A.2d 722, 726 (Me. 1990); State v. Turner, 550 N.W.2d 622, 628 (Minn. 1999).

130 *See, e.g.*, Opinion of the Justs., 117 N.H. 386, 389 (1977).

131 *See, e.g.*, McKevitt v. Pallasch, 339 F.3d 530, 532–33 (7th Cir. 2003) (critiquing generous lower court readings of *Branzburg*). *See also* Erik Ugland, *The New Abridged Reporter's Privilege: Policies, Principles, and Pathological Perspectives*, 71 Ohio St. L.J. 1, 4 (2010) (describing this shift in the federal courts' approach to the reporter's privilege).

132 Of course, state privileges don't extend protection in the context of federal subpoenas. However, such subpoenas are rarer. *See* RonNell Andersen Jones, *Avalanche or Undue Alarm? An Empirical Study of Subpoenas Received by the News Media*, 93 Minn. L. Rev. 585, 654 (2008) (showing that media organizations receive substantially more subpoenas from state governments than from the federal government).

declined to do so.[133] In the 1978 case *KQED v. Houchins*, for example, the Court rejected the press's claim to a First Amendment right to access prison facilities.[134] After multiple inmates died at a prison in California, the county sheriff curtailed journalists' access to the facilities.[135] A group of journalists sued, arguing that they had a constitutional right to access the prison. The Court denied the claim, holding that there is no First Amendment right of access to "all sources of information within government control."[136]

Two years later, in *Richmond Newspapers v. Virginia*, the Court did recognize a First Amendment right to access criminal trials.[137] But it made clear that the privilege extended to the public as a whole rather than to the press exclusively.[138] Moreover, the lower courts have largely limited the privilege to the judicial branch.[139] With a few exceptions for trial-like administrative proceedings like immigration hearings, the lower federal courts have not extended the right of access to the executive or legislative branches.[140]

Many states, in contrast, have extended constitutional access rights more broadly. A handful have enshrined rights of information access directly into the state constitutional text. At least six state constitutions contain explicit "right-to-know" provisions, which impose constitutional obligations on governments to provide public access to government records and proceedings.[141] These rights are often articulated in expansive terms. Louisiana's constitution, for example, provides that "no person shall be denied the right to observe the deliberations of public bodies and examine public documents, except in cases established by law."[142] These state right-to-know provisions can be used by courts to expand access rights beyond the federal minimum. Courts in these states often reference these constitutional provisions to

[133] *See, e.g.*, Pell v. Procunier, 417 U.S. 817, 822, 834 (1974); Saxbe v. Washington Post Co., 417 U.S. 843, 850 (1974); Houchins v. KQED, Inc., 438 U.S. 1, 7–8, (1978).

[134] *KQED*, 438 U.S. at 14.

[135] *Id.* at 3–5.

[136] *Id.* at 9.

[137] Richmond Newspapers, Inc. v. Virginia, 448 U.S. 555, 580 (1980).

[138] *Id.* at 575.

[139] *See* Rep. Comm. for Freedom of the Press, The Roots of Access Rights, https://www.rcfp.org/open-court-sections/a-the-roots-of-access-rights/ (describing the evolution of constitutional right of access law in the various circuits).

[140] *See, e.g.*, *See* Christopher Dunn, *Column: Rediscovering the First Amendment Right of Access*, N.Y.C.L. Union (Aug. 4, 2011), https://www.nyclu.org/en/publications/column-rediscovering-first-amendment-right-access-new-york-law-journal (describing a handful of court decisions extending constitutional access rights to administrative proceedings like immigration hearings).

[141] Cal. Const. art. I, § 3; Fla. Const. art. I, § 24; La. Const. art. XII, § 3; Mont. Const. art. II, § 9; N.H. Const. pt. 1, art. 8; N.D. Const. art. XI, § 6. Another two states contain more narrow provisions providing access to state financial records and expenditures. *See* Ill. Const. art. VIII, § 1; Mich. Const. art. IX, § 23.

[142] La. Const. Ann. art. XII, § 3.

underscore the sweeping nature of the transparency obligations imposed on state and local governments.[143]

Some state constitutions contain broader legislative transparency requirements as well. For example, Article I, § 5 of the U.S. Constitution provides that legislators may close proceedings when "in their Judgment" the discussion "require[s] Secrecy."[144] But equivalent state provisions do not always permit state legislatures this same discretion to close legislative doors.[145] Further, some state legislative access provisions expressly contemplate the unique position of the press. Alabama's constitution, for example, provides that under certain conditions the legislative houses may exclude the public from its proceedings, but they may not exclude "representatives of the press."[146]

There are other salient distinctions between federal and state constitutional access provisions as well. While the federal constitutional right of access is derived from the text of the First Amendment,[147] for example, roughly half of state constitutions contain express "open courts" provisions.[148] State courts, moreover, have often interpreted these requirements broadly. For instance, in Washington, the courts have held that the constitutional open-courts provision requires judges to proceed through a rigorous five-step analysis before they may exclude the public from access to certain court proceedings.[149]

State rights of access may also reach a greater set of government actors. The First Amendment right of access is limited to the judicial branch.[150] But many state constitutional access provisions extend further. At times this is explicit. For example, Missouri's constitution expressly states that legislative records are public records.[151] Voters made the change in 2018 after the legislature tried to exempt itself from the state public records law.[152] And Kentucky's constitution provides that a governor who grants pardons or commutes sentences must make the supporting records available

[143] *See, e.g.*, Herrmann v. Superior Ct. of Imperial Cnty., 75 Cal. App. 5th 535, 543, 290 Cal. Rptr. 3d 597, 603 (2022); Bd. of Trustees, Jacksonville Police & Fire Pension Fund v. Lee, 189 So. 3d 120, 125 (Fla. 2016).

[144] U.S. Const. art. I, § 5.

[145] *See* Idaho Const. art. III, § 12; Mo. Const. art. III, § 19; Nev. Const. art. IV, § 15; Or. Const. art. IV, § 14; Tex. Const. art. III, § 16.

[146] Ala. Const. § 57.

[147] Richmond Newspapers, Inc. v. Virginia, 448 U.S. 555, 580 (1980).

[148] App'x B, State Constitutional Open Government Provisions, https://knightcolumbia.org/documents/1aod4m2wyq. These clauses, too, are generally framed in broad terms, providing that courts shall be open to "every person." *Id.*

[149] Seattle Times Co. v. Ishikawa, 97 Wash. 2d 30, 37 (1982).

[150] *See* discussion *supra* notes 140–141 and accompanying text.

[151] Mo. Const. art. III, § 19.

[152] *See* Jason Hancock, *Bill Carving Some Legislative Records out of Missouri Sunshine Law Advances in Senate*, Missouri Independent (Feb. 27, 2023), https://missouriindependent.com/2023/02/27/bill-carving-some-legislative-records-out-of-missouri-sunshine-law-advances-in-senate/.

to the public.[153] Such provisions make clear that constitutional access requirements extend beyond the judicial branch.

Finally, implicit state constitutional rights of access – those that derive from explicit press and speech provisions – may also sweep more broadly than the federal constitutional right of access. For example, the Utah Supreme Court has held its state constitution requires additional factual showings before a court may order the press not to disseminate information about a trial, beyond what the First Amendment requires.[154] Taken together, these various state-level constitutional rights of information access can have important implications for the press's ability to engage in newsgathering efforts.

13.1.3.3 Prior Restraints

Under the First Amendment, prior restraints against publication are presumptively unconstitutional. But they are not prohibited outright. In *Near v. Minnesota*, the U.S. Supreme Court struck down a prior restraint on the publication of a magazine.[155] But it recognized there may be times where such restrictions were permissible, such as when protecting "the number and location of troops" in wartime.[156] Decades later, the Court reaffirmed its holding in the Pentagon Papers case,[157] holding once again that prior restraints are constitutionally disfavored but not categorically prohibited.[158]

A handful of states have taken a different approach. They have interpreted state constitutional free expression provisions to create an absolute prohibition against prior restraints. As early as 1805, for example, the Pennsylvania Supreme Court read the state's press provision to mean that citizens were free to "publish as [they] please in the first instance without control."[159] Later that century, the California Supreme Court held that the state constitution's speech and press provision forbids all prior government restraints on speech.[160] It reasoned that the First Amendment and the state constitution contained very different textual provisions. The state constitutional provision provided that "every citizen may freely speak, write, and publish his sentiments on all subjects." And the state supreme court concluded that the plain

[153] Ky. Const. § 77.

[154] KUTV, Inc. v. Wilkinson, 686 P.2d 456, 461–62 (Utah 1984) ("In addition, for purposes of our own constitutional direction that "[n]o law shall be passed to abridge or restrain the freedom of speech or of the press," Utah Const. art. I, § 15, we add a fourth test pertaining to during-trial publicity.")

[155] 283 U.S. 697, 715 (1931).

[156] *Id.* at 716.

[157] New York Times Co. v. United States, 403 U.S. 713, 714 (1971).

[158] *Id.*

[159] Respublica v. Dennie, 1805 WL 911, at *3 (Pa. 1805).

[160] Dailey v. Superior Ct. of City & Cnty. of San Francisco, 112 Cal. 94, 97 (1896).

language of this provision made clear that a citizen "shall have no censor over him to whom he must apply for permission."[161]

Other states followed suit, rooting their decisions in textual distinctions between the federal and state speech and press provisions. Arizona's constitution, for example, provides that "every person may freely speak, write, and publish on all subjects."[162] The state supreme court has read this language to mean that "there can be no censor appointed to whom the press must apply for prior permission to publish."[163] Similarly, the Washington Supreme Court has read its free expression provision to "rule out prior restraints under *any* circumstances."[164] And the Missouri Supreme Court has read its constitutional protections for speech and the press to operate as "an affirmative prescription against any exception."[165]

These decisions do not rule out the possibility of post-publication liability. To the contrary, most state constitutions provide that individuals are "responsible for the abuse" of speech and press rights.[166] But in terms of ex ante restraints on speech, some state supreme courts have held that their state constitutional free speech and press provisions sweep more broadly than the First Amendment.

13.1.3.4 Defamation

Some state constitutions also extend broader protections against defamation liability than those provided by the First Amendment. In *The New York Times Co. v. Sullivan*, the Supreme Court held that the First Amendment required government officials to show "actual malice," or either knowledge of the truth or reckless disregard for the truth, in order to prevail in a defamation suit.[167] The Court reasoned that aggressive libel lawsuits by government officials would have the effect of chilling public speech and criticism.[168] A decade later in *Gertz v. Welch*, the Court extended the requirement to public figures more broadly.[169]

In the decades since, *Sullivan* and its progeny have offered broad protections for the media to aggressively critique the government. They have also made it difficult for many defamation plaintiffs to prevail. The lower courts have expanded the definition of "public figure" to encompass many private figures unwittingly dragged

[161] *Id.*
[162] Ariz. Const. art. II, § 6.
[163] Phoenix Newspapers, Inc. v. Superior Ct. In & For Maricopa Cnty., 101 Ariz. 257, 259 (1966).
[164] *See* State v. Coe, 101 Wash. 2d 364, 374 (1984).
[165] Marx & Haas Jeans Clothing Co. v. Watson, 168 Mo. 133, 67 S.W. 391, 393 (1902). *See also* Lindsay & Co. v. Montana Fed'n of Lab., 37 Mont. 264, 96 P. 127, 131 (1908) (reading state constitution to prohibit all prior restraints).
[166] *See* discussion *supra* notes 77–78 and accompanying text.
[167] New York Times Co. v. Sullivan, 376 U.S. 254, 280 (1964).
[168] *Id.* at 282.
[169] 418 U.S. 323, 344–47 (1974).

into a public controversy.[170] At the same time, the media landscape has also changed in important ways in recent years.[171] Some critics have pointed to these legal and societal changes to argue that *Sullivan* should be overturned. Most notably, Justices Clarence Thomas and Neil Gorsuch have attacked *Sullivan* on both historical and empirical grounds, arguing that the press no longer deserves such insulation against defamation liability.[172]

There is no indication that *Sullivan* is at imminent risk of being reversed.[173] But if it were to be overturned, state constitutional defamation law would take on new salience. Any loss of federal constitutional rights would put new pressure on the equivalent state constitutional provisions.[174] State constitutional speech and press provisions could act as a partial safety net against the threat of federal constitutional retrenchment of First Amendment rights.

Many state courts would likely retain actual malice requirements under their state constitutions, even if *Sullivan* were to be cast aside. Actual malice requirements originated in the states.[175] Although these early state court decisions were mostly rooted in common law rather than in state constitutional protections, these decisions predate *Sullivan* and would likely survive its repeal.[176] Further, state supreme courts have not had reason to weigh in on whether their state constitutions independently require actual malice. The First Amendment sets the constitutional floor, and any equivalent state law defamation protections would be redundant.[177] But the repeal of *Sullivan* would force state courts to confront this question. And it is likely that many would find that actual malice requirements persisted under state constitutional law, especially in states with a long tradition of extending broad speech and press protections.[178]

This is not the only way that state constitutions implicate defamation liability. State courts have also interpreted state free expression provisions to provide broader protections against defamation suits. One example is state constitutional protection

[170] *See* Berisha v. Lawson, 141 S.Ct. 2424, 2425 (2021) (Thomas, J., dissenting from denial of certiorari) (critiquing this line of cases in part for extending the definition of public figure too far).

[171] *See* Penelope Muse Abernathy, The State of Local News (2023), https://localnewsinitiative.northwestern.edu/projects/state-of-local-news/2023/report/.

[172] Berisha v. Lawson, 141 S.Ct. 2424, 2425–30 (2021) (Gorsuch, J., dissenting).

[173] *See id.* (garnering only two votes); Counterman v. Colorado, 600 U.S. 66, 143 S.Ct. 2106, 2109 (2023)(affirming *Sullivan*).

[174] *See* discussion *supra* notes 29–31 and accompanying text.

[175] *See* New York Times Co. v. Sullivan, 376 U.S. 254, 280 n.20 (1964) (listing these decisions).

[176] *See id.* Further, some of these state court decisions did address the state press and speech clauses in the context of actual malice. *See, e.g.*, Coleman v. MacLennan, 98 P. 281, 284 (Kan. 1908).

[177] *See* New York Times Co. v. Sullivan, 376 U.S. 254 (1964).

[178] *See, e.g.*, Beach v. Shanley, 62 N.Y.2d 241, 255, 465 N.E.2d 304 (1984) ("This State has long provided one of the most hospitable climates for the free exchange of ideas.") (Wachtler, J., concurring).

for statements of opinion. Until the 1980s, the federal lower courts offered extensive protections under the First Amendment.[179] The leading case was a U.S. Court of Appeals for the District of Columbia Circuit opinion that held that the First Amendment provided absolute immunity from defamation liability for opinion-based claims.[180] The D.C. Circuit case also articulated a four-part test for determining whether a statement qualified for this opinion-based protection.[181] Many other federal circuits and state supreme courts adopted this approach.

But the Supreme Court overruled the D.C. Circuit opinion in 1990, in *Milkovich v. Lorain Journal*.[182] It articulated a narrower conception of opinion protection instead, one that turned on whether a statement was provably false.[183] The decision sowed confusion in the lower courts.[184] And a number of state supreme courts eschewed this new approach, adhering instead to the more press-protective D.C. Circuit standard when it came to state constitutional defamation protections.[185]

Notably, these state courts often rooted these decisions in textual and historical features unique to their state. New York's highest court, for example, reasoned that the state constitution's free expression provision articulates protection in "strong affirmative terms," unlike the First Amendment's negative prohibition against government interference.[186] The state court also described the state's long history of press protection and New York City's role as the "cultural center for the Nation."[187] Such textual, historical, and cultural features distinct to the state, the court reasoned, weighed in favor of broader state constitutional protection against defamation liability.[188]

Other state courts adopted similar reasoning. They held that their state constitutions, too, provided more robust protection against defamation liability. They likewise rooted these decisions in their states' unique history and distinct constitutional texts. The Rhode Island Supreme Court, for example, emphasized that its colony had been founded by religious "dissenters" and that the "free flow of opinion and debate" had been especially "vital" to the state.[189] And the Utah Supreme Court cited the state's tradition of aggressive editorial dissent between newspapers representing Mormon and non-Mormon interests when justifying

[179] Olman v. Evans, 750 F.2d 970 (D.C. Cir. 1984), *cert. denied*, 471 U.S. 1127 (1985).
[180] *Id.* at 971.
[181] *Id.* at 979–84.
[182] Milkovich v. Lorain J. Co., 497 U.S. 1 (1990).
[183] *Id.* at 19–20.
[184] *See* Kraus, *supra* note 44, at 94.
[185] *See, e.g.*, Immuno AG. v. Moor-Jankowski, 77 N.Y.2d 235, 261 (1991); West v. Thomson Newspapers, 872 P.2d 999, 1014 (Utah 1994); Dow v. New Haven Indep., Inc., 41 Conn. Supp. 31, 44 (Ct. Super. Ct. 1987).
[186] Immuno AG. v. Moor-Jankowski, 77 N.Y.2d 235, 249 (1991).
[187] *Id.*
[188] *Id.* at 249–52.
[189] Beattie v. Fleet Nat. Bank, 746 A.2d 717, 724 (R.I. 2000).

recognizing broader defamation protections for statements of opinion than the First Amendment provided.[190]

13.2 THE FUTURE OF CONSTITUTIONAL PRESS PROTECTIONS

State constitutions already operate as a source of independent protection for the press. Press advocates could do more to capitalize on these constitutional provisions. They could utilize state constitutions to extend new or expanded protections for the press. They could also mine the experience of the states and the history of state constitutional experimentation to bolster arguments for expanded federal press protections.

13.2.1 *The Future of State Constitutional Press Protections*

Textual and historical distinctions between federal and state constitutions have sometimes yielded broad protections for the press, beyond what the First Amendment provides. Further, certain states have also developed strong traditions of press protection, ones rooted in the distinct cultural or political features of the state.[191] But these efforts could be expanded. Press advocates could be more aggressive in raising state constitutional claims.[192] State courts could interpret these textual and historical distinctions to offer broader constitutional protections for the press. And voters could amend state constitutions in response to new or growing threats to journalism.[193]

When it comes to state constitutional texts, there is significant overlap in the fifty state constitutional free expression provisions.[194] States that have already offered broader protections can serve as a roadmap for other states to follow. Decisions expanding press protections in one state can be utilized when advocating for similar recognition in another, especially when the textual language is closely aligned. For example, New York's supreme court invoked the state's "strong affirmative" right to "speak, write, and publish on all subjects" when extending strong protections for statements of opinion.[195] Thirty-nine other state constitutions contain this same

[190] West v. Thomson Newspapers, 872 P.2d 999, 1014 (Utah 1994).

[191] *See, e.g.*, Beach v. Shanley, 62 N.Y.2d 241, 255, 465 N.E.2d 304 (1984) ("This State has long provided one of the most hospitable climates for the free exchange of ideas.") (Wachtler, J., concurring).

[192] *See, e.g.*, Robert I. Berdon, *Freedom of the Press and the Connecticut Constitution*, 26 CONN. L. REV. 659, 669 (1994) (describing the problem of litigants not raising possible state constitutional press claims).

[193] *See* Jessica Bulman-Pozen & Miriam Seifter, *The Right to Amend State Constitutions*, 133 YALE L.J. FORUM 191, 195–201 (2023) (describing these amendment rights).

[194] *See* App'x A, State Constitutional Free Expression Provisions, *supra* note 8.

[195] Immuno AG. v. Moor-Jankowski, 77 N.Y.2d 235, 249 (1991).

provision, articulated in the same affirmative terms.[196] Yet only a few have followed suit. Press advocates in those other states could look to New York's decision for guidance when raising similar claims.[197]

Press advocates could also raise novel claims for protection, ones rooted in the unique textual or structural features of the state constitutions or the state's distinctive histories and traditions. They could better capitalize on existing right-to-know protections, for example.[198] While state supreme courts often gesture to these provisions when discussing the state's strong support for open government, they rarely interpret these clauses to offer meaningful expansions of the state-level rights of access. Press advocates could take up this cause. They could argue, for instance, that the constitutional right of access reaches government actors or entities not covered by public records statutes.

Press advocates could also utilize textual provisions that clearly assign the press a structural democratic role. They could draw upon constitutional language that emphasizes the role of the press in overseeing government – for example, provisions that stipulate the "printing presses shall be free to everyone who undertakes to examine the proceedings of the legislature or any branch of government."[199] They could also invoke constitutional language that makes explicit the link between the suppression of the press and autocratic government, such as those declaring that freedom of the press "can never be restrained except by despotic governments."[200] Such textual provisions make a powerful constitutional statement about the democratic role and responsibility of the press.

Press advocates could also lean more heavily on the affirmative nature of state press protections.[201] These affirmative provisions could be cited to support a set of expanded positive rights and obligations that flow from state press and speech protections. They could be used to argue in favor of more affirmative and active government interventions – ones that would proactively ensure a vibrant and healthy information ecosystem. These could include, for example, expanded newsgathering protections. A more radical interpretation of these positive rights provisions might be that they impose affirmative obligations on the government to support local news institutions – for example, through tax breaks or subsidies.[202] The collapse of the local press has lent new urgency to such projects.

[196] *See* App'x A, State Constitutional Free Expression Provisions, *supra* note 8.

[197] Kraus, *supra* note 44, at 95 (advancing this argument in the context of Maryland's free expression provision).

[198] *See supra* note 142 and accompanying text.

[199] *See, e.g.*, Ky. Const. § 8; Pa. Const. art. I, § 7; Tenn. Const. art. I, § 19.

[200] Va. Const. art. I, § 12.

[201] *See* discussion *supra* notes 71–73 and accompanying text.

[202] *See* Christina Koningisor and Jacob Noti-Victor, *Innovation Policy and the Press*, *in* The Future of Press Freedom: Democracy, Law, and the News in Changing Times 437 (RonNell Andersen Jones & Sonja R. West eds., 2025).

State constitutional structural design could also be used to support expanded press protections. For instance, Rhode Island's constitution enshrines protection for speech and the press in separate constitutional provisions.[203] The U.S. Supreme Court has interpreted these federal speech and press rights to overlap, leaving the Press Clause with little independent meaning.[204] Yet in the state constitutional context, such structural separation cuts against developing this same type of textual redundancy between press and speech rights.[205] Press advocates could better capitalize upon these types of distinctions.

Relatedly, variations in state constitutional drafting histories could also offer opportunities for press advocates. Many of the debates of the earliest state constitutions have been preserved.[206] Further, these original constitutions have all been amended or replaced, often repeatedly.[207] This introduces a range of methodological questions and complexities when it comes to state constitutional interpretation.[208] But it also means that there is a larger set of state-level drafting materials to draw upon.[209] These later state constitutions often have more detailed and better-preserved records of the drafting debates.[210] They, too, can be mined to support broader state-level press protections.

Finally, state constitutional processes can be used to expand protections for the press. State constitutions are more easily amended than the U.S. Constitution.[211] This permits voters to respond to new or emerging threats to the press through ballot initiatives and amendments. In this way, states' bill of rights provisions serve a distinct political function from the federal Bill of Rights. These state constitutional processes allow state voters to respond more quickly to "particular government failures."[212]

Consider the example of California's constitutional reporter's privilege shield. Voters responded to specific threats to the press by elevating statutory reporter's privilege protections to constitutional status.[213] Other states could follow suit. They could respond to new or emerging threats to the press through ballot initiatives and

[203] R.I. Const. art. I, § 20 (freedom of the press); R.I. Const. art. I, § 21 (freedom of speech).

[204] *See* West, *supra* note 3, at 1028.

[205] *See also* Ark. Const. art. II, § 6 (never mentioning speech protections at all).

[206] *See* Marshfield, *supra* note 33, at 886–93 (describing these debates).

[207] *See* The Book of the States, General Information on State Constitutions (as of Jan. 1, 2022), https://bookofthestates.org/tables/general-information-on-state-constitutions-as-of-january-1-2022/.

[208] *See* discussion *supra* notes 29–32 and accompanying text.

[209] *See* Marshfield, *supra* note 33, at 876–77 (noting that there have been 233 state constitutional conventions between 1776 and 2020, and drafting records exist for 114 of them).

[210] *See id.*

[211] *See* Dinan, *supra* note 84 (comparing the 27 amendments of the U.S. Constitution to the more than 7,000 amendments of state constitutions).

[212] *See* Marshfield, *supra* note 33, at 860.

[213] *See supra* notes 122–127 and accompanying text.

amendments. They could amend state constitutions to enshrine all manner of press protections into the constitutional text – not just confidential sources but also expanded protections against defamation liability, prior restraints, government surveillance of journalists, and more. To the extent that existing statutory press provisions seem imperiled, voters could constitutionalize them, making them more difficult to ignore or circumvent in the future.

13.2.2 *The Future of Federal Constitutional Press Protections*

State-level constitutional experimentation might also hold important lessons for ongoing debates about federal protections for the press. This is not universally true. Different political, historical, and legal considerations are in play at the federal versus state levels. Some state-level protections – for example, absolute prohibitions against prior restraints – might be ill-suited to the federal context, given the unique national security and military considerations at stake at the federal level.[214] Moreover, there are important textual distinctions between federal and state press and speech provisions that limit the extent to which state constitutional interpretations can be adopted wholesale into the federal context.

Yet some state-level innovations might still be helpful in informing federal press-advocacy efforts. Specifically, the experience of the states could be mined to refute some of the Court's policy-based justifications for declining special First Amendment protections for the press. The Supreme Court has repeatedly declined to engage in the task of defining who qualifies for press-specific protections, for example. In *Branzburg v. Hayes*, the Court wrote: "Sooner or later, it would be necessary to define those categories of newsmen who qualified for the privilege," a task made complicated because the "informative function asserted by representatives of the organized press in the present cases is also performed by lecturers, political pollsters, novelists, academic researchers, and dramatists."[215] In other words, the definitional questions are simply too difficult for the courts to untangle.

The experience of the states undermines this claim. Forty-nine states extend some form of reporter's privilege to journalists through a mix of common law, constitutional, and statutory protections.[216] This has required defining who qualifies for protection. The states have taken various approaches – some functional, others more formal.[217] But overall, the experience of the states suggests that this definitional concern may be overblown. The states have managed the task largely without controversy, often finding that the person asserting the privilege is so clearly a

214 *See, e.g.*, Near v. State of Minnesota ex rel. Olson, 283 U.S. 697, 716 (1931).
215 Branzburg v. Hayes, 408 U.S. 665, 704–05 (1972).
216 *See* Koningisor, *supra* note 18, at 1202.
217 *See* West, *supra* note 3, at 1063–68 (reviewing these various legislative approaches).

journalist that they don't need to define the outer boundaries of its scope. As Professor Sonja West has argued, the experience of the states shows that "defining 'the press' can be done."[218]

We can also imagine how state experimentation might hold additional lessons for federal Press Clause constructions in the future. The Supreme Court has been hesitant to endow the federal Press Clause with any independent meaning. State constitutional examples can be used to illuminate new and different paths forward. These contrary experiences and histories of the states can be cited when urging the Court to revisit its holdings in such cases as *Branzburg* and *Milkovich*, for example.[219] State constitutional experimentation can be used to offer the Court a concrete set of examples for alternative options. And they can be used to help imagine a more expansive First Amendment – one that supports a more robust set of press rights.

13.3 CONCLUSION

The Roberts Court has curtailed the scope of various constitutional rights provisions in recent years. In response, scholars and activists have increasingly looked to state constitutions as an alternative source of protection. Across substantive areas like abortion and climate change, state courts have interpreted state constitutions to provide more expansive rights than the U.S. Constitution.[220] This chapter argues that members of the press should look to state constitutions as an alternative source of legal protection as well.

The U.S. Supreme Court has consistently declined to interpret the First Amendment in ways that extend special privileges to the press. But state constitutions can be used to fill in these federal constitutional gaps, operating as a powerful and independent source of protection for the media. Some states have already done so. They have extended greater protection under the state constitution when it comes to prohibitions against prior restraint, reporter's privilege shields, rights of information access, and protections against defamation liability.[221] These decisions are rooted in textual, structural, and historical distinctions between the federal and state constitutions, as well as differences in the federal and state political experiences.[222]

But more can be done. Press advocates could better capitalize on these distinctions going forward. They could look to the comparatively stronger texts of state constitutions to support stronger press rights. They could draw upon structural

[218] *Id.* at 1063.
[219] *See* discussion *supra* Section 13.1.3.
[220] *See supra* notes 43–44 and accompanying text.
[221] *See supra* Section 13.1.3.
[222] *Id.*

distinctions in state constitutions to avoid interpreting state-level press clauses to be wholly duplicative of state speech clauses. They could amend state constitutions in response to new and growing threats to the press. And they could hold up the examples of state constitutional experimentation to help imagine a new and more expansive First Amendment. These fifty "other press clauses" could step in where the federal Press Clause has failed.

14

The Long Shadow of *Food Lion*

Alan K. Chen

While attending a conference a few years ago, I had a private conversation about undercover investigations with the deputy general counsel of one of the nation's leading newspapers. When I asked about what I perceived to be a significant decrease in news media conducting such investigations, the person responded something to the effect of, "Well, *Food Lion* pretty much ended all that." The reference was to the U.S. Court of Appeals for the Fourth Circuit's 1999 decision in *Food Lion, Inc. v. Capital Cities/ABC, Inc.*,[1] one of the most important lower federal court cases shaping freedom of the press under the First Amendment in the past twenty-five years. The case involved a lawsuit by a large grocery store chain against ABC News and two of its producers, who had conducted an undercover investigation revealing that some stores' employees engaged in unsanitary, and possibly unlawful, food handling practices.[2] Although the ultimate outcome of the Fourth Circuit's decision was on balance favorable to the press, it flatly rejected the news network's contention that the First Amendment in any way limits tort claims against journalists engaged in this form of newsgathering.[3]

This chapter discusses the continuing shadow of the *Food Lion* case, which looms over the efforts of journalists and, increasingly of other citizens, to engage in undercover investigations to discover and disseminate truthful information on matters of profound public concern. At a time when many impediments to freedom of the press have emerged, legal barriers to undercover investigations suppress a key

Thanks to the Knight First Amendment Institute for inviting me to contribute to this important project. I am also grateful to RonNell Andersen Jones, Enrique Armijo, Rebecca Aviel, Evelyn Douek, Sarah Haan, Daphne Keller, Christina Koningisor, Matthew Schafer, David Schulz, Amanda Shanor, Mia Speier, Alexander Tsesis, Sonja West, and Marshall Van Alstyne for their thoughtful comments, with special thanks to Professors Andersen Jones and West for their organization of this Symposium. Nina Christensen, Karina Condon, and Charlotte Rhoad provided valuable research support.

1 194 F.3d 505, 510 (4th Cir. 1999).

2 *Id.*

3 *Id.* at 520–22. By "newsgathering," I mean the act of "seeking out news of public interest for the purpose of disseminating it to an audience." Erik Ugland, *Demarcating the Right to Gather News: A Sequential Interpretation of the First Amendment*, 3 Duke J. Const. L. & Pub. Pol'y 113, 137 (2008).

newsgathering tool that was once an important part of the news media ecosystem. Section 14.1 provides a brief overview of undercover investigations in American journalism and then explores how the Food Lion investigation was developed internally and carried out by Susan Barnett and Lynne Dale, producers at ABC's "Primetime Live" newsmagazine show.

In Section 14.2, the chapter describes the extensive litigation battle that followed ABC's national broadcast of the Food Lion story and surveys the major legal objections to undercover investigations. It contends that the *Food Lion* decision created a significant degree of uncertainty about whether and when such investigations may be carried out without violating the law. The case never reached the U.S. Supreme Court, making it technically binding only in the five states governed by the Fourth Circuit. But because the Supreme Court has never taken up the specific First Amendment question implicated by the *Food Lion* case, the lower court's decision continues to have widespread, arguably outsized, influence on the law governing undercover investigations.

Section 14.2 goes on to argue that *Food Lion* is responsible for a palpable chilling effect on those who might otherwise engage in undercover investigations, particularly those involving an investigator who secures employment with the target of an investigation. But *Food Lion* is more than just a legal precedent. Its deterrent effect also flows from the fact that it has shaped, and continues to shape, the journalism profession's internal ethical debates about undercover investigations. Sections 14.1 and 14.2 are based in part on interviews conducted with Barnett and Dale, as well as with Nathan Siegel, one of ABC's key legal counsel in the *Food Lion* case.[4]

Section 14.3 proceeds to call for reconsideration of the *Food Lion* framework and articulation of a meaningful constitutional protection for some aspects of newsgathering, which are long overdue. It lays out a tentative framework for a limited First Amendment privilege to protect undercover investigators from both targeted and generally applicable criminal and civil laws, and it addresses the limitations on and concerns with recognition of such a privilege.

14.1 THE NEWS MEDIA, UNDERCOVER INVESTIGATIONS, AND FREE SPEECH

14.1.1 *Undercover Investigations in American Journalism*

As I have written about extensively in other forums,[5] undercover investigations have been a fundamental component of newsgathering by the institutional press at

[4] Zoom interview with Susan Barnett and Lynne Dale, former producers, ABC "Primetime Live" (Jan. 8, 2024) [hereinafter *Barnett/Dale Interview*]; Zoom interview with Nathan Siegel (Jan. 11, 2024) [hereinafter *Siegel Interview*].

[5] Much of my work in this area was done in conjunction with my colleague, Justin Marceau. *See, e.g.*, Alan K. Chen & Justin Marceau, Truth and Transparency: Undercover Investigations in the Twenty-First Century (2023); Alan K. Chen & Justin Marceau,

various times throughout American history. Undercover investigations are actions taken by journalists who seek access to places, persons, and actions, when the investigative targets would otherwise not welcome investigators.[6] They typically involve two features that are sometimes questioned as problematic, unethical, or even illegal. First, the journalists gain access to the investigative target by using some form of deception – lying about their true identity, their news media employer, and their motives for seeking access to the target (or at least omitting relevant information about those things) – in order to gather information on matters of public concern.[7] One common undercover reporting tactic involves the journalist obtaining employment with the investigation's target.

Second, those who engage in undercover investigations also often use hidden cameras or recording devices to memorialize the conduct or information they are seeking to expose. The recordings verify what would otherwise be only the investigator's narrative account, thus lending substantial credibility to the information disclosed to the public. As Susan Barnett, one of the producers who went undercover for the Food Lion investigation told me, recording can be important to address a public increasingly skeptical of the press: If "[the viewers] don't see it, they don't believe it."[8]

American journalists began employing undercover investigative tactics before the Civil War, when northern newspapers sent reporters to the South to report on the abhorrent conditions of slavery.[9] During the war, undercover methods were also important tools for journalists from the North, who would have risked great danger reporting from the battlefields in the South had their true identities been known.[10] Since that time, the popularity of such investigations has ebbed and flowed, depending in part on historical context, changes in relevant legal and ethical principles, and the availability (or lack thereof) of other newsgathering methods.[11]

Developing a Taxonomy of Lies Under the First Amendment, 89 U. COLO. L. REV. 655 (2018); Justin Marceau & Alan K. Chen, *Free Speech and Democracy in the Video Age*, 116 COLUM. L. REV. 991 (2016); Alan K. Chen & Justin Marceau, *High Value Lies, Ugly Truths, and the First Amendment*, 69 VAND. L. REV. 1435 (2015). *See also* Alan K. Chen, *Investigative Deception Across Social Contexts*, https://knightcolumbia.org/content/investigative-deception-across-social-contexts; Alan K. Chen, *Cheap Speech Creation*, 54 U.C. DAVIS L. REV. 2405 (2021).

6 As such, they are distinct from two other important tools of information gathering and disclosure – investigative reporting and whistleblowing. For an explanation of the differences among these methods, *see* CHEN & MARCEAU, TRUTH AND TRANSPARENCY, *supra* note 5, at 214–15.

7 For a more extensive definition, *see* CHEN & MARCEAU, TRUTH AND TRANSPARENCY, *supra* note 5, at 18.

8 *Barnett/Dale Interview*, *supra* note 4. *See also* Marceau & Chen, *Video Age*, *supra* note 5, at 1029 ("A recording provides a self-authenticating and easily reproduced memorialization of one's encounters or experiences.").

9 BROOKE KROEGER, UNDERCOVER REPORTING: THE TRUTH ABOUT DECEPTION 15–30 (2012).

10 J. CUTLER ANDREWS, THE NORTH REPORTS THE CIVIL WAR 6–34 (1985).

11 CHEN & MARCEAU, TRUTH AND TRANSPARENCY, *supra* note 5, at 36–74.

Undercover investigations appear to have thrived during two periods in American history. The first high point was during the Progressive Era. By some accounts, the method was first popularized in the late 1800s and early 1900s by women seeking opportunities to break into what was then the male-dominated journalism profession. To the extent they could get newspaper jobs at all, women were hired primarily to write about issues that their editors believed were of concern only to women, such as fashion.[12] Women seeking to be treated as serious journalists turned to undercover investigations. But they were pejoratively dubbed "girl stunt reporters" for their exploits, suggesting that they were engaged in a kind of sensationalist journalism perhaps unworthy of "real" (i.e., male) reporters. Despite that label, these intrepid journalists exposed shocking misconduct across a wide range of the public and private sectors.[13]

In an attempt to break into the profession with hard news stories, some female reporters went undercover to gather information and then write about many of the day's most important social issues. The journalist most closely associated with this movement is Elizabeth Cochran, who wrote under the pen name Nellie Bly. Bly conducted numerous undercover investigations over the course of her impressive career but is best known for feigning symptoms causing her to be institutionalized at the Blackwell's Island Insane Asylum for Women, where she discovered systematically inhumane treatment of its residents. She took this information and first documented these conditions in the pages of the New York World newspaper, and later in her book, *Ten Days in a Mad-House*.[14]

Upton Sinclair, the writer who is perhaps most associated with undercover investigations, used similar methods to investigate conditions in the Chicago meatpacking industry in 1904. Though he initially undertook this work to expose the greed and excesses of the animal agriculture industry and the poor treatment of meatpacking workers, his investigation quickly turned to the stomach-turning conditions of food sanitation and handling, issues that later became the focus of his bestselling novel, *The Jungle*.[15] As Brooke Kroeger wrote, Sinclair:

> . . . intended to provide a searing examination of Big Beef, its power and corruption, and the grisly working conditions of the immigrant poor. But his story soon began to

[12] Jean Marie Lutes, Front-Page Girls: Women Journalists in American Culture and Fiction, 1880–1930 2 (2006) ("for men, participatory journalism was a choice; for women, it was one of the few ways to break out of the women's pages."). Unfortunately, the high-profile stories produced by women conducting undercover investigations did little to eradicate these types of gender biases in the profession. Amanda Svachula, *When the Times Kept Female Reporters Upstairs*, N.Y. Times (Sept. 20, 2018), https://www.nytimes.com/2018/09/20/insider/times-womens-section-female-reporters.html (noting that between 1955 and 1971, The New York Times ran a separate section on "Food, Fashions, Family, and Furnishings" written by women and directed at a female audience).

[13] Chen & Marceau, Truth and Transparency, *supra* note 5, at 4–6.

[14] Nellie Bly, Ten Days in a Mad-House (1887).

[15] Upton Sinclair, The Jungle (1906).

> turn on his stark depictions of how contaminated meat was making its way from the packinghouses of Chicago to the dinner tables of the world.[16]

In order to gather information for their stories, Sinclair and others who conducted undercover investigations during the Progressive Era used either overt or implicit forms of deception to gain access to people, places, and conduct that would otherwise have been inaccessible to them. In each case, that information was conveyed to the public and meaningfully informed public discourse and policy debates. Of course, given the technology of the day, they did not, like contemporary journalists, use hidden recording equipment. Rather, they relied on their memories and surreptitious notetaking to memorialize their findings. Sinclair reportedly would retire to his living quarters each evening to write down his notes while his memory was still fresh.[17] Given that his investigation spanned a period of seven weeks, he had to find some way to ensure that his information was documented without being detected.

Although the earlier work of the women undercover journalists and Sinclair are often linked, Kroeger suggested that by Sinclair's time, the standards for conducting such investigations and reporting the stories had evolved significantly. By the early twentieth century, journalists' undercover investigations were more sophisticated and reporters "went to great lengths to verify and analyze their findings."[18] Thus, at this early stage, the tactics of undercover investigations were maturing in accordance with the best standards of professional journalism.

Following the Progressive Era, "there seems to be a lull in undercover investigations, or at least ones that received national attention, from the mid-twentieth century until the 1970s."[19] Although journalists conducted undercover investigations intermittently from the Progressive Era to contemporary times, their use became much more prevalent after the Watergate scandal in the early 1970s, which placed investigative journalism front and center in the public's eye. Although it is unclear whether Washington Post reporters Bob Woodward and Carl Bernstein ever engaged in the tactics used by most undercover investigators, many other journalists began expanding the use of undercover investigations during the years surrounding Watergate.[20] Professional journalism organizations began focusing on creating or updating ethics codes for the industry during this period as well.[21]

[16] KROEGER, *supra* note 9, at 84.

[17] ANTHONY ARTHUR, RADICAL INNOCENT: UPTON SINCLAIR 49 (2006). Even reporters conducting undercover investigations more recently have resorted to similar tactics. KROEGER, *supra* note 9, at 172–76 (describing how Pulitzer Prize-winning Chicago Tribune reporter William Gaines, posing as a janitor to investigate a local private hospital, wrote notes on paper towels that he stashed away until he could safely recover them).

[18] KROEGER, *supra* note 9, at 83.

[19] CHEN & MARCEAU, TRUTH AND TRANSPARENCY, *supra* note 5, at 7.

[20] *Id.* at 54–55.

[21] *Id.* at 56–58.

The late 1960s and early 1970s also witnessed the introduction of a new form of journalism, the television newsmagazine. The first such program to receive national attention, CBS's still-popular show, "60 Minutes," began airing in 1968.[22] A type of long-form journalism, "television newsmagazine shows . . . allowed television journalists to go beyond reporting on discrete stories of the day to taking on broader, more time-consuming, and more expensive investigations."[23] They were in part the networks' reaction to the high costs and lack of advertising support for full-length documentaries, with executives believing that a single broadcast including multiple segments might be more successful.[24] Although some of the content was (and continues to be) "soft" news stories, television newsmagazines also evolved into a successful vehicle for airing the results of undercover investigations, as the *Food Lion* case illustrates. In addition, television newsmagazines benefited from the evolving technology making it easier to engage in secret recording, though not nearly as easy as it has become today.

Undercover investigations by American journalists have led to the discovery of information critical to public discourse about matters ranging from public corruption to food safety to sweatshop labor conditions, to name just a few. Although these investigative techniques originated in the journalism profession, they have since been adopted, and even celebrated and legally authorized, in other contexts. Fair housing investigators have long engaged in civil rights testing, where investigators using false identities and financial backgrounds are sent in to detect evidence of illegal racial steering and often document their findings with secret recordings.[25] Union activists may lawfully lie about their affiliation with unions to obtain jobs with employers whose workers they want to organize.[26] Law enforcement officers use the same tactics as undercover journalists to expose criminal activity through undercover sting operations.[27] And, more recently, political advocacy groups across the ideological spectrum have adopted undercover investigations to expose what they believe to be wrongful conduct.[28] As such, undercover investigations are an important vehicle for promoting transparency, accountability, and democracy, one of the central functions of the First Amendment.[29]

[22] *Television News Magazines*, in 4 Encyclopedia of Journalism 1385 (Christopher H. Sterling ed., 2009).

[23] Chen & Marceau, Truth and Transparency, *supra* note 5, at 58.

[24] *Television News Magazines*, *supra* note 22.

[25] Havens Realty Corp. v. Coleman, 455 U.S. 363, 373–74 (1982). *See also* Chen & Marceau, Truth and Transparency, *supra* note 5, at 10–12.

[26] James L. Fox, *"Salting" the Construction Industry*, 24 Wm. Mitchell L. Rev. 681, 683–84 (1998). *See also* Chen & Marceau, Truth and Transparency, *supra* note 5, at 15–16.

[27] *See, e.g.*, Hoffa v. United States, 385 U.S. 293, 303 (1966). *See also* Chen & Marceau, Truth and Transparency, *supra* note 5, at 16–18.

[28] Chen & Marceau, Truth and Transparency, *supra* note 5, at 12–14, 30–31. For example, undercover investigations have been used by animal rights activists and anti-abortion advocates, among others.

[29] Alexander Meiklejohn, Free Speech and Its Relation to Self-Government 88–89 (1948).

Undercover investigations may be even more central to promoting those goals in the current political and news environment.[30] The United States is currently living through a time of increasing partisan divide as well as mistrust of government and other institutions. Relatedly, the nation seems to be experiencing a period of epistemic chaos, with some people disputing the very nature of truth while misinformation and disinformation campaigns thrive in part because of the speed with which information can be transmitted over the internet.

In other times, one natural response to this environment might have been a thriving, independent press that could investigate and report on the most critical issues of the day, checking and exposing abuses of truth by government actors, political candidates and organizations, and foreign government interlopers. But the American press is itself experiencing an existential crisis. The institutional news media is struggling through both internal and external threats to its existence. American newspapers have been substantially impaired because their business model has been undermined by the emergence of the internet as a less expensive and more widely viewed platform for news and advertising.[31] A recent study by researchers at Northwestern's Medill School of Journalism projects that by the end of 2024, the nation will have lost a third of its newspapers since 2005.[32]

Shrinking revenues have also caused even the surviving major newspapers to cut budgets, sometimes in areas crucial to newsgathering. As discussed in greater detail below, conducting journalistically sound undercover investigations requires substantial resources.[33] The reduction in resources has also affected another important newsgathering tool, the pursuit of information through open records laws. One report indicated that, with the exception of The New York Times, legacy media companies have substantially reduced the number of requests they submit under the federal Freedom of Information Act.[34]

Nor is the news media immune to the fundamental loss of public trust that plagues other institutions. Multiple sources may be contributing to this loss of trust, from the sustained performative attacks on the news media by high-profile politicians to the emergence of the perception that "fake news" now pervades the media landscape (even though many of these stories come not from mainstream media but from individuals, organizations, and even foreign governments spreading

[30] Chen & Marceau, Truth and Transparency, *supra* note 5, at xiii–xvii.

[31] RonNell Andersen Jones & Sonja R. West, *The Disappearing Freedom of the Press*, 79 Wash. & Lee L. Rev. 1377, 1382–84 (2022)

[32] Penelope Muse Abernathy, *The State of Local News: The 2023 Report*, Executive Summary, https://localnewsinitiative.northwestern.edu/projects/state-of-local-news/2023/report/#executive-summary.

[33] *See infra* note 200 and accompanying text.

[34] Greg Munno, *FOIA Suits Jump in 2014*, The FOIA Project, Dec. 22, 2014, https://foiaproject.org/2014/12/22/foia-suits-jump-in-2014/ (reporting that between 2005 and 2012, traditional media brought between three and nine FOIA suits per year, but than in 2014, no legacy media outlet other than The New York Times filed a FOIA lawsuit).

disinformation across social media platforms).[35] There is also an increasing sense, it appears, that people believe the media is no longer "objective," even though news entities have never been entirely neutral.[36]

Finally, attacks on the media have also been literal, rather than metaphorical, with acts of violence or threats of such violence becoming tragically commonplace around the world.[37] The United States is not immune to the rise in violence against journalists. According to the U.S. Press Freedom Tracker, there were 593 assaults against journalists in the United States in 2020, which was an almost 1,400 percent increase over the prior year.[38] And those are just reported incidents. As Erin Carroll has observed, "Online insults and threats against journalists – particularly against women – exploded. According to one recent study, abuse is so rampant that it is part of the 'daily work lives' of women journalists. Researchers worry that the line between online attacks and offline violence is faint."[39]

One reaction to the challenges facing professional journalism in the United States might be to reinvigorate its newsgathering capacity to shore up its important role in promoting democracy. This might include devoting greater resources to reporting important stories through undercover investigations. Instead, we are witnessing increasing legal and ethical objections to this once important investigative practice.

14.1.2 *ABC's Investigation of Food Lion*

During the heyday of television newsmagazines' undercover investigations, producers at ABC's popular "Primetime Live" learned from a couple of different sources about concerns with practices at some branches of the Food Lion grocery store chain, which operates stores mostly in the southeastern United States.[40] The investigation and story were the project of two producers, Susan Barnett and Lynne Dale, who had never previously worked together.[41] Barnett and Dale initially came at the story from different angles. Barnett had recently completed a well-received

35 Andersen Jones & West, *supra* note 31, at 1388.

36 For a thoughtful response to the objectivity issue, *see* A. G. Sulzberger, *Journalism's Essential Value*, Colum. Journalism Review, May 15, 2023, https://www.cjr.org/special_report/ag-sulzberger-new-york-times-journalisms-essential-value-objectivity-independence.php.

37 Andersen Jones & West, *supra* note 31, at 1386–87. *See also Threats to Freedom of Press: Violence, Disinformation & Censorship*, May 11, 2023, https://www.unesco.org/en/threats-freedom-press-violence-disinformation-censorship (reporting that according to the United Nations Educational, Scientific, and Cultural Organization, a journalist somewhere in the world is killed every four days).

38 Erin Carroll, *Obstruction of Journalism: A New Way to Combat Violence Against Journalists*, Colum. Journalism Review, Jan. 13, 2022, https://www.cjr.org/analysis/obstruction-journalism-violence.php.

39 *Id.*

40 *Barnett/Dale Interview*, *supra* note 4.

41 The narrative about the initiation of the investigation comes from my Zoom interview of Barnett and Dale. *See Barnett/Dale Interview*, *supra* note 4.

"Primetime Live" story about the meatpacking industry and reached out to her source on that story – the Government Accountability Project (GAP),[42] a nonprofit organization dedicated to protecting and advocating for whistleblowers. GAP shared with her reports from Food Lion workers who had indicated that employees at some stores were adulterating food sold to consumers. Dale had independently been gathering information about labor violations at Food Lion, which prompted her to pitch that element of the story. "It wasn't about rotten meat, it was about [Food Lion stores] working employees off the clock."[43]

Notwithstanding what critics have suggested about undercover investigations, journalists do not typically undertake such investigations as fishing expeditions, sweeping broadly while hoping to uncover some unsavory conduct by their targets. Rather, this undercover work is usually just one component of an extensive, meticulous investigation using a combination of more traditional journalistic techniques, which may have already revealed a reasonable suspicion that an undercover investigation will lead to the discovery of additional newsworthy information. This was the case with the Food Lion investigation.

The Food Lion investigation was conducted consistent with the network and producers' professional journalistic standards. First, investigations were not conducted unless there was first credible information that undercover work would turn up newsworthy information. Importantly, substantial background reporting and sourcing took place as part of the investigation. The Food Lion investigation involved several months of traditional reporting before the undercover investigation began.[44] As Barnett said: "We do all the paper trail work. It's not like that doesn't happen and we just go undercover."[45] Nor is the story done when the undercover investigation has been completed. The producers worked for at least an additional six months between the investigation and the time the story was aired on national television.[46] In the end, the producers had obtained information from over 120 sources, all of whom were current or former Food Lion employees.[47] In addition, Barnett and Dale noted that it was important that an undercover story be one of "national importance" and have "national implication," and that hidden cameras not be used if there were other ways to obtain the relevant information.[48] The consideration of both the importance of the story and the availability of less intrusive means of gathering relevant information parallels

42 https://whistleblower.org/.

43 *Barnett/Dale Interview*, *supra* note 4. Coincidentally, as discussed above, Upton Sinclair also first began his undercover investigation of the meatpacking industry focused on labor practices, but also changed direction to instead examine food safety and sanitation.

44 *Barnett/Dale Interview*, *supra* note 4.

45 *Id.*

46 *Id.*

47 *Id.*

48 *Id.*

some of the journalism profession's published ethical standards relating to undercover investigations.[49]

While Barnett had done undercover investigations before, this was Dale's first foray into this newsgathering tactic. Barnett pitched going undercover as Food Lion employees to corroborate the information they had already received. As they designed their investigation, they worked closely with ABC News's legal counsel.[50] ABC approved the producers getting jobs at Food Lion stores, not disclosing their affiliation with ABC, and using hidden cameras. But the network stipulated that Barnett and Dale were to use their real names and Social Security numbers when they applied for their jobs at Food Lion, though it approved of them modifying significant aspects of their backgrounds on their resumes.[51] The trial court noted that Dale lied about having prior experiences as a meat wrapper and that both Barnett and Dale provided false references, employment histories, and addresses, and omitted any reference to their employer, ABC.[52]

To conduct the undercover part of the investigation, Barnett and Dale successfully obtained jobs at different Food Lion stores. Dale worked for two weeks as a meat wrapper in two different stores and Barnett worked as a delicatessen clerk for one week in one store. While working, they both performed their jobs in compliance with their assigned duties, and also engaged in an investigation to confirm the reports about food handling and labor practices.[53] They both wore hidden cameras that they were able to turn on at appropriate times to document problems with the stores' practices and recorded a total of about 45 hours of video between them.[54]

ABC aired the story on national television on its "Primetime Live" newsmagazine program on November 5, 1992. As the Fourth Circuit described the practices revealed by the report:

> The broadcast included . . . videotape that appeared to show Food Lion employees repackaging and redating fish that had passed the expiration date, grinding expired beef with fresh beef, and applying barbeque sauce to chicken past its expiration date in order to mask the smell and sell it as fresh in the gourmet food section. The program included statements by former Food Lion employees alleging even more serious mishandling of meat at Food Lion stores across several states. The truth of the PrimeTime Live broadcast was not an issue in the litigation.[55]

[49] *See, e.g.*, Society of Professional Journalists, *Society of Professional Journalists – 1996 Code of Ethics*, https://spjnetwork.org/quill2/codedcontroverscy/cthics-code-2009.pdf [hereinafter 1996 *SPJ Code of Ethics*] ("Avoid undercover or other surreptitious methods of gathering information except when traditional open methods will not yield information vital to the public.").

[50] *Id.*

[51] *Id.*

[52] Food Lion, Inc. v. Cap. Cities/ABC, Inc., 984 F. Supp. 923, 927 (M.D.N.C. 1997), *aff'd in part, rev'd in part*, 194 F.3d 505 (4th Cir. 1999).

[53] *Barnett/Dale Interview*, *supra* note 4.

[54] *Id.*

[55] *Food Lion*, 194 F.3d at 511.

Both before and after the story aired, however, there was a protracted legal battle over the legality of ABC's investigation and the subsequent broadcast. Section 14.2 describes that litigation and the important legal questions surrounding undercover investigations that it framed but did not necessarily answer.

14.2 THE FOOD LION LITIGATION AND POTENTIAL LEGAL BARRIERS TO UNDERCOVER INVESTIGATIONS

As valuable as undercover investigations can be to promoting democracy, transparency, and public discourse, there have long been objections to the secretive tactics necessary to carry them out. Targets of such investigations have been predictably upset when a journalist exposes their illegal or otherwise unsavory conduct to public scrutiny. During the Progressive Era, critics would describe intrepid women reporters with the pejorative label "girl stunt journalists" in order to convey a lack of journalistic legitimacy and to place them below their male peers on some sort of professional hierarchy.[56] This suggested that this type of important journalistic work was sensationalist and unprofessional. Perhaps not surprisingly, current critics of undercover investigations attack investigators with comparable epithets.[57] But at least in the earlier years, criticisms of such investigations were confined to simple rhetorical attempts to undermine journalists' professional credibility. Beginning sometime in the 1990s, however, investigative targets began turning to the courts in an effort to legally punish and chill undercover investigations.[58]

14.2.1 *Legal Theories Regarding Undercover Investigations*

In its case against ABC, Food Lion invoked all three of the potential common law claims typically brought against undercover investigators – fraud, trespass, and violation of the duty of loyalty. Before recounting the course of the *Food Lion* litigation, therefore, a brief overview of each of these theories is warranted. To a significant extent, these claims overlap. They each require us to examine whether one who

56 Kirkus Reviews, Feb. 15, 2021 ("'By writing these reporters back into history,' Todd writes, 'I aim to highlight the double standard that labels women as 'stunt reporters' while men are 'investigative journalists,' even as they do the same work.'") (reviewing KIM TODD, SENSATIONAL: THE HIDDEN HISTORY OF AMERICA'S "GIRL STUNT REPORTERS" (2021)), https://www.kirkusreviews.com/book-reviews/kim-todd/sensational-stunt/.

57 JAMES L. AUCOIN, THE EVOLUTION OF AMERICAN INVESTIGATIVE JOURNALISM 3–4 (2005). In states that have enacted Ag Gag laws, the legislative histories have revealed some colorful insults directed at undercover investigators, who have been called "jack wagon[s]," Animal Legal Def. Fund v. Herbert, 263 F. Supp. 3d 1193, 1198 (D. Utah 2017), "vigilantes," and been compared to "marauding invaders." Animal Legal Def. Fund v. Otter, 44 F. Supp. 3d 1009, 1024 (D. Idaho 2014).

58 Barry Meier & Bill Carter, *Undercover Tactics by TV Magazines Fall under Attack*, N.Y. TIMES (Dec. 23, 1996), www.nytimes.com/1996/12/23/business/undercover-tactics-by-tv-magazines-fall-under-attack.html.

engages in investigative deception has violated a common law duty that causes tangible harm to the investigation's target. Importantly, the relevant tort law operates against a background First Amendment doctrine governing the regulation of lies.

14.2.1.1 Fraud

At first glance, common law fraud is arguably the worst fit when it comes to undercover investigations. In *Food Lion*, the court applied the law of North Carolina and South Carolina, the two jurisdictions where the investigation took place.[59] Fraud in those states generally requires the plaintiff to show that the defendant intentionally made a false statement to the plaintiff, with the intent that the plaintiff rely on that statement, and that the plaintiff suffered injury by reasonably relying on the statement.[60] The Restatement (Second) of Torts' definition of fraud is narrower, applying only where the false statement is used to either lead someone to make decisions related to a business transaction or give a gift to the fraudster or a third party.[61]

The paradigm case of fraud is the use of false statements to induce the listener to make a purchase or financial investment. In the *Food Lion* case, however, the argument was that the producers made false statements in order to induce Food Lion to hire them as employees. Notably, even if one could argue that an undercover investigator is inducing someone to make the "business transaction" of hiring the investigator, that hiring decision still must damage the plaintiff. Yet most undercover investigators who conduct employment-based investigations are hired as lower level, at-will employees. Thus, the target is paying them a salary for their labor, and, assuming the investigators actually perform the job for which they were hired, the target is not harmed.

Furthermore, to recover for fraud, the plaintiff must show that the fraud was the cause of the harm. When the target of an investigation sues a journalist, it typically asserts that its damages flow not from the act of hiring the investigator, but from the disclosure of information discovered during the investigation. That is, they seek publication damages. As discussed below, however, under a fraud theory, the investigation's target cannot succeed on the theory that the fraud led to damages from the publication of truthful information acquired through the fraud.

A related theory is that when journalists mislead a target in an employment-based investigation, they are committing "resume fraud." The most obvious implication from the term resume fraud is that it applies to someone who inflates or exaggerates her credentials.[62] Journalists and others who seek employment to carry out an

59 *Food Lion*, 194 F.3d at 512.

60 *Id.*

61 Restatement (Second) of Torts §§552–53 (1995).

62 Moreover, it is unclear that any state recognizes an independent common law tort action for resume fraud. Rather, resume fraud appears to come up almost exclusively in the context of

undercover investigation are usually qualified to do the jobs, otherwise they would likely be quickly discovered. If they are qualified and perform their duties satisfactorily, there would be no damages other than, again, the harm from any resulting publication damages. Courts are divided on this point. The trial court in *Food Lion* agreed that Barnett and Dale committed resume fraud, but on this point the Fourth Circuit disagreed.[63]

The question of whether lying to get a job to conduct an undercover investigation is protected by the First Amendment turns on the United States Supreme Court's decision in *United States v. Alvarez*.[64] In *Alvarez*, the Court invalidated the Stolen Valor Act, a federal criminal law prohibiting a person from falsely claiming to have been awarded high military honors. In doing so, the Court held that false statements of fact are protected under the First Amendment unless they cause a legally cognizable harm or provide a material gain to the speaker.[65] In dicta, the *Alvarez* plurality identified lies to secure "offers of employment" as not protected, because obtaining a job constituted securing a valuable consideration.[66]

It is unlikely that the Court was contemplating undercover investigators when it included this language. From the context of this paragraph, the Court is describing paradigmatic cases of common law fraud in which people lie with the intent to secure a financial benefit. "It seems clear that the phrase 'material gain' as used in *Alvarez* is meant to be a synonym for fraud or injury-causing lie. Material gain in this context implies that the prevaricator is deriving some tangible benefit from the deceived party – that is to say, it is a species of unjust enrichment."[67]

However, in *Animal Legal Defense Fund v. Wasden*, the U.S. Court of Appeals for the Ninth Circuit held that there is no First Amendment protection for an undercover investigator who lies to gain employment with an investigative target. In *Wasden*, the plaintiffs argued that this language from *Alvarez* meant only to address those who falsely inflate their qualifications for a job, which more closely resembles common law fraud. They claimed that someone who *understates* their education or experience or omits their political affiliation to gain a job for the purpose of exposing wrongdoing does not fall within the *Alvarez*'s "offers of employment" language. The Ninth Circuit rejected that argument on a couple of grounds. First, it noted that someone who seeks employment with the intent to harm the employer is in "breach of the covenant of good faith and fair dealing that is implied

serving as a defense to wrongful termination and employment discrimination claims. *See, e.g.*, Cicchetti v. Morris Cnty. Sheriff's Off., 194 N.J. 563, 579 (2008).

63 Indeed, in the context of its evaluation of Food Lion's trespass claim, the court observed "if we turned successful resume fraud into trespass, we would not be protecting the interest underlying the tort of trespass – the ownership and peaceable possession of land." 194 F.3d at 518.

64 United States v. Alvarez, 567 U.S. 709 (2012).

65 *Id.* at 719, 723 (plurality opinion). *See also id.* at 734–36 (Breyer, J., concurring in the judgment) (stating general agreement with the majority's framework).

66 567 U.S. at 723.

67 Chen & Marceau, *High Value Lies*, *supra* note 5, at 1492 n.313.

in all employment agreements in Idaho."[68] Second, and perhaps more importantly, the court wrote that:

> Although it may be true that "the goal of undercover employment-based investigations is not to 'secure moneys or other valuable considerations' for the investigator, but rather to expose threats to the public," ALDF ignores that the Supreme Court singled out offers of employment and that *these undercover investigators are nonetheless paid by the agricultural production facility as part of their employment.*[69]

Other courts, including the Fourth Circuit in *Food Lion* (albeit before *Alvarez* was decided), have disagreed.[70] The implication of *Wasden* is that states may, without violating the First Amendment, punish even lies that understate one's qualifications or omit one's motivations in order to gain employment. If that is the case, then journalists will rarely if ever be able to engage in an employment-based investigation. But even if the Supreme Court narrows this language in *Alvarez* so that undercover investigators may lie to get jobs for the purpose of undercover journalism, there are other barriers under the common law of tort that would continue to deter them.

14.2.1.2 Trespass

Investigative targets sometimes sue undercover investigators for common law trespass. The Restatement defines trespass as the intentional entry onto the land of another "irrespective of whether [the trespasser] thereby causes harm to any legally protected interest of the other."[71] Two features of trespass law make it especially complicated to apply to undercover investigators. First, consent is an affirmative defense to trespass.[72] In the case of an undercover investigation, the target has given the investigator consent to enter the property, even if they have done so unaware of the investigator's true identity and motive. In other words, the property owner knows they have consented to *someone* entering their land. In some jurisdictions, consent is vitiated if the alleged trespasser has secured it through fraud;[73] in others, however, consent induced by fraud is valid, and no trespass has occurred.[74] As I have written elsewhere, it is problematic for the *Alvarez* First Amendment standard to turn on a

68 *Wasden*, 878 F.3d at 1201.

69 *Id.* at 1201–02 (emphasis added).

70 Animal Legal Def. Fund v. Herbert, 263 F. Supp. 3d 1193, 1206 (D. Utah 2017).

71 Restatement (Second) of Torts §652B (1995).

72 *See, e.g.*, Grygiel v. Monches Fish & Game Club, Inc., 328 Wis. 2d 436, 461 (2010).

73 Belluomo v. KAKE TV & Radio, Inc., 3 Kan. App. 2d 461 (1979); People v. Segal, 358 N.Y.S.2d 866 (Crim. Ct. 1974).

74 Keyzer v. Amerlink, Ltd., 173 N.C. App. 284 (2005), aff'd, 360 N.C. 397 (2006); Am. Transmission, Inc. v. Channel 7 of Detroit, Inc., 239 Mich. App. 695 (2000). *See also First Amendment – "Ag-Gag" Laws – Eighth Circuit Upholds Law Criminalizing Access to Agricultural Production Facilities under False Pretenses.* – Animal Legal Defense Fund v. Reynolds,8 *F.4th* 781 *(8th Cir. 2021)*, 135 Harv. L. Rev. 1166, 1169 (2022).

particular jurisdiction's state law, both because there would not be a uniform free speech standard across states and because uncertainty about the nature of state law in a particular jurisdiction may create a chilling effect on investigators.[75]

In some states, however, legislators have begun invoking trespassory interests as a justification for the enactment of criminal laws directed at undercover investigations. In recent years, for example, some states have crafted legislation targeting animal rights groups, who have adopted the undercover tactics of journalists to expose extreme abuses of farmed animals at industrial agriculture production facilities. These statutes, often referred to as "Ag Gag" laws, appear to be a direct response to several highly publicized undercover investigations by groups such as People for the Ethical Treatment of Animals (PETA). These laws impose criminal penalties on any person who either seeks access to animal facilities using deception or engages in secret recording at those facilities, or both. Such laws could also be used to prosecute journalists who conduct undercover investigations at such facilities.

Ag Gag laws target activists who, like journalists conducting undercover investigations, gain employment or otherwise gain access to agricultural facilities by lying or omitting information about their identities, motives, and affiliation with animal rights organizations. There has been extensive litigation about the constitutionality of such laws, with the plaintiffs asserting that the laws interfere with their First Amendment free speech rights. Those cases have led to mixed results, with some laws having been struck down in whole[76] or in part[77] and others upheld.[78]

The state law trespass question is also relevant to whether there is any First Amendment protection for undercover investigators. As we have seen, the Supreme Court's decision in *Alvarez* holds that lies are protected by the First Amendment unless they cause a legally cognizable harm to the listener or produce a material gain for the liar.[79] Trespass is a strict liability tort, however, so even a nonconsensual entry onto the land of another may lead to a tort judgment even if no actual harm has occurred. Thus, a lie that leads to a trespass (in a jurisdiction where fraud vitiates consent), may only be protected under the First Amendment if it causes no legally cognizable harm, but the Restatement says a trespass occurs "irrespective of whether [the trespasser] thereby causes harm to any legally protected

75 Chen, *Investigative Deception*, *supra* note 5.

76 People for the Ethical Treatment of Animals, Inc. v. N. Carolina Farm Bureau Fed'n, Inc., 60 F.4th 815 (4th Cir. 2023) (cleaned up); Animal Legal Def. Fund v. Kelly, 9 F.4th 1219 (10th Cir. 2021); Animal Legal Def. Fund v. Herbert, 263 F. Supp. 3d 1193 (D. Utah 2017). The author discloses that he serves or served as counsel to the plaintiffs in most of the Ag Gag cases cited in this chapter.

77 Animal Legal Def. Fund v. Reynolds, 8 F.4th 781 (8th Cir. 2021) ("Reynolds I"); Animal Legal Def. Fund v. Wasden, 878 F.3d 1184 (9th Cir. 2018).

78 Animal Legal Def. Fund v. Reynolds, 89 F.4th 1065, 1067 (8th Cir. 2024) ("Reynolds II").

79 United States v. Alvarez, 567 U.S. 709, 719, 723 (2012) (plurality opinion).

interest of the other."[80] Whether undercover investigations constitute a trespass or involve constitutionally protected speech turns on how to read these two seemingly contradictory legal rules together.

14.2.1.3 Duty of Loyalty

Finally, because successful undercover investigators often obtain employment with their targets to gain access to the information they seek, targets have sometimes also turned to a less common legal claim under the duty of loyalty. The duty of loyalty, which is recognized in some form in all jurisdictions, finds its roots in the law of agency, under which agents have a fiduciary duty to act loyally for the principal's benefit.[81] In the context of an undercover investigation, an employer can sue an undercover journalist under the theory that because the journalist is also working for their media employer, the employee is being disloyal to the target employer. The duty of loyalty is often described as being rooted in the long-standing, and somewhat anachronistic, biblical admonition against serving "two masters."[82] Because it is central to the Fourth Circuit's analysis in *Food Lion*, we will return to the duty of loyalty in greater detail below.

14.2.1.4 Defamation, Privacy, and Other Less-Viable Theories

Other causes of action not raised in Food Lion might conceivably be raised in response to undercover investigations, but are even more clearly not viable paths to liability. First, an employer might claim that an investigation violates its right of privacy. The only common law privacy torts that could conceivably apply in the context of undercover investigations would be intrusion upon seclusion and public disclosure of private facts. Intrusion upon seclusion relates to the types of personal privacy we all value, as it requires the tortfeasor to have interfered with the plaintiff's private space in a way that intrudes on a person or their private affairs or concerns, of a kind that would be highly offensive to a reasonable person.[83] Because undercover investigations seek information of public concern that can inform public discourse, they do not seem susceptible to this type of claim unless the investigator exceeds the

80 Restatement (Second) of Torts §652B (1995).

81 Marian K. Riedy & Kim Sperduto, *At-Will Fiduciaries? The Anomalies of a "Duty of Loyalty" in the Twenty-First Century*, 93 Neb. L. Rev. 267, 272 (2014). A related, but distinct concern, might be that an undercover investigator might intentionally or inadvertently reveal an employer's trade secrets. There are, of course, already many legal restrictions against stealing trade secrets, and this chapter is not suggesting the privilege would extend to exemption from such laws. Even beyond legal restrictions, the best practices for undercover investigations could explicitly prohibit even the unintentional public disclosure of trade secrets.

82 Food Lion, Inc. v. Cap. Cities/ABC, Inc., 951 F. Supp. 1224, 1230 (M.D.N.C. 1996). For the biblical citation, *see* Matthew 6:24 (New American Standard Bible).

83 Restatement (Second) of Torts §652B (1995).

reasonable bounds of the investigative plan. Public disclosure of private facts does not likely fit with undercover investigations because it only applies where the alleged tortfeasor reveals private information about the plaintiff that would be highly offensive to a reasonable person and the information is not of legitimate public concern.[84] Indeed, the public concern limitation seems uniquely suited to protect newsgathering generally.

A related concern is that an investigation could intrude on the legitimate privacy interests of fellow employees, who may be captured on video or whose conduct or remarks may be collected by the journalists.[85] While there may be cases in which this is true, as long as an employee is acting in the presence of the journalist and other employees, there is at least a more limited expectation of privacy in that they are at the very least aware that someone else is watching or listening to them. But there is, of course, a material difference between whispering a private thought or secret to a coworker and announcing that same information on national television. And in such an environment, confiding in a coworker is certainly not unlikely; Barnett and Dale fully acknowledged that they liked their fellow employees and found most of them to be nice people during their short tenures.[86]

But there are reasonably easy ways to protect the privacy of fellow employees during an undercover investigation. First, any video that is used in a broadcast can blur out the faces and other identifying information of the other employees. Second, there can be clear boundaries on what is newsworthy and what is not, with the latter including private personal information disclosed or revealed by other employees during an undercover investigation that are not germane to the topic being investigated. Third, there could be protections against undercover investigators "doxxing," revealing employees' private identifying information that may subject them to violence, threats, harassment, or embarrassing exposure to the public's eye. For example, suppose an undercover investigation reveals an employee to have engaged in morally abominable or illegal behavior, and the investigator then published that person's home address or other ways to locate them. Even if those employees have engaged in misconduct, there are legal avenues for addressing that without revealing their personal information and subjecting them to abuse. Doxxing can be prohibited under ethical regulations or best practices designed to limit the scope of undercover investigations.

One reason that investigative targets have invoked these particular common law claims is that they are unable to sue for defamation. Undercover investigations typically lead to the publication of truthful information, and truth is an affirmative

84 Restatement (Second) of Torts §652D (1995).

85 Typically, employee privacy concerns relate to intrusion by the employer, not by fellow employees. But in this context, there are conceivable privacy interests that may be implicated by an undercover investigation, so I address them here.

86 *Barnett/Dale Interview*, *supra* note 4.

defense to defamation claims under American law.[87] The Fourth Circuit even recognized this in the *Food Lion* case, when it described part of Food Lion's claim as "an end-run around First Amendment strictures."[88]

The only other way that investigative targets could sue their investigators for the publication of truthful information is if the targets can establish a theory of publication damages. But again, publication of truthful information cannot lead to liability under defamation law. Still, those who have been embarrassed by undercover investigations have tried to assert damages claims even for the publication of truthful information if the information was obtained through means that violated tort law. Those claims have typically faltered on causation grounds, with courts concluding that the cause of any reputational harm from the publication of truthful information is the underlying wrongdoing rather than the disclosure of information about that wrongdoing.[89]

14.2.2 *The Food Lion Litigation and Decision*

Following good journalistic practice, before ABC aired the Food Lion story, it contacted the grocery store company to notify it about the forthcoming broadcast and asked for a response. When Food Lion learned of ABC's plan, it immediately filed a lawsuit in Forsyth County Superior Court in North Carolina. Though Food Lion did not seek a prior restraint on the entire broadcast, its complaint argued that Barnett and Dale had obtained the hidden camera footage illegally and its prayer for relief requested a preliminary and permanent injunction barring the network from using any of that material in its broadcast.[90] The news media defendants removed the case to federal court on diversity grounds and successfully blocked the injunction.[91] After the story was broadcast, Food Lion continued its suit, seeking money damages for the harm allegedly caused by the investigation and broadcast. Its three central claims represent the most common legal theories used to sue undercover investigators – common law fraud, trespass, and breach of the duty of loyalty.

The ensuing litigation at the federal trial court level was an intense battle lasting four years and four months from the time the case was removed to federal court until the end of the trial.[92] The parties fought over discovery questions, sought protective orders, asserted privileges, produced expert witnesses, and filed countless pretrial

[87] *See, e.g.*, Grygiel v. Monches Fish & Game Club, Inc., 328 Wis. 2d 436, 461 (2010).

[88] *Food Lion*, 194 F.3d at 522.

[89] Chen & Marceau, *High Value Lies*, *supra* note 5, at 1502–05; Nathan Siegel, *Publication Damages in Newsgathering Cases*, 19 COMM. LAW, Summer 2001, at 11, 15 (2001).

[90] Complaint, Food Lion, Inc. v. Capital Cities/ABC, Inc., No. 92 CVS 5513 (Forsyth Co. Super. Ct. Sept. 17, 1992) (copy on file with author).

[91] This information was obtained from the Bloomberg docket database for Food Lion, Inc. v. Capital Cities/ABC, et al., U.S. District Court for the Middle District of North Carolina, No. 6:92-cv-00592 [hereinafter *Bloomberg Docket*].

[92] *Id.*

motions. Food Lion also sought sanctions against the defendants and their attorneys relating to some of the discovery fights.[93] There were serious disputes about how to conduct the trial as well. It is unclear whether this was a result of a court order or the parties' agreement, but the actual "Primetime Live" story was never presented to the jury.[94] This may have been the case because, as the trial court recognized, "Food Lion made no defamation claim and, therefore, did not challenge the truthfulness of the broadcast."[95]

Finally, more than four years after the "Primetime Live" broadcasts, the case went to trial.[96] After a multiweek trial on liability, the jury found all defendants liable for fraud and found Dale and Barnett liable for trespass and violating the duty of loyalty. The district court also found, based on the jury's findings, that the defendants had violated the state unfair and deceptive trade practices statute. It ruled, however, that Food Lion could not recover damages for lost profits, lost sales, or other economic harms associated with the broadcast on the ground that those damages were not proximately caused by the defendants' conduct.[97]

With that limit, the compensatory damages phase of the trial proceeded, with the jury awarding $1,400 in compensatory damages for fraud, two $1 nominal damage awards against both Barnett and Dale for trespass and breach of the duty of loyalty, and $1,500 in damages for violation of the state statute.[98] Finally, after the third phase of the trial, the jury awarded a stunning $5,545,750 in punitive damages against ABC and two of its executive producers.[99] Though the trial court reduced the punitive damages award to $315,000 on remittitur,[100] the verdicts were a substantial blow to the network, its producers, and the future of undercover investigations.

The defendants appealed, arguing on several grounds that the verdict should be overturned.[101] In a significant victory for the defendants, the Fourth Circuit reversed several aspects of the trial court's rulings. First, the court reversed the trial court's judgment that all defendants had committed fraud. In a creative variation on resume fraud, Food Lion claimed that it relied to its detriment on the belief that Barnett and Dale would continue in their jobs past the short period in which they worked. It argued that it suffered administrative costs relating to the need to find, hire, and

93 As one indication of the battle's intensity, the Bloomberg trial docket trial has 671 entries. *Id.*

94 Food Lion, Inc. v. Cap. Cities/ABC, Inc., 964 F. Supp. 956, 964 n.5 (M.D.N.C. 1997), *aff'd on other grounds*, 194 F.3d 505 (4th Cir. 1999).

95 *Id.* at 962.

96 *Bloomberg Docket*, *supra* note 91.

97 194 F.3d at 511.

98 *Id.* at 517. The trial court required Food Lion to elect whether to receive damages under the state statutory claim or the fraud claim. Food Lion elected to receive $1,400 under the latter. *Id.* at 511.

99 *Id.*

100 *Id.* at 511.

101 Food Lion cross-appealed on the denial of publication damages, but the court affirmed the district court's decision to reject that remedy. *Id.* at 522–24.

administratively process new employees to replace Barnett and Dale. Noting that neither of the producers represented that they would work at Food Lion indefinitely and that they were at-will employees, the court held that Food Lion could not have reasonably relied to its detriment on the misrepresentations made by Barnett and Dale to secure their jobs.[102] Most importantly, because the punitive damages award was tied to the fraud claim, the invalidation of that claim meant that the $315,000 verdict on that part of the case was vacated.[103]

Next, the Fourth Circuit reversed one of the two theories on which Food Lion's trespass claim rested. As discussed earlier, the states are divided on the question of whether a person who induces a landowner's consent to enter property by misrepresentation has committed a trespass. Food Lion asserted that such misrepresentation did vitiate its consent, but the Fourth Circuit disagreed. While noting that the Restatement states that consent induced by misrepresentation is not valid, the court nonetheless observed that "the various jurisdictions and authorities in this country are not of one mind in dealing with the issue."[104]

On this point, the Fourth Circuit followed the U.S. Court of Appeals for the Seventh Circuit's decision in *Desnick v. American Broadcasting Companies, Inc.*[105] In *Desnick*, a news station and its reporters conducted an undercover investigation by pretending to be patients in need of cataract surgeries to investigate an eye doctor who was reported to recommend such surgeries when they were not medically necessary. Though the reporters engaged in deception, the Seventh Circuit rejected the doctor's claim that they had trespassed. In an opinion by Judge Posner, the court held that the reporters' entry into a business that is open to customers is not a trespass because "consent to an entry is often given legal effect even though the entrant has intentions that if known to the owner of the property would cause him for perfectly understandable and generally ethical or at least lawful reasons to revoke his consent."[106] The court noted that in such a case, "[t]here was no invasion … of any of the specific interests that the tort of trespass seeks to protect."[107] But other federal courts have disagreed on this critical point.[108]

But the appellate court's decision was not a complete win for journalism. The Fourth Circuit upheld liability against Barnett and Dale on the duty of loyalty claim

[102] *Id.* at 512–13. In a partial dissent, Judge Niemeyer disagreed with the majority on this point. *Id.* at 524 (Niemeyer, J., concurring in part and dissenting in part).

[103] 194 F.3d at 522.

[104] *Id.* at 517.

[105] Desnick v. Am. Broad. Companies, Inc., 44 F.3d 1345 (7th Cir. 1995).

[106] *Id.* at 1351.

[107] *Id.* at 1352.

[108] *Compare Wasden*, 878 F.3d at 1196 (holding that a trespass does not occur when an investigator secures consent to enter a business property by deception); *Food Lion*, 194 F.3d at 518 (same); *Desnick*, 44 F.3d at 1352 (same) *with* Animal Legal Def. Fund v. Reynolds, 8 F.4th 781, 786 (8th Cir. 2021). Two federal judges have dissented in Ag Gag cases, taking the position that misrepresentation vitiates consent to enter land. *See Kelly*, 9 F.4th at 1250 (Hartz, J., dissenting); *Wasden*, 878 F.3d at 1211 (Bea, J., dissenting in part and concurring in part).

and on a distinct trespass theory. First, it concluded that under state law, the producers had violated the duty of loyalty. The Fourth Circuit conceded that under existing case law in North Carolina and South Carolina, the duty of loyalty had only been recognized where "an employee competes directly with her employer," "the employee misappropriates her employer's profits, property, or business opportunities," or "an employee breaches her employer's confidences," none of which were true here.[109] Nevertheless, the court predicted that, if faced with the issue, the courts of those states would have found a violation of the duty of loyalty on these facts. As it explained:

> The interests of the employer (ABC) to whom Dale and Barnett gave complete loyalty were adverse to the interests of Food Lion, the employer to whom they were unfaithful. ABC and Food Lion were not business competitors but they were adverse in a fundamental way. ABC's interest was to expose Food Lion to the public as a food chain that engaged in unsanitary and deceptive practices. Dale and Barnett served ABC's interest, at the expense of Food Lion, by engaging in the taping for ABC while they were on Food Lion's payroll. In doing this, Dale and Barnett did not serve Food Lion faithfully, and their interest (which was the same as ABC's) was diametrically opposed to Food Lion's. In these circumstances, we believe that the highest courts of North and South Carolina would hold that the reporters – in promoting the interests of one master, ABC, to the detriment of a second, Food Lion – committed the tort of disloyalty against Food Lion.[110]

The court also upheld the nominal damages verdicts against Dale and Barnett for trespass. Although it found that their initial entry on to Food Lion's property through "resume fraud" was not a trespass in itself,[111] it concluded that a trespass occurs when "*a wrongful act is done in excess of and in abuse of authorized entry*."[112] That wrongful act was the producers' violation of the duty of loyalty. The Fourth Circuit thus bootstrapped the producers' violation of the duty of loyalty as the requisite wrongful act that converted their initially consensual entry into a trespass. The overall outcome of the appeal was that only the two $1 nominal damages awards against both Dale and Barnett were ultimately upheld.

Furthermore, while the court reduced the defendants' financial liability to almost nothing, it rejected their contention that the First Amendment protected the producers from even that liability because the suit was targeting them for engaging in behavior that was indisputably newsgathering. The Fourth Circuit disagreed with the defendants' First Amendment arguments, noting that the Supreme Court has held on more than one occasion that journalists are not constitutionally entitled to exemption from generally applicable laws, even when they are engaged in

[109] 194 F.3d at 516.
[110] *Id.*
[111] *Id.* at 518.
[112] *Id.* at 517 (emphasis added). The Fourth Circuit also overturned the jury's fraud verdict on Food Lion's common law and statutory fraud claims. *Id.* at 512–13, 519–20.

newsgathering.[113] Neither the tort of trespass nor the duty of loyalty, it concluded, "targets or singles out the press."[114]

Moreover, it's noteworthy that the litigation lasted nearly seven years and likely cost ABC several million dollars to defend. ABC is a national television news network with substantial assets, but the chilling effect of this level of litigation costs would likely be more than enough to give pause to a local newspaper or television station that might have otherwise hoped to conduct an undercover investigation. In this way, litigation by the targets of undercover investigations has deterrent effects similar to those created by the prospect of costly defamation claims. Notwithstanding that in defamation cases, journalists have the extra First Amendment protection from *New York Times Co. v. Sullivan*[115] and may ultimately prevail in most cases, the litigation costs alone may shape journalists' decisions about what to investigate and what to publish.

Without some constitutional protection for undercover newsgathering, an important vehicle for facilitating the discovery and disclosure of information vital to democracy may be forever lost. Although some recent lower court decisions have offered hope for the development of some type of First Amendment privilege, other cases seem to foreclose that possibility. In the next part, I argue that *Food Lion* and its shadow have deterred journalists from engaging in employment-based undercover investigations. And I make a preliminary case for reconsidering *Food Lion* under certain conditions.

14.2.3 *Food Lion's Legal Deterrent Effect*

Despite a seemingly good outcome and the relatively benign impact of nominal damages awards, *Food Lion* continues to have a chilling effect on undercover investigations. Its ruling on the duty of loyalty has more significant effects than it might at first seem. This is particularly so because many consider employment-based undercover investigations to be the most effective type of undercover investigations because they permit investigators to access people and places beyond the eyes of the general public.[116]

First, although the *Food Lion* court did not directly accept the argument that consent to enter property induced by deception is a trespass, that area of the law continues to evolve. Courts upholding Ag Gag laws have been generally sympathetic to states' claims that gaining access or employment to private property by deception

[113] 194 F.3d at 520–22 (*citing* Cohen v. Cowles Media Co., 501 U.S. 663, 669 (1991); Branzburg v. Hayes, 408 U.S. 665, 684 (1972)).

[114] 194 F.3d at 521.

[115] New York Times Co. v. Sullivan, 376 U.S. 254, 278 (1964).

[116] *See generally* Cody Carlson, *The Ag Gag Laws: Hiding Factory Farm Abuses from Public Scrutiny*, The Atlantic, Mar. 20, 2012, https://www.theatlantic.com/health/archive/2012/03/the-ag-gag-laws-hiding-factory-farm-abuses-from-public-scrutiny/254674/.

interferes with the government interest in preventing trespass.[117] The plaintiffs in these cases have argued that although gaining access to private property by consent induced by false statements is a trespass under some states' laws, the trespass harm in cases of investigators is de minimis and therefore does not constitute the type of legally cognizable harm that *Alvarez* contemplates. While some courts that have struck down Ag Gag laws have agreed,[118] others have decided the cases without addressing that specific argument.[119] This leaves that important legal question in limbo.

Even if the trespass theory asserted by investigative targets were to be ultimately rejected, *Food Lion*'s interpretation of the duty of loyalty may make that irrelevant. Recall that the Fourth Circuit ruled that even a person who has received the landowner's consent to enter property as an employee may subsequently be engaged in a trespass if they breach the duty of loyalty by committing a wrongful act in excess of their authority to enter the premises.[120] The wrongful act, according to the court, was the act of "filming in non-public areas ... adverse to Food Lion."[121] But that describes virtually every single person who conducts an employment-based undercover investigation, thus exposing them to trespass liability via their inevitable violation (in the Fourth Circuit's view) of the duty of loyalty. Thus, the $1 verdicts notwithstanding, the impact of this part of the holding cannot be overstated. Undercover investigators always engage in deception when they conduct an employment-based investigation. They must lie or obscure their true identity, the sponsor of their investigation, and their motives whenever they try to get a job in this situation. The Fourth Circuit's conclusion that this constitutes a trespass when their *subsequent* conduct breaches the duty of loyalty effectively reverses its holding that "resume fraud" does not constitute a trespass. It also effectively undermines its earlier conclusion that consent to enter property induced by misrepresentation does not constitute a trespass. This seems to slice the onion a little too thin.

Similarly, even if *Alvarez* is ultimately interpreted to allow First Amendment protection for investigative deception, *Food Lion*'s conclusion about the duty of loyalty would render that pro-speech holding a nullity. According to the Fourth Circuit, the duty of loyalty is breached not by "resume fraud" but by the very fact that the employee is simultaneously working for the sponsor of the investigation and its target.[122] Thus, under any interpretation of *Alvarez*'s "offers of employment" dictum, under *Food Lion*, the breach of the duty of loyalty would still represent a legally cognizable harm.

[117] *See, e.g.*, Reynolds I, 8 F.4th at 786. Dissenting judges in some of the other cases asserted this same position. Kelly, 9 F.4th at 1250 (Hartz, J., dissenting); *Wasden*, 878 F.3d at 1211 (Bea, J., dissenting in part and concurring in part).

[118] Animal Legal Def. Fund v. Herbert, 263 F. Supp. 3d 1193 (D. Utah 2017).

[119] Animal Legal Def. Fund v. Kelly, 9 F.4th 1219 (10th Cir. 2021).

[120] 194 F.3d at 518.

[121] *Id.*

[122] *Id.* at 516.

It is not surprising, therefore, that Food Lion's trial strategy was to focus on Barnett and Dale's supposed acts of disloyalty. Both before and during the trial, Food Lion's lawyers attempted to portray Barnett and Dale as having staged some parts of the report that showed food sanitation or handling problems.[123] One incident described in the report was about a meat grinder that was not cleaned before the store closed one night, and that employees simply began using the uncleaned equipment the next day. Food Lion lawyers suggested that this was misleading, falsely alleging that Dale had sabotaged the store's water heater so that it would be unavailable for cleaning – a charge that was later found by the jury to be untrue.[124] Siegel reported that the focus of Food Lion's trial strategy was based on these "pseudo-staging allegations," attempting to show that Barnett and Dale were not only failing to do their jobs as Food Lion employees but also actively interfering with Food Lion's operations.[125] In a pretrial ruling, the district court found that allegations of "staging" were relevant to Food Lion's duty of loyalty claim, but those staging claims were later ruled inadmissible by the judge, who found they had no merit.[126]

To be sure, it isn't clear that *Food Lion* is even correct that the duty of loyalty applies in this context. First, the Fourth Circuit appears to have been incorrect even as a matter of state law. Just two years after *Food Lion* was decided, the North Carolina Supreme Court held that the district court in *Food Lion* had "incorrectly interpreted our state case law" and that "although our state courts recognize the existence of an employee's duty of loyalty, we do not recognize its breach as an independent claim."[127] Moreover, in many jurisdictions that do recognize a duty of loyalty cause of action, liability turns on whether the employee has a fiduciary duty to the employer.[128] As previously discussed, most undercover investigators take lower level, at-will employment jobs, which are generally not entrusted with the type of duties from which a fiduciary relationship is created.[129]

Furthermore, the Supreme Court has rejected this same type of agency law claim when directed at another type of undercover investigator. In *N.L.R.B. v. Town & Country Electric, Inc.*,[130] the Court considered an employer's claim that an employee who was also a paid union organizer was not an "employee" within the meaning of the National Labor Relations Act. In doing so, the employer invoked the common law of agency, which it maintained prohibited a person from

[123] *Barnett/Dale Interview*, *supra* note 4.

[124] *Id. See also* Food Lion, Inc. v. Cap. Cities/ABC, Inc., 964 F. Supp. 956, 964 (M.D.N.C. 1997), *aff'd on other grounds*, 194 F.3d 505 (4th Cir. 1999).

[125] *Siegel Interview*, *supra* note 4.

[126] Food Lion, Inc. v. Cap. Cities/ABC, Inc., 951 F. Supp. 1224, 1230 (M.D.N.C. 1996).

[127] Dalton v. Camp, 353 N.C. 647, 653 (2001).

[128] Riedy & Sperduto, *supra* note 81, at 272.

[129] *Id.*

[130] 516 U.S. 85 (1995).

simultaneously serving "two masters," the union and the employer.[131] But the Court disagreed with the employer's argument, concluding that the common law did not prohibit this particular type of disloyalty. In an opinion by Justice Breyer, the Court stated that it is a "hornbook rule" that a "person *may* be the servant of two masters . . . at one time as to one act, *if the service to one does not involve abandonment of service to the other*."[132] That seems to be the case with the investigation in *Food Lion*. In rejecting Food Lion's claim that it should recover the wages it paid to Barnett and Dale, the Fourth Circuit observed that:

> Dale and Barnett were paid because they showed up for work and performed their assigned tasks as Food Lion employees. Their performance was at a level suitable to their status as new, entry-level employees. Indeed, shortly before Dale quit, her supervisor said she would "make a good meat wrapper." And, when Barnett quit, her supervisor recommended that she be rehired if she sought reemployment with Food Lion in the future.[133]

Thus, it would appear that Barnett and Dale's work for ABC did not "involve abandonment of service to" Food Lion. Notwithstanding this conclusion on damages, however, the court found that "it is possible to perform the assigned tasks of a job adequately and still breach the duty of loyalty."[134]

14.2.4 *Food Lion's Influence on Journalism Ethics*

But *Food Lion*'s deterrent effect on undercover investigations derives not only from its status as a legal precedent but also because it has significantly influenced debates about the ethics of undercover investigations in the journalism profession. In recent years, there has been extensive criticism of undercover journalism from within the profession, with many claiming that the tactics necessary to carry out a successful undercover investigation demean the profession and undermine its credibility. Unlike other professions, journalism does not have a state licensing scheme, which would be severely problematic for freedoms of the press because it would grant the government too much control over journalists and might even be viewed as a form of prior restraint. But in other professions, ethical standards are set by professional licensing institutions. In journalism, each individual news institution, whether it be a newspaper or television network, sets its own internal ethical standards. While there are ethical codes published by professional journalism organizations, they are not binding. Ethical decisions are therefore decentralized, leaving substantial room for disagreement.

With regard to undercover investigations, this disagreement has been manifest. While some journalists defend undercover investigations as a critical tool for

[131] *Id.* at 93.
[132] *Id.* at 94–95 (quoting Restatement (Second) of Agency §226, at 498) (emphasis by the Court).
[133] *Food Lion*, 194 F.3d at 514.
[134] *Id.*

newsgathering, particularly to discover information that would not otherwise see the light of day, others argue that journalistic honesty cannot have exceptions and that truth is a central tenet of what it means to be a journalist. As Justin Marceau and I have written about extensively, this debate largely turns on the different schools of thought about the foundations of journalism ethics.[135] But the debate among journalists continues and is likely to persist.

While I cannot identify any empirical data or systematic examination of *Food Lion*'s impact on undercover investigations, there is a fair amount of anecdotal evidence that it has influenced the journalism ethics debate. First, as the quote from the beginning of this chapter suggests, in contemporary times, print newspapers have shown a great reluctance to undertake such investigations. Many of them have well-publicized ethical codes that forbid their employees from engaging in deception or using hidden cameras in their newsgathering.[136] It is unclear exactly when these codes went into effect, but my prior research suggests that the emergence of general professional objections to undercover investigations began in the late 1990s, roughly coinciding with the *Food Lion* decision.[137] For example, the Society of Professional Journalists (SPJ) first addressed undercover investigations explicitly in its 1996 revision to its Code of Ethics.[138] The prior 1973 version of SPJ's Code of Ethics does not mention undercover investigations,[139] but the 1996 revision states that journalists should "Avoid undercover or other surreptitious methods of gathering information except when traditional open methods will not yield information vital to the public" and further advises that "Use of such methods should be explained as part of the story."[140]

Indeed, the Food Lion company itself tried to expand the reach of its courtroom victory by trying to influence university journalism curriculums.[141] In a highly

[135] Chen & Marceau, Truth and Transparency, *supra* note 5, at 36–74. We argue in favor of a journalistic ethics standard grounded in the liberal theory and interpretation and activism theories, which both match well with a utilitarian model that weighs the value of the information discovered against any social harms that might be caused by an undercover investigation. Having said this, I do not take the counterarguments on the ethics of undercover investigations lightly. After all, utilitarian arguments can be highly subjective and tied to the value judgments of the person making them. One person may value newsgathering more highly than property and privacy interests, even in a business setting, while another may simply disagree. This makes it difficult to center an ethical claim on any form of general consensus. On the other hand, at least utilitarian arguments are transparent about their justifications, enabling society and individuals ultimately to make their own judgments.

[136] *See, e.g., Ethical Journalism: A Handbook of Values and Practices for the News and Editorial Departments – Pursuing the News*, N.Y. Times, www.nytimes.com/editorial-standards/ethical-journalism.html#. The Times does not indicate an initial publication date for the Handbook though it references a Newsroom Integrity Statement, published in 1999.

[137] Chen & Marceau, Truth and Transparency, *supra* note 5, at 60–62.

[138] *1996 SPJ Code of Ethics*, *supra* note 49.

[139] Society of Professional Journalists, *Society of Professional Journalists – 1973 Code of Ethics*, https://spjnetwork.org/quill2/codedcontroversey/ethics-code-1973.pdf.

[140] *1996 SPJ Code of Ethics*, *supra* note 49.

[141] Jacqueline Sharkey, *Taking the Fight to the Classroom*, 20 Am. Journalism Rev. 12 (1998); *Barnett/Dale Interview*, *supra* note 4.

controversial effort, shortly after the Fourth Circuit's decision, Food Lion prepared materials about the case and sent them to around 200 journalism professors around the country.[142] "The grocery chain's educational kit included a self-produced report, 'Fakes, Lies and Videotape,' and a 15-minute video prepared by a public relations firm, which uses unaired ABC footage to support the company's contention that ABC's report was untrue."[143] The company also apparently engaged a journalism professor to assist them in their efforts.[144] It is unclear what, if any, influence Food Lion's propaganda efforts had on journalism curricula, and many journalism faculty were quite skeptical about the effort. One professor noted that the materials prioritized Food Lion's viewpoint but did not provide the counterpoint from ABC's perspective that the investigation was consistent with journalism philosophy and norms.[145]

There is also anecdotal evidence from commentators about *Food Lion*'s impact on undercover investigations. Seth Stern, advocacy director for the Freedom of the Press Foundation, recently observed a drop in undercover investigations. As he noted, the *Food Lion* case has been "often presented to young journalists as a cautionary tale," and "the landmark case significantly slowed the once relatively common practice of 'undercover' journalism."[146] Notwithstanding the fact that *Food Lion* ultimately resulted in only nominal damages, Stern suggested that the case made lawyers recognize a substantial risk of "punitive damages based on newsgathering methods."[147] He suggested that because of the *Food Lion* case, many mainstream news outlets stopped engaging in hidden-camera and other undercover investigations.[148] As Stern observed, "There's no telling how many stories the public missed out on as a result of the changes to journalism – both legal and cultural – brought about by Food Lion."[149]

My interviews with the ABC producers and lawyer in the *Food Lion* case support Stern's observations and provide anecdotal support for my theory that *employment-based* investigations are decreasing. Although Susan Barnett and Lynne Dale went on to conduct multiple undercover investigations with different national television networks after the *Food Lion* case concluded, neither of them has done one requiring them to secure a job with the investigation's target.[150] Dale reported that "we couldn't get a job. That was off the table and had been off the table ever since

[142] Sharkey, *supra* note 141, at 12.
[143] *Id.*
[144] *Id.*
[145] *Id.*
[146] Seth Stern, *Is It Time to Revisit Undercover Journalism?*, Freedom of the Press Foundation (Oct. 31, 2023), https://freedom.press/news/is-it-time-to-revisit-undercover-journalism/
[147] *Id.*
[148] *Id.*
[149] *Id.*
[150] *See Barnett/Dale Interview*, *supra* note 4.

Food Lion sued us."[151] Similarly, media lawyer Nathan Siegel, who represented Barnett, Dale, and ABC during the *Food Lion* litigation, confirmed that there have been very few "undercover investigations since [*Food Lion*] that have turned on actually obtaining employment."[152]

Stern observed that not only have major journalism companies steered away from undercover investigations, but also that such investigations are "now often associated with fringe (and often disreputable) platforms,"[153] such as the far-right activist group Project Veritas. In response, he suggests that more mainstream journalists should (after consulting with lawyers) seize this tactic back from such groups, noting that the Fourth Circuit's recent favorable decision in *People for the Ethical Treatment of Animals v. North Carolina Farm Bureau Federation*[154] could be a catalyst.[155]

Another commentator has also framed the debate against the backdrop of groups with questionable credibility, but, unlike Stern, argues that the influence moves in the other direction. Erik Wemple, The Washington Post's media critic, has argued that the fringe groups' efforts to use undercover investigation have proven that the tactics are dishonorable.[156] Wemple wrote that before James O'Keefe established Project Veritas in 2011, "*American journalists were falling out of love with undercover tactics – a breakup aided by Food Lion's 1995 suit against* ABC *News* for its clandestine exposé on the grocery behemoth's unsavory meat-handling practices."[157]

Wemple goes on to say that "Mainstream outlets, accordingly, have spent the past couple of decades either swearing off undercover work or narrowing the circumstances when it's warranted."[158] He continued:

> Project Veritas must not have been spending enough time reading Poynter.org for ethics guidance. "Especially since the Food Lion misrepresentation and hidden-camera stuff, news organizations don't do the [full range]" of clandestine tactics, "where they put them all together at the same time," says Lee Levine, a longtime First Amendment attorney. Contemporary examples of undercover stories are harder and harder to come by these days, says Levine – and even in the years when the practice was tapering off, he continues, news organizations that did embrace it were "very careful not to lie."[159]

[151] *Id.*

[152] *Siegel Interview*, *supra* note 4.

[153] Stern, *supra* note 146.

[154] People for the Ethical Treatment of Animals, Inc. v. N. Carolina Farm Bureau Fed'n, Inc., 60 F.4th 815 (4th Cir. 2023) (cleaned up).

[155] Stern, *supra* note 146.

[156] Erik Wemple, *Verdict Upends Project Veritas's Journalism Defense in Infiltration Case*, WASH. POST (Sept. 23, 2022), https://www.washingtonpost.com/opinions/2022/09/23/project-veritas-democracy-partners-verdict/.

[157] *Id.*

[158] *Id.*

[159] *Id.*

14.3 RECONSIDERING FOOD LION

14.3.1 *Legal Hurdles to Reconsidering Food Lion*

The case for reconsidering *Food Lion* must begin with some existing barriers under current First Amendment doctrine. As has long been documented and criticized, the Supreme Court has never recognized a substantive constitutional right for the press distinct from the First Amendment right of free speech.[160] Notwithstanding the First Amendment's text, which specifically establishes a freedom of the press, the Court has ignored this and held that the press's rights are coextensive with the rights recognized under the Speech Clause.[161] Even in cases where the Court has recognized important freedoms for the press, such as in cases holding that the First Amendment embodies a right to access certain types of criminal proceedings in court, those rights have been understood as belonging to the public, not to the press per se.[162]

Furthermore, to date, the Court has consistently held that journalists are not entitled to exemptions from generally applicable criminal and civil laws, even if the enforcement of such laws directly impairs critical press functions.[163] More specifically, the Supreme Court has never recognized in any type of First Amendment right for journalists or others to protect them from laws or government action that inhibits their newsgathering. In *Branzburg v. Hayes*, the Court rejected the First Amendment claims of journalists who sought an exemption from testifying before grand juries and disclosing their confidential sources.[164] The reporters involved in that case argued that revealing their sources in grand jury proceedings would undermine their ability to engage in newsgathering because such sources would no longer trust that their identities would remain secret. While they did not seek an absolute privilege from grand jury subpoenas, the reporters argued that journalists should not be compelled to testify unless the State showed "sufficient grounds . . . for believing that the reporter possesses information relevant to a crime the grand jury is investigating, that the information the reporter has is unavailable from other sources, and that the need for the information is sufficiently compelling to override the claimed invasion of First Amendment interests occasioned by the disclosure."[165]

Rejecting the journalists' privilege claim, the Supreme Court noted that the Constitution does not call for treating journalists differently from the average citizen, who must appear before a grand jury and testify when subpoenaed, even if

[160] Sonja R. West, *Awakening the Press Clause*, 58 UCLA L. Rev. 1025, 1027 (2011).

[161] *Id.*

[162] Press-Enterprise Co. v. Superior Ct, 478 U.S. 1 (1986); Richmond Newspapers, Inc. v. Virginia, 448 U.S. 555 (1980) (plurality opinion).

[163] Cohen v. Cowles Media Co., 501 U.S. 663 (1991).

[164] Branzburg v. Hayes, 408 U.S. 665 (1972).

[165] *Id.* at 680.

the relevant information they have was obtained in confidence.[166] Key to the Court's reasoning was its concern that journalists not be permitted to be exempt from every "incidental" burden on their professional work from generally applicable laws.[167] While the Court stated it was not holding that newsgathering does not qualify for First Amendment protection, it did not articulate when such protection would be available and has not done so in the fifty years since it decided *Branzburg*.[168]

The Court also declared that members of the press are not exempt from generally applicable laws in *Cohen v. Cowles Media Co.*[169] In *Cohen*, a confidential source sued a newspaper for breach of contract and misrepresentation after it published a story disclosing the source's identity. The newspaper asserted a First Amendment privilege, arguing that it should not be subject to liability for the publication of truthful information that is lawfully obtained.[170] While the Court accepted that proposition in the abstract, it held that "generally applicable laws do not offend the First Amendment simply because their enforcement against the press has incidental effects on its ability to gather and report the news … The press may not with impunity break and enter an office or dwelling to gather news."[171]

These precedents would seem to present insurmountable barriers to the recognition of even a limited privilege for undercover investigations. But while they may set the baseline for claims to be exempt from otherwise generally applicable laws, there is nonetheless still room to assert some privileges. First, notwithstanding *Branzburg*'s holding, many lower federal courts have subsequently recognized a "qualified privilege" permitting journalists to refuse disclosure of confidential sources if potential negative impact on newsgathering outweighs the public's need for the information.[172] These courts seem to have taken to heart *Branzburg*'s recognition that the First Amendment provides "some protection" for newsgathering.[173] Nor is *Cowles*'s seemingly categorical rejection of a press exemption from generally applicable laws a complete bar to some constitutional protection for newsgathering. In some recent

[166] *Id.* at 682.
[167] *Id.*
[168] *Id.* at 681. It's also worth noting that there is a seamless connection between *Branzburg* and undercover investigations that has heretofore gone unrecognized. To the extent that no constitutional privilege exists to protect confidential informants, the law places greater pressure on journalists to find other ways to gather and disseminate information of broad public concern. Undercover investigations might at least partially fill that information gap, but only if there is some constitutional protection for conducting them.
[169] Cohen v. Cowles Media Co., 501 U.S. 663 (1991).
[170] *Id.* at 668–69.
[171] *Id.* at 669.
[172] *See, e.g.*, Bruno & Stillman, Inc. v. Globe Newspaper Co., 633 F.2d 583, 595–96 (1st Cir. 1980); Silkwood v. Kerr-McGee Corp., 563 F.2d 433, 436–37 (10th Cir. 1977).
[173] *Branzburg*, 408 U.S. at 681.

cases, lower courts have held that statutes that apply to a range of conduct are not exempt from First Amendment scrutiny where those statutes are applied to speech.[174]

14.3.2 *The Shape of a Legal Privilege for Undercover Investigations*

A legal privilege to engage in investigative deception and secret recordings to gather information on matters of public concern might be established by the Supreme Court as part of the First Amendment's Speech Clause or Press Clause. If the Court is unwilling to do so, such a privilege could be created at the local level by state supreme courts interpreting and applying their own speech and press clauses. Finally, as has occurred with shield laws that protect journalists from being compelled to disclose confidential sources, it could happen through state legislatures. The following sections discuss my proposal for possible ways to construct such a privilege.

14.3.2.1 Unconditional Privilege with Industry Self-regulation

If courts or legislatures were to recognize a newsgatherer's privilege to engage in deception and secret recording to conduct undercover investigations, one approach they could take is to make it an unconditional privilege, but rely on the news media's practice of self-regulation in other areas of press freedom in which broader public interests counsel against publication.[175] Despite the fact that news outlets are incentivized to pursue high circulation, ratings, and profits, the press counterbalances that demand with other concerns, such as maintaining credibility with its audience.[176]

One might reject an approach relying on industry self-regulation on the grounds that it insufficiently protects against the potential invasion of property, privacy, and loyalty interests that undercover investigations are said to compromise. But in several areas, the journalism profession has engaged in self-regulation and resisted publication of newsworthy information that may technically be published without restriction because such publication is protected by the First Amendment. For example, at least where the media obtain the information from publicly available sources, the Supreme Court has established that the news media may publish the names of

[174] People for the Ethical Treatment of Animals, Inc. v. N. Carolina Farm Bureau Fed'n, Inc., 60 F.4th 815, 825–26 (4th Cir. 2023) (cleaned up); Animal Legal Def. Fund v. Wasden, 878 F.3d 1184, 1190 (9th Cir. 2018).

[175] Blake D. Morant, *The Endemic Reality of Media Ethics and Self-Restraint*, 19 Notre Dame J.L. Ethics & Pub. Pol'y 595, 618 (2005) ("As a generalized rule, self-regulation diminishes the need for external regulation of the [news media] industry.").

[176] *Id.* at 609.

crime victims.[177] Yet it is recognized that because of internal ethics standards, the vast majority of media outlets generally do not report such information.[178] Similarly, self-regulation in journalism typically means that, despite the newsworthiness of these matters, the press does not report the names of juveniles involved in judicial proceedings, the results of presidential elections prior to the polls closing in western time zones, and information that might compromise national security interests.[179]

Relying on the journalism profession to self-regulate regarding undercover investigations may not, however, accomplish the goal of expanding such investigations because there is substantial and ongoing disagreement about the ethics of such investigations among the American media.[180] Many major newspapers prohibit their reporters from conducting undercover investigations regardless of whether there is any legal protection for such conduct.[181] However, the recognition of a constitutional or other legal privilege to engage in deception and secret recording might influence the internal professional standards that prohibit such conduct.

Another significant disadvantage of the unconditional privilege coupled with industry self-regulation is that it relies on professional standards that may not be generally accepted outside of the institutional news media. That is, it might limit the privilege to only those in the newsgathering profession and thereby exclude undercover investigators working with nonprofit organizations to support their political advocacy. By definition, those groups and their investigators would not be bound by the standards of professional journalism. Some would argue that this is a feature, not a bug, of a profession-based standard – under this view, the trade-off necessary to recognize a privilege that outweighs other legal interests, such as trespass or the duty of loyalty, can only be justified if that privilege is limited to those who agree to be bound by the journalism profession's ethical standards and are therefore professionally accountable. While I acknowledge this concern, the cost of a privilege limited to professional journalists would be the loss of information that might otherwise be uncovered through undercover investigations by non-journalists. And, as I argue below, ethical considerations may be accounted for by conditioning the privilege on adherence to a set of best practices, without regard to the identity of the investigator.

This version of the privilege would also arguably not apply to the increasingly common practices of citizen journalists, who are also not technically governed by professional journalistic standards. It is for this reason that I have previously argued that constitutional protection for undercover investigations be grounded in the

[177] *See, e.g.*, The Fla. Star v. B.J.F., 491 U.S. 524 (1989); Cox Broad. Corp. v. Cohn, 420 U.S. 469 (1975).

[178] Morant, *supra* note 175, at 609.

[179] *Id.* at 609–11.

[180] For a comprehensive discussion of these ethical debates, *see* Chen & Marceau, Truth and Transparency, *supra* note 5, at 36–74.

[181] *See, e.g.*, *Ethical Journalism*, *supra* note 136.

Speech Clause rather than the Press Clause.[182] But recognizing a Press Clause privilege in this form would at the very least ensure the protection of important undercover investigations by the professional news media.[183]

14.3.2.2 Conditional Privilege

An alternative model that courts or legislatures could consider is establishing a newsgatherers' privilege to be exempt from criminal or civil liability for engaging in undercover investigative tactics conditioned on two distinct grounds. First, it would only apply to the extent the person conducting the investigation is involved in newsgathering activities. Second, the privilege would apply only where investigators have adhered to a set of best practices or ethical norms that would safeguard against intrusion on some of the interests that would otherwise be promoted by enforcement of such laws.

The newsgathering limitation would provide some flexibility to courts examining a First Amendment newsgathering defense in criminal or civil litigation because it would permit them to reject the enforcement of such laws only as applied to newsgathering. There is obviously nothing unconstitutional about a generally applicable law requiring employees to be loyal (however defined) to their employers. But it is equally obvious, I think, that when employers dust off this tort to be used only when they have been the target of an undercover investigation, some First Amendment scrutiny should be applied.

In one of the most recent Ag Gag cases, the Fourth Circuit invalidated North Carolina's Property Protection Act, which created a new private right of action for employers to sue employees who entered "nonpublic areas of an employer's premises," captured the employer's data, paper, records, or other documents or recording images or sound occurring within that premises, and used that information "to breach the person's duty of loyalty to the employer."[184] The law was challenged as

182 There is an ongoing and important scholarly debate about the meaning of the Press Clause. Some legal scholars have argued for a more functional approach to applying the Press Clause, meaning that the constitutional protections extend to any person engaged in newsgathering, rather than only those who work for the institutional press. *See, e.g.*, Ugland, *supra* note 3, at 137; Linda L. Berger, *Shielding the Unmedia: Using the Process of Journalism to Protect the Journalist's Privilege in an Infinite Universe of Publication*, 39 Hous. L. Rev. 137, 137 (2003). Under that view, the Press Clause could be read to protect undercover investigations by the institutional media and other actors. Others contend that a functional approach is too broad, erasing the distinction between the Speech and Press Clauses, and paradoxically undermining the rights of the press and the distinct role the press plays in promoting democracy. *See, e.g.*, West, *supra* note 160, at 1032. This view, of course, is more consistent with the First Amendment's text.

183 *See* West, *supra* note 160, at 1056 (observing that a narrower reading of the Press Clause's scope might actually lead to more expansive, albeit not unlimited, constitutional protection for the press).

184 N.C. Gen. Stat. Ann. § 99A-2

unconstitutional on its face and as applied to animal rights investigators and others who wished to get jobs and disclose wrongdoing by their employers. The Fourth Circuit, however, invalidated the statute only as applied to the newsgathering activities of the animal rights organizations who challenged the law.[185] This is somewhat similar to a standard that Ashutosh Bhagwat has proposed. He has argued that while content-neutral regulations of the production of speech "are presumptively constitutional on their face," they "may be challenged as applied to speech that contributes in some substantial way to democratic self-governance."[186]

This condition has the further advantage of applying the privilege to any person engaged in legitimate newsgathering activities, rather than just professional journalists. As described in much of my other work, undercover investigations by political groups contribute to public discourse in ways that are comparable to those conducted by members of the press.[187] If we conceptualized the privilege as grounded in the Speech Clause, it would apply to all investigators. And even if the protection was located in the Press Clause, that Clause has sometimes been understood to protect the actions of people who undertook their actions with the intent to disseminate the information they obtained to the public, rather than to a particular class of professional journalists.[188]

The best practices condition would, like the newsgathering condition, allow the privilege to extend to both professional journalists and others, so long as the investigations adhere to best practices. Thus, civil rights investigators, animal rights activists, and labor organizers could assert the privilege even though they are not affiliated with the institutional press.

In our recent book on undercover investigations, Justin Marceau and I articulate a set of such practices.[189] Under our model, undercover investigations should follow several protocols as a safeguard against investigations that are unimportant, unnecessary, or overly intrusive. These standards are set forth in greater detail in our book, but a basic summary should suffice for the purposes of this chapter. First, the investigators must have "specific evidence" that an undercover investigation will "reveal misconduct, illegality, or wrongdoing on the part of [the] investigation's target" and should be limited to seeking information on matters of public concern.[190] Next, the information should not be otherwise available, or not available at a

185 People for the Ethical Treatment of Animals, Inc. v. N. Carolina Farm Bureau Fed'n, Inc., 60 F.4th 815, 821 (4th Cir. 2023) (cleaned up).

186 Ashutosh Bhagwat, *Producing Speech*, 56 Wm. & Mary L. Rev. 1029, 1065 (2015).

187 *See, e.g.*, Chen & Marceau, Truth and Transparency, *supra* note 5; Chen, *Investigative Deception*, *supra* note 5; Marceau & Chen, *Video Age*, *supra* note 5; Chen & Marceau, *High Value Lies*, *supra* note 5.

188 Eugene Volokh, *Freedom for the Press as an Industry, or for the Press as a Technology? From the Framing to Today*, 160 U. Pa. L. Rev. 459, 524 (2012).

189 Chen & Marceau, Truth and Transparency, *supra* note 5, at 264–65.

190 *Id.*

sufficiently detailed level, through more conventional sources.[191] Deception, including affirmative misrepresentation about "the investigator's identity, political affiliations, and motivations for gaining access to the investigation site" should be permissible, but only for the purpose of conducting the investigation.[192] Where an investigation is employment based, "the investigator should not exaggerate or inflate their credentials" and "must be able to competently perform their assigned job functions."[193] Additionally, any secret recording "must be reproduced truthfully in reports to the public. No alterations or editing to mislead the listener or viewer are permissible," although editing for "brevity, coherence, and to protect the privacy interests of the individuals recorded is permissible."[194] Investigators must not "cause physical harm, theft (including intellectual property), or other harms to the property of the investigation's target or to any person on the premises during the investigation" and should not "induce, solicit, or entrap others to engage in misconduct."[195] Finally, investigators should not "deprive individuals who are associated with the investigation site of their dignity, privacy, or autonomy unless that is the direct result of those individuals' participation in the suspected misconduct being investigated," and investigations involving access to "commercial properties are preferable to investigations that involve access to private homes or spaces."[196]

Conditioning the privilege on compliance with these best practices has a couple of advantages. First, and probably most importantly, it substantially limits the possibility that any such investigation will cause the types of tangible harms that are the basis of criminal and civil regulations of deception and secret recording. Thus, while it does not completely discount those potential harms, it uses them to define the limits of the privilege. Second, imposing this set of conditions on the exercise of the privilege means that the privilege can extend to both professional journalists and non-journalists who are careful to adhere to these standards.

14.3.3 *Addressing Concerns About an Undercover Investigations Privilege*

There are, of course, many potential objections to the recognition of a newsgatherers' privilege for undercover investigations. First, skeptics might argue that recognizing even a limited privilege would open the door to additional claims of privilege to violate other generally applicable laws. If undercover investigations are privileged, why shouldn't journalists be permitted to violate laws against breaking and entering into spaces where information of public concern can be found? And why wouldn't such privilege also extend to journalists who engage in computer

[191] *Id.* at 265.
[192] *Id.*
[193] *Id.*
[194] *Id.*
[195] *Id.*
[196] *Id.*

hacking, accessing private databases to troll for information hidden on a company's hard drive?

The interests compromised by break-ins and computer hacking, however, are far more tangible than those at stake in undercover investigations. The paradox of undercover investigations is that they take place secretly, but also in the open. In contrast to physical break-ins or computer hacks, in undercover investigations, the target knows that *someone* is observing questionable behavior on their property; they are just unaware of that person's true identity or motives. While investigative targets may claim that their rights are being violated because the trust they place in the investigator has been violated, the expectation of privacy in such a situation is much lower or, in some cases, may be nonexistent. Professor Marceau and I have argued elsewhere that this reduced expectation of privacy is analogous to the third-party doctrine in criminal procedure. As we observed, "in talking to other persons or inviting them into parts of your life, one always assumes the risk that the person might turn out to be a reporter, a cop, or some other form of false friend."[197] The same violation of trust might also arise with a current employee who engages in whistleblowing.[198] In other words, unlike with burglary or hacking, targets of undercover investigations assume the risk that the behavior they freely engage in while another person is present will later be revealed to others.

Another concern is that granting of legal permission for undercover investigations will lead to a massive expansion of such investigations, many of which may exceed the scope of legitimate newsgathering and result in serious privacy invasions and interference with businesses' ability to maintain a functioning workplace. The fear is that the recognition of a legal privilege would create a kind of atmosphere in which newsgatherers recklessly conduct undercover investigations as fishing expeditions hoping to find something worth reporting. There are a couple of natural impediments, however, to such a massive expansion. First, some news outlets are likely to retain their internal ethical prohibitions against their employees engaging in the type of conduct necessary to carry out an undercover investigation. As the ethical debates reflect, some journalists and media companies are viscerally opposed to undercover journalism.[199] Although I strongly disagree with this approach and hope that the recognition of a privilege would influence those beliefs, individual news entities may still decide to act more conservatively if they so choose.

Second, as reflected by the details of the Food Lion investigation,[200] properly conducting undercover investigations requires enormous resources. Investigations are complex, time consuming, and demand a large number of personnel hours for

[197] Chen & Marceau, *High Value Lies*, *supra* note 5, at 1463.

[198] Of course, employers may require their employees to sign nondisclosure agreements that may address this confidentiality concern. Whether an undercover investigation privilege might render such agreements unenforceable is beyond the scope of this chapter.

[199] *Barnett/Dale Interview*, *supra* note 4.

[200] *See supra* notes 44–47 and accompanying text.

background reporting, planning, conducting the investigation, post-investigation researching, and producing and editing the story that goes out to the public. This type of investigation cannot be undertaken lightly, even by a national news network. It is accordingly unlikely that recognition of a privilege will open the floodgates to an unreasonable number of new investigations.

Moreover, there are serious personal costs to journalists. The work is stressful. Barnett and Dale recounted their fear of being discovered by Food Lion employees during their undercover investigations. For example, Barnett recalled an instance when she was working at a Food Lion delicatessen. While instructing her, Barnett's supervisor "patted me on the stomach to show me how you kind of put the sandwich next to your stomach and you roll it in the Saran wrap. Anyway, when she patted my stomach, she hit [recording] gear. And I remember just catching my breath at that moment."[201]

Undercover journalists can also suffer serious physical burdens. During the Food Lion investigation, the producers had to carry heavy equipment concealed under bulky clothing. This was physically taxing, so much so that Barnett threw out her back from wearing the recording equipment while trying to do her Food Lion job.[202] Today, technology has developed so that cameras can be hidden in something the size of a button, alleviating the bulk problem. But there were also specific hazards from the large battery packs necessary to supply the hidden cameras with power. Dale suffered severe burns from the battery she was carrying, something she could not do anything about until the end of her shift.[203] The extent to which this problem has been alleviated by technology is less clear. These physical challenges can not only create a risk of physical harm but also significantly increase the chances that journalists will be discovered.

14.4 CONCLUSION

For a relatively narrow, mostly pro-press freedom opinion, the Fourth Circuit's decision in *Food Lion* has had a continuing and long-lasting deterrent effect on undercover investigations, both as a legal precedent and as an influence on journalists' ethical debates about such tactics. Its invocation of the relatively obscure common law duty of loyalty in some ways supersedes the importance of the law of undercover investigations that has developed since it was decided. Repudiating *Food Lion* and recognizing a limited form of newsgatherer's privilege for undercover investigations would be a useful reform that could restore an important journalistic tradition that has frequently led to the discovery and publication of information critical to public discourse and, in turn, to our democracy. At a time when many external and internal impediments already threaten the future of press freedom, perhaps taking this narrow but important step toward expanding the ability to engage in newsgathering could move the law in a promising direction.

[201] *Barnett/Dale Interview*, *supra* note 4.
[202] *Id.*
[203] *Id.*

15

The Enduring Significance of *New York Times v. Sullivan*

Samantha Barbas

One of the Supreme Court's most significant First Amendment rulings may be in peril. For the past sixty years, the landmark 1964 decision of *New York Times Co. v. Sullivan* and the cases that followed have secured strong First Amendment protections for the press and others who speak on public affairs. Under these cases, public officials and public figures must show that the speaker acted with "actual malice" or "reckless disregard" of the truth in order to win a libel suit.[1] Scholars and advocates have long celebrated *Sullivan* as one of the most important Supreme Court rulings for the protection of press freedom.

But in 2016, then-presidential candidate Donald Trump announced that he wanted to "open up" libel laws[2] to make it easier for him to sue his critics in the press.[3] Since then, attacks on *Sullivan* have taken on a new – and highly partisan – tenor. In 2017, former Republican vice-presidential candidate Sarah Palin brought a high-profile defamation case against The New York Times in which she called *Sullivan* "obsolete in the modern speech landscape."[4] Soon after, two Supreme Court justices, Clarence Thomas and Neil Gorsuch, urged the Court to reconsider *Sullivan* and its progeny.[5] Judge Laurence H. Silberman of the U.S. Court of

[1] New York Times Co. v. Sullivan, 376 U.S. 254, 273 (1964). This chapter draws heavily on my book ACTUAL MALICE: CIVIL RIGHTS AND FREEDOM OF THE PRESS IN NEW YORK TIMES V. SULLIVAN (2023).

[2] Michael M. Grynbaum, *Trump Renews Pledge to "Take a Strong Look" at Libel Laws*, N.Y. TIMES (Jan. 10, 2018), https://www.nytimes.com/2018/01/10/business/media/trump-libel-laws.html.

[3] Michael M. Grynbaum, *Trump Sues CNN for Defamation, Seeking $475 Million*, N.Y. TIMES (Oct. 3, 2022), https://www.nytimes.com/2022/10/03/business/media/trump-cnn-lawsuit.html.

[4] Bruce D. Brown & Gabe Rottman, *Sarah Palin's Fight Against The New York Times Shows the Free Press Isn't Safe*, TIME (Oct. 19, 2022, 4:04 PM), https://time.com/6223268/sarah-palin-wants-weaker-protections-for-the-press/.

[5] Berisha v. Lawson, 141 S.Ct. 2424, 2424–25 (2021) (Thomas, J., dissenting); *id.* at 2425–30 (Gorsuch, J., dissenting); Adam Liptak, *Two Justices Say Supreme Court Should Reconsider Landmark Decision*, N.Y. TIMES (July 2, 2021), https://www.nytimes.com/2021/07/02/us/supreme-court-libel.html; *see also* McKee v. Cosby, 139 S.Ct. 675, 676 (2019) (Thomas, J., concurring).

Appeals for the District of Columbia Circuit agreed, penning a sharply worded dissent that called for the Court to overrule *Sullivan*, declaring that the press is "bias [ed] against the Republican Party" and stating that The New York Times and The Washington Post "are virtually Democratic Party broadsheets."[6] A number of other litigants have also asked the Court to take a new look at *Sullivan*'s holdings, arguing that the ruling insufficiently protects the interest in personal reputation and awards the purportedly biased, liberal press with an unwarranted "subsidy" for untruthful publications.[7]

Any reconsideration of *Sullivan* and its legacy, however, must not be done in a historical vacuum. The story of *Sullivan* is a powerful illustration of the unique functions the press fulfills in American democracy and the importance of *Sullivan*'s protections of those functions. The history of *Sullivan* demonstrates how, when provided with sufficient constitutional protections, the press embodies key democracy-enhancing roles, such as reporting on public affairs, transmitting newsworthy information to the public, monitoring the conduct of public officials, and holding officials accountable to the citizenry. Arising out of the Civil Rights Movement, the history of *Sullivan* also shows us how a free press can serve as a voice for underrepresented groups and shine light on matters of importance that might otherwise go unseen.

Yet, as this chapter demonstrates, this history also lays bare the high stakes of losing the First Amendment protections recognized in *Sullivan*. Prior to the Court's ruling in *Sullivan*, government officials and other public figures routinely weaponized libel laws to suppress their critics, particularly members of the press. Journalists were arrested and assaulted. Major newspapers pulled their reporters out of the sites of ongoing public battles, leaving the public in the dark about significant newsworthy events. Libel law, to use Justice William Brennan's words in *Sullivan*, had a silencing, "chilling" effect on press.[8] This chapter uses history to explain how and why *Sullivan* nearly eliminated those overwhelming threats to the press. If *New York Times Co. v. Sullivan* and related cases are overruled, libel suits could again become weapons of blatant political suppression.

15.1 LIBEL AND THE PRESS

Libel is a civil cause of action that protects personal reputation against false and defamatory statements. A defamatory statement is one that seriously lowers a person's

[6] Tah v. Global Witness Publishing, Inc., 991 F.3d 231, 251 (D.C. Cir. 2021) (Silberman, J., dissenting). Jeremy W. Peters, *Sarah Palin's Libel Claim Against The Times Is Rejected by a Jury*, N.Y. Times (Feb. 15, 2022), https://www.nytimes.com/2022/02/15/business/media/new-york-times.html; Lawrence Hurley, *Supreme Court Turns Away Coal Baron's Defamation Claim*, NBC News (Oct. 10, 2023, 9:51 AM), https://www.nbcnews.com/politics/supreme-court-turns-away-coal-barons-defamation-claim-news-companies-rcna118036.

[7] *Id.*

[8] *Sullivan*, 376 U.S. at 300.

reputation; it exposes a person "to hatred, shame, obloquy, contumely, odium, contempt, ridicule, aversion, ostracism, degradation or disgrace [and] deprives one of their confidence and friendly intercourse in society."[9] It "injures [a person] in his profession or trade, [and] causes him to be shunned or avoided by his neighbors."[10]

Before 1964, a person who sued for libel didn't have to prove that the statement in question was false; rather, falsity was presumed. The plaintiff didn't have to show actual injury to their reputation, only that the statement had the potential to harm their reputation. Libel was judged under the rule of strict liability, meaning that a publisher was responsible for its statements regardless of the publisher's intent or state of mind at the time of publishing. The only ways a publisher could defend itself were by proving that the statement fell into one of a few narrow categories of statements that were "privileged," legally justified or excused, or, more commonly, by proving the truth of the statement "in all its particulars."[11] Truth was a complete defense to libel, but as a practical matter, proving the truth of a statement "in all its particulars" was difficult even if the statement was true. Prior to 1964, the Supreme Court had said repeatedly that defamation law did not implicate the First Amendment. Defamatory speech had no redeeming social value, the Court said, and its regulation could be left wholly to the states.[12]

Under these rules, publishing criticism – even truthful criticism – of public officials was a dangerous undertaking for a newspaper. Public officials routinely saddled their critics in the press with libel claims (claims that would today be considered meritless), often recovering considerable damage awards. Libel lawsuits against newspapers were a regular feature of American politics prior to the 1960s. Political officials and other powerful figures frequently harassed and intimidated their critics in the press through retaliatory libel suits. At the turn of the century, for example, railroad magnate James Fisk sued The Springfield Republican for $100,000, followed by lawsuits against two other newspapers for the same sum and a third claiming $1 million in damages. In 1916, Henry Ford brought a spurious lawsuit against the Chicago Tribune for calling him an "ignorant idealist" and an "anarchist."[13] Presidents even sued the press. In 1916, former President Theodore Roosevelt brought claims against a Michigan newspaper that accused him of being a

9 Kimmerle v. N.Y. Evening J., Inc., 186 N.E. 217, 218 (N.Y. 1933).

10 William Blake Odgers, A Digest of the Law of Libel and Slander with the Evidence, Procedure, Practice, and Precedents of Pleadings, Both in Civil and Criminal Cases 21 (1896).

11 *Sullivan*, 376 U.S. at 267.

12 Chaplinsky v. New Hampshire, 315 U.S. 568, 572 (1942); Beauharnais v. Illinois, 343 U.S. 250, 266 (1952).

13 David L. Lewis, The Public Image of Henry Ford: An American Folk Hero and His Company 106 (1987); *Henry Ford Files $1,000,000 Libel Suit; Resents Chicago Tribune's Charge of Anarchy in Connection with Enlistment of His Employees*, N.Y. Times, Sept. 8, 1916, at 18.

drunk.[14] Libel lawsuits sent the muckraking newspaper The New York World, published by Joseph Pulitzer, into bankruptcy in the early twentieth century. Fear of devastating libel suits led editors to routinely hold back critical commentary about public officials. Under the law at the time, a newspaper could only be sure of escaping a libel suit when the facts were entirely confirmable "in every detail."[15]

Despite strict libel laws and the risk of being sued, some major press outlets, such as The New York Times, did find ways to publish. The Times used specialized lawyers and conducted extensive fact-checking and vetting procedures, reviewing all copy for possible libel.[16] As a result of its aggressive tactics and well-trained lawyers, The Times rarely paid out judgments in libel cases. But few newspapers had the financial and legal muscle of The Times. And libel remained a formidable latent threat, even for The Times.

As I describe in my book *Actual Malice: Civil Rights and Freedom of the Press in New York Times v. Sullivan*, libel suits almost destroyed The Times in the 1960s, when officials in the South figured out how to weaponize libel law to attack newspapers that criticized segregation and exposed official violence against civil rights protesters. This "libel attack" on the press, which produced a series of lawsuits, including the *Sullivan* case, illustrated how libel law could be exploited by vengeful public officials. It demonstrated to the Supreme Court, and the public more generally, how existing libel laws were anathema to the robust public discourse on public affairs that is the "central meaning" of the First Amendment.

15.2 THE ATTACK ON THE NORTHERN PRESS

The South's libel attack on the northern press was a blatant attempt to halt media criticism of segregation and press coverage of the Civil Rights Movement more generally. The libel attack grew out of the southern campaign of "massive resistance," its defiance of the Supreme Court's 1954 decision in *Brown v. Board of Education*.[17] Segregationists feared the power of the press, and its power to sway public opinion toward integration and civil rights, with good reason. Media coverage of civil rights protests, and the violent backlash those protests generated, would prove critically important in building national support for civil rights that would lead to the Civil Rights Act of 1964. Images of civil rights activists being attacked by police and pictures of protesters being ejected from segregated lunch counters would illuminate the cruelties of the South's racial system and the courage of those who defied it.[18]

[14] *Roosevelt, Winning Libel Suit, Is Awarded 6 Cents*, San Francisco Call, June 1, 1913, at 1.

[15] Barbas, *supra* note 1, at 23.

[16] *Id.* at 24.

[17] David Wallace, Massive Resistance and Media Suppression: The Segregationist Response to Dissent during the Civil Rights Movement (2013).

[18] Barbas, *supra* note 1, at 36; Gene Roberts & Hank Klibanoff, The Race Beat: The Press, the Civil Rights Struggle, and the Awakening of a Nation 185–91 (2006).

The catalyst to the libel suit at issue in *Sullivan* was the lunch counter sit-in movement that took off in the South in 1960. When sit-in protesters in Montgomery, Alabama, were assaulted by white mobs, Public Affairs Commissioner L. B. Sullivan, who supervised the police, did nothing to stop the attack. Shortly after, a civil rights organization called the Committee to Defend Martin Luther King and the Struggle for Freedom in the South published a full-page fundraising advertisement in *The Times*, titled Heed Their Rising Voices, which accused officials in Montgomery and other southern cities of inflicting violence on civil rights protesters. The ad was endorsed by sixty-four eminent figures in the arts and politics, whose names appeared on the ad. Also listed at the bottom of the ad were the names of twenty ministers who were leaders of King's civil rights organization, the Southern Christian Leadership Conference. In reality, the ministers hadn't endorsed the ad; their names were added at the last minute by the Committee to Defend Martin Luther King.[19] This advertisement would form the basis of the *Sullivan* case.

The ad, it turned out, contained minor errors of fact. For example, it incorrectly reported the names of the songs protesters had sung on the steps of the Capitol in Montgomery. The most serious error was the claim that officials in Montgomery had padlocked the dining hall of the Alabama State College to starve and punish the protesters, which wasn't true.[20] The Times hadn't fact-checked the ad before running it and thus had failed to adhere to its own well-established policy of vetting all copy for accuracy. Although Sullivan wasn't mentioned by name in the ad, he claimed that he'd been defamed by statements in the ad implicating Montgomery "authorities" and "police" in violence against civil rights protesters.[21]

The essence of the charges, however, was true: Sullivan had been complicit in violence, although perhaps not in all the specific acts described in the ad.[22] But Sullivan's reputation wasn't harmed. At the time, being known for committing violence against civil rights protesters would have only enhanced his reputation among whites in Montgomery. Sullivan and three Montgomery commissioners sued The New York Times and four ministers whose names appeared on the ad for $500,000 each.[23] Shortly after, the governor of Alabama, John Patterson, also sued The Times, the ministers, and King for $1 million, claiming he'd been defamed by the ad's references to Alabama "authorities."[24]

Authorities in Birmingham likewise wasted no time in bringing libel suits against The Times over its news reporting on racial violence in the city – violence that had

[19] *Sullivan*, 376 U.S. at 260.

[20] *Id.*

[21] *Id.*

[22] Sullivan appears to have permitted white mobs to assault protesters, turning his police on them only after they had attacked the protesters. *Police Thwart Negro Services at Capitol*, Montgomery Advertiser, Mar. 7, 1960, at 1; Claude Sitton, *Negroes Dispersed in Alabama March; Attacked by Whites*, N.Y. Times, Mar. 7, 1960, at 1.

[23] *Sullivan*, 376 U.S. at 256.

[24] *Alabama Governor Sues for* $1,000,000, N.Y. Times, May 31, 1960, at 20.

been abetted by local officials, including Bull Connor, Birmingham's notorious commissioner of public safety.[25] These seven additional libel suits added $3.5 million in potential damages to The Times' burden.[26] A Times reporter was even brought up on charges of criminal libel for his reporting on Birmingham, which could have led to six months' imprisonment.[27] This use of libel law to enact a coordinated, state-sponsored attack on a disfavored newspaper was unprecedented in the history of the press.[28]

The Alabama libel suits presented an existential threat to The Times, which operated on a low profit margin and was barely breaking even in 1960.[29] The libel suits threatened to bankrupt The New York Times.[30] In response, The Times' lawyers made the historic decision of ordering all personnel to stay out of Alabama to avoid further libel trouble.[31] Because of the libel suits, the nation's newspaper of record didn't have a single reporter in one of the major sites of civil rights activity during the critical years of the Civil Rights Movement. The libel suits were having a chilling effect on the press.

In November 1960, an all-white jury in Montgomery concluded that the statements in the ad could be understood as defaming Sullivan and awarded him $500,000.[32] At the time, it was the largest-ever libel verdict in the country.[33] The Chicago Tribune noted that "even the most intrepid publisher must be intimidated into silence" by this use of libel law.[34] These successful libel suits, moreover, spurred a wave of copycat lawsuits. By 1964, southern officials had brought seventeen libel suits against northern media outlets seeking damage awards of more than $288 million.[35]

Notable examples include a lawsuit brought by arch-segregationist Edwin A. Walker. Walker was a retired Army general who led a segregationist mob that

[25] The offending articles were Harrison E. Salisbury, *Fear and Hatred Grip Birmingham*, N.Y. TIMES, Apr. 12, 1960, at 1, 28, and *Race Issues Shakes Alabama Structure*, N.Y. TIMES, Apr. 13, 1960, at 1, 33.

[26] BARBAS, *supra* note 1, at 85.

[27] *Id.* at 98–99.

[28] Samantha Barbas, *New York Times v. Sullivan: Perspectives from History*, 30 GEO. MASON L. REV. F. 1 (2023), https://lawreview.gmu.edu/forum/new-york-times-v-sullivan-perspectives-from-history/.

[29] ALEX JONES & SUSAN TIFFT, THE TRUST: THE PRIVATE AND POWERFUL FAMILY BEHIND THE NEW YORK TIMES 320 (1999).

[30] James Goodale, *Is the Public "Getting Even" with the Press in Libel Cases?*, 188 N.Y.L.J. 29 (1982).

[31] Freedom Forum Institute, *Silencing the Press*, NEWSEUMED, https://newseumed.org/tools/video-page/silencing-press (last visited June 30, 2024).

[32] *Sullivan*, 376 U.S. at 255.

[33] *$500,000 Damages Awarded Sullivan by Times Suit Jury*, MONTGOMERY ADVERTISER, Nov. 4, 1960, at 1.

[34] Brief for Trib. Co. as Amicus Curiae Supporting Petitioner at 12, New York Times Co. v. Sullivan, 376 U.S. 254 (1964) (No. 39).

[35] John Herbers, *Libel Actions Ask Millions in South: 17 Suits by Public Officials Are Pending in Courts*, N.Y. TIMES, Apr. 4, 1964, at 12.

assaulted reporters and federal officers to protest the admission of James Meredith, a Black student, to the University of Mississippi. Walker sued the Associated Press and ten other media outlets for $33 million in damages over accurate accounts that he had encouraged the rioting. The director of the Mississippi Highway Patrol, T. B. Birdsong, then sued The Saturday Evening Post over an article titled What's Next in Mississippi, which imputed "official misconduct" to patrolmen during the Ole Miss riots, alleging that state troopers failed to help federal marshals rein in the mob and that patrolmen stood by while a white vigilante posse beat up a news photographer. Birdsong sought $276 million in damages – $1 million for himself and $1 million for each of the state's 275 highway patrolmen. The sheriff of Etowah County, Alabama, sued the publisher of the Ladies' Home Journal, Curtis Publishing, for $3 million for an article that accused the sheriff and his deputies of brutality in racial demonstrations. Tom King, a candidate for mayor of Birmingham, threatened a libel suit against The Saturday Evening Post for describing Birmingham as the most "backwards" city in America on race.[36]

Many "publications are now under the shadow of potentially expensive [libel] actions," noted the *Columbia Journalism Review* in 1963. "The characteristic actions of the 1960s appear to be suits growing out of local or regional retaliation for reporting or comment by a national news organization," it observed. "Large awards and wide publicity seem to be encouraging more and more of the offended to sue."[37] This was putting it rather mildly.

15.3 APPEAL TO THE U.S. SUPREME COURT

After losing their appeal before the Alabama Supreme Court in 1962, The Times and the ministers appealed separately to the U.S. Supreme Court. The ministers' appeal focused on segregation in the trial proceedings and the racial animus that had given rise to the libel prosecutions.[38] The Times, represented by eminent Columbia University Professor Herbert Wechsler, focused on libel law's threat to freedom of the press and on the freedom of citizens to criticize their government more generally.

To avoid confrontation with the Supreme Court's well-established position on the constitutionally unprotected status of libel and the thorny issue of how reputation and free speech should be balanced, Wechsler brilliantly shifted the focus of the appeal from the right to protect reputation to the right of citizens to criticize the government. Wechsler argued that permitting Sullivan to recover on the theory that he was defamed by criticism of the "police" in Montgomery was akin to the defunct crime of seditious libel. That crime, under which a government may punish its

[36] Barbas, *supra* note 1, at 154.

[37] *Libel or Revenge?*, 2 Colum. Journalism Rev. (Fall 1963), at 2.

[38] Abernathy v. Sullivan, 376 U.S. 254 (1964).

critics, had long been assumed to be unconstitutional.[39] "The decision of the Supreme Court of Alabama gives a scope and application to the law of libel so restrictive of the right to protest and to criticize official conduct that it abridges the freedom of the press, as that freedom has been defined by the decisions of the Court," Wechsler's brief argued.[40] "It transforms the action for defamation from a method of protecting private reputation to a device for insulating government against attack. If the judgment stands, its impact will be grave – not only upon the press but also upon those whose welfare may depend on the ability and willingness of publications to give voice to grievances against the agencies of governmental power."[41]

The brief continued, "We submit that such a rule of liability cannot be reconciled with this Court's rulings on the scope of freedom of the press safeguarded by the Constitution. Those rulings start with the assumption that one of the prime objectives of the First Amendment is to protect the right to criticize 'all public institutions.' ... We do not see how ... criticism of an elected, public official may consistently be punished as a libel on the ground that it diminishes his reputation."[42] Criticism of public officials, Wechsler argued, was protected absolutely by the First Amendment.[43]

In March 1964, the Court threw out Sullivan's verdict and placed constitutional limits on libel laws in the form of the "actual malice" rule. A public official could not recover damages for libel unless they could show that the statement was false and made with "actual malice" – knowledge that the statement was false, or "reckless disregard of whether it was false or not."[44] Brennan created the "actual malice" rule, in part, to address the extreme and unusual facts of the case. He knew that a negligence standard, a standard of carelessness – which is the usual fault standard in personal injury cases and might have been the obvious standard to apply – wouldn't have protected The Times, since it admitted that it had been careless in publishing the ad without checking the facts. Brennan, the consummate negotiator, also created actual malice as a compromise to please different blocs of justices on the Court, including the three "absolutist" justices, Black, Goldberg, and Douglas, who would have taken Wechsler's extreme, absolutist position, and those justices who preferred less sweeping, balancing approaches.[45]

Brennan saw another reason for adopting actual malice. Inspired by Wechsler's analysis, Brennan offered the most extensive reading of the meaning of the First Amendment and its relationship to democracy in Supreme Court history to that

[39] *Sullivan*, 376 U.S. at 276.
[40] Brief for the Petitioner at 2, New York Times Co. v. Sullivan, 376 U.S. 254 (1964) (No. 39).
[41] *Id.*
[42] *Id.*
[43] *Id.*
[44] *Sullivan*, 376 U.S. at 286.
[45] Barbas, *supra* note 1, at 200–15.

time. Adopting Wechsler's views of freedom of expression, Brennan wrote that the ability of citizens to engage in debate of public issues, debate that may include caustic and sharp attacks on government and public officials, was the "central meaning" of the First Amendment.[46] The essence of the First Amendment is the right of citizens to engage in "uninhibited, robust, and wide open" public discourse, which was the essence of self-governance.[47] Libel law's rules of strict liability and the requirement that the defendant prove the truth had a "chilling effect" on public debate by producing self-censorship, Brennan wrote. Presented with rules that were overly strict, speakers would "steer . . . wide of the unlawful zone."[48]

Even a negligence standard, Brennan believed, didn't provide adequate "breathing room" for speech, because "erroneous statement is inevitable in free debate."[49] The Court adopted the actual malice standard as a way of providing First Amendment protection for speakers who criticized public officials, while at the same time allowing protection for reputation.[50] Brennan recognized that under the actual malice rule, harms caused by some false statements that were not made with reckless disregard for the truth would go unremedied. But this was the price of freedom of expression, he wrote. The urgent situation in Alabama had called on the Court to take a fresh look at an entire area of law and to reexamine the principles and values of the First Amendment.

15.4 FREEING THE PRESS

The Supreme Court saved the nation's newspaper of record from ruin. The *Sullivan* decision not only reversed L. B. Sullivan's judgment but turned back the segregationists' "libel attack." It freed the press to report fully and freely on the Civil Rights Movement, coverage that could have been undermined if the next wave of libel suits had gone through the courts without *Sullivan*'s protections.

After the Court handed down its opinion in *Sullivan*, media coverage of the Civil Rights Movement was indeed "robust and wide-open."[51] Reporting on protests in Selma, Alabama, the following year helped facilitate the national consensus on civil rights that led to the passage of the Voting Rights Act of 1965. Scholars agree that the success of the Civil Rights Movement can be attributed in large part to direct action protests and media coverage of those protests. *Sullivan* was one of the most important Supreme Court decisions facilitating the advance of the Civil Rights Movement.[52]

46 *Sullivan*, 376 U.S. at 273.
47 *Id.* at 270.
48 *Id.* at 282.
49 *Id.* at 271.
50 *Id.* at 279.
51 *Id.* at 270–71.
52 Anders Walker, *Neutral Principles: Rethinking the Legal History of Civil Rights, 1934–1964*, 40 Loy. U. Chi. L.J. 385 (2009).

More broadly, *Sullivan* facilitated a sea change in journalism, permitting the press to fulfill its constitutional function of reporting on public affairs without fear of devastating libel judgments. Prior to the 1960s, the press had relied on the assertions of the government on critical issues such as national security. But with the Vietnam War, journalists began publishing unauthorized versions of the facts. Such reporting, and investigative journalism more generally, would not have been possible without *Sullivan*. The protections of *Sullivan* facilitated the rise of investigative reporting as a genre. "The allowance of room for honest mistakes of fact encouraged the press to challenge official truth on two subjects so hidden by government secrecy, Vietnam and Watergate, that no unauthorized story could ever have been 'absolutely confirmable,'" in the words of journalist Anthony Lewis.[53] It was *Sullivan* that permitted the free flow of information "through the press so that the public would be informed about the government and its actions."[54]

If today's opponents of *Sullivan* and related cases succeed, it would become substantially riskier for speakers, including the press, to comment on public affairs. Without the protections of *Sullivan*, the press would be greatly limited in its ability to engage in its "watchdog" function, monitoring the conduct of public officials and holding them accountable to their constituents. A rollback of *Sullivan*, moreover, could herald a return to the "libel warfare" that existed before 1964. As the *Sullivan* story suggests, fewer protections for speakers in libel law would undermine the ability of the press and citizens to engage in the "uninhibited, robust, and wide-open" discourse that is central to public deliberation in a democratic society. The Supreme Court in 1964, and the American public more broadly, saw how libel law could be used to persecute critics of the status quo speaking out on behalf of social justice – persecution that could easily occur today in the absence of *Sullivan*'s protections. *Sullivan* changed the course of history, and in our contentious times, its protections matter more than ever.

[53] Anthony Lewis, Make No Law: The Sullivan Case and the First Amendment 158 (1991).
[54] *Id.*

16

Returning FOIA to the Press

Margaret B. Kwoka

In the popular imagination, a right to information is foundational. Democracy depends on an informed electorate, and the press, as a representative of and an intermediary for the public, should be able to access the information it needs to tell the rest of us what our "[g]overnment is up to."[1] Yet a right of the public or the press to access government information is not enshrined in our Constitution. While the U.S. Supreme Court has interpreted the First Amendment to guarantee some limited access to judicial proceedings, it has never expanded this right to include federal agency records.[2] For two hundred years of our nation's history, in fact, nothing did.

That all changed in 1966 when Congress enacted the Freedom of Information Act (FOIA), which is now the signature government transparency law in the United States.[3] The press, specifically, was at the forefront of the decade-long advocacy struggle that led to the passage of FOIA. Journalists and their associations provided Congress with significant input during the drafting of the legislation.[4] In congressional hearings, moreover, elected representatives repeatedly articulated their vision that the press would vigorously use FOIA to the benefit of the public.[5] Still, Congress has never limited the use of the law to the press; indeed, FOIA provides that any person may request any agency record for any reason. The government must respond within twenty business days and provide the record unless it falls within one of nine enumerated exemptions.[6]

Portions of this chapter were adapted from a Keynote Address given by the author at the Access and Accountability Conference at Yale University in 2021.

1 Nat'l Archives & Recs. Admin. v. Favish, 541 U.S. 157, 171–72 (2004).

2 *See generally, e.g.*, Gannett Co. v. DePasquale, 443 U.S. 368 (1979); Richmond Newspapers, Inc. v. Virginia, 448 U.S. 555 (1980); Globe Newspaper Co. v. Super. Ct., 457 U.S. 596 (1982); Press-Enterprise Co. v. Super. Ct. (1984).

3 5 U.S.C. § 552.

4 *See* Margaret B. Kwoka, Saving the Freedom of Information Act 23–25 (2021).

5 *Id.*

6 5 U.S.C. § 552(a)(6)(A)(i); *id.* § 552(b).

Today, the federal government receives nearly a million FOIA requests a year.[7] Many celebrate this level of engagement as a sign of the law's success. Yet the story looks different if we focus on the first-order FOIA users, namely the press (alongside watchdog groups, nonprofits, and community organizations), who are using the law to inform the broader public. When asked about FOIA's implementation, journalists, who now make less than 3 percent of all federal government-wide requests, may cite instances of success but generally give the law's implementation a failing grade.[8]

What, then, are the law's problems from the perspective of the press? Journalist FOIA requesters (or would-be requesters) typically encounter two sets of problems: first, extreme agency delay in responding to requests and, second, the practical inability of most reporters to obtain recourse when the agency wrongly denies their requests.[9] These problems are both long-standing and well known, and Congress has tried to address them through amendments to the law that have, for example, created new carrots and sticks for agencies to meet deadlines or established mediation services for requesters who are dissatisfied with the agency response.[10] Yet if these incremental reforms have made a difference, it is only at the margin.

In this chapter, I will lay out a case for structural, not incremental, reforms that have the potential to "return" FOIA to the press. That is to say, Congress could structurally reshape FOIA to better serve its first-order users, the news media, for the benefit of the public. To be clear, I would never advocate limiting FOIA rights to the press or other oversight requesters. But if FOIA isn't working for those requesters, then it is not doing the government transparency work we want it to do. Moreover, if it's not working for the press, then it's probably also not working well for others who are seeking government-held information.

7 U.S. Dep't of Just., Off. of Info. Pol'y, Summary of Annual FOIA Reports for Fiscal Year 2022, at 2 (2023), https://www.justice.gov/oip/page/file/1581856/dl?inline [hereinafter OIP Report].

8 Kwoka, *supra* note 4, at 3, 175–78; Paul McMasters, *FOIA: It's Always There*, Soc'y of Pro. Journalists (Oct. 1996), https://www.spj.org/foiabout.asp; *Delayed, Denied, Dismissed: Failures on the FOIA Front*, ProPublica (July 21, 2016), https://www.propublica.org/article/delayed-denied-dismissed-failures-on-the-foia-front. *Cf.* Jake Lucas, *How Times Reporters Use the Freedom of Information Act*, N.Y. Times (July 21, 2018), https://www.nytimes.com/2018/07/21/insider/information-freedom-reporters-pruitt.html (while purporting to describe successful uses of FOIA, quoting one frequent requester reporter as saying, "FOIA is basically useless if you don't file a lawsuit to force the government to act.").

9 FOIA Project Staff, *FOIA Suits Rise Because Agencies Don't Respond Even as Requesters Wait Longer to File Suit*, FOIA Project (Dec. 15, 2019), https://foiaproject.org/2019/12/15/foia-suits-rise-because-agencies-dont-respond-even-as-requesters-wait-longer-to-file-suit [hereinafter *FOIA Suits Rise*]; Nat'l Archives & Recs. Admin., 2020–2022 Freedom of Information Act Federal Advisory Committee Final Report and Recommendations 25 (2022), https://www.archives.gov/files/ogis/assets/foiaac-final-report-and-recs-2022-07-05.pdf; Knight Found., Forecasting Freedom of Information 8 (2017), https://knightfoundation.org/wp-content/uploads/2020/03/FOI-final-unlink.pdf.

10 *See* FOIA Improvement Act of 2016, Pub. L. No. 114-185, 130 Stat. 538 (2016); OPEN Government Act of 2007, Pub. L. No. 110-175, 121 Stat. 2524 (2007).

16.1 RETHINKING INFORMATION DELIVERY

Any conversation about journalists' use of FOIA must start with a conversation about delay. Delay is one of the most intractable problems in FOIA administration. Even for those requests designated as being on the "simple" rather than the "complex" track, government-wide average processing times in the last reported year were more than twice the statutory deadline, and some agencies' averages far exceeded that.[11] A congressional report titled "FOIA is Broken" documented, among other problems, that "[m]any agency FOIA offices have abandoned the statutory requirement to make a determination within 20 working days."[12] A recent Government Accountability Office (GAO) report described backlogged requests as "a perennial problem for many federal agencies," noting that in fiscal year 2022 the government-wide backlog of requests had reached more than 200,000.[13]

Delay is also the news media's biggest complaint and the reason journalists most often cite for not using the law more frequently. For example, ProPublica, an outlet that does use FOIA to great effect on a regular basis, nonetheless reports that delays "now routinely last longer than most journalists can wait – or so long that the information requested is no longer useful."[14] In a series of interviews that I conducted with journalists, reporters uniformly cited delay as a top concern in using FOIA.[15]

There is no doubt a variety of factors that contribute to delay. Agencies often cite resource constraints as a key factor, and there are many structural reasons why agencies are likely to have underfunded FOIA offices.[16] And, to be sure, there may be some level of agency recalcitrance in fulfilling particularly hot button requests.[17] But Congress's recent attempts to address delay have missed the mark; reforms have adjusted fee structures, reporting requirements, and other incentives,[18]

[11] OIP Report, *supra* note 7, at 12.

[12] Staff of H.R. Comm. on Oversight & Gov't Reform, 114th Cong., FOIA Is Broken: A Report iv (2016), https://oversight.house.gov/wp-content/uploads/2016/01/FINAL-FOIA-Report-January-2016.pdf.

[13] *FOIA Backlogs Hinder Government Transparency and Accountability*, U.S. Gov't Accountability Off. (Mar. 14, 2024), https://www.gao.gov/blog/foia-backlogs-hinder-government-transparency-and-accountability.

[14] *Delayed, Denied, Dismissed*, ProPublica, *supra* note 8.

[15] Kwoka, *supra* note 4, at 175–76.

[16] Margaret B. Kwoka, *An Information Commission*, 112 Geo. L.J. 841, 855–57 (forthcoming 2024).

[17] U.S. Dep't of Interior, Off. of Inspector Gen., No. 2019-ER-057, Lack of Tracking and Unclear Guidance Identified in the U.S. Department of the Interior's Awareness Review Process for Freedom of Information Act Requests (2022), https://www.oversight.gov/sites/default/files/oig-reports/DOI/Final-Report-FOIAAwareness.pdf.

[18] *See, e.g.*, OPEN Government Act of 2007, Pub. L. No. 110-175, 121 Stat. 2527 (2007) (codified as amended at 5 U.S.C. § 552(a)(4)(A)(viii)(I) (2007)) (providing that "an agency shall not assess any search fees (or in the case of a requester described under clause (ii)(II) of this subparagraph, duplication fees) under this subparagraph if the agency has failed to comply with any time limit under paragraph (6).")

implying that recalcitrance is the primary reason for delay and that if we simply punish late responses or reward timely ones, agencies' performance will improve.

Yet my research suggests there is another, much greater contributing factor that cannot be overlooked: the volume of non-oversight requesters. In the most comprehensive empirical account ever compiled, detailed in my book, *Saving the Freedom of Information Act*, I documented that the vast majority of requesters are not using FOIA for public oversight purposes but rather to advance private interests.[19] To be sure, these private interests are sometimes very compelling, and using FOIA for such purposes is neither illegitimate nor unlawful. Still, my look inside various FOIA offices revealed that FOIA processing is largely designed for and caters to whatever kind of request is dominating FOIA practice at a given agency. That is to say, agencies are essentially specializing in serving non-oversight requesters simply because they make up the vast majority of requesters.

To begin, some agencies, particularly law enforcement and benefits agencies, are inundated by first-person requests, or requests made by individuals who are seeking information or files about themselves. Take, for example, the Department of Homeland Security (DHS), which now receives more than half of the federal government's total requests every year, outpacing every other agency by an order of magnitude and clocking in at more than 500,000 requests.[20] Nearly all – more than 95 percent – of the requests DHS receives consist of noncitizens' first-person requests for their own immigration records, typically because they are needed in conjunction with either a pending or threatened deportation case or an application for a new visa or for citizenship.[21] Similarly, at the Federal Bureau of Prisons (FBOP), more than half of all requests are first-person in nature, with most individuals in this category requesting their own medical records.[22] Many other agencies also experience high volumes of first-person requests, making first-person requests the most frequent type of FOIA request government wide.[23]

Agencies that receive high volumes of first-person requests have processes that specialize in serving those requesters. One top official explained that the DHS is, in

19 Kwoka, *supra* note 4, at 136–48.

20 OIP Report, *supra* note 7, at 3. While DOJ has yet to compile a government-wide summary report for FY 2023, DHS's own FY 2023 Annual FOIA report shows even higher numbers of total requests received. U.S. Dep't of Homeland Sec., Fiscal Year 2023 Freedom of Information Act Report to the Attorney General of the United States and the Director of the Office of Government Information Services 13 (Mar. 2024), https://www.dhs.gov/sites/default/files/2024-03/23_0325_fy23-FOIA_Annual_Report.pdf.

21 Kwoka, *supra* note 4, at 172 (describing a characterization made by James Holzer, Deputy Chief FOIA Officer at DHS, that 96 percent of the agency's FOIA requests are first-person). My own data gathering suggested the same. At the three largest components of DHS, the percentage of first-person requests in the data I sampled was even higher. *See id.* at 81 (providing figures suggesting first-person requests made up approximately 99 percent of requests at USCIS, 98 percent at ICE, and 97 percent at CBP).

22 *Id.* at 103.

23 *See id.* at 93–115 (documenting many such examples).

his words, "trying to build a system that speaks to ninety percent of the requests that we get" and that the agency is "trying to drive down the response time for routine requests as far as possible."[24] At the Bureau of Prisons, a top FOIA official in charge of agency FOIA policy echoed this sentiment: "I put a lot of emphasis in processing simple requests quickly because it is one of the few things we have a lot of control [over] with our metrics."[25] This strategy is oftentimes very visible. At U.S. Citizenship and Immigration Services (USCIS) – the component agency of the DHS that receives the highest volume of requests – certain personnel do nothing but process noncitizens' requests for immigration files. Those individuals, who make up the vast majority of the agency's 250 or so FOIA processors, aren't even trained or qualified to answer any other types of requests, such as ones from reporters.[26]

Designing FOIA operations to best serve the largest FOIA constituency at a given agency is an entirely rational strategy. Agencies' FOIA performances are judged by the metrics they have to report, such as aggregate statistics on the number of requests received and processed, average processing times, and types of responses.[27] The best way to improve performance is naturally to focus on the bulk of routine and predictable requests, not on the comparatively tiny fraction of requests from journalists, which are often more topical and unique.

This phenomenon is not limited to agencies with high volumes of first-person requests. At other agencies, typically large regulatory agencies like the Securities and Exchange Commission (SEC), the Environmental Protection Agency (EPA), or the Food and Drug Administration (FDA), FOIA offices spend the vast majority of their time processing requests from commercial requesters seeking routine, discrete records such as inspection reports, financial filings, or government contract information.[28] To compound this dynamic, at many of these agencies with high-volume commercial requesting, a significant subset of those commercial requesters are businesses I classify as information resellers, which are businesses that request a high volume of records from the federal government and resell them, at a considerable profit, to private parties.[29] FOIA offices with these kinds of commercial requesters may have impressive performance statistics, particularly regarding the speed of their responses, but only because each request requires looking up a single record.[30] When those comprise 75, 85, or 95 percent of the requests received,

[24] Kwoka, *supra* note 4, at 172–73.

[25] *Id.* at 173.

[26] *Id.*

[27] 5 U.S.C. § 552(e). *See also Annual FOIA Reports*, U.S. Dep't of Just., Off. of Info. Pol'y, https://www.justice.gov/oip/reports-1.

[28] *See generally* Margaret B. Kwoka, *FOIA, Inc.*, 65 Duke L. J. 1361 (2016) (documenting the variety of commercial uses of FOIA, including at these named agencies).

[29] *See id.* at 1376–77.

[30] *See, e.g.*, U.S. Sec. & Exch. Comm'n, *FOIA Annual Report* 10 (2023), https://www.sec.gov/files/arfoia23.pdf (reporting that the SEC took a median of four days to process simple requests and twenty-seven days to process complex requests in fiscal year 2023).

agencies have little incentive to do anything but prioritize these requests and hire and train processors who specialize in addressing them.

In short, the sheer volume of non-oversight requesters necessarily affects journalists' and watchdog groups' requests in a negative way. These requesters not only create huge numbers of FOIA requests that strain agency resources but also distort the priorities of agency FOIA offices to incentivize catering to these much more frequent uses. As a consequence, the agencies lose, or fail to attain, the knowledge and skills necessary to serve the news media. That is to say, journalists' requests are likely to face worse outcomes in FOIA processing simply because they do not fit neatly into the process the agency has designed for more routine and predictable information requests.

The unfortunate reality, though, is that FOIA serves these other interests poorly, too. In the cases of individuals with a pending law enforcement proceeding or benefits application, FOIA may not provide the records they need in time to help them in their underlying case.[31] For businesses that want a database of all facilities inspection reports, building such a repository by requesting those records one at a time through individualized letter writing is highly inefficient.[32] These requesters are only turning to FOIA because there is no better alternative.

To return FOIA to the press, Congress could and should mandate that agencies consider alternative information delivery mechanisms for sets of records routinely needed by the public. While no one should be denied the option to avail themselves of FOIA, they wouldn't have to rely on FOIA if they had better alternatives, such as public access databases with affirmatively available records or individual portals for personal information or discovery in administrative proceedings. Examining the constituencies currently served by FOIA reveals the possibilities of serving those constituencies better outside of the FOIA system, saving FOIA for the first-order uses imagined.

16.2 RETHINKING OVERSIGHT

The second big structural problem for journalists seeking public information is that agencies' FOIA violations are relatively insulated from independent review or practical consequence. Put differently, the right to file a federal lawsuit to challenge agency denials under the Act is simply inadequate as an oversight mechanism.

When FOIA was originally enacted in 1966, Congress understood the importance of independent oversight of agency decisions to withhold records, and it focused on judicial review as the remedy for that concern. As a result, unlike in other administrative law contexts, Congress provided that courts should review agency decisions to

[31] Margaret B. Kwoka, *First-Person FOIA*, 127 Yale L.J. 2204, 2244, 2249 (2018). *See also generally* Nightingale v. U.S. Citizenship & Immigr. Servs., 507 F. Supp. 3d 1193 (N.D. Cal. 2020).

[32] Kwoka, *supra* note 28, at 1389–91, 1430.

withhold records de novo, without any deference to the agency's position.[33] And when the Supreme Court ruled that federal courts' powers to review were limited in some areas of national security in *EPA v. Mink*, Congress legislatively overruled the court and reinstated true de novo review in the statute.[34] In other words, Congress doubled down on the idea that the best protection against an executive agency's wrongful decision to withhold records is a full, independent adjudication by the courts.

The idea of de novo judicial review sounds good on paper. But in practice, judicial review has proven woefully inadequate. To begin with, getting into court is quite difficult. Hiring a lawyer is expensive, and litigation is resource-intensive. Most oversight requesters, including reporters and news media organizations, cannot afford legal fights over records. And the changing nature of news media means there are fewer and fewer legacy outlets that would potentially have the kind of resources required to litigate denials on behalf of their reporters. One study by James Hamilton documented that FOIA use generally is declining among smaller local news outlets.[35]

The fact that few reporters can go to court to challenge an agency's failure to comply with the law is particularly troubling because reporters who have brought FOIA suits have observed the power of independent review. In a series of interviews I conducted with journalists who are using FOIA particularly effectively, many stressed the value of going to court. Science journalist and New York University Professor Charles Seife said that he only started finding FOIA valuable when he found lawyers willing to fight his FOIA cases pro bono, including in a law school clinic.[36] Independent journalist Seth Freed Wessler was so motivated by the success of litigating some of his requests that he cofounded a nonprofit dedicated to linking freelance reporters with pro bono counsel in FOIA cases.[37] The New York Times provides another perfect example of the power of litigation. The newsroom's top lawyer David McCraw told me that he often sues agencies over their long delays simply to force the agency to respond.[38] Just filing a case can make a difference, even without the court making a decision.

But the truth is, these reporters are outliers. Federal litigation is slow, and it can sometimes take years to reach a conclusion, compounding the problems of delay.

[33] 5 U.S.C. § 552(a)(4).

[34] Margaret B. Kwoka, *Deferring to Secrecy*, 54 B.C. L. Rev. 185 (2013); *EPA v. Mink*, 410 U.S. 73 (1973); Freedom of Information Act, Pub. L. No. 93-502, 88 Stat. 1561 (1974) (codified as amended at 5 U.S.C. § 552).

[35] James T. Hamilton, *FOIA and Investigative Reporting: Who's Asking What, Where, When – And Why It Matters*, in Troubling Transparency: The History and Future of Freedom of Information 116, 121–23 (David E. Pozen & Michael Schudson eds., 2018).

[36] Telephone Interview with Charles Seife, Professor, N.Y.U. (Feb. 15, 2019).

[37] Telephone Interview with Seth Freed Wessler, Freelance Investigative Reporter (Apr. 10, 2019).

[38] Telephone Interview with David McCraw, Deputy Gen. Counsel, N.Y. Times, and Al-Amyn Sumar, First Amendment Fellow, N.Y. Times (May 3, 2019).

And the problem may be getting worse over time. A recent report by the Transactional Records Access Clearinghouse (TRAC) documented that FOIA litigation was facing longer and longer delays with a pending backlog of FOIA cases dragging on for years.[39]

Access to the courts and the length of the litigation process are not the only problems with judicial review. Even those requesters who make it into court and go through the lengthy litigation process find they do not always receive a truly independent federal court decision. Despite the mandate of de novo review, many FOIA scholars, including myself, have documented the various ways in which courts nonetheless defer to agency positions by, for example, invoking a special "substantial weight" standard for reviewing government affidavits in the national security context or by using various procedural shortcuts only in FOIA litigation that advantage the government, such as curtailing discovery.[40]

The US experience stands in stark contrast to a plethora of other countries around the world that have successfully implemented independent administrative oversight frameworks rather than relying on judicial review.[41] These bodies are typically styled as information commissions, and some of them have been operating for decades.[42]

For example, Mexico's information commission, known as INAI for its initials in Spanish, is one of the world's most celebrated among such institutions.[43] During a nine-month research stay in Mexico on a Fulbright grant, I studied INAI and its role in Mexico's transparency system.[44] I concluded that five pillars of its work are central to its success.[45] First, it operates a National Transparency Platform, a one-stop portal for requesters to submit, track, and appeal requests, along with a repository of previously released information and all records required to be made proactively

39 *FOIA Suits Rise*, *supra* note 9.

40 Kwoka, *supra* note 34; Meredith Fuchs, *Judging Secrets: The Role Courts Should Play in Preventing Unnecessary Secrecy*, 58 Admin. L. Rev. 131, 163–68 (2006); Susan Nevelow Mart & Tom Ginsburg, *[Dis-]Informing the People's Discretion: Judicial Deference Under the National Security Exemption of the Freedom of Information Act*, 66 Admin. L. Rev. 725 (2014).

41 Margaret B. Kwoka & Michael Karanicolas, *Overseeing Oversight*, 54 Conn. L. Rev. 655, 659 (2022).

42 *Id.* at 679–88.

43 Vivek Ramkumar & Diego de la Mora, *Mexico's Battle for Transparency*, U.S. News & World Rep. (Feb. 13, 2016), https://www.usnews.com/news/best-countries/articles/2016-02-13/mexicos-battle-for-transparency; Paul Lagunes & Oscar Pocasangre, *Dynamic Transparency: An Audit of Mexico's Freedom of Information Act*, 97 Pub. Admin. 162, 162–63 (2019).

44 My work at INAI was conducted pursuant to a cooperative work agreement between myself and INAI, as well as two rulings by The Ohio State University Institutional Review Board that my interviews both of government officials and journalists were exempt from IRB approval procedures. *See* Letter from INAI, Propuesta de Proyecto de Cooperación con Margaret Kwoka (Oct. 24, 2022) (on file with author); Letter from Ohio State University, Office of Responsible Research Practices to Margaret Kwoka, Study No. 2022E0709 (Aug. 4, 2022); Letter from Ohio State University, Office of Responsible Research Practices to Margaret Kwoka, Study No. 2022E0696 (Aug. 4, 2022).

45 Margaret B. Kwoka, Transparency Guardians (2024) (unpublished manuscript) (on file with author).

available by government entities.[46] This platform also facilitates all back-end work by government bodies and INAI. Second, it operates as an adjudication machine, deciding some 20,000 cases a year very quickly and ruling for the requester more than three-quarters of the time.[47] Third, it engages in affirmative monitoring of compliance by following the enforcement of its own orders, sampling responses to unappealed requests to review, and auditing compliance with affirmative disclosure obligations.[48] Fourth, it engages in concerted outreach and education, inside and outside of government, promoting a culture of understanding the fundamental human right to information as being inextricably linked with the exercise of other basic rights.[49] And finally, the leadership body – the seven members of the commission itself – sets a tone and an expectation around transparency that touches everything the institution does.[50] This well-funded institution is staffed with 800 employees and has separate state counterparts in every state in the country.[51]

My interviews with journalists who interact with INAI demonstrate the potential of an information commission to return transparency laws to the press. Uniformly, the reporters I spoke with praised INAI, despite occasional qualifications. One reporter summarized it this way: "I do think it's a very strong tool that we have as citizens, and as journalists, and academics. And I think it mostly works … I feel it is super important to have INAI."[52] Another said: "I think the fact that there's a centralized institution through which you can submit all requests is amazing."[53] When I asked one journalist if she was satisfied with INAI, she said, "[T]he truth is, despite everything, yes, I am satisfied. You can't deny that it works well … if you see journalism in Mexico in the last 10 years, the key [to success] has been the transparency system."[54]

46 Plataforma Nacional De Transparencia (PNT), https://www.plataformadetransparencia.org.mx.

47 INAI, Informe De Labores 58 (2022), https://micrositios.inai.org.mx/informesinai. A subset of those decisions are ones in which the requester wins in part.

48 *See generally id.*; *see also* Interview with Ileana Hidalgo Rioja, Secretaria del Acceso de la Informacion [Secretary of Access to Information], INAI, in Mexico City, Mex. (Mar. 9, 2023), at 6–7 (transcript on file with author).

49 Ley Federal de Transparencia y Acceso a la Información Pública (Federal Law of Transparency and Access to Public Information), at art. 43. *Cf. Estrena INAI la serie 'Derecho a saber' que se transmitirá en el canal del Congreso*, El Heraldo de México (Mar. 23, 2022), https://heraldodemexico.com.mx/nacional/2022/3/23/estrena-inai-la-serie-derecho-saber-que-se-transmitira-en-el-canal-del-congreso-389703.html.

50 As INAI's YouTube channel shows, the commissioners often make public appearances as part of their role. *See* INAI, YouTube, https://www.youtube.com/@ifaimexico/videos.

51 INEGI, Censo Nacional de Transparencia, Acceso a la Información Pública y Protección de Datos Personales 2023, at 19, 22 (May 2024), https://www.inegi.org.mx/contenidos/programas/cntaippdpf/2023/doc/cntaippdpf_2023_resultados.pdf.

52 Interview with Alejandra Ibarra Chaoul, Periodista & Autora, in Mexico City, Mex. (May 24, 2023), at 8 (transcript on file with author).

53 Interview with Anonymous Journalist, in Mexico City, Mex. (May 12, 2023), at 16 (transcript on file with author).

54 Zoom Interview with Gabriela Villegas Ramirez, Journalist, Univision Texas (May 30, 2023), at 5 (interview conducted in Spanish; transcript on file with author). *See also* Interview with

A couple of journalists I talked to had experiences making information requests in both the United States and Mexico. They highlighted some important differences. For example, they saw the simplicity of the process in Mexico as a huge advantage, both in making requests and in appealing decisions. One reporter said, "I'm surprised to see [that] other people's requests [are] often just a sentence that describes what they're asking for without reference to law or anything, and sometimes that sentence will be a little bit hard to interpret, or a little bit ... maybe they're using informal language, and then I'll look at the response and it will be like a very good response ... Whereas in the United States, I feel like it would be an automatic denial."[55] Another journalist, who makes similar requests in Guatemala, Mexico, and the United States, ranked Mexico as the best of the three by far.[56]

Journalists routinely use INAI's appeal process. One journalist said he appeals nearly every time he doesn't receive everything he wanted, and he estimated that he wins the appeal 90 percent of the time.[57] Another similarly reported appealing essentially every unsatisfactory response but estimated a lower success rate, around half of the time.[58] Still, there was broad agreement that the process was both fast and easy to engage with.[59]

The news media also praised INAI's role in facilitating proactive transparency, or acting as an archive or document repository. One journalist described her process of searching through past requests and responses to find information she needed for stories. She downloads databases of all past requests to a certain body for a certain period of time, then looks through them for key terms, and studies the data that was already released or uses that data to formulate her own, better-informed request.[60] Another journalist also cited the National Transparency Platform as crucial, particularly in ensuring that proactive disclosures are available from state and local institutions.[61]

To be sure, journalists lodged complaints about some of INAI's failures. One cited his perception that INAI does not sufficiently weigh public interest in disclosure as allowed by the law.[62] More than one noted that even once they won an appeal at INAI, sometimes the responding government entity did not comply with INAI's

Efraín Tzuc Salinas, Periodista de Datos, Quinto Elemento Lab, in Mexico City, Mex. (May 30, 2023), at 9 ("I think that the Institute [INAI] is important that it exists.") (interview conducted in Spanish; transcript on file with author).

55 Anonymous Journalist, *supra* note 53, at 3–4.

56 Gabriela Villegas Ramirez, *supra* note 54, at 5.

57 Efraín Tzuc Salinas, *supra* note 54, at 4–5.

58 Interview with Iván Benumea Gómez, Coordinador del Programa de Justicia Fiscal [Coordinator of the Tax Justice Program], FUNDAR, in Mexico City, Mex. (June 8, 2023), at 3 (interview conducted in Spanish; transcript on file with author) (author's translation).

59 Efraín Tzuc Salinas, *supra* note 54, at 4–5; Iván Benumea Gómez, *supra* note 58, at 3.

60 Anonymous Journalist, *supra* note 53, at 1.

61 Gabriela Villegas Ramirez, *supra* note 54, at 7.

62 Iván Benumea Gómez, *supra* note 58, at 3.

order.[63] One journalist had even brought a lawsuit to challenge an order determining that compliance was achieved.[64] Another asserted that, despite the ease of the process, it still advantaged sophisticated requesters and represented parties.[65] Still, the overwhelmingly positive assessment of INAI and the repeated drumbeat of its indispensability in newsgathering were heartening themes of my interviews.

Unfortunately, INAI eventually became a victim of its own success. After public spats with the commission, former Mexican President Andrés Manuel López Obrador engaged a years-long campaign against INAI, culminating in recent constitutional reforms led by President Claudia Sheinbaum that will eliminate the commission entirely.[66] While citing costs and inefficiencies as the impetus for reform, López Obrador and his successor took aim only after INAI acted as a meaningful check on government power, demonstrating, perhaps, the very power of the model itself.

One way to think about an information commission like INAI is that it acts as a public support or even a public subsidy to ensure that high-quality journalism continues. Subsidies or public funding for the news media, particularly local journalism, have been considered by policymakers, academics, and advocates.[67] The investment in maintaining public information, in facilitating broad access to requests and to appeals, and in monitoring compliance with transparency laws government wide is a way to support journalism without direct monetary grants or other direct forms of subsidy. It is, in short, a way to return public records requests to the press.

In the United States, many of us hoped that the Office of Government Information Services (OGIS), which Congress created as part of the 2007 amendments to FOIA, would serve this sort of role.[68] Unfortunately, despite some

[63] Alejandra Ibarra Chaoul, *supra* note 52, at 2; Iván Benumea Gómez, *supra* note 58, at 4; Efraín Tzuc Salinas, *supra* note 54, at 6.

[64] Efraín Tzuc Salinas, *supra* note 54, at 8.

[65] Alejandra Ibarra Chaoul, *supra* note 52, at 7.

[66] *See* James Wagner & Emiliano Rodríguez Mega, *Why Mexico Is Eliminating Independent Watchdog Agencies*, N.Y. Times (Nov. 28, 2024), https://www.nytimes.com/2024/11/28/world/americas/mexico-senate-watchdog-agencies.html.

[67] *See, e.g.*, Local Journalism Sustainability Act, H.R. 3940, 117th Cong. (2021); S. 2434, 117th Cong. (2021) (proposing tax credits for supporting local media as well as payroll tax credits for journalism outlets to pay employees); Christina Koningisor & Lyrissa Lidsky, *First Amendment Disequilibrium*, 110 Va. L. Rev. 1, 67 (2024) (suggesting a variety of creative funding models for the press, including philanthropic support and public funding); Press Release, MacArthur Foundation, $48 Million in Support of Local News, Initial *See*ding of Press Forward Collaborative (Dec. 18, 2023), https://www.macfound.org/press/press-releases/macarthur-announces-$48-million-in-support-of-local-news-initial-*see*ding-of-press-forward-collaborative (announcing a grant program for local media). Authors in this series have made similar suggestions. *See, e.g.*, Lili Levi, *Countering the Mosaic of Threats to Press Functions*, *in* The Future of Press Freedom: Democracy, Law, and the News in Changing Times 79 (RonNell Andersen Jones & Sonja R. West eds., 2025).

[68] Kwoka & Karanicolas, *Oversight*, *supra* note 41, at 675–78.

strengthening of that institution over time, it has never been given the resources or power necessary to fulfill the kind of role I envision. To begin, it does not have the power to issue binding orders but, rather, was designed to make policy recommendations and offer mediation services to resolve disputes between requesters and agencies. But recommendations are not orders, and at the end of the day, OGIS has no power to compel agencies to comply with the law. Moreover, OGIS is decidedly not an independent body. It is housed in the National Archives, itself an executive branch agency, and has already been beholden to some administration politics during its short life. Finally, it operates on a shoestring budget and with a tiny staff, woefully insufficient for the kind of demand we would expect for the services of a full-fledged information commission.

We should consider the formation of an information commission to administer and enforce FOIA obligations in the United States. I have previously described how such a body is possible within our current legal constraints and traditions and how it could be designed to withstand political pressure and facilitate access to information for the press and beyond.[69]

The time to return FOIA to the press is now. We are seeing the dangers of unchecked executive power around the world.[70] Scholars, policymakers, and advocates are increasingly focused on questions of democratic and constitutional renewal. While FOIA is a statutory right, it has rightly been described as quasi-constitutional or foundational. Accordingly, the reforms needed to return FOIA to the press are not small ones: They, too, are foundational.

69 Kwoka, *supra* note 16, at 873–85.

70 *See* Int'l Inst. for Democracy & Electoral Assistance, The Global State of Democracy 2022: Forging Social Contracts in a Time of Discontent (2022), https://www.idea.int/democracytracker/sites/default/files/2022-11/the-global-state-of-democracy-2022.pdf (exploring global trends putting democracy at risk and setting out policy recommendations to "reinvigorate" democratic reform).

PART V

Identifying Performers of the Press Function

17

From Bloggers in Pajamas to the Gateway Pundit

How Government Entities Do and Should Identify Professional Journalists for Access and Protection

Richard L. Hasen

One of the potential impediments to having the government grant special access or protection to "the press" is identifying who counts as a journalist. Over the past few decades, changes in digital technology have dramatically lowered barriers to entry for those who gather and publish information or provide commentary.[1] One news scoop might appear in *The New York Times* while the next might come from the proverbial blogger in pajamas who is breaking news from bed. As we learned when a teenager in Minneapolis recorded the police murder of George Floyd in 2020,[2] images recorded by ordinary citizens and posted on social media can spark reform and even catalyze a social movement.

If these changes in who reports news and how it is disseminated mean that everyone is "the press,"[3] or at least that it is impossible to identify today who counts as "the press," then any system of press exceptionalism that grants professional journalists special access or privileges is doomed to fail as potentially unconstitutional for being arbitrary or discriminatory.[4]

The data collection for this project would not have been possible without a research team led by UCLA Law Librarian Sherry Leysen and UCLA law student Sam Hall. Other researchers include Grace Cannell, Joseph Druckman, Whitney Forbis, Kyler Mcvoy, and Catherine Valloso. Thanks to all of them for their meticulous and important research. Thanks to RonNell Andersen Jones, Eugene Volokh, and Sonja West and to the staff of the Knight First Amendment Institute for useful comments and suggestions.

1 On the rise of this "cheap speech," *see* RICHARD L. HASEN, CHEAP SPEECH: HOW DISINFORMATION POISONS OUR POLITICS – AND HOW TO CURE IT (2022).

2 Rachel Treisman, *Darnella Frazier, Teen Who Filmed Floyd's Murder, Praised for Making Verdict Possible*, NPR (Apr. 21, 2021, 11:15 AM), https://www.npr.org/sections/trial-over-killing-of-george-floyd/2021/04/21/989480867/darnella-frazier-teen-who-filmed-floyds-murder-praised-for-making-verdict-possib [https://perma.cc/EV4B-QEBA].

3 *See* Timothy E. Cook, *Freeing the Presses: An Introductory Essay*, in FREEING THE PRESSES: THE FIRST AMENDMENT IN ACTION 1, 8 (Timothy E. Cook ed., 2005) (explaining one view of the Press Clause as that "all individuals have a right to disseminate their viewpoints for general consideration").

4 Arbitrary government conduct potentially violates the Due Process Clause of the Fifth and Fourteenth amendments. *See infra* note 58 (discussing *Dunleavy* case).

In fact, despite two decades of pajama-wearing bloggers and even with billions of TikTok, X, Facebook, Instagram, and other social media users regularly posting audio, video, photos, and text, government entities continue to generally have little trouble differentiating between professional journalists – those who regularly gather, report, and disseminate information to the public – and others. Government entities regularly identify members of the press. They do so in order to grant them special access to court proceedings, emergency scenes such as fires or riots, the White House, and government briefings; to give them a special "shield" against testifying in court or turning over evidence about conversations with others gathered in the process of reporting; and to grant them exceptions from other rules applicable to others, such as the usual disclosure and other campaign finance rules that apply to those who disseminate candidate speech in cooperation with candidates.

These special press privileges are rarely subject to successful litigation, at least so far as is evident through reported court cases. And they tend to protect professional journalists, as they are the ones most often and likely fulfilling the core functions of the press in educating the public and checking the government for excess, corruption, and incompetence.[5]

The biggest problem today for this type of "press exceptionalism" is not distinguishing between those who occasionally make or report news and those who do it as a profession. Government entities seem more than competent to draw those distinctions in ways that the courts have permitted. Instead, it is figuring out how to deal with those who are professional *faux* journalists: They act as though they are following journalistic standards and reporting the news, but they regularly and intentionally distribute false information for profit or political reasons or both. The

This argument is separate from the constitutional question whether, assuming it is possible to rationally identify "the press," giving preferential treatment to the press over others who gather or share information violates the First Amendment or the Equal Protection Clause of the Fifth and Fourteenth Amendments. For example, Professor Eugene Volokh argues that the Press Clause in the First Amendment protects the press as a technology rather than as an industry. Eugene Volokh, *Freedom for the Press as an Industry, or for the Press as a Technology? From the Framing to Today*, 160 U. PA. L. REV. 459 (2012); *but see* Sonja R. West, *The "Press," Then & Now*, 77 OHIO ST. L.J. 49 (2016) and Sonja R. West, *Press Exceptionalism*, 127 HARV. L. REV. 2434 (2014).

It might be argued (although Professor Volokh has not argued) that press exceptionalism violates the Equal Protection Clause for treating professional journalists better than others. This point was suggested by the Supreme Court in Citizens United v. Federal Election Commission, 558 U.S. 310, 352 (2010), which rejected a federal limitation on corporate spending on speech promoting candidates in elections but one that exempted media corporations. For a response, *see* Sonja R. West, *Favoring the Press*, 106 CALIF. L. REV. 91 (2018). I do not delve into this separate question in this chapter.

5 Sonja R. West, *Awakening the Press Clause*, 58 UCLA L. REV. 1025, 1069–70 (2011) ("I suggest that the press fills two primary roles that go beyond the values served by our basic free speech rights. The first is that the press gathers and conveys information to the public about newsworthy matters; and the second is that the press serves as a check on the government by conveying information to the voters about 'what [their] Government is up to.'" (internal citation omitted)).

question of how to treat sources like the website The Gateway Pundit that produce "real 'fake news'" – "fabricated stories designed to achieve particular ends, whether of political strategy or financial gain or both,"[6] – threatens the continued vitality of press exceptionalism.

This chapter examines how government entities determine who is a journalist to allocate resources under conditions of scarcity and ensure that the press can conduct their functions without undue government regulation and interference. Using a new data set of 172 laws, rules, and procedures that different government entities have used to define the press, Section 17.1 describes the most common tests government entities employ to identify journalists and compares them to each other. Although the definitions and tests differ in their particulars – and some rules simply say they apply to "journalists," "news media," or similar such terms without further definition – most of the definitions appear aimed at identifying the class of professionals who regularly gather, report, and disseminate news.

Section 17.2 describes the relatively rare reported litigation around these press-defining rules, teasing out the potential dangers of relying on particular definitions of journalists. Much of the litigation easily distinguishes between professional and nonprofessional journalists, and a few cases have dealt with the exclusion of journalists for permissible reasons, such as disruptive behavior. But not every issue is easy. Using the example of litigation over Maricopa County, Arizona's decision to exclude a faux journalist for The Gateway Pundit from an area where ballots were being tabulated following the 2022 elections, Section 17.2 focuses particularly on the line between unconstitutional viewpoint discrimination and permissible extension of the press exemption only to those who engage in legitimate professional journalism.

Section 17.3 then makes four normative recommendations about the tests government entities *should* use to define journalists. First, government entities should have explicit and meaningful standards for press exceptionalism. Entities should produce a set of written rules that are easily accessible and fairly applied. Second, most press exceptionalism should be limited to professional journalists who regularly produce news stories or commentary. It should not apply to the occasional blogger or poster on social media who is not regularly gathering, reporting, and disseminating news. Third, applicability of press exceptionalism should not turn on the type of technology, such as the use of digital technology, used to disseminate content. Fourth, and most controversially, government entities should continue to have the power to grant press exceptionalism to "bona fide correspondents of repute in their profession"[7] (a standard incorporated into some government press policies) so long as they do not engage in viewpoint discrimination. The key here is to exclude those who

[6] Lili Levi, *Real "Fake News" and Fake "Fake News,"*16 First Amend. L. Rev. 232, 248 n.55 (2018).

[7] *See infra* Sections 17.3 and 17.4.

violate basic journalism norms by having no track record of consistently gathering, reporting, and disseminating truthful information or with a track record of consistently and intentionally reporting and disseminating empirically verifiable false claims as true.

The normative standards I suggest are consistent with the reasons for press exceptionalism: The press plays socially important functions in providing citizens, voters, and others with valuable information and checking the power of government. Rules should assure preferential access for professional journalists, regardless of the medium in which they work, who are most likely to fulfill these functions, without giving a government entity the opportunity for viewpoint discrimination among the class of professional journalists. The most difficult questions concern how to deal with faux journalists without slipping into viewpoint discrimination.

17.1 THE PRINCIPLES AND PRACTICES OF GOVERNMENT PRESS DEFINITIONS

17.1.1 *The Purposes of Defining the Press: Allocating Scarce Resources and Protecting the Press Function*

The two primary reasons why government entities recognize press exceptionalism are allocation of space or other resources under conditions of scarcity and crafting exceptions to generally applicable rules so that the press can do its job unfettered by government regulation and limits.

Scarcity. Not everyone who wants to attend oral arguments in person at the U.S. Supreme Court can get in. There are three lines for attendance: one for lawyers who are admitted to the bar, another for the general public, and a third for people who are guests of the justices. There is a separate admission procedure for those who are credentialed members of the press. There are 439 seats, with 50 allocated to the public and 36 allocated to the press.[8]

The Supreme Court maintains a press gallery in the courtroom where note taking and artist sketching is permitted. Access requires a Supreme Court "hard pass" or "day pass" issued by the Public Information Office (PIO).[9] Members of the press get additional access to other parts of the Supreme Court building. The Court maintains a pressroom and even has limited space for audio and video broadcasts.

[8] Amy Howe, *Courtroom Access: The Nuts and Bolts of Courtroom Seating – and the Lines for Public Access*, SCOTUSBLOG (Apr. 1, 2020, 1:06 PM), https://www.scotusblog.com/2020/04/courtroom-access-the-nuts-and-bolts-of-courtroom-seating-and-the-lines-to-gain-access-to-the-courtroom/ [https://perma.cc/3C6N-54TG].

[9] *The Public Information Office*, U.S. SUP. CT. 5–6, https://www.supremecourt.gov/publicinfo/PIOServices.pdf [https://perma.cc/WM3H-LE9N].

The Court has issued three single-spaced pages of rules and four pages of commentary for obtaining the two types of press passes.[10] The Court revised the rules in 2015 "to address changes in the journalism profession."[11] Early in its set of rules, the Court's PIO explained its goals and the scarcity constraint it faces:

> The PIO's seven-member staff must carefully allocate the limited space and resources available for press usage. The Courtroom has a limited number of seats set aside exclusively for the media, and the press room has 18 carrels for the media's use. To ensure efficient allocation of space and resources, the PIO has traditionally reserved hard passes for full-time professional journalists employed by media organizations that have records of substantial and original news coverage of the Court and a demonstrated need for regular access to the Court's press facilities. The PIO makes no assessment of the content or quality of a journalist's coverage in the credentialing process. But because the Court's fundamental function is adjudication of important issues, the PIO must ensure that press credentialing does not create any appearance of partiality or unfair advantage among litigants or attorneys engaged in the Court's judicial processes. And because a press credential provides access to non-public spaces, the PIO must also be attentive to security concerns.[12]

The Supreme Court is not the only government entity that must deal with scarcity. To consider a few other common examples, the U.S. Department of Defense limits access to the Pentagon and nearby buildings only to approved journalists who apply, provide evidence that they are working as journalists with a bona fide need for access, and undergo a "security-awareness briefing."[13] The city of Chicago limits "access to areas reserved for the news media for the purpose of gathering and editing spot news or photographing news events"[14] while the Riverside County Fire Department in California asks members of the press to wear press credentials if they are not otherwise easily identifiable as members of the press, such as through the presence of a television news van. "We realize that you have a job to do, and we will help facilitate that as long as you are not in the way of our operation. We know that you want to cover the story, not become a part of the story … Generally, you will have unlimited access to an emergency scene. The only reason a fire department in

10 *Requirements and Procedures for Issuing Supreme Court Press Credentials*, U.S. Sup. Ct., https://www.supremecourt.gov/publicinfo/press/Media_Requirements_And_Procedures_Revised_071023.pdf [https://perma.cc/GZL7–7S8W]; *Commentary*, U.S. Sup. Ct., https://www.supremecourt.gov/publicinfo/press/Media_Credential_Commentary_February_2015_mod.pdf [https://perma.cc/99ZC-3EU8].

11 *Requirements and Procedures for Issuing Supreme Court Press Credentials*, *supra* note 10, at 1.

12 *Id.*

13 *For the Media: Badges & Passes*, U.S. Dep't of Defense, https://www.defense.gov/Resources/For-the-Media/ [https://perma.cc/XHR5-UB5A].

14 Chi., Ill., Municipal Code § 4-328-010 (2023), https://codelibrary.amlegal.com/codes/chicago/latest/chicago_il/0-0-0-2638039 [https://perma.cc/8F9T-DHV2].

California can limit the media's access is to prevent the media from interfering with the firefighters ability to do their job."[15]

Exceptions to Generally Applicable Rules. Sometimes a government law or policy will define the press not to secure access to a scarce resource but instead to exempt news media from otherwise generally applicable laws that, if applied to news media, could interfere with the press functions of informing the public and providing a check on government.

The most common example of these rules are media "shield" laws, which give the media a privilege against testifying about certain information, such as confidential sources. For example, under West Virginia law,

> No reporter may be compelled to: (1) Testify in any civil, criminal, administrative or grand jury proceeding in any court in this state concerning the confidential source of any published or unpublished information obtained by the reporter in the course of the above described activities without the consent of the confidential source, unless such testimony is necessary to prevent imminent death, serious bodily injury or unjust incarceration; or (2) Produce any information or testimony that would identify a confidential source, without the consent of the confidential source, unless such testimony or information is necessary to prevent imminent death, serious bodily injury or unjust incarceration.[16]

But laws protecting the press function go far beyond media shields. For example, the Federal Election Campaign Act imposes certain disclosure requirements and limits on corporate activity for those who make "expenditures" in relation to federal campaigns. The term "expenditure" is defined very broadly to include "anything of value, made by any person for the purpose of influencing any election for Federal office."[17] However, applying the expenditure rules to media activities could ensnare news reporting and editorial writing into the realm of campaign finance law. Simply spending resources reporting and writing about a candidate running for federal office could count as an expenditure if it is intended to help the public decide whether the candidate is fit for office.

For this reason, the same law exempts from the definition of "expenditure" "any news story, commentary, or editorial distributed through the facilities of any broadcasting station, newspaper, magazine, or other periodical publication, unless such facilities are owned or controlled by any political party, political committee, or candidate."[18]

Congress enacted this press exemption to generally applicable campaign finance laws because it did not intend to "limit or burden in any way the First Amendment

[15] *Public Affairs and Community Education Bureau: Additional Resources*, Riverside Cnty. Fire, https://www.rvcfire.org/about-us/pio [https://perma.cc/9SZM-YBA9].

[16] W. Va. Code § 57-3-10(b) (2024).

[17] 52 U.S.C. § 30101(9)(A)(i) (2024).

[18] *Id.* § 30101(9)(B)(i).

freedoms of the press and of association." The exemption "assures the unfettered right of the newspapers, TV networks, and other media to cover and comment on political campaigns."[19]

Likely for similar reasons of not interfering with the press function, government entities sometimes exempt the press from definitions of lobbying. For example, Michigan law exempts from the definition of "lobbyist" a "publisher, owner, or working member of the press, radio, or television while disseminating news or editorial comment to the general public in the ordinary course of business."[20]

To consider one more example, an Oregon law regulating the types of mail that may be sent and received by patients in state institutions exempts "journalist mail" from certain restrictions, which the law defines as:

> Any mail sent by a patient to a news media organization such as, but not limited to a newspaper, a magazine and a television station's news department, or sent to a patient from a news media organization, and which is clearly labeled "journalist mail" on the addressee side of the envelope, set apart from the return and mailing addresses for ease of recognition, and where the news media organization is verifiable.[21]

Sometimes, government entities enact rules that have the effect of subsidizing the press function. For example, the Federal Communications Commission has a set of detailed rules for determining how to respond to requests for documents under the Freedom of Information Act. These rules are derived from Congress's FOIA rules contained in a federal statute, including a requirement to treat news media more favorably than the general public when it comes to public records requests.[22] The agency charges fees to search for documents and also fees for "review" of documents by government employees to determine if such documents are exempt from disclosure under complex FOIA rules. Charges for such document "review" apply to any "commercial use request," a definition which otherwise could cover journalists who work for press entities (at least those press entities that run for-profit). The FCC rules, however, exempt from the definition of "commercial use" requests made by the news media.[23] This exemption means the government bears the cost of reviewing FCC documents sought by the news media, but other commercial enterprises pay for such document review.

[19] H.R. Rep. No. 93-1239, at 4 (1974).

[20] MICH. COMP. LAWS ANN. § 4.415(7)(a) (West 2024).

[21] OR. ADMIN. R. § 309-102-0110(13) (2024).

[22] *See* 5 U.S.C. § 552(a)(4)(A) (2024). *See also* Price v. Garland, 45 F.4th 1059, 1075 (D.C. Cir. 2022) (rejecting challenge to fee requirements for commercial filming on National Park Service land that includes exceptions for, among other things, filming by the news media).

[23] *See* 47 C.F.R. §0.466(a)(4) (2024); *see also id.* §0.467 (2024). On the potential problems with the FOIA's dysfunction being driven by non-journalists inundating government agencies with requests, *see* MARGARET B. KWOKA, SAVING THE FREEDOM OF INFORMATION ACT (2021).

17.1.2 *Examples of How Government Entities Define the Press*

Government officials must implement any rules providing for press exceptionalism, meaning that government officials must somehow identify who counts as the press for purposes of the relevant rule. As we will see, some laws, rules, and regulations do not define who counts as a journalist, leaving significant discretion in the hands of government officials. But most rules do offer some definitions or criteria.

Consider again the Supreme Court, which has particularly detailed and onerous rules given a situation of both great demand and a stark scarcity of space. To qualify for a Supreme Court press "hard pass" – which provides the greatest access and privileges to the Court – an applicant must be a "full-time journalist" who "operates or is employed by a media organization, and the applicant's primary professional work is for the media organization through which the applicant seeks a hard pass." Further, the "applicant or the applicant's media organization [must have] a record of substantial and original news coverage of the work of the Court" and the applicant must attest that he or she "will be present at the Court regularly for reporting purposes." Even meeting those requirements is not enough. The applicant cannot "practice law before the Court and [must be] independent of individuals and entities that practice law before the Court" and cannot have been a Court employee for the prior two years.[24]

Perhaps because these rules come from an institution with leaders and a staff comprising elite lawyers, the "Commentary" to the Supreme Court's rules provides additional guidance. For example, "We expect that an applicant will normally be able to satisfy the 'full-time journalist' requirement through the affirmation of the applicant's employer or supervisor. To determine whether this requirement has been satisfied, we may also ask applicants if they hold active press credentials from another government entity, such as the Congressional or White House press galleries."[25] And on the question of "substantial and original" news coverage of the Court, the commentary provides:

> Journalists and organizations with records of substantial and original coverage of the Court are more likely to disseminate information about the Court's work to the public. This requirement may be satisfied by documentation of past reporting. For journalists who have not previously covered the Court, the requirement may be

[24] *Requirements and Procedures for Issuing Supreme Court Press Credentials*, *supra* note 10, at 2. The rules are somewhat more lax for getting a (less valuable) "Day Pass":

> Day Passes. To qualify for a day pass, an applicant must demonstrate:
>
> The applicant is a journalist affiliated with a media organization or, as space allows, a writer who is not affiliated with a media organization; and
>
> The applicant has a need to report from the Court on, or to observe, a particular Court session.
>
> Exceptions. Applicants may be relieved of the need to meet the requirements listed above when necessary to address new or unanticipated situations, to prevent undue hardship, or to ensure fairness in the application of these requirements.

Id.

[25] *Commentary*, *supra* note 10, at 1.

satisfied if the applicant's media organization – rather than the applicant – has regularly published substantial and original reporting about the Court.[26]

For its October 2023 term, the Supreme Court reported that there were twenty-three hard pass holders (and two artists). All the hard pass holders were from major news outlets, like the Associated Press and the Washington Post, except for one: Amy Howe, of the Howe on the Court website and, much more prominently, of the widely respected SCOTUSblog website.[27] Indeed, it was the status of SCOTUSblog's reporters that led the Supreme Court to revise its rules in 2015. Howe's husband and SCOTUSblog co-founder, Tom Goldstein, was a regular Supreme Court practitioner. No doubt this circumstance led the Court to adopt the criterion of journalistic independence from lawyers appearing before the Court as a prerequisite to a Supreme Court hard pass.[28]

Similarly, the Federal Election Commission (FEC) has provided guidance through its regulations and advisory opinions on the applicability of the media exemption. One regulation expands on the statutory provision exempting costs incurred by news media as an "expenditure," which was written in 1974 as part of amendments to the Federal Election Campaign Act.[29] The regulation explicitly expands statutory language to cover newer forms of media not in existence when Congress crafted the press exemption:

> Any cost incurred in covering or carrying a news story, commentary, or editorial by any broadcasting station (including a cable television operator, programmer or producer), *website*, newspaper, magazine, or other periodical publication, *including any Internet or electronic publication*, is not an expenditure unless the facility is owned or controlled by any political party, political committee, or candidate, in which case the cost for a news story:
>
> (a) That represents a bona fide news account communicated in a publication of general circulation or on a licensed broadcasting facility; and
>
> (b) That is part of a general pattern of campaign-related news account that give reasonably equal coverage to all opposing candidates in the circulation or listening area, is not an expenditure.[30]

[26] *Id.*

[27] *Hard Pass Holders for the October 2023 Term*, U.S. Sup. Ct., https://www.supremecourt.gov/publicinfo/Hard_Pass_List_OT_23.pdf [https://perma.cc/W4GA-KESX].

[28] For more on the SCOTUSblog controversy, *see* Richard L. Hasen, Plutocrats United: Campaign Money, the Supreme Court, and the Distortion of American Elections 142 (2016); Sam Hananel & Mark Sherman, *Supreme Court Notebook: SCOTUSblog Denied Press Credential*, Associated Press (Feb. 9, 2015, 6:42 PM), https://apnews.com/article/bb8e6893b47c44b38a46fbf47bc96d5c [https://perma.cc/2662-J5ZA].

[29] The statute, currently codified at 52 U.S.C. § 30101(9)(B)(i) (2024), exempts from the definition of "expenditure" "any news story, commentary, or editorial distributed through the facilities of any broadcasting station, newspaper, magazine, or other periodical publication, unless such facilities are owned or controlled by any political party, political committee, or candidate."

[30] 11 C.F.R. § 100.132 (effective Mar. 1, 2024) (emphasis added); *see also id.* § 100.73 (effective Mar. 1, 2024) (similar exemption to Federal Election Campaign Act definition of "contributions").

Federal Communications Commission regulations, in exempting news media from costs of reviewing documents requested under FOIA, similarly recognize that technology advances affect the definition of "news media." It lists examples of the news media, entities such as:

> television or radio stations broadcasting to the public at large and publishers of periodicals (but only if such entities qualify as disseminators of news) who make their products available for purchase or subscription by, or free distribution to, the general public. These examples are not all-inclusive. Moreover, *as methods of news delivery evolve (for example, the adoption of electronic dissemination of newspapers through telecommunications services), such alternative media shall be considered to be news-media entities.*[31]

One of the more entertaining examples of an FEC advisory opinion discussing the scope of the press exemption concerned comedian Stephen Colbert's creation of a "super PAC" (called "Americans for a Better Tomorrow, Tomorrow"), which he used to criticize campaign finance rules as part of his television show, "The Colbert Report." The show appeared on the Comedy Central cable television channel owned by a corporation, Viacom. Colbert asked the FEC whether he could engage in certain political activities under the press exemption despite Viacom's status as a corporation and given spending limits then in effect on corporations. In a lengthy opinion, the FEC applied its earlier precedents, cited congressional legislative history in creating the press exemption, and considered court cases in concluding that some of the activities proposed by Colbert and to be funded by Viacom would fall under the press exemption and other activities would not.[32]

The Supreme Court and the FEC apply very different criteria in defining who can benefit from press rules, in part because the Supreme Court must deal with

[31] 47 C.F.R. §0.466(a)(7) (emphasis added). The full subsection reads:

> The term representative of the news media refers to any person or entity that gathers information of potential interest to a segment of the public, uses its editorial skills to turn the raw materials into a distinct work, and distributes that work to an audience. In this clause, the term news means information that is about current events or that would be of current interest to the public. Examples of news-media entities are television or radio stations broadcasting to the public at large and publishers of periodicals (but only if such entities qualify as disseminators of news) who make their products available for purchase or subscription by, or free distribution to, the general public. These examples are not all-inclusive. Moreover, as methods of news delivery evolve (for example, the adoption of electronic dissemination of newspapers through telecommunications services), such alternative media shall be considered to be news-media entities. A freelance journalist shall be regarded as working for a news-media entity if the journalist can demonstrate a solid basis for expecting publication through that entity, whether or not the journalist is actually employed by the entity. A publication contract would present a solid basis for such an expectation; the Commission may also consider the past publication record of the requester in making such a determination.

[32] Fed. Election Comm'n, Advisory Opinion 2011-11 (June 30, 2011), https://www.fec.gov/files/legal/aos/2011-11/AO-2011-11.pdf [https://perma.cc/V57P-3C4G].

conditions of physical scarcity – only so many people can be present in the courtroom to watch the facial expressions and gestures of the justices, lawyers, and others – while there is no limit under FEC rules on how many entities and persons may be entitled to an exemption from generally applicable campaign finance laws. But the FEC is concerned that companies that own media but are not engaging in press functions in relation to certain election-related activities may try to use the exemption. It therefore must draw sensible and administrable lines to protect the press function while not allowing the exception to swallow up all of campaign finance law.

More generally, there are many ways to define the press, driven in part by the reasons for the definitions. For example, there is a legitimate government interest in keeping people away from an active fire scene. But it is also important that the government allow a limited number of qualified people access to the scene to provide the public with valuable and accurate reports about the conditions at the scene of the emergency. Likewise, allowing every blogger or Instagram poster to claim the media shield would end compelled testimony in court, which is vital for the courts' role in determining truth. But giving professional news media a shield from testifying in court is also a good thing because it enables the press to protect confidential sources who provide information valuable to the public.

17.1.3 *An Empirical Look at How Government Entities Define the Press*

Here, I offer the first systematic analysis of how government entities define the press.[33] Thanks to the great efforts of a team of UCLA Law researchers led by Sherry Leysen and Sam Hall, we have compiled a database of 172 examples of government entities defining the press for one government purpose or another, and we have categorized how the government entities have done so.

The research team found the examples of government rules that define the press through a variety of searches of electronic databases including Westlaw, Google searches, and examinations of government entity websites.[34] The database is not comprehensive – for example, it leaves out some redundant rules concerning FOIA requests and similar procedures under state and local law – but does cover a wide spectrum of federal, state, and local government entities including agencies, courts, and police and fire departments. A methodological appendix, posted online,

[33] Before this study, Professor Sonja West offered numerous helpful examples of press exceptionalism contained in various state and federal statutes. *See* West, *supra* note 5, at 1062–68. West provided four general categories: "Medium of Communication or News Affiliation," "News-Related Activities," "Circulation or Regularity of Publication," and "Wage Earning or Livelihood." *Id.* The current study offers more examples, and not just of legislatively enacted rules.

[34] The database, including explanations of coding, is posted at https://electionlawblog.org/wp-content/uploads/Hasen-Journalist-Definitions-Database-as-posted.xlsx [https://perma.cc/A49W-G96J].

describes in greater detail the methodology for identifying and classifying these rules.[35]

The major categories of rules in the 172-item database are: media shield laws and privileges (63 examples), media credentialing (27 examples), rules related to obtaining public records (24 examples), rules for student journalists (19 examples), rules related to emergencies or public safety (12 examples), and lobbying or campaign finance rules (8 examples).

Of the 172 rules, 95 expressly provide a definition or definitions of "the press" or a variant on the term and 112 (partially overlapping with the first group of rules) define "journalist" or a variant of the term. Consider, for example, the detailed rules for media accreditation at NASA. Its main rule provides access for "Professional News Media." It provides:

> Applicant must be employed or performing work on behalf of such news-gathering and distribution organizations as: newspapers, magazines, trade newsletters, television and radio stations, independent production companies with approved projects, and internet news sites. To be given NASA media credentials, individuals from these organizations must be full or part-time professional media (i.e. receive external payment for researching and reporting news/commentary/analysis/informational content). Media must report for the outlet they are credentialed under. Individuals not employed by such organizations will be considered freelancers.[36]

Subsidiary rules govern accreditation by freelancers as well as for determining which internet organizations can qualify for the media accreditation. Among other things, applicants from internet organizations must show they are more than content aggregators, that content on the organization's website is "accurate and updated regularly," that content is "not solely to sell a product or service separate from the news/commentary/analysis/information," that content "is not solely available and distributed on social media platforms, including, but not limited to blogs," and that the "website exercises editorial oversight (i.e. runs corrections, updates)."[37]

Of the 172 rules in the database, 33 define neither a journalist nor the press. However, some of these 33 rules still require some proof that the applicant is working as a professional journalist. For example, the U.S. Department of State does not define explicitly who is a journalist for the purpose of issuing a foreign individual a press pass. But the application process asks the applicant for, among other things, the name of the journalist's organization, "a short (2–4 sentence) biography describing your work and experience as a journalist," the "type of

[35] The methodological appendix is posted at https://electionlawblog.org/wp-content/uploads/Journalists-and-The-Press-Methodology-as-posted.pdf [https://perma.cc/NE3Q-4SNB].

[36] Brian Dunbar, *NASA Agencywide Media Accreditation Policy*, NASA (Apr. 7, 2023), https://www.nasa.gov/general/nasa-agencywide-media-accreditation-policy/ [https://perma.cc/7DXW-W92E].

[37] *Id.*

Media (magazine, newspaper, TV, radio, online, news agency, other)," the media's audience size and its website address, "an original letter addressed to the State Department's Foreign Press Centers … from the director of the media organization for which you work, written in English, on the organization's letterhead, and dated no more than 30 days prior to your application, confirming the details of your assignment to the United States," and "three articles, images, or other media produced by the applicant and run by foreign news organizations within the last sixty days that credit the applicant."[38]

A few rules leave the issue of determining who is a journalist in the hands of a government employee without much guidance and without recognition of changing technology. Consider Ohio's media shield statute, which allows nondisclosure of sources by a "person engaged in the work of, or connected with, or employed by any newspaper or any press association for the purpose of gathering, procuring, compiling, editing, disseminating, or publishing news."[39] Aside from the vagueness of terms such as being "connected with" a newspaper, how broadly should the term "newspaper" be read? Ohio judicial precedent suggests quite narrowly. A 1960 Ohio court case held that the statute did not include "periodicals" such as the Dun & Bradstreet financial reports.[40] The case is old but appears to remain good law. I have found no reported Ohio cases considering whether this privilege applies to full-time, online-only political websites or blogs, for example, if

[38] *Foreign Press Center Media Credential Application Guidelines (Washington, D.C.)*, U.S. DEP'T OF STATE, https://www.state.gov/foreign-press-center-media-credential-application-guidelines-washington-dc/ [https://perma.cc/5EP6–7C7A].

[39] OHIO REV. CODE ANN. § 2739.12 (West, Westlaw through File 18, 135th Gen. Assemb. 2023–24).

[40] Deltec v. Dun & Bradstreet, Inc., 187 F. Supp. 788 (N.D. Ohio 1960). For cases raising similar questions about how broadly to construe statutory language protecting journalists, especially in light of changing technology, *see* Toll v. Wilson, 453 P.3d 1215 (Nev. 2019); Gubarev v. Buzzfeed, Inc., No. 17-cv-60426, 2017 WL 6547898 (S.D. Fla. Dec. 21, 2017); Forensic Advisors, Inc. v. Matrixx Initiatives, Inc., 907 A.2d 855, 863 (Md. Ct. Spec. App. 2006); Price v. Time, Inc., 416 F.3d 1327 (11th Cir. 2005); *In re* Burnett, 635 A.2d 1019 (N.J. Super. Ct. Law Div. 1993); Cepeda v. Cohane, 233 F. Supp. 465 (S.D.N.Y. 1964).

In Tripp v. Department of Defense, 284 F. Supp. 2d 50 (D.D.C. 2003), a federal court held that a reporter for the newspaper *Stars and Stripes* was entitled to assert a reporter's privilege even though the newspaper was under the control of the U.S. Department of Defense: "both the DOD and Congress intend for the *Stars and Stripes* to operate like other commercial newspapers, and enjoy First Amendment protections and prohibitions. While it is true that *Stars and Stripes* is within DOD control, the legislative history of the National Defense Authorization Act reveals that Congress intended the information gathered by editors and reporters and published in *Stars and Stripes* to be free of interference from the DOD chain of command, provided it is balanced, accurate, and of interest to the readership." *Id.* at 56.

For a good general overview of the history of media shield laws and their status in federal and state courts, *see* 23A CHARLES A. WRIGHT, KENNETH W. GRAHAM, JR. & ANN MURPHY, FEDERAL PRACTICE AND PROCEDURE § 5426 *General Rule – Journalist Privilege* (Supp. 2023). For an early look on how changes in technology should affect who is entitled to assert the journalist's privilege, *see* Mary-Rose Papandrea, *Citizen Journalism and the Reporter's Privilege*, 91 MINN. L. REV. 515 (2007).

they might be considered "newspapers," similar to when the FEC added websites to the statutory definition of what entities are covered by the campaign finance press exemption.[41]

In looking through the definitions of "journalist," "news media," and the like among the rules in the database, the most common aim appears to be identifying people whose profession is journalism: those who gather, report, and disseminate news as their (full or part-time) jobs. For example, twenty rules in the database require the applicant to list the type of journalist employer for whom they work and/or provide a letter from this employer verifying employment. Eight rules require that the applicant attest or prove independence from lobbyists, with five of those also requiring independence from control of political parties. Seven rules require attestation that the reporting will cover the subject matter relevant to the requester's access (as the Supreme Court rules do), and eleven rules require evidence of the requester's standing or list as a standard the "bona fides" of the journalist or of the produced journalism.

Some of the rules rely at least in part on an external source of authority, such as a committee of journalists that helps police access. Under the rules for admission to the U.S. Senate gallery, a "Standing Committee of Correspondents," elected by those who are already admitted with press privileges into the Senate, determines admission for "bona fide correspondents of repute in their profession." This is a key standard, discussed more fully below.

In making such a showing, applicants for the U.S. Senate gallery must show that they are full-time paid correspondents, that they work for a "news organization" with daily publication and mailing privileges under U.S. Postal Service rules or "whose principal business is the daily dissemination of original news and opinion of interest to a broad segment of the public, and which has published continuously for 18 months."[42] Further,

[41] A separate privilege applies to those "engaged in the work of, or connected with, or employed by any noncommercial educational or commercial radio broadcasting station, or any noncommercial educational or commercial television broadcasting station, or network of such stations, for the purpose of gathering, procuring, compiling, editing, disseminating, publishing, or broadcasting news." OHIO REV. CODE ANN. § 2739.04 (Westlaw). It is doubtful whether this provision would apply to podcasters or others who are professional journalists working in video or audio but who do not work for a radio or television "broadcasting station, or network of such stations."

[42] *Governing Rules*, U.S. SENATE PRESS GALLERY, https://www.dailypress.senate.gov/membership/gallery-rules/ [https://perma.cc/PFY9-3USP].

Some government entities engage in bootstrapping, whereby permission to serve as a journalist for one government entity satisfies the conditions for the other. For example, in determining whether someone is a "full-time journalist" for the purposes of the Supreme Court rules, "we may also ask applicants if they hold active press credentials from another government entity, such as the Congressional or White House press galleries." *Commentary*, *supra* note 10. For some criticism of the lack of transparency surrounding the U.S. Senate Gallery's treatment the request for a press credential by SCOTUSBlog's then-reporter, Lyle Denniston, *see* Jonathan Peters, *Why Can't SCOTUSBlog Get a Credential?*, COLUM. JOURNALISM REVIEW,

> the applicant must reside in the Washington, D.C. area, and must not be engaged in any lobbying or paid advocacy, advertising, publicity or promotion work for any individual, political party, corporation, organization, or agency of the U.S. Government, or in prosecuting any claim before Congress or any federal government department, and will not do so while a member of the Daily Press Galleries.
>
> Applicants' publications must be editorially independent of any institution, foundation or interest group that lobbies the federal government, or that is not principally a general news organization.[43]

Rules for student media unsurprisingly refer to recognition by the university where the student is engaging in journalism. For example, a Hawaii law protecting student journalists from certain adverse consequences for controversial reporting defines a student journalist as "a student who determines, gathers, compiles, writes, edits, photographs, records, or prepares information or advertising for inclusion in university-sponsored media."[44] The statute also defines what counts and what is excluded from the definition of "university-sponsored media."[45]

17.2 LITIGATION OVER GOVERNMENT PRESS EXCEPTIONALISM

Litigation over who is entitled to press exceptionalism is relatively rare. Of the 172 rules in the database, 136 did not lead to reported decisions over who is entitled to exercise the exemption.[46] This section considers the cases that have led to reported decisions and concludes that they are generally unremarkable and involved people or entities who either are not professionals or are journalists who were excluded from certain press privileges for not meeting certain objective criteria. The exception is the recent case of *TGP Communications, LLC v. Sellers*, which

Apr. 29, 2014, https://www.cjr.org/behind_the_news/why_cant_scotusblog_get_a_credential.php [https://perma.cc/92HR-CL8D].

43 *Governing Rules*, *supra* note 42.

44 HAW. REV. STAT. § 304A-951(h) (2023).

45 *See id.*:

> "University-sponsored media" means any material:
>
> (1) Prepared, written, published, or broadcast in any media by a student journalist in the university system;
> (2) Distributed or generally made available, either free of charge or for a fee, to members of the student body; and
> (3) Prepared under the direction of a student media advisor, regardless of whether the material is supported financially by the university or by use of facilities of the university or produced in conjunction with a class for which the student is enrolled.
>
> "University-sponsored media" does not include material intended for distribution or transmission for classroom purposes only.

46 In the database, 36 of the rules were cited in litigation. Two of the rules in the database, listed last, involve courts applying non-statutory (or non-constitutional) standards. Together that makes 38 of the 172 examples involving court decisions.

involved The Gateway Pundit, a far-right outlet known for spreading disinformation. This case raised difficult questions about the line between determining bona fide journalist qualifications and impermissible viewpoint discrimination.

17.2.1 *People or Entities Who Are Not Professionals*

A good number of the cases involve people who are not members of the professional media claiming a press privilege.[47] For example, in *Borden v. Bare*, a federal district court held that Fresno County, California, sheriffs did not violate the constitutional rights of a person who was not a member of the media and who attempted to stand in the "designated media area" around a county courthouse to make a cellphone recording of the courthouse's lobby and security area. She was arrested when she would not leave after being asked to do so. In this case, even the plaintiff did not contend that she was a member of the news media.[48]

Similarly, in *Campaign Legal Center v. Federal Election Commission*,[49] a super PAC supporting Hillary Clinton's presidential campaign argued that it was entitled to the media exemption from limits on campaign contributions to a candidate. The PAC claimed the press exemption because one of the things it did was write op-eds in support of Clinton's candidacy. Treating the matter as self-evident, the district court concluded that the PAC could not qualify for the exemption because the media exemption "is for the media." It held the Federal Election Commission acted in an arbitrary and capricious manner in concluding otherwise.[50]

Along similar lines, a Texas appellate court denied media status to a labor union operating a website. In *Service Employees International Union No. 5 v. Professional Janitorial Service of Houston, Inc.*,[51] a labor union was sued for defamation and other torts by PJS, a janitorial service, for statements made on the union's website. The union regularly communicated through its website, which had over 4,000 visitors

[47] A number of cases concern the question whether as a matter of statutory construction a particular jurisdiction's rule for press exceptionalism could be applied to bloggers or operators of a YouTube video channel. *See* Benvenuto v. Brookman, No. HHD-CV-106119733S, 2020 WL 8024760 (Conn. Super. Ct. Nov. 13, 2020) (blogger not entitled to media shield law where legislature did not intend law to protect bloggers and blog allowed for posting of unedited comments by its subscribers); Green v. Pierce County, 487 P.3d 499 (Wash. 2021), *cert. denied*, 142 S.Ct. 1399 (2022) (not determining whether operator of a YouTube channel constitutes "news media" for purpose of Washington state public records requests because operator YouTube channel did not have a separate legal existence apart from the operator; dissenter would have found operator entitled to be considered news media).

[48] Borden v. Bare, No. 20-cv-01103, 2022 WL 4586231 (E.D. Cal. Sept. 29, 2022). The Ninth Circuit affirmed in an unpublished opinion on qualified immunity grounds. Borden v. Bare, No. 22-16569, 2023 WL 6937410 (9th Cir. Oct. 20, 2023).

[49] Campaign Legal Ctr. v. FEC, 466 F. Supp. 3d 141 (D.D.C. 2020). The case remains ongoing. 646 F. Supp. 3d 57 (D.D.C. 2022), *appeal filed*, No. 22-5336 (D.C. Cir. Dec. 23, 2022).

[50] 466 F. Supp. 3d at 159.

[51] Serv. Emps. Int'l Union Loc. 5 v. Pro. Janitorial Serv. of Hous., Inc. 415 S.W.3d 387 (Tx. Ct. App. 2013).

per day. When the trial court denied the union summary judgment on its claims, it sought to take an interlocutory appeal before the case went to trial. Such an appeal before trial in a defamation case is allowed under Texas law only for members of the news media, including electronic media. The union claimed its website counted as electronic media, but the appeals court disagreed, concluding in an extensive analysis that "although the record establishes that the union publishes information concerning political and social issues to the public through its websites, the record does not establish that the union's primary business is reporting the news or that it was acting in the capacity of a journalist or news reporter in publish[ing] its statements about PJS. Thus, the union does not qualify as a 'member of the electronic media.'"[52]

17.2.2 *Journalists Excluded for Not Meeting Objective Criteria*

Some cases involve journalists who argue that they were improperly excluded from press access.[53] Most of these cases are unsuccessful. In one, a journalist complained that he was being excluded from press conferences held by Chicago's mayor on the grounds that he was asking difficult questions, but the journalist's own evidence showed that his "aggressive and irate" behavior in government offices was the reason for his exclusion.[54]

In *Ateba v. Jean-Pierre*,[55] Simon Ateba, a journalist working for Today News Africa, complained when he and about 500 other journalists lost "hard pass" access to the White House when the White House reinstated an earlier policy requiring that applicants for a hard pass show they held a press credential from the Supreme Court or the press gallery of one of the Houses of Congress. Ateba had some history of interrupting White House press conferences to complain that he was not getting answers to his press inquiries about issues concerning US-Africa relations, and he claimed viewpoint discrimination.

A federal district court rejected his arguments. The court held that the "bona fide correspondents of repute in their profession" standard from the Senate Press gallery

52 *Id.* at 402.

53 For cases concerning applicability of a requirement that a journalist be "independent" in some way, *see* Simon v. Northwestern Univ., 321 F.R.D. 328, 331 (N.D. Ill. 2017) (documentary filmmaker who was also an attorney waived Illinois reporter's privilege by joining prisoner's legal team as an attorney); Aberdeen City Council v. Bloomberg, L.P., No. 23 Misc. 70, 2023 WL 5489064, at *5 (S.D.N.Y. Aug. 25, 2023) (personal relationship between journalist Stephanie Ruhle and CEO of company that Ruhle wrote about for Bloomberg did not vitiate Second Circuit's journalist privilege for Ruhle and Bloomberg absent evidence "that Ruhle made any changes to a story at Plank's direction, attempted to circumvent her editors, or sought any special treatment from Bloomberg for Under Armour").

54 Kelly v. Lightfoot, No. 22-cv-4533, 2023 WL 5720988, at *5 (N.D. Ill. Sept. 5, 2023) ("Based on these facts plead[ed] by Plaintiff, it is implausible that Plaintiff's questions were the reason for his credential revocation. Second, Plaintiff's exhibits and attached evidence demonstrate that Plaintiff's conduct (pushing through Mayor Lightfoot's security team, demonstrating aggressive and irate behavior) was the reason for his credential revocation.").

55 Ateba v. Jean-Pierre, No. 23-cv-02321, 2023 WL 8469743 (D.D.C. Dec. 7, 2023), *appeal filed*, No. 24-05004 (D.C. Cir. Jan. 11, 2024).

as administered by the Standing Committee of Correspondents (discussed above) imposed professional standards that did not violate the First Amendment. "Importantly, reliance on a professional credentialing body also tends to reduce the risk Ateba apparently fears most – that the White House will discriminate against journalists based on their relationship with the White House."[56]

The *Ateba* case stands in marked contrast to clashes between the Trump White House and journalists Jim Acosta and Brian Karem, both of whom had their hard press passes suspended on grounds of supposedly unprofessional behavior. Federal courts ordered the press passes restored because the White House violated the journalists' due process rights in not providing sufficient notice of the kind of conduct that could merit a suspension.[57] Similarly, in *Alaska Landmine, LLC v. Dunleavy*,[58] a federal district court held that an Alaska governor's decision of who to include in or exclude from press conferences likely violated due process because of the failure of the governor's office to articulate an "explicit and

[56] *Id.* at *26.

[57] *See* Karem v. Trump, 960 F.3d 656 (D.C. Cir. 2020). The Acosta dispute is described at page 661. The Karem incident arose from the following dispute:

> In July 2019, President Trump hosted a Social Media Summit attended by various internet influencers and personalities, including former presidential advisor Sebastian Gorka. At the Summit's conclusion, the President delivered prepared remarks in the Rose Garden, which the White House press corps, Appellee Brian Karem included, covered. Like other reporters, Karem listened to the remarks from a roped-off press area that surrounded the rows of chairs where Summit attendees, including Gorka, sat.
>
> After concluding his remarks, President Trump walked back towards the White House, at which point Karem shouted a question at the President, who ignored it and went inside. Several Summit attendees, however, reacted to Karem's question: one shouted, "He talked to us, the real news," and another said sarcastically, "Don't be sad, don't be sad." Karem smiled, gestured to the attendees, and declared, "This is a group eager for demonic possession." Although several people laughed, Gorka "took it differently." He "turned around in his chair and yelled, 'And you're a 'journalist,' right?' – making air quotes with his hands." As Gorka began to stand, Karem shouted in response, "Hey come on over here and talk to me, brother, or we can go outside and have a long conversation," while motioning backward with his right thumb over his shoulder. Gorka then walked briskly toward Karem, shouting, "Are you threatening me now in the White House? In the Rose Garden? You are threatening me in the Rose Garden?" With the two men now standing face to face, Karem, his voice lowered, stated, "I said I'd be happy to talk to you." Gorka, still yelling, responded, "You are a punk! You're not a journalist! You're a punk!" Gorka then walked away, and, as he did, Karem twice shouted in his direction, "Go home," and then, "Hey Gorka, get a job!"
>
> Several minutes after this initial incident, Karem again encountered Gorka, this time in the White House Palm Room. Placing his hand on Gorka's arm, Karem "tried to explain that, in making his earlier comment, he had only meant that he wanted to talk." "Gorka … disagreed," prompting Karem to repeat, "I said 'talk.'" As staffers began ushering press out of the Palm Room, Gorka repeatedly told Karem, "You're done." Before walking away, Karem tried to shake Gorka's hand, but Gorka refused.

Id. at 662 (citations omitted).

[58] Alaska Landmine, LLC v. Dunleavy, 514 F. Supp. 3d 1123 (D. Alaska 2021).

meaningful standard" for inclusion or exclusion of those seeking press access.[59] The plaintiff was a political blogger who previously was invited to governor press conferences but was then excluded.

17.2.3 *Exclusion of Potentially Faux Journalists Who Are Not "Bona Fide Correspondents of Repute in Their Profession"*

By far the most difficult issue today on the question of press exceptionalism concerns not the line between professionals and nonprofessionals but between professionals who adhere to journalistic standards and faux journalists who are employed to regularly produce real "fake news."[60] In the era of cheap speech, it is easy to produce content that appears to be journalism but in fact complies with no journalistic norms, such as verification of facts, and is instead intentional propaganda shared solely for political motives or profit.[61]

A recent case, *TGP Communications, LLC v. Sellers*, illustrates the problem. In an unpublished order (not citable as precedent under the court's rules),[62] a U.S. Court of Appeals for the Ninth Circuit panel granted an injunction pending appeal to Jordan Conradson, a "reporter" for the website The Gateway Pundit, after Conradson was denied a press pass to observe the counting of ballots after the 2022 midterm elections by Maricopa County, Arizona.[63] Maricopa County rules for issuing a press pass had much in common with other rules covered in this chapter, and the county copied the rules used for press passes by Wisconsin's governor and upheld against First Amendment challenge at the U.S. Court of Appeals for the Seventh Circuit (in a case discussed later in this section).[64] The rules included these requirements:

e. Is the petitioner a bona fide correspondent of repute in their profession, and do they and their employing organization exhibit the following characteristics?

[59] *Id.* at 1134. *See* also the recent settlement of a case brought by Laura Belin, who operated a political blog in Iowa for seventeen years but was denied a press credential by the Iowa legislature. The credential was first denied for no reason, and then denied on grounds that Belin was not "nonpartisan." As part of the settlement, the legislature removed that criterion. Tyler Jett, *Bleeding Heartland Journalist Wins 50K Settlement in Suit Challenging Press Pass Denial*, Des Moines Register, Apr. 2, 2024, https://www.aol.com/bleeding-heartland-journalist-wins-50k-193247516.html.

[60] *See* Levi, *supra* note 6.

[61] *See generally* Hasen, *supra* note 1.

[62] *See* 9th Cir. R. 36-3(a).

[63] TGP Commc'ns, LLC v. Sellers, No. 22-16826, 2022 WL 17484331 (9th Cir. Dec. 5, 2022), *appeal dismissed*, No. 22-16826, 2023 WL 3698762 (9th Cir. May 1, 2023).

[64] Answering Brief, TGP Commc'ns, LLC v. Sellers, No. 22-16826, 2022 WL 17980262, at *8 (Dec. 19, 2022) ("When creating the Policy, the County did not create a new standard from whole cloth. Instead, the County adopted the Policy essentially verbatim from a press pass policy already used in the Office of the Governor of Wisconsin. As discussed below, the County felt safe adopting this Policy because it had already been examined by the Seventh Circuit and determined to be constitutionally valid." (citation omitted)).

i. Both avoid real or perceived conflicts of interest;
ii. Both are free of associations that would compromise journalistic integrity or damage credibility;
iii. Both decline compensation, favors, special treatment, secondary employment, or political involvement where doing so would compromise journalistic integrity; and
iv. Both resist pressures from advertisers, donors, or any other special interests to influence coverage.[65]

Maricopa County had determined that Conradson did not qualify for a press pass because he and The Gateway Pundit "(a) do not avoid real or perceived conflicts of interest and (b) are not free of associations that would compromise journalistic integrity or damage credibility." And the county found that Conradson is "not a bona fide correspondent of repute in [his] profession."[66]

The Ninth Circuit, stressing the preliminary nature of the review of denial of a temporary restraining order, held that Conradson and The Gateway Pundit would likely succeed on appeal because the county likely engaged in viewpoint discrimination in violation of the First Amendment.[67]

In support of its argument that Conradson had a conflict of interest violating the rules, the county noted that Conradson attended political party events, but it presented no other evidence of conflicts of interest. The Ninth Circuit held that this was insufficient evidence of a conflict.[68] More importantly, the county pointed to what it saw as Conradson's unprofessionalism, demonstrating that he was not a journalist of good repute:

> As part of the application process, Mr. Conradson submitted three links to work examples. Those three articles ... do little more than proselytize *The Gateway Pundit*'s views. Each article germinates from a news report or press release (such as the County's announcement of Press Pass criteria). Mr. Conradson then expresses an opinion about the news report or press release and supports that opinion by referencing like-minded social media posts, prior articles by *The Gateway Pundit*, and allying websites that express the same viewpoints. Moreover, each article uses inflammatory and/or accusatory language, such as "Fake News Media," "globalist elitist establishment," and "highly flawed 2022 Primary Elections." And while Mr. Conradson is certainly entitled to express his opinions, his poorly sourced, researched, and reported work lacks the journalistic integrity and credibility required by the Press Pass criteria.[69]

65 *TGP Commc'ns*, LLC, 2022 WL 17484331, at *2 (quoting county rules).
66 *Id.*
67 *Id.* at *4–5.
68 *Id.*
69 *Id.* at *5.

Instead of viewing the county's evidence as proof of Conradson's lack of bona fide standing among journalists, the Ninth Circuit saw it as an indication that the county was engaged in viewpoint discrimination:

> It is the County's politically-tinged assessment of Conradson's prior reporting that appears to have led it to deny him a press pass. That type of viewpoint-based discrimination is exactly what the First Amendment protects against. Because it appears at this preliminary stage that the County engaged in viewpoint discrimination, it is likely that the County's denial of a press pass will not survive review when considering Conradson's as-applied challenge.[70]

The Ninth Circuit also rejected the relevance of other evidence of Conradson's unprofessional behavior as probative of his lack of bona fides:

> The county noted that "Conradson appeared at press conference on October 13, 2022, with a hidden camera. On November 10, 2022, he showed up at [the Maricopa County Tabulation and Election Center] under the guise of being there to pick up his credentials." He allegedly became disruptive, and the County had to remove him from the facility. Such conduct is troubling. None of these subsequent acts, however, could have influenced the County's previous denial of the press pass.[71]

This case later settled and so the record was not more fully developed. At the early stages of the litigation, the county did not appear to present more evidence about whether Conradson and The Gateway Pundit were engaged in legitimate journalism.

A more fully developed record might well have led the courts to conclude that The Gateway Pundit should be considered faux journalism and not comprised of "bona fide correspondents of repute in their profession." One academic study of websites purporting to present news, for example, found the organization to be one of the leading sources of false claims online in the United States,[72] including the incendiary false claim that the 2020 US presidential election was stolen. The fact-checking organization PolitiFact examined 26 claims made by The Gateway Pundit and rated 23 of the 26, or 88 percent of them, "mostly false," "false," or "pants on fire" false.[73] Both Facebook and Twitter removed and demoted content from the website and its founder on grounds of persistent spread of disinformation.[74]

70 *Id.* (footnote omitted).

71 *Id.* at *4 n.2.

72 Produktentwicklung Analyse, *Media Analysis of the US Election: September 2020*, PRESSRELATIONS: KNOWLEDGE DISCOVERY (Oct. 30, 2020), https://www.pressrelations.com/blog/en/media-analysis-of-the-2020-us-election [https://perma.cc/888E-4GHQ].

73 *PolitiFact Scorecard: The Gateway Pundit*, POLITIFACT, https://www.politifact.com/personalities/gateway-pundit/ [https://perma.cc/2E5M-EPX6].

74 Peter Eisler, *Facebook's Struggle with Gateway Pundit Highlights Challenge of Containing Disinformation*, REUTERS (Dec. 3, 2021, 3:12 PM), https://www.reuters.com/business/media-telecom/facebooks-struggle-with-gateway-pundit-highlights-challenge-containing-2021-12-03/; Alexis Benveniste, *Twitter Banned Gateway Pundit Founder Jim Hoft*, CNN (Feb. 8, 2021,

In briefing on the appeal, Maricopa County further claimed that items posted on The Gateway Pundit and by Conradson encouraged threats of violence against county workers: "For example, Mr. Conradson published a blog post wherein he falsely accused an election worker of improperly accessing and deleting election data, and he included the election worker's name and photograph in the post. This post directly led to the election worker in question receiving death threats, including statements such as 'hang that crook from [the] closest tree so people can see what happens to traitors,' in the comments to Mr. Conradson's post."[75]

The county claimed it was motivated by security concerns rather than viewpoint discrimination in excluding Conradson, noting that the county had given press passes to companies it considered ideologically similar, such as Newsmax, the Western Journal, and the Epoch Times.[76] The Gateway Pundit countered that the county had not raised security concerns in denying Conradson a press pass, that evidence of such threats was not in the record, that the threats did not come from defendants, and that there was insufficient evidence as to the similarity between The Gateway Pundit and others given press passes.[77]

More significantly for the purposes of this chapter, some supporters of The Gateway Pundit argue that it is unconstitutional to award press passes only to journalists who are bona fide professionals of repute. For example, the group FIRE (Foundation for Individual Rights and Expression) filed an amicus brief along with another organization in the *TGP Communications* case attacking the very idea that government entities are permitted to consider standards such as repute in the profession or commitment to objectivity as a legitimate basis to decide who gets a press pass. FIRE wrote that "terms like 'repute,' 'associations,' 'journalistic integrity,' and 'credibility'" are vague and standardless. It further argued that it "is highly questionable whether the government even *could* devise non-viewpoint discriminatory criteria to decide whether a journalist

12:27 PM), https://www.cnn.com/2021/02/07/media/twitter-ban-gateway-pundit-founder-jim-hoft/index.html [https://perma.cc/XY6E-A8C8].

75 Answering Brief, *supra* note 64, at *10–11 (citations omitted).

76 *Id.* at *32. There is additional discussion of the security concerns in the district court opinion denying a temporary restraining order (that was later overturned by the Ninth Circuit). TGP Commc'ns LLC v. Sellers, 642 F. Supp. 3d 957, 961 (D. Ariz. 2022), *rev'd*, No. 22-16826, 2022 WL 17484331 (9th Cir. Dec. 5, 2022), *appeal dismissed*, No. 22-16826, 2023 WL 3698762 (9th Cir. May 1, 2023).

77 Appellants' Reply Brief, TGP Commc'ns, LLC v. Sellers, No. 22-16826, 2022 WL 18024026, at *24–25 (Dec. 23, 2022). On the viewpoint discrimination point, appellants countered:

> The County attempts to absolve itself of viewpoint discrimination by claiming that it "granted press passes to several other organizations with a similar viewpoint, such as Newsmax, the Western Journal, and the Epoch times." The only valid portion of this statement is the use of the Oxford Comma. What are these other publications' viewpoints? The record is void of any finding in that regard. Are their viewpoints the same as *one another*? Are their viewpoints even internally consistent amongst even their own journalists and editors? They certainly are not the same viewpoints as the Appellants.

Id. at *13–14.

demonstrates 'objectivity,' because requiring a journalist to be 'objective' inherently requires him to meet the government's conception of a particular viewpoint ('objectivity') and punishes him for reporting from other viewpoints (such as a conservative slant)."[78]

In making its argument, FIRE sought to have the Ninth Circuit reject a contrary holding of the U.S. Court of Appeals for the Seventh Circuit in *John K. MacIver Institute for Public Policy v. Evers*.[79] That case concerned an application by the Wisconsin governor's office of the same standards later adopted by Maricopa County to exclude someone from a press conference on grounds of not meeting the standards. The Seventh Circuit defended the governor's standards as reasonable, viewpoint neutral, consistent with public policy in informing the public, and in line with similar standards used by the U.S. Congress and many others.[80] *Ateba* too is a case where a federal district court appeared to uphold the general permissibility of a "bona fide repute in the profession" standard.[81]

17.3 HOW GOVERNMENT ENTITIES SHOULD DEFINE THE PRESS IN LIGHT OF FIRST AMENDMENT VALUES FOR PRESS EXCEPTIONALISM

In this final section of the chapter, I turn from describing and analyzing how government entities *actually determine* who is the press for purposes of press

[78] Brief of Amici Curiae Foundation for Individual Rights and Expression and the Marion B. Brechner First Amendment Project in Support of Plaintiffs-Appellants and Reversal, TGP Commc'ns, LLC v. Sellers, No. 22-16826, 2022 WL 17869087, at *9–10 (Dec. 16, 2022).

[79] *Id.* at *11; John K. MacIver Inst. for Pub. Pol'y, Inc., v. Evers, 994 F.3d 602 (7th Cir. 2021).

[80] *See* 994 F.3d at 610–11:

> We find that the Governor's media-access criteria are indeed reasonable and not an effort to suppress MacIver's expression because of its viewpoint. The Governor contends that its criteria are intended to consider limited space constraints, address security concerns, and ensure that those in attendance will maximize the public's access to newsworthy information, and be more likely to abide by professional journalistic standards such as honoring embargoes and off-the-record communications. The resulting list of qualified media personnel includes a wide variety of news organizations and journalists from across the state and nation. The first three of the criteria listed in the memorandum are reasonably related to the viewpoint-neutral goal of increasing the journalistic impact of the Governor's messages by including media that focus primarily on news dissemination, have some longevity in the business, and possess the ability to craft newsworthy stories. The list prioritizes access by journalists whose reporting will reach wider audiences, while also allowing room for smaller media outlets (such as tribal publications). The criteria listed in numbers four and five of the memorandum are reasonably related to the viewpoint-neutral goal of increasing journalistic integrity by favoring media that avoid real or perceived conflicts of interest or entanglement with special interest groups, or those that engage in advocacy or lobbying. Similar standards are also used by other governmental bodies such as the U.S. Congress. There is nothing inherently viewpoint-based about these criteria, and MacIver has not provided any evidence that the Governor's office manipulates these neutral criteria in a manner that discriminates against conservative media.

[81] *See supra* notes 55–56 and accompanying text.

exceptionalism to the question of how they *should* do so. In setting forth four principles, I am guided by the normative view that press exceptionalism benefits the public when it facilitates the press function of providing the public regularly with valuable information and serving as a check on government overreach, corruption, or unconstitutional action. (Following Sonja West, I believe that First Amendment protection for freedom of speech, properly understood, should provide great protection for those not able to take advantage of press exceptionalism who occasionally engage in newsgathering, reporting, and disseminating information.[82])

First, consistent with the *Dunleavy* case,[83] government entities should articulate *explicit and meaningful standards* for enforcing press exceptionalism. The entity should publish a set of written rules that are easily accessible and fairly applied. Without such standards, arbitrary government action becomes too likely. Lack of written standards can also create the appearance of favoritism even if unwritten rules are being applied consistently. As the D.C. Circuit held in a 1977 case, the White House's "failure to articulate and publish an explicit and meaningful standard governing denial of White House press passes for security reasons, and to afford procedural protections to those denied passes, violates the First and Fifth Amendments."[84]

Second, most *press exceptionalism should be limited to professional journalists who regularly produce news stories or commentary*. Especially under conditions of scarcity, those who are most likely to regularly provide the public with reliable information and serve as a check on the government should be the ones with the greatest access and freedom from otherwise applicable government regulation. Professionalism does not require that the person is necessarily paid by a news organization, although that is strong evidence of working in the journalism profession. The key is the regularity of gathering, reporting, and disseminating information. Such a standard protects student journalists working with university-affiliated media, for example. It does not, however, cover bloggers or social media posters who only on rare occasions make or break news or who rarely provide news analysis or commentary.

Third, the question of applicability of a rule of press exceptionalism *should not turn on the type of technology used to disseminate journalism*. Today, even many long-standing respected local newspapers publish most or all of their news digitally, and many, to save costs, have eliminated print editions. There is no reason to believe that content published via new technology should be subject to different standards than content produced for newspapers, magazines, radio, or television.

Digital media did not exist when government officials crafted many of the press exceptionalism rules in my database. Some government entities have read language

82 West, *supra* note 5, at 1058.
83 Alaska Landmine, LLC v. Dunleavy, 514 F. Supp. 3d 1123 (D. Alaska 2021).
84 Sherrill v. Knight, 569 F.2d 124, 131 (D.C. Cir. 1977).

broadly – such as reading the term "newspaper" to encompass new forms of news media. When possible as a matter of statutory interpretation, this type of broad reading of rules benefits society. When such interpretation is not fairly possible, legislatures or government entities should revise or rewrite the rules to account for changes in technology.

Saying that technology of dissemination should not be relevant to press exceptionalism is different from arguing that every blogger or poster on social media is entitled to press exceptionalism. In fact, the focus on professional journalism would mean that in the current moment, most bloggers and social media posters would not be entitled to such an exception. But professional journalists working in new media should be treated the same as professional journalists working in legacy media. NASA's ban on all "bloggers," for example (which it classifies incorrectly as a type of "social media"), should be changed. People who work as professional journalists should qualify, whether they write their professional journalism for a blog or another website or not.

Fourth, and most controversially and delicately, *government entities, or journalistic societies given powers by government entities, should continue to have the power to identify the press by reference to a "bona fide correspondents of repute in their profession" standard, so long as they do not engage in viewpoint discrimination.*

We should reject the nihilism of a post-truth world, insisting that we cannot distinguish between The New York Times and The Gateway Pundit and that there is no way of measuring objectivity in reporting. In contrast to the arguments of FIRE and others, there *are* empirically verifiable facts in the world, and entities purporting to be journalists that systematically deny those facts or regularly present empirically false claims as facts should not be considered journalists entitled to press exceptionalism. The best way to enforce such rules is by examining whether the entity claiming press privileges complies with journalistic practices, such as fact-checking, giving those written about a chance to respond, and not reporting empirically false facts as proven. These issues can be examined in a systematic way without inviting arbitrary government action.

The key is to avoid slipping into viewpoint discrimination, particularly if the viewpoints expressed by the person seeking press exceptionalism are controversial. Someone who proves employment as a professional journalist should be denied press privileges only if the person seeking press status has *no track record of consistently gathering, reporting, and disseminating truthful information*, or if the person has *a track record of consistently reporting and disseminating empirically verifiable false claims as true*. This standard takes away most discretion on the part of government entities, giving them something specific and empirically verifiable to focus on, and such a decision may be meaningfully reviewed by courts.

This standard unavoidably puts government bodies in the position of deciding whether those purporting to be journalists are regularly peddling lies rather than the truth, and this no doubt presents some dangers.[85] What would stop a deceptive government entity from declaring real professional journalists to be faux journalists peddling fake news? Here, we must rely upon the courts to look over the shoulder of those government officials to ensure that the inquiry is not a pretext for viewpoint discrimination.

Judicial review appeared to work in the *TGP Communications* case. Maricopa County should not have relied on the fact that Conradson "expresse[d] his opinion" in his articles or that he used "inflammatory and/or accusatory language, such as 'Fake News Media,' 'globalist elitist establishment,' and 'highly flawed 2022 Primary Elections'"[86] to deny press access. These criteria indeed appear aimed at discriminating against the journalist and his publication for his viewpoint. These criteria do not point to whether Conradson was gathering and reporting true facts, regardless of his political spin or ideology.

But if the county could have demonstrated that Conradson showed no track record of consistently gathering, reporting, and disseminating truthful information, or if he had had a consistent track record of reporting and disseminating empirically verifiable false claims as true, then the county reasonably could have denied him press privileges without violating the First Amendment.[87]

This line between determining a journalist's bona fides and engaging in viewpoint discrimination requires a careful look at the record of the person seeking the press exemption, and doubtful cases should be resolved in favor of press exceptionalism.[88] But there are cases where press privileges could and should be properly denied when a full-time professional faux journalist is not engaged in the act of journalism, and government entities should be allowed to say so in appropriate cases and act on this conclusion. Denial of press privileges to faux journalists furthers the reasons for having press exceptionalism in the first place.

Finally, it is worth recognizing the potential political backlash that may come from allowing government entities to exclude faux journalists from press

85 *See* RonNell Andersen Jones & Lisa Grow Sun, *Freedom of the Press in Post-Truthism America*, 98 Wash. U.L. Rev. 419, 466–67 (2020), for a discussion of an alternative approach focused more on process questions (such as whether the organization checks its facts) than on making a substantive judgment.

86 TGP Commc'ns, LLC v. Sellers, No. 22-16826, 2022 WL 17484331, at *5 (9th Cir. Dec. 5, 2022).

87 More recent reporting revealed that even within The Gateway Pundit organization, employees were worried about the truthfulness of Conradson. He was instrumental in spreading lies about two Georgia election workers, falsely claiming they had stolen the 2020 presidential election in Georgia for Joe Biden. Sam Levine, *Workers at Far-Right Site Gateway Pundit Feared Credibility Issues, Filing Shows*, The Guardian (May 1, 2024), https://www.theguardian.com/us-news/2024/may/01/gateway-pundit-2020-election-lies [https://perma.cc/2GYU-BNQ3].

88 The case of "pink slime" local "news" websites presents some especially difficult questions about who should count as a professional journalist. *See* Tow Center for Digital Journalism, *"Pink Slime": Partisan Journalism and the Future of Local News* (Jan. 2024), https://towcenter.columbia.edu/sites/default/files/content/%E2%80%9CPink%20Slime%E2%80%9D_%20Partisan%20journalism%20and%20the%20future%20of%20local%20news%20%281%29.pdf [https://perma.cc/4Y33-C3TE].

exceptionalism. The Gateway Pundit, for example, has consistently spread false statements, such as about rigged or stolen elections, favored by right-wing populists. A decision to exclude The Gateway Pundit from observing Maricopa County's ballot-counting process, particularly when election denialists were falsely claiming that such counting was "rigged," likely would be seen by some as viewpoint discrimination even if the exclusion was based solely upon the website's failure to adhere to basic journalistic practices.

To mitigate this risk, government entities, as noted above, should resolve close cases in favor of press exceptionalism. A partisan press is becoming increasingly the norm again in American journalism,[89] and government entities should be careful not to confuse the question of the political views of a journalist (or the journalist's employer) with whether a person posing as a journalist is actually a journalist. Journalists and entities can hold and write from whatever point of view they like without risking the benefits of press exceptionalism. What people claiming to be journalists cannot do if they want the benefits of press exceptionalism is consistently present empirically verifiable false statements as true or consistently deny the truth of empirically verifiable true statements. In the end, how government entities handle this difficult question could reflect not only on the legitimacy of journalism but on the legitimacy of government and US democracy as well.

[89] Andersen Jones & Sun, *supra* note 85, at 472–79.

18

A Professional Wrestler, Privacy, and the Meaning of News

Amy Gajda

In October of 2012, something momentous happened in the clash between the law of privacy and the law of press: Gawker, a website that specialized in sensational news often involving celebrities – one that promoted itself as making "today's gossip … tomorrow's news" – published professional wrestler Hulk Hogan's sex tape without his permission.

It was momentous because the not-safe-for-work post illustrates how difficult it can be to define news, how the meaning of "the press" has changed in an internet age, and how legal protections for traditional newsgatherers can be imperiled if the words "news" and "press" are stretched too broadly to include all truth and all publishers. Those matters are the focus of this chapter.

The two-minute-long, black-and-white, grainy Hogan sex tape was not at all Hollywood-esque; it showed Hogan[1] completely nude, very much engaged in explicit sexual activity with a woman on a bed in someone else's house, handling himself in a way that indicated that he was quite unaware that he was being filmed (not that that would matter). Gawker headlined its scoop: "Even For a Minute, Watching Hulk Hogan Have Sex in a Canopy Bed Is Not Safe For Work, But Watch It Anyway." Millions did.

Within days, Hulk Hogan's lawyers announced that they would sue Gawker on behalf of their client and would stake their claim on the "basic concept" of "invasion of privacy."[2] Publishing another's explicit sexual activity, the attorneys said, "cannot be tolerated by a civil society."[3]

Gawker's lawyers came out swinging in response: "Tabloid journalism in America is protected under the newsworthy standard every day," they argued, and they maintained that the tape had real news value.[4] Gawker's *journalists* even more

[1] I will refer to him as Hulk Hogan throughout this chapter for ease of reader understanding. Hogan's real name is Terry Bollea, and his lawsuit was brought under the Bollea name.

[2] Nancy Dillon, *Hulk Smash*, N.Y. Daily News (Oct. 16, 2012), https://www.pressreader.com/usa/new-york-daily-news/20121016/281509338423024.

[3] *Id.*

[4] José Patiño Girona, *Hogan Seeks to Copyright His Sex Tape*, Tampa Trib., Nov. 9, 2012.

vehemently argued that the First Amendment protected their decision to publish, that the Constitution unambiguously "afford[ed] [them] the right to publish true things about public figures," and that any other legal decision would be "risible and contemptuous of centuries of First Amendment jurisprudence."[5]

I had heard about the sex tape very early on because a student had sent me a link to Gawker's original not-safe-for-work post. The student's sharing wasn't salacious; it was academic. I had been predicting in my media-related law classes for years that a gossip-type website would someday publish a sex tape featuring a celebrity and would suggest that the tape had news value protected by the Constitution. It had finally happened.

A brief bit of background is in order here. I became a law professor at the dawn of the internet age after an initial career in journalism. For nearly a decade, both before and during law school (and at some points after), I worked in journalism, mainly as a television news anchor, reporter, and producer in Toledo, Ohio; Salisbury, Maryland; Charlottesville, Virginia; Harrisburg, Pennsylvania; and Detroit, Michigan. I learned much in those newsrooms and television stations about the craft of journalism and about the ethics, principles, and gut feelings that stopped journalists from publishing many things that most people would consider deeply private. I recall learning from police precisely how a public figure had died, for example, which involved sexual information that would have mortified his family; I of course did not include such detail in news stories about his death. The fact that we had *video* of newsworthy tragedies like car accidents and plane crashes made such ethics decisions all the more routine and often easy because what we had on tape was so troubling. Our newsroom rule was that there would be no gruesome images of people and no death images. When Pennsylvania's state treasurer died by suicide at a press conference, I played a key role in our newsroom decision to freeze the video at the moment that he pulled the gun from his briefcase, even though our cameras had captured everything that transpired that tragic day. We would at times unintentionally capture video of embarrassing things, such as a clothing malfunction on a windy day or a person who fell on the street, and those videos were off limits too.

Many newsrooms like mine had their own ethics codes that guided such news decisions. The main one that journalists across the United States followed and continue to follow was drafted by the Society of Professional Journalists. "Only an overriding public need can justify intrusion into anyone's privacy," the SPJ Code read. It told reporters to "[a]void pandering to lurid curiosity" too.

That's why, when I joined the permanent faculty at the University of Illinois College of Media and its College of Law, I jumped at the chance to teach journalism ethics and I chose privacy as the main focus for my scholarship. I was

[5] John Cook, A *Judge Told Us to Take Down Our Hulk Hogan Sex Tape Post. We Won't.* Gawker, Apr. 25, 2016.

particularly interested in the conflict between privacy and the freedom to publish truth. I knew my own sensibilities, I knew journalism's ethics provisions, and I was intrigued when judges opined on the newsworthiness of journalistic decisions, at times deferring to publishers even in surprising situations.

That was in the early 2000s, and it soon became clear that the democratization of the internet and the ease of publishing had changed things. Suddenly, ethics-abiding gatekeepers of information like the journalists I had worked with for years – those commonly deferred to by judges – were not the norm. Suddenly, anyone could assess the public interest in anything (or not) and instantly publish whatever they believed would satisfy it, including the graphic or embarrassing visuals and information that would have never made it to any one of our newscasts.

That, then, is the background inspiration for my two decades of scholarship. I've written, for example, about the strikingly critical description of journalism in the famous law review article, titled The Right to Privacy, published in 1890 by Samuel Warren and Louis Brandeis, and argued that sensationalistic coverage both of Warren's family and his friend Grover Cleveland (a president with a scandalous past) had been the main spark for the piece.[6] I wrote in the California Law Review about a shift in court decisions in favor of privacy and against press freedoms, comparing journalism's ethics provisions with what at the time was far more permissive law.[7]

My first media-focused book, *The First Amendment Bubble: How Privacy and Paparazzi Threaten a Free Press*, explored the press-privacy clash even more deeply.[8] And my most recent book, *Seek and Hide: The Tangled History of the Right to Privacy*,[9] named by The New York Times as one of the 100 Notable Books for 2022, looked at the press-privacy clash over time, all the way back to the earliest days when Massachusetts was a colony and shut down a newspaper in part for reporting that the King of France was having an affair with his daughter-in-law. So, back in 2012, when that former student sent me a link to the Hulk Hogan sex tape, I instantly recognized the constitutional clash – and I also suspected that Hulk Hogan would ultimately win.

18.1 A BRIEF HISTORY OF PRIVACY AND NEWS

When Gawker journalists argued in the wake of Hulk Hogan's invasion-of-privacy lawsuit that a legal decision in favor of Hulk Hogan would be "risible and

6 Amy Gajda, *What If Samuel D. Warren Hadn't Married a Senator's Daughter?: Uncovering the Press Coverage That Led to the Right to Privacy*, 2008 MICH. ST. L. REV. 35 (2008) (symposium).

7 Amy Gajda, *Judging Journalism: The Turn Toward Privacy and Judicial Regulation of the Press*, 97 CALIF. L. REV. 1039 (2009).

8 AMY GAJDA, THE FIRST AMENDMENT BUBBLE: HOW PRIVACY AND PAPARAZZI THREATEN A FREE PRESS (2015).

9 AMY GAJDA, SEEK AND HIDE: THE TANGLED HISTORY OF THE RIGHT TO PRIVACY (2022).

contemptuous of centuries of First Amendment jurisprudence," they weren't exactly right. From the very beginning of the United States, even before the First Amendment was ratified, there was recognition – sometimes troubling recognition – that not all bits of truthful information had equal news value. Back then, what we might today call invasion of privacy was known in part as "truthful libel," called that because, judges and other thought leaders said, truthful information could be more harmful at times to a person's reputation and emotions than falsity. Blackstone's Commentaries on the Laws of England had supported that idea to some extent, suggesting that, despite the essentiality of freedom of the press, those who published things that were "improper, mischievous, or illegal," including non-justifiable information about extramarital affairs, it was suggested, "must take the consequence of [their] own temerity."[10]

At least some of the Founders seemed to agree. Consider the discussion about the boundaries of press freedom between William Cushing and John Adams, who were particularly concerned that the Constitution might protect newspapers that reported on what they called politicians' "instances of male conduct" – their extramarital immoral behavior. Cushing, who would later become a justice on the U.S. Supreme Court, suggested that the *person* should be protected in such instances, not the *publisher*. "My question is this," Cushing's letter to Adams read, "[W]hether it is consistent with [the First Amendment], to deem & adjudge any publications of the press, punishable as libels, that may arraign the conduct of persons in office, charging them with instances of male conduct repugnant to the duty of their offices & to the public good & Safety; – *when such charges are supportable by the truth of fact?*"[11] "Doubtless," he added, the liberty of the press "may & ought to be restrainable" in some of those cases.[12]

Adams agreed. "You may easily conceive a Case, when a *Scandalous Truth* may be told of a Man, without any honest motive, and merely from malice,"[13] he replied to Cushing. "[I]n Such a Case, Morality and religion would forbid a Man from doing Mischief merely from Malevolence, and I thought that Law would give damages."

Thereafter, a court in New Orleans in 1811 sided with a man who'd written a love letter and against a newspaper that had threatened to publish it.[14] Whatever press freedoms existed in the publication of the letter, the court explained, paled in comparison to the plaintiff's privacy interests, and it repeatedly condemned the

[10] 3 William Blackstone, Commentaries on the Laws of England 125 (1765); United States v. Fries, 9 F. Cas. 826, 839 (C.C.D. Pa. 1799) (No. 5,126) (quoting Blackstone at 152).

[11] Letter from William Cushing to John Adams (Feb. 18, 1789) (founders.archives.gov) (emphasis added).

[12] *Id.*

[13] *Id.*

[14] Denis v. Leclerc, 1 Mart. (o.s.) 297 (La. Sup. Ct. 1811).

publisher who would share such truthful information. Any constitutional promise of a free press, it said, would not protect the publisher of personal secrets:

> If [the First Amendment] can be invoked to support the defendant, in the right of . . . violating the secrets of his correspondence, it will protect the propagation of any slander or libel. Neither Congress, nor the Circuit Court of the United States, seem to have ever considered this article as susceptible of so strange a construction.

A little more than a century later, the first Restatement on Torts protected privacy in a similar way. "A person who unreasonably and seriously interferes with another's interest in not having his affairs known to others," the provision read in 1939, was liable for what was called "Interference with Privacy."[15] Such protection for privacy included seemingly newsworthy situations; those Restatement authors would have held a newspaper liable for publishing a photograph taken in public of a "hideously deformed" person harmed at birth by inexpert medical care, even when that photograph accompanied an article about the need for better medical care for newborns.[16]

Forty years later, when the American Law Institute published the Second Restatement on Torts, it included a parallel provision titled Publicity Given to Private Life.[17] "One who gives publicity to a matter concerning the private life of another," the provision read, "is subject to liability to the other for invasion of his privacy, if the matter publicized is of a kind that (a) would be highly offensive to a reasonable person, and (b) is not of legitimate concern to the public." As for what would be both highly offensive and not of legitimate concern, the Restatement authors suggested that "[s]exual relations . . . are normally entirely private matters" and that "even the actress . . . is entitled to keep to herself . . . such intimate details of her life."[18]

But the American Law Institute added an important note to this new publication-related privacy tort:

> It has not been established with certainty that liability of this nature is consistent with the free-speech and free-press provisions of the First Amendment to the Constitution, as applied to state law through the Fourteenth Amendment.[19]

That warning note made sense for several reasons. Once journalism turned away from scandal and started to abide by ethics standards more generally[20] (a shift that

[15] Restatement of Torts § 867 (Am. Law Inst. 1934).

[16] *Id.*

[17] Restatement (Second) of Torts § 652D (Am. Law Inst. 1977).

[18] *Id.*

[19] *Id.*

[20] I looked at this history of journalism and law first in *Judging Journalism*, *supra* note 7, and amplified the coverage in both The First Amendment Bubble, *supra* note 8, and in Seek and Hide, *supra* note 9.

occurred mainly in the 1920s and 1930s), court decisions increasingly deferred to journalism's news judgment in many cases that involved claimed invasion of privacy, sometimes even in a constitutional sense. The Supreme Court wrote in *Gertz v. Robert Welch, Inc.*, a 1974 defamation case concerning the assessment of matters of general public interest, for example, that it doubted the wisdom of committing such an assessment task to judges.[21] In another case that same year, the justices worried even more strongly about judicial interference with the news judgment of journalists, suggesting that "government regulation of this crucial process" was inconsistent "with First Amendment guarantees."[22] And then, in 1975, in *Cox Broadcasting v. Cohn*,[23] the Court held that a television station that had broadcast the name of a deceased rape victim would not be liable for a privacy invasion despite her grieving father's emotional pain and a state statute that allowed punishment for such a publication. It seemed that much, if not all, truthful information, even emotionally harmful information, would be protected.

The already deferential lower courts generally followed suit. Four years after *Cox Broadcasting*, in 1979, the Iowa Supreme Court held that "[i]n determining whether an item is newsworthy, courts cannot impose their own views about what should interest the community."[24] Judges, the court added, "do not have license to sit as censors."[25] Federal courts suggested the same: "[J]udges, acting with the benefit of hindsight," the First Circuit wrote in 1989, should not assess journalistic news judgment aggressively, because "[e]xuberant judicial blue-penciling after-the-fact would blunt the quills of even the most honorable journalists."[26]

But shortly thereafter, in the mid-to-late 1990s, the internet exploded in a very real way. Rather suddenly, it was not at all clear which publishers qualified as journalists and what truthful publications qualified as journalism. If there were indeed honorable journalists whose sharp quills needed judicial defenders and if indeed the law protected a journalistic judgment of newsworthiness, what about the bloggers and the social media posters and the others who created websites filled with a reality that wreaked emotional harm? Would those assessors of information of public interest and publishers of truth be protected too?

By 2007, the answer, at least in many places, appeared to be no. "Ethical standards regarding the acceptability of certain discourse have been lowered," the Ohio Supreme Court wrote in a case that recognized for the very first time in the state the privacy tort of false light, even though the justices had rejected it in the past as being too similar to defamation.[27] "[A]s the ability to do harm has grown," those

21 418 U.S. 323 (1974).

22 Miami Herald Publishing Co. v. Tornillo, 418 U.S. 241 (1974).

23 Cox Broadcasting v. Cohn, 420 U.S. 469, 487 (1975).

24 Howard v. Des Moines Register & Tribune Co., 283 N.W.2d 289 (1979).

25 *Id.* at 302.

26 Ross v. Midwest Communications, Inc. 870 F.2d 271 (5th Cir. 1989).

27 Welling v. Weinfeld, 886 N.E.2d 1051, 1058–59 (Ohio 2007).

justices wrote, referring to the internet, "so must the law's ability to protect the innocent."[28]

That same sort of shift seemed to be happening at the United States Supreme Court too.

18.2 *BARTNICKI V. VOPPER* AND HULK HOGAN

In 2001, eleven years before Gawker published the Hulk Hogan sex tape, the Supreme Court decided *Bartnicki v. Vopper*.[29] The decision was an important one for media; the justices had found that a radio station would not be liable for publishing a cellphone conversation that had been surreptitiously recorded by an unknown person and had been given to the radio station by someone who did not work there. On the tape, an official who represented the local teachers' union had suggested that violence might be used against school board officials in order to influence a labor dispute. The Supreme Court held that such a discussion was in itself a matter of public concern. Even though the revelation of the wiretapped conversation violated federal law, the justices reasoned, the later broadcast of that recording was not unlawful because the First Amendment protected the station's decision to publish such "unquestionably" newsworthy information. "[S]tate action to punish the publication of truthful information seldom can satisfy constitutional standards," the Court wrote, quoting its own language from 1979's *Smith v. Daily Mail Publishing*.[30]

There were three wrinkles in *Bartnicki*, however, and each suggested that, like the lower courts, the Supreme Court might also be shifting away from broad protection for publishers – a shift springing in part from willy-nilly publication decisions.

The first wrinkle was that the *Bartnicki* decision did not sweep broadly. The radio station had not been involved in the surreptitious recording of the information itself; it had been given the tape by a person unaffiliated with the station and, therefore, was innocent of any wrongdoing. There remained a "still-open question," the Court wrote, and that was "whether, in cases where information has been acquired *unlawfully* by a newspaper or by a source, government may ever punish not only the unlawful acquisition, but the ensuing publication as well."[31] (Later decisions, including those from federal appellate courts,[32] have indeed held publishers liable for information that they obtained unlawfully, although the issue remains open at the Supreme Court.)

The second wrinkle was that the word "seldom" in the *Daily Mail Publishing* quote – that "state action to punish the publication of truthful information *seldom*

[28] *Id*. at 1059.
[29] Bartnicki v. Vopper, 532 U.S. 514 (2001).
[30] 443 U.S. 97, 102 (1979).
[31] *Bartnicki*, 532 U.S. at 528.
[32] Dahlstrom v. Chicago Sun-Times, 777 F.3d 937 (7th Cir. 2015).

can satisfy constitutional standards" – seemed an important limitation in *Bartnicki*. In other words, the *Bartnicki* Court could have chosen language that was more sweepingly protective of news, for example, by declaring that state action to punish the publication of truthful information can *never* satisfy constitutional standards. But it did not. Instead, the justices in the *Bartnicki* majority wrote that the outcome could well be different in cases involving different facts, such as those in which there had been the revelation of non-newsworthy "domestic gossip or other information of purely private concern."[33] Moreover, the justices in *Bartnicki* noted that the Court had, over time and in the sorts of decisions that included *Cox Broadcasting*,[34] repeatedly refused "to answer categorically whether truthful publication may ever be punished consistent with the First Amendment."[35] Quoting *Florida Star v. B.J.F.*,[36] the Court wrote that "the future may bring scenarios which counsels our not resolving anticipatorily" this "ultimate question," because of the "sensitivity and significance of the interests presented between [the] First Amendment and privacy rights."[37]

The third wrinkle appeared in *Bartnicki*'s concurring and dissenting opinions. Justices Breyer and O'Connor in concurrence suggested that the Constitution tolerated certain privacy-protective laws because of the right of privacy's importance and called it an "interest[] of the highest order."[38] They suggested too that even *public* figures retained some rights to "private communication," especially in an age involving "challenges" that "technology may pose to the individual's interest in basic personal privacy."[39] And then they listed as among "truly private matters," what they called "sexual relations" between two public figures that had been recorded.[40] In other words, a celebrity sex tape.

Three justices dissented in *Bartnicki*; they would have ruled against the radio station's claimed First Amendment interests. They too were worried about the "significant privacy concerns" arising from technological advances that allowed others to access personal communications. "Even where the communications involve public figures,"[41] Justices Rehnquist, Scalia, and Thomas wrote, the conversations are nonetheless private and worthy of protection. That third wrinkle, therefore, means that in 2001 at least five of the justices on the Supreme Court would

33 *Bartnicki*, 532 U.S. at 533.
34 420 U.S. 469 (1975).
35 *Bartnicki*, 532 U.S. at 529.
36 491 U.S. 524 (1989).
37 *Bartnicki*, 532 U.S. at 529.
38 *Id.* at 536 (quoting *id.* at 518).
39 *Id.* at 541.
40 The concurrence cited Michaels v. Internet Entertainment Group, Inc., 5 F. Supp. 2d 823 (C.D. Cal. 1989), a case involving the actress Pamela Anderson and her husband, rock star Tommy Lee.
41 *Bartnicki*, 532 U.S. at 554–55.

surely have sided with Hulk Hogan and against Gawker's publication of the sex tape featuring him.

It also suggests that Bartnicki, although a 6-3 decision in favor of media, was ultimately a 5-4 decision against it – a decision against media's own discretion to determine newsworthiness in situations that involve personal privacy. Just as *Bartnicki* itself suggested, this had been hinted at in a more nuanced reading of those earlier seemingly pro-publication decisions, including the word "seldom" in *Daily Mail Publishing*. "[T]here *is* a zone of privacy surrounding every individual," the Court had written in *Cox Broadcasting v. Cohn*, for example, "a zone within which the State may protect him from intrusion by the press, with all its attendant publicity."[42] And in *Florida Star*, the justices had written: "We do not hold that truthful publication is automatically constitutionally protected, or that there is no zone of personal privacy within which the State may protect the individual from intrusion by the press, or even that a State may never punish publication of the name of a victim of a sexual offense"[43] because there is "sensitivity and significance" in privacy interests that are just as profound as those inherent in press interests.

In other words, if anything, centuries of jurisprudence seemed to tip Hulk Hogan's way.

18.3 THE LEGACY OF GAWKER'S PUBLICATION OF HULK HOGAN'S SEX TAPE

The pretrial litigation over Hulk Hogan's sex tape was contentious. Gawker argued that the First Amendment protected its right to publish the tape as news, while Hogan claimed the explicitness of the tape violated his privacy. Although two preliminary court decisions found that any restriction on publishing the tape would be an unconstitutional prior restraint,[44] neither of these opinions addressed the graphic nature of the nudity and sexual intercourse. In fact, it was not clear whether the judges had even seen the video excerpts that Gawker published. In 2016, the case proceeded to a Florida jury.

[42] *Cox Broadcasting*, 420 U.S. at 487.

[43] *Florida Star*, 491 U.S. at 541.

[44] In 2012, a federal trial court rejected Hogan's request for a preliminary injunction to force removal of the tape, noting that his "public persona," composed of, among other things, reality television appearances, a biography, and discussion of his sex life, made the video "a subject of general interest and concern to the community." Bollea v. Gawker Media, 2012 U.S. Dist. Lexis 162711 (M.D. Fla. Nov. 13, 2012). Further, in 2014, a Florida appellate court overturned a trial court injunction and ruled that Hogan's "extramarital affair and the video evidence of such" were linked to "a matter of public concern" and, in the preliminary injunction context, were "within Gawker Media's editorial discretion to publish." Gawker Media v. Bollea, 129 So. 3d 1196 (Fla. App. 2014).

At trial, jurors heard the Gawker reporter who wrote the post admit that there was no news value in the graphic nudity shown in the tape,[45] and thereafter they decided that Gawker should pay Hogan $140 million, an astonishing amount that ultimately drove Gawker to bankruptcy. The case settled for $31 million, but even that sum was large enough to create quite a stir in the plaintiffs' bar. The Washington Post suggested that there was a new disorder, which it called "Hulk Hogan Syndrome" that was suddenly afflicting plaintiffs who'd been wronged by media, leading to these plaintiffs and their attorneys "winning big."[46] The headline theorized that such verdicts might well reflect hostility toward more modern publishers.

Since then, various courts have decided other cases in ways suggesting that Hulk Hogan Syndrome is real and that judges also might have it. Put another way, modern court decisions show that judges are both worried about privacy interests and fed up with the breadth of the newsworthiness defense – and, in turn, they have pivoted to positions that disfavor publishers. In 2022, for example, the federal district court for Oregon decided that a famous author's stepdaughter had a valid claim against her stepfather's biographer who had described in rather graphic terms the sexual abuse she had suffered at the hands of her birth father.[47] The Supreme Court of Indiana in 2023 decided that a patient's diagnosis and prescribed treatment were private information; the publisher had mistakenly received the information meant for another and had posted it to Facebook.[48] And, in 2023, a federal district court in Indiana held that Netflix producers who had shared on social media the identities of people conceived by a prolific sperm donor as part of a promotional campaign for a documentary could be liable for invasion of privacy.[49]

But, notably, in each of those examples – just as in the Hulk Hogan case – it is not clear whether any of those publishers should be considered journalists or whether those truthful publications should be considered journalism. It's possible to argue that such labels are appropriate in each, of course: that the biographer and the Facebook poster and the Netflix producers were all journalists and that each bit of truth that they published was news. But looking at those decisions from the *ethics* provisions that often inform journalists' decisions regarding what is appropriately published and what isn't – what newsworthiness means in a journalistic sense – the labels "journalist" and "news" are not at all clear. Many journalists, I would think, would say these decisions to publish were utterly inappropriate given the facts. And

[45] Eriq Gardner, *Gawker Trial: Editor Admits Hulk Hogan's Penis Isn't Newsworthy*, Hollywood Rep. (Mar. 16, 2016), https://www.hollywoodreporter.com/business/business-news/gawker-trial-editor-admits-hulk-875098/.

[46] Paul Farhi, *Rolling Stone Verdict May Reflect Hostility Toward Media*, Wash. Post, Nov. 6, 2016.

[47] Conroy v. Mewshaw, 2022 WL 2981453 (D. Ore. July 28, 2022).

[48] Z.D. v. Community Health Network, 217 N.E.3d 527 (Ind. 2023).

[49] Doe v. Netflix, 2023 WL 3848379 (S.D. Ind. June 6, 2023).

these, in part, are the reasons that judges who once deferred to the judgments of publishers of truth are less likely to do so today. Perhaps the greatest worry in all of this is that such decisions can now affect what might be considered "real" journalists, those in legacy journalism who might well decide after sincere newsroom introspection that a more graphic description of sexual abuse on different facts was appropriate to a news story, or that an individual's medical diagnosis was newsworthy, or that the precise names of people involved in something that had news value was an important part of the story. It is not going too far to suggest here that journalists like those who worked and continue to work in my old newsrooms can be chilled by such outcomes that involve people who published truth under very different standards.

This modern pushback against the broad invocation of newsworthiness in privacy cases can help inform discussions about who or what qualifies as press for constitutional purposes too. If law has created deferential carveouts for journalism over the years on the assumption that the journalistic entities would be operating within professional ethics strictures that decided questions of newsworthiness in a way that balanced important social norms and interests, what happens to those carveouts when those assumptions are no longer true? And how might this backlash against the actions of fringe actors who are eager to justify their behaviors as newsworthy lead to scalebacks that remove constitutionally valuable protections from those who are actually performing the press function?

It seems clear that a more sacrosanct approach to terms like "press" and "news" would ultimately benefit the whole – that more exclusive definitions would help protect the publishers that matter most. Privacy's history teaches that lesson. And a $140-million-dollar jury verdict is surely a very big lesson too.

19

Reconstructing the First Amendment

Teaching Disenfranchised Perspectives on Press Freedom

Meredith D. Clark

In journalism education, the First Amendment's guarantee of press freedom is typically taught as a cornerstone of American democracy. Yet this approach too often fails to grapple with the historical and ongoing realities of racial inequality and the experiences of marginalized communities, particularly Black Americans, in relation to press freedom. The traditional emphasis on teaching journalists to be strictly "objective" often leads the press to report in ways that perpetuate the status quo and fail to hold those in power accountable.

The prevailing standards in journalism education, moreover, tend to give educators conflicting directives. Taken at face value, these standards seem to encourage journalism educators to teach the First Amendment as a neutral principle that protects press freedom and encourages journalists to strive for objectivity and balance in their reporting. However, the standards also tell educators to emphasize the profession's multicultural history and to promote communication that empowers and centers the voices of marginalized communities – an approach that might require journalists to take a more active stance on issues of social justice. Recent debates over "journalistic objectivity" on issues of Black protest, editorial witnessing, and journalistic authority during the Movement for Black Lives have illustrated how these principles can clash with each other in newsrooms.

In this chapter, I argue for a critical reexamination of how the First Amendment and press freedom are taught in journalism classrooms. I draw on historical analysis, legal case studies, and contemporary examples to advocate for a "reparative journalism" approach. By centering the voices and experiences of those who have been systematically excluded from the full protections of the First Amendment and by interrogating the complex relationship between race, power, and the press, this approach seeks to develop a more inclusive, historically grounded, and forward-looking vision of journalism's role in society. Ultimately, this chapter contends that reckoning with the racial dynamics of press freedom is essential, not only for journalism education but also for the practice of journalism itself, as a means of fulfilling its democratic purpose and holding power to account.

19.1 WHAT IS REPARATIVE JOURNALISM?

Two hundred fifty years of slavery. Ninety years of Jim Crow. Sixty years of separate but equal. Thirty-five years of racist housing policy. Until we reckon with our compounding moral debts, America will never be whole.

—Ta-Nehisi Coates, "The Case for Reparations"[1]

Scholars have extensively written about and debated the merits of reparations in a number of countries and contexts. Coates' 2014 essay, "The Case for Reparations," brought the conversation out of scholarly and legislative domains and planted it more firmly into public discourse. Decades of reports on the topic have attempted to quantify the impact of stolen wages and physical and psychological assaults on Black families, but most attempts to map the complicity of systems that have normalized Black subjugation focus on the obvious players of education, government, labor, law, medicine, and property ownership.[2] Media, particularly the news media, binds all of these together. As we read and listen to news reports, we develop a sense of our shared social reality, an understanding of who we are and how the world works. So influential is the news media that the founders of the Black press in the United States used their very first editorial in 1827 to condemn other publishers for their role in positioning Black people as deviant and irredeemable.[3] More than 150 years later, the Kerner Commission, tasked with identifying the cause of race riots in inner cities throughout the country, also implicated the news media for its failure to present a full and accurate picture of what Black life was like and warned that should our social systems continue down the same path, we would move toward "two Americas, one Black and one White, separate and unequal."[4] The compounding moral debt that Coates spoke of has quietly accumulated in journalism and journalism education as well. In the years before, during, and after World War II, the practice moved from one of vocation to occupation, professionalized through the creation of post-secondary degree programs that were generally exclusive to white males. The country's oldest journalism program, the University of Missouri, repeatedly denied

1 Ta-Nehisi Coates, *The Case for Reparations*, Atl. (June 2014), https://www.theatlantic.com/magazine/archive/2014/06/the-case-for-reparations/361631/.

2 Randall Robinson, The Debt: What America Owes to Blacks (2001); Rashawn Ray & Andre M. Perry, *Why We Need Reparations for Black Americans*, Brookings Inst. 1–5 (Apr. 15, 2020), https://www.brookings.edu/articles/why-we-need-reparations-for-black-americans/; William Darity, Jr & A. Kirsten Mullen, From Here to Equality: Reparations for Black Americans in the Twenty-First Century (2022); Ruti G. Teitel, Transitional Justice (2000).

3 *Freedom's Journal*, PBS, https://www.pbs.org/blackpress/news_bios/newbios/nwsppr/freedom/freedom.html (last visited June 30, 2024).

4 National Advisory Commission on Civil Disorders, Report of the National Advisory Commission on Civil Disorders 1 (1968), https://www.hud.gov/sites/dfiles/FHEO/documents/kerner_commission_full_report.pdf (last visited June 30, 2024).

Lucile Bluford, a Black woman, entry to its graduate program.[5] The school went so far as to temporarily shutter the program (ostensibly because of the demands on students and faculty being called to serve in World War II) and to create a separate program at Lincoln University in order to maintain segregation.[6]

From antebellum days to the Civil Rights Movement and beyond, newspaper publishers used their platforms to fix Black people as subhuman in the American imagination. Pre-Emancipation-era papers bankrolled themselves by selling slave ads.[7] Outlets such as the Raleigh News & Observer and the Wilmington Morning Star incited race riots to silence the Black press.[8] News editors refused to hire and promote Black staffers, only reluctantly moving to do so after being publicly shamed by the Association of Newspaper Editors in the 1970s. Until 2019, the Associated Press Stylebook, considered the "Journalist's Bible," lacked guidance on identifying and naming racism and racists.[9] The addition of the entry was prompted by the largest racial justice movement in American history.[10] If there is an American institution thought to contribute to democratic ideals while directly denying Black people and other marginalized folks equal treatment, it is journalism. If there is an American institution in need of a commitment to reparative work with Black communities, it is journalism. For the purpose of this chapter, I focus on Pablo de Greiff's articulation[11] of three goals that define the concepts of reparations: recognition of harms, restoration of civic trust, and the development of social solidarity. Reparative journalism education must first admit how and where our pedagogies and practices have contributed to harm. It must focus on strategies for restoring civic trust by identifying places where we have caused this segment of the public to rightfully doubt our commitment to equity. And we must use the classroom as a space to model a nonexclusive understanding of how journalists and members of the public outside of the newsroom must share in a right to free expression as a means of building solidarity.

5 *The Legacy and Leadership of Lucile Bluford*, Kansas City Pub. Libr. (June 29, 2022), https://kclibrary.org/news/2022-06/leadership-and-legacy-lucile-bluford.

6 *Id.*

7 Jordan E. Taylor, *Enquire of the Printer: Newspaper Advertising and the Moral Economy of the North American Slave Trade, 1704–1807*, 18 Early Am. Stud. 287 (2020), https://www.jstor.org/stable/27077808.

8 Jennifer L. Larson, *Early African American Perspectives on the Wilmington Race Riots of 1898*, Documenting the Am. S., https://docsouth.unc.edu/highlights/riots_1898.html (last visited June 30, 2024).

9 Dorie Truong, *AP Stylebook Update: It's OK to Call Something Racist When It's Racist*, Poynter (Mar. 29, 2019), https://www.poynter.org/reporting-editing/2019/ap-stylebook-update-its-ok-to-call-something-racist-when-its-racist/.

10 Gabriel R. Sanchez, *Americans Continue to Protest for Racial Justice 60 Years After the March on Washington*, Brookings Inst. (Aug. 25, 2023), https://www.brookings.edu/articles/americans-continue-to-protest-for-racial-justice-60-years-after-the-march-on-washington/.

11 Pablo de Greiff, *Justice and Reparations*, in The Handbook of Reparations 451 (Pablo de Grieff ed., 2006), https://doi.org/10.1093/0199291926.003.0013.

As a point of disambiguation, note that the concept of reparative journalism should not be conflated with media reparations, the economic program advanced by policy coalition Media 2070.[12] Reparative journalism is a complement and refers to a set of educational and vocational values, norms, and practices iteratively applied to address the wounds from prior eras while building a responsible apparatus for the social construction of news in the twenty-first century. The framework demands recognition of the foundational flaws in the construction of American social systems, with a central focus on the impact of anti-Black racial hierarchy as reflected in the adoption of chattel slavery, the imposition of Jim Crow and segregation, and the retrenchment of white supremacy as normative in contemporary culture. Thus, this chapter sets forth the operationalization of a particular educational practice: teaching the First Amendment in the twenty-first century with a commitment to recognizing how and where it intersects with anti-Black racism.

The organizing principle of reparative journalism is that social institutions that shape the construction of reality in the United States must directly confront how the legacy of slavery has shaped the institution's norms, customs, and values and resituate its practices by centering the perspectives of the vulnerable. In practice, this means acknowledging the presence and influence of racial discrimination in journalism. For instance, our contemporary news media workforce, which has for decades struggled to attract, retain, and promote non-white journalists, is characterized by the exclusion of Black students in journalism schools (and, more broadly, most institutions of higher learning) during the period in which the journalism evolved from a vocation to a profession.[13]

I articulated its core commitments in 2020:

Reparative journalism must be visionary, rather than reactionary.
Reparative journalism must be grounded in the history of the ignored.
Reparative journalism must be critically intentional.
Reparative journalism must be comprehensive.
Reparative journalism requires alternative funding and production models.
Reparative journalism requires the redistribution of power.
Reparative journalism will require an unfathomable commitment of time – more than any of us may have in this life.[14]

[12] Joseph Torres et al., Media 2070: An Invitation to Dream Up Media Reparations (2020), https://mediareparations.org/essay/.

[13] Federica Cherubini & Ramaa Sharma, *Changing Newsrooms 2023: Media Leaders Struggle to Embrace Diversity in Full and Remain Cautious on AI Disruption*, Reuters Inst. for the Study of Journalism (Dec. 5, 2023), https://reutersinstitute.politics.ox.ac.uk/changing-newsrooms-2023-media-leaders-struggle-embrace-diversity-full-and-remain-cautious-ai; Peregrine Frissell et al., *Missed Deadline: The Delayed Promise of Newsroom Diversity*, Asian Am. Journalists Ass'n's Voices (July 27, 2017), https://voices.aaja.org/stories/philadelphia-2017/missed-deadline-the-delayed-promise-of-newsroom-diversity.

[14] Meredith D. Clark, *The Year Journalism Starts Paying Reparations*, NiemanLab, https://www.niemanlab.org/2020/12/the-year-journalism-starts-paying-reparations/ (last visited June 30, 2024).

If news media creators – from student journalists working in campus media to veterans working on investigative stories and features – were to adhere to these commitments, it would shift news narratives from their focus on political and social elites and move the plight of marginalized people into the center. A vision of reparative journalism is one that covers the political economy of poverty from the perspective of those who live it rather than the policymakers who decide how their lives unfold. The framework requires that such reporting be grounded in history. Thus, it would begin by working backward through the federal, state, and local reforms and customs that have created nearly intractable inequalities in our society.

The Accrediting Council for Education in Journalism and Mass Communication (ACEJMC), formed in 1945, is the largest accrediting body for journalism programs in the United States. To date, 120 programs have some level of accreditation through the organization.[15] Although ACEJMC does not prescribe particular curriculum or pedagogical approaches, it sets forth several criteria for evaluating the rigor of programs. The first three criteria are stated here as a clear articulation of a schema for understanding why critical examination and reinterpretation of the First Amendment are necessary for contemporary journalism education. Alongside eight other core competencies, graduates of ACEJMC programs should have the ability to:

- apply the principles and laws of freedom of speech and press, in a global context, and for the country in which the institution that invites ACEJMC is located;
- demonstrate an understanding of the multicultural history and role of professionals and institutions in shaping communications;
- demonstrate culturally proficient communication that empowers those traditionally disenfranchised in society, especially as grounded in race, ethnicity, gender, sexual orientation, and ability, domestically and globally, across communication and media contexts.[16]

A purposive search and brief review of syllabi from media law, media ethics, and related courses that satisfy the First Amendment criteria from ACEJMC-accredited schools reflects a pattern in the literature assigned and modules taught about the First Amendment, including the Speech and Press Clauses. A journalism law and ethics class at a mid-size public university in the Northeast is described as "a foundation course in personal freedom and professional protection" that will equip students to "understand the foundation for freedom of expression" and link judicial values to "the work of mass media professionals and the free expression of citizens."[17]

[15] *Accrediting Standards*, Accrediting Council on Educ. in Journalism and Mass Commc'ns, http://www.acejmc.org/policies-process/accrediting-standards/ (last visited June 30, 2024).

[16] *Principles of Accreditation*, Accrediting Council on Educ. in Journalism and Mass Commc'ns, http://www.acejmc.org/policies-process/principles/ (last visited July 1, 2024).

[17] Syllabus on file with author.

Another course from a large public university in the Southeast "analyzes media policies and practices with respect to their political and practical generation, Constitutional foundation, ethical enactment and social impact, including such topics as government regulation of the media, the influence of pressure groups, media influence, and libel and privacy laws."[18] A third course, Media Law and Ethics, at a large private university on the West Coast vows "students will learn about their legal rights and obligations" and that the course will teach them "how to publish information without violating defamation and invasion of privacy, how to gather information to avoid legal and/or ethical trouble and how to deal with subpoenas ..." with a goal of "keep[ing] you and your employer out of trouble."[19] The common theme among the syllabi is clear: The First Amendment is being taught as a tangible license of rights and responsibility with an emphasis on market risks and demands. The descriptions rest on key assumptions about the First Amendment and its application: that this law confers legible power to the journalism profession and extends an egalitarian privilege to the masses; that all enjoy these privileges equally; and, foundationally, that the intention of the law was entered into the historical ledger under an expression of collective sentiment. That is, that commitment to pluralist democracy, as articulated in the preamble to the Constitution, was developed from a place of altruism and justice for all.

Nothing could be further from the truth.

In the examples that follow, I encourage educators to teach about the abolitionist press as the first real challenge of the First Amendment and to connect the threat of abolition in the pre-Civil War era to contemporary threats to First Amendment freedoms. I then use the foundational *New York Times Co. v. Sullivan* case to illustrate how traditional journalism education erases critical insight into how First Amendment law was weaponized in attempts to silence Black liberation workers. I close with a brief provocation of how contemporary conceptions of who is a journalist, and thus protected by the First Amendment, have implications for anyone who bears witness to civil rights violations and publishes them in the social media age.

19.2 PRESS FREEDOM, ABOLITIONISM, AND THE FIRST RECONSTRUCTION

Reparative journalism education must first acknowledge the *potential* for harm in our failure to critically interrogate the development and application of the First Amendment in a historical context. Students of the First Amendment must first develop a basic understanding that the rights guaranteed by the Constitution did not legally apply to anyone other than white men until the ratification of the Thirteenth,

[18] *Id.*

[19] *Id.*

Fourteenth, Fifteenth, and later the Nineteenth Amendments. Some courses addressing the First Amendment note that its robust protections for speech were not fully established by the Supreme Court until the mid-twentieth century, as the Court gradually came to recognize the importance of protecting dissenting views, including those of Communists and antiwar activists.

Thus, a consideration of the dire, dangerous conditions in which early Black publishers worked would further enrich students' understanding of the complicated history of the incomplete protections of the First Amendment. Periodicals including Freedom's Journal, The Colored American, The North Star, and The People's Advocate risked physical safety and economic ruin to provide Black communities with news and information in the service of racial uplift as a means of uplifting a nation and the nation.[20] Abolitionist allies such as Elijah Lovejoy – who was eventually martyred for the cause – were run out of town, their presses repeatedly destroyed.[21] Black writers, like David Walker, were subject to bounties for violating Black codes by encouraging the formerly enslaved to fight for their freedoms.[22] The early existence of the Black press highlighted tensions between the existence of the First Amendment and its practical accessibility for non-whites.

William M. Carter Jr.'s work on the First Amendment and the ratification of the Thirteenth, Fourteenth, and Fifteenth Amendments – the Second Founding – offers a framework ripe for exploration by historians, journalism scholars, and journalism educators committed to researching and teaching critical perspectives on press freedom.[23] As Carter writes, the question of the abolitionist press presented one of the earliest tests of the nation's commitment to free speech and press freedom in the pre-Civil War era:

> The Sedition Act of 1798 sparked the nation's first sustained controversy regarding the First Amendment's guarantee of freedom of speech. The national controversy over slavery presented the second such major free speech moment. Legislators and judges, public intellectuals, the popular press, and ordinary citizens discussed and debated whether abolitionist speech represented such a danger that it could be suppressed consistent with state and national guarantees of free speech.[24]

Revisiting and focusing on press freedom and the Second Founding as part of our pedagogy on the First Amendment would require students to engage with centuries-old assumptions about institutional and personal freedoms and rights that have proven ephemeral in recent years. Recent Supreme Court decisions have radically

[20] Benjamin Quarles, Frederick Douglass (1948).

[21] *Today in History – November 7*, Libr. Cong., https://www.loc.gov/item/today-in-history/november-07 (last visited June 30, 2024).

[22] David Walker, Appeal to the Coloured Citizens of the World (Great Neck Publishing 2017).

[23] William M. Carter, Jr, *The Second Founding and the First Amendment*, 99 Tx. L. Rev. 1065 (2021), https://texaslawreview.org/the-second-founding-and-the-first-amendment/.

[24] *Id.* at 1083.

changed the scope of various constitutional rights that were long thought inviolable.[25] How should our understanding of press freedom, and its defense, change in an era when it is no longer inconceivable that a court may rescind rights without warning? How secure is our ongoing ability to access the full promise of the First Amendment, especially when current legal challenges threaten to plunge us back into states' rights doctrines? What might a more judicially limited grant of press freedom mean for the publication of journalism that is out of favor with the ruling class, including journalism that is community-run or self-published? How might all of this change how students conceive of the role of the journalist in the future?

A classroom discussion on these questions might draw upon the tradition of Cone's Black Liberation Theology, where one's "heart, mind, body, and soul are where the dispossessed are."[26] Students might be invited to see how the journalist shares a sense of precarity with Black people in America: the ever-present threat of dispossession. This commonality is a point of invitation to consider the First Amendment from the vantage point of Black journalists and, more specifically, Black people in America. This sense of positionality moves our consideration beyond mere acceptance of the First Amendment and requires an interrogation of its development and application, including how it is taught.

19.3 *NEW YORK TIMES CO. V. SULLIVAN*: THE FIRST AMENDMENT AND THE SECOND RECONSTRUCTION

No course on media law, media ethics, or the First Amendment is complete without a mention of *New York Times Co. v. Sullivan*, the Supreme Court case that clarified the watchdog function of the press.[27] Most who have taken a course about free expression could probably recall with little effort that the case sets forth a high bar for holding publishers liable for defamation and perhaps even define what "actual malice" is without having to look it up. They might even be able to recall that Birmingham Police Commissioner L. B. Sullivan sued the paper over an ad, claiming the text portrayed him in an unflattering light. But what often goes unmentioned in the journalism classroom is the racialized nature of the case.

Beneath the text of "Heed Their Rising Voices," the advertisement placed by the Committee to Defend Martin Luther King and the Struggle for Freedom in the South in The New York Times on March 29, 1960, were the names of activists, celebrities, and clergy members seeking moral and financial support for Committee

[25] Dobbs v. Jackson Women's Health Organization, 597 U.S. 215 (2022); Mary Ziegler, *If the Supreme Court Can Reverse Roe, It Can Reverse Anything*, ATL. (June 24, 2022), https://www.theatlantic.com/ideas/archive/2022/06/roe-overturned-dobbs-abortion-supreme-court/661363/.

[26] JAMES H. CONE, A BLACK THEOLOGY OF LIBERATION: 50TH ANNIVERSARY EDITION (Orbis Books 2020).

[27] 376 U.S. 254 (1964).

to Defend Martin Luther King and the Struggle for Freedom in the South.[28] The Revs. Ralph Abernathy, Joseph Lowery, Solomon S. Seay, and Fred L. Shuttlesworth's names were listed among the signatories of the statement, although the ministers testified in court that they were added by Bayard Rustin without their knowledge or consent.[29]

Sullivan sued The Times and the ministers and was initially granted a $500,000 judgment (about $5.25 million in 2024 dollars).[30] The lawsuit was part of a repertoire of suppressive actions designed to curb the reach of communications that shed light on the struggles for integration in the South. At the time, news organizations, including The Times, faced civil suits that numbered in the millions of dollars, as powerful segregationists and their allies attempted to leverage market forces to silence the national press coverage by bankrupting them.[31] But if the target were simply the news outlets themselves, why name four ministers?

Scholars Samantha Barbas[32] and Aimee Edmondson[33] have both written extensively about the racial and socioeconomic implications of the *Sullivan* case for the four Alabama ministers who were named as co-defendants with The Times but whose experiences are often lost to history. Resituating *Sullivan* from a reparative journalism standpoint requires educators to consider the impact of the case and its outcomes on the most vulnerable individuals and groups involved. While the libel suit brought against The Times was part of a larger strategy designed to bankrupt news organizations in the North, their corporate structures delayed and shielded them from economic and social harms in ways that left individuals unprotected. As Barbas writes, by 1964, national news organizations were confronting more than $288 million in damages from libel suits brought by segregationists.[34] But in between *Sullivan*'s initial decision in an Alabama courtroom and the Supreme Court ruling, The Times' co-defendants' personal property was seized as an outcome of being convicted of libel.[35]

The ministers' inclusion was both a matter of legal maneuvering – necessary to keep the lawsuit in Alabama's jurisdiction – and an indication of how the law can be weaponized to suppress the speech of marginalized Others. Considering *Sullivan* through this lens is not only valuable for offering a more complete history of the

28 *Id.* at 256–57.

29 *Id.* at 260; *see also* Garrett Epps, *The Civil Rights Heroes the Court Ignored in* New York Times v. Sullivan, ATLANTIC (Mar. 20, 2014), https://www.theatlantic.com/national/archive/2014/03/the-civil-rights-heroes-the-court-ignored-in-em-new-york-times-v-sullivan-em/284550/.

30 *Id.* at 256.

31 AIMEE EDMONDSON, IN SULLIVAN'S SHADOW: THE USE AND ABUSE OF LIBEL DURING THE CIVIL RIGHTS MOVEMENT (2019); *Sullivan, supra* note 27, at 278 n.18 and 294–95.

32 SAMANTHA BARBAS, ACTUAL MALICE: CIVIL RIGHTS AND FREEDOM OF THE PRESS IN NEW YORK TIMES V. SULLIVAN (2023).

33 EDMONDSON, *supra* note 31.

34 BARBAS, *supra* note 32; *see also* Samantha Barbas, *New York Times v. Sullivan: Perspectives from History*, 30 GEO. MASON L. REV. F. 1 (2023).

35 BARBAS, *supra* note 32, at 127–28.

case's circumstances and significance in the Civil Rights era but also for studying the parallels between that moment and the present political era.

A reparative approach to teaching media law prompts us to map various modes and loci of power in *Sullivan*. Jennifer Brandel explains multiple considerations for power-mapping exercises.[36] We might consider historical and contemporary forms of power: the channels, flow, and means of justifying power, and classic definitions of hard or soft power – that is, the binary of force versus enticement. "What if every news story, no matter the form, helped people understand the foundational and systemic structures that are keeping things as is, creating conflict, or enabling new power to flow and, therefore, create new realities?" Brandel asks.[37] Reparative journalism encourages an expansion of the question such that racial hierarchies and the practices of domination that enforce them are considered part of this power analysis. Thus, teaching on the case would encourage students to abandon so-called color-blind thinking and consider why Sullivan named not only The New York Times as the injurious party in the lawsuit but also four other Alabamans known to be at the forefront of the antisegregation movement.[38] A recognition of power beyond the scope of the free press in this case would prepare students to anticipate strategies of domination that use the law and other levers of control to compound oppression. Ideally, this lens would encourage news workers to investigate similar contemporary legal, statutory, and executive actions for what they are – a means of fixing historically marginalized and comparatively subjugated peoples to new forms of oppression and control.

Discussing *Sullivan* in this context also invites consideration of the protections and resources available to the corporate press that do not extend to the individual, a useful framework for thinking about current debates over who qualifies as a journalist and what infrastructure must be in place for them to enjoy press protections. These questions should direct our attention to news workers and publishers who do not enjoy the protections of permanent employment with a corporate news organization. We might consider how press freedom differs for a media startup versus a legacy publication or for a staff writer versus a freelancer. What short- and long-term material risks do individuals outside of traditional news media structures face when they engage in advocacy as part of their First Amendment rights? Each of the ministers' vehicles was seized and sold by the state of Alabama, with the intention of not only causing financial hardship but also creating obstacles to their participation in racial justice work.[39] Ultimately, Shuttlesworth and Lowery would leave the state of Alabama and pursue their work elsewhere.[40]

36 Jennifer Brandel, *A Sneak Peak at Power Mapping, 2073's Top Innovation*, NiemanLab, https://www.niemanlab.org/2020/12/an-sneak-peak-at-power-mapping-2073s-top-innovation/ (last visited June 30, 2024).

37 *Id.*

38 Anthony Lewis, Make No Law: The Sullivan Case and the First Amendment 12 (1992).

39 Barbas, *supra* note 32, at 128.

40 *Id.*

A power analysis of the motivations, techniques, and function of social values and institutions involved in the *Sullivan* case will help underscore that the decision to bring the suit was not simply a matter of Sullivan attempting to defend his reputation but an attempt by segregationists and sympathizers to intimidate civil rights activists into silence by wounding or chilling the press. Threats to press freedom often emerge first as threats to the most vulnerable in society. Thus, the implications of the case have enduring relevance for those who struggle against authoritarian regimes, be they informed by racism, nationalism, theism, or other organizing themes.

19.4 THE COMPLEX RELATIONSHIP BETWEEN JOURNALISM AND SOCIAL CHANGE

Mainstream journalists and publishers often position press freedom, and the act of engaging in journalism, as vital to democracy and portray the press as part of the vanguard of movements for social change. In this telling, journalists work tirelessly to fulfill two proverbial goals: to "give voice to the voiceless" and to "speak truth to power."[41]

A reparative journalism approach to teaching about press freedom would critically examine this depiction of the press, its work, and its successes. Again, a consideration of the history of race and journalism in the United States would provide a useful frame. Scholars have shown that only within the last two decades have news organizations begun to seriously examine and acknowledge their amplification of narratives that fixed Black people at the bottom of the country's racial hierarchy.[42] The fantasy of being "a voice for the voiceless" extends to the position journalists imagined they have taken with respect to freedoms for those included in aforementioned groups as well.[43] But as John Nerone noted in an essay about journalism's hegemonic crisis, news workers reshaped their collective orientation to the ideal of racial equality only *after* political elites began to understand and respond to its implications for the future of electoral politics.

> Journalism's hegemony in the domain of news has a relationship within the hegemonic order in the larger society, in other words. The example of the Civil Rights movement is the best available case in US history that journalism can challenge the hegemonic order, but even in that case the decisive nature of journalism's intervention is unclear. Granted, by the 1960s national news

[41] *SPJ Code of Ethics*, SOC'Y PRO. JOURNALISTS, https://www.spj.org/ethicscode.asp (last updated Sept. 6, 2014).

[42] Nisha Sridharan & Angeline Taylor, *Sorry Seems to Be the Hardest Word: Reinforcing Institutional Identities Through Newspaper Apologies for Racist Past*, 24 JOURNALISM STUD. 2053 (2023).

[43] LEWIS RAVEN WALLACE, THE VIEW FROM SOMEWHERE: UNDOING THE MYTH OF JOURNALISTIC OBJECTIVITY (2019).

> organizations had overwhelmingly come to embrace a post-segregationist order, but this was only after the national political parties had changed their positions in response both to a mass popular movement among African-Americans, a Supreme Court-led change in the judicial order, and a new calculation of electoral realities that showed the possibility of winning national power while slighting southern white dead-enders. But granting the Civil Rights movement exceptional status, it remains an exception that proves the rule. In the normal run of modern history, journalism's hegemony over news has worked to support the general hegemonic order. The people and interests who run things did so more effectively because journalism made it seem natural.[44]

In order to propel our students toward a reparative journalism consideration of the First Amendment, we must consider the enduring impact of racial subjugation within the country's institutions, including the Fourth Estate. We must also interrogate how effectively journalists have historically "spoken truth to power," as opposed to supporting existing systems, as Nerone noted.

The concept of "fearless speech," introduced by Mary Anne Franks, provides a framework for the latter discussion.[45] In a 2018 essay, Franks draws upon Michel Foucault's articulation of the Greek concept of parrhesia, or fearless speech, and his argument that it emphasizes candor, mortal risk, and a commitment to the social duty of truth-telling above all that might be gained from engaging in more flattering or complementary speech. Contemporarily, fearless speech is that which refuses to exchange the ability to win favor and influence others (which seems to be the currency of the twenty-first century) for the responsibility of upholding unflinching truths. We may, perhaps, find examples of fearless speech in difficult spaces, such as confronting the realities of surveillance, war, and genocide in Gaza. We may also find examples of fearless speech in journalism, but asking students to consider the response of institutions – including media organizations – to the fearless speech of individual journalists offers a fruitful path for discussion.

The contestation over journalistic works such as Nikole Hannah Jones' reporting on the re-segregation of US public schools via school choice, charter schools, and redistricting policies is an example of fearless journalistic speech that confronts structural oppression.[46] The 1619 Project, an in-depth narrative exploration of the indelible effect of chattel slavery on multiple American institutions, might similarly be deemed an example of fearless speech.[47] The project, designed to contest hegemonic and unchallenged narratives about American history, was met with

[44] John Nerone, The Media and Public Life: A History 322 (2015).

[45] Mary Anne Franks, *Fearless Speech*, 17 First Amend. L. Rev. 294 (2018).

[46] Katie Robertson, *Nikole Hannah-Jones Denied Tenure at University of North Carolina*, N.Y.Times (July 15, 2022), https://www.nytimes.com/2021/05/19/business/media/nikole-hannah-jones-unc.html.

[47] *1619 Project*, N.Y. Times Mag., https://www.nytimes.com/interactive/2019/08/14/magazine/1619-america-slavery.html (last visited June 30, 2024).

censorial response by lawmakers at the federal and state levels. In July 2020, Senator Tom Cotton (R-Ark.) filed S.4292, the "Saving American History Act," during the 116th Congressional Session, which would have expressly prohibited elementary and secondary schools from teaching the project's curriculum under threat of withdrawn federal funding.[48] The bill's text was echoed in bills introduced in Arkansas, Iowa, and Mississippi in 2021.[49] Had Cotton's bill passed and been signed into law, schools would have been forced to consider the cost of engaging with the curriculum, as the restrictions demanded that no school that taught 1619 content receive federal funding for professional development.[50] Additionally, the bill would have required that the secretaries of agriculture, education, and health and human services create a formula to prorate decreased federal funding for any school that implemented the curriculum.[51] These measures could arguably have had a "chilling effect" on the speech of teachers, students, and support staff, pushing them to err on the side of caution and reject the curriculum outright rather than risk the loss of a school's federal funding.[52] According to the National Center for Education Statistics, US public school districts received anywhere from 5 percent to 20 percent of their annual revenue from federal sources as of 2021.[53]

In keeping with a reparative journalism framework, educators would also consider the political and social context of threats against fearless speech, such as the proposed bans on the 1619 Project curriculum. Each of these measures was introduced during a period in which federal and state governments were considering legislation to ban teaching antiracism and critical race theory (CRT).[54] The CRT

48 Saving American History Act of 2020, S. 4292, 116th Cong. (2020); Bryan Armen Graham, *Tom Cotton Calls Slavery "Necessary Evil" in Attack on New York Times' 1619 Project*, The Guardian (July 26, 2020, 5:54 PM), https://www.theguardian.com/world/2020/jul/26/tom-cotton-slavery-necessary-evil-1619-project-new-york-times.

49 Harmeet Kaur, *Bills in Several States Would Cut Funding to Schools that Teach the 1619 Project. But They Mostly Aren't Going Anywhere*, CNN (Feb. 10, 2021, 7:29 PM), https://www.cnn.com/2021/02/10/us/1619-project-school-funding-cut-bills-trnd/index.html.

50 Press Release, Senator Tom Cotton, Cotton Bill to Defund 1619 Project Curriculum (July 30, 2020), https://www.cotton.senate.gov/news/press-releases/cotton-bill-to-defund-1619-project-curriculum (announcing Senator Cotton introduced a bill that would "prohibit the use of federal funds to teach the 1619 Project by K-12 schools or school districts. Schools that teach the 1619 Project would also be ineligible for federal professional-development grants.").

51 *Id.* ("Under the bill, the Secretaries of Education, Health and Human Services, and Agriculture would be required to prorate federal funding to schools that decide to teach the 1619 Project – determined by how much it costs to plan and teach that curriculum.").

52 Jonathan Friedman & James Tager, *Educational Gag Orders: Legislative Restrictions on the Freedom to Read, Learn, and Teach* (Nov. 2021), https://pen.org/report/educational-gag-orders/.

53 *Public School Revenue Sources*, Nat'l Ctr. Educ. Stat., https://nces.ed.gov/programs/coe/indicator/cma/public-school-revenue (last updated May 2024).

54 Leah M. Watson, *The Anti-"Critical Race Theory" Campaign – Classroom Censorship and Racial Backlash by Another Name*, 58 Harv. Civil Rights–Civil Liberties L. Rev. 487 (2023); Taifha Natalee Alexander, *Tracking the Attack on Critical Race Theory in Education*, U.S. News & World Rep. (Apr. 11, 2023, 3:21 PM), https://www.usnews.com/opinion/articles/2023-04-11/tracking-the-attack-on-critical-race-theory-in-education.

Forward Project, housed at UCLA Law School's Critical Race Studies Center, tracked more than 560 government-related measures of this sort.[55] The documents range from carefully worded executive orders, including one signed by President Trump in September 2020 that outlawed the teaching of "divisive concepts"[56] on race and gender; to state-level legislation, such as the Stop WOKE Act[57] signed into law by Florida Governor Ron DeSantis in April 2022; to district policies, such as the Temecula Valley Unified School District's anti-CRT resolution approved in December 2022.[58]

Considering the rules and guidelines that are applied within institutions to manage media employees provides another useful starting point for a discussion of the meaning of fearless speech in journalism. Such examples include the perennial conflicts around student journalism, including administrative budget cuts that restrict funding and ultimately impact the ability of student journalists to do their work.[59] In 2018, for instance, the student government association at Wichita State University cut the student newspaper's budget by two-thirds following reporting on the university administration's business affairs.[60] Similar cuts were aimed specifically at student journalists' salaries in 2007 when the student legislature slashed The Missouri Miner's budget at the University of Missouri at Rolla.[61] The Student Press Law Center has designated such actions as Red Flags, highlighting the ways in

[55] Taifha Alexander et al., CRT Forward: Tracking the Attack on Critical Race Theory (2023), https://crtforward.law.ucla.edu/wp-content/uploads/2023/04/UCLA-Law_CRT-Report_Final.pdf.

[56] Exec. Order No. 13,950, 85 Fed. Reg. 60,683 (Sept. 28, 2020).

[57] Press Release, Governor Ron DeSantis, Governor DeSantis Announces Legislative Proposal to Stop W.O.K.E. Activism and Critical Race Theory in Schools and Corporations (Dec. 15, 2021), https://www.flgov.com/2021/12/15/governor-desantis-announces-legislative-proposal-to-stop-w-o-k-e-activism-and-critical-race-theory-in-schools-and-corporations/ (initial announcement); Press Release, Governor Ron DeSantis, Governor Ron DeSantis Signs Legislation to Protect Floridians from Discrimination and Woke Indoctrination (Apr. 22, 2022), https://www.flgov.com/2022/04/22/governor-ron-desantis-signs-legislation-to-protect-floridians-from-discrimination-and-woke-indoctrination/ (news that it was signed into law).

[58] Vania Patino, *Anti-CRT, Parental Notification Policies at Temecula Valley Unified School District Lawsuit Heads to Court*, Spectrum News 1 (Jan. 23, 2024, 2:45 PM), https://spectrumnews1.com/ca/la-west/education/2024/01/23/anti-crt-policy-at-temecula-valley-unified-school-district-headed-to-court.

[59] *Tag: Red Flag*, Student Press L. Ctr., https://splc.org/tag/red-flag/ (last visited June 30, 2024).

[60] Madeline Deabler, *How Threats to The Sunflower's Funding Have Closely Followed Coverage of the University, Innovation Campus*, Sunflower (Feb. 26, 2018), https://thesunflower.com/25077/opinion/how-threats-to-the-sunflowers-funding-have-closely-followed-coverage-of-the-university-innovation-campus/; Gabriel Greschler & Taylor Potter, *Wichita State University President John Bardo Approves Major Cuts to Student Paper, The Sunflower*, Student Press L. Ctr. (Mar. 2, 2018), https://splc.org/2018/03/sunflower-proposed-funding-cuts/.

[61] Brian Hudson, *Missouri Newspaper Threatens University with Lawsuit to Restore Funding*, Student Press L. Ctr. (Feb. 14, 2007), https://splc.org/2007/02/missouri-newspaper-threatens-university-with-lawsuit-to-restore-funding/.

which budget cuts may amount to censorship if undertaken disproportionately and in response to coverage.[62]

The reactive media codes of conduct that police and silence journalists are another point of entry for operationalizing fearless speech. On matters of journalism ethics and public critique of issues, educators could point to the examples of The New York Times writers Jazmine Hughes and Jaime Keiles, who were forced to resign after signing a protest letter about Palestinian genocide in Gaza.[63] Arguments, of course, will be made about the appropriateness of allocating university funding to support student media or about requiring journalists to adhere to an organization's code of conduct, but both serve the same function: They are disciplinary measures that manufacture the illusion of the journalists' consent to self-censor under penalty of material expulsion from the organization. Certainly, journalists who wish to engage in conduct that counters the cultural demands of an organization, be it a university's journalism program or a corporate newsroom, are free to do their work elsewhere. But the inability to "stand on business" while maintaining one's professional standing and having equal access to resources exposes the charade of free speech as we've conceived it vis-à-vis the First Amendment.

A discussion of fearless journalistic speech might also ask students to critically examine the different levels of protection enjoyed by the press as opposed to "citizen journalists," even in cases where the First Amendment rights are theoretically the same. This discussion might invite students to consider the different levels of risk incurred by those engaging in fearless speech. For example, the right to record police activity in public spaces has been widely recognized by courts as a right shared by everyone, not only the press. And in the past decade, two incidents of police brutality that sparked nationwide protests and debate were initially recorded and shared not by professional journalists but by individuals recording on their smartphones: Ramsey Orta, who filmed the NYPD officers who put Eric Garner in a stranglehold that killed him, and Darnella Frazier, whose recording of George Floyd's police murder sparked some of the largest protests ever seen in the United States. In both cases, their First Amendment right to record the incident was clearly protected by law. But in both cases, the resulting attention upended their lives, made them fear for their safety, and made them potential targets for retaliation by police.[64] (Classroom instructors might also consider linking these examples back to the *Sullivan* case and its consequences for the four Alabaman civil rights activists named as defendants.)

[62] *Tag: Red Flag*, *supra* note 59.

[63] Amy Goodman & Juan González, *NY Times Writers Jazmine Hughes & Jamie Keiles Resign After Signing Letter Against Israeli War on Gaza*, Democracy Now! (Nov. 14, 2023), https://www.democracynow.org/2023/11/14/nyt_magazine.

[64] Chloé Cooper Jones, *Fearing for His Life*, Verge (Mar. 13, 2019, 10:00 AM), https://www.theverge.com/2019/3/13/18253848/eric-garner-footage-ramsey-orta-police-brutality-killing-safety; Giulia McDonnell Nieto del Rio, *Darnella Frazier, the Teenager Who Recorded George Floyd's Murder, Speaks Out*, N.Y. Times (July 7, 2021), https://www.nytimes.com/2021/05/25/us/darnella-frazier.html.

19.5 CONCLUSION

The interpersonal domain of oppression prompts us to consider how we teach journalists to conceive of themselves and their roles in the field. The notion of a fearless speech orientation acknowledges warnings that the First Amendment rests on an ephemeral foundation. For if we were to reconceptualize our responsibilities as journalists from the perspective of those who, by their own expression, would benefit from having their messages amplified and, at times, clarified by our profession, we would move toward recognition that there are few truly voiceless individuals in our society and that the pursuit of broad press protections, rather than those limited to a specific professional class/designation, is in our collective best interest. It follows that people from structurally marginalized social positions are among those who need protection the most. The rest of society will undoubtedly benefit.

20

Journalism and Academia

Knowledge Institutions Buttressing Constitutional Democracy

Vicki C. Jackson

Knowledge institutions play a critical role in maintaining constitutional and democratic guardrails, encouraging the pursuit of reliable knowledge, providing the public with accurate information, and fostering informed debate about office-holders, candidates, and public policies. For this reason, authoritarian leaders often attack knowledge institutions (alongside other common targets like political opponents, and independent government bodies) in efforts to consolidate power, suppress dissenting voices, and control public narratives.[1] Among the key, often-targeted knowledge institutions are a free truth-seeking press and independent universities.

Knowledge institutions are public and private entities that have a central purpose of pursuing knowledge – creating, disseminating, and preserving it.[2] They include universities, libraries, museums, the press, government offices charged with collecting and reporting data, and independent research institutes. As organized entities with continuity over time, they pass on to new generations their cultures of knowledge-seeking and verification. Knowledge institutions and their active members seek to apply standards of a wide range of intellectual disciplines, differing across fields and institutions. They aspire to apply these standards autonomously, not

With deep thanks to Lincoln Caplan, RonNell Andersen Jones, Martha Minow, and Sonja West for their helpful comments, and to Peter Morgan and Dino Hadziahmetovic, Harvard JDs 2024, and Jenna Bao and Joyce Yun, Harvard JDs expected 2026, for their able research assistance. Remaining errors are the responsibility only of the author.

[1] *See generally* Aziz Huq & Tom Ginsburg, *How to Lose a Constitutional Democracy*, 65 UCLA L. Rev. 78 (2018).

[2] For my earlier work on this idea, *see* Vicki C. Jackson, *Knowledge Institutions in Constitutional Democracies: Preliminary Reflections*, 7 Can. J. Comp. & Cont. L. 156 (2021); Vicki C. Jackson, *Knowledge Institutions in Constitutional Democracy: Reflections on "the Press,"* 14 J. Media L. 275 (2022) [hereinafter *On "the Press"*]. Whether public or private, knowledge institutions must have the independence to apply relevant disciplinary standards for the pursuit of truth. In the US, the press is predominantly private, while public universities now enroll more than twice as many students as private ones. *See* Veera Korhonen, *College Enrollment in Public and Private Institutions the U.S. 1965–2031*, Statista, https://www.statista.com/statistics/183995/.

to reach results tailored to satisfy government or business preferences, but with independence according to the professional norms of their field and institution.[3]

As institutions, they offer protection to knowledge-related values that go beyond those secured by individual freedoms of expression. They do so for several reasons, described at length in my earlier work. First, such institutions help define, in ways no individual can, the best disciplinary tools and practices oriented to discovering or verifying knowledge. Second, institutions transmit cultures of knowledge-seeking across generations – again, in ways that individuals by themselves cannot. Third, institutions provide "focal points"[4] for organizing around the protection of those individual freedoms so essential to the free inquiry on which searches for better truths are founded. Fourth, institutions have legal and financial resources that can be deployed to help protect the knowledge-seeking efforts of their members. Finally, institutions, on the whole, have stronger functional and normative claims than individuals do to act with authority as intermediaries in an ocean of information and misinformation.

In recent years, however, the authority of the press and universities as knowledge institutions has increasingly come under scrutiny – and not just from rising populists. Critics are asking questions such as: Are these institutions genuinely devoted to producing and disseminating knowledge, or are they primarily focused on protecting and aggrandizing their own reputations or economic interests? Is the press overly fixated on sensationalism and short-term news coverage at the expense of deeper and more substantive reporting? Are universities too preoccupied with maintaining "politically correct" stances to be trusted to perform their knowledge-seeking roles and to maintain a free and open campus environment for all students? Can these knowledge institutions truly claim independence from the powerful forces that control so much of society? Are the ethical norms they espouse admirable or despicable? Are their ethical norms sufficiently adhered to in practice to warrant their continued recognition as guiding principles of the press and universities?

This chapter sketches some tentative responses to these questions. It considers how the press and universities are similar as knowledge institutions and how they differ. It explores the nature of journalistic and academic topics and judgments, their independence in the pursuit of knowledge, the time frames of their work, and their ethics. It aims to draw attention to how these two institutions use overlapping but not

[3] Both academia and journalism have a central purpose of developing new knowledge; academic institutions also seek to disseminate and preserve existing bodies of knowledge. Libraries and museums also function as knowledge institutions, with the central purposes of preserving and disseminating knowledge. Trial courts might also be thought of as knowledge institutions insofar as they have the goal, using disciplinary procedures of the law of evidence, to determine the (likely) facts as between two or more contesting parties, although this knowledge-creation may also be viewed as more contingent, and, to the extent it turns on factual findings about some broad phenomenon like drug use, may be subject to unsettlement in other litigations between different parties.

[4] *See* Adam Chilton & Mila Versteeg, How Constitutional Rights Matter (2020).

identical tools to develop shared knowledge and test knowledge claims, and how sustaining the independent competencies necessary towards this goal is challenged by rising polarization and mistrust and by diminishing public and private financial support. I close with some reflections on the relationships among knowledge institutions and why the interdependent infrastructure of knowledge institutions matters so much to constitutional democracy.

Constitutional democracies are not necessarily self-sustaining. They must safeguard the independence and integrity of elections, government structures, and knowledge institutions, including universities and the free press. Doing so requires honest assessment of their strengths and weaknesses, adequate funding for their central tasks, and appropriate degrees of institutional autonomy to preserve the reliability of their knowledge functions.

20.1 PROFESSIONAL JUDGMENT IN PURSUIT OF GENUINE KNOWLEDGE

Constitutional democracies depend on knowledge to sustain their governments. Whether conceptualized as the need for competence,[5] expertise,[6] or effectiveness,[7] governments depend on the development of shared conceptions of reliable knowledge. Knowledge institutions, including academia and the press, play key roles in the development of this shared knowledge.[8]

Ideally, both the institutional press and higher education institutions seek to protect the exercise of professional judgment by those who do knowledge work within them. For the press, the core knowledge work is done by journalists (including reporters and editors).[9] For academia, the core knowledge work is done by

5 *See generally* Robert C. Post, Democracy, Expertise and Academic Freedom: A First Amendment Jurisprudence for the Modern State (2012).

6 *See generally* Bruce Ackerman, *The New Separation of Powers*, 113 Harv. L. Rev. 633 (2000).

7 *See generally* Constitutionalism and a Right to Effective Government? (Vicki C. Jackson & Yasmin Dawood eds., 2022).

8 *See* Huq & Ginsburg, *supra* note 1, at 130 (on the importance of a shared epistemic base).

9 On the key role of editors, *see, e.g.*, Jacqui Banaszynski, *The Core Role of Editors in Trustworthy Journalism*, Nieman Storyboard (Nov. 7, 2023), https://niemanstoryboard.org/stories/editing-journalism-accuracy-bias-gaza/ (arguing that editors provide several crucial quality control functions); Allison Baker & Viviane Fairbank, *Fact-Checking as Part of the Editorial Process*, *in* The Truth in Journalism Fact-Checking Guide (2022), https://thetijproject.ca/guide/the-editorial-process/) (on the editorial process in Canada); *Journalistic Guidelines*, PBS, https://www.pbs.org/wgbh/frontline/about-us/journalistic-guidelines/ (last visited May 21, 2024) (on the editorial process at PBS); Max van Drunen, *Editorial Independence in an Automated Media System*, 10 Internet Pol'y Rev. 1 (2021), https://policyreview.info/articles/analysis/editorial-independence-automated-media-system (on editorial independence in Europe); Emmett Lindner, *Editing with a Reporter's Instinct*, N.Y. Times (June 30, 2022), https://www.nytimes.com/2022/06/30/insider/editing-with-a-reporters-instinct.html (on editing at the N.Y. Times); *see also* Evelyn Douek & Genevieve Lakier, *Rereading "Editorial Discretion,"* Knight First Amendment Institute at Columbia University (Oct. 24, 2022), https://

individual faculty members, sometimes alone, sometimes working with others, and subject to the more indirect and less collaborative constraints of peer review and evaluation.

For the press, a classic concept of the editorial process embraces the active involvement of editors as internal checks throughout the entire news production cycle. In serious press organs, the relationship between editors and reporters (and other kinds of journalists) is collaborative. It often begins with the selection of which stories to pursue, continues with discussions about when stories are sufficiently established by the facts, and ends with editing of the final article. Editors can be an integral part of the process of reporting a story at many junctures, reflecting a degree of joint venturing between reporters and editors as allies in the development and production of news stories.

The growth of new outlets for reporting through social media sites and blogs may pose a challenge to the continued viability of the model of editors who act as internal intermediaries checking what journalists write and reinforcing disciplinary norms of good investigative journalism.[10] Yet, the idea of internal checks remains an important aspect of contemporary journalism. The most respected newer journalism sites, such as ProPublica,[11] as well as "legacy" organs, continue to rely on editors to protect the integrity of their journalistic process, though empirical work on the extent of this practice remains to be done.

In academia, such partnerships between editors and researchers in developing scholarly works are less common than in journalism. Editors of scholarly journals or books may sometimes – but need not – play a role similar to news editors in deciding what themes or subjects authors should pursue. Some invited scholarly collections or journal symposia, for example, are framed by the scholarly editors' careful guidance on what topics different chapters should seek to cover. But many scholarly books are conceived entirely by their authors and are submitted to a publisher only after they are complete or well set on course. The checks of peer review are thus both less sustained and more independent than those of an editor in a journalistic institution working with reporters.[12]

knightcolumbia.org/blog/rereading-editorial-discretion (arguing that U.S. Supreme Court has recognized editorial discretion as protected by the First Amendment).

10 Other changes in the work of journalism may follow from increased streaming of public events, diminishing the perceived need for in-person attendance, and the possibility of artificial intelligence to generate reports of public meetings. *See, e.g.*, Sophie Culpeper, *AI Will Soon Be Able to Cover Public Meetings. But Should It?*, NiemanLab (June 15, 2023), https://www.niemanlab.org/2023/06/ai-will-soon-be-able-to-cover-public-meetings-but-should-it/.

11 *See* Jason Grotto, *How Do We Verify Anonymous Sources?*, ProPublica (Aug. 28, 2018), https://www.propublica.org/article/ask-propublica-illinois-vetting-anonymous-sources ("Editors play a crucial role in the decision to use an anonymous source. Our code of ethics says editors 'have an obligation to know the identity of unnamed sources' so they can 'assess the appropriateness of using their information.'").

12 In academia, a separate institutional body, the Institutional Review Board (IRB), will scrutinize projects that entail "human subject research," but primarily with a focus on the adequacy of

In contrast to journalism's collaborative editorial process, academia relies on peer review in assessing quality both in granting tenure and, for journals, in deciding whether to accept articles for publication. Although the specific practices vary across disciplines, peer review is a key part of academia's decisional processes.[13] The review process for publication in a peer-reviewed journal may be quite substantive and contribute materially to improving the published work. (Publication in peer-reviewed journals is important in many academic fields; a possible exception, however, is the field of law in the United States, where prestigious reviews are often edited by students, not peer-reviewed.) Publication-specific peer review is part of the academic process of knowledge production; it operates in a more arm's-length manner than the process of editors checking journalists' work.

While a faculty mentor may feel some sense of engagement with junior faculty, it would be unusual for that relationship to be seen by either party as the kind of alliance journalists often share with an editor. Faculty members may be able to obtain additional peer feedback and critique from workshopping their papers or sending them out for critical comment from colleagues, which can be an important and helpful part of the scholarly process. But the relationship is not that between an editor and a reporter. Other faculty members offering feedback (rather than as part of a peer review

procedures for consent, and risk minimization and selection criteria for human participants. *See* GAO REPORT, INSTITUTIONAL REVIEW BOARDS 9 (Jan. 2023), https://www.gao.gov/assets/d23104721.pdf (identifying three main purposes: assuring that "risks to participants are minimized, … participants will have sufficient information to decide whether to consent to the research, and … participants will be selected fairly (e.g., not selected because of ease of availability or manipulability).").

[13] For discussions of peer review in the sciences, *see, e.g.*, Peyman Sardari Nia et al., *Behind the Curtain of the Editorial Process: How Editors Decide!*, 36 INTERDISC. CARDIOVASCULAR & THORACIC SURGERY 2 (2023), https://www.ncbi.nlm.nih.gov/pmc/articles/PMC9977384/ (detailing improvements to journal's peer review process); The ISME Journal, *Editorial Process: Summary of the Editorial Process*, SPRINGER NATURE, https://www.nature.com/ismej/authors-and-referees/editorial-process (last visited May 22, 2024) (providing an overview of the submission and peer review process for journal); Simon Wessely, *Peer Review of Grant Applications: What Do We Know?*, 352 THE LANCET 301 (1998), https://www.thelancet.com/journals/lancet/article/PIIS0140673697111291/fulltext (assessing criticisms of peer review of grant applications). For peer review in the humanities and social sciences, *see* THE BRITISH ACADEMY, PEER REVIEW: THE CHALLENGES FOR THE HUMANITIES AND SOCIAL SCIENCES (2007), https://www.thebritishacademy.ac.uk/documents/197/Peer-review-challenges-for-humanities-social-sciences.pdf (reviewing the practices and difficulties of peer review in the UK in the social sciences and humanities). For more general treatment of peer review in academic publishing, *see* Kristy Law, *The Peer Review Process – A Complete Guide*, OXFORD ABSTRACTS (Jan. 10, 2023), https://oxfordabstracts.com/blog/what-is-the-peer-review-process/ (offering a generalized guide to the history, process, and strategies of peer review); *Understanding the Peer Review Process*, TAYLOR & FRANCIS GRP. (2024), https://authorservices.taylorandfrancis.com/publishing-your-research/peer-review/ (last visited June 9, 2024) (describing peer review for journals published by Taylor & Francis). For a skeptical treatment of proposals to pay for peer review, *see* Tim Vines & Alison Mudditt, *What's Wrong with Paying for Peer Review?*, THE SCHOLARLY KITCHEN (June 16, 2021), https://scholarlykitchen.sspnet.org/2021/06/16/whats-wrong-with-paying-for-peer-review/.

process) do not operate as gatekeepers to the publication of academic work in the same way a traditional news editor could be a gatekeeper to journalists' work. However, some scholars do work in very large collaborative groups on work having many coauthors; this surely provides opportunities for review and checking, although it also raises predictable temptations for individual contributors to focus only on the aspects of the work to which they directly contributed, rather than on the entire project.

The comparisons between how the institutions of academia and journalism create knowledge raise a number of questions warranting further consideration. For example, does the insulation of much academic work, as compared to the ongoing (theoretical) relationship of reporters and editors, have any implications for their knowledge-producing roles? Or, is what matters the overall cluster of opportunities for checking and incentives for accurate work? Are there more such opportunities for checking and incentives for accuracy in academia, given its longer time frame for production and extended period during which critiques, modifications, and even retractions can occur? Or are there more such opportunities in journalism, where a wider readership may be quick to point out flaws or questions?[14] Alternatively, is what matters more the commitment of participants to truth-seeking modes of work? How significant is the presence of legal and practical protections for the independence of the overall process – in journalism, for reporting and editing, in academia, for researching, writing, teaching, and publishing of scholarship?

Both news media and academic journals have suffered embarrassing and very public failures of their truth-checking processes in recent years.[15] Academia has

[14] For one well-known example *see* Molly A. Dugan, *Journalism Ethics and the Independent Journalist*, 39 McGeorge L. Rev. 801 (2007) (describing correction, by citizen journalists and bloggers, of Dan Rather's mistaken accusation that President Bush received favorable treatment in the National Guard).

[15] On news media, *see, e.g.*, Laura Kukkonen, *The Finnish Fabulist*, Colum. Journalism Rev. (Apr. 23, 2024), https://www.cjr.org/analysis/the-finnish-fabulist.php (discussing a Finnish journalist who disclosed that he had made up details in his published work, whose work has been largely pulled); Dan Gillmor, *Can Our Corrections Catch Up to Our Mistakes as They Spread Across Social Media?*, NiemanLab (Mar. 15, 2019), https://www.niemanlab.org/2019/03/can-our-corrections-catch-up-to-our-mistakes-as-they-spread-across-social-media/. On academic work, there have been numerous documented incidents of plagiarism; *see, e.g.*, Helayna Schafer, *Plagiarism as a Recurrent Issue*, 48. J. C.& U.L. 71, 74–81 (2023), as well as suspicion that asserted documentation for historical claims did not exist, *see, e.g.*, Columbia University Board of Trustees, *The Bancroft and Bellesiles*, History News Network (Dec. 13, 2002), https://www.hnn.us/article/the-bancroft-and-bellesiles (reprinting Columbia University Trustees' announcement in December 2002 that the Bancroft prize in history, which had been awarded to a professor at Emory for a book on gun ownership in the colonial period, was being withdrawn based on "evidence of falsification" and other departures from scholarly practice as determined by a panel of historians from other universities). On much discussed failures of replication of studies in psychology, in particular, but also in other social sciences, pharmacology, neurology, and medicine, *see* Edith Beerdsen, *Litigation Science after the Knowledge Crisis*, 106 Corn. L. Rev. 529, 530–33 (2021) (describing as illustrative two studies in 2010 and 2011 that, by 2017, had been discredited); *see also* Mark Filip, Report of the Scientific Panel of the Special Committee of the Stanford University Board of Trustees

sought to develop measures to prevent systemic problems in reliability.[16] The declining numbers of journalists and immense financial pressures faced by news organizations of all sizes may inhibit devoting more resources to improving accuracy, yet some journalists, academics, and organizations engage in regular critiques of what they see as flawed journalism.[17] Ideological commitments may impair, or be seen to impair, an institution's willingness to adhere to truth-seeking practices, including open inquiry.[18]

(July 17, 2023), https://boardoftrustees.stanford.edu/wp-content/uploads/sites/5/2023/07/Scientific-Panel-Final-Report.pdf (reviewing allegations of scientific misconduct by Stanford President Marc Tessier-Lavigne and finding manipulation of data by others; finding that he was unaware of the manipulation, but also that he "failed to decisively and forthrightly correct mistakes in the scientific record"); Stephanie Saul, *Stanford University President Will Resign After Report Found Flaws in His Research*, N.Y. Times (July 19, 2023), https://www.nytimes.com/2023/07/19/us/stanford-president-resigns-tessier-lavigne.html. *See generally Board of Directors*, Retraction Watch, https://retractionwatch.com/the-center-for-scientific-integrity/board-of-directors (last visited June 9, 2024) (sponsored by the Center for Scientific Integrity).

16 *See* Beerdsen, *supra* note 15, at 546–47 (describing massive efforts by researchers to explore extent of replication failures, reasons therefor (including manipulability of "statistical significance" measures), and how research communities are developing remedial tools to combat methodological weaknesses that lead to unreliability, including by diminishing "analytical flexibility" as study goes along).

17 For critical stances on particular pieces of reporting, *see, e g.*, Laura Wagner, *Journalism Professors Call on New York Times to Review October 7 Report*, Wash. Post (Apr. 29, 2024) (journalism professors calling for independent review of New York Times story alleging significant sexual violence during the October 7 Hamas attacks on Israel); Jeff Gerth, *The Press Versus the President, Part One*, Colum. Journalism Rev. (Jan. 30, 2023), https://www.cjr.org/special_report/trumped-up-press-versus-president-part-1.php (critically reviewing The New York Times's and other newspapers' reporting on Trump and Russia). For an organized effort to "provide reliability ratings for news outlets based on transparent journalistic criteria," *see* NewsGuard, at https://www.newsguardtech.com/ (last visited May 25, 2024). For examples of the considerable debate over how to characterize Fox News, *see, e.g.*, A. J. Bauer et al., *What Is Fox News? Partisan Journalism, Misinformation, and the Problem of Classification*, 16 Elec. News 18 (2022), https://journals.sagepub.com/doi/pdf/10.1177/19312431211060426 (suggesting the need to expand categories of news media to include partisan reporting sources like Fox); Eric Alterman, *Altercation: Not Now, Not Ever, Has Fox News Been Journalism*, Am. Prospect (June 18, 2021), https://prospect.org/politics/altercation-not-now-not-ever-has-fox-news-been-journalism/.

18 In the press, NewsGuard's ratings suggest that both Fox News and MSNBC have failed to adhere to journalistic criteria for reporting much of the time. *See* NewsGuard, *Statement by NewsGuard on the Updated Ratings for the Websites of Fox News and MSNBC* (July 22, 2022), https://www.newsguardtech.com/press/newsguard-statementfox-news-msnbc-rating-updates/ ("For the first time since NewsGuard launched in 2018, both the Fox News and MSNBC sites are rated red, meaning they have earned an overall score of less than 60 out of 100. Their readers are urged to proceed with caution when they encounter content from these websites."). In academia, questions have been raised about one-sidedness in classroom teaching at major secular universities and about the political commitments of some religious universities, such as Liberty University, with a "Christian" identity according to its website. *See About Liberty*, Liberty Univ., https://catalog.liberty.edu/graduate/about-liberty/ (last visited June 9, 2024); *see, e.g.*, Jennifer Schuessler, *The Fight over Academic Freedom*, N.Y. Times (Feb. 16, 2024), https://www.nytimes.com/2024/02/16/arts/academic-freedom-harvard-universities.html; Nick Anderson, *Virginia's Liberty University: A Mega-College and Republican Presidential Stage*, Wash. Post (Mar. 23, 2015, 10:16 AM),

These are human institutions, and failures at some levels are to be expected. These failures should be critiqued when they result from deviations from truth-seeking norms and corrected going forward. My point, for now, is that each type of institution employs distinctive mechanisms designed to sort good, accurate reporting from bad, unreliable reporting or good, reliable scholarship from bad, unreliable scholarship. Each knowledge institution has internal mechanisms designed both to reinforce the goal of accuracy at the outset and to provide checks when that goal is not met. At a time when both institutions face serious threats, attention to these mechanisms is of particular importance.

20.2 INDEPENDENCE AND THE IDEAL OF OBJECTIVITY IN THE APPLICATION OF PROFESSIONAL JUDGMENT

Biased precommitments are antithetical to the aspirations for objectivity, impartiality, or fairness associated with good scholarship and good journalistic reporting.[19] Even opinion journalism, which may be quite partisan or advocacy-oriented, should rely on a reasonable factual basis.[20] The search for genuine knowledge must be conducted independently of commercial or governmental interests in predetermined answers.

For most reputable journalists and academics, their perceived and actual independence – including from powerful influences of friends, family, business, or government – is an important element of professional self-understanding.[21] Press

https://www.washingtonpost.com/news/grade-point/wp/2015/03/23/virginias-liberty-university-a-mega-college-and-republican-presidential-stage/.

19 A revolt against the ideal of "objectivity" in journalism may be more a rejection of a stance too accepting of official accounts, *see* Michael Schudson, Journalism: Why it Matters 48 (2020), or of assumptions that perfect knowledge is possible, rather than a rejection of efforts to provide better accounts of the world through critical attention to what is likely to be true and what is likely to be biased – whether that attitude is called "fair" or "objective." *See id.* at 52–58 (arguing that journalists should try to "forget" their prior knowledge and check their biases, while engaged in evidence gathering to provide not their own "views" but rather "reporting"). *Cf.* Stephen J. A. Ward, The Invention of Journalism Ethics (2d ed. 2015) (arguing for what he terms "pragmatic objectivity").

20 Although this idea is oft asserted, *see, e.g.*, Parker Molloy, *Opinion Journalism Is Broken*, Dame Mag. (Apr. 13, 2022), https://www.damemagazine.com/2022/04/13/opinion-journalism-is-broken/ ("Good opinion writing is heavily fact-checked, thoroughly edited, and strives to make whatever arguments are available with the facts as they are."); Matthew M. Reavy, *Objectivity and Advocacy in Journalism*, 25 Media Ethics (2013) (describing advocacy journalism as "endeavor[ing] to be fact-based"), many critics of journalism fear that opinion writing now detracts from the role of more objective news reporting. *See, e.g.*, Molloy, *supra* note 20; Jakob Moll, *Opinion Pieces (Including This One) Are Ruining the Internet*, Nieman (June 3, 2022), https://nieman.harvard.edu/articles/opinion-pieces-online-news/.

21 *See, e.g.*, A. G. Sulzberger, *Journalism's Essential Value*, Colum. Journalism Rev. (May 15, 2023), https://www.cjr.org/special_report/ag-sulzberger-new-york-times-journalisms-essential-value-objectivity-independence.php.

and academic institutions deploy various methods, some overlapping, some distinctive, to protect that independence.

Some academics enjoy "tenure," that is, a guarantee of their position absent extraordinary justification for removal. Tenure is believed to contribute to the desired independence of thinking, research, writing, and teaching. Yet increasingly, teaching loads at colleges and universities are filled by nontenure track faculty, many of whom are part-time workers with relatively little job security or bargaining power.[22] Many journalists likewise work without any institutional guarantees of tenure or even long-term contracts in an increasingly shrinking part of the economy. Even without tenure protections, though, other factors may help sustain commitments to journalistic independence. These include working as part of a team, collaborating with an editor, and operating in a journalistic culture that values independence and accuracy of reporting.

Job tenure is not the only source of independence. Ethical norms in academia also insist on intellectual independence and integrity. The first principle in the American Association of University Professors's (AAUP) Statement of Professional Ethics provides that professors' "primary responsibility . . . is to seek and to state the truth as they see it . . . [and] practice intellectual honesty," while not allowing "subsidiary interests" to "seriously hamper or compromise their freedom of inquiry."[23] The ethos of objectivity or impartiality in professional judgment remains an important aspect of both academia and professional journalism, and it may be as dependent on institutional cultures as it is on structural protections of job security.[24] Institutional cultures in academia and journalism nurture norms about what it means to value accuracy, knowledge, and independent judgment.

The New York Times' *Ethical Journalism* handbook, for example, discusses several situations of apparent conflicts of interest that might threaten "the

[22] *See* USC Rossier Pullias Center for Higher Education, *Off the Track: The Rising Number of Non-Tenure-Track Faculty and What It Means for Students in Our Colleges and Universities*, https://pullias.usc.edu/download/off-the-track-the-rising-number-of-non-tenure-track-faculty-and-what-it-means-for-students-in-our-colleges-and-universities/ (last visited June 9, 2024) (In 1969, 78.3 percent of university professors were tenured or tenure track, but only 33.5 percent in 2009, with close to 48 percent employed as part-time faculty); *see also* Jacques Berliner Blau, *They've Been Scheming to Cut Tenure for Years. It's Happening*, CHRONICLE OF HIGHER EDUCATION (Feb. 1, 2023) (reporting that a 2020–21 survey shows that 24 percent of faculty are tenured and another 9 percent are on a tenure track, with a trend toward replacing tenure track with contingent faculty positions).

[23] *See Statement of Professional Ethics*, AM. ASS'N OF UNIV. PROFESSORS, https://www.aaup.org/report/statement-professional-ethics (last visited June 9, 2024).

[24] Professional aspirations are even reflected in union positions in journalism and academia, which articulate the importance of "protecting academic freedom," Collective Bargaining, AM. ASS'N OF UNIV. PROFESSORS, https://www.aaup.org/programs/collective-bargaining (last visited June 9, 2024), and promoting "honesty" in "news, editorials, advertising, and business practices" and raising "the standards of journalism and ethics of the industry," The News Guild–CWA Constitution Art. 1, Sec. 2, https://newsguild.org/constitution/ (last visited June 9, 2024).

impartiality and neutrality of The Times and the integrity of its report."[25] It prohibits accepting "free or discounted lodging and transportation except where special circumstances give little or no choice" and includes a sample letter to return gifts, along with a policy forbidding acceptance of all but "trinkets of minor value."[26] The Times also forbids accepting "anything that could be construed as a payment for favorable coverage or as an inducement to alter or forgo unfavorable coverage."[27]

Similarly motivated rules appear elsewhere in news organs and associations. The Guardian's Editorial Code of Practice and Guidance requires news staff to disclose financial interests that might "create the impression of a conflict of interest,"[28] prohibits journalists from holding public office,[29] and substantially limits the receipt of "freebies."[30] The Global Charter of Ethics for Journalists likewise provides for the avoidance of conflicts of interests by journalists and asserts that the "right of the public to truth is the first duty of the journalist."[31] (The contrast here with the alleged conduct of the tabloid National Enquirer in paying to "kill" a news story and keep it from the public is obvious.[32])

[25] *See Ethical Journalism*, N.Y. Times, https://www.nytimes.com/editorial-standards/ethical-journalism.html# (last visited Apr. 28, 2024) [hereinafter N.Y. Times Ethics].

[26] *Id.*

[27] *Id.*

[28] Guardian News & Media, Editorial Code of Practice and Guidance (2023), https://uploads.guim.co.uk/2023/07/27/GNM_editorial_code_of_practice_and_guidance_2023.pdf (last visited Apr. 28, 2024).

[29] *See id.* ("[I]t is important that outside interests do not come into conflict with journalists' work for GNM in any way that could compromise, or appear to compromise, the editorial integrity and reputation of individual journalists or GNM."; also requiring disclosures of personal or financial activities that might create impressions of potential conflicts and prohibiting public office holding while a journalist).

[30] *Id.* (prohibiting "any payment, gift or other advantage" that would "undermine accuracy, fairness or independence"). The policy requires reporting to the "senior duty editor" of attempts "to induce favourable editorial treatment through the offer of gifts or favours"; and requires reporting in footnotes "when an airline, hotel or other interest has borne the cost of transporting or accommodating a journalist" and states, "[a]cceptance of any such offer is conditional on GNM being free to assign and report, or not report, any resulting story as it sees fit."

[31] *See* International Federation of Journalists, Global Charter of Ethics for Journalists, https://www.ifj.org/who/rules-and-policy/global-charter-of-ethics-for-journalists (last visited Apr. 28, 2024) ("The journalist shall not use the freedom of the press to serve any other interest and shall refrain from receiving any unfair advantage or personal gain because of the dissemination or non-dissemination of information. He/she will avoid … any situation that could lead him/her to a conflict of interest in the exercise of his/her profession.… He/she will refrain from any form of insider trading and market manipulation."). This is not to say such ethical precepts are always adhered to. For a discussion of "envelope journalism," where reporters are paid by nonemployers to write particular things, *see, e.g.*, Katrin Voltmer, The Media in Transitional Democracies 208 (2013); Bahtiyar Kurambayev & Eric Freedman, *Ethics and Journalism in Central Asia: A Comparative Study of Kazakhstan, Kyrgyzstan, Tajikistan and Uzbekistan*, 35 J. Media Ethics 31 (2019).

[32] On the National Enquirer's "catch and kill" approach to suppress news stories disadvantageous to Trump's campaign, *see, e.g.*, Julia Reinstein et al., *David Pecker Testified that Trump Stories*

Some traditional news media have reflected their concern for independence by separating the reporting divisions from the business divisions – a separation that has come under strain in recent years as the economic challenges for legacy news media have increased.[33] For example, The New York Times forbids consultation between the news and business division, *except when* advertising needs are "directly related to the business of the news department;" the Times also limits and regulates (rather than prohibits) information exchange between the news and advertising departments.[34] Such consultations can play a critical role in helping news media navigate great economic challenges and maintain enough financial viability to be able to report independently on the news.[35] Yet if a particular story is shown to have been "pulled" or held back because of political or economic influence, it reflects badly on the press organ's reputation.[36]

Academia faces similar concerns about conflicts, although it handles them differently. In the last decades of the twentieth century, commercial and governmental collaborations in university-based research increased substantially, creating heightened opportunities for conflicts of interest.[37] Universities have developed policies and structures to help manage these new relationships,

Were "National Enquirer Gold." He Said He Killed Them to Help Trump, ABC NEWS (Apr. 29, 2024), https://abcnews.go.com/US/david-pecker-testified-trump-stories-national-enquirer-gold/story?id=109708606.

33 *See, e.g.*, Alessio Cornia et al., *'We No Longer Live in a Time of Separation': A Comparative Analysis of How Editorial and Commercial Integration Became a Norm*, 21 JOURNALISM 172 (2020), https://doi.org/10.1177/1464884918779919; Ira Basen, *Breaking Down the Wall*, CTR. FOR JOURNALISM ETHICS (Dec. 19, 2012), https://ethics.journalism.wisc.edu/2012/12/19/breaking-down-the-wall/. *See generally* MARTHA MINOW, SAVING THE NEWS (2021).

34 *See* N.Y. Times Ethics, *supra* note 25.

35 *See* ADAM NAGOURNEY, THE TIMES 388–97 (Kindle, 2023) (describing discussions between news and editorial staff about whether to have a paywall for The N.Y. Times' online stories).

36 *See, e.g.*, Michael Calderone & Jason Schwartz, *Wall Street Journal Staffers Accuse Editor of Suppressing Story*, POLITICO (Mar. 29, 2018), https://www.politico.com/story/2018/03/29/wall-street-journal-editor-story-suppression-accusations-492393; David Folkenflik, *'Washington Post' CEO Tried to Kill a Story About Himself. It Wasn't the First Time*, NPR (June 7, 2024), https://www.npr.org/2024/06/07/nx-s1-4995105/washington-post-will-lewis-tries-to-kill-story-buzbee.

37 *See, e.g.*, Peter J. Harrington, *Faculty Conflicts of Interest in an Age of Academic Entrepreneurialism: An Analysis of the Problem, the Law and Selected University Policies*, 27 J. COLL. & UN. L. 775 (2001); Peter Lee, *Patents and the University*, 63 DUKE L. J. 1 (2013) (discussing case law "reflecting a new normative vision of universities as commercial entities" with the same obligations under the patent laws as other commercial actors). For a recent example of academic collaboration with business and government in scientific innovation, *see* Anne J. Manning, *Glimpse of Next Generation Internet*, HARV. GAZETTE (May 15, 2024) (describing the work reflected in a new paper on two-node quantum networking as "supported by the AWS [Amazon Web services] Center for Quantum Networking's research alliance with the Harvard Quantum Initiative, the National Science Foundation, the Center for Ultracold Atoms (an NSF Physics Frontiers Center), the Center for Quantum Networks (an NSF Engineering Research Center), the Air Force Office of Scientific Research, and other sources").

including technology transfer offices and offices of sponsored programs.[38] These programs can involve policies that, in contrast to general academic norms of openness, permit researchers to withhold their findings, for example, to allow time for patenting. In some fields, individual faculty members may develop separate consulting businesses related to research work patented by the university, which complicates their roles as members of the academic community.[39] In these respects, scholars may be much more financially involved with outside influences than are journalists.

Universities and press organizations increasingly adopt conflict of interest policies designed to prevent – or at least disclose – influences that might undermine the independence of professional judgment. At some news media companies, policies limit involvement between journalists and the subjects they are writing about, and editors may reassign reporters if involvements create the appearance of partiality.[40] In academia, the scholar herself may be the primary judge of whether her work presents conflicts of interest.[41] And in some fields of research, such as anthropology, the role of participant observation as a research method is relatively well-established. While news media may tightly control what other entities their reporters can work for (for example, prohibiting freelance work for competitors[42]), academics – especially in the sciences – frequently collaborate with faculty at other institutions. Competition among journalistic media is the norm; academia can be very competitive, but there are also major areas of collaborative work. Scholarly journals increasingly require a statement either disclaiming or disclosing potential conflicts of interest, and many universities have policies requiring disclosure of potential conflicts of interest.[43]

[38] *See* Christopher J. Ryan, Jr, et al., *The Hidden Cost of University Patents*, 21 Berk. Bus. L. J. 203, 208 (2024).

[39] *Cf.* Peter Lee, *Innovation and the Firm: A New Synthesis*, 70 Stan. L. Rev. 1431, 1482–87 (2018) (describing a range of arrangements involving universities, firms, and faculty inventors); Brenda M. Simon, *Preserving the Fruits of Labor: Impediments to University Inventor Mobility*, 89 Tenn. L. Rev. 1 (2021).

[40] N.Y. Times Ethics, *supra* note 25, at Pursuing the News.

[41] *See, e.g.*, *Conflict of Interest/Commitment Policy*, Carnegie Mellon Univ., https://www.cmu.edu/policies/administrative-and-governance/conflict-of-interest-commitment.html (last updated Mar. 27, 2012) ("The first and most important line of defense against conflicts of interest or commitment must be the university members themselves.").

[42] *See* N.Y. Times Ethics, *supra* note 25, at Work Outside the Times.

[43] For policies at Carnegie Mellon, *see, e.g.*, *Conflict of Interest/Commitment Policy*, *supra* note 41. For policies at Harvard, *see, e.g.*, Harvard University Office of Labor and Employee Relations, *Conflicts of Interest or Commitment*, *in* Staff Personnel Manual (dated 2007), https://hr.harvard.edu/staff-personnel-manual/general-employment-policies/conflicts-interest-or-commitment (last visited June 22, 2024); Harvard University Office of the Vice Provost for Research, *Conflicts of Interest and Commitment*, *in* Research Policies & Compliance (dated 2012), https://research.harvard.edu/researchpolicies-compliance/financial-conflicts-of-interest/; Harvard University Institutional Conflicts of Interest Policy (2020), https://bpb-us-e1.wpmucdn.com/websites.harvard.edu/dist/f/106/files/2023/10/icoi_policy.pdf (last visited June 22, 2024). For a more recent reiteration of disclosure requirements, *see*, e.g., Office of the Vice Provost for Research, Conflict of Commitment Policy (June 1, 2024) chrome-

Disclosure is no panacea,[44] but it is a recognition of the importance of upholding ethical norms of independent judgment.

Both journalists and academics may be influenced in their choice of research or writing topic by incentives from outside and within their institutions. In academia, the interests of leading journals, or the availability of grants, may influence scholars' topics of inquiry. Some academics may choose topics regarded as easier to publish on, in the interest of obtaining tenure or other academic benefits. Grants are more likely to be available for novel findings (at least in some scientific fields), which may influence the incentives of the researcher – discouraging replication studies, for example, despite their importance for the continued verification of initial results. In law, there are "popular" topics in which student editors (who play an important role in the US scholarly legal literature) or even academic editors are deemed more likely to have an interest.

In the press, the increased conjoining of business with reporting concerns reflects the reality that the press (whether traditional legacy press or new blogs or websites that want to be viewed as impartial news sources) must attract sufficient audience share to sustain themselves. Publishers care, as they usually have, about net revenue; reporters care about how many followers they have on Twitter or Facebook. Thus, financial and popular incentives may influence reporters in what kinds of topics they pursue, as may the ideological commitments of their employer. (This raises the question of whether stronger norms of impartiality and independence exist in what is reported in a story than in the selection of what topics to pursue or report on.[45])

While the ideal of independence is important, it is unsurprising that neither academic research nor news reporting, as human institutions in a world of finite resources and attention, are conducted based only on the abstract importance of the subject or the internal interests of the researcher. For the press, the combined, related pressures of current popular interest, the role of clickbait and unseen algorithms, and financial sustainability (which may favor what those who are advantaged in society are interested in) may play a larger day-to-day role on topic choice than in parts of academia. For academics, the rise of untenured faculty in the US may threaten both the time and the independence faculty have for research. Yet

extension://efaidnbmnnnibpcajpcglclefindmkaj/https://research.harvard.edu/files/2024/05/Conflict-of-Commitment-Policy-June-2024.pdf.

44 *See generally* Omri Ben-Shahar & Carl E. Schneider, *The Failure of Mandated Disclosure*, 159 U. Pa. L. Rev. 647, 652 (2011). Note that in order for disclosure to mean much, watchdogs – like journalists – are needed to follow and report on the disclosures.

45 *Cf.* Cornia et al., *supra* note 33 (describing the new norm of integration as influencing in some areas what topics to cover more and what topics to cover less, without necessarily being told what they "have to follow," and keeping political reporting distinct from business interests of news outlet). For related discussion, *see* Anya Schiffrin, *Same Beds, Different Dreams?: Charitable Foundations and Newsroom Independence in the Global South*, Center for International Media Independence 17–19 (2017), https://www.cima.ned.org/resource/beds-different-dreams-charitable-foundations-newsroom-independence-global-south/ (describing differing views on donor designation of topics to be covered and editorial independence).

journalists and academics retain considerable freedom on what topics to write on. The aspiration for independence of judgment in what is reported or what is written remains an important distinguishing feature of both. A major challenge for years to come is how to sustain both forms of independence as they face pressures from economic change, political controversies, and unusually virulent attacks.

20.3 TIME, RESOURCES, AND THE NATURE OF KNOWLEDGE DEVELOPMENT

The different time scales of journalism and academia influence the kind of topics and the depth of coverage that academic and journalistic work produce. Universities – major ones, at least – will provide a depth of knowledge-related resources in libraries, access to scholarly databases, scientific equipment, and the collective presence of scholarly experts in many fields. Press organizations are likely to be quite differently and perhaps more thinly resourced, but journalists may be able to more readily gain access to information from current officeholders than academics.

Daily or even weekly journalists report on sudden, unexpected events[46] and look for "scoops" – that is, important newsworthy developments that have not been discovered or reported by others. This task is becoming more challenging given the widespread public sharing of breaking news on social media, including reporting by noninstitutional reporters. Professional journalists who develop networks of reliable information providers are still able to produce such scoops, especially in areas in which information is tightly controlled and not accessible to casual observers.[47] Daily reporters, moreover, regularly work against very tight deadlines. Even feature reporters for newspapers and magazines may be working on deadlines related to the topicality of their subjects. Investigative journalists may work on a time frame of months pursuing a story in depth – but if they are associated with news media, typically not years, as many academics may spend on a single book or article.

Academics face different time pressures than do members of news media. As noted above, writing even a single good article for publication in an academic journal can take months or even years; academic books can take even longer. Moreover, most faculty in the United States also have teaching responsibilities; devoting time to good teaching means that most faculty usually cannot devote their work life exclusively to research.[48] Untenured academics who are hoping for tenure

[46] On the value of such event-driven reporting, *see* Michael Schudson, *Why Democracies Need an Unlovable Press*, *in* Freeing the Presses: The First Amendment in Action (Timothy E. Cook ed., 2005).

[47] *See generally* National Security, Leaks and Freedom of the Press: The Pentagon Papers Fifty Years On (Geoffrey R. Stone & Lee C. Bollinger eds., 2021).

[48] This teaching obligation is a key difference between university faculties and journalists. Unlike leading journalists, university faculty members are expected to teach students as well as develop

face definite time pressures to produce published scholarship before tenure consideration; in systems with regular review of all faculty, pressures to show regular research publications continue throughout an academic career. Junior faculty and those outside the United States with competitively ranked systems based on regular review of faculty publications have serious incentives to frequently produce scholarship that is placed in well-rated journals.[49]

It continues to be the case that academic life allows more time for reading and reflection than most journalism positions do. Yet commentators have expressed concerns about the prioritizing of quantity over quality in articles in academia. Professors in highly competitive fields are facing increased pressure to produce more papers in shorter time periods, although this is not the same type of time pressure as is faced by journalists who work under daily deadlines. Academic time scales allow – or, in some cases, require[50] – more time for deep research, reflection, and multiple drafts in ways that journalism often does not. This gives rise to an expectation of fewer errors in academic work than in daily journalism. Nonetheless, although the time pressures differ, they exist in both fields.

The analytical tasks that can be expected of academic work and journalism also differ, though there are areas of overlap. Some areas of academic inquiry, such as in the physical sciences, are simply beyond the capacities of those who do not have a quality lab to work in. Some areas of academic inquiry are not sufficiently contemporary, or take too long to research, to be possible (or of interest) for journalists.

The press is better situated than academia to quickly produce daily or weekly reporting and in-depth investigations that are published close in time to the events being investigated. Unlike academics, press outlets typically do not have processes that can delay, sometimes by many months, even being able to start interviewing sources.[51] Yet the search for the popular (or sensational) does not always correspond with what is important to public well-being; commercial incentives may be at war

knowledge. The obligation to teach students both constrains time for developing new knowledge and, at least for classroom teaching, may impose a different set of obligations on faculty than would apply to, say, "opinion" journalism. *See* Edward Shils, The Academic Ethic 99–100 (1984) (arguing that classroom faculty have obligations "not to pretend that what is controversial is not controversial," and to be "scrupulous to recommend reading which will make the idiosyncratic bent of [their own] teaching obvious," presumably by introducing the range of views on contested subjects that have reasonable degrees of support). By contrast, journalistic opinion writing does not have the same obligation of fair presentation of competing views but can offer more particular views of a subject.

49 On regular publication assessments in the UK, *see* REF 2029: Research Excellence Framework, https://www.ref.ac.uk/ (last visited May 22, 2024).

50 Academic research on "human subjects" involving interviewing living persons, having living persons participate in social or cognitive experiments, or even surveying living persons, as well as the testing of medical drugs, devices, or approaches may require approval in advance of undertaking the research by IRBs. *See supra* note 12.

51 On IRB review, which can delay research involving human subjects while awaiting approval, *see supra* notes 12 and 50.

with reporting that informs citizens about events relating to government policy. The topicality that news media see – reporting on current developments in government in regulation, in politics, and in events and trends affecting people's daily lives – is wide, but under these pressures, still limited.

In contrast, the choice of topics for academic research in universities is quite broad and not constrained by subjects of current topical interest. Classicists pore over ancient texts in languages no longer spoken; archeologists explore understandings of peoples and societies' lives from the past; historians pursue improved understandings of different periods of history of different peoples and countries around the world; physicists seek to improve understanding of the smallest particles in the universe and the largest distances between objects in the universe; biologists and chemists work to improve understandings of processes of physical change. Scholars can pursue research into more lasting forms of knowledge than journalists, deepening or challenging existing understandings in philosophy, history, literature, and art, or testing the continued validity of scientific beliefs or mathematical propositions and developing new ones. Sometimes these avenues of research yield interesting perspectives on current topics, but often they do not, yet they contribute to the development of valuable human knowledge by engaging with the world and existing understandings in an epistemically open and (hopefully) rigorous way.

In areas of overlapping interests, which may arise in fields of social sciences, scholars may be better – in part because they have more time – at developing and testing theoretical explanations for phenomena, periodizing large amounts of historical data, and more generally identifying patterns across time and societies. Journalism, on the other hand, is superior to most academic work in its currency, which can provide raw material for historians and other academics by offering a daily diffusion of new information on contemporary life, government, elections, candidates for and incumbents in public office, emerging problems, conflicts, and trends. Journalism also continues to provide a forum for curated public discussion through letters to the editor and opinion pieces, a feature not so available with respect to academic work. Occasionally, journalism has also risen to provide astonishingly deep levels of research requiring immense collaboration in the acquisition and presentation of data, as exemplified by The New York Times' daily charts on the COVID pandemic.[52]

The time constraints and substantive work of journalists and academics share some characteristics but also differ in important ways. Do journalists chase stories that have little long-term value but appeal to currently popular obsessions? Do academics pursue topics of interest only to a small number of other academics,

[52] *See Coronavirus in the U.S.: Latest Map and Case Count*, N.Y. Times, https://www.nytimes.com/interactive/2021/us/covid-cases.html (last updated Mar. 23, 2023) (reporting on the end of its daily COVID data reporting).

or, alternatively, write in "safe" or "politically correct" well-ploughed veins? Yes, all of these occur, as well as more concerning conduct.

Yet, both academics and journalists regularly produce highly valuable reports, discoveries, and analyses, which may inform the public of major problems with government or business (often being concealed by those who benefit from them) or offer the kind of medical discoveries that have extended life spans dramatically. History suggests that only free and open fields of inquiry – that will inevitably include some low-value or mistaken research and reporting – will produce these and other such valuable results. Increased awareness of these benefits, increased attention to the resources needed to sustain knowledge institutions, and constructive critique to help institutions improve their own work will benefit both knowledge institutions and the constitutional democracies to which they are so important.

20.4 ETHICAL CONSTRAINTS SUPPORTED BY PROFESSIONAL OR RELATED ORGANIZATIONS

Books about universities tout these organizations' importance to advances in science, cross-cultural knowledge, competitiveness (in business and more generally), amelioration of poverty, and government policy or public administration.[53] Some also emphasize their contributions to democracy more generally and to social equality.[54] Books about the press tout its importance to civic knowledge, communication among readers, "watchdogging" those in positions of (private or public) power, and holding them to account.[55] Yet these books do not as often claim that the press facilitates effective government or business competitiveness, even though some of the origins of the European press in newsletters concerning commercially valuable information plainly existed to serve business interests[56] and even though there is a long linkage between the press and government functions (and a link between local "news deserts" and corruption).[57] Notably, writers do not call on the press to develop innovations that enable better business practice or governance, while they do assign this task to universities. The ethos of the press as independent

[53] *See, e.g.*, DEREK BOK, UNIVERSITIES AND THE FUTURE OF AMERICA (1990).

[54] *See, e.g.*, RONALD J. DANIELS ET AL., WHAT UNIVERSITIES OWE DEMOCRACY (2021).

[55] *See generally* SCHUDSON, *supra* note 19.

[56] For descriptions of the development of commercial newsletters in Europe in the seventeenth and eighteenth centuries, *see* David H. Tucker et al., *The First Newspapers*, BRITANNICA (last updated May 20, 2024), https://www.britannica.com/topic/publishing/The-first-news papers; PAUL STARR, THE CREATION OF THE MEDIA: POLITICAL ORIGINS OF MODERN COMMUNICATIONS 31 (2004).

[57] *See* TIMOTHY E. COOK, GOVERNING WITH THE NEWS (1998) (arguing that the press as a whole was an institution and that it had a principal function of serving as a tool of government policymaking by those in government or concerned with government policy). On how loss of local newspapers is associated with a rise in corruption, *see, e.g.*, Ted Matherly & Brad N. Greenwood, *No News Is Bad News: The Internet, Corruption, and the Decline of the Fourth Estate*, 48 MISQUARTERLY 699 (June 2024).

and as reporting on rather than "making" the news would resist such instrumentalization. Consequently, a quite different ethos animates academia and journalism.

Despite this and other differences, both journalism and academia have commitments to pursuing genuine knowledge, and both have developed ethical principles, which may be reinforced by standards of conduct adopted by specific institutions (that is, specific newspapers or universities). The ethical standards of both entities include an emphasis on transparency, accuracy, and truth-seeking. I have discussed the ethical, truth-seeking, and information-verification norms of the press in earlier writing.[58] Below I discuss academic ethics.

The AAUP Statement on Professional Ethics asserts, as a basic obligation of faculty: "Their primary responsibility to their subject is to seek and to state the truth as they see it ... They accept the obligation to exercise critical self-discipline and judgment in using, extending and transmitting knowledge. They practice intellectual honesty."[59] In succeeding paragraphs, the statement addresses obligations to students, colleagues, the institution, and their community.[60]

Discrete disciplinary associations of faculty across universities often reflect on the ethics of scholarship in their fields. For example, the publishing arm of the American Institute of Physics sets technical precepts for authors, including the expectation that "results of research should be recorded and maintained in a form that allows analysis and review, both by collaborators before publication and by other scientists for a reasonable period after publication."[61] The Institute also establishes norms, including that "fabrication of data is an egregious departure from the expected norms of scientific conduct, as is the selective reporting of data with the intent to mislead or deceive, as well as the theft of data or research results from others."[62] Similarly, in the humanities, the American Historical Association says that while historians have much they disagree on, they all agree on some precepts: "All historians believe in honoring the integrity of the historical record. They do not fabricate evidence. Forgery and fraud violate the most basic foundations on which historians construct their interpretations of the past."[63]

[58] Jackson, *On "the Press," supra* note 2 at 289–91.

[59] Statement on Professional Ethics, Am. Ass'n of Univ. Professors, https://www.aaup.org/report/statement-professional-ethics (last updated 2009).

[60] For the AAUP's Statement on Professional Ethics, *see supra* note 59. As the AAUP statement also notes, the enforcement mechanism for academia differs from that in law and medicine: it points out that, unlike in law and medicine, where there are statewide professional associations that enforce codes of conduct, in academia the expectation is that the individual institution of higher education will enforce. *Id.* On the professions as "knowledge communities," *see* Claudia E. Haupt, *Professional Speech*, 125 Yale L. J. 1238, 1248–49 (2016).

[61] *Ethics for Authors*, AIP Publ'g, https://publishing.aip.org/resources/researchers/policies-and-ethics/authors/ (last visited May 8, 2024).

[62] *Id. See also id.* ("Proper acknowledgment of the work of others used in a research project must always be given.").

[63] *Statement on Standards of Professional Conduct*, Am. Hist. Ass'n, https://www.historians.org/jobs-and-professional-development/statements-standards-and-guidelines-of-the-discipline/statement-on-standards-of-professional-conduct (last updated 2023).

Some ethical norms differ between journalists and academics. Journalists typically name their sources, and they generally contend that the sources a reporter relies on for a story should only be kept confidential in special circumstances. In contrast, social scientists who do survey research are expected to take measures to maintain the confidentiality of their survey respondents. For both reporters and academics, the obligation to protect the confidentiality of a source once a promise of confidentiality has been given may raise conflicting moral and legal obligations.[64] On occasion, journalists have gone to jail rather than comply with a subpoena and reveal an anonymous source without the source's consent. Some condemn those journalists for obstructing justice, while others hail them as heroes. Most US states provide some protection for journalists from forced disclosure of confidential sources. Although similar protection for academics is less well established, they have sought it on similar grounds and on occasion been successful.[65] As many state journalist-shield laws recognize, sometimes confidentiality assurances are the only way to verify and get an important story of government or private malfeasance out to the public.

The aggressive critique that follows public disclosure of departures from ethical standards suggests the continued relevance of these norms in both journalism and academia. There are too many such departures. But they attract controversy and critique – through which norms of honest, truth-oriented work can be upheld.

20.5 KNOWLEDGE INSTITUTIONS' INTERDEPENDENCE AND CONSTITUTIONAL DEMOCRACY

The shared aspiration of journalism and academia to honesty and to "extending … knowledge"[66] is reflected in their intellectual *interdependence*. In earlier work, I have provided examples of how the press, universities, and government offices that collect and provide data draw from one another's work and are, in a sense, parts of an interdependent epistemic infrastructure; the press may play an important role in circulating new ideas from academia.[67] However, the interdependence of

[64] *See generally* Michael Farrell, *Anonymous Sources*, Soc'y of Pro. Journalists, https://www.spj.org/ethics-papers-anonymity.asp (last visited June 9, 2024).

[65] *See, e.g.*, Frank Murray, *Boston College's Defense of the Belfast Project: A Renewed Call for a Researcher's Privilege to Protect Academia*, 39 J.C. & U.L. 659 (2013); Cusumano v. Microsoft Corp., 162 F.3d 708, 714 (1st Cir. 1998) (upholding lower court decision refusing to compel discovery for, inter alia, confidential information academic researchers had obtained and stating: "Academicians engaged in pre-publication research should be accorded protection commensurate to that which the law provides for journalists.").

[66] AAUP Statement, *supra* note 59.

[67] *See Jackson, On "the Press," supra* note 2 at 319–20, nn.193–200. For additional examples, *see, e.g.*, Richard L. Hasen, *Racial Gerrymandering's Questionable Revival*, 67 Ala. L. Rev. 365, 380 n.79 (2015) (citing the work of journalist Jason Zengerle); Frank D. LoMonte & Daniel Delgado, *The Importance of Accessible Government Data in Advancing Environmental Justice*, 47 Wm. & Mary Env't L. & Pol'y Rev. 827, 864–65 (2023) (discussing series in the Tampa Bay Times, which won a Pulitzer in 2022 for investigative journalism, on conditions inside a lead

knowledge institutions goes beyond these kinds of instances of direct utilization by one kind of institution of the work of another. Historically, increases in education and literacy helped promote press readership.[68] More generally, knowledge institutions can play a role of supporting overarching values that benefit society and government in constitutional democracies – of "truth, science, morality and arts in general," as the Continental Congress proclaimed about the role of the press in 1774,[69] and the ideals of disciplined truth-seeking searches for better knowledge.

These overarching values include a commitment to rationality in decision-making. This commitment, in turn, requires that people have skills of critical inquiry and understanding, including skills in evaluating evidence that bears on important public questions. These values also include the importance of public knowledge of government – not just knowledge of what the institutions are but understanding of how government actually works – appreciating the need for trade-offs in desired ends, for example, or developing an ability to distinguish abuses of power from ordinary disagreements. For these tasks, President Washington and many other US presidents thought a national university was required.[70] The national universities that exist today, created through more decentralized mechanisms, continue to be urged to consider whether they are providing the education that participants in our constitutional democracy need.[71]

From the earliest days, the press has been viewed as playing a central role in serving as a watchdog that could criticize government officials, providing a forum for letters and opinions from a range of readers, and promoting public knowledge of government. A postal subsidy for newspapers was provided in the 1792 Act establishing the postal service.[72] Even earlier, in September 1789, the very first Congress mandated the secretary of state to receive all enacted laws and to assure their publication in "at least three public newspapers."[73]

smelting plant). Journalists may also benefit from academic work that provides a context for understanding more specific incidents or trends on which they report.

68 Paul Horwitz, First Amendment Institutions 147 (Kindle 2014).

69 Starr, *supra* note 56, at 76 (quoting from the Continental Congress "address to the Inhabitants of Quebec").

70 *See* George Thomas, The Founders and the Idea of a National University: Constituting the American Mind 2–6 (2014) (arguing that for its proponents, a national university would help inculcate the habits of mind and knowledge that would enable the organs of our constitutional government to work).

71 *See* Daniels et al., *supra* note 54, at 86–130 (discussing "free minds" and "educating democratic citizens").

72 *See* https://about.usps.com/who/profile/history/periodicals-postage-history.htm (noting "rock bottom rate" for newspaper delivery specified by Congress in 1792 Act).

73 1 Stat 68, Sept. 15, 1789, an Act for the Safekeeping of Records of the United States. One might contrast this statute with what Stephen Ward reports was an action by the British House of Commons in 1660 making it a criminal offense to report on parliament. Ward, *supra* note 19, Kindle p. 147.

Finally, these knowledge institutions and others together help promote the idea that the truth, or truths, or better understandings of the world, are worth pursuing. Without the idea that there *is* knowledge – that at any given time, there are better (more accurate) and worse (less accurate) understandings of facts and trends, physical and social processes and causes; and that study, reason, and consideration of evidence can help arrive at ever better understandings – it is almost impossible to find a shared epistemic space for democratic self-governance. There are also necessarily uncertainties in the real pursuit of knowledge, which both universities and journalists can help us understand. But trying to have a democracy without some shared basis for establishing what is, at least contingently, accepted as usable knowledge is almost impossible to imagine.

Whether the press or universities will retain their current institutional and economic forms is a serious question.[74] The press, in particular, has undergone a dramatic economic and professional shift over the last two decades; governments in recent years have "disinvested" in public universities; and public trust in both news media and universities has declined markedly.[75] But the functions these institutions serve – of attempting honestly and accurately to report on daily events and attempting honestly and accurately to understand the human and natural world in all its manifestations – are essential to good societies. In helping to hold governments accountable, they are of particular importance to constitutional democracies, where decisions by an informed citizenry are at the theoretical foundation of the legitimacy of the state.

[74] New models of journalism are struggling to emerge. *See*, e.g., Ellen Clegg & Dan Kennedy, What Works in Community News: Media Startups, News Deserts and the Future of the Fourth Estate (2024); Alexandra Bruell, *How the Atlantic Went from Broke to Profitable in Three Years*, Wall St. J. (Mar. 28, 2024).

[75] *See*, e.g., William C. Kirby, *Introduction: International Innovation & American Challenges*, Daedalus 7 (Spring 2024) ("[F]orty-three of all fifty states have disinvested in higher education since 2008"); Gallup, Confidence in Institutions (reflecting decline from 37 percent in 2000 to 18 percent in 2023 of persons with a "great deal" or "quite a lot" of confidence in newspapers, and a similar decline for television news; for universities, reflecting a decline of 57 percent to 36 percent of those with "great deal" or "quiet a lot" of confidence in higher education), https://news.gallup.com/poll/1597/confidence-institutions.aspx. The causes of these declines are too complex to fully explore here, but likely include well-publicized lapses by these institutions (or their members) from standards of independence, competence, and impartiality, as well as unprecedentedly sustained attacks on the institutions as such by high public officials.

21

Policing Press Freedom

Hannah Bloch-Wehba

For many years, press freedom advocates have seen law enforcement as a threat to journalism's autonomy and independence. But the nature of that threat is changing. In the past, press freedom concerns typically centered on the risk that law enforcement might compel or coerce journalists to become unwilling participants in prosecutions and investigations of third parties. Statutory, constitutional, and regulatory interventions have been developed in response to stave off that possibility. Yet those protections, while still meaningful, do not address the potential criminal liability that reporters face in gathering and reporting the news. Today, the prospect of journalists facing arrest and prosecution is not as far-fetched as it might once have seemed.

Consider a few representative incidents. In December 2017, prosecutors charged citizen journalist Priscilla Villarreal with violating Texas' prohibition on "misuse of official information" after she got a tip from a Laredo police officer.[1] In March 2019, San Francisco police searched freelance journalist Bryan Carmody's home and office, confiscating his devices, as they investigated who had leaked information about the sudden death of Public Defender Jeff Adachi.[2] In December 2021, sheriff's deputies arrested citizen journalist Justin Pulliam as he recorded a mental health check outside Houston.[3] In August 2023, police raided the newsroom and the home of the publisher of the Marion County Record, a local newspaper that was investigating a business owner's application for a liquor license.[4]

There are two competing ways of seeing these kinds of episodes. In the first vision, these kinds of occurrences are affronts to press freedom and show that press-specific

[1] Leif Reigstad, *Lagordiloca's Arrest Raises Constitutional Concerns*, Texas Monthly (Dec. 21, 2017), https://www.texasmonthly.com/articles/lagordilocas-arrest-laredo/.

[2] *Police to Acknowledge Press Protections After Disputed Raid*, AP News (May 26, 2020), https://apnews.com/general-news-2c00861e7b3da4d7276f43c065b71ffb.

[3] *Fort Bend Retaliation*, Inst. for Just., https://ij.org/case/fort-bend-retaliation/.

[4] Sherman Smith et al., *Police Stage "Chilling" Raid on Marion County Newspaper, Seizing Computers, Records and Cellphones*, Kansas Reflector (Aug. 11, 2023), https://kansasreflector.com/2023/08/11/police-stage-chilling-raid-on-marion-county-newspaper-seizing-computers-records-and-cellphones/.

legal protections are necessary to blunt law enforcement's ability to target and harass the media. Faced with the question of how best to protect journalism and a free press, many scholars have zeroed in on what is sometimes called "press exceptionalism," calling for special protections for the press against generally applicable laws. Special protections constitute "targeted statutory and constitutional protection of the press functions."[5] A basic premise of press exceptionalism is that, although the press faces particular challenges in exercising its constitutional rights, it is treated the same as an ordinary individual or business.[6]

In the second vision, these incidents are disturbing examples of widespread dysfunction in law enforcement. Broad and vague laws are commonplace, overcriminalization runs rampant, and law enforcement enjoys substantial discretion in how to investigate, deter, and prevent crime.[7] Although the press may have particular complaints about these dynamics, these are not problems unique to the press. Perhaps these incidents underscore the unique and disproportionate effects of criminal charges and investigations on the press. But they also illustrate the fundamental inability of distinctive legal protections to shield the media from law enforcement activity that is, for a large number of Americans, simply expected and routine.[8]

As with all ailments, how we diagnose the problem will shape how we think about the right treatment. If the problem is press specific, then the law should address these challenges by treating the press differently, perhaps by conferring special advantages or relieving general burdens, enabling the press to engage in its constitutionally recognized functions in ways that it currently cannot. If the press's woes are symptomatic of a more systemic problem in law enforcement, however, then the press ought to prioritize limiting law enforcement's power and discretion in ways that would benefit the press alongside many others as well.

This chapter reflects on the limitations of press exceptionalism. In my view, even if press-specific interventions are valuable in other domains, they are unlikely to be effective remedies for most law enforcement activities that target the press. My reasons for pessimism have more to do with criminal law and procedure than with free expression. Because criminal law is so broad, many routine newsgathering activities might run afoul of any number of state and federal statutes.[9] Reporters might also be accused of soliciting unlawful disclosures or aiding sources who violate

5 RonNell Andersen Jones & Sonja R. West, *An Introduction to Our Project: The Future of Press Freedom*, Knight First Amend. Inst. (Oct. 16, 2023), https://knightcolumbia.org/blog/an-introduction-to-our-project-the-future-of-press-freedom.

6 Sonja R. West, *Press Exceptionalism*, 127 Harv. L. Rev. 2434, 2436 (2014) ("The underlying problem journalists face is that they are treated by the law as being no different than the subjects they are covering or, perhaps, mere curious bystanders.").

7 Debra Livingston, *Police Discretion and the Quality of Life in Public Places: Courts, Communities, and the New Policing*, 97 Colum. L. Rev. 551 (1997).

8 Amna A. Akbar, *Toward a Radical Imagination of Law*, 93 N.Y.U. L. Rev. 405, 436 (2018) ("In cities big and small, rich and poor, north and south, police violence is routine.").

9 For example, failure to obey/disperse, resisting arrest, trespass, interference with police duties.

substantive criminal laws.[10] Even where law enforcement may not intend to pursue charges against a journalist, the existence of broad criminal liability enables police and prosecutors to evade procedural restrictions on investigations of the press.

Press-specific protections are not well matched to these law-enforcement dynamics. Even the strongest procedural defenses for the press are likely to falter in the face of substantive law that criminalizes the acts that constitute newsgathering. Press-specific status rules are also hard for law enforcement to administer on the fly. And experience has shown that existing remedies do little to disincentivize unconstitutional conduct by law enforcement agencies. Furthermore, and perhaps most important of all, a model of protection that relies on the press to litigate its rights on a case-by-case basis is almost by definition ill-suited to systemic law enforcement dysfunction.

Even assuming that special press protections are valuable, they also have significant, underappreciated costs. Enabling the press to claim special legal status may entrench distrust of press actors. Recognizing special press rights to be free of surveillance and monitoring, for example, can help to consolidate and legitimate law enforcement's substantial power to surveil and monitor everybody else. In the name of creating legal certainty and stability for newsgatherers, conferring special rights on the press also invites a different form of instability and uncertainty as decision-makers determine what terms like "newsgathering" and "press" mean. At least with respect to law enforcement – the focus of this chapter – press-specific protections are at best only mildly helpful and at worst counterproductive. The protections the press really needs are the same general safeguards against government overreach and broad law-enforcement discretion that all speakers should enjoy, not specific rules narrowly focused on the press.

The rest of the chapter proceeds in three main sections. First, I trace the existing protections for journalism – and those that are absent – to make the case that the press is relatively unprotected from law enforcement. Second, I argue that special protections are ill-equipped to solve systemic law enforcement problems. Finally, I point to some paths for the press to take a more aggressive role in reshaping law enforcement without using special protections to do so.

21.1 THE CURRENT LANDSCAPE

Many scholars have identified problems for press freedom that arise out of criminal law and procedure. Historically, a particular concern for the press was that it might

[10] Ann E. Marimow, *Justice Department's Scrutiny of Fox News Reporter James Rosen in Leak Case Draws Fire*, Wash. Post (May 20, 2013, 6:55 PM), https://www.washingtonpost.com/local/justice-departments-scrutiny-of-fox-news-reporter-james-rosen-in-leak-case-draws-fire/2013/05/20/c6289eba-c162-11e2-8bd8-2788030e6b44_story.html; David Snyder & Duffy Carolan, *Fifth Judge Sides with FAC, Orders Release of Records in Bryan Carmody Raid*, First Amend. Coal. (Sept. 3, 2019), https://firstamendmentcoalition.org/2019/09/fifth-judge-sides-with-fac-orders-release-of-records-in-bryan-carmody-raid/.

be dragged into investigations or prosecutions of its sources because it possessed information obtained in confidence that was evidence of criminality.[11] As a result, and in response to the lack of constitutional protection, a variety of statutory and regulatory constraints have developed to shield the press from being made to comply with these sorts of demands.

21.1.1 *Press-Specific Protections*

Many of the extant press-specific protections in state and federal law sprung up in the aftermath of the Supreme Court's decisions in *Branzburg v. Hayes* and *Zurcher v. Stanford Daily*, two germinal cases involving attempts to seek evidence in the possession of the press for use in prosecutions of third parties. In *Branzburg*, the Supreme Court held that the First Amendment does not confer an unqualified reporter's privilege that would prevent a journalist from being compelled to reveal the identity of their source before a grand jury. *Branzburg* prompted Congress to introduce dozens of shield bills, none of which were ultimately enacted.[12] *Branzburg* also stimulated state legislation: Before *Branzburg* was decided, seventeen states had enacted shield laws recognizing some version of a reporter's privilege.[13] Today, according to the Reporters Committee for Freedom of the Press, forty states have shield statutes, and eight more have recognized a reporter's privilege grounded either in common law or the state constitution.[14] In addition, a federal shield bill, the PRESS Act, was reintroduced in 2023; I return to that bill below.

In *Stanford Daily*, the Supreme Court upheld the constitutionality of a newsroom search and seizure conducted after police obtained a search warrant based on probable cause. In response to the *Stanford Daily* decision, Congress enacted the Privacy Protection Act of 1980, which typically bars law enforcement from searching journalists' work product and documentary materials using a search warrant and requires them to use a subpoena instead.[15] Similarly, Department of Justice (DOJ) guidelines impose additional requirements when law enforcement uses compulsory process to seek information from or relating to the news media.[16]

These statutory and regulatory protections are particularly important because journalists and press institutions often have information that is relevant to criminal and national security investigations. The threat of subpoenas and other compulsory

[11] RonNell Andersen Jones, *Rethinking Reporter's Privilege*, 111 MICH. L. REV. 1221, 1222 (2013) (describing the reporter's privilege as "what journalists *see* as the First Amendment issue most critical to the flow of information in our democracy").

[12] Christina Koningisor, *The De Facto Reporter's Privilege*, 127 YALE L. J. 1176, 1198 (2018).

[13] *Id.* at 1201 n.131 (*citing* Branzburg v. Hayes, 408 U.S. 665, 689 n. 27 (1972)).

[14] *Reporter's Privilege Compendium*, REPS. COMM. FOR FREEDOM OF THE PRESS, https://www.rcfp.org/reporters-privilege/ (last visited May 25, 2024).

[15] 42 U.S.C. § 2000aa.

[16] 28 C.F.R. § 50.10.

process can deter sources from coming forward and otherwise chill reporting.[17] In other words, it is precisely the press's performance of its checking and watchdog functions that makes it an appealing target of compulsory process, and the threat of compulsory process is an effective way of managing the press's reporting and "silencing political dissent."[18]

Of particular relevance here, legal protections can mean that law enforcement agencies treat journalists differently than other individuals, shielding them from certain law enforcement methods and demands. Criminal procedure is replete with examples of this kind of differential treatment. If law enforcement has probable cause to believe that evidence of a crime is present in someone's office, they can ordinarily obtain a warrant to search the premises.[19] But if law enforcement wants to search a newsroom, it is barred by federal law from getting a warrant.[20] If law enforcement wants to subpoena an individual's cell phone or email records from a third-party communications provider, it can ordinarily do so without notice to the individual.[21] But if the Federal Bureau of Investigation (FBI) wants to subpoena a journalist's records, it must give the journalist notice and an opportunity to be heard.[22] If prosecutors want to call someone to testify before a grand jury, they are ordinarily entitled to "every man's evidence."[23] But if prosecutors want to call a journalist to testify, they must comply with state shield laws governing how they do so.[24]

21.1.2 *Substantive Criminal Law*

The special protections I outlined above limit law enforcement's ability to coerce the press to participate in investigations of others. What about when criminal law enforcement targets the press itself? Press-specific protections play a smaller and less robust role than we might expect in limiting law enforcement abuses. With few exceptions, press freedom laws are procedural rather than substantive. They tell us what kinds of rules law enforcement must abide by when they interact with the press. Surprisingly, however, there are many open questions about how criminal law can be used against the press.

17 Koningisor, *supra* note 12, at 1251–53; RonNell Andersen Jones, *Media Subpoenas: Impact, Perception, and Legal Protection in the Changing World of American Journalism*, 84 Wash. L. Rev. 317, 393 (2009) (describing the "nationwide chill" created by an uptick in media subpoenas).

18 Koningisor, *supra* note 12, at 1254.

19 Zurcher v. Stanford Daily, 436 U.S. 547 (1978).

20 42 U.S.C. § 2000aa.

21 Hannah Bloch-Wehba, *Exposing Secret Searches: A First Amendment Right of Access to Electronic Surveillance Orders*, 93 Wash. L. Rev. 145, 159 (2018).

22 28 C.F.R. § 50.10.

23 Rebecca Wexler, *Ignorance of the Rules of Omission: An Essay on Privilege Law*, 76 Vand. L. Rev. 1609, 1615 (2023).

24 *Reporter's Privilege Compendium*, *supra* note 14.

Some things are clear: For decades, it has been plain that the government must meet an exceptionally high bar in order to prevent the press from publishing even highly classified information.[25] Likewise, a similar, "exceedingly stringent" standard must be satisfied to justify criminal prosecution for the publication of "truthful materials of public concern."[26] These demanding standards limit government action against all speakers, not only press actors. On the other hand, the First Amendment affords "few, if any, protections" to sources who leak to the press.[27] This "mixed approach" generally confers substantial protection on the publishers of information, regardless of whether they are members of the press, and exceedingly limited protection on their sources.[28]

The press's potential criminal and civil liability for newsgathering activities is much murkier than its liability for publication. Indeed, the broad questions of whether and to what extent state and federal governments can choose to punish or constrain newsgathering activities are largely unresolved. First Amendment doctrine has long held that "generally applicable laws do not offend the First Amendment simply because their enforcement against the press has incidental effects on its ability to gather and report the news."[29] If a law can generally be enforced against an ordinary speaker, it can also be enforced against the press.

To a limited extent, special protections prevent law enforcement from interfering with newsgathering. Special protections for the press might confer particular rights on journalists, such as when a press pass enables a journalist to attend a meeting or a hearing from which the general public is excluded. Special protections might also relieve reporters from generally applicable burdens, like when a curfew order contains an exemption permitting journalists to stay out when the general public must be off the streets.[30] However, these protections are typically local, piecemeal, and haphazard.

Criminal law, by and large, contains no exceptions for journalists or reporters. This explains why, in recent years, journalists have been arrested in droves while covering widespread protests and unrest.[31] In response to uprisings against police injustice, lawmakers in states across the country have also undertaken a new drive to

[25] N.Y. Times v. United States, 403 U.S. 713 (1971).

[26] Yochai Benkler, A *Free Irresponsible Press: Wikileaks and the Battle over the Soul of the Networked Fourth Estate*, 46 HARV. C.R.-C.L. L. REV. 311, 354 (2011).

[27] Heidi Kitrosser, *Leak Prosecutions and the First Amendment: New Developments and a Closer Look at the Feasibility of Protecting Leakers*, 56 WM. & MARY L. REV. 1221, 1226 (2015).

[28] *Id.*

[29] Cohen v. Cowles Media Co., 501 U.S. 663, 669 (1991).

[30] Sasha Peters & Linda Moon, *Curfew Orders Without Media Exemptions May Be Unconstitutional Under First Amendment*, REPS. COMM. FOR FREEDOM OF THE PRESS (June 12, 2020), https://www.rcfp.org/curfew-order-special-analysis/.

[31] U.S. Press Freedom Tracker, https://pressfreedomtracker.us/; JOEL SIMON, COVERING DEMOCRACY: PROTEST POLICE, AND THE PRESS, KNIGHT FIRST AMEND. INST. (June 20, 2023), https://knightcolumbia.org/research/covering-democracy.

criminalize protest and immunize private violence against protestors, endangering journalists still further.[32]

Other lingering questions concern potential liability for publishing information that was obtained unlawfully. While "news gathering is not without its First Amendment protections,"[33] it remains an open question "whether, in cases where information has been acquired *unlawfully* by a newspaper or by a source, government may ever punish not only the unlawful acquisition, but the ensuing publication as well."[34] Meanwhile, the prosecution of Julian Assange continues to raise questions about the potential liability of press actors who might be complicit in violations of the Espionage Act or other federal or state laws.[35]

Of course, this does not mean that there are no substantive First Amendment limits on criminal law. But proactive constitutional challenges appear to be more successful than post hoc assertions that arresting, prosecuting, or punishing journalism violates the First Amendment. For example, courts in several circuits have struck down so-called "ag gag" laws "aimed at stifling undercover investigations or whistleblowing" regarding animal welfare, environmental concerns, and working conditions.[36] Similarly, in upholding the material-support statute, the Supreme Court in *Holder v. Humanitarian Law Project* suggested that regulations of "independent speech" supporting terrorism or "material support" of domestic organizations would likely fail constitutional scrutiny.[37]

The legal risks for newsgathering are real. Consider the classic example: the Espionage Act.[38] The Espionage Act makes it a crime to receive or disseminate national defense information "to any person not entitled to receive it."[39] For decades, questions about potential criminal liability for news organizations that possess and publish classified information have plagued press institutions as well as scholars, advocates, and the courts.[40]

To date, the government has largely refrained from charging journalists under the Espionage Act, with only rare exceptions. Historically, the Espionage Act has been

[32] International Center for Not-For-Profit Law, US Protest Law Tracker, https://www.icnl.org/usprotestlawtracker/.

[33] *Branzburg*, *supra* note 13, at 707.

[34] Florida Star v. B.J.F., 491 U.S. 524, 535 n.8 (1989).

[35] Benkler, *supra* note 26; *An Open Letter from Editors and Publishers: Publishing Is Not a Crime*, N.Y. Times (Nov. 28, 2022), https://www.nytco.com/press/an-open-letter-from-editors-and-publishers-publishing-is-not-a-crime/.

[36] Alan K. Chen & Justin Marceau, *High Value Lies, Ugly Truths, and the First Amendment*, 68 Vand. L. Rev. 1435, 1439 (2015).

[37] Holder v. Humanitarian Law Project, 561 U.S. 1, 39 (2010).

[38] Stephen L. Vladeck, *Inchoate Liability and the Espionage Act: The Statutory Framework and the Freedom of the Press*, 1 Harv. L. & Pol'y Rev. 219 (2007).

[39] 18 U.S.C. § 793(d)–(e).

[40] David McCraw & Stephen Gikow, *The End to an Unspoken Bargain? National Security and Leaks in a Post-Pentagon Papers World*, 48 Harv. C.R.-C.L. L. Rev. 473, 478 (2013) ("[T]he Espionage Act remains dense, contradictory, and essentially unexplored as to whether it can be applied to publishers ... and how.").

chiefly enforced against those who *leak* defense information rather than against those who publish it.[41] The Espionage Act has been invoked to prosecute a third-party publisher of classified information only twice. In 1942, the United States attempted to prosecute the Chicago Tribune for publishing a story that revealed that the United States had "cracked a Japanese communications code," but the grand jury did not indict the paper.[42] More recently, Julian Assange, the founder of Wikileaks, pleaded guilty to a charge under the Espionage Act in exchange for a sentence that permitted him to return to Australia without serving additional time in a United States prison.[43]

The Espionage Act is far from the only statute under which prosecutors can charge journalists. Reporters covering protests are frequently charged with trespass or violating curfew or dispersal orders.[44] Journalists have also been charged for reporting on law enforcement under other state laws that criminalize obstruction or interference.[45]

Consider, too, the case of Priscilla Villarreal, perhaps better known as "Lagordiloca."[46] Villarreal is a citizen journalist from Laredo, Texas, where she "live-streams raw footage from local crime scenes – shootings, gruesome traffic accidents, tense hostage situations, immigration raids, and whatever else she comes across – to more than 80,000 loyal Facebook followers."[47] In 2017, Villarreal was arrested and charged with "misuse of official information" after she texted a source inside the Laredo Police Department to corroborate the details of a Border Patrol worker's suicide and a fatal car accident.[48] Under Texas criminal law, anyone who

[41] *Id.* at 474; Kitrosser, *supra* note 27, at 1240 (2015) (describing the "mixed approach" to leak prosecutions that affords few protections to leakers but substantial protection to third parties who publish leaked information).

[42] Michael E. Ruane, *Unsealed 75 Years after the Battle of Midway: New Details of an Alarming WWII Press Leak*, Wash. Post (June 5, 2017, 8:00 AM), https://www.washingtonpost.com/news/retropolis/wp/2017/06/05/unsealed-75-years-after-the-battle-of-midway-new-details-of-a-critical-wwii-press-leak/.

[43] Mari Yamaguchi et al., *WikiLeaks' Assange Pleads Guilty to Publishing US Military Secrets in Deal that Secures His Freedom*, Associated Press (June 25, 2024, 11:38 PM), https://apnews.com/article/assange-justice-department-plea-wikileaks-saipan-australia-00eb380879ff636cc9b916f82f82ed40.

[44] U.S. Press Freedom Tracker, *supra* note 31.

[45] Gregory Royal Pratt, *Calumet City Drops Citations Against Daily Southtown Reporter Who Called Workers Seeking Comment*, Chicago Tribune (Nov. 6, 2023, 7:54 p.m.), https://www.chicagotribune.com/2023/11/06/calumet-city-drops-citations-against-daily-southtown-reporter-who-called-workers-seeking-comment/; Shant Shahrigian, *Daily News Reporter Arrested While Covering New Year's Eve Protest Near Times Square, Is Held Overnight*, N.Y. Daily News (Jan. 1, 2024, 9:44 p.m.), https://www.nydailynews.com/2024/01/01/daily-news-reporter-arrested-covering-new-years-eve-protest-midtown-manhattan/.

[46] Villarreal v. City of Laredo, Texas, 94 F.4th 374, 382 (5th Cir. 2024).

[47] Leif Reigstad, *For Lagordiloca, Live-Streaming Crime Scenes Is Just a Night's Work*, Texas Monthly (Jan. 2018), https://www.texasmonthly.com/true-crime/lagordiloca-livestreams-laredo/.

[48] *Villarreal*, 94 F.4th at 382.

"solicits or receives from a public servant" nonpublic government information "with intent to obtain a benefit" is guilty of a felony.[49] Although a trial court found the statute under which Villarreal was charged unconstitutionally vague, Villarreal's First Amendment suit ultimately foundered in the Fifth Circuit on qualified immunity grounds.[50] In October 2024, the United States Supreme Court vacated the Fifth Circuit's decision and remanded the case for further consideration.[51]

Complicating matters further, the threat of substantive criminal liability can also be used to circumvent heightened procedural requirements constraining how law enforcement obtains information from the press. Return to the Espionage Act: Although direct prosecutions of news media actors have been rare, leak prosecutions and investigations have soared.[52]

Law enforcement can circumvent procedural limits on investigations by dangling substantive criminal charges for journalists. For example, in 2013, Fox News reporter James Rosen was named an unindicted co-conspirator in an indictment of a government leaker, enabling government investigators to "seize his e-mails to build their case against the suspected leaker."[53] By naming Rosen as an unindicted co-conspirator, law enforcement could avoid the limitations imposed by the Privacy Protection Act of 1980, which made it unlawful for the government to search for or seize a journalist's work product or documentary materials unless probable cause existed that the journalist "has committed or is committing the criminal offense to which the materials relate."[54] Although Rosen was never charged, his emails were important to the investigation of the leaker, Stephen Jin-Woo Kim, who ultimately served time in federal prison.[55]

Property laws can also be used to criminalize newsgathering and facilitate law enforcement searches that would otherwise be barred. In Bryan Carmody's case, law enforcement was investigating a leak about the suspicious death of Jeff Adachi, the longtime San Francisco public defender. Carmody, a freelance reporter, had obtained the death investigation report from the San Francisco police. In applying for a search warrant for Carmody's home and office, the police swore an affidavit that they were investigating state felony charges of receiving stolen property.[56]

49 Tex. Penal Code Ann. § 39.06.

50 Villarreal, 94 F. 4th at 384.

51 Villarreal v. Alaniz, 2024 WL 4486343 (mem.).

52 *See, e.g.*, McCraw & Gikow, *supra* note 40, at 492 (noting the rise in Espionage Act prosecutions under the Obama Administration); Charlie Savage & Eileen Sullivan, *Leak Investigations Triple Under Trump, Sessions Says*, N.Y. Times (Aug. 4, 2017), https://www.nytimes.com/2017/08/04/us/politics/jeff-sessions-trump-leaks-attorney-general.html.

53 Marimow, *supra* note 10.

54 42 U.S.C. § 2000aa.

55 Peter Maass, *Destroyed by the Espionage Act*, The Intercept (Feb. 18, 2015, 6:38 AM), https://theintercept.com/theintercept/2015/02/18/destroyed-by-the-espionage-act/.

56 In re Search Warrants, Case No. MISC-2516764 (Cal. Super. Ct. S.F., Aug. 30, 2019), https://firstamendmentcoalition.org/wp-content/uploads/2019/09/Quinn-affidavit.pdf; *see also* Snyder & Carolan, *supra* note 10.

Collectively, these developments suggest that the dominant legal mechanisms for guaranteeing press freedom are not well equipped to address criminal law enforcement. This is in part, to be sure, because of legal uncertainty or indeterminacy. But as I describe below, the real problem is that special protections for the press simply are not effectively backstopped by substantive limits on law enforcement.

21.2 THE LIMITS OF SPECIAL PROTECTIONS

Special protections such as shield laws and rules barring newsroom searches have operated somewhat well to protect press actors from being obligated to participate in criminal proceedings. To be sure, these protections do not function as well as many would like.[57] Indeed, the practical value of special protections is an open question, because they often fail to deliver on their promise. Calls for reaffirming the press's special protections are often loudest when existing protections fall short.

But press advocates are too optimistic about the potential of extending special protections to meaningfully constrain law enforcement. Indeed, special protections are both structurally and substantively ill-suited to the problems posed by law enforcement entanglements with the press.

21.2.1 *Practical Problems*

Many of the proposals to limit law enforcement investigations of journalists are simply underinclusive. Start with the low-hanging fruit, the federal shield law. In 2023, Congress reintroduced a federal shield bill meant to prevent law enforcement from compelling journalists to reveal their sources.[58] The bill would have prevented federal law enforcement from compelling journalists to disclose "protected information" and from compelling third-party service providers to disclose journalists' records.[59] Essentially, it would have codified the DOJ guidelines covering media subpoenas, limiting the possibility that future administrations could repeal or reverse those rules.[60] After incoming President Donald Trump urged congressional Republicans not to pass the bill, the PRESS Act died in the 188th Congress.[61]

Even if the PRESS Act had not suffered the same fate that has befallen every other proposal for a federal shield law, it would have been wildly underinclusive.

[57] West, *supra* note 6, at 2435 ("On a day-to-day basis, American journalists deal with legal uncertainties in the pursuit of news.").

[58] Protect Reporters from Exploitative State Spying Act, H.R. 4250, 118th Cong. (2023).

[59] *Id.* §§ 3, 4.

[60] Oliver Darcy, *A Bipartisan Bill Aims to Protect Journalists from Being Forced to Reveal Their Sources*, CNN (June 22, 2023, 10:46 PM), https://www.cnn.com/2023/06/22/media/bipartisan-bill-journalism-protections-reliable-sources/index.html.

[61] Charlie Savage, *Trump Tells Republicans to 'Kill' Reporter Shield Bill Passed Unanimously by House*, N.Y. Times (Nov. 20, 2024), https://www.nytimes.com/2024/11/20/us/politics/trump-press-act-freedom-reporters.html.

It overlooked the many other avenues that federal law enforcement has for acquiring and searching data: by purchasing records from private vendors, for example,[62] or by conducting searches of data that have already been acquired by other means, including through bulk national security surveillance.[63] Indeed, the FBI may and frequently does query data acquired under national security surveillance authorities for evidence of crimes without judicial oversight.[64]

This is not a problem that one can solve with simple statutory fixes. There is a more profound mismatch between the mechanism of a federal shield bill and contemporary law enforcement practices. Tactics of proactive and preventive policing, coupled with new technologies of data acquisition, storage, and interpretation, "produce dramatically different ways of identifying suspects."[65] These shifts in law enforcement techniques and technologies have produced new methods of investigation and identification that make traditional subpoenas and compulsory process less critical, although not entirely obsolete. The result is that much of the same information protected by shield laws is readily attainable by other means. The same problem animating the shield bill – the risk that compulsory process will lead sources and journalists to self-censor – also pervades bulk surveillance.[66]

In an era of bulk surveillance, retail protections for individual journalists from targeted compulsory process remain important, but they simply don't go far enough. The individualized protections offered by shield statutes do not, and cannot, address the shift in policing from reactive investigation of crime to models oriented toward proactive data acquisition, mining, and prevention.[67] Press-specific constitutional rights are not going to prevent the government from secretly acquiring and searching

[62] Matthew Tokson, *Government Purchases of Private Data*, 59 Wake Forest L. Rev. 269 (forthcoming 2024).

[63] Section 702 *Backdoor Searches: Myths and Facts*, Brennan Ctr. for Just., https://www.brennancenter.org/our-work/research-reports/fisa-section-702-backdoor-searches-myths-and-facts (last updated Nov. 30, 2023).

[64] Elizabeth Goitein, *The Year of Section 702 Reform, Part II: Closing the Gaps and Completing the Modernization of FISA*, Just Sec. (Apr. 18, 2023, https://www.justsecurity.org/86011/the-year-of-section-702-reform-part-ii-closing-the-gaps-and-completing-the-modernization-of-fisa/).

[65] Elizabeth E. Joh, *The New Surveillance Discretion: Automated Suspicion, Big Data, and Policing*, 10 Harv. L. & Pol'y Rev. 15, 16 (2016).

[66] Leonard Downie, Jr & Sara Rafsky, *The Obama Administration and the Press: Leak Investigations and Surveillance in Post-9/11 America*, Comm. to Protect Journalists (Oct. 10, 2013), https://cpj.org/wp-content/uploads/2013/10/us2013-english.pdf; Human Rights Watch, *With Liberty to Monitor All: How Large-Scale U.S. Surveillance Is Harming Journalism, Law, and American Democracy* (July 28, 2014), https://www.hrw.org/report/2014/07/28/liberty-monitor-all/how-large-scale-us-surveillance-harming-journalism-law-and; Jesse Holcomb & Amy Mitchell, *Investigative Journalists and Digital Security*, Pew Rsch. Ctr. (Feb. 5, 2015), http://www.journalism.org/2015/02/05/investigative-journalists-and-digital-security/; PEN Amer. Ctr., Chilling Effects: NSA Surveillance Drives U.S. Writers to Self-Censor (Nov. 12, 2013), https://www.pen.org/chilling-effects.

[67] Tom Tyler, *Police Discretion in the Twenty-first Century Surveillance State*, 2016 U. Chi. Legal F. 579, 581 (2016) (raising "questions about the ability of traditional legal concepts to effectively restrain modern criminal justice systems").

"vast stores of data about all of us, which they then can scrutinize whenever the fancy strikes them."[68] For one thing, there is no process or opportunity for individuals to intervene to object to the government's acquisition of information about them. In theory, legislation could require additional substantive or procedural standards to be met before the government could use data about or of the press, but, to date, restrictions on how lawfully acquired information can be used are rare.[69] In addition, the long-standing rule that the First Amendment is not offended as long as surveillance takes place in a manner consistent with the Fourth Amendment calls into question whether special rights would ever meaningfully constrain law enforcement's acquisition and use of information.[70]

More importantly, procedural protections such as the PRESS Act leave open law enforcement's ability to investigate journalists for substantive criminal violations. The PRESS Act appears to constrain law enforcement's ability to draw journalists into investigations of their sources, but because the avenues for substantive criminal liability remain quite broad, it may in fact create a perverse incentive to charge journalists directly as a way of avoiding the application of the special procedural rules that protect them. Journalists who publish government information are at risk of direct liability under a number of different statutes, including the Espionage Act, as well as the federal prohibition on receipt of stolen property.[71] The PRESS Act explicitly provides that it should not be construed to prevent law enforcement from investigating journalists who are "suspected of committing a crime."[72] In this respect, the PRESS Act is actually weaker than the DOJ guidelines that it is meant to codify; those guidelines apply whenever a reporter is "acting within the scope of newsgathering," defined to include the "receipt, possession, or publication" of information or the establishment of a way of receiving that information from a source.[73] In short, the DOJ guidelines explicitly provide that newsgathering is not a criminal act.[74]

Similarly, the Privacy Protection Act of 1980 generally requires law enforcement to use a subpoena instead of a warrant to conduct a newsroom search.[75] However, the Act contains a complicated, nested series of exceptions providing that a government official *may* conduct a search if there is probable cause that the journalist "has committed or is committing the criminal offense to which the materials relate," except if the offense is "receipt, possession, communication, or withholding" of the materials being sought.[76] In an exception to the exception to the exception, the

68 Barry Friedman, *Lawless Surveillance*, 97 N.Y.U. L. Rev. 1143, 1145 (2022).

69 Andrew Guthrie Ferguson, *Surveillance and the Tyrant Test*, 110 Geo. L.J. 205, 276 (2021).

70 *See infra* text accompanying notes 89–92.

71 18 U.S.C. § 641; Vladeck, *supra* note 38, at 228–31.

72 Protect Reporters from Exploitative State Spying Act, *supra* note 58, at Sec. 6.

73 28 C.F.R. pt. 50.10(b)(2)(ii)(A).

74 28 C.F.R. pt. 50.10(b)(2)(ii)(B).

75 42 U.S.C. § 2000aa.

76 42 U.S.C. §§ 2000aa(a)(1), (b)(1).

government *may* use a search warrant if there is probable cause to believe that the journalist violated the Espionage Act, the Atomic Energy Act, or child pornography laws.[77]

Even these exceptions may be underinclusive, however. Journalists may also face charges under theories of "third-party inchoate liability" for soliciting the disclosure of leaked information.[78] At the risk of repetition: The Privacy Protection Act does not apply to journalists who are charged with aiding and abetting or conspiring to violate the law. Procedural protections meant to prevent the state from using the press as a *source of evidence* in prosecutions of others do little to protect the press from opportunistic criminal prosecution. Instead, they simply submerge definitional questions about the scope of protection for newsgathering.

In this way, the PRESS Act highlights the problematic relationship between substance and process in criminal law enforcement. As William Stuntz noted almost thirty years ago, "[p]rocedural rules make broader criminal liability more attractive, since the latter can be used as a device for evading the costs of the former."[79] Special procedural protections reduce the risk that high costs of criminal sanctions might be "imposed for no reason (i.e., on the whim of some government official) or for a bad reason (e.g., the defendant's race or politics)."[80] In other words, Stuntz wrote, "[i]f the rights work, the specter of punishment for no reason or for evil reasons vanishes."[81] But as Stuntz points out, procedural protections are not enough: Substantive law must also draw lines between those who "deserve punishment" and those who do not.[82]

But substantive criminal law often sweeps incredibly broadly.[83] The prevalence of very broad laws, investigative power, and discretion calls into question the notion that the problem for press freedom is special rather than general. Perhaps the problem is different: Perhaps the underlying problem is that a powerful state, armed with nearly unfettered power to enforce the law in discretionary and discriminatory ways, may exercise that power against the press and against its critics. Even if and when it chooses not to do so, the threat of potential enforcement becomes a "sword of Damocles," generating anxiety and potentially leading the press to pull its punches in response.[84]

77 *Id.*

78 Vladeck, *supra* note 38, at 221. In my reading, even the DOJ guidelines do not effectively resolve whether soliciting disclosure of information from a source might amount to conspiracy.

79 William J. Stuntz, *Substance, Process, and the Civil-Criminal Line*, 7 J. CONTEM. LEGAL ISSUES 1, 10 (1996).

80 *Id.* at 7.

81 *Id.*

82 *Id.*

83 Kiel Brennan-Marquez, *Extremely Broad Laws*, 61 ARIZ. L. REV. 641 (2019).

84 Kiel Brennan-Marquez & Stephen E. Henderson, *Fourth Amendment Anxiety*, 55 AM. CRIM. L. REV. 1, 25 (2018).

21.2.2 *Doctrinal Problems*

Special protections are of limited value, in part, because their enforcement almost always depends on press institutions and journalists to pursue litigation after the fact. Start with a basic premise that recognizing special rights and privileges for the press would "offer them reliable protection from prosecution," deter government officials from searching and seizing journalists' electronic devices, and otherwise shelter newsgathering from law enforcement meddling.[85] At bottom, the argument for special constitutional protections must hinge on the belief that recognizing rights under the Press Clause would create meaningful incentives for government actors to behave differently.

The problem is that the existing special protections that we have, although strong on paper, are not strong enough to prevent misconduct. Consider, again, the search of Bryan Carmody's office. Both California law and the federal Privacy Protection Act prevent law enforcement from using search warrants to acquire journalists' unpublished work product.[86] Yet that is precisely what the San Francisco police did in Carmody's case. And once they did so, what was Carmody's remedy? Though Carmody received a $369,000 settlement after the fact, the existence of precise, long-standing legal protections did not deter the police.[87] Similarly, the Marion County Record and some of its employees have filed lawsuits against city and police officials in Marion, Kansas, arguing that the newsroom searches there violated their First Amendment rights.[88]

While prosecutors and judges might act differently in a world with more special protections, the incentives for police are unclear. A major doctrinal problem is that, in multiple areas of criminal procedure, Fourth Amendment standards for government conduct subsume First Amendment protections for free expression. Take searches and seizures, for example: In *Stanford Daily*, the Court held that the Fourth Amendment's warrant requirement was sufficient to vindicate the First Amendment interests implicated by a newsroom search.[89] As Alex Abdo has observed, courts usually consider the constitutionality of government surveillance

[85] Sonja R. West, *Awakening the Press Clause*, 58 UCLA L. REV. 1025, 1043–44 (2011).

[86] 42 U.S.C. § 2000aa; Cal. Evid. Code § 1070; Cal. Penal Code § 1524(g).

[87] Tim Cushing, *Documents Show SFPD Ignored the Press Pass the Department Had Issued to Brian Carmody in Order to Place Him Under Surveillance*, TECHDIRT (Jul. 13, 2020, 1:56 PM), https://www.techdirt.com/2020/07/13/documents-show-sfpd-ignored-press-pass-department-had-issued-to-brian-carmody-order-to-place-him-under-surveillance/.

[88] Sherman Smith, *Kansas Newspaper That Was Raided by Marion Police Sues Officials for Attack on Free Press*, KANSAS REFLECTOR (Apr. 1, 2024, 11:51 AM), https://kansasreflector.com/2024/04/01/kansas-newspaper-that-was-raided-by-marion-police-sues-officials-for-attack-on-free-press/; Katie Moore, *'Caught in the Crossfire': Third Lawsuit Filed After Police Raid on Kansas Newspaper*, THE KANSAS CITY STAR (May 29, 2024, 1:46 PM), https://www.kansascity.com/news/state/kansas/article287220630.html.

[89] Zurcher v. Stanford Daily, 436 U.S. 547, 565–66 (1978).

programs "primarily in Fourth Amendment terms."[90] The result is that, for many law enforcement demands, the existence of probable cause that a crime has occurred defeats a First Amendment claim that a search or seizure is overly intrusive. Similarly, the existence of probable cause supporting arrest typically trumps a claim that law enforcement unlawfully retaliated against an individual, including a journalist, for exercising their First Amendment rights.[91] Because the substantive criminal law is so broad, probable cause will often exist.[92]

A second problem relates to remedies. Ex post remedies are not particularly effective at deterring constitutional violations.[93] The key remedy for law enforcement conduct that is unconstitutional under the Fourth Amendment is the "widely reviled" exclusionary rule.[94] For many reasons, including because prosecutions of journalists are relatively rare, the exclusionary rule is unlikely to benefit the press. Civil rights lawsuits are also meant to deter police misconduct, but civil liability is difficult to come by. Qualified immunity shields from liability "all but the plainly incompetent or those who knowingly violate the law."[95] Money damages are also unlikely to meaningfully deter misconduct: Direct sanctions are rare, officers are often indemnified, and violations that cause "psychic injury" as their primary harm are hard to monetize.[96] Meanwhile, there are also barriers to injunctive relief: In *Los Angeles v. Lyons*, the Supreme Court held that litigants lack standing to get prospective injunctive relief unless they can demonstrate a "real and immediate threat" of future unlawful conduct by police.[97]

A third problem relates to the willingness of the press to litigate at all. In order for special protections to deter misconduct, the press would need to assert its newfound rights.[98] This is a familiar posture for press actors: In the past, press institutions have sometimes played the role of "legal instigators and enforcers" in both constitutional and statutory domains.[99] Indeed, the public's constitutional right of access to

[90] Alex Abdo, *Why Rely on the Fourth Amendment to Do the Work of the First?*, 127 YALE L.J. F. 444, 450 (2017–18).

[91] Nieves v. Bartlett, 139 S.Ct. 1715, 1726 (2019) ("The presence of probable cause should generally defeat a First Amendment retaliatory arrest claim.").

[92] Atwater v. City of Lago Vista, 532 U.S. 318, 354 (2001) ("If an officer has probable cause to believe that an individual has committed even a very minor criminal offense in his presence, he may, without violating the Fourth Amendment, arrest the offender.").

[93] Oren Bar-Gill & Barry Friedman, *Taking Warrants Seriously*, 106 NW. U. L. REV. 1609, 1613 (2012).

[94] *Id.* at 1626.

[95] Malley v. Briggs, 475 U.S. 335, 341 (1986).

[96] Bar-Gill & Friedman, *supra* note 93, at 1628.

[97] 461 U.S. 95 (1983).

[98] Mark Tushnet, *An Essay on Rights*, 62 TEX. L. REV. 1363, 1380 (1984) ("Because rights have a social context, their realization as a fact of social life rather than their mere recognition in political and legal rhetoric requires that right-holders have the material and psychological resources that will allow them to exercise their rights.").

[99] RonNell Andersen Jones, *Litigation, Legislation, and Democracy in a Post-Newspaper America*, 68 WASH. & LEE L. REV. 557, 559 (2011).

government proceedings was developed in litigation brought by newspapers.[100] But the news industry is also sometimes unwilling to assert itself. In part, of course, this is because shrinking budgets make costly litigation a luxury good.[101] In part, too, news industry participants are sometimes unwilling to litigate because the professional devotion to objectivity in journalism has made the press "reluctant to aggressively confront abuses of power."[102]

This is a particular problem in the context of law enforcement. As Oren Bar-Gill and Barry Friedman observe, "To achieve its deterrent effect, litigation over Fourth Amendment violations must occur regularly enough to be a plausible threat and to develop the law necessary to provide rules for police officials."[103] But even if they had the resources, most press institutions do not want to repeatedly sue the police. By doing so, they risk losing access to sources and places they need for reporting, as well as more targeted forms of retribution, and they may well become part of the story.[104]

21.2.3 *Conceptual Problems*

One problem with special protections of particular relevance to this volume is identifying who ought to receive them.[105] An exemption-based structure requires decision-makers (and, ultimately, courts) to determine whether a would-be claimant is entitled to protections intended for "the press" or not.[106] As Sonja West has described it in the context of campaign finance law, the structure immediately confronts the objection that "there is no acceptable way to identify which speakers should be allowed to claim a media exemption and which should not."[107]

Institutions have differing capacities to apply these exemptions. The stakes of identifying "the press" are undoubtedly higher as legacy media outlets have cratered and web publications, social media, podcasts, and other forms of content production have taken their place. In settings with ample time to consider whether an individual or an organization is a member of "the press," I think the identification hurdle, as it has been construed, is overstated: Courts and other decision-makers have been

[100] Richmond Newspapers, Inc. v. Virginia, 448 U.S. 555 (1980); Press-Enter. Co. v. Super. Ct. of Cal., Riverside Cnty., 464 U.S. 501 (1984); Press-Enter. Co. v. Super. Ct. of Cal., Riverside Cnty., 478 U.S. 1 (1986).

[101] Andersen Jones, *supra* note 99; *see also* Knight Foundation, *In Defense of the First Amendment* (2016) (reporting that "the news industry is weaker in its ability to pursue legal activity around First Amendment-related issues than it was 10 years ago").

[102] Hannah Bloch-Wehba, *The Ideology of Press Freedom*, 14 UC Irvine L. Rev. 1, 7 (2024).

[103] Bar-Gill & Friedman, *supra* note 93, at 1631.

[104] Bloch-Wehba, *supra* note 102, at 7.

[105] West, *supra* note 6, at 2437 ("Then there are the bloggers.").

[106] Sonja R. West, *Favoring the Press*, 106 Calif. L. Rev. 91, 115–20 (2018).

[107] Sonja R. West, *The Media Exemption Puzzle of Campaign Finance Laws*, 164 U. Pa. L. Rev. Online 253, 255 (2016).

administering press-specific statutory exemptions for decades without much trouble.[108]

For police-making decisions on the fly, identifying journalists is a more serious challenge but still a manageable one.[109] Consider the uprisings against racial violence that occurred after George Floyd's murder in 2020. For over 100 days straight, people demonstrated in Portland, Oregon, frequently coming into conflict with city and federal law enforcement.[110] Soon after the uprisings began, a group of local legal observers and press actors filed a complaint in federal court alleging that law enforcement was targeting journalists and other "neutrals."[111] The district court issued a temporary restraining order barring city police from "arresting, threatening to arrest, or using physical force directed against any person whom they know or reasonably should know is a Journalist or Legal Observer. . ., unless the Police have probable cause to believe that such individual has committed a crime."[112] The result was that, after the order was issued, protestors and bystanders could be arrested for failing to disperse, but press and legal observers could not.[113] In a chaotic situation, the police needed some way of identifying the press in order to afford them special protections, so the court defined "indicia of being a Journalist" – official press passes or "distinctive clothing that identifies the wearer as a member of the press."[114] In short, there were administrable ways of distinguishing "the press" from ordinary speakers even under challenging conditions.

The newly dynamic nature of the press makes the identification problem more difficult, however. As press functions become more widely distributed, the costs of protecting the press also rise. In part, the costs of protection are higher because the press industry is harder to contain as its powerful gatekeepers shrink and vanish. A full sketch of the news industry's downward turn is beyond the scope of this chapter. The short version is that the advertising-based business model of the press has been ill-equipped to compete with platform-based advertising.[115] The rise of programmatic advertising "disrupted the distribution model for news, took over the

108 Richard L. Hasen, *From Bloggers in Pajamas to the Gateway Pundit: How Government Entities Do and Should Identify Professional Journalists for Access and Protection in* The Future of Press Freedom: Democracy, Law, and the News in Changing Times 271 (RonNell Andersen Jones & Sonja R. West eds., 2025) [hereinafter The Future of Press Freedom].

109 *See* Simon, *supra* note 31, at Ch. 4 (describing LAPD and LASD's position that only law enforcement-issued credentials could serve as identification for a journalist).

110 Luke Mogelson, *Revisiting Portland's "Summer of Rage,"* The New Yorker (June 20, 2023), https://www.newyorker.com/culture/photo-booth/revisiting-portlands-summer-of-rage.

111 Complaint at 1, Index Newspapers LLC v. City of Portland, Case No. 3:20-cv-1035-SI (D. Or. June 28, 2020).

112 Temporary Restraining Order at 8, Index Newspapers LLC v. City of Portland, Case No. 3:20-cv-1035-SI, (D. Or. July 2, 2020), ECF No. 33.

113 *Id.*

114 *Id.* at 9.

115 Nikki Usher, News for the Rich, White and Blue: How Place and Power Distort American Journalism 134–35 (2021).

creation and the pricing of the advertising market, and colonized audience attention."[116] Newspapers and legacy press outlets suffered from diminishing ad dollars. Many folded.

The same advances in information and communication technology that reshaped commercial advertising also changed journalism itself. The emergence of social media platforms redistributed the power to communicate from legacy news media institutions to individuals, nonprofits, civil society organizations, and others. Indeed, the digital age was widely heralded for its "democratization" of communications.[117] As Jack Balkin has observed, "changes in technology and the economics of mass communication" have fundamentally reshaped journalism.[118]

Technological shifts that "democratized" communications and demolished the news industry made it both easier and harder to identify press functions.[119] On the one hand, new platforms with new business models increasingly fulfilled some of the traditional functions of the press industry.[120] Partly as a result, methods of identifying the press based on business structure or medium would be underinclusive, leaving out freelance journalists or those who publish exclusively online.[121] At the same time, the profusion of online platforms and publications has made it easier for individuals to "act at times as a casual journalist."[122] As Sue Robinson and Cathy DeShano write, "Seldom has such a disruptive phenomenon penetrated the inner echelons of the press."[123]

The redistribution of the press function among so many different actors also makes press-specific protections more costly to law enforcement and to society at large. In a world in which the major press freedom cases were about reporters affiliated with recognized, mainstream news organizations, the press was not only easy to identify, it was also small and elite. Today, the elite press might be even smaller, but it is much more difficult to identify. The disintermediation of press activities, such as gathering and disseminating information, means that many other people can plausibly claim to be exercising at least some press functions. Some of them, as Professor Rick Hasen notes, are better described as faux journalists than real ones.[124]

[116] *Id.* at 141.

[117] Jack M. Balkin, *Old-School/New-School Speech Regulation*, 127 Harv. L. Rev. 2296, 2304 (2014); Reno v. ACLU, 521 U.S. 844, 870 (1997).

[118] Balkin, *supra* note 117, at 2302.

[119] Emily Bell & Taylor Owen, *The Platform Press: How Silicon Valley Reengineered Journalism*, Colum. Journalism Rev. (Mar. 29, 2017), https://www.cjr.org/tow_center_reports/platform-press-how-silicon-valley-reengineered-journalism.php/.

[120] *Id.*

[121] West, *supra* note 6, at 2449.

[122] *Id.* at 2448.

[123] Sue Robinson & Cathy DeShano, *"Anyone Can Know": Citizen Journalism and the Interpretive Community of the Mainstream Press*, 12 Journalism 963 (2011).

[124] Hasen, *supra* note 108.

Administering press freedoms is therefore not only harder because the press is more difficult to identify. Rather, any press-protective rule will need to be farther-reaching, both to reach individuals who may not resemble legacy journalists and to accommodate a new mode of thinking about the press's functions, instead of its identity. In other words, the concern is not just about administrability or the extent to which a press-specific rule might violate the First Amendment; it's rather about the social costs that press-specific protections might produce once they are broadened to capture all the press's functions.

21.2.4 *Costs*

Special protections are not only disappointingly ineffective. Adopting them may also impose additional costs. The first is political: The recognition of press-specific rights may, perversely, reinforce distrust and resentment of the press. When we create special privileges for the in-group, we reinforce the inferiority of the out-group. As Jamal Greene points out, to the extent the recognition of constitutional rights hinges on a binary choice between those who do and do not hold rights, "it places us in an adversarial rather than a cooperative posture vis-à-vis other members of the polity."[125] This is, of course, always a concern, but is perhaps particularly salient amid widespread distrust of the press. My worry is that emphasizing the exceptional nature of the press may actually accentuate the tendency to "delineat[e] the press as an enemy . . . that ought to be distrusted, countered, and perhaps ultimately stripped of ordinarily observed rights and liberties."[126]

The second cost is that recognizing and protecting press rights can legitimate law enforcement activities that suppress others' rights.[127] In a sense, this is a cost related to the prevailing way in which press rights have been framed as examples of "negative liberty" to be free of government interference.[128] When we create special rights for the press, we enable certain individuals and institutions to be free of forms of government intrusion that are otherwise expected. We also forego the opportunity to recognize *positive* expressive rights for the broader public.[129]

[125] Jamal Greene, *Rights as Trumps?*, 132 Harv. L. Rev. 28, 80 (2018) ("If my assertion of rights depends strictly on your lack thereof, and vice versa, it is natural for me to *see* you not as a friend whose different commitments must be reconciled with mine but rather as an enemy who is, in too real a sense, out to destroy me.").

[126] RonNell Andersen Jones & Lisa Grow Sun, *Enemy Construction and the Press*, 49 Ariz. St. L.J. 1301, 1308 (2017).

[127] *Cf.* Bloch-Wehba, *supra* note 102, at 49.

[128] Tushnet, *supra* note 98, at 1393 ("[T]he predominance of negative rights creates an ideological barrier to the extension of positive rights in our culture.").

[129] Daryl J. Levinson, *Framing Transactions in Constitutional Law*, 111 Yale L.J. 1311, 1363 (2002); Victor Pickard, *Legal Foundations for Non-Reformist Media Reforms: A Positive-Rights Paradigm for Guaranteeing a Universal Press System*, *in* The Future of Press Freedom, *supra* note 108 (describing how the framing of press rights as negative rights "disproportionately benefit[s] media corporations' rights over the public's").

Consider one example: Andrea Sahouri, a reporter for the Des Moines Register, was covering a Black Lives Matter protest in 2020 when she was arrested along with dozens of protestors. Unlike nearly every other reporter who was arrested during that summer, Sahouri was actually prosecuted on misdemeanor charges of failure to disperse and interference with an official act.[130] Sahouri, the Register, and amici argued that, as working press, Sahouri should not be prosecuted because her activities were fully protected by the First Amendment. She was ultimately acquitted.

Imagine that Sahouri had a unique right not to comply with a lawful order to disperse. What are the consequences of recognizing Sahouri's right for all of those other individuals who are expected to comply? There are, as I noted above, expressive consequences – the recognition of Sahouri's rights suggests that ordinary protestors have none and thus places the press and the public on unequal footing. It confers a privilege on Sahouri to engage in expressive activities while the public is simultaneously denied an ability to do so. There are thus distributional consequences. Protecting press actors may lead to more police time and resources being dedicated to arresting protestors instead of journalists.

Recognizing special rights will always create some inequality between rightsholders and non-rightsholders. But if recognizing special rights also aggravates unequal treatment by focusing law enforcement energies elsewhere, then the press not only benefits from but becomes a participant in a broader injustice. Moreover, once the press has received special rights that benefit it directly, it is less likely to act in solidarity with other speakers or advocate for the expressive rights of others.[131] Perhaps most alarming, then, is the fact that special rights, by separating press actors from other speakers and conferring special privileges upon them, make it less likely that the press industry will act in solidarity with other speakers.

21.3 NEW APPROACHES

The usual framing of press-specific protections – as special rights, privileges, or defenses that only press actors can invoke – is reactive rather than proactive. It assumes that the existence of press-specific protections will deter abuses and infringements on press freedom, and it relies on individuals and press institutions to litigate and pursue claims against powerful actors after violations have occurred.

The assumption that special protections will work to curtail the gravest threats to journalism is rooted in a fundamental faith that individual rights effectively

[130] Ryan J. Foley, *Reporter Faces Trial in Case Seen as Attack on Press Rights*, AP NEWS (Mar. 5, 2021, 2:14 PM), https://apnews.com/general-news-domestic-news-domestic-news-3a3ad2a4765852832c2eab841ff2824b.

[131] Jonathan R. Macey, *Public Choice: The Theory of the Firm and the Theory of Market Exchange*, 74 CORNELL L. REV. 43, 46 (1988) (summarizing basic insight of public choice theory that legislation is a product of influence by "pressure groups").

safeguard government accountability. At bottom, they are designed for a different time, one in which the press and the government occupied a relatively stable "equilibrium," and each institution served as a check on the excesses of the other.[132] As Christina Koningisor and Lyrissa Lidsky have demonstrated with respect to government secrecy in particular, the "underlying beliefs that the press is sufficiently powerful and the government is sufficiently constrained" underpin many of the core features of press freedom jurisprudence.[133] Today, however, both elements of that equilibrium are under strain, with the diminishment of journalism and the rise in government power altering the balance in favor of the state.[134] Meanwhile, these shifts are occurring against a background of substantial uncertainty about the scope and reach of First Amendment protections.

Without dramatically limiting the discretion afforded to criminal law enforcement agencies, doctrinal exceptionalism will not provide sufficient protection to the press function. Yet we most often see narrow and procedural protections instead of broad and substantive ones. The reason is, at least in part, ideological: The appeal of special procedural protections is in part that they enable the press to claim legal protection without outright challenging or critiquing substantive criminal law. Press institutions often prefer not to challenge law enforcement power outright, as doing so "could be seen to undermine journalistic objectivity by inserting press institutions into a broader debate."[135] Instead, the press has embraced a strategy of "seeking specific protections for journalists or 'neutral' actors" while leaving broader substantive criminal law intact.[136] Press institutions have historically been reluctant to take a position on substantive issues related to criminal law enforcement. As I argue in earlier work, the press's commitment to journalistic objectivity has also influenced its legal strategy and shaped its choices about advocacy.[137] Because of a combination of scarce resources and institutional values, press institutions often prioritize litigation about issues such as government transparency or newsgathering rights instead of broader accountability-oriented litigation.

All of this is to say that I share the press exceptionalists' concern that reporters and journalists face unacceptable levels of uncertainty about their legal protections as they gather and report the news. Where we part ways is with respect to the appropriate solutions. If my account so far is correct, then special protections are not the right path forward. So how can we effectively constrain government meddling and interference with the press function without special rights?

Part of the answer must be that any rights-based approach to press freedom has to be backed up by meaningful police reforms that decrease law enforcement's ability

[132] Christina Koningisor & Lyrissa Lidsky, *First Amendment Disequilibrium*, 110 VA. L. REV. 1, 18–19 (2024).

[133] *Id.* at 28.

[134] *Id.*

[135] Bloch-Wehba, *supra* note 102, at 48.

[136] *Id.* at 50.

[137] *Id.* at 43–44.

to interfere with press functions. These reforms are more likely to be holistic than press-specific. To date, however, the press industry has typically stayed out of debates about police authority unless they directly implicate journalism.[138] The press has been short-sighted about the potential threats that criminal law enforcement may pose to cherished constitutional values.

If the press were to change strategies – if the industry were to pursue greater limits on law enforcement power to ensure that newsgathering could operate with fewer inhibitions – it would reshape their advocacy efforts. The press is a powerful interest group capable of influencing policymaking, but it has chosen not to engage in many legislative debates that have deep implications for newsgathering.

A primary area on which the press ought to take a more aggressive position is the policing of protest. As one press freedom advocate has put it, "[C]overing protests routinely is the most dangerous activity for journalists."[139] Mass arrests at protests are common, and law enforcement often uses aggressive techniques to maintain order that have dramatic implications for journalists' safety and ability to gather the news. For selfish reasons, then, the press industry ought to support meaningful reductions in law enforcement's power to curtail protest.

Some changes to law enforcement practices are already afoot to restrict police discretion in controlling demonstrations and protest. In the last several years, political pressure and court-ordered settlements have compelled some of the nation's largest law enforcement agencies to change how they police protests, including by creating new systems to respond to demonstrations[140] and restricting the use of "less-lethal" munitions.[141]

Although these changes undoubtedly benefit the journalists and reporters who interact with law enforcement, they are largely not "special rights" – they reflect that broader changes to the policing of dissent are necessary to protect expressive freedoms.[142] As Joel Simon pointed out in his report for the Knight First Amendment Institute at Columbia University, "Many of the most serious press freedom violations that have occurred in recent years do not stem from any difficulty on the part of the police in distinguishing who is and who is not a journalist."[143]

[138] *Id.* at 48.

[139] Simon, *supra* note 31, at Ch. 4.

[140] Maria Cramer, *N.Y.P.D. Must Rewrite Rules for Policing Protests After Sweeping Deal*, N.Y. Times (Sept. 5, 2023), https://www.nytimes.com/2023/09/05/nyregion/nypd-settlement-protesters-penning.html.

[141] *See, e.g.*, A.B. 48, State Assemb., Reg. Sess. (Ca. 2021); S.B. 20-217, Gen. Assemb., Reg. Sess. (Colo. 2020); S 2963, 191st Gen. Court (Mass. 2020).

[142] In some jurisdictions, police treatment of journalists is governed by explicit special statutory requirements. Even there, however, special protections frequently fail to work as intended. Kevin Rector, *LAPD Treatment of Journalists Denounced, Again, After Abortion Rights Protest Downtown*, L.A. Times (June 25, 2022, 2:46 PM), https://www.latimes.com/california/story/2022-06-25/lapd-treatment-of-journalists-denounced-again-after-abortion-rights-protest-downtown.

[143] Simon, *supra* note 31, at Preface and Introduction.

Instead, intentional targeting of press actors by law enforcement appears increasingly and disturbingly common.

The impediments to recovery of monetary damages for civil rights violations also suggest that the press ought to take a more aggressive and proactive role. The press could, for example, call for an end to qualified immunity, which often stands in the way of recovery for civil rights violations.[144] Return for a moment to *Villarreal v. City of Laredo*, the case in which Lagordiloca was charged with misdemeanor solicitation of nonpublic information. While the U.S. Court of Appeals for the Fifth Circuit conceded that Villarreal had the right to publish the information that she received, the majority held that the city of Laredo was entitled to qualified immunity because it was not "clearly established" that Villarreal had a right to solicit nonpublic information from a government source – in other words, that she had a right to gather the news.[145] The court suggested that Lagordiloca should have "followed Texas law, or challenged that law in court," before engaging in newsgathering.[146] As I write, the Fifth Circuit is reconsidering Villarreal's case after the Supreme Court remanded it.

Despite lingering uncertainty about the outcome for Lagordiloca, *Villarreal* suggests that press institutions should affirmatively seek legal clarity about the scope of newsgathering and thus invites the press to consider what such a litigation strategy could look like. In particular, there are two areas in which the law of newsgathering could be developed. First, the press could employ a coordinated litigation effort to clarify and develop newsgathering protections. Numerous states have laws that affect newsgathering. While Texas' prohibition on the solicitation of nonpublic information seems unique, many states have criminalized other elements of newsgathering through prohibitions on trespass, interference with official acts, or the receipt of stolen property. A litigation strategy oriented toward limiting the impact of these criminal laws on the free flow of information may produce some certainty about constitutional newsgathering protections. It may even produce major benefits for press freedom. It need not, however, be press specific or even centered on the press.

One such strategy might center on the role of subjective intent as a limit on broad criminal statutes that affect newsgathering. For First Amendment scholars, the role of intent in circumscribing potential civil and criminal liability is familiar: In cases involving obscenity, defamation, and true threats, the Supreme Court has required that, even in cases involving utterly unprotected speech, prosecutors must demonstrate that a defendant acted with subjective intent to produce the danger that the law is meant to prevent.[147] But many statutes criminalizing newsgathering already include mens rea requirements, limiting this strategy's utility. A further-reaching

[144] *See, e.g.*, Ending Qualified Immunity Act, H.R. 2847 118th Cong. (2023).
[145] *Villarreal*, 94 F.4th at 395.
[146] *Villarreal*, 94 F.4th at 381.
[147] Counterman v. Colorado, 600 U.S. 66, 76–78 (2023).

strategy might be modeled on the successful effort to secure judicial recognition and protection of the right to record government officials in public.[148] That effort involved a mix of pre-enforcement challenges and Section 1983 suits.[149] Notably, although the ability to record is of critical importance to journalists and the press, the right to do so is not limited to those exercising the press function: It is a right possessed by all.[150]

Another area for development is the use of class action lawsuits against law enforcement agencies that systematically engage in actions that infringe on press freedom. Litigation over racial profiling in traffic enforcement provides a useful model: Class actions alleging a pattern or practice of discriminatory enforcement that violates the Fourth and Fourteenth Amendments have overcome some of the many barriers to police reform and resulted in ongoing court-ordered monitoring.[151] If press actors have compelling evidence that a police agency is purposefully engaging in practices to stifle newsgathering and retaliate against First Amendment-protected activity, law enforcement reform litigation can be a powerful tool. Indeed, police reform litigation is doubly significant for the press because it not only relies on government information (which the press might be skilled at uncovering) but also frequently uncovers additional information of significant public concern (which the press could use in its news reporting).[152]

Nevertheless, it is not at all obvious that efforts to "settle the law" through litigation will necessarily advance press freedom.[153] *Villarreal* itself reveals a circuit court that is highly deferential to criminal law enforcement. Efforts to clarify and strengthen the law of newsgathering may risk undermining the tenuous protections that currently exist. Indeed, in the context of the Espionage Act, some have suggested that "benign indeterminacy" ultimately may be preferable to settling the question.[154]

Broader restrictions are necessary to reshape police authority and law enforcement's relationship with the press. But legal action is unlikely to accomplish these goals without sustained pressure and community involvement. In this respect, it is a real problem that many press institutions have taken the position that objectivity

[148] Margot E. Kaminski, *Privacy and the Right to Record*, 97 B.U. L. Rev. 167 (2017).

[149] *See, e.g.*, Am. Civil Liberties Union of Ill. v. Alvarez, 679 F.3d 583 (7th Cir. 2012); Glik v. Cunniffe, 655 F.3d 78 (1st Cir. 2011); Fields v. City of Phila., 862 F.3d 353 (3d Cir. 2017).

[150] Jocelyn Simonson, *Beyond Body Cameras: Defending a Robust Right to Record the Police*, 104 Geo. L.J. 1559 (2016).

[151] *See, e.g.*, Sunita Patel, *Jumping Hurdles to Sue the Police*, 104 Minn. L. Rev. 2257 (2020) (discussing barriers to structural police reform).

[152] Hannah Bloch-Wehba, *Visible Policing: Technology, Transparency, and Democratic Control*, 109 Cal. L. Rev. 917 (2021).

[153] Simon, *supra* note 31, at Ch. 4 ("The obvious solution is to try to settle the law.").

[154] William H. Freivogel, *Publishing National Security Secrets: The Case for "Benign Indeterminacy*,"3 Journal of Nat'l Sec. L. & Pol'y 95 (2009); Harold Edgar & Benno C. Schmidt, Jr, *The Espionage Statutes and Publication of Defense Information*, 73 Colum. L. Rev. 929, 936 (1973).

requires reporters to act apolitically. Indeed, many news organizations bar their employees from engaging in political activism or supporting political causes.[155] These policies inhibit the ability of journalists and reporters to challenge how law enforcement clamps down on free expression. Ironically, the objectivity paradigm prevents journalists from participating in grassroots organizing alongside others who are advocating for their First Amendment rights.

Even so, press institutions can take a more aggressive tack in addressing law enforcement agencies' choices in interacting with the communities they serve. Press institutions might take the lead in advocating for new training, policies, and regulations for how law enforcement engages with First Amendment rightsholders, for example. Or they might call for meaningful constraints on law enforcement surveillance, in recognition of pervasive monitoring's implications for free expression.[156]

21.4 CONCLUSION

As mainstream news outlets wither and the job of producing press coverage is distributed more broadly, the classic protections for press freedom are becoming less effective at protecting journalists. The distribution of press work means that journalists are harder to identify, and it is therefore more difficult to determine whether an individual is entitled to special protections or not. Meanwhile, very broad substantive criminal laws also permit law enforcement to investigate, monitor, threaten, and ultimately punish press actors, regardless of special protections that may apply. This dynamic is especially concerning as states have acted to criminalize protest activities,[157] undercover investigations,[158] and other expressive conduct.[159] Broad statutes are proliferating; at the same time, First Amendment doctrine supplies only limited avenues for effectively challenging them.

In short, the problem that press freedom faces is not simply a problem of insufficient protections; rather, it is that any procedural protections are likely to be less effective against a very powerful state.[160] Press freedom advocacy needs to become bolder, braver, and more aggressive if it is to ensure that the values of journalism remain viable amid threats to democratic discourse and critical news coverage.

[155] Bloch-Wehba, *supra* note 102, at 38.

[156] Press Release, Brennan Ctr. for Just., Senate Approves Massive Expansion of Government Surveillance Power; Brennan Center Reacts (Apr. 19, 2024) https://www.brennancenter.org/our-work/analysis-opinion/senate-approves-massive-expansion-government-surveillance-power-brennan.

[157] International Center for Not-For-Profit Law, *supra* note 32.

[158] Animal Legal Defense Fund v. Wasden, 878 F.3d 1184 (9th Cir. 2018); Animal Legal Defense Fund v. Reynolds, 8 F.4th 781 (8th Cir. 2021).

[159] Dream Defenders v. Governor of the State of Florida, 57 F.4th 879 (11th Cir. 2023); Oklahoma State Conference of NAACP v. O'Connor, 569 F. Supp.3d 1145 (W. D. Okla. 2021); McKesson v. Doe, 601 U.S. __ (2024).

[160] *Cf.* Brennan-Marquez, *supra* note 83.

PART VI

Supporting the Press Function

22

The Right to Know

Wesley Lowery

In June 1945, the U.S. Supreme Court issued a 4,900-word opinion that significantly curbed the power of an aspiring monopoly known as the Associated Press (AP).[1]

The case arose out of the wire service's adoption of two new bylaws. The first allowed its 1,200 member newspapers to block their competitors from joining the service, thus denying a large number of news outlets access to the vital information provided by the wire. The second banned member newspapers from selling their content directly to any nonmember newspaper. In short, news organizations that were members of the AP had access to news from around the country and the world, but those that were not part of the news agency were denied not only the AP's wire content but also all content produced by the member papers themselves. If one of their competitors managed to gain AP membership, then they were banned from joining as well. The Supreme Court, however, ruled that these new policies were antitrust violations under the Sherman Act, which, among other things, explicitly prohibits businesses from banding together to undercut their competition.

Among its defenses, the AP had argued the government was infringing on its constitutionally protected press freedoms. But Justice Hugo Black, writing for the Court, rejected that argument and held that the First Amendment did not allow the AP to run nonmember papers out of business. In fact, he asserted that the constitutional provision functioned to ensure the opposite. The First Amendment, Black wrote, "rests on the assumption that the widest possible dissemination of information from diverse and antagonistic sources is essential to the welfare of the public," and "a free press is a condition of a free society."

Rather than simply a ban on government interference, Black identified in the First Amendment an *affirmative* right, held by each American, to have access to the breadth and depth of information that only a robust and diverse press can provide. Black's son would later recall that his father believed press freedom meant more to "the preservation of our democratic republic than" any other part of the

[1] Associated Press v. United States, 326 U.S. 1 (1945).

Constitution, even as he believed it was necessary to break up concentrated media power and "(disperse) that power more equably."[2]

Black's contention that there is a public right to robust, accurate information has been a core value held by many of America's most consequential journalists, who understood it to be a central prerequisite of any nation that aspires to be equal, equitable, and just: "The people must know before they can act. And there is no educator to compare with the press," wrote Ida B. Wells.[3]

Half a century later, Ralph McGill expounded on this idea, declaring, "Freedom of the press is not the personal property of any one editor or publisher, or of any association of them. It is not something that can be locked in the safe at night . . . It is merely one of the guarantees to the people. It is their property."[4]

Most often taken as ensuring a freedom *of* the press as an industry, Black's ruling suggests a more proper reading of the First Amendment provides an individual right *to* the press, namely, that citizens in our democracy will have access to reliable, accurate, and comprehensive information in order to empower their full enfranchisement in our democracy, with the promise that each citizen has a *right to know*.

A free press is often heralded as a key cornerstone of American democracy, functioning as a vital institution tasked with informing the public and holding those in power accountable. Yet, as the industry faces an existential crisis, with the collapse of traditional business models and the rise of deep political polarization amid a sea of misinformation and propaganda, it has become increasingly clear that thinking of press freedom only as a market that must be protected from government interference cannot sustain the kind of robust, diverse, and accessible press that a healthy democracy requires. This chapter argues that to truly fulfill the promise of a "right to know" for all people, we must reimagine the relationship between the press and the public and consider bold new forms of public support for journalism.

***

By the time of Black's opinion in *Associated Press*, the American press had evolved far beyond what it was 150 years earlier, when James Madison first crafted the language that would become the First Amendment. In his later writings, Madison argued that in a representative republic in which citizens elect their leaders, care of the public opinion is a paramount concern. "Without the rule of public opinion, government cannot rightfully be considered free," wrote historian Colleen A. Sheehan of Madison's ideology, noting that he and other founders took it as a given that there would be a vibrant, diverse, privately owned American press and that the government had a proactive obligation to ensure that it remained so. "In Madison's understanding of free government, the representative is thus made

[2] Hugo Black, Jr., My Father: A Remembrance (1975).

[3] Ida B. Wells, *Self-Help*, *in* Southern Horrors: Lynch Law in All Its Phases (1892).

[4] Ralph McGill, *There Is Time Yet*, The Atlantic, Sept. 1944.

responsible for influencing and guiding public opinion … Because public opinion is sovereign in a free society, the republican statesman is obliged to advance its formation and expression."[5]

By the late 1800s and early 1900s, the American press had transformed from a relatively niche industry in which men of letters debated the vital issues of the day into loyal organs of competing political parties and then, finally, into an increasingly powerful form of mass communication. "Far more important than any part they ever played in politics, newspapers finally established themselves in an indispensable role as journals of vital information," opined Ken Cooper, the longtime chief executive of the Associated Press.[6]

From the beginning, however, this new form of the press, charged with disseminating nonpartisan information, faced criticism for failing to live up to the nobility of its mission. As the century turned, newspaper titans Joseph Pulitzer and William Randolph Hearst pioneered "yellow journalism" – a sensationalist style that blended fact and fiction in order to maximize profits. In turn, Adolph S. Ochs founded The New York Times on the promise that its news reports would be unbiased, staid, and impartial. Yet, in response to The Times' failures to live up to its own stated standards, critics like Walter Lippmann lambasted the paper, noting that for all its vows of impartiality, its reports often depicted a version of reality skewed by its journalists' establishmentarian biases. "The current theory of American newspaperdom is that an abstraction like the truth and a grace like fairness must be sacrificed whenever anyone thinks the necessities of civilization require the sacrifice,"[7] Lippmann wrote, accusing The Times of censoring views and ignoring facts that cut against status quo beliefs.

Newspaper editors largely rejected Lippmann's calls for rigorous journalistic methods (even as they later developed a self-mythology in which they claimed him as their patron saint). Generations of critics echoed Lippmann and other early twentieth-century press dissidents concerning the dangers of a greedy, lazy, irresponsible commercial press and were similarly dismissed.[8]

[5] Colleen A. Sheehan, *The Politics of Public Opinion: James Madison's "Notes on Government,"* 49 Wm. & Mary Q. 609 (1992).

[6] Kent Cooper, The Right to Know: An Exposition of the Evils of News Suppression and Propaganda (1956).

[7] Walter Lippmann, Liberty and the News (1920).

[8] *History*, News Leaders Association, https://members.newsleaders.org/asne-history (last visited June 26, 2024) (noting that the American Society of News Editors, now the News Leaders Association, was founded in 1922 by newspaper editors angry and defensive about similar criticisms leveled by NAACP president Moorfield Storey and journalist Frederick Lewis Allen that called for a more considerate, responsible press); Ben H. Bagdikian, The New Media Monopoly (2004) ("The news media suffer from built-in biases that protect corporate power and consequently weaken the public's ability to understand forces that create the American scene. These biases in favor of the status quo … do not seem to change materially over time.").

During World War II, University of Chicago President Robert Hutchins and Time magazine founder Henry Luce convened a thirteen-member panel of prominent scholars to examine the state of the press. In its 1947 final report, the Hutchins Commission observed and warned that

> [News] agencies can facilitate thought and discussion. They can stifle it. They can advance the progress of civilization or they can thwart it. They can debase and vulgarize mankind. They can endanger the peace of the world; they can do so accidentally, in a fit of absence of mind. They can play up or down the news and its significance, foster and feed emotions, create complacent fictions and blind spots, misuse the great words, and uphold empty slogans ... [t]heir scope and power are increasing every day as new instruments become available to them. These instruments can spread lies faster and farther than our forefathers dreamed.[9]

If the charge of the press is to nurture our public opinion, which in turn powers our democracy, then the performance of the press can be judged by the health of that democracy. By that measure, then as now, there is no question our press has fallen desperately short.

The Hutchins Commission noted that the American press was controlled by private businessmen who too often utilized their presses to spread divisiveness, misinformation, and political propaganda. Its members warned that an irresponsible press that prioritized profits over the public good would result in an American populace willing to support significant governmental impositions on press freedom. Today, the leader of one of our country's major political parties proclaims the press "the enemy of the people," vows to alter libel and defamation laws in order to undercut press freedoms, and directs his raucous crowds to target individual journalists who fail to indulge him. We are living the Hutchins Commission's nightmare.

***

The technological innovations of the last century – from broadcast radio and television to cable and then the digital revolution ushered in by the internet – have upended the media industry, the public square, and the geopolitical order. Ultimately, cellphones, broadband internet, and social media have placed publishing and distribution power in the hands of every individual citizen, giving each the equivalent of their own printing press and the possibility that their dispatches, no matter how factual or farcical, could be consumed by the world.

We, furthermore, live in an era of significant media consolidation. Locally owned newspapers beat out and bought out their cross-town competitors, before themselves combining into regional and then national chains. Many of those companies then shifted from being privately owned to publicly traded companies, requiring them to optimize profit at the expense of the information needs of the public. The internet

[9] Commission on Freedom of the Press, A Free and Responsible Press (1947).

ripped the heart out of the print advertising business and upended the general-interest news bundle, forcing publishers to chase online traffic and decode ever-changing tech algorithms.

A handful of innovative media outlets have managed to thrive in this challenging environment, often by serving niche audiences, such as political obsessives or high-income finance workers. Others, however, have resorted to monetizing divisiveness and propaganda. As journalist George Packer observed in The Atlantic, "[v]enerable outlets perish or self-mutilate; newer ones come and go in a flash; mountains of bait are thrown into the water to see what rises to the surface."[10] Packer's assessment leads to a damning, if understated, verdict: "This exhausting effort consumes so much time and talent that it's difficult to face the obvious truth: The for-profit model of journalism shows signs of being broken."[11]

These signs are not small ones but rather billboards projecting a dire warning from high above the graveyard that houses a century's worth of corpses.

In the 1940s, America was a nation of about 133 million residents with 44 million newspaper subscriptions among them – nearly a newspaper per household. Circulation continued to climb through the mid-1980s before leveling off and then, with the spread of the internet in the 2000s, plummeted into the abyss. By 2022, there were just 20.9 million American newspaper subscriptions, including digital subscribers – less than one for every 20 of the country's 333 million residents.[12] "It is clear that the for-profit model cannot be sustained except at a few national news brands," asserts Neal Zuckerman, a media analyst with the Boston Consulting Group. "Consumers' and advertisers' willingness to pay is not sufficient to cover the costs of creating, distributing, and operating local newspapers."[13]

The most recent study by Northwestern University found that since 2005 the country has lost nearly 2,900 newspapers and almost two-thirds of its newspaper journalists. "The last 20 years of local news have been grim, a narrative told in verbs such as demise, decimate, devastate, and decline,"[14] according to political scientists Danny Hayes and Jennifer Lawless. They further assert, "No part of the business has gone unaffected, with some newspapers disappearing altogether and others reduced to such shells that it just seems like they've disappeared."[15]

[10] George Packer, *Is Journalism Ready?*, The Atlantic, Dec. 2023.

[11] *Id.*

[12] *Newspapers Fact Sheet*, Pew Research Center (Nov. 10, 2023), https://www.pewresearch.org/journalism/fact-sheet/newspapers/.

[13] Neal Zuckerman, *The Cost of Sustaining Local Journalism: A Working Paper*, Medium (June 6, 2023), https://medium.com/@neal.zuckerman/the-cost-of-sustaining-local-journalism-a-working-paper-5e2d14b52882.

[14] Penelope Muse Abernathy & Sarah Stonbely, *The State of Local News: The 2023 Report*, Nw. Medill Local News Initiative (2023), https://localnewsinitiative.northwestern.edu/assets/slnp/the_state_of_local_news_2023.pdf.

[15] Danny Hayes & Jennifer L. Lawless, News Hole: The Demise of Local Journalism and Political Engagement (2021).

Notably, there are a few national mainstream media outlets that have managed to turn our current moment into a financial boon. Take CNN for example. Between 2016 and 2022, as the network's on-air reporters and anchors were (accurately) proclaiming that the fate of American democracy was imperiled, CNN's corporate owners and their shareholders pocketed more than $1 billion a year in profit.[16] Along similar lines, in November 2023, an article headlined Uncertain Times Have Been Good for Dow Jones explained that the corporate owners of the Wall Street Journal and Barons were on pace to make the most money of any quarter since Rupert Murdoch acquired them in 2007.[17] That same year, The New York Times projected that the paper would earn close to $100 million in profits, despite it being one of the American media's worst years in recent history, with thousands of journalism jobs lost.[18]

Our nation needs organizations like The Times which, despite others' best efforts, has no journalistic peer. To its credit, The Times has for years been among the leading chroniclers of the demise of local newspapers. The Times has also invested in significant investigative partnerships with local outlets, sponsoring rigorous journalism in places where market forces long ago forced such work to extinction. But this corporate charity cannot change the fact that The Times and its would-be peers are, first and foremost, businesses with financial interests that will always clash, at least to some extent, with their stated values. No matter its newsroom's ethics, The Times' primary institutional prerogative will always be making (or at least not losing) money. The Times has nobly declared its editorial independence from political causes, movements, and ideologies,[19] but actual independence – true freedom – cannot be achieved by an outlet that remains a slave to the market; its decisions are necessarily dictated by the demands of advertisers, online traffic trends, and the sensibilities of its subscribers. The Times and its peers are not actually, as former managing editor Gerald Boyd was known to call them, "a public trust."[20] At their best, they provide a vital service to society, but they remain, at their core, profit-seeking private enterprises. "The *Times* goes to great lengths to assert its independence; it's practically the company's mission statement. Some of this, undoubtedly, is

[16] Benjamin Mullin, *Profits Slump at CNN as Ratings Plummet*, N.Y. TIMES (Aug. 2, 2022), https://www.nytimes.com/2022/08/02/business/media/cnn-profit-chris-licht.html.

[17] Dominic Ponsford, *Uncertain Times Have Been Good for Dow Jones, a Rare 2023 Publishing Success Story*, PRESS GAZETTE (Nov. 30, 2023), https://pressgazette.co.uk/north-america/dow-jones-almar-latour-interview-2023/.

[18] Angela Fu, *2023 Was the Worst Year for the News Business Since the Pandemic*, POYNTER (Dec. 27, 2023), https://www.poynter.org/business-work/2023/2023-was-the-worst-year-for-the-news-business-since-the-pandemic/.

[19] A. G. Sulzberger, *Journalism's Essential Value*, COLUM. JOURNALISM REV. (May 15, 2023), https://www.cjr.org/special_report/ag-sulzberger-new-york-times-journalisms-essential-value-objectivity-independence.php.

[20] GERALD BOYD, MY TIMES IN BLACK AND WHITE: RACE AND POWER AT THE *NEW YORK TIMES* (2010).

driven by business interests . . . it wants the largest possible audience,"[21] media critic Margaret Sullivan, who spent four years as the paper's public editor, has observed. "A big tent, if the entry fee is high enough, is a lucrative tent. That's one of many reasons for this emphasis on 'independence.'"[22]

Even within the most professional newsrooms, journalistic decisions are made based on the concept of "news values" – what assignments, headlines, and story framings will attract the most readers, drive the most clicks, and sell the most newspapers by being the most attractive and compelling to readers – which is a capitalistic incentive, not a journalistic one. In 1987, Pamela Shoemaker offered (and critiqued as tools of the status quo) what remains the widely accepted list of "news values."[23] Shoemaker listed timeliness, proximity, impact, interest, conflict or controversy, sensationalism, prominence, and oddity. These values, or built-in biases, underscore the extent to which our news ecosystem is not based on providing the public what it actually needs to know to nurture a healthy democracy. "News values can be seen less as a reflection of what type of information citizens want or need,"[24] researchers Tony Harcup and Deirdre O'Neill have argued, "[a]nd more as a reflection of organizational, sociological and cultural norms combined with economic factors."[25]

Most "sensational" stories hold little tangible relevance to citizens' lives and livelihoods. Timeliness, by its nature, prioritizes speed over rigor. Proximity precludes thoughtful coverage of consequential events from across the country and around the world, thus denying readers the broad base of knowledge needed to fully participate in the democratic process and to influence not just local matters but global ones. A focus on how many people are "impacted" by a story or event provides a means of dodging the responsibility to accurately document the realities of minority communities. A bias toward framing stories through the lens of controversy or conflict is a recipe for removing necessary context, complication, and nuance. An emphasis on audience "interest" is pure capitalism – defining something as news if people are willing to consume it.

Through that lens, it should not be surprising to see studies like a recent report published in the *Columbia Journalism Review*, which examined political coverage that appeared on the front pages of The Times and its chief rival The Washington

[21] Margaret Sullivan, *Some Unsolicited Advice for Joe Kahn of* The New York Times *and Other Editors*, AM. CRISIS (May 10, 2024), https://margaretsullivan.substack.com/p/some-unsolicited-advice-for-joe-kahn.

[22] *Id.*

[23] Pamela J. Shoemaker, *All the Deviance That's Fit to Print: Newsworthiness and Social Change* (Aug. 1985) (paper presented at the *68th Annual Meeting of the Association for Education Journalism and Mass Communication*), https://files.eric.ed.gov/fulltext/ED257128.pdf.

[24] Tony Harcup & Deirdre O'Neill, *What Is News? Galtung and Ruge Revisited*, 2 JOURNALISM STUD. 261 (2001).

[25] *Id.*

Post during the months leading up to the 2022 midterm elections.[26] The study found that our nation's leading news organizations had provided coverage that offered "little insight into policy."[27] Researchers found that, out of The Times' 219 frontpage articles about domestic politics, just 10 "explained domestic public policy in any detail."[28] On the frontpage of The Post, just four pieces out of 215 "discussed any form of policy," and not a single one probed the "policies that candidates aimed to bring to the fore."[29] During a vital election year, amidst a historic battle for the future of our multiracial liberal democracy, our leading journalistic outlets produced reams of political "news," yet, by at least this measure, managed to offer the public little in terms of vital knowledge and information necessary for self-government.

Of course our leading journalistic organizations provide more political theater criticism and horse race analysis than they do substantive coverage about the stakes of public policy. This is because they operate in a market that has made it clear what it is willing to pay for and what it is not. For decades, press critics, with Jay Rosen at the forefront, have been detailing the democracy-corroding norms of most mainstream political journalism. In 2008, Rosen aptly described the pervasive "who's-gonna-win" mentality: "'Who's-gonna-win?' is portable, reusable from cycle to cycle, and easily learned by newcomers to the press pack."[30] It's a mentality, Rosen explained, that "generates an endless series of puzzles toward which journalists can gesture as they display their savviness, which is the unofficial religion of the mainstream press."[31]

Such journalism has continued largely unaltered not because most journalists disagree with the substance of these critiques, though some, of course, do. Rather, it persists because of the underlying financial realities. For the companies that control our media, journalism befitting our democracy – focused on substance and complexity, not ephemeral scoops and partisan conflict – is not a viable business plan. It can't win ratings wars, it doesn't sell papers and drive traffic, and it certainly doesn't produce the kind of profits needed in order to keep owners, executives, shareholders, and their offspring firmly planted within the American aristocracy. Adequately informing the whole of the public and maximizing profits are incompatible aims. We've convinced ourselves our goal is the former, yet we've constructed our democracy's information ecosystem around the latter.

26 Gideon Heltzer et al., *Warped Front Pages*, COLUM. JOURNALISM REV. (Nov. 20, 2023), https://www.cjr.org/analysis/election-politics-front-pages.php.

27 *Id.*

28 *Id.*

29 *Id.*

30 Jim Romenesko, *Jay Rosen: Why Horse Race Journalism Works for Journalists*, POYNTER (Jan. 21, 2008), https://www.poynter.org/reporting-editing/2008/jay-rosen-why-horse-race-journalism-works-for-journalists/.

31 *Id.*

It is necessary to draw a distinction between a media system that prioritizes "news" and one that aims to disseminate "information." All news contains some information. But not all information or journalism is "news." The most vital information – how to participate in democracy, what public services are available and how to procure them, what your government is actually doing and not doing, how to best understand and contextualize daily societal occurrences – is almost never relayed in our "news." Instead, most "news" consists of context-lacking micro-updates, singular scenes cut from an ongoing public soap opera that are nearly incomprehensible to anyone who has missed the last episode and that will be proven inaccurate, irrelevant, or both by the airing of the next one. As famed writer Gay Talese recalled of his childhood impression of the press, "[n]ews" was not information, facts, or even knowledge but was "ephemeral."[32] "News is a commodity, not a mirror image of reality,"[33] economist James T. Hamilton wrote in 2004. "Focusing on media economics shows how consumers' desires drive news coverage and how this conflicts with the ideal of what the news ought to be."[34] Or, as Lippmann noted a century ago: The truth and the news are not the same thing. "The function of news is to signalize an event,"[35] he wrote, and "[t]he function of truth is to bring to light the hidden facts."[36]

Truth has tangible value; it decodes complexity and equips the citizenry with the ability to navigate an ever-complicated world. *News* is now produced at an unprecedented clip by social media influencers, podcasters, and virtually every person with access to the internet. *News* sows distrust because most news is sensational, lacking rigor, and incomplete. What American democracy needs, what it craves, is *quality information*: vetted, trustworthy, and complete. "Citizens need journalists more than ever, precisely because there is so much information available, of such varying quality and relevance,"[37] Thomas E. Patterson wrote in 2013's *Informing the News*, in which he argued that the journalism required for healthy democracy must be reflective, not reflexive. Patterson called for "knowledge-based journalism," in which journalists develop expertise and deploy slow, rigorous methods.[38] "There are plenty of conscientious journalists. But their efforts are diminished by what other reporters are doing."[39]

* * *

32 Gay Talese, Bartleby and Me: Reflections of an Old Scrivener (2023).

33 James T. Hamilton, All the News That's Fit to Sell (2004).

34 *Id.*

35 Walter Lippmann, Public Opinion (1965).

36 *Id.*

37 Thomas E. Patterson, Informing the News: The Need for Knowledge-Based Journalism (2013).

38 *Id.*

39 *Id.*

Although there have been American news organizations operating as nonprofits for more than a century, the post-Watergate era witnessed the birth of a small but influential wave of nonprofit outlets that set the stage for the sector's current explosion. The movement began with the founding of Mother Jones magazine in 1976 and the Center for Investigative Reporting in 1977. These outlets were explicit about their mission: to tell the types of stories that corporate-owned media were disincentivized from producing by deploying the kind of journalistic rigor often absent from daily news coverage. "As news organizations have reduced their commitment to serious journalism, there has been an incalculable cost to communities, to citizens' ability to monitor those in power, and of course to those professionals directly impacted in the profession of journalism itself,"[40] wrote Charles Lewis, a pioneer of the nonprofit journalist model. In 1989, Lewis founded the Center for Public Integrity,[41] and in 1997 he launched the International Consortium of Investigative Journalists. He would later be among the co-founders of the Institute for Nonprofit News and launch the Investigative Reporting Workshop.[42] "The question was," Lewis wrote in 2006, "Is there a way to create a modest attempt at a journalistic utopia ...?"[43]

Once an outlier in the journalistic landscape – for much of the last century, nonprofit media consisted primarily of National Public Radio and its various local affiliates – the sector ballooned in the 2000s, as the bottom finally fell out of the newspaper industry. Over the last two and a half decades, a number of high-profile nonprofit newsrooms have been launched, including ProPublica in 2008, the Texas Tribune in 2009, the Marshall Project in 2015, the 19th* in 2020, and a wave of lesser-known news organizations that have sprouted up across the country. In many cases, these organizations have framed their missions not as replicating the corporate media outlets that they hope to replace but as explicitly offering a public service that those organizations refuse to provide. In 2015, the Institute for Nonprofit News had about 120 members.[44] Today, it represents more than 400 nonprofit news organizations, about 300 of them local newsrooms.

The nonprofit news ecosystem is primarily bankrolled by a handful of major philanthropic organizations and includes structural support, consisting of, among others, programs that help these publishers establish membership programs, run end-of-the-year giving campaigns, and share editorial and business best practices. These noble efforts have unquestionably bettered our field and resulted in a

40 Charles Lewis, *The Growing Importance of Nonprofit Journalism*, Harv. U. Shorenstein Ctr. Working Paper Series (Apr. 2007), https://dash.harvard.edu/bitstream/handle/1/37375928/2007_03.pdf?sequence = 1&isAllowed = y.

41 Since 2020, I have been a member of the Center for Public Integrity's board of directors. I am currently co-chair.

42 In July 2023, I succeeded Lewis as the Investigative Reporting Workshop's executive editor.

43 Lewis, *supra* note 40.

44 *Annual Report 2015*, Inst. for Nonprofit News (2015), https://inn.org/wp-content/uploads/2022/09/2015-INN-AnnualReport.pdf.

nonprofit media sector that produces meaningful journalism. Indeed, to some, nonprofit journalism is the coveted answer to the failings of the commercial press, especially at the local level.

Reality, however, suggests that we remain far from the utopia Lewis envisioned because there simply is not enough money available to finance a nonprofit journalistic nirvana. The best estimates suggest that rebuilding the local news and information ecosystem will require between $1 billion and $3 billion each year.[45] As of 2023, the Boston Consulting Group estimated that current philanthropic giving to local journalism totals about $150 million a year.[46] A coalition of longtime journalism funders, led by the MacArthur Foundation and Knight Foundation, has recently launched a campaign called "Press Forward," which aims to mobilize $500 million over the course of five years toward rebuilding, revitalizing, and reimagining local news.[47] It is a noble, unprecedented effort that is undoubtedly already the largest fundraising campaign for news and information in American history.

It's also a band-aid being frantically fastened over a gaping bullet hole. Even if Press Forward reached its goal of pumping half a billion dollars into local nonprofit news over the course of five years, and even if every single one of those were new, previously uncommitted dollars, that would bring the total of philanthropic funding for local news and information to about $250 million a year – somewhere between 8 and 25 percent of what has been deemed necessary, and nowhere close to the amount needed to stabilize American democracy.

And there are legitimate concerns, often voiced quietly by those unwilling to risk earning the ire of such prominent and important potential funders, that such a centralization of nonprofit funding could in fact create a more risk-averse, stylistically monochromatic nonprofit press. In April 2024, Richard Logan, a leading journalism funder, warned attendees of an investigative journalism conference at UC Berkeley that, intended or not, such consolidation of foundation giving would have the same disastrous effects that corporate media consolidation had over the course of the previous century, leading to a nonprofit press corps too terrified of upsetting its wealthy benefactors and powerful foundations to do its job: "The writing has been on the wall for a long time,"[48] Logan declared, according to the notes I took from the audience. "If you think life without freedom and democracy is worth living, then well I guess when we're in the camps we'll have very little to talk about."[49]

[45] Steve Waldman, *Size of the Gap*, Rebuild Local News (Apr. 4, 2023), https://www.rebuildlocalnews.org/size-of-the-gap/.

[46] Zuckerman, *supra* note 13.

[47] *Press Forward Will Award More Than $500 Million to Revitalize Local News*, MacArthur Found. (Sept. 7, 2023), https://www.macfound.org/press/press-releases/press-forward-will-award-more-than-500-million-to-revitalize-local-news.

[48] Richard Logan, *Remarks at 16th Annual Reva and David Logan Symposium on Investigative Reporting* (Apr. 19–21, 2024) (notes on file with author).

[49] *Id.*

And those nonprofit news organizations who succeed in earning the favor of philanthropies and foundations are then tasked with completing the same puzzle that for-profit media failed to solve for a century, namely convincing a sizable-enough portion of the public to pay sufficient money to support an information system that can effectively serve the masses before this philanthropic seed money runs out. "No one in the foundation world wants to think these nonprofits are going to be dependent on foundations for a long time,"[50] an employee of a major foundation remarked in 2010. "Journalism startups have got to figure out some way to get people to pay for them."[51] More recently, when announcing support for a new local nonprofit news organization in Houston, a major journalism funder described philanthropy's role as supporting the Fourth Estate "until the industry finds its footing"[52] – as if the flailing information system undermining our democracy were a younger sibling in need of some cash to cover their housing deposit.

The assumption at the heart of the push for nonprofit media "sustainability" is that, despite a century of available evidence, local markets across the country are not only capable of but willing to support healthy information ecosystems. But unacknowledged in this formulation is the fact that many of the core components of the local news bundle that kept newspapers, magazines, and television news profitable for much of the twentieth century – sports scores, classified ads, weather predictions, crosswords, coupons, and comics – are now readily available, for free, to would-be news consumers via the internet.

Also unacknowledged in this plan is the reality that all too often the communities most in need of healthy civic information are also those least able to pay for it, even if they wanted to. "Business models for local news ... simply don't work for outlets serving low-income communities,"[53] observed Madeleine Bair, who in 2017 founded El Timpano, which serves Latino and Mayan immigrants in the Bay Area of California. "Sustainability has become a core focus for many journalism funders, who want to see that a news outlet will not rely on philanthropy for the long term,"[54] Bair continued,

> But in a context in which the one common denominator of sustainable digital outlets is that they serve affluent audiences, this metric becomes a bias in favor of news that serves the well-to-do, and in the end a self-fulfilling prophecy: There are

50 Mary Walton, *The Nonprofit Explosion*, Am. Journalism Rev. (Sept. 2010), https://ajrarchive.org/article.asp?id=4906.

51 *Id.*

52 *Houston Foundations to Launch Nonprofit Newsroom*, Philanthropy News Dig. (Jan. 24, 2022), https://philanthropynewsdigest.org/news/houston-foundations-to-launch-nonprofit-newsroom.

53 Madeleine Bair, *Toward Equitable Models of Journalism Sustainability*, JSK Fellows (Dec. 11, 2023), https://jskfellows.stanford.edu/toward-equitable-models-of-journalism-sustainability-f0b76f864cf5.

54 *Id.*

few models of sustainable outlets that serve low-income audiences, so funders don't take a chance investing in such outlets.[55]

If there is one lesson the last one hundred years of the American press has taught us, it is that the type of rigorous information ecosystem required of a healthy democracy is *not* sustainable as a market-supported enterprise – at least not in many of the communities that most desperately need accurate news and information, and certainly not at scale. Yes, some local nonprofit news efforts have – through subscription, sponsorship, membership, events, and foundation money – found innovative ways to fill information gaps. But we cannot allow small successes to distract from inescapable conclusions. Through its focus on the unachievable aspiration of local news sustainability, philanthropy has made clear it is unwilling and unable to support democracy's long-term information needs. So too have the consumers. National Public Radio – described as public media but more accurately understood as a nonprofit outlet with some public support – has spent decades attempting to build a membership model. It is currently in a crisis, with at least one industry watcher predicting all of "public radio" could collapse within a decade.[56]

Amid these realities, many of the journalists most successful at building nonprofit organizations have explicitly called for a non-market-based remedy. "More ambitious philanthropy and business model improvements will not be enough to reverse the loss of local news, let alone build a better, more robust, more inclusive local news sector than we've had before. Government must play a role,"[57] argued Steve Waldman, the co-founder and former president of Report for America and his Rebuild Local News coalition colleague Anna Brugmann. Sewell Chan, the outgoing editor-in-chief of the Texas Tribune and incoming editor of the Columbia Journalism Review, wrote an essay pleading for urgent investments not just from philanthropy and citizens but from the government in order to stem what he described as an "information apocalypse":

> Proposals for any kind of government intervention will raise hackles among journalists who believe the First Amendment rules out a role for public support of journalism. I know the danger of state control of broadcasting … I hear, as well, warnings of negative unintended consequences of government action … But most

[55] *Id.*

[56] Benjamin Mullin & Jeremy W. Peters, *Inside the Crisis at NPR*, N.Y. Times (Apr. 24, 2024), https://www.nytimes.com/2024/04/24/business/media/inside-the-crisis-at-npr.html ("I believe that public radio has five to seven years to reimagine itself before it's simply unsustainable," said Eric Nuzum, a former NPR executive and co-founder of the audio consulting and production company Magnificent Noise; he continued, "And they can't take two or three years of that time debating a business model.").

[57] Anna Brugmann & Steven Waldman, *Testimony Submitted to the California Senate Judiciary Committee on Local Journalism in the Digital Age*, Rebuild Local News (Dec. 5, 2023), https://www.rebuildlocalnews.org/testimony-submitted-to-the-senate-judiciary-committee-on-local-journalism-in-the-digital-age/.

journalists do not have the luxury of temporizing as their institutions and livelihoods crumble.[58]

Or, as Elizabeth Green, the CEO and co-founder of Chalkbeat, has put it: "We have to subsidize reporting if we want democracy to survive."[59]

***

In American democracy, innovative and provocative ideas – from abolition to suffrage to desegregation to marriage equality to drug legalization to redress and reparations – often begin in states before eventually marching their way to Washington. And recent years have seen a movement, largely led by Waldman and his colleagues, to convince local and state governments to provide public funding as a means of infusing resources into our dying media ecosystem.

If a free press is truly a vital public good, with the best media outlets vowing to serve as a public trust, then we must create an *actual* federal public trust to ensure every American has access to the news and information they need to be full citizens in our democracy. The aim would not be a government-run media but rather a government-ensured one. Rather than create a centralized public media that could be punished by politicians who dislike its coverage – or commandeered as a propaganda tool by a demagogue president – we could instead direct federal news and information money directly to local communities.

If Congress were to create such a trust, it could, for example, pledge to provide $10 million in annual federal public information grants to each of the country's 435 congressional districts. This would channel urgent public resources to every community in the country, instantly transforming the news and information landscape for the relatively modest, by federal budgeting standards, price tag of $4.35 billion per year. Such a program would place money directly in the hands of local media outlets, neighborhood organizations, and civic institutions that reflect the demographics, values, and sensibilities of America's various communities.

Such a program could follow the successful, widely accepted model of the U.S. National Science Foundation, a federal agency established in 1950, which in fiscal year 2023 distributed more than $7 billion in taxpayer money to researchers at US colleges and universities.[60] And there is precedent, in the Corporation for Public Broadcasting (CPB), for the independent administration and distribution of government dollars to support a free press. The $4.25 billion allotment for public

58 Sewell Chan, *A Lost Decade: Policymakers Fiddled as Newsrooms Burned*, 707 ANNALS OF THE AM. ACAD. OF POL. & SOC. SCI. 62 (2023).

59 Sara Fischer, *Pandemic Drives Nonprofit Media Boom*, AXIOS (Feb. 23, 2021), https://www.axios.com/2021/02/23/covid-newspapers-nonprofit-media.

60 *FY 2025 Budget Request to Congress*, NATIONAL SCIENCE FOUNDATION (Mar. 11, 2024), https://nsf-gov-resources.nsf.gov/files/00_NSF_FY25_CJ_Entire%20Rollup_web.pdf?VersionId=cbkdqD_UMweHEIsZwPjtVgcQRwMccgvu.

information could be administered through the creation of a new agency, governed by a charter that ensures and insists it is operated in a way that is, as President Lyndon B. Johnson vowed when he authorized the creation of the CPB, "carefully guarded from Government or from party control. It will be free, and it will be independent – and it will belong to all of our people."[61]

Federal public information money could be limited to news and information efforts, excluding pure opinion journalism, and available to any institution that proposes innovative efforts to expand the availability of rigorous, factual information in order to empower citizens to fully participate in our democracy. Eligible institutions could include for-profit and nonprofit newsrooms, other nonprofit organizations, colleges and universities, libraries, and other civic institutions. It is easy to imagine a host of projects, carried out by news organizations, civic institutions, or partnerships between both, that would meet such criteria. These projects could ensure that every citizen has access to information about registering to vote, polling locations, and local candidates and political issues on their ballot, as well as their community's local history and contemporary challenges. This money could also guarantee that an accessible public record is created of every government meeting, that a transcript is taken and archived of every court proceeding, and that there are trained professional journalists in every city hall and statehouse to help sift through and interpret all of this information. Importantly, at a time when news organizations face, among other things, a *distribution* crisis, the funds would ensure that such information is actively disseminated to citizens in order to inform public opinion.

Just as the point of a public library is not to replace or compete with the bookstore, such an agency would not aspire to construct a public media system to replace or displace commercial and nonprofit media. Rather, it would provide for a suite of services that the market will never incentivize for-profit businesses to create on their own – services that compile and curate information while also working to ensure that all citizens, regardless of means, have access to that information. "Americans need accurate, contextual news and information to make decisions that help our communities thrive. It's tempting to think that means news leaders need only focus on gathering and publishing facts. But local news has other essential roles that complement and enhance reporting,"[62] Samantha Ragland and Kevin Locker of the American Press Institute have argued, highlighting public information efforts, including the "solutions circles" convened by the Mississippi Free Press to brainstorm ways of addressing community problems, public forums held by the Cardinal News in Virginia, and storytelling events run by The Tennessean that help

[61] President Lyndon B. Johnson, *Remarks upon Signing the Public Broadcasting Act of 1967* (Nov. 7, 1967) (transcript available in the LBJ Presidential Library, https://www.lbjlibrary.org/object/text/remarks-upon-signing-public-broadcasting-act-11-07-1967).

[62] Samantha Ragland & Kevin Loker, *Journalism Has Many Roles. It's Time to Embrace the Role of Convener*, Ky. Press Ass'n (May 9, 2024), https://members.kypress.com/articles/journalism-has-many-roles-its-time-to-embrace-the-role-of-convener/.

community members share their own experiences, among others. "Media should also be a force for social connection," asserted Ragland and Locker, and further, media should be "[a] convener of people across differences and a facilitator for what to do after the facts are laid bare."[63]

What those who champion such public information (also referred to as civil information and, in the mid-1990s, "public journalism"[64]) understand is that democracy will not be saved by fact-checks, investigations, or view-from-nowhere-coded news dispatches alone – not even if today's media organizations possessed a means of distributing them to a majority of the population (which they do not) and not even if that population trusted our media organizations (which it does not). In fact, decades of social science tell us that presenting people with facts that contradict their beliefs and opinions is not enough to change their minds or eradicate falsehoods.[65]

"No one is ever forced by just the collection of facts to accept a particular theory of their meaning,"[66] philosopher John Dewey wrote in 1927. "The imagination of the founders did not travel beyond what could be accomplished and understood in a congeries of self-governing communities,"[67] Dewey continued, calling for us to consider democracy, especially a geographically vast and racially diverse one, impossible without the development of a shared "great community." A similar framing was echoed, decades later, in the final book published by the Rev. Dr. Martin Luther King Jr. prior to his assassination, which wrestled with how, following the 1965 Voting Rights Act, Americans could best build cohesive multiracial democracy. "Where Do We Go From Here," asks the book's title, "Chaos or Community?"[68]

While often framed as having been in ideological "debate," Dewey and Lippmann are better read together, as an argument for *democratic cohesion*: the belief that a healthy public opinion, and thus a functioning democracy, requires both that the public have access to reliable, rigorously compiled and honestly presented facts *as well as* thriving local communities, well-tended by reliable institutions (the press chief among them), for that information to be digested and debated. A democracy fails if it has one but not the other. Currently, our democracy has neither.

As Richard Young, the founder and executive director of CivicLex, a media organization in Lexington, Kentucky, put it:

> If we want people to value local news, we must demonstrate its importance to young people early in their life. If we want people to trust our data and sources, we must help them know how to navigate that data themselves. If we want people to be open

63 *Id.*

64 Alicia C. Shepard, *The Gospel of Public Journalism*, 16 Am. Journalism Rev.28 (1994).

65 Richard Sima, *Why Do Our Brains Believe Lies? Correcting Lies and Misinformation Is Difficult Because Learning the Truth Doesn't Delete Them From Our Memory*, Wash. Post (Nov. 3, 2022), https://www.washingtonpost.com/wellness/2022/11/03/misinformation-brain-beliefs/.

66 John Dewey, The Public and Its Problems (1927).

67 *Id.*

68 Martin Luther King, Jr., Where Do We Go From Here: Chaos or Community? (1967).

> to different perspectives in our publications, we must build spaces where they actually interact with people who are different from them. If we want the information and reporting we produce to compel people to participate in the decision-making that shapes their communities, we must build a civic life worth participating in.[69]

***

There will likely be a powerful, vocal opposition from within journalism and the media, not just to the particulars of this proposal but to any step toward providing significant public funding to support the American press. The core of this is an ideological rejection of anything that could threaten the perception that our media is independent of the government that it covers.[70] And there is no question that there is significant reason for vigilance to prevent political figures and partisans from wielding indiscriminate power over the press that holds it to account.

Yet the American market is as powerful a force in American life as the American government. We've spent centuries worrying that some president or king will seize our presses when all along it has been our own owners, publishers and editors – ever anxious about the sensibilities of advertisers, readers, and subscribers – who are those most likely to halt them and most often actually halting them. It has been a press that is hopelessly wedded to that market that incentivizes our industry's worst professional instincts and has helped bring our democracy to the brink. As poll after poll shows trust in the American press at the lowest levels on record,[71] too many industry leaders and journalistic practitioners insist that the only potential solution is more of the same. Surely, we can survive a mild resetting of the scales. Because the market, left to its own devices, does not build community. It sows chaos.

There is a growing movement in favor of more market regulation, especially as it relates to technology companies who now hold near monopolies on the distribution of information. And there are arguments being made for a more robust, fully funded public media. Both are based in the same principle, namely, that the government must play a proactive role in encouraging and facilitating a healthy information

69 Richard Young, *Local News Must Help "Build a Civic Life Worth Participating In,"* The Objective (Dec. 5, 2023), https://objectivejournalism.org/2023/12/richard-young-local-news-building-civic-life/.

70 No matter the historical reality that the US government has provided significant financial support to the press at various junctures.

71 Art Swift, *Americans' Trust in Mass Media Sinks to New Low*, Gallup (Sept. 14, 2016), https://news.gallup.com/poll/195542/americans-trust-mass-media-sinks-new-low.aspx; Megan Brenan, *Americans' Trust in Media Remains Near Record Low*, Gallup (Oct. 18, 2022), https://news.gallup.com/poll/403166/americans-trust-media-remains-near-record-low.aspx ("At 34%, Americans' trust in the mass media to report the news 'fully, accurately and fairly' is essentially unchanged from last year and just two points higher than the lowest that Gallup has recorded, in 2016 during the presidential campaign. Just 7% of Americans have 'a great deal' of trust and confidence in the media, and 27% have 'a fair amount.' Meanwhile, 28% of U.S. adults say they do not have very much confidence and 38% have none at all in newspapers, TV and radio. Notably, this is the first time that the percentage of Americans with no trust at all in the media is higher than the percentage with a great deal or a fair amount combined.")

ecosystem, as the argument for the creation of a public trust to sponsor public information. Such government investment should not be seen as a replacement for the growing philanthropic support for journalism but rather as a welcome supplement to it. Nothing in this chapter should be taken as an argument in favor of centralized, government-run media. Instead, it is an endorsement of a news and information ecosystem composed of countervailing forces: a healthy, properly regulated market-based press; an ascendant nonprofit press sector; and a properly funded public media. All of those distinct forces would then, in this system, be buoyed by the possibility of receiving government support in exchange for providing vital public information they would otherwise be disinclined by market forces to produce.

Imagine an American information ecosystem constructed as a stool with three distinct legs. When one wobbles or falters, the others are able to carry its weight. But the stool itself cannot stand if it is constructed on top of sand. A healthy press requires a firm foundation, a minimum flow of healthy information available to all, and communal venues in which all can gather to digest and debate it. A public trust for the press would help ensure that foundation, incentivizing each pillar of our press toward its better angels.

Legal scholar Martha Minow has argued, "Government action always carries risks and need to comport with constitutional guarantees, but government inaction can also jeopardize constitutional guarantees."[72] Minow has also opined that,

> If the infrastructure for gathering, reporting, and distributing news is absent in many communities, if readers and viewers are overwhelmed by distractions designed to take their attention, and if no recourse is available through the accountability mechanisms designed for either government or private enterprises, it is time to return to the Constitution's text and basic principles.[73]

If there truly is, as Justice Black argued, an American right to know, then there is little choice *but* to subsidize our news and information ecosystem. Our society has a long-established solution for public entitlements that the free market will not support equitably: We have the government pay for them. Such a system would not be a government-controlled press but rather a government-ensured one. And such public investment would ensure every American has news and information providers that, as journalist Darryl Holliday has put it, "strengthen democracy rather than erode it."[74] If we aspire to be a true multiracial and multicultural society, then we must ensure that each American has an equal claim to public goods and protected rights, and, perhaps most crucially, their right to know.

[72] Martha Minow, Saving the News: Why the Constitution Calls for Government Action to Preserve Freedom of Speech (2021).

[73] *Id.*

[74] Darryl Holliday, *Journalism's Civic Media Moment Could Be a Movement*, in Reinventing Journalism to Strengthen Democracy: Insights From Innovators (P. Dallas & P. Ellis eds., 2023).

23

Distorting the Press

Heidi Kitrosser

American journalism is an essential public good. Representative democracy would mean little were the people not capable of informing themselves, sharing ideas with one another, and overseeing those who govern them. It was this understanding, along with a hard-won knowledge of the lengths to which powerful actors will go to suppress the free flow of information and ideas, that led Revolutionary-era thinkers "routinely [to] suggest[] that the 'Liberty of the Press' was 'a great Bulwark of the Liberty of the People'...."[1] These lessons have been relearned generation after generation throughout American history. In the 1970s, for instance, Justice Stewart spoke approvingly of investigative journalists' dogged pursuit of abuses of power, like those that brought down the Nixon presidency.[2] Relating those examples back to the pre-Revolutionary Crown's efforts to stymie the press, Stewart remarked that the Crown understood all too well that "the free press meant organized, expert scrutiny of government."[3] Today, with authoritarianism on the march at home and abroad and with misinformation and disinformation as growing problems,[4] we need a vibrant, professional press more than ever.

I am very grateful to RonNell Andersen Jones, Sonja West, Katy Glenn Bass, and the Knight First Amendment Institute for inviting me to participate in a wonderful project on press freedom. For very helpful edits and insights, I owe much thanks to the aforementioned people as well as to my fellow Knight press freedom "pod" members, to other participants in the Knight press freedom conference of May 2024, and to participants in a workshop at Northwestern – Pritzker School of Law.

1 RonNell Andersen Jones, *Press Speakers and the First Amendment Rights of Listeners*, 90 U. Colo. L. Rev. 499, 537–38 (2019) (quoting Leonard W. Levy, Legacy of Suppression: Freedom of Speech and Press in Early American History 69 (1960) (internal citations omitted)).

2 Potter Stewart, *Or of the Press*, 26 Hastings L.J. 631, 631 (1975).

3 *Id.* at 634.

4 *See generally, e.g.*, Masha Gessen, Surviving Autocracy (2020); Sophia Rosenfeld, Democracy and Truth: A Short History (2019); Steven Levitsky & Daniel Ziblatt, How Democracies Die (2018); Aziz Huq & Tom Ginsburg, *How to Lose a Constitutional Democracy*, 65 UCLA L. Rev. 78 (2018).

And yet, just as we need it most, the American press is in crisis. The troubles are partly sociopolitical, fueled by the same antidemocratic forces that make journalism so essential today.[5] The crisis also has a substantial economic component. As Victor Pickard put it recently, "We no longer have a commercial market that can support the levels of journalism that democracy requires."[6] He elaborates that the collapse of the traditional revenue model for journalism has had dire consequences: Since 2005, "the U.S. has lost almost one-third of its newspapers and nearly two-thirds of its newspaper journalists ... [M]ore than one half of American counties have little or no access to local news."[7] Pickard aptly concludes that "[t]his isn't just a journalism crisis: it's a democracy crisis."[8]

Although no single elixir will save the American press, enhanced public funding is among the tools needed to address its existential crisis. In a sense, this is an old idea. As Martha Minow observes, "[p]ublic resources to support journalism and news have been a feature of American life since shortly after the founding of the nation. Early postal subsidies permitted newspapers to be sent through the mail at reduced rates," and "[t]axpayer dollars ... support public broadcasting."[9] Still, public support for journalism in the United States is paltry compared to state financial investments in news media in other democratic nations.[10] Pickard and Timothy Neff note, for example, that "[a]t $465 million dollars, 2020 federal funding of US public media amounted to just $1.40 per capita. By comparison, countries such as the UK, Norway, and Sweden devote around $100 or more per capita toward their public media."[11] Relative to other democracies – indeed, relative to countries that considerably outrank the United States in a leading index of world democracies[12] – the United States has ample room for growth in public media funding.

[5] *See, e.g.*, Levitsky & Ziblatt, *supra* note 4, at 198–203; RonNell Andersen Jones & Sonja R. West, *The Fragility of the American Press*, 112 Northwestern U. L. Rev. 567, 571–72, 580–93 (2017).

[6] Niala Boodhoo, *Victor Pickard: A New Business Model for Journalism*, 1 Big Thing (Feb. 22, 2024) (transcript and recording available at https://www.axios.com/2024/02/22/victor-pickard-a-new-business-model-for-journalism).

[7] Victor Pickard, *Taking Media Out of the Market*, LPE Project (Jan. 31, 2024), https://lpeproject.org/blog/taking-media-out-of-the-market/.

[8] *Id.*

[9] Martha Minow, Saving the News: Why the Constitution Calls for Government Action to Preserve Freedom of Speech 138 (2021).

[10] *See* Minow, *supra* note 9, at 138; Timothy Neff & Victor Pickard, *Raising the Bar for Journalism*, Media Ineq. & Change Ctr., https://www.asc.upenn.edu/sites/default/files/2021-06/MIC_Infographic_Authors.pdf (last visited June 22, 2024); Victor Pickard & Timothy Neff, *Op-Ed: Strengthen Our Democracy by Funding Public Media*, Colum. Journalism Rev. (June 2, 2021), https://www.cjr.org/opinion/public-funding-media-democracy.php; Catherine Buni, *Four Ways to Fund – and Save – Local Journalism*, NiemanReports (May 7, 2020), https://niemanreports.org/articles/4-ways-to-fund-and-save-journalism/.

[11] Pickard & Neff, *Op-Ed*, *supra* note 10.

[12] *See EIU Democracy Index* 2023, Economist Intel. Unit 9, Table 2 (2024), https://www.eiu.com/n/campaigns/democracy-index-2023/.

However, public funding raises the specter of state capture. The concern is a legitimate one, but it is hardly insurmountable. Indeed, as just noted, the United States has maintained some form of support for the news media since shortly after its founding, and some of the world's strongest democracies far exceed the United States' level of investment in public media. The solution is not to abandon the idea of public support but to ensure that protections are in place to shield public journalism from partisan or political capture. Such protections necessarily are multi-faceted, with aspects that evolve over time as conditions shift. They include funding-source decisions, legislative and regulatory directives, and informal norms. The governing constitutional framework, too, is a matter of no small importance. In this chapter, I focus on the latter.

Specifically, I explore First Amendment tools to protect publicly subsidized journalism against state capture. Although I emphasize judicial decisions and arguments, I urge readers to keep in mind the larger legal, social, and political frameworks within which such decisions and arguments exist. In other words, courts and litigation comprise but one piece of the anti-capture infrastructure. Furthermore, although constitutional arguments typically center on courts, they can and should be made in other venues as well. First Amendment considerations, including those that I raise here, ought to be weighed not only by courts but also by legislators crafting funding legislation.

My constitutional arguments center primarily on what I call the "anti-distortion principle." To be clear, the principle I discuss here is different from the similarly named concept that was raised in some campaign finance cases. I say more about the distinction between the two in the accompanying footnote.[13] As I use the term here, the anti-distortion principle is the notion that the government may not impose conditions on subsidized speech that would distort the very nature of the type of speech at issue or the process through which it is created. For example, should a state create a program to fund "investigative journalism on state and local issues important to the community" but prohibit using the funds for stories that "cast the governor in a negative light," the prohibition would raise valid anti-distortion concerns. The state, one could reasonably object, is purporting to fund investigative

[13] Proponents of restricting corporate political expenditures long have argued that corporate wealth distorts electoral debates. The Supreme Court adopted this reasoning in the 1990 case of Austin v. Michigan Chamber of Commerce, citing the "'corrosive and distorting effects of immense aggregations of wealth that are accumulated with the help of the corporate form and that have little or no correlation to the public's support for the corporation's political ideas.'" Austin v. Michigan Chamber of Commerce, 494 U.S. 652, 660 (1990) (quoted in Richard L. Hasen, *Citizens United and the Orphaned Antidistortion Rationale*, 27 GA. ST. L. REV. 989, 991 (2011)). Twenty years later, the Court rejected this anti-distortion rationale and overruled *Austin* in Citizens United v. Federal Election Commission, 558 U.S. 310, 348–52 (2010). *See also* Hasen, *supra* at 996–97. The anti-distortion interest cited in the campaign finance cases is obviously quite different from the one that I embrace in this chapter. As I explain in this chapter's text, I use the term to describe conditions on government funding or employment that distort the nature of the funded expressive enterprises.

journalism while short-circuiting the reporting and editing processes that characterize it. This would enable political actors to use a discipline – investigative journalism – associated with rigorous information-gathering and corroboration practices to launder political messaging. Such message laundering undermines key values associated with the Speech and Press Clauses, including government distrust and checking the powerful.

Neither the concept of anti-distortion nor the importance of public funding is unique to the press. Rather, each is part of a larger phenomenon that I call public knowledge production and that I explored in earlier work.[14] Public knowledge producers – which I define very similarly to Vicky Jackson's definition of "knowledge institutions" – are "those government entities, officials, or employees who, in the ordinary course of their work, engage in 'knowledge production or dissemination … according to disciplinary norms.' This includes government scientists, economists, and other disciplinary experts."[15] It also includes publicly employed or subsidized journalists and teachers. As with publicly supported journalism, public knowledge production on the whole fills informational and educational gaps that the commercial marketplace alone cannot provide. Its existence does, however, demand vigilance against state capture.

Given the presence of public knowledge production in the United States – within and outside of the realm of journalism – and given the risks of state capture, it is unsurprising that the foundations of an anti-distortion principle already exist in aspects of free speech case law. Still, the principle requires substantial elaboration, both because its articulation in judicial precedent is underdeveloped and because there are countertendencies in the case law that must be addressed.

The principle's justification – that is, the reason why distortion is concerning from a First Amendment perspective – is only thinly gestured at in existing precedent. The same is true of the principle's implementation – in other words, of how one can determine the nature of a type of speech or of an expressive institution and assess whether it has been distorted. Furthermore, applying anti-distortion analysis to journalism implicates the First Amendment's Press Clause as well as its Free Speech Clause. It also is far from clear where the anti-distortion principle ends and the "government speech doctrine" begins. The latter is the notion that when the government employs personnel or subsidizes private speakers to convey the

[14] Heidi Kitrosser, *Protecting Public Knowledge Producers*, 22-17 Knight First Amend. Inst. (Dec. 16, 2022), https://knightcolumbia.org/content/protecting-public-knowledge-producers, *reprinted in* 4 J. Free Speech L. 473 (2023) (subsequent citations will use the pagination from the Journal of Free Speech Law reprinting)). *See also* Heidi Kitrosser, *"A Government That Benefits from Expertise": Unitary Executive Theory & the Government's Knowledge Producers*, 72 Syracuse L. Rev. 1473 (2022).

[15] Kitrosser, *"A Government That Benefits from Expertise," supra* note 14, at 1491. *See also* Kitrosser, *Protecting Public Knowledge Producers*, *supra* note 14, at 481.

government's own message, the First Amendment simply does not apply; the government may impose whatever restrictions it likes on the resulting speech.

In Section 23.1 of this chapter, I elaborate on what the case law presently has to say about both anti-distortion and government speech. Sections 23.1.1 and 23.1.2 discuss cases that entail public knowledge production apart from journalism, whereas Section 23.1.3 focuses entirely on cases involving the press. In Section 23.2, I aim to build out the anti-distortion principle's theoretical underpinnings, elaborating on why distortion undermines key values associated with speech and press freedoms. In Section 23.3, I draw from existing cases, particularly those involving public or subsidized news media, to identify guidelines that courts and legislatures can use to determine when distortion is afoot.

23.1 WHAT JUDICIAL PRECEDENT CURRENTLY SAYS ABOUT DISTORTION, GOVERNMENT SPEECH, AND STATE-SUBSIDIZED JOURNALISM

23.1.1 *Traces of an Anti-distortion Principle in the Case Law*

Although it is far from a coherent or well-theorized concept in the case law, traces of an anti-distortion principle can be detected in various areas of judicial precedent. Perhaps the best-known example to this effect is the standard for evaluating speech conditions in limited public forums. In such cases, courts ask whether the restriction is viewpoint-neutral and reasonable in light of the forum's nature and purpose.[16]

The Supreme Court offered its most overt and detailed embrace of an anti-distortion principle in *Legal Services Corporation v. Velazquez*.[17] The *Velazquez* Court held unconstitutional a statutory restriction limiting the arguments that federally funded legal services corporation attorneys ("LSC attorneys") could make in litigation. Pursuant to the restriction, LSC attorneys could argue only that state or federal statutes had been misapplied in their clients' cases; they were barred from challenging the laws themselves as unconstitutional or, in the case of the state laws, as violating federal law.[18] Writing for the Court, Justice Kennedy emphasized that LSC attorneys were not engaged in "government speech."[19] Their role, rather, was

[16] *See, e.g.*, Rosenberger v. Rector, 515 U.S. 819, 829 (1995) ("[o]nce it has opened a limited forum ... the State must respect the lawful boundaries it has itself set. The State may not exclude speech where its distinction is 'not reasonable in light of the purpose served by the forum,' nor may it discriminate against speech on the basis of its viewpoint") (internal citations omitted). *See also* Legal Services Corp. v. Velazquez, 531 U.S. 533, 544 (2001) (describing *Rosenberger* as premised on the idea that the government "could not elect to use ... a college publication structure in a regime which prohibits speech necessary to the proper functioning of [that] system[] ....").

[17] 531 U.S. 533 (2001).

[18] *Id.* at 537–39.

[19] *Id.* at 541–43, 547–48.

to speak on behalf of their private, indigent clients.[20] Crucially, they were charged to do so through "an existing medium of expression" – the legal system.[21] However, in limiting the stock of arguments from which LSC attorneys can draw to advise and advocate for their clients, the government impermissibly "distorts the legal system by altering the traditional role of the attorneys" as zealous advocates for their clients.[22] Among the problems with such distortion is that it "prohibits speech and expression upon which courts must depend for the proper exercise of the judicial power."[23] The Court stressed that "[a]n informed, independent judiciary presumes an informed, independent bar."[24] Justice Kennedy thus relied partly on descriptive reasoning, observing that the restriction conflicts with "the traditional role of the attorneys" and with the judiciary's expectation that lawyers will conform to that role.[25] He also invoked normative concerns about the impact of such distortion on the legal system. Indeed, he suggested that normative considerations were especially strong in this case because the restriction "insulate[d] the Government's interpretation of the Constitution from judicial challenge,"[26] thus implicating "central First Amendment concerns."[27]

An anti-distortion principle also can be discerned in several cases involving free speech on university campuses. Echoing *Velazquez*, the Court in these cases drew on descriptive understandings of what university life and academia entail and on normative views regarding the features that imbue them with constitutional value. In *Rosenberger v. Rector and Visitors of the University of Virginia*,[28] for example, the Court held that the University of Virginia's (UVA) system for subsidizing student groups is akin to a limited public forum; as such, the subsidies cannot constitutionally be allocated on the basis of viewpoint or in a manner unreasonable in light of the subsidy program's purpose.[29] UVA had breached these limits by denying funds on the basis of viewpoint.[30] The Court stressed the denial's incompatibility with the nature and mission of universities, positing: "In the university setting . . . the State acts against a background and tradition of thought and experiment that is at the center of our intellectual and philosophic tradition."[31]

The constitutional salience of an anti-distortion principle for public academia is also reflected in *Garcetti v. Ceballos*.[32] *Garcetti* established that public employees

[20] *Id.*
[21] *Id.* at 542–43.
[22] *Id.* at 544.
[23] *Id.* at 545.
[24] *Id.*
[25] *See supra* text accompanying notes 23–25.
[26] 531 U.S. at 548.
[27] *Id.* at 547.
[28] 515 U.S. 819 (1995).
[29] *Id.* at 823–24, 829–30.
[30] *Id.* at 830–32, 834–35.
[31] *Id.* at 835.
[32] 547 U.S. 410 (2006).

receive no First Amendment protection against termination or other job-related penalties for speech that they convey in the course of doing their jobs. The *Garcetti* rule is of a piece with government speech doctrine and thus largely antithetical to anti-distortion principles. However, the *Garcetti* Court left the door open to an exception for the expressive work of public school academics, acknowledging that "[t]here is some argument that expression related to academic scholarship or classroom instruction implicates additional constitutional interests that are not fully accounted for by this Court's customary employee-speech jurisprudence."[33] An academic freedom exception is necessarily grounded in an anti-distortion principle, specifically in the notion that the state may not create or fund an institution of a type ordinarily characterized by academic freedom but then curtail that freedom.

Garcetti and *Rosenberger* stand on the shoulders of several McCarthy-era cases that extoll the virtues of academic freedom and suggest that its compromise distorts pedagogy and scholarship. In *Keyishian v. Board of Regents*, for example, the Court invalidated New York statutes "barring employment on the basis of membership in 'subversive' organizations. . . ."[34] The suit had been brought by a group of state university faculty members, and the Court stressed the laws' incompatibility with academic freedom. "The classroom," it wrote, "is peculiarly the 'marketplace of ideas.'"[35] The laws would distort the classroom's very nature. The Court framed this point partly in descriptive terms, telling readers what the classroom "*is*."[36] But it also invoked normative concerns about the free speech value served by an undistorted classroom. For example, the Court quoted an earlier case to the effect that "[n]o one should underestimate the vital role in a democracy that is played by those who guide and train our youth . . . Teachers and students must always remain free to inquire, to study and to evaluate . . . otherwise our civilization will stagnate and die."[37]

Courts also have touched on anti-distortion reasoning in cases involving public libraries. For example, in *United States v. American Library Association*,[38] a plurality of the Supreme Court, as well as the two concurring justices, all relied partly on their understanding of ordinary library practices to assess the constitutionality of a statutory condition on federal funding for public libraries. The statutory provisions required public libraries that receive federal funding for internet access to use blocking software to prevent patrons from accessing child pornography, obscenity, and other "visual depictions" harmful to minors.[39] The libraries were permitted to

33 *Id.* at 425.

34 Keyishian v. Bd. of Regents, 385 U.S. 589, 605–06 (1967), *quoted in* Connick v. Myers, 461 U.S. 138, 144 (1983).

35 *Id.* at 603.

36 *Id.* (emphasis added).

37 *Id.* at 603 (citing Sweezy v. New Hampshire, 354 U.S. 234, 250 (1957)).

38 539 U.S. 194 (2003).

39 *Id.* at 201.

disable the blocking software during periods of lawful adult usage and, in some cases, juvenile usage.[40] Writing for the plurality, Chief Justice Rehnquist reasoned that the law's constitutionality could not be resolved without "first examin[ing] the role of libraries in our society."[41] In performing this assessment, Rehnquist mixed a descriptive understanding of what libraries do with a normative take on what they should do to fulfill their "worthy missions of facilitating learning and cultural enrichment."[42] He concluded that libraries must make content-based judgments as to which materials "have 'requisite and appropriate quality.'"[43] In the same vein, public libraries should be free to offer patrons the "vast amount of valuable information" on the internet without also being forced to give them access to obscenity or child pornography.[44] The plurality thus upheld the statutory conditions. The two concurring justices – Kennedy and Breyer – cited the constitutional significance of the fact that the law permitted libraries to unblock the software upon request by adult patrons.[45] Justice Breyer also elaborated on the nature of libraries from both descriptive and normative perspectives, citing their role as "critically important sources of information"[46] and comparing their traditional practices – including content selection and the employment of closed stacks – to the challenged statutory condition.[47]

As these examples demonstrate, traces of an anti-distortion principle are scattered throughout First Amendment case law. Yet the idea remains undertheorized, and two points especially call for development. First, the *why*. That is, why it matters, from a First Amendment perspective, whether government conditions distort the nature of funded speech or speech institutions. Second, the *how*. That is, how interpreters should determine the nature of certain types of speech or expressive institutions. Lack of clarity on these points heightens the anti-distortion principle's vulnerability to an encroaching government speech doctrine.

23.1.2 *Government Speech Doctrine*

There is indeed tension between the anti-distortion principle and the Supreme Court's widening embrace of the "government speech doctrine." Government speech doctrine is typically traced to the 1991 case of *Rust v. Sullivan*.[48] In *Rust*, the Supreme Court upheld federal regulations barring family planning clinics from

[40] *Id*. at 198–201.
[41] *Id*. at 203.
[42] *Id*.
[43] *Id*. at 204.
[44] *Id*. at 200. Indeed, Chief Justice Rehnquist observed that numerous public libraries had already begun to use filtering software before the statutory provisions at issue were enacted. *Id*.
[45] *Id*. at 214 (Kennedy, J., concurring); *id*. at 219 (Breyer, J., concurring).
[46] *Id*. at 216 (Breyer, J., concurring).
[47] *Id*. at 217–20 (Breyer, J., concurring).
[48] 500 U.S. 173 (1991).

mentioning abortion in the course of providing federally subsidized counseling.[49] The *Rust* Court characterized the regulations as doing nothing more than setting boundaries on the scope of a government-funded program.[50] It was the *Rosenberger* Court that first framed *Rust* as a government speech decision.[51] *Rust*, it said, had "recognized that when the government appropriates public funds to promote a particular policy of its own it is entitled to say what it wishes."[52]

Rust itself embodies the tension between the government speech doctrine and anti-distortion. Critics of *Rust* have argued that the challenged conditions forced medical providers to choose between funding and professional and ethical norms. As Robert Post put it, the regulations sought to "override [physicians'] necessary exercise of independent professional judgment."[53] They also upended patients' expectations of the care that they would receive from a funded clinic: "In a world where physicians routinely exercise independent judgment, patients come to expect and rely on that judgment."[54] Post's insights help to illuminate the distorting effect of the regulation on the speech of subsidized medical professionals. Five years after Post's article was published, the Supreme Court issued its opinion in *Velazquez*, recognizing the distorting effect of the challenged restrictions on LSC attorneys. Although the *Velazquez* Court made some effort to distinguish *Rust*, explaining that the latter involved a "programmatic [governmental] message,"[55] that distinction failed to account for the distorting effect of directing medical professionals to convey the government's messaging. *Velazquez* and *Rust* thus represent two strains in the case law – the anti-distortion principle and government speech doctrine – and the tension between them.

In the years since *Rust* was decided, government speech doctrine has expanded considerably. This has prompted commentators and jurists to express alarm, much of it over the risk that government largesse will be leveraged to silence disfavored private voices and views.[56] For example, the Supreme Court held in *Walker v. Tex. Div., Sons of Confederate Veterans*[57] that specialty license plates in Texas, even those designed by private groups to reflect private hobbies and interests, constitute

49 *Id.* at 191.

50 *Id.* at 196.

51 *Rosenberger*, 515 U.S. at 833.

52 *Id. See also Velazquez*, 531 U.S. at 541 (explaining that "*Rust* did not place explicit reliance" on the government speech rationale, but that, "when interpreting the holding in later cases . . . we have explained *Rust* on this understanding.").

53 Robert C. Post, *Subsidized Speech*, 106 YALE L.J. 151, 173 (1996).

54 *Id.* at 174.

55 *Velazquez*, 531 U.S. at 548.

56 *See, e.g.*, Matal v. Tam, 137 S.Ct. 1744, 1758 (2017); Walker v. Tex. Div., Sons of Confederate Veterans, 576 U.S. 200, 221 (2015) (Alito, J., dissenting); Mary-Rose Papandrea, *The Government Brand*, 110 NORTHWESTERN U. L. REV. 1195, 1197–98, 1226–34 (2016); Caroline Mala Corbin, *Government Speech and First Amendment Capture*, 107 VA. L. REV. ONLINE 224, 231–41 (2021).

57 576 U.S. 200 (2015).

government speech.[58] Dissenting on behalf of himself and three other justices, Justice Alito lamented the Court's "capacious understanding of government speech"[59] that "threatens private speech that government finds displeasing."[60] As *Walker* demonstrates, the risks of a growing government speech doctrine are not limited to distortion,[61] but they very much include distortion.

The government speech development most conducive to distortion is the *Garcetti* rule – that is, the holding of *Garcetti v. Ceballos* to the effect that public employees have no First Amendment protection for expression that they convey in the course of doing their jobs. Although the *Garcetti* Court's reasoning is murky and at points even contradictory,[62] it relies at least partly on a government speech rationale, characterizing public employee work product speech as speech that "the employer itself has commissioned or created."[63] To support this point, it cites *Rosenberger*'s description of *Rust*'s holding: "When the government appropriates public funds to promote a particular policy of its own it is entitled to say what it wishes."[64] The assumption that government employees invariably convey a government-crafted message when they speak runs headlong into distortion concerns in the many cases in which employees are hired to provide professional judgment and expertise. Recall that the *Garcetti* Court itself implicitly acknowledges this insofar as it suggests the possible necessity of an exemption for public academics.

The clash between government speech doctrine and anti-distortion aims is cast in especially sharp relief in litigation regarding *Garcetti*'s academic exception. For example, in *Pernell v. Florida Board of Governors* – a case currently pending on appeal before the U.S. Court of Appeals for the Eleventh Circuit – the defendants urged the District Court for the Northern District of Florida to reject an academic exception to *Garcetti*, noting that the *Garcetti* Court had not definitively established one. The defendants characterized professorial classroom speech as "heartland government speech."[65] As such, they argued, a state legislature may dictate its contents.[66] The district court rejected this position, deeming it incompatible with the Supreme Court's "clear constitutional concerns," reflected in *Garcetti* and

58 *Id.* at 204–05, 214–15; *id.* at 221–22, 225–26 (Alito, J., dissenting).
59 *Id.* at 222 (Alito, J., dissenting).
60 *Id.* at 221.
61 *See also, e.g.*, *Matal*, 137 S.Ct. at 1758 (drawing the line at treating the grant of a trademark as an event that transforms private speech into government speech and observing, "[i]f private speech could be passed off as government speech by simply affixing a government seal of approval, government could silence or muffle the expression of disfavored viewpoints.").
62 *See* Heidi Kitrosser, *The Special Value of Public Employee Speech*, 2015 Sup. Ct. Rev. 311, 332–36 (2015).
63 *Garcetti*, 547 U.S. at 422.
64 *Id.* (citing *Rosenberger*, 515 U.S. at 833).
65 Defendants' Memorandum of Law in Support of Motion to Dismiss at 10, Pernell v. Fla. Bd. of Governors, No. 4:22-cv-304 (N.D. Fla. Sept. 22, 2022).
66 *Id.*

elsewhere, for academic freedom.[67] Thus far, every federal appellate court to have considered the issue similarly has exempted scholarly and pedagogical speech in higher education from *Garcetti*'s reach.[68]

23.1.3 *State-Subsidized Journalism in Existing Case Law*

Courts have also considered the reach of government speech doctrine and anti-distortion principles in the context of public journalism and state subsidies for private press entities. A leading Supreme Court case in this regard is *Arkansas Educational Television Commission v. Forbes*.[69] Writing for the *Forbes* Court, Justice Kennedy held that a public television station had not violated the First Amendment by refusing to include Ralph Forbes in a televised candidates' debate for a congressional seat. Justice Kennedy found that the debate was a nonpublic forum but concluded that the station's decision to exclude Forbes was viewpoint-neutral and reasonable in light of the forum's purpose.[70] Given Forbes' lack of public and financial support as a candidate, the station's decision "was a reasonable, viewpoint-neutral exercise of journalistic discretion."[71]

A few aspects of *Forbes* are especially relevant to our inquiry. First, the majority relied on its descriptive understanding of the natures, respectively, of broadcast journalism and of candidate debates. With respect to the former, Justice Kennedy repeatedly invoked the notion that editorial discretion is a core feature of journalism. As such, he explained, it typically is inappropriate for courts to treat broadcast programs as forums at all.[72] On the other hand, the nature of a candidate debate – specifically, the fact that in airing it, a broadcaster traditionally implies "that the views expressed [are] those of the candidate, not its own"[73] – makes it "a nonpublic forum, from which AETC could exclude Forbes in the reasonable, viewpoint-neutral exercise of its journalistic discretion."[74] Second, the majority considered normative factors in concluding that candidate debates are forums, albeit nonpublic ones, and thus not entirely outside the reach of First Amendment analysis. It cited the "exceptional significance" of candidate debates "in the electoral process," observing that "[d]eliberation on the positions and qualifications of candidates is integral to our system of government, and electoral speech may have its most profound and widespread impact when it is disseminated through televised debates."[75] Third, the majority left open a question that is especially germane to

67 *Pernell* at *9–*10.
68 *See* Heim v. Daniel, 81 F.4th 212, 224–28 (2d Cir. 2023)
69 523 U.S. 666 (1998).
70 *Id.* at 682.
71 *Id.* at 683.
72 *Id.* at 673–75.
73 *Id.* at 675.
74 *Id.* at 676.
75 *Id.* at 675–76.

this chapter: the extent to which Congress, rather than courts, has leeway to impose access demands on public broadcasters. Justice Kennedy explained that the First Amendment would not necessarily "bar the legislative imposition of neutral rules for access to public broadcasting."[76] However, "in most cases, the First Amendment of its own force does not compel public broadcasters to allow third parties access to their programming."[77] The Court's discussion and the underlying controversy all took place against the backdrop of a statutory scheme that imposed duties on broadcasters "to schedule programming that serves the 'public interest, convenience, and necessity.'"[78]

The Supreme Court did grapple with congressional restraints on public broadcasters in a series of mid-twentieth-century cases. Although these cases preceded the development of modern government speech doctrine, they reflect an instinct to reconcile the government's ability to define its own projects with the editorial independence that the Court associated, descriptively and normatively, with the news media. The government benefits at stake in these cases included both subsidies and broadcast spectrum. The latter was a limited commodity, and Congress had conditioned its use on broadcasters' serving the "'public interest, convenience, and necessity.'"[79] Writing for the majority in 1984's *FCC v. League of Women Voters* ("*LWV*"), Justice Brennan explained that "given spectrum scarcity," broadcast licensees could be treated "as fiduciaries for the public...."[80] Using this rationale, the Court in previous cases had rejected First Amendment challenges to both the FCC's "Fairness Doctrine"[81] and a "limited right of 'reasonable' access" to the broadcast airwaves for "legally qualified federal candidates."[82] Still, the Court maintained that broadcasters retained "'the widest journalistic freedom consistent with their public [duties]."[83] "Indeed," Brennan wrote, "if the public's interest in receiving a balanced presentation of views is to be fully served, we must necessarily rely in large part upon the editorial initiative and judgment of the broadcasters who bear the public trust."[84] The *LWV* Court paired these words with action, holding that Congress had exceeded constitutional limits when it barred broadcasters who received any funding from the congressionally created Corporation for Public Broadcasting from airing editorials.[85] In the Court's view, the editorial ban violated

76 *Id.* at 675.
77 *Id.*
78 Indeed, the *Forbes* Court's discussion and the underlying controversy took place against the backdrop of this requirement. *Id.* at 673 (quoting 47 U.S.C. § 309(a)).
79 *Id.* (quoting 47 U.S.C. § 309(a)).
80 468 U.S. 364, 377 (1984).
81 *Id.* at 378 (citing Red Lion Broad. Co. v. FCC, 395 U.S. 367, 396 (1969)). The Fairness Doctrine "require[d] broadcasters to provide adequate coverage of public issues and to ensure that this coverage fairly and accurately reflect[ed] the opposing views." *Id.*
82 CBS v. FCC, 453 U.S. 367, 396 (1981), *cited in LWV*, 468 U.S. at 378.
83 *LWV*, 468 U.S. at 378 (quoting *CBS*, 453 U.S. at 395) (additional internal citation omitted).
84 *Id.* (citing CBS v. DNC, 412 U.S. 94, 124–27 (1973)).
85 *Id.* at 366, 395.

the First Amendment because it forced licensees to refrain from behavior that descriptively constituted a core part of journalism and normatively bore substantial free speech value. As to the latter, Justice Brennan wrote for the majority that "the expression of editorial opinion ... lies at the heart of First Amendment protection."[86] Preserving it "is part and parcel of 'a profound national commitment ... that debate on public issues should be uninhibited, robust, and wide open.'"[87] The majority also melded its normative reasoning with descriptive observation, suggesting that the press is essential to democracy in part because of its tradition of editorial speech: "[T]he special place of the editorial in our First Amendment jurisprudence simply reflects the fact that the press ... carries out a historic, dual responsibility in our society of reporting information and of bringing critical judgment to bear on public affairs."[88]

Finally, a recent U.S. District Court case from the District of Columbia – 2020's *Turner v. U.S. Agency for Global Media*[89] – directly tackles the tension between government speech doctrine and anti-distortion concerns regarding the press. Although *Turner* was never appealed, having been mooted by a change in administrations, it is remarkable in that it takes the view that *Garcetti*'s reasoning about a potential academic freedom exception extends to public news media. Specifically, Judge Beryl Howell concludes that "*Garcetti* does not apply to the core editorial or journalistic functions of government-employed journalists"[90] for the same reason that it ought not to apply to academics: "Freedom of the press holds an equally exalted place in the First Amendment firmament" as does academic freedom.[91] She follows this point with a long list of citations and quotations from Supreme Court opinions extolling the "essential role" of the press "in our democracy."[92] Judge Howell's analysis assumes that when the government creates or manages certain knowledge-producing institutions, including journalism and academia, the constitutional value of those institutions can limit the government's ability to distort the features that make them valuable.

Three additional aspects of *Turner* are instructive. First, because Judge Howell found *Garcetti* inapplicable to publicly employed journalists, she ordinarily would have proceeded to the so-called "*Pickering* balance test," whereby courts determine whether speech is on a matter of public concern and, if so, weigh "the employee's interest in protected speech against the government's interest in promoting efficiency. ..."[93] However, because of procedural limits on federal employees' ability

86 *Id.* at 381.
87 *Id.* at 382 (quoting New York Times Co. v. Sullivan, 376 U.S. 254, 270 (1964)).
88 *Id.* (internal citation omitted).
89 502 F. Supp. 3d 333 (D.D.C. 2020).
90 *Id.* at 376.
91 *Id.* at 375.
92 *Id.* at 375 (quoting N.Y. Times Co. v. United States, 403 U.S. 713, 717 (1971) (Black, J., concurring)); *id.* (citing several additional Supreme Court cases).
93 *Id.* at 376.

to bring First Amendment claims directly in federal courts, the *Turner* court could consider only some of the plaintiffs' claims on the merits.[94] Specifically, Judge Howell limited her merits review to the plaintiffs' First Amendment challenge to the defendants' alleged breach of a statutory and regulatory firewall between the U.S. Agency for Global Media's (USAGM) political leadership and its professional journalists in editorial decision making.[95] Because the acts that comprised the alleged breach were "'generally applicable'" policies and practices rather than "'particularized disciplinary action[s],'" Judge Howell concluded that another legal standard – from *United States v. National Treasury Employees Union* (*NTEU*) – had to be imported into her application of the *Pickering* balance test.[96] Judge Howell thus asked, pursuant to *NTEU*, whether "the restrictions … allegedly imposed on [plaintiffs'] speech are no more restrictive than '"reasonably necessary to protect" various government interests.'"[97] The *Turner* Court rightly framed its use of the *NTEU* standard as premised partly on the greater reach – including the potential chilling effects – of broadly applicable policies and practices as opposed to post hoc, individualized employment actions.[98] Yet the *NTEU* standard might independently be justified as reflecting the lesser deference due to a nonexpert political appointee's ex ante policy decision as opposed to a post hoc, individualized determination by a supervisor who is an expert in the relevant field.

Second, in assessing the reasonable necessity of the challenged actions, the *Turner* court implicitly conducts an anti-distortion analysis. This is an intuitive move, as reasonable necessity cannot be determined without assessing an institution's characteristic needs and goals and the practices typically employed to meet those ends. Given the practical nature of this inquiry, Howell focuses on descriptive aspects of USAGM, its stations, and journalistic institutions generally. She compares the challenged acts to USAGM's statutory guidelines, including the directive that "U.S.-funded international broadcasting 'be conducted in accordance with the highest professional standards of broadcast journalism'"[99] and the statutory firewall that gives "evaluative and review responsibilities" to USAGM while leaving "day-to-day control … to the stations themselves."[100] She also consults Voice of America's

94 *Id.* at 363–64 (explaining that alleged "personnel actions" must first be challenged through administrative channels under the Civil Service Reform Act).

95 *Id.* at 366–68. *See also* Amended Complaint at ¶¶ 173–79, Turner v. U.S. Agency for Global Media, Case No. 20-cv-2885 (D.D.C. Nov. 4, 2020) (detailing plaintiffs' third cause of action, the constitutional claim regarding firewall breach).

96 *Id.* at 377 (citing United States v. National Treasury Employees Union [NTEU], 513 U.S. 454 (1995)).

97 *Id.* at 378 (quoting Weaver v. U.S. Info. Agency, 87 F.3d 1429, 1436 (D.C. Cir. 1996) (citing *NTEU*, 513 U.S. at 474)). Before conducting this balancing test, Judge Howell determined that the plaintiffs' journalistic work plainly entailed "'matters of public concern.'" *Id.* at 376 (citing Pickering, 391 U.S. at 568).

98 *Id.* at 377–78.

99 *Id.* at 378 (quoting 22 U.S.C. § 6202(a)(5)).

100 *Id.* (quoting Ralis v. RFE/RL, Inc., 770 F.2d 1121, 1125 (D.C. Cir. 1985)).

Best Practices Guide and USAGM's ethics policy in evaluating whether the defendants' alleged firewall breaches were "reasonably necessary," or whether alternative procedures were available to achieve their ends.[101] Additionally, Judge Howell compares some of the requirements imposed by USAGM on personnel to "standard journalistic practices."[102]

Third, the facts underlying *Turner* highlight the complexity that can arise in reconciling anti-distortion goals with legitimate government line-drawing concerning the scope of state projects. Yet *Turner* also illustrates that such difficulties are not insurmountable. The heightened complexity stems from the fact that USAGM oversees international broadcasting stations, most famously the Voice of America (VOA).[103] US international broadcasting efforts plainly are designed to serve diplomatic purposes; indeed, it is no coincidence that VOA began in the midst of World War II, with its first broadcast transmitted in Germany in 1942.[104] Accordingly, USAGM networks are charged by statute to ensure that their broadcasts are "consistent with the broad foreign policy objectives of the United States."[105] The networks also "shall include" in their broadcasts "a balanced and comprehensive projection of United States thoughts and institutions."[106] At the same time, the governing statutory authorities – and long-standing US and network representations as to the characters of the networks – demand journalistic independence in day-to-day operations and best journalistic practices.[107] Judge Howell reconciled these competing considerations by finding that the reasonable necessity standard was met with respect only to those managerial decisions that did not directly intrude into or threaten to chill day-to-day journalistic and editorial decision making.[108]

23.2 WHY DISTORTION IS A FIRST AMENDMENT PROBLEM

The precedent described above reflects two things about existing free speech case law. First, government speech doctrine is potentially a very expansive means to empower federal and state legislative and executive bodies to cloak political messaging in the vestments of professional expertise – whether journalistic, pedagogical, scientific, or otherwise. Second, extant judicial doctrine contains the makings of an important counter-force – the anti-distortion principle – to guard against such expansion. However, the latter is currently lacking in two important respects. First, the *why* of anti-distortion – specifically, why distortion is a problem from a First

[101] *Id.* at 382.
[102] *Id.* at 383.
[103] *Id.* at 343–47.
[104] *Id.* at 341–44.
[105] *Id.* at 345 (quoting International Broadcasting Act § 303(a)(1)).
[106] *Id.* (quoting International Broadcasting Act § 303(b)(2)).
[107] *See, e.g., supra* text accompanying notes 100 and 101.
[108] *Turner*, 502 F. Supp. 3d at 378–85 (assessing specific firewall breach allegations under the reasonable necessity standard).

Amendment perspective – is not explained with depth or consistency across the cases. Second, the *how* of the principle – that is, how one determines whether and when distortion exists – has not been considered with deliberateness, although aspects of it can be inferred from existing cases.

In this section, I consider the *why* question raised by the anti-distortion doctrine. I explain that distortion is a First Amendment problem for reasons involving both negative First Amendment theory, which focuses on the dangers of speech regulation, and positive First Amendment theory, which focuses on the affirmative benefits of speech and press freedoms. With respect to negative theory, distortion enables the government to pull the wool over the people's eyes, leveraging its largesse to present political, even partisan messaging as the product of disciplinary expertise. This is a cause for alarm whenever it impacts the expression of public employees or subsidized private actors. There are special bases for concern when the government claims to be funding journalism. Second, when the government purports to fund knowledge production but conditions its subsidies on speech restrictions that have a distorting effect, it undermines the affirmative First Amendment values of the very enterprise that it claims to subsidize. In the case of funded journalism, distortion undercuts journalists' ability to perform core First Amendment and structural constitutional functions: overseeing the actions of society's most powerful actors, including government actors, and educating the American public about important issues and events that impact their community and the larger world.

23.2.1 *Distortion and the Negative Theory of Speech and Press Freedoms*

Efforts to launder political messaging – that is, to pass it off as expertise by imposing pressure on public employees or subsidy recipients – are antithetical to one of the core values underlying the First Amendment's protections for free speech: distrust of government power.[109] As Helen Norton explains:

> While courts and commentators have long posited that speech deserves constitutional protection when it is affirmatively valuable in facilitating democratic self-governance, enlightenment, and individual autonomy, the First Amendment tradition also relies on what many call a negative theory of the Free Speech Clause. Under this approach, the Constitution protects speech not so much because it is so valuable, but instead because the government is so dangerous in its capacity to abuse its regulatory power.[110]

Negative theory is not mutually exclusive from positive theories of free speech, which include the notions that free speech facilitates the search for truth, is essential

[109] *See, e.g.*, Helen Norton, *Distrust, Negative First Amendment Theory, and the Regulation of Lies*, 22-07 Knight First Amend. Inst.3 (Oct. 19, 2022), https://knightcolumbia.org/content/distrust-negative-first-amendment-theory-and-the-regulation-of-lies.

[110] *Id.*

to a democratic system, and enhances individual autonomy.[111] Indeed, Frederick Schauer has demonstrated that negative free speech theory lies at the core of all major theories of free speech value.[112] For example, the democracy theory of free speech might at first blush seem a contradiction in terms: a democracy-based argument for limiting the majority's power to restrict free speech. What makes sense of the theory is the reality of human, and hence governmental, fallibility. As Schauer writes: "We wish to preserve the freedom to criticize the policies of the majority because those policies may be wrong, just as any other judgment may be wrong."[113] Incompetence is not the only risk; those who govern us may be corrupt or abusive and may suppress or manipulate speech to shield themselves from criticism or unwelcome revelations.[114]

Heightened alert against government abuse or incompetence is well warranted when distortion is afoot. Although political actors generally are free to craft and convey whatever messages they like, it is another story when they use public employees or subsidized private actors as vehicles to convey those messages and present them to the public as products of professional judgment and expertise. In such cases, there is reason to fear either that the political actors who crafted the messages believe that they themselves have resolved the scientific or other question at issue, a conclusion that raises fallibility concerns, or that they are abusing their power by cloaking political messaging as expertise.

Negative free speech theory packs an additional punch when it is applied to the press, and the Constitution's Press Clause provides an additional textual hook for it as well. As Helen Norton writes, "[n]egative theory can help us understand the press clause as providing an especially robust shield from the government's retaliation,"[115] given the press's oversight role and its structurally and historically antagonistic relationship to the powerful actors, including government actors, whom it oversees.[116] There are distinct reasons to fear governments' efforts to leverage their largesse to dress self-scripted plaudits in the vestments of hard-hitting journalism or to squash critical reporting.[117]

[111] *Id.* at 3–4; *see also, e.g.*, Frederick Schauer, Free Speech: A Philosophical Enquiry 33–34, 44–46, 71–72, 86 (1982).

[112] Schauer, *supra* note 111, at 33–34, 44–46, 71–72, 86 (1982).

[113] *Id.* at 45.

[114] *See* Norton, *supra* note 109, at 3–4, 6–8.

[115] Helen Norton, *Reinvigorating the Press Clause Through Negative Theory*, *in* The Future of Press Freedom: Democracy, Law, and the News in Changing Times 161, 162 (RonNell Andersen Jones & Sonja R. West eds., 2025).

[116] *Id. See also, e.g.*, Andersen Jones, *supra* note 1, at 2443–44.

[117] *See also* Andersen Jones, *supra* note 1, at 546 ("The government knows that as listeners 'we value the press for telling us what our elected officials are up to, so that we can, in turn, have an informed dialogue about their performance and make informed decisions about whether we wish to elect them again.' It has every incentive to attempt to use its power to shape and even forcibly control that content to make it favorable to the government.").

One might argue that negative theory counsels against the government's financing journalism at all, given the dangers of abuse or error. Even if this view were a sound one, it would not detract from the importance of protecting against government capture through distortion when the government does fund press activities. More importantly, the argument against public financing overlooks two points: first, the affirmative value, indeed the essentialness of an active and robust press in American life; and second, the importance of public financing, perhaps today more than ever, as one of the tools with which to ensure the survival of the American press. I elaborate on both points in the next subsection.

23.2.2 *Distortion and the Affirmative Benefits of Speech and Press Freedoms*

Courts and scholars have long relied on speech's affirmative value, often bolstered by negative theory, to justify and interpret First Amendment protections. To take a classic example, the Supreme Court in *New York Times Co. v. Sullivan* famously established a high bar for public official plaintiffs in defamation cases.[118] The majority opinion by Justice Brennan invoked the value of speech and press freedoms in enlightening and informing the people and thus in serving democracy and checking governmental power. Brennan quoted James Madison to the effect that, "If we advert to the nature of Republican Government, we shall find that the censorial power is in the people over the Government, and not in the Government over the people."[119] Brennan also approvingly described Madison's view that "[t]he right of free public discussion of the stewardship of public officials was … a fundamental principle of the American form of government."[120] The *Sullivan* Court bolstered its discussion of these benefits with a nod to negative theory, quoting Justice Brandeis to the effect that "the occasional tyrannies of governing majorities" demand constitutional guarantees for free speech.[121]

Distortion robs expression of its affirmative First Amendment value. The problem is well illustrated by the example of the press. As reflected in *Sullivan* – which was technically a Free Speech Clause case but invoked the press's constitutional significance extensively in its reasoning[122] – courts and scholars frequently associate the press with democratic and oversight values.[123] These values cannot be served, however, by journalism that is compromised by distortion. This is particularly obvious with respect to journalism's checking or oversight function. A journalist

[118] New York Times Co. v. Sullivan, 376 U.S. 254 (1964).

[119] *Id.* at 275 (quoting 4 ANNALS OF CONG. 934 (1974)).

[120] *Id.*

[121] *Id.* at 270 (quoting Whitney v. California, 274 U.S. 357, 375–76 (Brandeis, J., concurring)).

[122] *See* Sonja R. West, *The Stealth Press Clause*, 48 GA. L. REV. 729, 730, 745 (2014) (characterizing *Sullivan* as a "stealth" press case because it embraced "the unique role of the press" while technically being "not really a 'press' case").

[123] *See* Vincent Blasi, *The Checking Value in First Amendment Theory*, 2 AM. BAR FOUND. RSCH. J. 521 (2977)

will obviously face a conflict in reporting on a person or entity who controls their substantive output. Distortion is also antithetical to the First Amendment's role in supporting democracy more broadly. To the extent that reporting involves politics or policy, it can be difficult to predict when it might entail checking – a journalist might, for example, stumble unexpectedly across a scandal – and the temptation for political interference thus remains a factor. Beyond checking, distortion intrinsically threatens to hijack features that make journalism central to a healthy democracy – its ability to spread information and ideas that are presumed to follow from fact-finding, corroboration, and learned analysis – to dress up and convey political messaging.

Furthermore, as noted earlier, it would not be desirable simply to write off government support for fear of distortion. American journalism is currently in a terribly precarious economic state, one that has decimated much investigative reporting and local news coverage.[124] Although public financing is not the only tool available for "saving the news,"[125] it is an essential part of the toolkit.[126] As current events demonstrate all too well, socially valuable reporting does not necessarily translate to commercial success. More so, private financial interests often will be antagonistic to investigative reporting or editorial commentary that oversees powerful public and private actors.[127] Public financing has its own problems, to be sure, not the least of which is the risk of state capture under even a robust anti-distortion framework. What is needed, ideally, is a diverse array of models for funding the news, ranging from the for-profit to the publicly funded to the private nonprofit. Yet if a publicly funded press is to possess the affirmative First Amendment values that make it worth supporting, anti-distortion principles are essential.

23.3 IDENTIFYING DISTORTION

Even if one supports the principle of anti-distortion in theory, there remains the practical question of how to determine when distortion is afoot. To make matters trickier still, identifying distortion is a two-step process. One must first define the baseline: What *is* the nature or ordinary practices of the knowledge institution or type of expression at issue? One then must ask whether the challenged condition or directive is reasonably compatible with that baseline.

These are not easy questions, but they are also not impassable ones. Because they are deeply fact-driven inquiries, there is no one-size-fits-all formula to resolve them. One can, however, identify factors for courts, legislatures, and other decision-makers to consider. The existing case law itself is a useful starting point toward this end.

[124] *See supra* notes 6–8.

[125] *See generally* Minow, *supra* note 9.

[126] *See supra* text accompanying notes 9–12.

[127] *See, e.g.*, Sonja R. West, *Press Exceptionalism*, 127 Harv. L. Rev. 2434, 2451 (2014) (citing the press' role in checking powerful private as well as public actors); West, *supra* note 122, at 754–55 (same).

Recall from Section 23.1 that although courts have not identified anti-distortion as a distinct legal principle, they have implicitly considered whether distortion exists on a number of occasions. In this section, I draw from those cases to suggest several factors that courts, legislatures, and other decision-makers can use to guide distortion inquiries.

23.3.1 *Descriptive Considerations*

23.3.1.1 The Government's Own Representations

In a sense, the anti-distortion principle amounts to a rule that the government cannot have its cake and eat it too in the realm of public knowledge production. That is, it cannot purport to sponsor expression grounded in disciplinary expertise but set conditions that sabotage that goal. In determining the nature of a given expressive enterprise or type of speech, then, the government's public representations as to what it is funding should loom large. Governments often make such assertions through statutory and regulatory authorities and other public pronouncements.

The *Turner* Court relied in part on such evidence. Judge Howell looked to statutory descriptions of the funded knowledge producer – in this case, USAGM and its networks – to determine its nature. For example, she emphasized the statutory directive that "U.S.-funded international broadcasting 'be conducted in accordance with the highest professional standards of broadcast journalism'"[128] and the statutory firewall that gives "'evaluative and review responsibilities'" to USAGM while leaving "'day-to-day control . . . to the stations themselves.'"[129] Although these provisions bear most directly on USAGM's statutory duties, Judge Howell also treated them as having First Amendment significance because they informed the "reasonable necessity" inquiry that she undertook pursuant to *NTEU*.[130]

I would add an additional rationale for treating these provisions as probative of the constitutionality of the defendants' actions: They bear on the nature of the broadcasting enterprise that the government purports to be funding. This enterprise is especially complicated given its diplomatic dimension, as discussed in Section 23.1.[131] Nonetheless, the United States repeatedly has indicated through the relevant statutory authorities and otherwise that "in contrast to the state-run propaganda that dominates media in the countries where VOA and its sister networks broadcast, US-funded international broadcasting outlets combat disinformation and deception with facts, told through an American lens of democratic values."[132] As the *Turner*

[128] 502 F. Supp. 3d at 378 (quoting 22 U.S.C. § 6202(a)(5)).
[129] *Id.* at 378 (quoting Ralis, 770 F.2d at 1125).
[130] *Supra* text accompanying notes 98–101.
[131] *See supra* text accompanying notes 104–109.
[132] 502 F. Supp. 3d at 342.

Court put it, quoting an earlier case by the D.C. Circuit, "'to transform' these outlets 'into house organs for the United States government' would be 'inimical to [their] fundamental mission.'"[133] If distortion offends First Amendment values, then such transformation is a First Amendment problem.

23.3.1.2 Structure and Decision-Maker Identity

Structural factors, including the source of challenged actions or directives, are also highly probative of distortion. To illustrate, consider how a twist in the facts of *FCC v. League of Women Voters* might have altered the outcome. Recall that in *LWV*, the Supreme Court invalidated a statutory provision that barred broadcasters who received certain federal funds from running editorials.[134] Suppose instead that there had been no such statutory bar but that the producer of a particular news program, a career professional, had decided to stop running editorials on the program. Structurally, these circumstances suggest that the producer might well have been applying professional judgment grounded in expertise about programming choices. This indicia of non-distortion might be overcome by other factors, for instance, if there were evidence that the producer had faced pressure from politically appointed supervisors who did not like the content of recent editorials. The fact that the decision appeared at first blush to constitute a programming call by an expert decision-maker would not necessarily be decisive. But it would weigh in favor of a non-distortion finding.

Two aspects of *Turner* also reflect structural considerations. First, the core free speech violation that Judge Howell identified was a structural one – the breach of the firewall between political supervisors and career journalists. Second, recall that Judge Howell incorporated the relatively demanding *NTEU* test into the *Pickering* balancing test because she was evaluating "generally applicable" policies and practices rather than post hoc employee discipline.[135] Judge Howell rightly justified this move by reference to the relatively long reach of ex ante policies.[136] I would also add a second, independent basis for applying *NTEU*: an ex ante policy decision by a nonexpert political figure warrants considerably less deference than a fact-driven, post hoc determination by a career supervisor who is a professional in the field.

Finally, implicit in my attention to structure and decision-maker identity is the notion that "the government" is many things. For simplicity's sake, I refer throughout this chapter to statements that "the government" made or to actions that it took. However, it is important to keep in mind that even a single governmental unit – say, the US federal government or the government of a particular state or locality – comprises countless functions, departments, and people. For purposes of a

133 *Id.* at 342 (quoting Ralis, 770 F.2d at 1125).
134 *See supra* notes 85–88.
135 *See supra* text accompanying notes 96–97 (citing *Turner*, 502 F. Supp. 3d at 377–78).
136 *Supra* text accompanying note 96 (citing *Turner*, 502 F. Supp. 3d at 377).

distortion inquiry, it matters a great deal who within the government issued a particular directive – whether, for example, they were elected or appointed politically, whether they were part of the career civil service, and whether their role is associated with a professional discipline.

23.3.1.3 Evidence of Standard Practices

Knowledge production takes place within broader social and professional contexts laden with meaning. Particular types of knowledge production are associated with distinct professional and ethical norms, standard practices, and training.[137] As we saw in Section 23.1, courts frequently tap into this fact when they ask whether conditions on subsidized expression are constitutional.

To determine the nature and standard practices of a particular type of knowledge producer, courts draw from a hodgepodge of factors, including their own impressions, statements made in judicial precedent, legislative assumptions, and record evidence. In *LWV*, for example, the Supreme Court described editorials as central to journalism, invoking the press's "historic, dual responsibility in our society of reporting information and of bringing critical judgment to bear on public affairs."[138] To support this point, it cited earlier case law as well as the fact that the FCC had "for the past 35 years actively encouraged commercial broadcast licensees to include editorials on public affairs in their programming."[139] Outside of the broadcasting realm, recall that the Supreme Court in *Velazquez* relied on "the traditional role of the attorneys," which it took to encompass "the proposition that attorneys should present all the reasonable and well-grounded arguments necessary for proper resolution of the case."[140] Finally, returning to the example of *Turner*, Judge Howell drew not only on statutory claims of allegiance to best journalistic practices and to a firewall between politics and journalism but also on other evidence of standard and best practices, including VOA's *Best Practices Guide* and USAGM's ethical code.[141] The *Turner* plaintiffs also provided testimony to the effect that best practices in private journalism include the use of firewalls between commercial and journalistic interests.[142]

23.3.2 *Normative Considerations*

Courts do not rely solely on descriptive factors to determine the nature of particular knowledge producers. They also lean heavily on normative considerations,

[137] *See supra* notes 14–15 and accompanying text.
[138] *See supra* text accompanying note 89.
[139] *LWV*, 468 U.S. at 382.
[140] *Velazquez*, 531 U.S. at 545.
[141] 502 F. Supp. 3d at 382.
[142] *See* Kitrosser, *Protecting Public Knowledge Producers, supra* note 14 and accompanying text (quoting Declaration of Amanda Bennett in Support of Plaintiffs' Motion for a Temporary Restraining Order and Preliminary Injunction at 3–4, ¶ 10, *Turner*, 502 F. Supp. at 333).

emphasizing the importance of protecting those features that carry First Amendment value. In *Forbes*, for example, the Court observed not only that candidate debates are best characterized descriptively as nonpublic forums but that categorizing them as such – which subjects them to viewpoint discrimination and reasonableness rules – is warranted given their "exceptional significance" "in the electoral process."[143] Similarly, in *LWV*, the Court described editorials as a core aspect of broadcast journalism but also emphasized their importance to values associated with speech and press freedoms. Editorials are, the Court stated, "part and parcel of 'a profound national commitment ... that debate on public issues should be uninhibited, robust, and wide open.'"[144] Finally, in *Turner*, Judge Howell spoke of the firewall both as something that the United States had effectively pledged to honor and as essential to preserving the integrity of USAGM's news coverage. For example, to support her conclusion that the plaintiffs likely would succeed in their First Amendment claims regarding the defendants' newsroom intrusions, Judge Howell observed that "journalists and editors have already refrained from engaging in certain speech" and are "less willing to take on controversial but important stories and exercise greater caution in making statements that may offend defendants."[145] The significance of these observations is particularly pronounced when they are juxtaposed with Judge Howell's rationales for exempting the press from *Garcetti*'s reach, including the notions that "[f]reedom of the press holds an ... exalted place in the First Amendment firmament" and that "[t]he press was [meant] to serve the governed, not the governors."[146]

23.4 CONCLUSION

Neither the First Amendment in its own right, nor courts interpreting it, can make publicly funded knowledge producers impervious to state capture. First Amendment case law does, however, contain a surprisingly rich set of arguments and ideas to grapple with the problem of capture. Most importantly, it contains the seeds of an anti-distortion principle to the effect that the government may not condition funding – whether through employment or through a subsidy on a private actor – in a manner that distorts the nature of the type of speech or expressive institution that it purports to fund. The anti-distortion principle is important in its own right, and as a tool to limit a risk factor for capture – government speech doctrine – that was created by the judiciary itself.

Of course, judicial doctrine and litigation can get us only so far. Anti-distortion arguments grounded in case law are but one tool to support public knowledge

143 *Forbes*, 523 U.S. at 675–76. *See also supra* text accompanying note 75.

144 *LWV*, 468 U.S. at 382 (quoting *Sullivan*, 376 U.S. at 270). *See also supra* text accompanying notes 86–88.

145 *Turner*, 502 F. Supp. 3d at 381.

146 *Id.* at 375 (quoting Time, Inc. v. Hill, 385 U.S. 374, 389 (1967)).

production and to protect against its capture by the state. Such arguments most obviously can be wielded in litigation. They can also be invoked in the legislative drafting process to help guide the design of statutes regarding public employment or funding of knowledge producers. More so, the underlying threats against which anti-distortion principles guard – particularly the danger that political actors will launder partisan or political messaging to pass it off as the product of disciplinary expertise – can be raised in public discourse.

Perhaps somewhat counterintuitively, anti-distortion arguments also provide occasion to encourage public knowledge production. This is so for at least two reasons. First, the anti-distortion principle is justified not only by the government distrust associated with negative speech theory but by the positive aspirations of affirmative free speech theories. Second, robust anti-distortion principles are responsive to an argument routinely made against state funding – that is, the risk of capture.

Journalism's existential crisis casts into sharp relief both the affirmative benefits that anti-distortion principles help to foster and the dangers against which they guard. With respect to the former, recall the arguments that an active press is essential to oversee powerful government and private actors and, more broadly, to make democracy function. Where the market alone cannot provide this public good, some state support is essential; that support itself must be subject to anti-distortion principles to protect the funded reporting's value. With respect to the latter, government capture of the media bears harms that an anti-distortion principle is essential to guard against. To be sure, the anti-distortion principle is far from sufficient to save journalism. But insofar as public funding is an essential part of any rescue mission, so too is the anti-distortion principle.

24

Legal Foundations for Non-reformist Media Reforms

A Positive-Rights Paradigm for Guaranteeing a Universal Press System

Victor Pickard

Elementary democratic theory holds that self-governance requires a free – and, by implication, a *functional* – press system.[1] However, today, much of the American press infrastructure is being dismantled by a deeply systemic market failure, with little hope for self-correction. While significant democratic deficits have always existed in American journalism, it is becoming glaringly obvious that a purely commercial press system cannot provide for a multiracial democratic society's basic information and communication needs. At the time of this writing, the United States has lost nearly one-third of its newspapers and two-thirds of its journalists since 2005 – a profound structural crisis that promises to significantly worsen in the coming years.[2] It is no longer debatable that the advertising-dependent business model that supported commercial journalism for well over a century has irreparably collapsed. Systemic alternatives are desperately needed.

If democracy requires a press regardless of its profitability, it is incumbent upon society to develop a rationale for why the government must guarantee a baseline level of news and information for *all* members of society, not just the privileged few who happen to live in affluent neighborhoods. Otherwise, we guarantee a future of informational redlining and market censorship in which entire communities will be consigned to living permanently in news deserts, effectively disenfranchised from media production, dissemination, and consumption – and from fully participating in everyday civic life.[3]

Providing universal public service journalism to everyone requires ambitious, long-term, structural reforms – most likely involving the creation of an entirely

[1] Under standard First Amendment theory, it is generally recognized that a key feature of speech and press freedoms is to cultivate an informed citizenry. *See, e.g.*, Robert Post, *Participatory Democracy and Free Speech*, 97 VA. L. REV. 477 (2011).

[2] Penny Muse Abernathy, *The State of Local News: The 2024 Report*, MEDILL LOCAL NEWS INITIATIVE (Nov. 16, 2023), https://localnewsinitiative.northwestern.edu/projects/state-of-local-news/2023/report/.

[3] I examine the structural roots of the journalism crisis and their implications for democratic self-governance in VICTOR PICKARD, DEMOCRACY WITHOUT JOURNALISM? CONFRONTING THE MISINFORMATION SOCIETY (2020).

new public media system.[4] Given the unlikelihood of a commercial solution emerging to support local journalism at a systemic level, only the federal government has the resources and political power to create such a system. Generating the political support needed for initiating this massive project obviously will require much discursive, ideological, and legal work to shift the prevailing market-libertarian "common sense." Toward this admittedly long-term project, we must first legitimize the federal government's intervention in the commercial media marketplace to ensure the existence of a press system.

With an eye toward such a lofty objective, this chapter aims to articulate a positive-rights paradigm that marshals contemporary, historical, and international legal frameworks to argue that government should have an *affirmative duty* to guarantee meaningful access to news and information for everyone. Drawing from democratic, legal, and economic theories, the chapter builds on a long lineage of argumentation – from Alexander Meiklejohn and Jerome Barron to more recent arguments advanced by C. Edwin Baker and Martha Minow – for why the First Amendment does not forbid government interventions that promote journalism. If we assume that press freedom is rendered meaningless without a press to protect, we arguably should go even further to compel the government to make targeted and democratically determined interventions into the media marketplace to guarantee public alternatives when private commercial media institutions fail to serve democratic needs.[5]

The aim of this chapter, therefore, is threefold. First, I discuss the special nature and necessity of positive rights for guaranteeing a viable press system within democratic societies. Then, I explore their manifestations in international, historical, and contemporary legal doctrines, especially in state constitutions, which arguably are the most promising sites for positive-rights formulations with respect to the press. Finally, I conclude with a discussion on an ambitious paradigm shift grounded in positive-rights discourse that envisions a structural transformation of the existing press system – what I refer to as "non-reformist media reforms."

24.1 WHY WE NEED POSITIVE RIGHTS

What do we mean by "positive rights," and why do we need them? Drawing a useful, if imperfect, dichotomy from Isaiah Berlin's classic essay Two Concepts of Liberty, we can understand discourses around speech and press freedoms as falling under either negative liberties ("freedom from") or positive liberties ("freedom to").[6]

[4] For a discussion about the necessity and feasibility of creating a new public media system, *see id.*

[5] *See, e.g.*, ALEXANDER MEIKLEJOHN, FREE SPEECH AND ITS RELATION TO SELF-GOVERNMENT (1948); Jerome A. Barron, *Access to the Press – A New First Amendment Right*, 80 HARV. L. REV. 1641 (1967).

[6] Isaiah Berlin, *Two Concepts of Liberty*, *in* FOUR ESSAYS ON LIBERTY (Henry Hardy ed., 1969).

Broadly speaking, negative rights are associated with the absence of obstacles to freedom, whereas positive rights aim to maximize individuals' full potential, allowing them to make their own decisions and exercise agency over their own lives.

Positive rights typically require state action to provide a particular service or benefit, whereas negative rights require the government to refrain from doing something. As political theorist Emily Zackin succinctly summarized: "Negative rights are the bases of demands for restraint by the government, while positive rights are the bases of demands for intervention."[7] In highly inegalitarian societies such as the United States, achieving positive rights necessitates redistributing power. The Australian legal scholar Andrew Kenyon observed that positive rights promote participatory democracy because they "aim to give voice to the marginalized and support material and social preconditions for participation [in society]."[8]

When applied to media, an emphasis on positive rights often seeks to protect collective rights held by publics and audiences as much as those held by individual persons or corporations as speakers. This position casts doubt on the question of whether unregulated market-based relationships alone could ever fully support essential positive freedoms, such as guaranteeing access to high-quality, diverse media. Therefore, protecting and promoting positive rights typically necessitates more direct government intervention.

In the United States, however, protecting speech and press freedoms historically has been framed in negative terms, as exemplified by the First Amendment, which states that "Congress shall make no law . . . abridging the freedom of speech, or of the press." This wording contains an implicit assumption that the only barrier to realizing such freedoms is the government. The prioritization of negative rights based on this interpretation has long impoverished American policy debates regarding positive press freedoms, which has, in turn, disproportionately benefited media corporations' rights over the public while rendering the government less likely to intervene.

An emphasis on negative rights notwithstanding, what does the legal and democratic theory literature actually tell us? It shows us that, in fact, a well-established, if somewhat lesser-known, body of legal theory values positive freedoms in our media at least as much as negative ones. Since the dawn of the American republic, a tacit assumption has existed that government must intervene to protect such rights. This tradition, which became more pronounced in the New Deal era and continues to the present day, has the potential to revitalize the American regulatory imagination and reorient policy agendas toward confronting systemic market failure and the ever-worsening journalism crisis.

7 Emily Zackin, Looking for Rights in All the Wrong Places: Why State Constitutions Contain America's Positive Rights 41 (2013).

8 Andrew Kenyon, Democracy of Expression: Positive Free Speech and Law 220 (2021).

Leading constitutional law scholars have long acknowledged the government's necessary role in promoting positive press freedoms that considered not just the freedoms of the press owners but also those of the public. For example, Thomas Emerson suggested that subsidies might be necessary to enable citizens to voice opinions in the commercial press and that the government had an "affirmative power" to support infrastructures that protected a public's "right to hear."[9] Elsewhere, he argued for an "affirmative First Amendment" through which government intervention could be justified if it promoted greater opportunity for expression and increased diversity of viewpoints and voices in the public sphere.[10]

More recently, former Harvard Law School Dean Martha Minow argues in her book, *Saving the News*, that while the First Amendment forbids abridgement of US citizens' freedoms, it does not forbid the government from intervening to ensure such freedoms exist. Minow also suggests, per a review of the extant literature, that "[t]he First Amendment's presumption of an existing press may even support an *affirmative obligation* on the government to undertake reforms and regulations to ensure the viability of a news ecosystem."[11]

Similar arguments for more positive rights vis-à-vis the press have accumulated in recent years. In 2010, for example, former Columbia University President Lee Bollinger authored an op-ed in *The Wall Street Journal* titled Journalism Needs Government's Help.[12] Around the same time, other legal scholars argued that press subsidies are not only consistent with US history and international standards but also constitutional.[13]

[9] Thomas I. Emerson, The System of Freedom of Expression 649 (1970). *See also* Kenyon, *supra* note 8, at 221; Mike Ananny, Networked Press Freedom Creating Infrastructures for a Public Right to Hear (2018).

[10] Thomas I. Emerson, *The Affirmative Side of the First Amendment*, 15 Ga. L. Rev. 795 (1981). It should be noted that Emerson advocated for a distinction drawn between "governmental promotion" (e.g., subsidies that enhanced private speech) as opposed to "governmental participation" (e.g., situations where the government continues to own and control).

[11] Martha Minow, Saving the News: Why the Constitution Calls for Government Action to Preserve Freedom of Speech 98 (2021) (emphasis added). *See also* Susan Bandes, *The Negative Constitution: A Critique*, 88 Mich. L. Rev. 2271 (1990); Gillian E. Metzger, *The Supreme Court 2016 Term – Foreword: 1930s Redux: The Administrative State Under Siege*, 131 Harv. L. Rev. 1 (2017); David P. Currie, *Positive and Negative Constitutional Rights*, 53 U. Chi. L. Rev. 864 (1986).

[12] Lee Bollinger, *Journalism Needs Government's Help*, Wall St. J. (July 14, 2010, 12:01 AM), http://online.wsj.com/article/SB10001424052748704629804575324782605510168.html.

[13] *See, e.g.*, David Schizer, *Subsidizing the Press*, 3 J. Legal Analysis 1 (2011); Brad Greenberg, *A Public Press? Evaluating the Viability of Government Subsidies for the Newspaper Industry*, 19 UCLA Ent. L. Rev. 189 (2012); *A New Age for Newspapers, Diversity of Voices, Competition and the Internet: Hearing Before the Subcomm. on Courts and Competition Policy of the H. Comm. on the Judiciary*, 111th Cong. 62 (2009) (statement of C. Edwin Baker, Professor, University of Pennsylvania Law School), *as reprinted in* Will the Last Reporter Please Turn out the Lights: The Collapse of Journalism and What Can Be Done About It 128–30 (Robert McChesney & Victor Pickard eds., 2011).

Similarly, scholars have long argued that the mere absence of state intrusion does not automatically guarantee press freedoms.[14] These arguments are buoyed by a continuous – if often overlooked – tradition of legal discourse that legitimates affirmative government intervention to protect the press. Moreover, this affirmative tradition sees such positive rights as superseding the protection of individual liberties and serving as a kind of social protection of the press.

These special protections are further evidenced by what appears to be a constitutional carve-out for the unique democracy-enabling status of the press as an institution – notably, the only private industry guaranteed such special constitutional protections. One often-cited example is Supreme Court Justice Potter Stewart's argument that First Amendment protections exceed individuals' speech freedoms to treat the press as an autonomous and necessary institution, thereby rendering support for a free press "a *structural* provision of the Constitution."[15] At the very least, press freedom, in this context, can be interpreted as serving society as a whole and not merely individual press owners.[16] Moreover, under this interpretation, the press can be seen as engaging in special institutional First Amendment activities and performing an important proxy role for broader publics.[17]

Such statements – some supporting positive rights more generally and others dealing directly with press freedoms – suggest that the First Amendment's primary purpose is not only to shield us from government tyranny but also to create greater potential for human freedom and to support democratic governance writ large. In other words, this doctrine also has the potential to serve as a commitment to protecting and expanding positive press rights for the collective good that, in turn, promotes and enhances greater capabilities for participatory democracy. This positive-rights project is further legitimated by situating it historically.

24.1.1 *Positive Rights in Historical Perspective*

Throughout history, a long-standing debate has centered on the intended meaning of the "or of the press" clause in the U.S. First Amendment, which is a categorical differentiation from "freedom of speech." For example, First Amendment scholar Steven Shiffrin notes that Supreme Court decisions notwithstanding, much existing jurisprudence and case law suggests that the Press Clause confers special privileges on the press. Shiffrin argues that "the *New York Times* is not a fertilizer factory," and it should not be treated like an ordinary business.[18]

14 Kenyon, *supra* note 8. *See also* Damian Tambini, Media Freedom (2021).

15 Justice Potter Stewart, *Address Before Yale Law School* (Nov. 2, 1974), *in* 26 Hastings L.J. 631, 633 (1975).

16 *See* Sonja R. West, *The Majoritarian Press Clause*, 2020 U. Chi. Legal F. 311, 314 (2020).

17 RonNell Andersen Jones, *Press Speakers and the First Amendment Rights of Listeners*, 90 Colo. L. Rev. 499 (2019).

18 Steven Shiffrin, What's Wrong with the First Amendment? 126–27 (2016).

Another leading First Amendment scholar, Robert Post, similarly argues that press freedoms require special considerations and protected rights in society. He observes four distinct constitutional values that are often attributed to the press, implying a wide array of rights: (1) the value of public discourse; (2) the Meiklejohnian value of distributing information; (3) the checking (against abuses of power) value; and (4) the value of the public sphere.[19] Likewise, some historical evidence suggests that the First Amendment's original framers considered the press to be an autonomous institution whose special constitutional protections went beyond supporting individuals' speech freedoms.[20]

Indeed, at the time when the Bill of Rights was drafted, the founders had already begun to recognize "the press" as a discrete institution based on specific political-economic arrangements with broader public responsibilities than typical businesses.[21] Leading figures of the early American republic argued for not only the importance of supporting the press as an institution but also the need for protecting the public's access to it. Advocating for a balanced range of diverse viewpoints, Benjamin Franklin suggested that members of the public should have a positive right to express themselves in the press.[22] Moreover, it is well known that prominent framers of the Constitution argued emphatically that the press plays a special role within a democracy and that, as an institution, it must be protected.[23]

Media historian Robert Martin refers to these assumptions as part of the "open press doctrine," which extended well beyond simply preventing state interference in news media to also considering the press's obligations to the public. He argues that newspapers were not seen merely as private property but also as collective goods. This positive-rights discourse, he suggests, was as much "in the air" at the time of the founding as were libertarian concerns about government encroachment on individual freedoms.[24]

One need not resort to originalist explanations to make the case for special press protections that exceed freedom of speech rationales. In more recent years, a growing body of research focusing on "press exceptionalism" convincingly shows that media institutions and individuals engaged in press-related activities deserve special protection and consideration under the law.[25] This work may lead to useful

[19] Robert Post, *The Press and American Democracy*, *in* The Future of Press Freedom: Democracy, Law, and the News in Changing Times 17 (RonNell Andersen Jones & Sonja R. West eds., 2025).

[20] Charles Clark, *The Press the Founders Knew*, *in* Freeing the Presses: The First Amendment in Action 33–50 (Timothy Cook ed., 2005).

[21] Freeing the Presses: The First Amendment in Action 8 (Timothy Cook ed., 2005).

[22] *Id.*

[23] *See, e.g.*, James Madison's assertion that "the means of acquiring [popular information]" was both tragic and farcical: James Madison, *James Madison to W.T. Barry*, *in* 1 The Founders' Constitution 103–09 (Philip Kurland & Ralph Lerner eds., 1987).

[24] Robert Martin, The Free and Open Press: The Founding of American Democratic Press Liberty, 1640–1800 (2001).

[25] *See, e.g.*, Sonja R. West, *Press Exceptionalism*, 127 Harv. L. Rev. 2434 (2014).

insights into the Press Clause that could bolster the argument that direct government support of the press is constitutional. For example, legal scholar Luke Morgan argues that the First Amendment should be interpreted as protecting an "institutional press," not just individual disseminators of press content, which could empower the government to make more aggressive interventions into the media marketplace that might otherwise be deemed unconstitutional under the Free Speech Clause.[26] Thus far, however, instead of expanding definitions of the press, the Supreme Court has progressively truncated its definition (and, indirectly, its protections) over time.[27]

Nonetheless, history more broadly shows us that the American government has *always* been centrally involved in the development and communication of information in both proactive and positive ways. The belief that Americans must have access to reliable and diverse information – and that the government had an affirmative duty to help provide such services, especially when the market alone fails to support news media – justified massive state investments in the country's first major communications network: the postal system. From its earliest days, this system served primarily as a news-delivery infrastructure, with newspapers constituting as much as 70 percent of mail delivered in the 1790s and 95 percent in the 1830s.[28]

During the first major national debate over American media policy, the founders of the US government concluded that they should not mandate that the postal service be financially self-supporting, thus prioritizing its educational purpose. In doing so, they rejected what the historian Richard John terms a "fiscal rationale."[29] Instead, they privileged the press system's essential service to democracy and helped finance it via massive postal and printing subsidies that today would translate to tens of billions of dollars. This viewpoint- and content-neutral commitment to subsidize news media not only required a particular normative vision of a press system's vital role within a democratic society, but it also recognized that the market alone could not provide the levels of journalism that an informed citizenry requires, thus demonstrating why preserving such positive rights require affirmative protections from the state.

24.2 AN UNFINISHED PROJECT

Throughout the twentieth century, democratic theorists, media critics, reformers, policymakers, and social movements wrestled with but largely failed to establish a

[26] Luke Morgan, *The Broken Branch, Capitalism, the Constitution, and the Press*, 125 Penn St. L. Rev. 1 (2020). *See also* Paul Horwitz, First Amendment Institutions (2013); Frederick Schauer, *Principles, Institutions, and the First Amendment*, 112 Harv. L. Rev. 84 (1998).

[27] RonNell Andersen Jones & Sonja R. West, *The U.S. Supreme Court's Characterizations of the Press: An Empirical Study*, 100 N.C. L. Rev. 375 (2022). Worryingly, the authors have found that the Court has in recent years stopped invoking the Press Clause.

[28] Richard John, Spreading the News: The American Postal System from Franklin to Morse 38 (1995).

[29] *Id.* at 47–48.

firm positive theory of press freedom.[30] This outcome was less the result of an ideological constraint or lack of political imagination – though in many cases, these deficiencies were certainly contributing factors – and more a consequence of the repressive backlash against a social democratic media reform project in the 1930s and 1940s.

The postwar 1940s witnessed a roiling debate around determining the normative role of the press in a democratic society. For example, the Hutchins Commission on Freedom of the Press convened a group of the nation's leading intellectuals to define press freedoms and formulate the best means of protecting them. Despite issuing clear articulations of valuing positive rights in defining press freedoms – especially those put forth by William Hocking, who, in his solo-authored contribution to the Commission, likened the press to that of a "public utility in private hands," speculating it should be treated as a common carrier and promising a public right to the press[31] – the Hutchins Commission ultimately fell back on mostly industry-friendly positions. Their conclusions later became narrated as the "social responsibility" model of the press, which, in many ways, recapitulated the libertarian model while holding out some hope for a more positive-rights-based model.[32]

The debates of the 1940s over defining press freedoms coincided with a reckoning around the failures of commercial broadcast media.[33] After reformers mostly failed in their efforts to establish a more social democratic vision for media, their policy battles over radio's normative role in a democratic society culminated in codifying some modest positive freedoms by the end of the decade, such as those represented by the much-maligned Fairness Doctrine.[34]

Seeing at least a partial turn toward positive rights, the mid twentieth century witnessed a kind of "greatest hits" for championing positive freedoms, especially in a couple of high-profile Supreme Court opinions. First is the Supreme Court's 1945 *Associated Press* (AP) decision, which considered the AP's contention that its First Amendment rights exempted it from federal antitrust restrictions. The Court dismissed this argument and instead asserted that the First Amendment assumes the "widest possible dissemination of information from diverse and antagonistic sources

[30] For book-length treatments of these histories and these debates, *see* Victor Pickard, America's Battle for Media Democracy: The Triumph of Corporate Libertarianism and the Future of Media Reform (2015); Sam Lebovic, Free Speech & Unfree News: The Paradox of Press Freedom in America (2016).

[31] William Hocking, Freedom of the Press: A Framework of Principle 174 (1947).

[32] Pickard, *supra* note 30, at 124–89. *See also* Victor Pickard, *"Whether the Giants Should Be Slain or Persuaded to Be Good": Revisiting the Hutchins Commission and the Role of Media in a Democratic Society*, 27 Critical Stud. Media Commc'n 391 (2010).

[33] For an essay about the 1940s battles over radio regulation and their contemporary implications, especially for social media regulation, *see* Victor Pickard, *The Great Reckoning*, 22-03 Knight First Amend. Inst. (Feb. 24, 2022), https://knightcolumbia.org/content/the-great-reckoning.

[34] Victor Pickard, *The Strange Life and Death of the Fairness Doctrine: Tracing the Decline of Positive Freedoms in American Policy Discourse*, 12 Int'l J. Commc'n. 3434 (2018).

is essential to the welfare of the public."[35] The Court further declared that it would be decidedly "strange" to assume that "the First Amendment should be read as a command that the government was without power to protect that freedom."[36]

More than two decades later, in its 1969 *Red Lion* decision, the Supreme Court again relied on a positive-rights framework to uphold the Fairness Doctrine. The Court held that, when considering First Amendment protections, "It is the right of the viewing and listening public, and not the right of the broadcasters, which is paramount."[37] The Court further stated that "[i]t is the right of the public to receive suitable access to social, political, esthetic, moral, and other ideas and experiences which is crucial here."[38] The Court's privileging of the collective public rights of audiences over those of private broadcasters was arguably the pinnacle of such positive-rights discourse.

This reasoning, however, did not prevail several years later with regard to print media in the *Tornillo* decision, in which the Supreme Court unanimously struck down a Florida law that granted the positive right of a "right to reply" for political candidates whose personal character had been impugned by newspapers.[39] Hence, positive rights did not extend as far to the press as they had with broadcasting. Other media, such as telecommunications, have seen a mixed legacy, including the pronouncement at times of government interventions to support positive freedoms, especially in the areas of state action doctrine, must carry obligations, and common carriage.[40] Positive-rights discourse also has been central to the ongoing debates over net neutrality, which the Federal Communications Commission recently reinstated.[41]

This long history notwithstanding – including landmark cases and court decisions that contained or implied positive-rights readings of First Amendment protections – legal theories featuring positive rights have not served as the foundation for extensive jurisprudence toward press protections. The negative-rights paradigm so prevalent in the United States is often assumed to be a natural fixture of the American legal and ideological landscape. Any attempt to establish positive rights backed up by redistributive, regulatory, and protective measures, according to the dominant view, is not constitutionally mandated and, at the very least, would require majoritarian congressional support.

35 Associated Press v. United States, 326 U.S. 1, 20 (1945).

36 *Id.*

37 Red Lion Broad. Co., Inc. v. FCC, 395 U.S. 367, 368 (1969).

38 *Id.* at 390.

39 Miami Herald Publ'g Co. v. Tornillo, 418 U.S. 241 (1974).

40 For an overview of this affirmative first amendment protections for telecommunications, *see* Dawn C. Nunziato, Virtual Freedom: Net Neutrality and Free Speech in the Internet Age (2009). *See also* Matthew Bunker & Charles Davis, *The First Amendment as a Sword: The Positive Liberty Doctrine and Cable Must-Carry Provisions*, 40 J. Broad. & Elec. Media 77 (1996).

41 Victor Pickard & David Berman, After Net Neutrality: A New Deal for the Digital Age (2019).

The US negative-rights orientation, with its focus on limiting government intrusion into people's everyday lives, differs from the approaches taken in the vast majority of democratic federal constitutions around the world. In most democratic countries, the government has an affirmative duty to guarantee positive rights. In the United States, however, the federal Constitution's First Amendment, which emphasizes negative freedoms, provides the primary legal protection for expressive rights, including speech and press-related freedoms.

Emily Zackin argues that the lack of "governmental protection from social and economic privation," where states intervene to protect their citizens from nongovernmental threats and harms, evidences an "American Constitutional Exceptionalism."[42] Although many have assumed that such anti-statist, classically liberal proclivities have always been hegemonic in the United States, stemming from a commitment to laissez faire capitalism, the protection of private property, and a deep suspicion of government interventions since the nation's earliest days, Zackin convincingly argues otherwise. In line with recent revisionist historical research, she suggests that the American libertarian tendency is more contingent and less culturally predetermined. In fact, ample evidence from the states reveals the existence of other American intellectual and democratic traditions founded on positive rights.

Likewise, Jessica Bulman-Pozen and Miriam Seifter recently argued that, unlike the federal Constitution's exclusive emphasis on negative rights, state constitutions are more likely to enshrine positive rights and affirmative government duties. They also note that state constitutions, in contrast to the federal Constitution's focus on individual liberties, "temper strong rights with attention to communal welfare … [and] treat rights as a means of guaranteeing democracy as well as personal freedom."[43] I look more closely at some of these formations in the next section.

24.3 POSITIVE RIGHTS IN STATE CONSTITUTIONS

In seeking out more expansive articulations of the necessity for protecting positive freedoms, especially as they relate to the press, we may look at how they are rendered in state constitutions.[44] Indeed, more positive equivalents of this doctrine are readily found in state constitutions across the country. Many state constitutions include articulations of positive rights protecting speech and press freedoms that were adopted prior to the existence of the federal First Amendment. Some of these

[42] Zackin, *supra* note 7, at 4–6.

[43] Jessica Bulman-Pozen & Miriam Seifter, *The Right to Amend State Constitutions*, 133 Yale L.J. 191, 194 (2024).

[44] I am indebted to Katherine Glenn Bass's suggestion and to Mia Speier's superb research assistance in writing this section. I am also indebted to Christina Koningisor for generously sharing her extensive research on positive articulations in state constitutions. For an examination of this research, please see her chapter "The Other Press Clauses," published as part of this collection.

statements and declarations offer greater protections than those grounded in the U.S. Constitution and sketch out a more expansive notion of the government's affirmative duties toward press provisions.

While language affirming positive rights often falls loosely under rubrics such as the public's "right to education" – nearly always implied rather than explicitly stated – support for press-related freedoms is more infrequent. Nonetheless, examples of positive-rights language in state constitutions are relatively common and suggest an underutilized potential for supporting journalism. And in some cases, support for positive press freedoms is relatively explicit.

The press-specific provisions of many state constitutions have mirrored the federal First Amendment, but some contain language that is considerably more grounded in positive rights. For example, Steven Calabresi and Sarah Agudo note that Missouri's "expression clause" states that "the free communication of thoughts and opinions is one of the invaluable rights of man, and that every person may freely speak, write and print on any subject."[45] Many other states have similar clauses that are remarkably expansive in their positive rights-oriented framing of expressive rights.

The Pennsylvania constitution goes so far as to feature language that seemingly guarantees public access to printing presses for government reporters. In Article 1, Section 7, the Pennsylvania constitution states: "The printing press shall be free to every person who may undertake to examine the proceedings of the Legislature or any branch of government...."[46] Specifically stressing the importance of public investigation into matters of public interest, this wording suggests special protections for the press's unique watchdog role. Such articulations of press freedoms in Pennsylvania, which emerged within discourses that imply the importance of an institutional press, inspired strong positive language in other state constitutions.[47] For example, the Kentucky state constitution also declares that "[p]rinting presses shall be free to every person who undertakes to examine the proceedings of the General Assembly or any branch of government."[48]

New York state courts have often gone beyond the boundaries delineated in the federal First Amendment to extend press freedom protections to journalists and media institutions.[49] Their embrace of positive rights is even more pronounced

[45] This clause is singled out for attention in Steven G. Calabresi & Sarah E. Agudo, *Individual Rights Under State Constitutions When the Fourteenth Amendment Was Ratified in 1868: What Rights Are Deeply Rooted in American History and Tradition?*, 87 TEX. L. REV. 7, 41 (2008).

[46] PA. CONST. art. I, § 7. Pennsylvania has what can be seen as dual press clauses: one appears as an individual right and the other is treated as part of the structure of the government. For a discussion of this case, *see* Sonja West, *The "Press": Then and Now*, 77 OHIO ST. L.J. 49 (2016), https://digitalcommons.law.uga.edu/fac_artchop/1067/.

[47] Seth F. Kreimer, *The Pennsylvania Constitution's Protection of Free Expression*, 5 U. PA. J. CONST. L. 12 (2002).

[48] KY. CONST. § 8.

[49] Erin M. Peradotto, *Safeguarding Freedom of Speech and of the Press in New York with Heightened State Constitutional Protection*, 92 N.Y. ST. BAR ASS'N J. 12 (2020).

around government guarantees for public education. For example, the New York Court of Appeals has interpreted the state constitution's Education Article to mean that the state is required to provide students with the opportunity for a "sound basic education."[50] It also seems clear that the New York state constitution directs the state to maintain and support a *system* of free common schools that serve a social, collective right and prevent education from being dictated by class-based inequities.

Some states' amenabilities to expansive interpretations of press freedoms might signal openness to new arguments even where positive-rights analysis has not yet been embraced. For example, California has long been a national leader in demonstrating greater protections for press freedom than federal law, especially for student journalists and student media.[51] While we might see protections for student journalists as an example of negative rights in protecting them from obtrusive government meddling and censorship, this case also demonstrates how states can provide greater press protections than the federal government. It also highlights states' capabilities for expanding the legal and statutory understanding of who qualifies as a protected member of the press. California also contains positive language for the public having a "right of access to information concerning the conduct of the people's business, and, therefore, the meetings of public bodies and the writings of public officials and agencies shall be open to public scrutiny. . . ."[52]

In light of these glimmers of more positive rights for the press, it is worth considering how we might go further to expand *public* rights whereby citizens can establish "standing" or a redressable claim for meaningful access to the press (just as they might with public education). Looking at the history of how public education became constitutionally protected in the states holds potential lessons for how we might create a new public media system – a point I plan to revisit in future research. At the very least, this history suggests the necessity of framing such arguments in terms of class-based and racial inequities, emphasizing that only wealthier and whiter neighborhoods have access to high-quality journalism.

For now, suffice it to say that regardless of our precise strategic vision, which I return to later in the chapter, one of the benefits of focusing on state-level initiatives is that they often reflect national priorities and advance important debates that have been stymied or given too little attention at the federal level. Moreover, they can offer proofs of concept that widen our political imagination regarding what the government can do in the face of a structural journalism crisis and, more specifically, how it can protect the press from systemic market failure, as well as provide public access to such institutions. International articulations of press rights – including those found in other countries' constitutions, international bodies, and

[50] Levittown Union Free Sch. Dist. et al. v. Nyquist, 57 N.Y. 2d 27, 48 (1982); Campaign for Fiscal Equality v. State of New York, 86 N.Y. 2d 307, 315 (1995).

[51] *See A Guide to California's Student Press Freedom Laws*, Student Press Law Ctr., https://splc.org/know-your-rights-california/ (last visited June 21, 2024).

[52] Cal. Const. art. I, § 3.

even US global media – are another key repository of positive-rights discourse and can help denaturalize the belief in US constitutional exceptionalism. I turn to these next.

24.4 POSITIVE RIGHTS IN INTERNATIONAL CODES AND LAWS

Generally speaking, positive freedoms are more established in press-related doctrines and codes internationally compared to the United States. One notable example is Article 19 of the United Nations Declaration of Human Rights – sometimes associated with the right to communicate – which codifies the right to "receive and impart information and ideas through any media."[53] This code has long inspired international media reform efforts, often used to advocate for expanding public access to media institutions.

However, perhaps counterintuitively, positive rights formulations are also present in some existing codes around US global media. Indeed, traces of similar principles are rearticulated in statements delineating the normative mission of US international broadcasting services.[54] For example, in its International Broadcasting Act of 1994, Congress stated the following in the first of five declarations about its commitments to international broadcasting: "It is the policy of the United States to promote the right of freedom of opinion and expression, including the freedom 'to seek, receive, and impart information and ideas through any media and regardless of frontiers,' in accordance with Article 19 of the Universal Declaration of Human Rights."[55]

Congress further defined its commitment to a positive mission of news media in language that championed the "[o]pen communication of information" that was "based on reliable information about its potential audience" and "designed so as to effectively reach a significant audience."[56] Moreover, professional standards for international broadcast journalism shall include the following:

> a balanced and comprehensive projection of United States thought and institutions, reflecting the diversity of United States culture and society ... programming to meet needs which remain unserved by the totality of media voices available to the people of certain nations; information about developments in each significant region of the world; a variety of opinions and voices from within particular nations

[53] Universal Declaration of Human Rights art. 19, G.A. Res. 217A, at 71, U.N. GAOR, 3d Sess., 1st plen. mtg., U.N. Doc. A/810 (Dec. 12, 1948). The European Convention on Human Rights, Article 10, has almost identical language. Convention for the Protection of Human Rights and Fundamental Freedoms art. 10, *opened for signature* Nov. 4, 1950, 213 U.N.T.S. 221 (entered into force Sept. 3, 1953).

[54] I am indebted to Matthew Conaty's research assistance with the following analysis on US international broadcasting.

[55] United States International Broadcasting Act of 1994, 22 U.S.C. § 6201.

[56] 22 U.S.C. § 6202.

> and regions prevented by censorship or repression from speaking to their fellow countrymen ... and training and technical support for independent indigenous media through government agencies or private United States entities.[57]

It must be noted, however, that these codifications of positive rights notwithstanding, stronger safeguards against government pressures on international broadcasting are still needed. A recent book by Kate Wright et al. carefully documents how such relatively vague and unenforceable language has helped create systemic vulnerabilities to state capture, which became more evident during the Trump administration.[58]

In terms of constitutional doctrine, compared to the United States, other democratic nations, especially in Western and Northern European social democracies, feature more pronounced positive-freedom articulations. To give one striking example, Germany's constitution offers strong positive-rights articulations. For example, in Article 5 of the Basic Law for the Federal Republic of Germany, the German constitution states:

> Every person shall have the right freely to express and disseminate his opinions in speech, writing and pictures and to inform himself without hindrance from generally accessible sources. Freedom of the press and freedom of reporting by means of broadcasts and films shall be guaranteed. There shall be no censorship.[59]

Political scientists have noted that Article 5 bears striking differences compared to the U.S. First Amendment.[60] Its protections clearly are not limited to prohibiting state interference, suggesting that its provisions could be invoked against nonstate actors beyond governments. Furthermore, Article 5 is much more specific in protecting rights of speech against censorship and mentions modern types of mediated communication, such as film and broadcasting.

The German constitution also devotes a fair amount of language to defining public broadcasting, even constitutionally mandating its existence, and conferring upon it a preferred status over private and commercial broadcasters to prevent market censorship.[61] This acknowledgement that a commercial media system is structurally ill-equipped to provide for a democratic society's information needs is strikingly absent in American legal doctrine. Drawing from international articulations of positive rights and the government's affirmative duty to protect them can

57 *Id.*

58 Kate Wright et al., Capturing News, Capturing Democracy: Trump and the Voice of America (2024).

59 Gesetz zur Änderung des Grundgesetzes [Law Amending Basic Law], Dec. 19, 2022, BGBl I at 2478 (Ger.), translation at https://www.gesetze-im-internet.de/englisch_gg/englisch_gg.html.

60 Donald P. Kommers & Russell A. Miller, The Constitutional Jurisprudence of the Federal Republic of Germany: Third Edition, Revised and Expanded 41 (2012).

61 C. Edwin Baker, Media Concentration and Democracy: Why Ownership Matters 161, 245 (2007). *See also* Peter Humphreys, Media and Media Policy in Germany: The Press and Broadcasting since 1945 (1994); Kenyon, *supra* note 8, at 243.

help denaturalize the US libertarian paradigm that continues to impede structural media reform and press protections.

24.5 POTENTIAL FOR REORIENTING THE FIRST AMENDMENT

The entire premise of press freedoms and protections under the First Amendment presupposes a functioning press system. However, US constitutional law has long had a blind spot toward creating *opportunities* for expression. Privacy rights and freedom of expression are founded on negative liberties that shield citizens from state tyranny, but a pro-democracy agenda must also include a strong case against other sources of tyranny (such as concentrated corporate power and market censorship) while legitimating government intervention to create greater public capabilities to produce and to access information.

In other words – it bears repeating – the mere absence of state interference does not sufficiently guarantee a democratic media system. To confront threats to democracy, such as rapidly expanding news deserts (as well as digital divides and unaccountable media monopolies), we must recalibrate the First Amendment to become a more progressive force in society.

The various traditions sketched above may contribute to a foundation for advocating for a more positive First Amendment. Arguably, the most promising angle toward advancing positive press freedoms is to draw from the examples found in state constitutions. In theory and in practice, the abstention doctrine, as well as principles associated with federalism in general, grant states the power to use their own constitutions in interpreting and effectuating state laws. State constitutions often provide more expansive rights, especially around issues such as public education, environmental protection, and labor. Although states must adhere to basic federal minimum standards and guidelines, the U.S. Supreme Court lacks authority to overturn state legal decisions in most cases.[62] As one legal textbook notes, courts have often interpreted state constitutions "to more broadly protect and supplement key fundamental rights and protections."[63] This check on the federal government is, in fact, an intended feature that allows states to exceed federal standards and to offer broader rules and protections.

This balance of legal power helps explain an increasing trend in recent years toward turning to state courts and state constitutions to protect individual rights. Certainly not all these legal movements have worked to advance positive freedoms, especially in cases involving reproductive rights. But some measures have been quite

[62] Exceptions exist. For example, the Due Process Clause of the 14th Amendment affords the Supreme Court the chance to overturn laws that run afoul of the First Amendment.

[63] Protections in the New York State Constitution beyond the Federal Bill of Rights 3 (Scott N. Fein & Andrew B. Ayers eds., 2017), https://www.nysenate.gov/sites/default/files/article/attachment/protections_in_the_new_york_state_constitution_beyond_the_federal_bill_of_rights.pdf.

progressive, such as targeting climate change in the state of Montana, where a state court judge argued in a 2023 case that it violated the public's state constitutional right "to a clean and healthful environment."[64]

Decades ago, Justice William J. Brennan Jr. advocated for the strategy of relying on state constitutions to advance rights far exceeding protections provided for in the Bill of Rights. He argued that federalism affords us with "a double source of protection for the rights of our citizens," and we can turn to state courts and constitutions – which should be seen as a "font of individual liberties" – when the Supreme Court is too limited in its legal interpretations.[65] Given the US federal government's caution and conservativism, it stands to reason that, in the near term, at least, we should focus on state-level initiatives based on a public right to the press that would mandate state governments to ensure the existence of local journalism in all communities. If such a protection were to take hold in several states, perhaps it would someday be embraced at the federal level.

While using a rights-based argument to advocate for guaranteed social benefits is open to reasonable criticism,[66] it nonetheless lends some hope. This is especially true once we look beyond the federal level, such as the recent spate of state-level laws aimed at protecting local journalism that state legislatures are considering or have already implemented in places like New Jersey, Washington, DC, California, New York, Illinois, and Wisconsin. Under these plans, news outlets prioritizing local journalism receive various kinds of public subsidies and grants from state governments, and more such initiatives will likely take root before long. But until we scale up these plans to cover all communities across the entire nation, we still need more far-reaching plans for the long term.

24.6 THE NEED FOR NON-REFORMIST MEDIA REFORMS

The legal thinking discussed thus far supports an argument for more robust government provision of the press and lays important groundwork for ambitious reforms. This is a first necessary step towards creating the systemic overhaul that is needed to support the level of journalism that democracy requires. However, the profound structural crisis that democratic society is facing warrants even greater urgency. Establishing a "public right to the press" behooves us to aim higher.

[64] For an overview of such state-level developments, *see* Marcia Coyle, *State Courts, Voters Increasingly Turning to State Constitutions to Protect Rights*, Const. Daily Blog (Aug. 18, 2023), https://constitutioncenter.org/blog/state-courts-voters-increasingly-turning-to-state-constitutions-to-protect-rights.

[65] William J. Brennan, Jr, *State Constitutions and the Protection of Individual Rights*, 90 Harv. L. Rev. 489, 491–503 (1977). For a discussion on how the terms of federalism must be renewed and worked out again every generation, *see* Neil D. McFeeley, *The Supreme Court and the Federal System: Federalism from Warren to Burger*, 8 Publius 5 (1978).

[66] *See, e.g.*, Samuel Moyn, Not Enough: Human Rights in an Unequal World (2018).

With this aim in mind, we might look to "non-reformist media reforms" that seek to ultimately transform journalism and significantly lessen, or remove altogether, the commercial pressures and logics that decimate and degrade our media at a structural level, from incentivizing low-quality journalism online to hollowing out newsrooms throughout the country.[67] Loosely derived from the political theories of André Gorz, this framework privileges social needs over profit imperatives.[68]

While this framework increasingly has been applied to social problems such as mass incarceration and other activist struggles, applying it to media can help bring into focus a long-term project aimed at "just transitions" and structural transformations. Such an approach looks beyond small-bore proposals to shore up commercial journalism – measures that at least inadvertently bolster the status quo and keep the existing institutional structures largely intact – to instead aim to radically restructure and democratize the system to include voices and viewpoints beyond traditional parameters.

Ultimately, such a policy agenda does not aim to prop up incumbents and status quo models within the ever-eroding commercial media sector. Rather, it endeavors to entirely reorient information and communication infrastructures in ways that align with serving human needs. While expanding the social imaginary for what is politically possible, this project necessitates building out nonmarket alternatives by either creating entirely new infrastructures or by restructuring already-existing systems such as public broadcasting and the postal system. Arguably, working towards such utopian scenarios for journalism's future is not only the most ethical program, but it is also the most practical course of action.

What might these reforms look like? Ultimately, our strategic vision must internalize that no long-term commercial viability exists for most kinds of journalism, especially when the market itself is a major part of the problem. The scale and scope of the current journalism crisis call for radical structural reforms that mitigate or eliminate the commercial pressures that prevent our news media from serving democratic needs. A major barrier to this kind of political project, however, is the failure to imagine structural alternatives outside the existing commercial media system.

And while the growing philanthropic commitments to supporting journalism are a positive development, one problem with relying on private capital is that funders tend to be mercurial and insufficiently committed for the long term. We need

67 For an earlier formulation of this "non-reformist media reforms" framework, *see* Victor Pickard, *Taking Media Out of the Market*, LPE PROJECT (Jan. 31, 2024), https://lpeproject.org/blog/taking-media-out-of-the-market/.

68 Mark Engler & Paul Engler, *André Gorz's Non-Reformist Reforms Show How We Can Transform the World Today*, JACOBIN (July 22, 2021), https://jacobin.com/2021/07/andre-gorz-non-reformist-reforms-revolution-political-theory. For an excellent discussion of a "non-reformist reforms" framework applied to criminal justice law reform and political strategy, *see* Amna A. Akbar, *Non-Reformist Reforms and Struggles over Life, Death, and Democracy*, 132 YALE L.J. 2497 (2023).

permanent, unconditional support for the local journalism that democracy requires. Nonetheless, the burgeoning nonprofit news sector illustrates what journalists can do if liberated from commercial constraints.

For example, nonprofit news institutions such as City Bureau, ProPublica, and Outlier Media exemplify traits often associated with high-quality journalism: collaborative, investigative, and community focused. They consistently produce reporting that exposes injustices committed against marginalized communities while drawing attention to urgent problems that society must address at a systemic level. Compared to commercial news organizations, these media institutions are often more engaged with their respective communities and devoted to progressive social missions. An infusion of philanthropic money into local news by Press Forward – more than $500 million over five years – suggests this sector will continue to expand. But much more is needed.

In the final analysis, guaranteeing media access for all members of society requires a robust public media system. Working towards this universal service mission, we can leverage already-existing public infrastructures as initial building blocks for a new public media system. These may include post offices, libraries, public access media, public broadcasting stations, universities, and other public spaces and institutions. However, given that the United States is a global outlier for how little it funds public media in general, more ambitious investments – as well as structural reforms – are still necessary.[69]

Toward this long-term objective, non-reformist media reforms have significant strategic value by directing policy interventions toward immediate goals while also seeking to expand future opportunities. In the short term, such plans can help mobilize diverse coalitions, build grassroots power from below, and open new terrains of struggle for structural reform. In the long term, these projects can shift popular common sense and lead to lasting systemic change. Based on this calculus, any reform that chips away at existing media institutions' antidemocratic and commercial designs can help engage news workers and local communities in rebuilding local journalism from the ground up. Such initiatives may include unionizing newsrooms, creating worker-owned cooperatives, transitioning commercial news organizations into non- or low-profit outlets, and incentivizing partnerships between public broadcasting stations and local print media. These more immediate and modest reforms can help establish the early foundations for greater transformative change in the coming decades.

24.7 THE LONG ROAD TO REFORM

The precise nature of today's media-related challenges and threats to democratic governance are distinct from those in years past. This is true even compared to those

69 For an analysis of US public media allocations in global comparison, *see* Timothy Neff & Victor Pickard, *Funding Democracy: Public Media and Democratic Health in 33 Countries*, 29 INT'L J. PRESS/POLITICS 1 (2021).

that existed fifteen or twenty years ago at a time when Jerome Barron's work was enjoying renewed attention and C. Edwin Baker's work was central to a resurgent media reform movement.[70] During this juncture in the early 2000s – a time of war and neoliberal hegemony – many media reformers and policymakers perceived the most severe threat to a democratic press as the increasing concentration of media ownership. More specifically, they decried the growing monopolistic power of media conglomerates as grossly limiting the diversity of the public sphere, and much of the strategic thinking was focused on how to reign in or crush these media monopolies.

Today's market censorship, however, is more subtle and yet more profound. Although run-amok corporate power certainly continues to play an outsized detrimental role in the pathologies plaguing our information and communication infrastructures – abuses of power from social media platforms like Facebook and Twitter, predatory hedge funds like Alden Global Capital, irresponsible cable television companies like Fox News, and propagandistic broadcasting networks like Sinclair Broadcasting, to name a few of the more egregious examples – the core problem facing the health of our news media today is deeply systemic and irreducible to bad actors. Essentially, what we are facing today are not just media monopoly problems; we are dealing with *capitalism* problems. Competition policy is necessary but insufficient in achieving a viable democratic press. Ultimately, our goal should be to remove entire sectors of our information and communication systems from the market altogether. We need a political horizon for journalism beyond unfettered capitalism.

In many ways, the market's hidden hand in media systems is that of a censor. As such, its pernicious effect on journalism must be minimized. This "market censorship" argument is central to making the case for government intervention. As C. Edwin Baker, James Curran, Sue Curry Jansen, and other political economists have argued for many years, the market actively and predictably filters out specific voices, distorts coverage, and underserves entire communities along socioeconomic and racial lines.[71] Government intervention on behalf of media that effectively ameliorates this discrimination would, in fact, be promoting a kind of negative liberty by preventing economic factors from silencing voices, discriminating against particular viewpoints, and barring entire groups from full participation in democratic society.

That the violence of the market against the press is routinely accepted as part of the natural order of things is striking. When authorities forcibly shut down

[70] Robert W. McChesney, *Freedom of the Press for Whom? The Question to Be Answered in Our Critical Juncture*, 35 Hofstra L. Rev. 1433 (2007).

[71] C. Edwin Baker, Advertising and a Democratic Press (2014); James Curran & Jean Seaton, Power without Responsibility (8th ed. 2018); Sue Curry Jansen, *Ambiguities and Imperatives of Market Censorship: The Brief History of a Critical Concept*, 7 Westminster Papers in Commc'n & Culture 12 (2010).

newsrooms and oppress journalists – as was the case when local police raided the offices of the Marion County Record, a small weekly newspaper in Kansas, in August 2023 – such actions justifiably draw intense outcry and condemnation from news organizations and from the public in general.[72] But when the commercial market does essentially the exact same thing – dismantling local media outlets and marching journalists out of newsrooms onto the street – we resign ourselves to this silencing of the press. It is unfortunate, we may tell ourselves, but the market has spoken, and there is little we can do.

Instead of accepting such fatalism, we can return agency to democratic society by treating our media's design as something based on inherently *political* choices. Accordingly, we must constantly remind ourselves that our media institutions are neither natural nor inevitable but rather the product of policy decisions – decisions that should be determined by us all, not just a small group of media owners and investors (typically white, wealthy men). To engage broader constituencies, these policy debates must be further politicized, which is a central aim of any major media reform movement.

Fortunately, even if often absent from the dominant liberal policy consensus, creative and large-scale ideas for structural reform are accumulating.[73] For example, increasing numbers of analysts and activists argue for transitioning platforms into public utilities by devolving platform ownership and control to tech workers or users as cooperatives.[74] While some advocates have called for breaking up platform monopolies into smaller firms or forcing them to share more advertising revenues with media producers, others have gone even further by advocating for an entire "public stack" in which each layer of our digital media system – including news media publishers, social media platforms, and even the pipes that bring internet services to our homes – is decommodified and radically democratized.[75]

[72] Steven Lee Myers & Benjamin Mullin, *Raid of Small Kansas Newspaper Raises Free Press Concerns*, N.Y. TIMES (Aug. 14, 2023), https://www.nytimes.com/2023/08/13/business/media/kansas-marion-newspaper-police-raid.html.

[73] For an overview and synthesis of these more ambitious policy plans, *see* Victor Pickard, *Another Media System Is Possible: Ripping Open the Overton Window from Platforms to Public Broadcasting*, 30 JAVNOST: THE PUBLIC 284 (2023).

[74] *See, e.g.*, K. Sabeel Rahman & Zephyr Teachout, *From Private Bads to Public Goods: Adapting Public Utility Regulation for Informational Infrastructure*, KNIGHT FIRST AMENDMENT INSTITUTE (Feb. 4, 2020), https://knightcolumbia.org/content/from-private-bads-to-public-goods-adapting-public-utility-regulation-for-informational-infrastructure. For some key historical background on this concept, *see* William J. Novak, *The Public Utility Idea and the Origins of Modern Business Regulation*, *in* CORPORATIONS AND AMERICAN DEMOCRACY 139 (Naomi R. Lamoreaux & William J. Novak eds., 2017). Of course, a danger is always that such arguments can open the door for the state being able to compel certain kinds of speech. For an overview of recent discussions, *see* Rachel Reed, *Compelling Speech*, HARV. L. TODAY (Feb. 21, 2024), https://hls.harvard.edu/today/supreme-court-preview-netchoice-v-paxton/.

[75] *See, e.g.*, Sanjay Jolly & Ellen P. Goodman, *A "Full Stack" Approach to Public Media in the United States*, GERMAN MARSHALL FUND (July 26, 2021), https://www.gmfus.org/news/full-stack-approach-public-media-united-states.

Towards this aim, one compelling model is the Local Journalism Initiative, which would enable people to vote on allocating funds to local news organizations of their choice, thereby guaranteeing competition between multiple newsrooms in every county.[76] To create the massive resources needed to launch such a program, the journalist John Nichols has called for a "Marshall Plan."[77] Similarly, The Washington Post columnist Perry Bacon recommends spending $10 billion annually to support 200 new journalists in each US congressional district.[78] I have called for establishing in every community a "Public Media Center," a new type of anchor institution that is federally guaranteed but locally owned and governed.

Suffice it to say that bold and innovative ideas already exist. What is still lacking is the public support and political will to implement them. Regardless of the precise model on which we aim our sites and the exact strategy that carries us there, our north star should remain firmly fixed: Everyone should be provided ample access to high-quality news and information from local media outlets that look like and are overseen by the communities they serve. And all community members should be empowered to create their own media and tell their own stories. None of this is possible, however, until we confront the systemic market failure that is driving journalism to ruin.

The drafters of the First Amendment could not have anticipated such a hypercapitalistic, corporate-dominated media system developing in the United States.[79] They could not have predicted systemic market failure because their political economy was so radically different from that which exists today. The eighteenth-century press was not nearly as market-driven and advertising-dependent as it would become in the twentieth century. From the framers' vantage point, it could be safely assumed that the publishers' interests and the public's interests (at least among those who were seen as full-fledged members of the polity) were one and the same against an all-powerful state.

Our contemporary moment calls for an unshakeable commitment to protect *both* negative and positive liberties. We must guarantee individual freedoms as well as meaningful democratic participation in political life. With the ongoing collapse of local journalism – marked by massive layoffs, expanding news deserts, and rising corruption – we may be reaching an inflection point. But to guide us down the

[76] Robert McChesney & John Nichols, *The Local Journalism Initiative: A Proposal to Protect and Extend Democracy*, COLUM. JOURNALISM REV. (Nov. 30, 2021), https://www.cjr.org/business_of_news/the-local-journalism-initiative.php.

[77] John Nichols, *Local News Has Been Destroyed. Here's How We Can Revive It*, NATION (Dec. 12, 2023), https://www.thenation.com/article/society/local-news-revival-plan/.

[78] Perry Bacon, Jr, *America Should Spend Billions to Revive Local News*, WASH. POST (Oct. 17, 2022, 7:00 AM), https://www.washingtonpost.com/opinions/2022/10/17/local-news-crisis-plan-fix-perry-bacon/. For a discussion of how such subsidies could be established, *see* Kyle Langvardt, *Structuring a Subsidy for Local Journalism*, 3 J. FREE SPEECH L. 297 (2023).

[79] The modern corporation simply did not exist at that time; collective enterprises were typically chartered to perform a specific function under the direct auspices of state legislatures.

correct path, we must avoid old libertarian assumptions about the government's inability to provide for the press.

Ultimately, we need a new paradigm founded on positive rights and driven by participatory democracy. While this paradigm shift is largely predicated on an ideological and intellectual project that moves common sense away from a market-fundamentalist, negative-freedom framework, the structural transformation that is necessary depends on social forces from below. At the same time, we also must ensure that our democratic theories and strategies for systemic change align with these social movement goals.

Given ongoing endemic market failures, any future for the kind of journalism that serves democratic needs will rise or fall with government interventions. To overcome libertarian biases, these forays into the commercial media marketplace must be justified by clearly articulated positive rights. Setting the stage for such policymaking will require much ideological, political, and discursive work. It is a long-term struggle, but one from which we cannot shy away.

25

Innovation Policy and the Press

Christina Koningisor and Jacob Noti-Victor

In colonial America, a small network of local newspapers proved crucial in the lead-up to the Revolutionary War. They facilitated the exchange of information between the colonies, fostering a collective sense of identity among politically distinct entities.[1] They also spread news of British injustices, creating a shared set of grievances that ultimately coalesced into more united opposition to foreign rule.[2] This circulation of news throughout the colonies "made the American Revolution possible."[3]

Yet these crucial information exchanges did not occur on their own. Rather, they were the product of deliberate government intervention. In 1754, Benjamin Franklin served as the postmaster general in the colonies under the British Crown.[4] He decided to exempt newspaper-to-newspaper exchanges from postage and delivery fees. Under this policy, printers could send their editions to one another through the mail at no cost.[5] Congress later codified this rule with the enactment of the Postal Act of 1792. The statute also permitted newspapers to send issues to their subscribers at a lower rate.[6] Collectively, these interventions facilitated the free exchange of

1 Jeffrey L. Pasley, The Tyranny of Printers: Newspaper Politics in the Early American Republic 33 (2001) ("It was a matter of consensus, then as now, that Patriot newspapers were one of the most important factors in turning American public opinion against Great Britain.").

2 Timothy E. Cook, *Public Policy Toward the Press: What the Government Does for the News Media*, in The Press 252 (Geneva Overholser & Kathleen Hall Jamieson 2005) ("Newspapers carried word of local problems and built consensus on collective grievances against the British.").

3 *Id.*

4 U.S. Postal Service, *About Us, Benjamin Franklin: Postmaster General*, https://about.usps.com/who-we-are/postal-history/pmg-franklin.pdf.

5 Cook, *supra* note 2, at 252.

6 Postal Act of 1792, Act of Feb. 20, 1792, ch. 7, 1 Stat. 232. The impact of this subsidy was significant. *See* Cook, *supra* note 2, at 38 ("By 1832 the circulation of newspapers constituted 95 percent of the weight of the mail but provided only 15 percent of total postal revenue.").

ideas and created a vibrant public sphere for intellectual discussion and debate.[7] The number of newspapers proliferated.[8]

Since then, the government has intervened in countless ways to support the press. It has offered various forms of financial support, such as tax subsidies and grants.[9] It has also recognized new property-like interests, such as "hot news," in order to allow media organizations to seek a return on their investments in newsgathering.[10] It has invested substantial resources in critical information infrastructure, such as telegraph and radio cables, satellites, broadband internet cable, and more.[11] And it has engaged in myriad forms of regulation that have facilitated growth in media, such as creating rules to manage and allocate broadcast spectrum.[12]

Yet this effort takes on new urgency today. The American press is in a period of decline. Since 2005, the nation has lost roughly a third of its newspapers and nearly two-thirds of its newspaper journalists.[13] Local newspapers have been especially hard hit, leaving large swaths of America without any local news coverage at all.[14] Members of the press have described it as an "extinction-level event."[15]

This has prompted a wave of new efforts to save the local press. Many of these have been undertaken voluntarily by the media. Press institutions have tried innovating to attract back advertisers and subscribers. These efforts have included increased investments in video and data-driven journalism,[16] new financial structures like journalism cooperatives or direct public offerings to subscribers,[17] and an

7 *See* Robert C. Post, *Data Privacy and Dignitary Privacy: Google Spain, the Right to Be Forgotten, and the Construction of the Public Sphere*, 67 DUKE L.J. 981, 1072 (2018).

8 Michael T. Gibson, *The Supreme Court and Freedom of Expression from 1791 to 1917*, 55 FORDHAM L. REV. 263, 293 (1986) (describing how the number of newspapers in the United States rose "from less than one hundred in 1825 to more than six hundred in 1850").

9 *See infra* Sections 25.2.2 and 25.2.4.

10 *See infra* Section 25.2.1.2.

11 *See* MARTHA MINOW, SAVING THE NEWS 52–54 (2021) (describing these investments).

12 *See* THE PUBLIC AND BROADCASTING 4–6, FEDERAL COMMUNICATIONS COMM. (2021), https://www.fcc.gov/sites/default/files/public_and_broadcasting_0.pdf.

13 Penelope Muse Abernathy, *The State of Local News: 2023 Report* (2023), https://localnewsinitiative.northwestern.edu/projects/state-of-local-news/2023/report/#:~:text=Since%202005%2C%20the%20country%20has,small%20and%20mid%2Dsized%20communities.

14 *Id.* Advertising revenue at local television stations has remained more consistent over time. *See Local TV News Fact Sheet*, PEW RES. CTR. (Sept. 14, 2023), https://www.pewresearch.org/journalism/fact-sheet/local-tv-news/.

15 *See* Paul Farhi, *Is American Journalism Headed Toward an 'Extinction-Level Event'?*, THE ATLANTIC (Jan. 30, 2024), https://www.theatlantic.com/ideas/archive/2024/01/media-layoffs-la-times/677285/.

16 *See, e.g.*, Lauren Easton, *The Future of Data Journalism in Local News*, ASSOCIATED PRESS (Feb. 4, 2019), https://blog.ap.org/industry-insights/the-future-of-data-journalism-in-local-news (describing how the AP is assisting local news outlets with expanding data-driven journalism efforts).

17 *See, e.g.*, Berkeleyside Staff, *First in the Nation: Berkeleyside Raises $1M from Readers in Direct Public Offering*, BERKELEYSIDE (Apr. 12, 2018), https://www.berkeleyside.org/2018/04/12/first-in-the-nation-berkeleyside-raises-1m-from-its-readers-in-a-direct-public-offering (example of direct

expansion of nonprofit, digital-only outlets.[18] They have also included the sale of struggling media institutions to wealthy individuals.[19] But these private-sector and internal reforms have had only limited success and have not yet stemmed the decline of the local press.[20]

In response, scholars, policymakers, and journalists have called for the government to take more aggressive steps to bolster the press, especially the local press. Many interventions have been proposed or adopted in recent years. They include intellectual property rights, tax credits, subsidies, prizes, and grants.[21] These reforms have also been proposed by a wide range of government actors, including international organizations; foreign countries; and federal, state, and local legislators.[22]

Yet there has been little effort to develop an overarching framework to compare and evaluate these many different policy interventions.[23] This chapter begins this work. It argues that the local news crisis should be understood as a kind of innovation failure, one that calls for solutions drawn from areas of the law that have long grappled with similar problems. In markets like pharmaceuticals and technology, policymakers often employ "innovation policy pluralism," or combinations of intellectual property protections and other government tools, such as prizes and

public offering); Banyan Project, *We Are Pioneering a New Model for Community-Energizing Journalism*, https://banyanproject.coop/ (example of news cooperative).

18 *See, e.g.*, Sarah Scire, *Now Nonprofit, the Salt Lake Tribune Has Achieved Something Rare for a Local Newspaper: Financial Sustainability*, Nieman Lab (Nov. 29, 2021), https://www.niemanlab.org/2021/11/now-nonprofit-the-salt-lake-tribune-has-achieved-something-rare-for-a-local-newspaper-financial-sustainability/ (describing a newspaper's conversion from for-profit to nonprofit status).

19 *See, e.g.*, Benjamin Mullin & Katie Robertson, *A Decade Ago, Jeff Bezos Bought a Newspaper. Now He's Paying Attention to It Again*, Wash. Post (July 22, 2023), https://www.nytimes.com/2023/07/22/business/media/jeff-bezos-washington-post.html.

20 *See* Abernathy, *supra* note 13. *See also* Ryan Mac, Benjamin Mullin & Katie Robertson, *Los Angeles Times Owner Clashed with Top Editor over Unpublished Article*, N.Y. Times (Jan. 26, 2024), https://www.nytimes.com/2024/01/26/business/media/los-angeles-times-owner-editor-clash.html (describing conflicts of interest that can arise when a wealthy owner purchases a media outlet).

21 *See* discussion *infra* Section 25.2.

22 *Id.*

23 Some have addressed the pros and cons of various government interventions through other policy lenses. *See, e.g.*, Leonard Downie, Jr & Michael Schudson, *The Reconstruction of American Journalism*, in Will the Last Reporter Please Turn Out the Lights: The Collapse of Journalism and What Can Be Done to Fix It (Robert W. McChesney & Victor Pickard eds., 2009) (describing the pros and cons of various interventions, and endorsing certain options like increased tax incentives for press institutions); Kyle Langvardt, *Structuring a Subsidy for Local Journalism*, 3 J. Free Speech L. 297, 316–18 (2023) (examining possible public news subsidy design in light of potential constitutional limitations); Minow, *supra* note 11, at 104–44 (proposing various government interventions to support the press); Neil Weinstock Netanel, *Mandating Digital Platform Support for Quality Journalism*, 34 Harv. J. L. & Tech. 473, 499 (2021) (critiquing three types of government initiatives to bolster journalism); David M. Schizer, *Subsidizing the Press*, 3 J. Legal Analysis 1, 2–3 (2011) (proposing a framework for analyzing press subsidies that focuses on how well editorial independence is preserved, how effectively a subsidy channels resources to "externality-generating activities," and political feasibility).

grants.[24] Such combinations harness both free-market forces and government regulation to foster socially valuable services in productive and efficient ways.[25]

Drawing on the work of scholars who have examined various combinations of innovation policy levers in other contexts, we map these existing and proposed press interventions onto this innovation policy rubric. Specifically, we rely on an innovation policy framework developed by scholars Daniel Hemel and Lisa Larrimore Ouellette. We adopt this framework to plot various press policy proposals across two indices: whether the interventions are government-sponsored or market-driven; and whether the innovation reward is allocated ex ante or ex post.[26]

Consider an example. The Postal Act of 1792[27] represents a government intervention designed to bolster innovation and, specifically, press innovation.[28] Congress set the price of the subsidy and determined who would shoulder the costs – in this case, private letter-senders who paid higher postage fees.[29] Further, the incentive was imposed ex ante: The government offered the subsidy in advance to any qualifying newspaper, regardless of their business model, focus, or level of success.[30] We argue that each press policy intervention can be plotted along these two dimensions. Further, we suggest that categorizing the various press policy interventions in this way permits a comparison among the different policy levers and an analysis of how these levers can be combined and layered to meet different innovation goals.[31]

After mapping out these various proposed press policy interventions, we conclude by suggesting that intellectual property and other market-driven mechanisms alone are insufficient to ensure continued local news creation in today's media landscape. Yet a pure government-funding model is also inadequate. Instead, intellectual property solutions should be combined with other government incentives like grants, subsidies, tax benefits, and prizes.[32] In future work, we intend to evaluate the benefits and drawbacks of combining them in different ways at various levels of the local news supply chain by drawing on interventions in other industries, such as

[24] *See* Daniel J. Hemel & Lisa Larrimore Ouellette, *Innovation Policy Pluralism*, 128 Yale L.J. 544, 549 (2019); Daniel J. Hemel & Lisa Larrimore Ouellette, *Beyond the Patents-Prizes Debate*, 92 Tex. L. Rev. 303, 316 (2013).

[25] Hemel & Ouellette, *Innovation Policy Pluralism*, *supra* note 24, at 549 (arguing that this lens allows policymakers to "identify a wide range of circumstances in which IP/non-IP combinations can advance the goals of innovation law").

[26] *Id.* at 547–51 (mapping out this framework).

[27] *See* Postal Act of 1792, Act of Feb. 20, 1792, ch. 7, 1 Stat. 232.

[28] We explain why the media should be considered a form of innovation below. *See infra* Section 25.1.

[29] Richard R. John, Spreading the News: The American Postal System from Franklin to Morse 39 (2009).

[30] *See* Postal Act of 1792, Act of Feb. 20, 1792, ch. 7, 1 Stat. 232. This is in contrast to an ex post intervention, which might have provided the subsidy as a reward for the creation of a specific kind of new story or based on the ultimate popularity of the news product.

[31] *See* discussion *infra* Section 25.3. *See also* Hemel & Ouellette, *Innovation Policy Pluralism*, *supra* note 24, at 549 (mapping out the innovation policy pluralism framework).

[32] *See* discussion *infra* Section 25.2.

pharmaceuticals, that have also suffered from innovation failures.[33] This chapter lays the descriptive groundwork that will allow us to advance these normative claims.

It does so in three sections. Section 25.1 describes the innovation policy framework. It then argues that this rubric can be a useful lens for evaluating press policy proposals. Section 25.2 applies this framework to various existing or proposed press policy interventions. It outlines five categories of regulatory interventions when it comes to the press: market-set, ex post rewards; market-set, ex ante rewards; government-set, ex post rewards; government-set, ex ante rewards; and hybrid approaches. It then concludes by briefly examining the implications of the press policy pluralism framework. It outlines our plans for future research by offering early lessons learned by mapping press policy innovations onto the policy pluralism rubric.

25.1 INNOVATION POLICY LEVERS

"Innovation" is a nebulous concept. Among policymakers and in popular discourse, it usually refers to the fostering of technological or scientific breakthroughs. But, as scholars of intellectual property contend, innovation can and should be a broad umbrella, referring to the production of all "knowledge goods." It encompasses anything that contains ideas and/or information, including but not limited to, "[b]ooks, blueprints, films, and pharmaceutical formulas."[34]

By adopting this approach, we treat journalism as a form of innovation.[35] As discussed further below, the market failures that have plagued the news industry correspond closely to the market failures known to occur in other innovation-focused industries, such as technology, pharmaceuticals, and entertainment.[36]

33 *See* Christina Koningisor & Jacob Noti-Victor, *Press Policy Pluralism* (draft on file with authors).

34 Daniel J. Hemel & Lisa Larrimore Ouellette, *Knowledge Goods and Nation-States*, 101 MINN. L. REV. 167, 168 n.1 (2016). *See also* Hemel & Ouellette, *Innovation Policy Pluralism*, *supra* note 24, at 549 (An innovation incentive "establishes the payoff structure for producers of knowledge goods."); Brett M. Frischmann & Mark A. Lemley, *Spillovers*, 107 COLUM. L. REV. 257, 301 n.4 (2007) (defining innovation "to refer to the process of research, invention, and development and refinement of new ideas").

35 *See* Hemel & Ouellette, *Innovation Policy Pluralism*, *supra* note 24, at 168 n.1 (referring to a "knowledge good" as "anything that can be digitized") (quoting HAL VARIAN, MARKETS FOR INFORMATION GOODS 3 (1999)). Newspapers clearly pass the minimum threshold of this test. Moreover, the social value of press products is particularly high when assessed through some of the normative frameworks that have been applied to copyright and other innovation-encouraging interventions. *Cf.* Neil Weinstock Netanel, *Copyright and a Democratic Civil Society*, 106 YALE L.J. 283, 288 (1996) ("Copyright provides an incentive for creative expression on a wide array of political, social, and aesthetic issues, thus bolstering the discursive foundations for democratic culture and civic association.").

36 *See infra* Section 25.2 (examining various government responses to market failures in the media).

Indeed, innovation in general is often understood to require some kind of legal or regulatory intervention to occur effectively. The law involves itself in innovation not simply because many innovations are socially desirable but because the production of knowledge goods commonly poses economic difficulties. Knowledge goods generally suffer from a classic public goods problem: They can be used simultaneously by many without leading to scarcity (nonrivalrousness) and their use cannot inherently be limited to some and not others (nonexcludability).[37]

In more concrete terms, a song or a pharmaceutical formula or a piece of investigative reporting can be copied and shared indefinitely without any inherent way for the creator to police such sharing. This runs in contrast to tangible goods – from apples to airplanes – that can only be used by one person at a time (rivalrousness) and, by virtue of the good's physical nature, can be protected from use by nonowners (excludability). Many contend that, because of the problems of nonrivalrousness and nonexcludability, innovators will lack an incentive to produce socially valuable knowledge goods unless they are guaranteed some possibility of financial reward for investing the time and money that innovation generally requires.[38]

Most notably, patent and copyright law provide this financial reward by granting innovators a limited right to exclude access to their innovations and, therefore, charge a market-based price. Without this property right, the theory goes, innovators would lack the incentive to produce valuable knowledge goods. But property-based interests are not the only way this innovation incentive can occur. The government can also directly reward innovators through grants, prizes, or tax credits.

Legal scholars, in particular Lisa Larrimore Ouellette and Daniel Hemel, have categorized the variety of ways that a government can facilitate "innovation policy."[39] Specifically, they note the distinctions between when the innovation reward is set temporally (ex post vs. ex ante) and who actually sets the reward amount (market vs. government).[40] A brief discussion of the four categories follows.

Market-Set, Ex Post Rewards. This category includes any intervention that grants an innovator the right to exclude and thus charge a market price. Patent, copyright, and other forms of intellectual property are all examples of such policy levers. Patent law, for example, grants inventors twenty years of exclusivity for nonobvious, useful innovations.[41] Thanks to this exclusivity, the patent owner can earn a financial reward through licensing the invention or through producing the invention itself.[42]

[37] William M. Landes & Richard A. Posner, The Economic Structure of Intellectual Property Law 13–14 (2003).

[38] *Id.*; Mark A. Lemley, *Property, Intellectual Property, and Free Riding*, 83 Tex. L. Rev. 1031, 1053 (2005).

[39] Hemel & Ouellette, *Innovation Policy Pluralism*, *supra* note 24, at 547–49.

[40] *Id.* at 554.

[41] Hemel & Ouellette, *Beyond the Patents-Prizes Debate*, *supra* note 24, at 319.

[42] *Id.* at 320.

The compensation structure of intellectual property is ex post because the innovator will only be able to demand compensation if they successfully produce a knowledge good that the public actually finds valuable. Simply *attempting* to write a novel or invent a new pharmaceutical is not sufficient; the innovator must actually produce something of value. The reward is market-set because the precise compensation will be dictated by market demand. The government itself is neutral as to the specific innovation and the kind of compensation it warrants.[43]

Market-Set, Ex Ante Rewards. This category includes tax preferences and other interventions that lower the costs of doing business for innovators. For example, the tax code explicitly allows researchers to deduct certain expenses related to research and development.[44] Through these preferences, innovators are incentivized to spend more money more quickly on research than would otherwise be financially feasible.

Tax preferences are ex ante because they are provided neutrally to anyone engaged in a specific form of innovation before the results of the innovative activity are known. But the reward is still dictated by the market because the benefits of a tax preference are meaningless if innovation does not ultimately yield a marketable product. The preference may enable a quicker route to that possibility, but it does not guarantee it.[45]

Government-Set, Ex Post Rewards. This category includes government prizes that promise compensation if a specific innovation goal is achieved. For example, if the government is concerned about a specific disease, it may set a prize for the successful development of a vaccine for that disease.[46]

A prize operates ex post because only successful achievement of the prize's criteria will yield a reward. But, unlike a patent, the reward is government-set; compensation can be received regardless of whether the innovation has market value.

Government-Set, Ex Ante Rewards. This category includes direct spending by the government on innovation. Such direct spending can be done through grants or through direct government ownership of entities engaging in research. Examples of the former include funding provided to private researchers by the National Institute of Health, and examples of the latter include direct government-funded research at the Department of Energy's National Laboratories.[47]

[43] Hemel & Ouellette, *Innovation Policy Pluralism, supra* note 24, at 553 (2019). The government is of course also involved in IP-based rewards because the government is responsible for creating the IP entitlement to begin with. But the market, not the government, dictates the actual *compensation amount*.

[44] I.R.C. § 174(a) (2006). *See also* Hemel & Ouellette, *Beyond the Patents-Prizes Debate, supra* note 24, at 321–26 (describing these tax provisions).

[45] Hemel & Ouellette, *Innovation Policy Pluralism, supra* note 24, at 553–54; Hemel & Ouellette, *Beyond the Patents-Prizes Debate, supra* note 24, at 328.

[46] Hemel & Ouellette, *Innovation Policy Pluralism, supra* note 24, at 553–54.

[47] *See generally* W. Nicholson Price II, *Grants*, 34 Berkeley Tech. L.J. 1, 17 (2019).

Through such direct funding, research and development can occur without regard to market-driven returns on investment. But, in contrast to prizes, the reward is not conditioned on a specific successful outcome. Thus, the reward is government-set because the government makes the compensation decision, but it is ex ante because the reward is given before the government knows whether the innovative activity has actually proven fruitful.

***

These categories provide a helpful heuristic for making sense of various innovation policy proposals in any industry focused on the production of knowledge goods, including, as the next section argues, the press. It is important to note, however, that the categories are more ideal types that can encompass a variety of policy arrangements. As Hemel and Ouellette note, many actual interventions operate on a spectrum between government-set and market-set rewards and even between ex ante and ex post reward settings.[48] Moreover, specific policy interventions can entail intricate combinations of different innovation strategies. For example, government-funded researchers may be permitted to also seek a patent – a mixing of patent and grant strategies. Or the government might license a pharmaceutical patent at a market-set price and then distribute the corresponding medicine for free – a matching of a market-set reward with government-driven allocation. In addition to discussing how the four primary innovation policy categories already operate in the press landscape, some of these combinations are also discussed in the next section.

25.2 INNOVATION POLICY AND THE PRESS

For much of the nation's history, the press has been governed largely by market forces.[49] Technological innovations throughout the 1800s caused publishing costs to fall, making newspapers more widely available to the masses.[50] By the end of the 1800s, media magnates like William Randolph Hearst and Joseph Pulitzer had established media empires through the sale of salacious and scandal-ridden "yellow journalism" papers.[51] The industry continued to grow from there. Newspaper advertising revenue grew from roughly \$3.7 billion in 1960, to \$14.8 billion in 1980, to \$48.7 billion in 2000.[52]

48 *See* Hemel & Ouellette, *Innovation Policy Pluralism*, *supra* note 24, at 554.

49 *See, e.g.*, Victor Pickard, Josh Stearns & Craig Aaron, Changing Media: Public Interest Policies for the Digital Age 252 (2009) (noting that Finland and Denmark spend 75 times more on public media than the United States). Of course, there are many exceptions. *See* Minow, *supra* note 11, at 36–57 (describing US government interventions to support the press).

50 *See* Bruce E. Boyden, *Regulating at the End of Privacy*, 2013 U. Chi. Legal F. 173, 191 (2013).

51 Ken Gormley, *100 Years of Privacy*, 1992 Wis. L. Rev. 1335, 135–51 (1992).

52 *Newspaper Fact Sheet*, Pew Res. Ctr. (Nov. 10, 2023), https://pewresearch.org/journalism/fact-sheet/newspapers/ ("Estimated advertising and circulation revenue of the newspaper industry" showing \$3.681 billion in 1960, \$14.794 billion in 1980, and \$48.78 billion in 2000).

Yet around the turn of the millennium, the press's long-standing financial model began to break down. The invention of the internet brought a series of cascading financial, technological, and cultural changes that disrupted the media's financial viability. Job and real estate listings had long subsidized news reporting.[53] But the internet allowed for the disaggregation of classified advertisements from journalism products.[54] Further, critical advertising revenue migrated online to other platforms.[55] Many newspapers and magazines also offered their publications for free online. Readers became accustomed to accessing news without paying for the content, and it became difficult to later reshape consumer expectations again.[56]

Local news outlets were hardest hit by these developments, especially local newspapers. Since 2005, 2,900 newspapers have closed.[57] Many that remain are now "ghost newspapers," with little or no staff and limited original reporting.[58] More than half of American counties now have no local newspaper or only a single paper,[59] and most of the existing local newspapers today are published only weekly.[60] The rise of digital-only outlets has not come close to making up for this loss.

Against this backdrop, governments have begun to experiment with new and expanded forms of financial support for the press. The press has always functioned with some measure of intervention and assistance from the government in the United States, although the government's support has traditionally been limited.[61] Given the depth and severity of the current local news crisis, however, many government actors, both domestically and abroad, have begun experimenting with new forms of press assistance. Many advocates have also proposed innovative new forms of support that have not yet been implemented. This section surveys these efforts, categorizing them according to the innovation policy pluralism framework developed by intellectual property and innovation law scholars.

25.2.1 *Market-Set, Ex Post Rewards*

A ubiquitous form of innovation policy consists of the various legal regimes that enable the press to successfully monetize content in the marketplace. These policy

[53] Jack Shafer, *Why Has Local News Collapsed? Blame Readers*, POLITICO (June 12, 2021), https://www.politico.com/news/magazine/2021/06/12/local-news-demand-493495.
[54] *See* Langvardt, *supra* note 23, at 299.
[55] MINOW, *supra* note 11, at 13, 25.
[56] *Id.*
[57] *See* Abernathy, *supra* note 13.
[58] *Id.*
[59] *Id.*
[60] *Id.*
[61] RODNEY BENSON & MATTHEW POWERS, PUBLIC MEDIA AND POLITICAL INDEPENDENCE: LESSONS FOR THE FUTURE OF JOURNALISM AROUND THE WORLD 8 (2011), https://www.issuelab.org/resources/13259/13259.pdf.

tools enable media companies to enforce a right to exclude, thereby preventing freeriding by rivals or by users.[62] Thanks to these protections, media companies can assert control over the ways in which the public can access new content, which in turn allows these companies to utilize a variety of monetization strategies: for example, direct charging for content via subscriptions or hard-copy purchases, licensing of content, or seeking payment from advertisers.[63]

We include in this category conventional forms of intellectual property, especially copyright, as well as media-specific regimes, such as "hot news misappropriation" or special licensing obligations for platforms. We also include the variety of laws that enable media companies to prevent circumvention of various technical protections, such as paywalls. This section discusses each of these regimes below.

25.2.1.1 Copyright

In the United States, copyright protects any original work – including textual works, audio works, or audiovisual works – from the moment of fixation.[64] News articles, television news, podcasts, or radio news broadcasts are all protected by copyright.[65] Newspapers, magazines, and websites are also protectable as a collective work or compilation.[66] Thanks to copyright protection, media companies can seek damages or injunctive relief for any unauthorized copying, distribution, or transmission of these materials.[67]

Copyright in news, however, is more limited than copyright in areas such as music, art, or literature. Copyright law does not extend to ideas or facts about the world. The Supreme Court has explicitly stated that "all facts – scientific, historical, biographical, and news of the day . . . may not be copyrighted and are part of the public domain available to every person."[68] In practice, then, copyright in news materials is limited to the specific ways these unprotectable facts are expressed. The wholesale copying of an entire, or a large portion of, a news article would be considered infringing, but the borrowing of facts for inclusion in a new work of journalism – even if such facts were previously unreported – would not be

62 *See* Landes & Posner, *supra* note 37, at 12–14.

63 *See generally* Pew Research Center, *State of the Media Project*, https://www.pewresearch.org/topic/news-habits-media/news-media-trends/state-of-the-news-media-project/.

64 17 U.S.C. § 102.

65 Though copyright vests in the "author" of the work, many news companies retain ownership of their reporters' works through copyright assignment agreements or the work for hire doctrine. U.S. Copyright Office, Copyright Protections for Press Publishers 29–30 (2022), https://www.copyright.gov/policy/publishersprotections/202206-Publishers-Protections-Study.pdf.

66 17 U.S.C. § 101 (defining compilation and collective work). *See also* U.S. Copyright Office, *supra* note 65, at 29 n.145.

67 17 U.S.C. § 106.

68 Feist Publications, Inc. v. Rural Tel. Serv. Co., 499 U.S. 340, 348 (1991) (internal quotations and citations omitted).

considered infringing. For a finding of infringement, an entire article need not be copied verbatim, but the copy must be highly similar, including, for example, utilizing "the same structure and organization, ... the same chronological and substantive grouping of facts ... [and some] identical phraseology and word choice."[69]

Protection for news material is further limited by some other areas of copyright. The simple copying of short phrases or headlines is generally not actionable.[70] The fair use doctrine can also prevent news organizations from asserting copyright in certain contexts. While fair use will generally not excuse a rival news organization's copying of protected material,[71] the doctrine allows members of the public to copy materials for many educational uses.[72]

Copyright, then, is primarily useful to media organizations for preventing the unauthorized dissemination of news articles and the like (in contrast to the reuse of factual materials from those articles in other reporting).[73] Actually asserting copyright, however, can carry some challenges. Registration of a work at the Copyright Office is a precondition to filing suit, and this process can prove onerous for news organizations that are constantly producing new content.[74] Broad unauthorized dissemination online by members of the public is also generally difficult and expensive to police.[75] Around a decade ago, some media organizations attempted to deal with these costs by assigning their rights to sue for infringement to a for-profit "copyright enforcement" entity called Rightshaven. But after a series of failed

69 Nihon Keizai Shimbun, Inc. v. Comline Bus. Data, Inc., 166 F.3d 65, 70 (2d Cir. 1999).

70 *See* U.S. Copyright Office, *supra* note 65, at 33–37 (noting application of merger doctrine and de minimis use doctrine in this context).

71 *See, e.g.*, Los Angeles News Serv. v. Reuters Television Int'l, Ltd., 149 F.3d 987, 993 (9th Cir. 1998), *as amended on denial of reh'g and reh'g en banc* (Aug. 25, 1998) (finding that Reuters copying of clips of Los Angeles riots was not fair use when Reuters did "not explain the footage, edit the content of the footage, or include editorial comment"); Harper & Row Publishers, Inc. v. Nation Enterprises, 471 U.S. 539, 540 (1985) (scooping of material from yet-to-be-published memoir was not fair use).

72 *See generally* Cambridge Univ. Press v. Patton, 769 F.3d 1232, 1267 (11th Cir. 2014) (exploring scope of fair use for educational purposes); *see also* 17 U.S.C. § 110(1)) (outlining explicit carve out for classroom uses).

73 Trademark law may additionally allow news organizations to assert a cause of action for the specific copying of brand-identifying information by an unauthorized competitor. *See, e.g.*, Washington Post Co. v. Total News, Inc., No. 97 Civ. 1190 (PKL) (S.D.N.Y., filed Feb. 20, 1997) (settled case in which several media companies brought trademark and copyright claims against a news aggregator website for, among other things, using "framed" in-line links in which the media companies' content and brand-identifying information appeared on the website).

74 *See* Andrew Deck, *The Intercept Charts a New Legal Strategy for Digital Publishers Suing OpenAI*, NiemanLab (Mar. 20, 2024), https://www.niemanlab.org/2024/03/the-intercept-charts-a-new-legal-strategy-for-digital-publishers-suing-openai/ (discussing this problem).

75 Dan Frosch, *Enforcing Copyrights Online, for a Profit*, N.Y. Times (May 2, 2011), https://www.nytimes.com/2011/05/03/business/media/03righthaven.html.

litigations against various bloggers and news aggregators, Rightshaven ultimately closed its operations.[76]

25.2.1.2 Hot News Misappropriation

The unprotectability of facts under copyright law has, historically, raised concerns for newspapers that their investments in gathering news would go unrewarded, since rivals could immediately co-opt and rewrite any breaking news stories. In reaction to this problem, the federal courts developed a special form of unfair competition tort: hot news misappropriation. As the Supreme Court elucidated in 1918, newspapers maintain a "quasi-property" interest in their time-sensitive, factual news reporting that they can assert against competitors.[77]

The later abolition of federal common law, however, relegated the cause of action to the common law of just a handful of states.[78] And the passage of the 1976 Copyright Act raised questions about whether the cause of action was preempted. In its 1997 decision in *NBA v. Motorola*, the Second Circuit held that preemption concerns limit the doctrine's applicability to a very narrow set of scenarios.[79] Since then, courts that have considered hot news misappropriation claims have generally not permitted them to go forward.[80]

Some courts and commentators have speculated that hot news misappropriation can survive if recharacterized as a kind of unfair competition or unjust enrichment claim, rather than an intellectual property interest.[81] Indeed, news organizations continue to assert such protection for their works. For example, in the litigation over OpenAI's use of The New York Times' materials, the parties are currently debating the applicability of a common law hot news misappropriation claim.[82]

[76] David Kravets, *Copyright Troll Righthaven Says It's Nearing Bankruptcy*, WIRED (Sep. 12, 2011), https://www.wired.com/2011/09/righthaven-nearing-bankruptcy/.

[77] Int'l News Serv. v. Associated Press, 248 U.S. 215, 242 (1918).

[78] Netanel, *supra* note 23, at 499.

[79] *See* Nat'l Basketball Ass'n v. Motorola, Inc., 105 F.3d 841, 845 (2d Cir. 1997) (describing these exceptional circumstances).

[80] *See, e.g.*, Fox News Network, LLC v. TVEyes, Inc., 43 F. Supp. 3d 379, 399 (S.D.N.Y. 2014); *see also* U.S. COPYRIGHT OFFICE, *supra* note 65, at 47 n.266 (surveying cases).

[81] *See* Barclays Cap. Inc. v. Theflyonthewall.com, Inc., 650 F.3d 876, 902 (2d Cir. 2011) (noting the requirement of direct competition between the plaintiff and defendant). *See also* Shyamkrishna Balganesh, *The Uncertain Future of "Hot News" Misappropriation After Barclays Capital v. Theflyonthewall.com*, 112 COLUM. L. REV. SIDEBAR 134, 135 (2012); Shyamkrishna Balganesh, *"Hot News": The Enduring Myth of Property in News*, 111 COLUM. L. REV. 419, 475–76 (2011).

[82] *See* Complaint at 1–4, The New York Times Co. v. Microsoft Corporation, Open AI Inc. (Dec. 27, 2023) (No. 23 Civ. 11195), https://nytco-assets.nytimes.com/2023/12/NYT_Complaint_Dec2023.pdf (asserting cause of action for "common law misappropriation"). *Cf.* Open AI Memorandum of Law in Support of Motion to Dismiss (Feb. 26, 2024) (No. 23 Civ. 11195), https://static01.nyt.com/newsgraphics/documenttools/82a013b9ba852548/9d4b1790-full.pdf (arguing that claim is preempted in light of *Barclays*) *with* New York Times Memorandum of

25.2.1.3 Press Publishers' Rights Against Platforms

The rise of online platforms and news aggregators has posed significant challenges for media organizations. In particular, platforms' role as both a gateway and (algorithmic) curator of consumers' access to news has led to significant decreases in news media revenue.[83] Rather than accessing news directly on a media organization's website, most consumers now encounter news articles via platforms, while accompanied by the highly precise targeted advertisements that these platforms enable through data accumulation and sophisticated algorithms. This has meant that news organizations' advertising revenue has decreased significantly, as advertisers have instead flocked to platforms.[84] Notably, from 2014 to 2018, Google and Facebook advertising revenue increased by 150 percent while newspapers experienced a 35-percent advertising revenue decline.[85] Moreover, platform-based news access has also eroded consumers' familiarity with distinct media brand identities, as consumers now access content through algorithmically driven curation that is mostly independent of specific media brands.[86]

Platforms' role in reducing media revenue has led to several interventions ostensibly designed to restore the status quo by requiring platforms to compensate news organizations for reproducing their content. Some of these interventions can be categorized as intellectual property-like ex post, market-based rewards. In particular, Article 15 of the 2019 European Union Copyright Directive provides that EU member states must grant press publishers an exclusive right to prevent platforms (including news aggregators, social media companies, and search engines) from reproducing excerpts of press publications without permission.[87]

This press publishers' right is independent of the copyright in the news story.[88] Thus, for example, a national law implementing Article 15 would require Facebook to obtain permission from a publisher before providing a headline and short snippet of a news story (even though such permission would not always be required under copyright law). Notably, the Copyright Directive explicitly justifies the creation of this new press publishers' right using the language of innovation incentives. It explains that the "organisational and financial contribution of publishers in producing press publications needs to be recognised and further encouraged to ensure the sustainability of the publishing industry." The Copyright Directive aims

Law in Opposition to OpenAI's Motion to Dismiss, https://ipwatchdog.com/wp-content/uploads/2024/03/NYT-v-OpenAI-Opp-Motion-to-Dismiss-3-11-2024.pdf (arguing that claim falls under narrow hot news exception and is not preempted).

[83] Netanel, *supra* note 23, at 479.

[84] *Id.* (describing rise in platform advertising revenue); Abernathy, *supra* note 13 (describing decline in newspapers' advertising revenue).

[85] Netanel, *supra* note 23, at 480–81.

[86] *Id.* at 482–83.

[87] Council Directive 2019/790, 2019 O.J. (L 130) 35, 57–59, 92, 118.

[88] Netanel, *supra* note 23, at 501.

to do so by providing "harmonised legal protection for press publications in respect of online uses by information society service providers."[89]

While the Article 15 press publisher right does not cover simply linking to press material (without the inclusion of any excerpt), some countries have implemented their own press publisher rights that also include linking. For example, Australia and Canada require payment for such uses. And in order to address perceived imbalances in bargaining positions,[90] Australian and Canadian laws require platforms to negotiate royalties with news organizations before the platforms can make their news content available. They also enable the government to step in to set rates if negotiations do not succeed.[91]

The United States has not enacted a press publishers' right, but California has proposed legislation modeled after some of the examples described above. Like the Canadian and Australian approaches, the proposed California Journalism Prevention Act would require that platforms engage in a negotiation, with the possibility of arbitration, to determine an amount the platforms must pay for a license to make available news content.[92]

Scholars have criticized press publishers' rights on a variety of grounds. The lack of government-mandated negotiation and rate-setting in the EU Directive raises concerns that large platforms will take advantage of their market power to demand the use of content for a low or no fee.[93] Approaches with mandatory arbitration or rate-setting attempt to resolve this competition problem but still raise concerns that platforms will deprioritize news content, or even pull it altogether, to lower or avoid royalty payments. For example, the Canadian government is still in negotiations with Facebook, which has threatened to pull all news content from its platform in Canada.[94]

89 Council Directive, *supra* note 87, at 104.

90 *See generally* U.S. Copyright Office, *supra* note 65, at 52–54 (discussing competition problems).

91 Treasury Laws Amendment (News Media and Digital Platforms Mandatory Bargaining Code) Bill 2021 (Cth) (Austl.), Div. 6–7, 9–10, https://parlinfo.aph.gov.au/parlInfo/download/legislation/bills/r6652_aspassed/toc_pdf/20177b01.pdf; Bill C-18, Online News Act, 1st Sess., Secs. 4, 18–22, 44th Parl., 2022 (first reading, Apr. 5, 2022) (Can.), https://www.parl.ca/DocumentViewer/en/44-1/bill/C-18/first-reading. *See also* Matthew Ingram, *Canada Imitates Australia's News-Bargaining Law, But to What End?*, Colum. Journalism Rev. (Marc. 16, 2023), https://www.cjr.org/the_media_today/canada_australia_platforms_news_law.php; U.S. Copyright Office, *supra* note 65, at 24–26.

92 Cameron Joseph, *Can Legislation Save Journalism in California?*, Colum. Journalism Rev. (Feb. 16. 2024), https://www.cjr.org/the_media_today/california_news_bill_buffy_wicks.php.

93 Netanel, *supra* note 23, at 504.

94 Vjosa Isai, *Google Agrees to Pay Canadian Media for Using Their Content*, N.Y. Times (Nov. 29, 2023), https://www.nytimes.com/2023/11/29/world/americas/google-canada-news-media-deal.html; Ashley Belanger, *Meta Won't Negotiate with Publishers, Will End Facebook News in Canada*, Ars Technica (June 23, 2023), https://arstechnica.com/tech-policy/2023/06/facebook-cutting-off-news-in-canada-to-avoid-paying-publishers-for-content/.

The California proposal has also received more specific criticism. Some media stakeholders have raised concerns that the royalty payouts would predominantly benefit large media organizations (or, even more troublingly, clickbait-focused entities), at the expense of small, local media outlets.[95] Finally, some commentators believe the California proposal could not survive a court challenge on First Amendment and/or copyright preemption grounds.[96]

Notwithstanding these criticisms, the direct payments from platforms to media organizations have begun to prove helpful to at least some in the news industry. In particular, in 2023, 33 percent of media leaders described payments from platforms as an "important revenue stream."[97]

25.2.1.4 Paywall Anti-circumvention

Many media organizations now use online paywalls, requiring a reader to create an online account and (usually) pay a fee in order to access content. Paywalls provide a source of direct revenue to media companies, while also attempting to ensure that users access content predominantly on the media company's website, which can bolster advertising revenue.[98]

Paywalls, however, are easily circumvented by specialized software, URL manipulation, or password sharing.[99] Several areas of law may provide protections for media companies that seek to prevent circumvention. Access to paywalled media content is

95 *See* Chris Jennewein, *Opinion: A Bill to Prop Up Legacy Media in California Is Bad News for Journalism*, Times of San Diego (Apr. 18, 2023), https://timesofsandiego.com/opinion/2023/04/18/a-bill-to-prop-up-legacy-media-in-california-is-bad-news-for-journalism/; Mike Rispoli, *Lawmakers Must Ensure That Preserving California Journalism Doesn't Enable Clickbait*, Cal Matters (Jan. 22, 2024), https://calmatters.org/commentary/2024/01/preserving-california-journalism-bill-clickbait/. *See also* Paul Matzko, *From Hot News to Link Tax: The Dangers of a Quasi-Property Right in Information*, 3 J. Free Speech L. 269, 286–93 (2023) (arguing that such informational closure will lead to industry consolidation, diminished competition, and censorship).

96 *See, e.g.*, Eric Goldman, *California's Proposed Fix to the Journalism Crisis Is Unconstitutional and Worse Than Socialism (Comments on the California Journalism Protection Act, CJPA)*, Tech. & Marketing L. Blog (June 22, 2023), https://blog.ericgoldman.org/archives/2023/06/californias-proposed-fix-to-the-journalism-crisis-is-unconstitutional-and-worse-than-socialism-comments-on-the-california-journalism-protection-act-cjpa.htm (explaining these arguments).

97 Nic Newman, *Journalism, Media, and Technology Trends and Predictions 2023*, Reuters Inst. (Jan. 10, 2023), https://reutersinstitute.politics.ox.ac.uk/journalism-media-and-technology-trends-and-predictions-2023#:~:text=Beyond%20paid%20content%2C%20the%20fastest,up%204pp%20on%20last%20year ("Google now pays more than 300 publishers for content across the European Union as well as in other parts of the world like Australia and Canada and Facebook has been paying up to $20 million to some large publishers for content it includes in its news section.").

98 *See* Hannah Farrow, *How Newsrooms Are Building Better Paywalls*, Local News Initiative (Mar. 9, 2021), https://localnewsinitiative.northwestern.edu/posts/2021/03/09/paywalls/.

99 *See, e.g.*, Chip Brownlee, *Google's New Chrome Makes It Easier to Bypass Newspaper Paywalls*, Slate (July 31, 2019), https://slate.com/technology/2019/07/google-chrome-update-incognito-mode-paywall-workaround.html.

usually accompanied by terms of service that may create contract remedies for misuse of the paywall or its underlying content.[100] Additionally, the Digital Millennium Copyright Act's (DMCA) prohibition against circumventing technical measures that control access to copyrighted works[101] may be implicated by efforts to bypass a paywall.[102] Such a theory remains untested, and the courts' differing interpretations of the DMCA may pose barriers.[103] That being said, at least one recent case attempted such a strategy: The owners of the Wall Street Journal brought a series of breach-of-contract and DMCA anti-circumvention claims against the owner of a commercial password sharing service.[104] The case, however, settled before any judgment on the merits.[105]

25.2.2 *Market-Set, Ex Ante Rewards*

A variety of ex ante, market-based rewards are also used to support the press. Most take the form of tax benefits. Through these tax initiatives, the government harnesses information held by the private sector. Government actors establish "general ground rules for the reward system without making tailored, technology-specific judgments."[106] The government offers up financial incentives but leaves private actors free to decide how to respond.[107]

There is a long history in the United States of using federal, state, and local tax incentives to support the press. A common example is the use of sales tax exemptions for news publishers. As far back as the nation's founding, states have excluded newspapers and other news products from general sales and use taxes.[108] This technique is still employed today as a form of government support for news institutions.[109] Federal, state, and local governments have also long provided tax breaks for items critical to the news manufacturing processes. They have exempted ink,

[100] U.S. Copyright Office, *supra* note 65, at 46.

[101] 17 U.S.C. § 1201.

[102] Theresa M. Troupson, *Yes, It's Illegal to Cheat a Paywall: Access Rights and the DMCA's Anticircumvention Provision*, 90 N.Y.U. L. Rev. 325 (2015) (making this argument).

[103] *Id.* (noting that this theory would require adoption of the Ninth Circuit's interpretation of Section 1201 articulated in MDY Indus., LLC v. Blizzard Ent., Inc., 629 F.3d 928, 950 (9th Cir. 2010)); *see also* U.S. Copyright Office, *supra* note 65, at 46 n.259. Some have also speculated that the Computer Fraud and Abuse Act (CFAA) would provide protection for paywall circumvention, though implementing such a theory would also face barriers. *Id.*

[104] Complaint and Jury Demand, Dow Jones & Co., Insupac., Plaintiff, v. Nic.kl, Inc., Defendant., 2022 WL 836871 (E.D. Pa. Mar. 21, 2022).

[105] Settlement Agreement, Dow Jones & Co., Inc., Plaintiff, v. Nic.kl, Inc., Defendant., 2:22-CV-01070.

[106] Hemel & Ouellette, *Beyond the Patents-Prizes Debate*, *supra* note 24, at 307.

[107] *Id.* at 308.

[108] Martha Minow, *The Changing Ecosystem of News and Challenges for Freedom of the Press*, 64 Loy. L. Rev. 499, 522 (2018).

[109] Geoffrey Cowan & David Westphal, *Public Policy and Funding the News* 10–11, USC Ctr. On Comm. Leadership & Pol. (2010), https://bpb-us-w1.wpmucdn.com/sites.usc.edu/dist/5/

newsprint, and newspaper machinery and related equipment from sales taxes.[110] They have also excluded broadcasting and other telecommunications equipment from sales taxes.[111]

Such benefits are less valuable today because news organizations print fewer hard copies or offer digital-only products. But new tax incentives could be fashioned to better address publishers' needs in the digital age. For example, President Joe Biden's 2020 Build Back Better Act proposed tax credits for the salaries of new journalism hires. The bill, if enacted, would have provided $25,000 for the salary of local journalists in their first year of employment and a $15,000 tax credit for the following four years.[112] Similarly, Washington state recently enacted a law that reduces newspaper publishers' tax rate under the state's business and occupation tax,[113] a move estimated to save the states' publishers around $1 million per year.[114]

Other tax-based proposals have focused on better utilizing existing tax advantages. For example, nonprofit press institutions already receive general tax breaks available to all nonprofit journalism entities.[115] Some scholars have argued that the government should make it easier for for-profit news organizations to convert into nonprofit ones in order to obtain the benefits of these existing tax-based incentives.[116] The downside is that nonprofit institutions are restricted from engaging in certain political activities, such as endorsing candidates.[117] But these costs might be outweighed by the financial advantages of securing nonprofit status. Similarly, scholars have suggested moving all for-profit journalism institutions into a lower tax bracket.[118]

6 ("[F]ederal and state tax laws forgive more than $900 million annually in taxes related to newspapers and magazines.").

[110] *Id.*

[111] Minow, *supra* note 108, at 522.

[112] Marc Tracy, *Local News Outlets Could Reap $1.7 Billion in Build Back Better Aid*, N.Y. TIMES (Nov. 28, 2021), https://www.nytimes.com/2021/11/28/business/media/build-back-better-local-news.html. *See also* STEPHEN GILLERS, JOURNALISM UNDER FIRE 150 (2018) (arguing that this approach won't assist media organizations that earn little money and already have low tax burdens).

[113] Wash. Rev. Code Ann. §§ 82.04.214; 82.04.759. *See also Washington State Grants Tax Exemption to Publishing Industry Leaders*, SALES TAX INST. (Dec. 27, 2023), https://www.salestaxinstitute.com/resources/washington-state-grants-tax-exemption-to-publishing-industry-leaders#:~:text=Gross%20Receipts%20Tax-,Washington%20State%20Grants%20Tax%20Exemption%20to%20Publishing%20Industry%20Leaders,and%20occupation%20(B%26O)%20tax (describing the effects of these legislative efforts).

[114] Brier Dudley, *Legislature Votes to Support Local News, New Capital Outlet Launching*, SEATTLE TIMES (Apr. 19, 2023), https://www.seattletimes.com/opinion/legislature-votes-to-support-local-news-new-capital-outlet-launching/.

[115] *See* ProPublica, *Donate*, https://give.propublica.org/give/346423/%23!/donation/checkout#!/donation/checkout (noting that donations are tax-deductible because the institution is a 501 (c)(3)).

[116] GILLERS, *supra* note 112, at 150; MINOW, *supra* note 11, at 141.

[117] GILLERS, *supra* note 112, at 150.

[118] *Id.* at 149 (outlining this proposal, but also noting that there is a risk that the money goes back to shareholders or to news executives rather than back into democracy-promoting journalism).

Scholars and policymakers have proposed modifying existing tax laws to incentivize the donation of legacy news institutions as well – for example, by eliminating capital gains when newspapers are sold or by providing enhanced federal tax deductions when newspapers are donated.[119] They also have focused on redistributive efforts among media institutions. For instance, they have proposed taxing wealthier news institutions that benefit from government information infrastructure like broadcast technology to subsidize other, less-profitable forms of journalism.[120]

Some of these proposals may not pass constitutional muster. At times, governments have imposed selective taxes on press institutions to silence political critics. The Supreme Court has struck down these efforts on First Amendment grounds.[121] In doing so, it has emphasized that the government should not use its powers of taxation to single out specific press institutions or the press as a whole for either beneficial or adverse treatment.[122] Yet the Court has permitted tax burdens that fall more heavily on some news industries than others. For example, it has upheld a tax on the receipts of the sales of services for cable television but not for newspaper and magazine subscriptions.[123]

As a result, generally applicable taxes will most likely not pose a constitutional problem. But those that burden the press specifically, favor certain press outlets over others, or discriminate against particular viewpoints may be found unconstitutional. It is unclear how these precedents would apply against some of the proposals described above, such as tax treatments that favor local press institutions over national or regional outlets. That said, tax incentives that do comply with First Amendment requirements offer a clear policy benefit. Such rewards incentivize news creation while still tethering its allocation to market forces.

25.2.3 *Government-Set, Ex Post Rewards*

Governments at all levels have also established rewards for which the government both sets the price and determines ex post how it is allocated. These innovation incentives mostly operate independent of market forces.[124] In the context of the press, these usually take the form of journalism prizes.

[119] *Solutions: Our Plan*, Rebuild Local News, https://www.rebuildlocalnews.org/solutions/our-plan/.

[120] Minow, *supra* note 11, at 142–43 ("The government could set aside for public media a portion of the proceeds from frequency auctions, or a portion of the application and renewal fee for broadcast licenses.").

[121] *See* Grosjean v. Am. Press Co., 297 U.S. 233, 240 (1936) (striking down a tax that targeted only newspapers with circulations larger than 20,000).

[122] *See, e.g.*, Minneapolis Star & Trib. Co. v. Minnesota Com'r of Revenue, 460 U.S. 575, 581 (1983); Arkansas Writers' Project, Inc. v. Ragland, 481 U.S. 221, 234 (1987). The Court has reasoned that even tax benefits selectively granted could be used to reward press allies and silence press critics. *Minneapolis Star*, 460 U.S. at 592.

[123] Leathers v. Medlock, 499 U.S. 439, 441 (1991).

[124] *See* Hemel & Ouellette, *Innovation Policy Pluralism*, *supra* note 24, at 554–55.

Governments have long used prizes to incentivize innovation, especially in areas like engineering, science, and medicine.[125] Among the best-known examples, the British government offered a prize in 1714 to whoever solved the long-standing problem of calculating longitude while at sea.[126] Press-based government prizes are distinct from those awarded in other contexts, in part because it is more difficult to create objective metrics against which to measure success and in part because there is a greater risk of viewpoint-based decision making by the government.[127]

Yet prizes already operate as a powerful incentive for the press. Awards like the Pulitzer Prize are among the nation's most prestigious and coveted domestic honors.[128] The financial benefits from these rewards are often modest compared to other forms of both government- and market-based interventions. The Pulitzer Prize, for example, provides award winners with $15,000.[129] But the nonmonetary benefits – including recognition, prestige, and potential future employment opportunities – are often highly valued.

Most journalism prizes are awarded by private nonprofit groups, such as the Pulitzer Prize Board[130] or the American Society of Magazine Editors, which awards the National Magazine Awards.[131] Yet some journalism prizes can be categorized as government or quasi-government initiatives. These are prizes awarded with government funds or administered through public universities. Among the best-known examples is the Peabody Award, which recognizes excellence in television, broadcast media, and radio journalism.[132] The University of Georgia and the National Association of Broadcasters jointly fund and administer this award.[133] Another example is the Livingston Award, which recognizes outstanding journalism by

[125] Hemel & Ouellette, *Beyond the Patents-Prizes Debate*, *supra* note 24, at 317–19 (describing this history).

[126] *See* M. Diane Burton & Tom Nicholas, *Prizes, Patents and the Search for Longitude*, 64 EXPLORATIONS IN ECON. HISTORY 21, 21–22 (2017), https://www.hbs.edu/ris/Publication%20Files/Longitude_e207c234-9b02-4be8-b5c2-252b42c04ec7.pdfhttps://www.hbs.edu/ris/Publication%20Files/Longitude_e207c234-9b02-4be8-b5c2-252b42c04ec7.pdf. *See also* Michael J. Burstein & Fiona E. Murray, *Innovation Prizes in Practice and Theory*, 29 HARV. J. L. & TECH. 401, 402–03 (2016) (examining how innovation prizes work in practice).

[127] *See* Nat'l Endowment for the Arts v. Finley, 524 U.S. 569, 580–85 (1998) (permitting content-based but not viewpoint-based choices when the government is making funding decisions to award arts grants to private recipients).

[128] THE PULITZER PRIZES, https://www.pulitzer.org/.

[129] THE PULITZER PRICES, *Frequently Asked Questions*, https://www.pulitzer.org/page/frequently-asked-questions#:~:text=What%20do%20Pulitzer%20Prize%20winners,cash%20award%20and%20a%20certificate.

[130] *Id.*

[131] NATIONAL MAGAZINE AWARDS, *ASME Awards 2024*, https://ellieawards.secure-platform.com/a/page/judges.

[132] THE PEABODY AWARDS, *83rd Peabody Winners*, https://peabodyawards.com/awards/winners/

[133] THE PEABODY AWARDS, *Our Story*, https://peabodyawards.com/our-story/; AM. ARCHIVE OF PUBLIC BROADCASTING, *History of the Peabody Award*, https://americanarchive.org/exhibits/peabody/history-peabody.

reporters under the age of 35.[134] The University of Michigan administers and partially funds this prize.[135]

There are many such examples. The University of Florida administers the Collier Prize for State Government Accountability, for example, which awards $25,000 for excellence in press reporting about state governance.[136] The University of Wisconsin administers the Anthony Shadid Award for Journalism Ethics, which recognizes ethical decisions made during the newsgathering process.[137] UCLA administers the Loeb Awards, which recognizes excellence in business and financial journalism.[138] And so on.[139]

In addition to prizes that public universities administer, government agencies also directly dispense a handful of awards. For instance, the U.S. Agency for Global Media, which oversees government-funded and directed media outlets like Voice of America and Radio Free Europe,[140] offers annual prizes to government journalists employed by affiliated press institutions.[141] A handful of government actors or agencies at the state or local levels also directly award journalism prizes. For instance, the Texas Governor's Committee on People with Disabilities issues an annual award recognizing excellence in reporting about individuals with disabilities.[142]

25.2.4 *Government-Set, Ex Ante Rewards*

Finally, the government provides ex ante awards to the press, or monetary incentives that the government dispenses before a news product has been created. Examples

[134] Wallace House Ctr. for Journalism, *Investing in the Future of Journalism*, https://wallacehouse.umich.edu/livingston-awards/about/.

[135] Wallace House Ctr. for Journalism, *Staff*, https://wallacehouse.umich.edu/wallace-house/staff/.

[136] *About Us*, Collier Prize for State Gov't Accountability, Univ. of Fl. College of Journalism and Comm., https://www.jou.ufl.edu/collier-prize-for-state-government-accountability/collier-prize-about/.

[137] *Shadid Award Nomination*, Ctr. for Journalism Ethics, Wisc. School of Journalism and Mass Comm., https://ethics.journalism.wisc.edu/shadid-award/shadid-award-nomination/.

[138] Press Release, UCLA School of Management, 2023 Gerald Loeb Award Finalists, Lifetime Honorees and Awards Event in New York City Announced by UCLA Anderson (Aug. 15, 2023), https://www.prnewswire.com/news-releases/2023-gerald-loeb-award-finalists-lifetime-honorees-and-awards-event-in-new-york-city-announced-by-ucla-anderson-301901255.html.

[139] *See, e.g.*, University of Oregon School of Journalism and Comm., *Ancil Payne Award for Ethics in Journalism*, https://journalism.uoregon.edu/payne (describing journalism award administered by the University of Oregon); Ariz. St. Univ., Walter Cronkite School of J. and Mass Comm., *Cronkite Award Honors David Muir*, https://cronkite.asu.edu/community/walter-cronkite-award/ (describing journalism award administered by Arizona State University); USC Annenberg School for Communication and Journalism, *The Selden Ring Award for Investigative Reporting*, https://annenberg.usc.edu/journalism/selden-ring (describing journalism award administered by the University of Southern California).

[140] U.S. Agency for Global Media, *David Burke Awards*, https://www.usagm.gov/awards/.

[141] *Id.*

[142] Office of the Tex. Gov., *Barbara Jordan Media Awards*, https://gov.texas.gov/organization/disabilities/barbara_jordan_media_awards.

include various types of grants and subsidies for media institutions. They also include direct funding to government-controlled media entities, such as the military publication Stars and Stripes or overseas government radio and broadcast stations like Voice of America.

25.2.4.1 Grants and Subsidies

The government has long supported the press in the form of both direct and indirect grants and subsidies. Historical examples include financial assistance with the purchase of newspaper manufacturing equipment,[143] shipping costs,[144] and more.[145]

Ex ante government rewards today come in different forms. Some are one-time or time-limited grants. They can look like prizes, but they operate as grants because the government dispenses them before press products are created. Examples include government-funded journalism fellowships like the Fulbright Program. Fulbright Germany, for instance, offers funding for early-career American journalists to conduct research and serve as interns in German media outlets.[146] Fulbright Japan offers a fellowship for early-career journalists to engage in a months-long reporting project in Japan.[147] And the Fulbright-National Geographic Award Program offers one-time grants for research and storytelling about conservation efforts in partnership with the National Geographic magazine.[148]

Some states have also begun experimenting with government-funded fellowships to compensate for the loss of local news reporting. In 2022, for instance, the California legislature allotted $25 million in state funding to a new state-sponsored reporting fellowship.[149] The program awards up to 40 two-year fellowship positions per year at news organizations throughout the state, with an emphasis on serving underrepresented communities.[150] Similar programs have been funded in New

[143] *See, e.g.*, Cowan & Westphal, *supra* note 109, at 10–11.

[144] *See, e.g.*, Postal Act of 1792, Act of Feb. 20, 1792, ch. 7, 1 Stat. 232.

[145] *See, e.g.*, Minow, *supra* note 11, at 52–54 (describing government research and development funding for communications infrastructure).

[146] Fulbright U.S. Student Program, Germany, 5 *Young Professional Journalist Program*, https://us.fulbrightonline.org/countries/europe-and-eurasia/germany/1686.

[147] Fulbright U.S. Student Program, Japan, 5 *Journalism (Research)*, https://fulbrightscholars.org/award/journalism-research.

[148] The Fulbright-National Geographic Award, *Fulbright U.S. Student Program*, https://us.fulbrightonline.org/applicants/types-of-awards/fulbright-national-geographic-award.

[149] Christa Scharfenberg, *More Public Funding for Local News*, Nieman Lab (2024), https://www.niemanlab.org/2023/12/more-public-funding-for-local-news/; *About the Fellowship*, U.C. Berkeley School of Journalism, https://fellowships.journalism.berkeley.edu/cafellows/.

[150] *About the Fellowship*, U.C. Berkeley School of Journalism, https://fellowships.journalism.berkeley.edu/cafellows/.

Mexico and Washington state,[151] and legislatures in other states are considering additional proposals.[152]

A related set of ex ante rewards provide annual or repeated financial grants to the press. Perhaps most significant is Congress's annual budgetary allotment to the Corporation for Public Broadcasting, which oversees public-funded media institutions like NPR and PBS.[153] Each year, Congress allots funding to the independent governing board. The board then disperses these funds to public radio and television stations across the nation.[154] These funds are significant. Congress provides over $500 million per year to public media.[155] Yet they still represent only a small part of public radio and broadcasting stations' spending. Congressional allocations comprise only around 7 percent of the average public radio's budget and 13 percent of the average public television station's budget today.[156]

Some states have followed the federal government's lead by enacting similar public media governance institutions. In 2018, for example, New Jersey created the New Jersey Civic Information Consortium.[157] This structure is similar to the federal model in that the state legislature awards a grant to the consortium, which then allocates the funds to different state and local media institutions.[158] But the funds have been dispensed differently and have been used to support a wider range of media outlets, including journalism translation services and training programs.[159]

The government awards many other, smaller grants annually to media institutions. For example, the Bay Journal is a small publication that covers environmental issues in the Chesapeake Bay.[160] The Clean Water Act of 1972 requires that the government make information about its progress on the bay cleanup available to the public.[161] Since the 1980s, the Environmental Protection Agency (EPA) has fulfilled

[151] Press Release, Sen. Karen Keiser, 33 Leg. District – Des Moines, WA Legislature Establishes Fellowship for Journalism in the Public Interest, https://senatedemocrats.wa.gov/keiser/2023/04/26/wa-legislature-establishes-fellowship-for-journalism-in-the-public-interest/.

[152] Scharfenberg, *supra* note 149.

[153] Corporation for Public Broadcasting, *About CBP*, https://www.cpb.org/aboutcpb.

[154] *Id.*

[155] Press Release, Corporation for Public Broadcasting, CPB Statement on Congress' Passage of Funding for Public Media, https://www.cpb.org/pressroom/CPB-Statement-Congress-Passage-Funding-Public-Media.

[156] Corporation for Public Broadcasting, *CFB Financial Information*, https://www.cpb.org/aboutcpb/financials. The remaining costs are covered by a combination of state and local government allocations, universities and foundations, and donations from listeners. *Id.*

[157] N.J. Civic Information Consortium, *About the Consortium*, https://njcivicinfo.org/about/.

[158] *Id.*

[159] New Jersey Civic Information Consortium, *Annual Report* (2023), https://njcivicinfo.org/wp-content/uploads/2023/11/2023-Annual-Report-New-Jersey-Civic-Information-Consortium.pdf.

[160] Bay Journal, *About Us*, https://www.bayjournal.com/site/about.html.

[161] 33 U.S.C.A. § 1267(B)(ii).

this obligation by awarding funding each year to the Bay Journal through a competitive grant.[162]

Scholars and advocates have also proposed new types of grant-funding institutions to support the press. One scholar has argued for the creation of a "National Endowment for Journalism," similar to the National Endowment for the Arts.[163] This program could be modeled after the federal government's arts program, accepting applications and dispensing funds on a project-by-project basis. Others have proposed an international journalism consortium, which would dispense journalism funds globally, allowing democratic nations to support journalism efforts in repressive or autocratic nations.[164] Still others have proposed the creation of a local news bank that would offer low-interest loans, no-interest loans, or loans-to-grant support for new or struggling local press institutions.[165]

A further set of ex ante government interventions come in the form of press subsidies used to defray press institutions' costs. Examples include the post office subsidies to newspapers. These began in colonial times, but they continue into the present. The value of these subsidies, however, has declined over time. Until the late 1960s, publishers received up to a 75-percent subsidy on mailed news products.[166] Today, the postal subsidy is around 11 percent.[167] The importance of this ex ante reward has decreased with the transition to digital publication. But the total amount of the postal subsidy was significant. At the program's height in 1967, the government was providing the equivalent of roughly $3.5 billion in today's dollars in postal subsidies to the press.[168]

Another form of government subsidy for the press comes in the form of reduced licensing fees for private media institutions that broadcast over government-owned

[162] Jacob Fenston, *The EPA Killed This Newspaper's Funding. Was It Something They Said?*, WAMU (Feb. 7, 2018), https://wamu.org/story/18/02/07/epa-killed-newspapers-funding-something-said/. The journal also illustrates the perils of government support for the press without proper safeguards in place against editorial interference. *See* Jon Allsop, *An Unusual First Amendment Fight on the Chesapeake Bay*, Colum. Journalism Rev. (Feb. 22, 2018), https://www.cjr.org/united_states_project/bay_journal_epa_funding.php (describing how the EPA threatened to cut funding in retaliation for unfavorable coverage).

[163] Gillers, *supra* note 112, at 163.

[164] Nishant Lalwani, *A Free Press Is the Lifeblood of Democracy – Journalists Must Not Be Silenced*, The Guardian (July 5, 2019), https://www.theguardian.com/global-development/2019/jul/05/a-free-press-is-the-lifeblood-of-democracy-journalists-must-not-be-silenced.

[165] Rebuild Local News, *Solutions: Policy Menu*, https://www.rebuildlocalnews.org/policy-menu/.

[166] Cowan & Westphal, *supra* note 109, at 1.

[167] *Id.*

[168] Steven Waldman, *There's Already a Solution to the Crisis of Local News. Just Ask This Founding Father*, Politico (Apr. 2, 2023), https://www.politico.com/news/magazine/2023/04/02/james-madison-subsidize-the-news-00090023. Different scholars have provided different estimates of the value of these 1960s-era subsidies. *See, e.g.*, Cowan & Westphal, *supra* note 109, at 1 (arguing that the subsidies were worth around 2 billion in today's dollars).

radio and broadcast frequencies.[169] Historically, the government has charged these commercial media institutions only nominal amounts, allowing private media institutions to construct their business on top of the public's airwaves.[170] In exchange, the government has imposed public-interest obligations on these private institutions. For example, the government has required licensees to air both sides of an issue and cover topics of public importance.[171] The government has also offered cable companies public rights of way for the laying of cable infrastructure as long as they open up free access channels for public, government, and educational access television.[172] Individuals and community groups can then use these stations to air programming at little or no cost.[173]

25.2.4.2 Government Press

Government-run media outlets can also be characterized as an extreme form of ex ante government reward.[174] While government actors mostly or entirely fund and administer these institutions, they still play an important role in the democratic information ecosystem, reporting from regions and telling stories that commercial outlets are no longer able to cover. They also have some mechanisms in place to safeguard journalistic independence and protect against editorial interference.

One well-known example is Stars and Stripes, a military newspaper that the Union Army began during the Civil War.[175] Today, the Defense Media Activity, a subset of the Department of Defense, administers the paper.[176] Roughly half of its funding comes from the Pentagon.[177] Under federal regulations, military interference in the editorial process is prohibited,[178] and the newsgathering and publishing process must proceed "in accordance with journalistic standards governing US daily commercial newspapers of the highest quality."[179]

Another example is the set of government-run radio and television stations that broadcast overseas. These include the federal entities of Voice of America and the

[169] MINOW, *supra* note 11, at 43.
[170] *Id.*
[171] *Id.*
[172] Public, Educational, and Governmental (PEG) Access Cable Television Channels: Issues for Congress, Cong. Res. Serv. Rep., R42044 (Jan. 4, 2013), https://www.everycrsreport.com/files/20130104_R42044_65f871bc221565c497baa74be4b6bb299ca5d718.pdf.
[173] *Id.*
[174] *Cf.* Rochelle Cooper Dreyfuss, *Tailoring Incentives: A Comment on Hemel and Ouellette's Beyond the Patents-Prizes Debate*, 92 TEX. L. REV. 131, 132 (2014) ("[G]overnment-conducted research has several unique features that make the option worthy of separate consideration.").
[175] STARS AND STRIPES, *About Stars and Stripes*, https://ww2.stripes.com/about-us#history/.
[176] *Id.*
[177] *Id.* The other half comes from advertisements and subscriptions. *Id.*
[178] 32 C.F.R. § 246.4.
[179] *Id.*

Office of Cuba Broadcasting.[180] They also include Radio Free Europe, Radio Free Asia, and the Middle East Broadcasting Networks, which operate as independent nonprofits but receive substantial funding from federal government grants.[181] Collectively, these radio and television stations broadcast in more than forty languages in countries around the globe.[182]

There are also some safeguards in place to protect against government interference with the editorial process. For example, by federal statute, the secretary of state must "respect the professional independence and integrity" of the stations.[183] Yet these institutions are not wholly independent. For instance, Voice of America must produce content that is "consistent with the broad foreign policy objectives of the United States."[184] Government-controlled journalism comes with risk, moreover, such as the threat that government actors will retaliate against press institutions for unfavorable coverage through funding cuts and other mechanisms.[185]

Even so, these outlets play an important role in the broader press ecosystem. Dozens of news outlets have closed their foreign bureaus since 2003, and the ones that still exist now employ fewer reporters.[186] Government press institutions cannot replace truly independent media. But in certain places overseas, such as many US military bases abroad, government journalists are the only American correspondents left reporting from the area.[187]

Together, government grants and subsidies at all levels offer substantial financial assistance to the press. Yet the amount of ex ante support the United States provides today is much lower than it has been in the past.[188] The United States also lags behind other Western democracies in the amount of press support that it provides.[189] While the United States spends around $1.40 per capita to fund public media, for example, the United Kingdom spends around $80 per capita, and Denmark spends more than $100 per capita.[190] The US government could still do more, especially when it comes to local media outlets.

180 U.S. Agency for Global Media, *Structure*, https://www.usagm.gov/who-we-are/organizational-chart/.

181 U.S. Agency for Global Media, *Radio Free Asia*, https://www.usagm.gov/networks/rfa/.

182 Voice of America, *Mission and Values*, https://www.insidevoa.com/p/5831.html.

183 22 U.S.C.A. § 6202(c)(1), 22 U.S.C.A. § 6204(c).

184 22 U.S.C.A. § 6202(a)(1).

185 *See, e.g.*, Riley Beggin, *The Fight over Defunding Stars and Stripes, Explained*, Vox (Sept. 5, 2020), https://www.vox.com/policy-and-politics/2020/9/5/21424085/trump-fight-defunding-stars-and-stripes-newspaper (describing threats to cut the funding of *Stars and Stripes*).

186 Anup Kaphle, *The Foreign Desk in Transition*, Colum. Journalism Rev. (Mar. 2, 2015), https://www.cjr.org/analysis/the_foreign_desk_in_transition.php.

187 *Ombudsman on the Pentagon's Order to Shut Down 'Stars and Stripes'*, On Media, NPR (Sept. 4, 2020), https://www.npr.org/2020/09/04/909793785/ombudsman-on-the-pentagons-order-to-shut-down-stars-and-stripes.

188 Waldman, *supra* note 168.

189 *See* Pickard, Stearns & Aaron, *supra* note 49, at 252.

190 Timothy Karr & Craig Aaron, Beyond Fixing Facebook 20 (2019), https://www.freepress.net/sites/default/files/2019-02/Beyond-Fixing-Facebook-Final.pdf.

25.2.5 *Hybrid Approaches*

Several existing or proposed media-related innovation policy levers incorporate aspects of the different interventions described above. Unlike grants and prizes, these interventions do not entail direct government funding of media organizations, but they also do not entail pure free market-driven rewards. Rather, the government intervenes at various stages of the press-to-consumer supply chain to promote purchasing, leading to compensation to media organizations without having to rely solely on consumer willingness or ability to pay.

One example of such an intervention is the practice of public libraries and educational institutions purchasing newspaper and magazine subscriptions.[191] These government institutions pay the media company's market price but then provide the public with access to these materials for free. This intervention is akin to what Hemel and Ouellette call a "matching" approach to innovation policy, in which an ex post market-based innovation reward is coupled with a government-controlled form of allocation.[192] Such combinations can be particularly valuable when the government wishes to rely on predominantly market-based innovation incentives but the public benefits of cheap or free dissemination are also high.[193] This is certainly true of the press, where the positive effects of citizen access to media are notably high.[194]

Another example of the government intervening in the media-to-consumer supply chain is through tax credits or subsidies to consumers. For example, a 2020 draft bill in Congress proposed giving each taxpayer a $250 credit for subscriptions to local newspapers.[195] The credit would have covered 80 percent of subscription costs in the first year and 50 percent of subscription costs in each of the next four years.[196] Similarly, the Massachusetts legislature has also proposed providing taxpayers with a credit of up to $250 to purchase subscriptions to "local community newspapers."[197]

[191] *See* Daniel A. Gross, *The Surprisingly Big Business of Library E-Books*, New Yorker (Sept. 2, 2021), https://www.newyorker.com/news/annals-of-communications/an-app-called-libby-and-the-surprisingly-big-business-of-library-e-books (describing the high costs publishers are charging libraries for access to e-books and digital magazine subscriptions).

[192] The main example of this trend is the government purchasing a patent at the market rate, and then distributing the patented intervention to the public at a free or discounted rate. But the strategy can be used in copyright markets as well. Hemel & Ouellette, *Innovation Policy Pluralism*, *supra* note 24, at 602–07 (citing public libraries' purchase of copyrighted works for free public consumption).

[193] *Id.*

[194] *See* discussion *infra* Section 25.3.

[195] Local Journalism Sustainability Act, 116th Cong., H.R.3940 (June 16, 2021), https://www.congress.gov/bill/117th-congress/house-bill/3940. *See also* Local Journalism Sustainability Act Summary, Rep. Ann Kirkpatrick & Dan Newhouse, https://www.rebuildlocalnews.org/wp-content/uploads/2023/01/kirkpatricknewhousesummary.pdf (summarizing the bill).

[196] Local Journalism Sustainability Act Summary, *supra* note 195.

[197] An Act to Establish a Local Community Newspaper Subscription Tax Credit, H.D. 1518, 193rd General Court of the Commonwealth of Massachusetts, https://malegislature.gov/Bills/193/HD1518.

Some foreign countries have already enacted such provisions. France, for instance, provides a tax deduction of up to 50 euros to anyone who purchases a new magazine or newspaper subscription.[198] Similarly, one United States nonprofit has suggested giving citizens vouchers to purchase news products.[199] All of these proposals would lower the costs of news for consumers, allowing them to purchase media products at the market price even if their willingness or ability to pay is otherwise low.

The government has also intervened in the media advertising market by creating tax exemptions for the sale of advertising services.[200] The goal of these initiatives is to return advertising dollars back to the press, especially to local press institutions. States have long exempted news advertising from general sales tax obligations.[201] But others have experimented with more novel approaches in recent years. In 2021, for instance, Wisconsin created an income and franchise tax credit for any business that purchased advertising in a local media outlet.[202] The credit can be used for 50 percent of the advertising expenditure up to a maximum of $5,000.[203] Likewise, in 2023, Maryland enacted a law permitting small- and medium-sized businesses to claim a tax credit for advertising through a news media organization based in the state.[204] Similar bills have been proposed in other states and in Congress, although they have yet to pass.[205] As with consumer tax benefits, these interventions preserve media companies' market-based revenue structure – in this case, advertising – but encourage greater purchasing than might otherwise occur.[206]

198 *France Gives Tax Credits to News Subscribers*, News Media Ass'n (July 2, 2020), https://newsmediauk.org/blog/2020/07/02/france-gives-tax-credits-to-news-subscribers/. *See also* Gov't of Can., *About the Digital News Subscription Tax*, https://www.canada.ca/en/revenue-agency/services/tax/individuals/topics/about-your-tax-return/tax-return/completing-a-tax-return/deductions-credits-expenses/deductions-credits-expenses/digital-news-subscription.html (describing a similar law in Canada).

199 Mark Histead, *Local News Dollars*, Democracy Pol. Network, https://democracypolicy.network/agenda/strong-people/strong-communities/local-news-dollars. This proposal is based on Seattle's "democracy voucher" program, in which residents get $25 credits to donate to any political campaign that they would like. *See* David Hyde, *Democracy Vouchers Are Back, But Do They Neutralize Big Money in Local Politics?*, KUOW (Feb. 21, 2023), https://www.kuow.org/stories/democracy-vouchers-are-back-but-do-they-neutralize-big-money-in-local-politics.

200 Cowan & Westphal, *supra* note 109, at 10–11 (describing state-level tax breaks for the sale of advertising services).

201 *Id.*

202 2021 Assembly Bill 762, AB 762, Wisconsin State Legislature (Dec. 9, 2021), https://docs.legis.wisconsin.gov/2021/related/proposals/ab762.

203 *Id.*

204 Income Tax – Local Advertising Tax Credit, Maryland General Assembly, 2023 Session, https://mgaleg.maryland.gov/mgawebsite/Legislation/Details/hb0540?ys = 2023RS.

205 *See, e.g.*, .R. 4756, 118th Cong. (July 19, 2023), https://www.congress.gov/bill/118th-congress/house-bill/4756/text; HB 1121, House Committee of Reference Amendment, Colorado General Assembly 2022, https://s3-us-west-2.amazonaws.com/leg.colorado.gov/2022A/amendments/HB1121_L.003.pdf.

206 A related strategy is the government's intervention as a participant in the advertising market itself. For example, some have argued that the government should prioritize purchasing of advertisement in media sources that need financial help, such as local news. *See Government*

25.3 CONCLUSION: TOWARDS A PRESS POLICY FRAMEWORK

A range of innovation policy levers are already at play in the press ecosystem. From copyright and other intellectual property protections, to tax credits, to grants, to prizes, the government has frequently intervened to encourage the creation of media products. As the last section explained, categorizing these interventions as ex post or ex ante and as government-based or market-based showcases that they fall within the innovation policy pluralism framework that has been used in other industries where innovation is prioritized.

We hope this categorization is valuable in and of itself, but we also believe that innovation policy pluralism provides a necessary path to tackling some of the biggest problems facing the press today. A full discussion of these issues – including analogizing to interventions in other industries that frequently suffer from innovation failures – will be the subject of future research. But we conclude here by briefly offering some preliminary observations.

First, and perhaps most obviously, the press must be understood as a form of innovation that can benefit from numerous, and overlapping, policy interventions. The choice here should not be between market-based remuneration and full government control of the media. Rather, a range of more subtle interventions can be used in combination to solve the specific problems facing the media. For example, just as financially lucrative pharmaceuticals – like weight loss drugs – can generally be incentivized solely using market-based interventions, like patents,[207] so too large, national media organizations may be able to survive primarily by using market-based interventions, like copyright or press publishers' rights.[208] But just as other pharmaceuticals, such as "orphan drugs" for rare diseases, often require direct government funding,[209] so too media in smaller, less established markets may require more direct grants in order to successfully operate.[210]

Second, paying attention to both the timing and institutional nature of a press policy intervention may help with weighing the pros and cons of an intervention, including First Amendment implications. While many are naturally skeptical of government control of the press,[211] not all government intervention is the same. The

Advertising and Local News, CENTER FOR COMMUNITY MEDIA, https://www.rebuildlocalnews.org/designing-the-program-introduction/.

[207] Hemel & Ouellette, *Beyond the Patents-Prizes Debate*, *supra* note 24, at 376–78.

[208] *See* discussion *supra* Section 25.1.1.

[209] *See, e.g.*, Orphan Drug Act, Pub. L. No. 97-414, 96 Stat. 2049 (1983) (codified as amended in scattered sections of 15, 21, 42 & 46 U.S.C.).

[210] *See* discussion *supra* Sections 25.1.3 and 25.1.4.

[211] *See, e.g.*, George F. Will, *Local Media Is Struggling. Government Subsidies Would Make It Worse.*, WASH. POST (Feb. 21, 2024), https://www.washingtonpost.com/opinions/2024/02/21/government-subsidies-newspapers/; Jeffrey M. McCall, *Keep Government Money Out of Journalism Industry*, THE HILL (Sept. 20, 2022), https://thehill.com/opinion/technology/3651235-keep-government-money-out-of-journalism-industry/. *See also* Hemel & Ouellette, *Innovation Policy Pluralism*, *supra* note 24, at 605–06 (arguing that for creative works, we may not want "the government dictating the substance of creative works, but we do want some subsidy for producers and consumers.").

government, for example, can intervene using broadly applicable tax credits for media organizations. If structured properly, such an approach can provide a necessary financial boost, while still trusting the market to ultimately allocate rewards to media products based on public demand.[212] This might help ensure the government does not engage in content- or viewpoint-based discrimination in choosing how to allocate funding, while still recognizing that the press cannot survive if forced to shoulder all of the harsh realities of a market-focused business model.

Third, the question of innovation incentives can and should be decoupled from the question of allocation. Scholars and policymakers have criticized intellectual property and other forms of market-based pricing for failing to account for distributive justice and other values.[213] Considering the role of the press in fostering democratic engagement, this concern certainly also applies to media products.[214] But the government can step in in subtle ways to enable broader distribution of press products, even if incentives are market focused. Just as the government may purchase a vaccine patent at the market price and then distribute the vaccine for free, the government can (and has, in the case of public libraries and education institutions) purchase press products at market-based prices and then allocated those products for free.[215] Such an approach may be particularly valuable since it frees the press's decision making from government supervision but still enables broad access to media products.[216]

Fourth, and finally, new interventions may be necessary to successfully solve the many financial problems facing the press, especially in an age of platform-based intermediation and increasing public distrust of the media in general. The numerous interventions in other innovation-intensive industries like pharmaceuticals, music, or technology – such as compulsory licensing, various grant and tax credit programs, and new or adapted intellectual property rights – could be mined to discover promising solutions to the crises facing the press. These examples demonstrate that innovation in general is rarely a one-size-fits-all policy problem, and solving the problems facing the media will be no exception.

[212] Hemel & Ouellette, *Beyond the Patents-Prizes Debate*, *supra* note 24, at 376 ("Patents . . . are most effective where potential innovators have ready access to the requisite financial capital and where the negative effects of risk aversion on innovators' incentives are limited . . . and where market signals provide reliable proxies for social benefits.").

[213] *See generally* Amy Kapczynski, *The Cost of Price: Why and How to Get Beyond Intellectual Property Internalism*, 59 UCLA L. Rev. 970, 978 (2012) ("Price can be a problematic way of distributing goods that are important to justice because the existing distribution of resources may be unjust.").

[214] *See, e.g.*, Victor Pickard, *Journalism's Market Failure Is a Crisis for Democracy*, Harvard Bus. Rev. (Mar. 12, 2020), https://hbr.org/2020/03/journalisms-market-failure-is-a-crisis-for-democracy (arguing that the local news crisis "arose because the news media's commercial imperatives never fully aligned with democratic objectives").

[215] *See* discussion *supra* Section 25.2.5.

[216] *Cf.* Hemel & Ouellette, *Innovation Policy Pluralism*, *supra* note 24, at 602–03 (looking to libraries as an example of "a match between an IP innovation incentive and a non-IP allocation mechanism").

26

Are We Saving the News?

Martha Minow

Reports of declining local news have become all too familiar.[1] The crises in the news ecosystem are numerous: The funding model for local news has collapsed as advertising and eyeballs have migrated to online social media platforms.[2] Digital platforms and partisan media outlets are enabling (not halting) the rise in misinformation and disinformation. Private equity companies, committed only to short-term profits, are purchasing and strip-mining even profitable local news outlets. As a result, the public's trust in conventional (and fast disappearing) news outlets is declining rapidly.[3] Meanwhile, these patterns of consumption and distrust of information sources are reflecting and contributing to our social and political divisions[4]

[1] This chapter draws on and updates issues explored in MARTHA MINOW, SAVING THE NEWS: WHY THE CONSTITUTION CALLS FOR GOVERNMENT ACTION TO PRESERVE FREEDOM OF SPEECH (2021). *See also* Martha Minow, *Does the First Amendment Forbid, Permit, or Require Government Support of News Industries?*, *in* CONSTITUTIONALISM AND A RIGHT TO EFFECTIVE GOVERNMENT (Vicki C. Jackson & Yasmin Dawood eds., 2022); *The Changing Ecosystem of News and Challenges for Freedom of Press*, 64 LOYOLA L. REV. 499 (2018), reprinted as *O ecossistema de notícias em mudança e os desafios para a liberdade de imprensa*, *in* ELEIÇÕES E DEMOCRACIA NA ERA DIGITAL (Paulo Gustavo Gonet Branco et al. eds., 2022).

[2] *E.g.*, Thomas E. Patterson, *News Crisis: Can Local Public Radio Help Fill the News Gap Created by the Decline of Local Newspapers?*, SHORENSTEIN CTR. ON MEDIA, POL. & PUB. POL'Y (Jan. 25, 2023), https://shorensteincenter.org/news-crisis-local-public-radio-report/; Margaret Sullivan, *What Happens to Democracy When Local News Dries Up?*, WASH. POST (Nov. 30, 2021), https://www.washingtonpost.com/magazine/2021/11/30/margaret-sullivan-the-local-news-crisis/. For a distinctive study of holes in local news coverage in one state, *see* Christopher Hanson, *Topography of a News Ecosystem: A First-of-Its-Kind Study Diagnoses the Local News Crisis in a Single State*, POYNTER (Apr. 19, 2024), https://www.poynter.org/locally/2024/university-maryland-merrill-college-journalism-local-news-crisis-study/.

[3] *More than Half of U.S. Counties Have No Access or Very Limited Access to Local News*, NW. MEDILL SCH. OF JOURNALISM, https://www.medill.northwestern.edu/news/2023/more-than-half-of-us-counties-have-no-access-or-very-limited-access-to-local-news.html (last visited June 18, 2024) [hereinafter *Access to Local News*].

[4] Ro'ee Levy, *Social Media, News Consumption, and Polarization: Evidence from a Field Experiment*, 111 AM. ECONOMIC REV. 831 (2021), https://doi.org/10.1257/aer.20191777; Flavia Roscini, *How the American Media Landscape Is Polarizing the Country*, B.U. PARDEE SCH. GLOBAL STUD. (May 28, 2024), https://sites.bu.edu/pardeeatlas/advancing-human-progress-initiative/back2school/how-the-american-media-landscape-is-polarizing-the-country/. *But see*

as digital platforms continue to expose people to disinformation and misinformation, with little progress in redressing these problems.[5]

Since I published on the issues a few years ago, these trends have only continued and, indeed, accelerated.[6] I argued then, and still believe, that the U.S. Constitution's First Amendment – including the Speech and Press Clauses – recognizes the functions of newsgathering and circulation as fundamental to the projects of self-government.

Practices that once sustained vibrant newsgathering and distribution ecosystems have now been disrupted and are in jeopardy in the wake of the practices of social media platforms, the behaviors of private equity investors, and the choices made by media entities themselves. With a particular focus on local news, this chapter first sketches federal constitutional and governmental support of newsgathering and circulation; then turns to current sources of disruption and potential constructive reforms; and finally identifies some promising developments and further questions that they present.

26.1 AFFIRMATIVE GOVERNMENTAL SUPPORT

Many of the Constitution's framers recognized the importance of free speech and the press to self-government and freedom from tyranny.[7] In their writings and in their actions, James Madison, John Adams, Thomas Paine, George Washington,

Chloe Wittenberg et al., *Media Measurement Matters: Estimating the Persuasive Effects of Partisan Media with Survey and Behavioral Data*, 85 J. Politics (2023), https://www.journals.uchicago.edu/doi/10.1086/724960 (experiment contrasting stated preferences with actual news consumption patterns showed that less frequent consumers of news tend to be more persuaded by partisan content). A survey examining the United States and several European countries indicated very low contact with actual news sources but also little influence of partisan sources on people's views. Magdalena Wojcieszak et al., *No Polarization from Partisan News: Over-Time Evidence from Trace Data*, 28 Int'l J. Press/Politics 601 (2023), https://doi.org/10.1177/19401612211047194.

5 Lisa Macpherson & Rajan Srinivasan, *"Lies All the Way Down" – Combating 2024 Election Disinformation*, Pub. Knowledge (Mar. 18, 2024), https://publicknowledge.org/lies-all-the-way-down/.

6 Michael Lipka & Elisa Shearer, *Audiences Are Declining for Traditional News Media in the U.S. – With Some Exceptions*, Pew Rsch. (Nov. 28, 2023), https://www.pewresearch.org/short-reads/2023/11/28/audiences-are-declining-for-traditional-news-media-in-the-us-with-some-exceptions/; Brandy Zadrozny, *Disinformation Poses an Unprecedented Threat in 2024 – And the U.S. Is Less Ready than Ever*, NBC News (Jan. 18, 2024), https://www.nbcnews.com/tech/misinformation/disinformation-unprecedented-threat-2024-election-rcna134290.

7 *See* David Wilson, *Freedom of the Press in the Eyes of the Founding Fathers*, Colonial Williamsburg (July 7, 2020), https://www.colonialwilliamsburg.org/learn/living-history/freedom-press-eyes-founding-fathers/. Benjamin Franklin – perhaps the founding father with the deepest ties to the press – expressed after the enactment of the Constitution some concerns about the unfettered press. *See* Arthur Milikh, *Franklin and the Free Press*, Heritage Found. (Apr. 4, 2017), https://www.heritage.org/american-founders/commentary/franklin-and-the-free-press.

and Thomas Jefferson emphasized the vital importance of the freedoms of speech and of the press to democracy and freedom.[8] The First Amendment's freedoms provide a distinct bulwark against autocracy and a foundation for self-government by the people, which are key rationales for their protection.[9]

The federal Constitution's guarantees of free speech and press curb governmental restrictions, but do they also entail positive duties? Courts may not be well-positioned to articulate or enforce governmental duties affirmatively to assist free speech and press, but the Constitution is not only directed to courts. Those who swear allegiance to the Constitution and all who take seriously the survival of the government it established should understand constitutional commitments as obliging actions that respect and support both speech and the press.[10] These duties could include taking steps to strengthen the viability and reliability of newsgathering and distribution, as demonstrated by the actions of the federal government from the start and through time.

[8] *See* Wendell Bird, The Revolution in Freedoms of Press and Speech: From Blackstone to the First Amendment and Fox's Libel Act 7–9, 221–38, 268–75, 330 (2020); Minow, Saving the News, *supra* note 1, at 38–41; Wilson, *supra* note 7. George Washington wrote in 1783, "the freedom of Speech may be taken away – and, dumb & silent we may be led, like sheep, to the Slaughter." *National Gazette*, George Washington's Mount Vernon, https://www.mountvernon.org/library/digitalhistory/digital-encyclopedia/article/national-gazette/ (quoting From George Washington to Officers of the Army, 15 March 1783).

[9] The drafters of the First Amendment were, of course, familiar with the protection of the press in the states, such as Pennsylvania and Virginia. *See* Bird, *supra* note 8, at 337–57; Paul Starr, The Creation of the Media: Political Origins of Modern Communications (2004). The Virginia ratifying convention directed that "[t]he people shall not be deprived or abridged of their right to speak, to write, or to publish their sentiments; and the freedom of the press, as one of the great bulwarks of liberty, shall be inviolable." *Id.*, at 73–74. Pennsylvania's Declaration of Rights specified that "the people have a right to freedom of speech, and of writing, and publishing their sentiments, therefore, the freedom of the press ought not to be restrained," and the Pennsylvania Constitution assured free use of printing presses by "any person who undertakes to examine the proceedings of the legislature, or any part of the government." *Id.* The Pennsylvania Constitution to this day directs: "The printing press shall be free to every person who may undertake to examine the proceedings of the Legislature or any branch of government, and no law shall ever be made to restrain the right thereof." Pa. Const., art. 1, § 7.

[10] For a thorough argument for an affirmative governmental "duty to guarantee meaningful access to news and information for everyone," *see* Victor Pickard, *Legal Foundations for Non-Reformist Media Reforms: A Positive-Rights Paradigm for Guaranteeing a Universal Press System*, *in* The Future of Press Freedom: Democracy, Law, and the News in Changing Times 415 (RonNell Andersen Jones & Sonja R. West eds., 2025) [hereinafter The Future of Press Freedom]. *See also* Minow, Saving the News, *supra* note 1, at 94–100; C. Edwin Baker, Media Concentration and Democracy 161, 245–62 (2006); Thomas I. Emerson, *The Affirmative Side of the First Amendment*, 15 Georgia L. Rev. 795 (1981); RonNell Andersen Jones, *Press Speakers and the First Amendment Rights of Listeners*, 90 Colo. L. Rev. 499 (2019); Sonja R. West, *The Majoritarian Press Clause*, 2020 U. Chi. L. Forum 309 (2020), https://legal-forum.uchicago.edu/print-archive/majoritarian-press-clause.

The Press Clause is the only provision in the Constitution that explicitly protects a private industry. But in practice, the federal government throughout history has done more than simply shield the press from governmental restrictions.[11] Congress established discounted postal rates for newspapers and the free exchange of newspapers between news printers and publishers.[12] Subsequent governmental support shaped communication, including the sharing of news, through the telegraph, telephone, computer, and the internet.[13] And the government constructed the system of broadcast licenses, the regulation of cable, the antitrust laws molding the communications industry, the Newspaper Preservation Act of 1970, the Freedom of Information Act, the Public Broadcasting System, and other federal policies.[14] State and local governments have also supported newsgathering and circulation.[15]

The constitutional guarantees of free speech and free press are primarily justified by their support of democratic self-governance, yet a nonviable press poses a grave threat to Americans' ability to engage in self-governance.[16] The goal of safeguarding democracy through the existence of countervailing powers underlies both the separation of powers among the three federal branches and the division of power between the federal government and the states. The press and the private sector

[11] Sonja R. West, *Favoring the Press*, 106 CAL. L. REV. 91 (2018), https://www.jstor.org/stable/44630787.

[12] MINOW, SAVING THE NEWS, *supra* note 1, at 43, 54. For both historical origins and more recent developments of such policies, *see* RICHARD KIELBOWICZ, NEWS IN THE MAIL: THE PRESS, POST OFFICE, AND PUBLIC INFORMATION, 1700–1860S (1989); Congressional Research Service, *Postage Subsidies for Periodicals: History and Recent Developments* (Jan. 22, 2009), https://www.everycrsreport.com/reports/R40162.html.

[13] *See* RICHARD R. JOHN, SPREADING THE NEWS: THE AMERICAN POSTAL SYSTEM FROM FRANKLIN TO MORSE (1998). *See* also KATIE HAFNER, WHERE WIZARDS STAY UP LATE: THE ORIGINS OF THE INTERNET (1996).

[14] LARRY SATKOWIAK, THE CABLE INDUSTRY (2015); TIM WU, THE CURSE OF BIGNESS: ANTITRUST IN THE NEW GILDED AGE (2018). *See* Geoffrey Cowan & David Westphal, *Public Policy and Funding the News*, USC ANNENBERG SCH. FOR COMMC'N & JOURNALISM 7 (2010), https://fundingthenews.usc.edu/report/ (noting the federal government has been a "watchdog of power among news business owners; consumer advocate championing the news and information needs of underserved or neglected communities; affirmative action catalyst for extending employment and ownership opportunities to minorities and women; regulator of the public airwaves; and provider of both direct and indirect subsidies that have been important pieces of the news industry's economic health."). *See also* AMERICAN BAR ASSOCIATION, TELECOM ANTITRUST HANDBOOK (2019); STEVE R. RIVKIN, A NEW GUIDE TO FEDERAL CABLE TELEVISION REGULATIONS (1978); MICHAEL J. ZARKIN, THE FCC AND THE POLITICS OF CABLE TV REGULATION, 1952–1980: ORGANIZATIONAL LEARNING AND POLICY DEVELOPMENT (2010).

[15] Cowan & Westphal, *supra* note 14, at 7 (noting state and local government support for news through income tax deductions and credits, local municipalities permission for newspaper vendor boxes on city sidewalks, state shield-law protection for reporters against prosecutors' subpoenas).

[16] *See* ALEXANDER MEIKLEJOHN, FREE SPEECH AND ITS RELATION TO SELF-GOVERNMENT (1948); Robert Post, *Participatory Democracy and Free Speech*, 97 VA. L. REV. 477 (2011).

serve as yet another countervailing power.[17] Moreover, state constitutions, many of which were drafted before the federal Constitution, embrace positive duties on government to support the press.[18] The duty to take action to safeguard the press hence has roots in this constitutional rationale, as well as in the long-standing history of governmental support for and involvement in news technologies and practices. A variety of policies and laws that undergird the circulation of news (and the human enterprises making it possible) are therefore both consonant with, and even bolster, these constitutional principles.

Some may view the federal Constitution solely as a set of restrictions on federal governmental power, but that misunderstands the commitment, which was motivated by the failure of the limited-government conception of the Articles of Confederation, to create and maintain an effective government.[19] How can there be effective self-government without access to news? And how can public and private power be held to account without workable journalism? These are the questions that the now undeniable crisis in the news world, especially in local news, urgently raises.

26.2 CAUSES AND RESULTS OF THE DECLINES IN LOCAL NEWS PRODUCTION

Since 2005, the United States has lost more than 2,900 newspapers, and as of 2023, it is losing them at an average of 2.5 a week.[20] Related trends have left 200 communities

[17] *See* The Federalist No. 51 (James Madison). *See also* John Kenneth Galbraith, *Countervailing Power*, 44 Am. Econ. Rev. 1 (1954), https://www.jstor.org/stable/1818317 (developing notion of "countervailing power").

[18] For a discussion of state constitutional laws that include affirmative duties as well as protections for the press, *see* Elijah O'Kelley, *State Constitutions as a Check on the New Governors: Using State Free Speech Clauses to Protect Social Media Users from Arbitrary Political Censorship by Social Media Platforms*, 69 Emory L. J. 111 (2019), https://scholarlycommons.law.emory.edu/elj/vol69/iss1/3/; Pickard, *supra* note 10; Christina Koningisor, *The Other Press Clauses*, *in* The Future of Press Freedom, *supra* note 10, at 182. The drafters of the First Amendment knew the protections of the press in the states, such as Pennsylvania and Virginia. *See* Starr, *supra* note 9.

[19] Noting ongoing controversy over whether the U.S. Constitution embraces only restrictions on government or also duties to enable people to exercise rights, *see* Emily Zackin, *Positive Rights*, *in* The Oxford Handbook of the U.S. Constitution (Mark Tushnet et al. eds., 2015) (ebook), https://doi.org/10.1093/oxfordhb/9780190245757.013.34. For analysis of the arguments over negative and positive liberty conceptions of the constitution, *see* David P. Currie, *Positive and Negative Constitutional Rights*, 53 U. Chi. L. Rev. 864 (1986), https://chicagounbound.uchicago.edu/cgi/viewcontent.cgi?article = 5993&context = journal_articles. Assertion of the commitment to an effective government even in the face of arguments about constitutional limits on its powers by a member of the founding generation informs the foundation Supreme Court decision affirming Congressional power to create a national bank, despite lack of relevant explicit authority. *See* McCulloch v. Maryland, 17 U.S. (4 Wheat.) 316 (1819).

[20] *Access to Local News*, *supra* note 3; *see* Sarah Grevy Gotfredsen, *US News Industry Faces Bleak Start to 2024*, Colum. Journalism Rev. (Feb. 20, 2024), https://www.cjr.org/tow_center/us-

with no local news coverage,[21] while half of all local communities in the United States now have only one newspaper, and most of these are published just once a week.[22] As local news rapidly loses audiences, newspapers and broadcasters in small cities and towns are merging or being sold to chains or private equity investors. These new owners pursue economic returns through cost reductions and restructuring.[23]

Advertising revenues have followed people to digital platforms, whose owners and managers often choose not to invest in news production. This means they do not pay even for copyrighted news reports posted by users. It also means that they do not participate in what once was a virtuous circle where publishers used revenue from subscriptions and advertisements to support additional reporting. These trends especially decimate what might be called "local government accountability reporting," such as reporting on the excessive reliance on fines and fees by Ferguson, Missouri, where the police shooting of Michael Brown, an unarmed Black man, triggered racial riots across the country.[24] It turns out that the city of Ferguson had no daily newspaper, no news blog focused on local government, no community radio station, and no local public-access television.[25] After the identification of lead in the water supply of Flint, Michigan, whistleblower and public health expert Dr. Mona Hanna-Attisha said to me, "Actually, we were lucky."[26] When I asked why, considering that the discovery of lead represented a major crisis of public health, law, and politics, her reply was unforgettable: "We have good local

news-industry-faces-bleak-start-to-2024.php. A recent source indicates 225 counties now have no local newspapers. *See* Frank Jacobs, *America's News Deserts Are Growing*, Big Think (Apr. 18, 2024), https://bigthink.com/strange-maps/counties-without-newspapers/; *see also* Penelope Abernathy et al., The State of Local News 2022, Northwestern Medill Local News Initiative 6, 18 (2022).

21 Penelope Muse Abernathy, The Rise of a New Media Baron and the Emerging Threat of News Deserts (2016), https://www.usnewsdeserts.com/wp-content/uploads/2016/09/07.UNC_RiseOfNewMediaBaron_SinglePage_01Sep2016-REDUCED.pdf. For a comprehensive study, *see* Margaret Sullivan, Ghosting the News: Local Journalism and the Crisis of American Democracy (2020).

22 *Access to Local News*, *supra* note 3.

23 C. W. Anderson et al., The News Media: What Everyone Needs to Know 137–40 (2016); Robert W. McChesney & John Nichols, The Death and Life of American Journalism: The Media Revolution that Will Begin the World Again (2010); Abernathy, *supra* note 21, at 12–14, 20–21.

24 Joseph Shapiro, *In Ferguson, Court Fines and Fees Fuel Anger*, NPR (Aug. 25, 2014), https://www.npr.org/2014/08/25/343143937/in-ferguson-court-fines-and-fees-fuel-anger.

25 Josh Wilson, *Fixing Journalism's Ability to Promote Civic Good Should Be the Focus of Philanthropic Giving*, Chron. Philanthropy (Nov. 1, 2017), https://www.philanthropy.com/article/Opinion-Fixing-Journalism-s/241610.

26 Conversation with Dr. Hanna-Attisha, at the MIT Media Lab Disobedience Award ceremony (July 20, 2017) (where Dr. Hanna-Attisha received a Disobedience Award for "defying conventions of peer review as they sought to bring attention to Flint's water crisis before more people were affected"). *See also* Mona Hanna-Attisha, What the Eyes Don't See: A Story of Crisis, Resistance, and Hope in an American City (2018).

news. There are hundreds of Flint, Michigans out there without local news, so we don't know about them."

The news ecosystems in this country were never perfect. Many communities had little coverage and faced biases affecting what was covered and how stories were reported or missed. News outlets often have neglected covering politics and abuses of power in their reporting and too frequently only reflect the interests of certain segments of the community. In the nineteenth century, political parties sponsored local news, and it was not until the turn of the twentieth century that journalists claimed to be objective.[27] Yet the loss of local journalism has palpable costs to democracy and community well-being. Communities lacking local news have higher rates of public and private corruption, as well as lower voter turnout than those with a steady supply of local news.[28]

There is a certain irony that it is local journalism facing the starkest challenges, because it has been among the most trusted sources of news – far more than national outlets.[29] Indeed, regions that lose local news become more

[27] *See* Michael Schudson, Discovering the News: A Social History of American Newspapers (1981); Michael Schudson, Journalism: Why It Matters (2020).

[28] On voting, *see* Martin Baekgaard et al., *Local News Media and Voter Turnout*, 40 Local Gov't Stud. 518 (2014), https://www.tandfonline.com/doi/abs/10.1080/03003930.2013.834253; Christopher Chapp & Peter Aehl, *Newspapers and Political Participation: The Relationship Between Ballot Rolloff and Local Newspaper Circulation*, 42 Newspaper Rsch. J. (2021), https://journals.sagepub.com/doi/10.1177/07395329211014968; Danny Hayes & Jennifer L. Lawless, *The Decline of Local News and Its Effects: New Evidence from Longitudinal Data*, 80 J. Politics (2018), https://www.dannyhayes.org/uploads/6/9/8/5/69858539/decline.pdf; David Hughes, *Does Local News Stimulate Voter Participation in State Supreme Court Elections?*, 8 J.L. & Cts. 8 (2020), https://www.cambridge.org/core/journals/journal-of-law-and-courts/article/abs/does-local-journalism-stimulate-voter-participation-in-state-supreme-court-elections/CE8E2CBDF4CF9C58DF08A013AE8B05A3. On declines in local news and increases in corruption, *see* Kriston Capps, *The Hidden Costs of Losing Your City's Newspaper*, Bloomberg (May 30, 2018), https://www.bloomberg.com/news/articles/2018-05-30/when-local-newspapers-close-city-financing-costs-rise, and even ideological identities demand more attention; Ted Matherly & Brad N. Greenwood, *No News Is Bad News: Political Corruption, News Deserts, and the Decline of the Fourth Estate*, Acad. Mgmt. Proc. (Aug. 2021), https://www.semanticscholar.org/paper/No-News-is-Bad-News%3A-Political-Corruption%2C-News-and-Matherly-Greenwood/545f14dc04ef25e3927cc940f43208b43b3c43e1; Steven Waldman, *The Local-News Crisis Is Weirdly Easy to Solve*, Atl. (Aug. 8, 2023), https://www.theatlantic.com/ideas/archive/2023/08/local-news-investment-economic-value/674942/.

[29] *See* Sarah Fioroni, *Local News Most Trusted in Keeping Americans Informed About Their Communities*, Knight Found. (May 19, 2022), http://knightfoundation.org/articles/local-news-most-trusted-in-keeping-americans-informed-about-their-communities/; Sarah Fioroni & Knight Foundation, *The Roles of Local News, Personal Networks, and Social Media in Local Political Engagement*, Knight Found. (May 19, 2022), https://knightfoundation.org/articles/the-roles-of-local-news-personal-networks-and-social-media-in-local-political-engagement/; *American Views 2022: Part 2, Trust Media and Democracy*, Knight Found. (Feb. 15, 2023), https://knightfoundation.org/reports/american-views-2023-part-2/; Dean Ridings, *Trusted and Reliable, Local Newspapers Matter to Their Communities*, Summerville J. Scene (Nov. 7, 2023), https://postandcourier.com/journal-scene/opinion/trusted-and-reliable-local-newspapers-matter-to-their-communities/article_70dfb06c-7c9e-11ee-976b-f3c80b717bba.html.

partisan.[30] Perhaps the lower partisan divisions in local communities reflect how local politics and local issues tend to be less partisan and divisive than national politics.[31] News organizations not only reflect but also help to constitute a "public," a community of interest.[32] Journalists invite people to identify with a community and also stand in for the polity in holding those in power accountable.[33] When the press loses its viability, when it disappears, or when trust in it fades, then social trust and the sense of participation in a shared community also dissipate. Understanding why local news providers are disappearing thus matters for larger issues of social trust and democracy's future, and the following discussion explores contributing factors.

26.2.1 *Actions by Owners*

Some owners of media, such as the Koch brothers and the Murdoch family, have used their position to advance particular ideologies affecting the journalistic pursuits of facts and truth.[34] Consolidation of ownership in broadcasting – Sinclair, as of 2024, owns 185 stations – has produced reductions in local coverage and perhaps diminished diversity in viewpoints.[35] Private equity companies buy

[30] *Did You Know? Regions That Lose News Outlets Become More Partisan*, News Literacy Project, https://newslit.org/tips-tools/did-you-know-loss-of-local-news-outlets/ (last visited June 18, 2024); Matthew P. Hitt et al., *Why Losing Our Newspapers Is Breaking Our Politics*, Sci. Am. (Mar. 26, 2019), https://www.scientificamerican.com/article/why-losing-our-news papers-is-breaking-our-politics/.

[31] Richard Florida, *Are Local Politics as Polarized as National? Depends on the Issue*, Bloomberg (Apr. 24, 2019), https://www.bloomberg.com/news/articles/2019-04-24/local-politics-aren-t-as-polarized-as-national-politics; Michael Williams, *Keeping Political Partisanship Out of Local Government*, ICMA (Aug. 1, 2021), https://icma.org/articles/pm-magazine/keeping-political-par tisanship-out-local-government.

[32] Charles B. Forcey, *Review of Schudson, Michael, The Power of News*, H-Review (Sept. 1997), https://www.h-net.org/reviews/showrev.php?id=1270; Michael Schudson, *Why Conservation Is Not the Soul of Democracy*, 14 Critical Stud. in Mass Commc'n 297, 304–05 (1997).

[33] Forcey, *supra* note 32.

[34] Sasha Chavkin, *The Koch Brothers' Media Investment (Updated)*, Colum. Journalism Rev. (Apr. 22, 2023), https://www.cjr.org/united_states_project/the_koch_brothers_media_invest .php; David McKnight, *Rupert Murdoch's News Corporation: A Media Institution with a Mission*, 30 Hist. J. Film, Radio & Television 303 (2010), https://doi.org/10.1080/01439685 .2010.505021. *See* Matea Gold, *The Mercers and Stephen Bannon: How a Populist Power Base Was Funded and Built*, Wash. Post (Mar. 17, 2017), https://www.washingtonpost.com/ graphics/politics/mercer-bannon/. Peter Thiel used his resources to bring lawsuits against one outlet (Gawker) and thereby destroy it. Andrew Ross Sorkin, *Peter Thiel, Tech Billionaire, Reveals Secret War with Gawker*, N.Y. Times (May 25, 2016), https://www.nytimes.com/2016/ 05/26/business/dealbook/peter-thiel-tech-billionaire-reveals-secret-war-with-gawker.html.

[35] Sarah Ellison, *Sinclair's Recipe for TV News: Crime, Homelessness, Illegal Drugs*, Wash. Post (Feb. 16, 2024), https://www.washingtonpost.com/politics/2024/02/16/sinclair-broadcasting-con servative-media-trump/; Lisa Marshall, *Media Consolidation Takes Toll on Local News But Doesn't Necessarily Bias Coverage*, https://www.colorado.edu/today/2021/10/20/media-consolida tion-takes-toll-local-news-doesnt-necessarily-bias-coverage; Levy, *supra* note 4.

local news outlets and typically proceed to cut reporters, original stories, and local coverage.[36]

Often, the entities are actually in the black, but the new owners strip-mine them, squeezing profits from subscriptions and sales while destroying their ongoing viability.

A few notable news enterprises have found wealthy investors who treat the enterprises in part as philanthropies, with commitments to editorial independence, but still seek to make them financially going concerns even if that means layoffs.[37] The chief examples are Jeff Bezos and The Washington Post and Patrick Soon-Shiong and the L.A. Times, who both pursued a civic mission but, over time, appear to be losing the willingness to foot the bills.

26.2.2 *Migration of Advertising Dollars to Social Media*

The elephant in the room is the devastation to the business model of private news enterprises posed by social media platforms. It probably started with Craigslist: The reliable revenue source of local advertising shifted from local media to online networks.[38] Social media sites have, over time, drawn the lion's share of advertising revenues while taking advantage of the technology to collect detailed data about the consumers and to target ads based on that data. The platforms also offer unlimited space, permitting videos and copy, along with metrics available to the sponsoring companies at any time. The data platforms – including Amazon, Google, Netflix, YouTube, Facebook (Meta), and TikTok – assemble audiences far larger than any local news outlet ever could. Even local retailers send their advertising to the platforms to follow the attention of consumers.[39]

[36] Margot Susca, Hedged: How Private Investment Funds Helped Destroy American Newspapers and Undermine Democracy (2024); Brier Dudley, *Study: Private Equity Firms Buying Newspapers Cut Local News*, Seattle Times (Feb. 18, 2022), https://www.seattletimes.com/opinion/study-private-equity-firms-buying-newspapers-cut-local-news/.

[37] Lukas I. Alpert, *How Biotech Billionaire Patrick Soon-Shiong's Los Angeles Times Investment Went Wrong*, MarketWatch (Jan. 23, 2024, 3:52 PM), https://www.marketwatch.com/story/how-biotech-billionaire-patrick-soon-shiongs-los-angeles-times-investment-went-wrong-ec1d916d; Noah Kirsch, *Journalists Are Angry About Layoffs at The Atlantic, Owned by Billionaire Laurene Powell Jobs*, Forbes (May 21, 2020, 7:37 PM), https://www.forbes.com/sites/noahkirsch/2020/05/21/journalists-are-angry-about-layoffs-at-the-atlantic-owned-by-billionaire-laurene-powell-jobs/; Benjamin Mullin & Katie Robertson, *A Decade Ago, Jeff Bezos Bought a Newspaper. Now He's Paying Attention to It Again*, N.Y. Times (July 22, 2023), https://www.nytimes.com/2023/07/22/business/media/jeff-bezos-washington-post.html.

[38] *The Evolution of Classified Ads*, ADvendio (June 27, 2022), https://www.advendio.com/evolution-classified-ads ("In the early 2000's the internet became more readily available to households which posed a bigger opportunity for digital classifieds to reach a larger audience and thus, increase profitability. With this jump from print to digital, the figure of newspaper ad revenue reduced by over half to 18%.").

[39] Ephraim Schwartz, *Ad Dollars Drive Online Move*, InfoWorld (Apr. 2, 2007, 5:00 PM), https://www.infoworld.com/article/2662445/ad-dollars-drive-online-move.html.

Digital technologies accelerate trends pursued by broadcasting and cable businesses: "narrowcasting," which focuses only on specific segments of potential viewers and users. Following advice from Roger Ailes, Rupert Murdoch created Fox Media as an enterprise that unabashedly serves as the cheerleader and propaganda machine for one political party rather than seeking to serve diverse audiences.[40] Digital media has further refined narrowcasting and unbundled content.[41] Rather than combining political news with sports, recipes, weather, and crossword puzzles, digital media allows consumers to bypass human editors, which disintegrates traditional media enterprises. Legacy media companies were slow to adapt, and when they did, they too often gave their content away, which contributed to the expectation that content could be found online for free. Advertising dollars shifted from newspapers and magazines to social media and digital search platforms. These platforms target people based on the data about their prior uses, which reveals their interests. This shift has decimated cross-subsidies and serendipity as features of the information ecosystem.

26.2.3 *Legal Treatment and Practices of Digital Media*

Online interactive networks invite people to participate in peer-to-peer communications and to access businesses, entertainment, and news sources with no fee other than sharing their personal data. Through these platforms, users can connect with friends and family, build larger social and professional networks, and find information.[42] These platforms offer users the ability to post and exchange information, photographs, and videos, as well as to become active producers, not just consumers, in the sharing networks.[43]

Individuals regularly embed copyrighted materials (and, perhaps with more legal safety, post links to the digital materials they find online), including copyrighted

[40] David Plotz, *Fox News Channel: It's Not Fair, It's Not Balanced. So What?*, SLATE (Nov, 23, 2000), https://slate.com/news-and-politics/2000/11/fox-news-channel.html; Kelefa Sanneh, *What Roger Ailes Figured Out*, NEW YORKER (May 24, 2017), https://www.newyorker.com/news/news-desk/what-roger-ailes-figured-out. For a media review of a media retelling of this media story, *see* Daniel D'Addario, *TV Review: "The Loudest Voice,"* VARIETY (June 26, 2019), https://variety.com/2019/tv/reviews/the-loudest-voice-review-roger-ailes-showtime-1203243626/.

[41] Cary A. Bolles, *How the Internet Evaporates the Middle: Unbundling Media*, MEDIUM (Oct. 17, 2014), https://medium.com/@gbolles/unbundling-media-6c3e79bc2d95; *Unbundled Media Poses a Challenge*, FORBES (Apr. 3, 2006), https://www.forbes.com/2006/03/31/media-content-tech-cx_0403oxford.html?sh = b5122e9cf4bf.

[42] Dylan Selterman, *Why Do People Even Use Social Media?*, PSYCH. TODAY (July 18, 2023), https://www.psychologytoday.com/us/blog/the-e-resistance-hypothesis/202307/why-do-people-even-use-social-media; Simon Kemp, *Digital 2024: Global Overview Report*, DATAREPORTAL (Jan. 31, 2024), https://datareportal.com/reports/digital-2024-global-overview-report (majorities of users identify social connection, finding information, and entertainment as key reasons for social media use).

[43] Abhisa Pal, *Motivations of Individuals Participating in Social Media: A Cultural Perspective*, 14 J. MODERN ACCT. & AUDITING 315 (June 2018), https://doi.org/10.17265/1548-6583/2018,06.003.

journalism. In practice, the platform companies do little to enforce copyrights held by the original creators of the materials, and the burden falls on the creators who are not well situated to monitor global social media networks.[44] In addition, copyright laws have complex exceptions, and the rules vary across jurisdictions.[45] In the United States, a further complication is the shield from liability Congress created for social media companies through Section 230 of the Communications Decency Act.[46] That provision also protects social media companies from liability for falsehoods, defamation, and other legal vulnerabilities faced by conventional media companies.[47]

At the same time, social media platforms work with algorithms designed to maximize people's "engagement," which boosts material that elicits outrage and polarization, including misinformation and disinformation.[48] The algorithms select and amplify materials while seeking to optimize the time people spend online and, hence, the number of ads they see. And outrage fuels "virality," or massive spread, which in turn increases profits.[49] But the casualties are public trust in news, individual thought, the health of the polity, and even individuals' health (due to misinformation and distrust related to health news).[50]

[44] Abou Naja, *Copyright Infringement on Social Media: How to Prevent*, Abou Naja Intell. Prop. (Apr. 25, 2024), https://abounaja.com/blogs/copyright-infringement-on-social-media; Matt D'Angelo, *How to Avoid Copyright Infringement in the Age of Social Media*, Bus. News Daily (Oct. 23, 2023), https://www.businessnewsdaily.com/4693-legal-image-usage.html.

[45] *See* sources cited in *supra* note 44.

[46] *See* Minow, Saving the News, *supra* note 1, at 53, 107–13; *Section 230 Protections*, Elec. Freedom Forum, https://www.eff.org/issues/bloggers/legal/liability/230 (last visited June 18, 2024).

[47] Congressional Research Service, *Section 230: An Overview* (Jan. 4, 2024), https://crsreports.congress.gov/product/pdf/R/R46751.

[48] Gizem Ceylan, *How Social Media Rewards Misinformation*, Yale Sch. Management (Mar. 31, 2023), https://insights.som.yale.edu/insights/how-social-media-rewards-misinformation; Anastasia Micich & R. J. Cross, *How Misinformation on Social Media Has Changed News*, U.S. PIRG Educ. Fund (Nov. 22, 2023), https://pirg.org/edfund/articles/misinformation-on-social-media/.

[49] *See* Jon Evans, *Facebook Isn't Free Speech, It's Algorithmic Amplification Optimized for Outrage*, TechCrunch (Oct. 20, 2019), https://techcrunch.com/2019/10/20/facebook-isnt-free-speech-its-algorithmic-amplification-optimized-for-outrage/. For further details and proposal for reforms, *see* Sara Bundtzen, *"Suggested for You": Understanding How Algorithmic Ranking Practices Affect Online Discourses and Assessing Proposed Alternatives*, Inst. for Strategic Dialogue (2022), https://www.isdglobal.org/wp-content/uploads/2022/12/Understanding-How-Algorithmic-Ranking-Practices-Affect-Online-Discourses-and-Assessing-Proposed-Alternatives.pdf.

[50] Camila Mont'Alverne et al., *The Trust Gap: How and Why News on Digital Platforms Is Viewed More Skeptically Versus News in General*, Reuters Inst. (Sept. 22, 2022), https://reutersinstitute.politics.ox.ac.uk/trust-gap-how-and-why-news-digital-platforms-viewed-more-sceptically-versus-news-general; Yasmim Mendes Rocha et al., *The Impact of Fake News on Social Media and Its Influence on Health During the COVID-19 Pandemic: A Systematic Review*, Z Gesundh Wiss. 1 (2021), https://www.ncbi.nlm.nih.gov/pmc/articles/PMC8502082/. On the jeopardy to thought, *see* Robert Post, *The Internet, Democracy, and Misinformation*, *in*

26.3 POTENTIAL RESPONSES

Policymakers can pursue several kinds of responses. The first approach would tackle the forces undermining the viability of local news by holding social media platform companies to the standards applied to responsible actors and by protecting the companies' readers and users. The second would bolster existing local newsgatherers and providers, as well as nurture potential ones, while also cultivating the public's demands and taste for their efforts. The third approach would promote innovations in business models for local news, in newsgathering and dissemination, and in the institutional arrangements affecting the news ecosystem.

26.3.1 *Responsibilities of Social Media Companies*

Amazon, Alphabet, and Meta, which operate social media activities, are among the companies with the largest market valuations in history.[51] They can and should be held to the same duties that apply to other companies, including paying for the use of copyrighted materials and meeting consumer protection responsibilities, such as guarding against fraud and defamation.[52] Efforts to ensure such payments are already underway in other countries. For example, Canada's Online News Act, adopted in 2022, and Australia's News Media Bargaining Code, passed in 2021,[53] are policies keyed to the negotiations between journalism entities and tech platforms. These laws aim to establish a bargaining code that requires social media companies to compensate news organizations for the use of content that they produce.

Tech companies resist efforts to hold them accountable, and in the United States, they successfully lobbied for and retained legal insulation from liability on their side. That legal insulation – provided in Section 230 of the Communication Decency Act – once could be justified as protection for fledging enterprises in the early days of the internet. That justification no longer makes sense, given the enormous success of large platform companies. Hence, Congress should amend the statutory immunity of platforms from legal liability.[54] If individual litigation to enforce laws imposing

Disinformation, Misinformation and Democracy (Ronald J. Krotoszynski, Jr. et al. eds., forthcoming 2024).

[51] Amazon is not only an online retailer, host of other retailers, and provider of cloud services; it increasingly provides social media functions. Kiri Masters, *Amazon Is Looking More Like a Social Media Platform. Here's How Brands Can Benefit*, Forbes (Aug. 29, 2022, 1:31 PM), https://www.forbes.com/sites/kirimasters/2022/08/29/amazon-is-looking-more-like-a-social-media-platform-heres-how-brands-can-benefit/.

[52] *See* Minow, Saving the News, *supra* note 1, at 104–12, 129–38.

[53] Selen Ozturk, *How Can Local Media Face the News Crisis?*, Ethnic Media Servs. (Feb. 5, 2024), https://ethnicmediaservices.org/news-exchange/how-is-local-media-facing-the-news-crisis/.

[54] Mountains of scholarship and policy proposals on the subject include *Danielle Draper, Section 230: Are Online Platforms Publishers, Distributors, or Neither?*, Bipartisan Pol'y Org. (Mar. 13, 2023), https://bipartisanpolicy.org/blog/section-230-online-platforms/; Rosie Moss, *The Future of Section 230: What Does It Mean for Consumers?*, Nat'l Ass'n Atty's Gen.

liability are inadequate or inefficient, legislative reform should make such duties clear and enforceable or condition the immunity on their fulfillment.[55] Alternatively, Congress could tax digital ads to support local journalism, which would place responsibility on critical activities underlying the financial challenges faced by local news outlets.[56] Currently, tech companies externalize the effects of their activities, but the government could use taxation to place the responsibilities on the shoulders of the internet companies as opposed to the community at large.

26.3.2 *Protect Users and Consumers*

In addition to enforcing terms of service agreements and consumer protection laws, new laws could protect digital media users from some of the platform companies' detrimental effects on local news without jeopardizing free speech.[57] Other potential reforms could shift power to users of digital media by requiring transparency and explanations of the algorithms companies use to select content or by putting content curation in the hands of users.[58] A thoughtful proposal along these lines would demand that internet companies permit users to install "middleware," or software that gives users more control over content selection and moderation, thus unbundling editorial control and the other functions of the social media platforms.[59]

(July 21, 2023), https://www.naag.org/attorney-general-journal/the-future-of-section-230-what-does-it-mean-for-consumers/; Elliot Sher, *Amending Section 230 to Reform Social Media and Address Political Extremism*, The Gate (University of Chicago) (April 11, 2023), http://uchicagogate.com/articles/2023/4/11/amending-section-230-reform-social-media-and-address-political-extremism/; Michael D. Smith & Marshall Van Alstyne, *It's Time to Update* Section 230, Harv. Bus. Rev. (Aug. 12, 2021), https://hbr.org/2021/08/its-time-to-update-section-230.

55 *See* Jessica Gutierrez Alm, *"Sharing" Copyrights: The Copyright Implications of User Content in Social Media*, 35 Hamline J. Pub. L. & Pol'y 104 (2014), https://digitalcommons.hamline.edu/jplp/vol35/iss1/2/.

56 *See* Julia Angwin, *Can Taxing Big Tech Save Journalism?*, Markup (July 16, 2022), https://themarkup.org/newsletter/hello-world/can-taxing-big-tech-save-journalism; Paul Romer, *A Tax That Could Fix Big Tech*, N.Y. Times (May 6, 2019), https://www.nytimes.com/2019/05/06/opinion/tax-facebook-google.html; Lucia Walinchus, *Opinion: We Need a News Utility*, Poynter (June 16, 2022), https://www.poynter.org/commentary/2022/national-tax-support-journalism/.

57 Reforms should avoid empowering actions by repressive governments in the name of cracking down on misinformation and disinformation. *See* Gabrielle Lim & Samantha Bradshaw, *Chilling Legislation: Tracking the Impact of "Fake News" Laws on Press Freedoms Internationally*, Ctr. Int'l Media Assistance (July 19, 2023), https://www.cima.ned.org/publication/chilling-legislation/.

58 Bundtzen, *supra* note 49.

59 Francis Fukuyama et al., *Middleware for Dominant Digital Platforms: A Technological Solution to a Threat to Democracy*, Stan. Cyber Pol'y Ctr. (2021), https://fsi-live.s3.us-west-1.amazonaws.com/s3fs-public/cpc-middleware_ff_v2.pdf. For a litigation effort on a related theme, *see* Ethan Zuckerman, *I Love Facebook. That's Why I'm Suing Meta*, N.Y. Times (May 5, 2024), https://www.nytimes.com/2024/05/05/opinion/facebook-court-internet-meta.html.

Congress has required broadcast and cable companies to carry local news, so might social media companies have similar duties? The immediate objection to this proposal is that the scarcity of the airwaves justified such regulations of broadcasting.[60] Yet the Supreme Court also upheld "must-carry" requirements on cable companies, despite the lack of scarcity, because it recognized the government's compelling interest in ensuring state and local content and public media options.[61] If governments lack the ability to impose similar duties on social media companies, perhaps some inducements – such as conditioning Section 230 immunity on such duties – could be enacted.

26.3.3 *Increasing Support for Local News by Amplifying Both Supply and Demand*

Financial support for local news can be increased through philanthropy. This is the strategy adopted by a coalition of foundations forming the "Press Forward" initiative.[62] Committing $500 million nationwide with a plan to raise another $500 million for local and regional efforts, Press Forward is devoted to strengthening trusted local newsrooms, improving the infrastructure for producing and disseminating local news, redressing inequities in coverage and practices, and developing policies to expand access to local news and information.[63] Converting for-profit news organizations to nonprofit status can open avenues for support by encouraging donations by individuals in addition to large-scale support from philanthropies.[64] In addition, for-profit news organizations can establish affiliated foundations for support.[65]

60 *See* Red Lion v. FCC, 395 U.S. 367 (1969).

61 *See* Turner Broad. Co. v. FCC, 520 U.S. 180 (1997); *Cable Television*, FEDERAL COMMC'NS COMM'N (Mar. 19, 2024), https://www.fcc.gov/media/engineering/cable-television.

62 *Democracy Flourishes When People Have Access to Reliable Information*, PRESS FORWARD, https://www.pressforward.news/; Alex Daniels, *After Shaky Start, Philanthropy Coalition's $500 Million Local News Effort Takes Shape*, CHRON. PHILANTHROPY (Apr. 25, 2024), https://www.philanthropy.com/article/after-shaky-start-philanthropy-coalitions-500-million-local-news-effort-takes-shape.

63 Press Release, MacArthur Foundation, $48 Million in Support of Local News, Initial Seeding of Press Forward Collaborative (Dec. 18, 2023), https://www.macfound.org/press/press-releases/macarthur-announces-$48-million-in-support-of-local-news-initial-seeding-of-press-forward-collaborative.

64 Kathleen McElroy et al., *Considerations for Community Newspaper Conversion to Nonprofit*, U. TEX. SCH. JOURNALISM (2024), https://journalism.utexas.edu/innovation/considerations-community-newspaper-conversion-nonprofit; Institute for Nonprofit News, *Quick Guide to Converting a For-profit to a Nonprofit News Outlet*, https://inn.org/research/guides/conversion-guide/ (last visited June 18, 2024); Margaret Renkl, *Can Nonprofit News Save the South from Itself?*, N.Y. TIMES (Apr. 29, 2024), https://www.nytimes.com/2024/04/29/opinion/nonprofit-media-journalism.html.

65 *See, e.g.*, Teresa Parker & Ed Miller, *About Us*, PROVINCETOWN INDEPENDENThttps://provincetownindependent.org/about-provincetown-independent/ (a beneficial corporation,

The government can also support the news ecosystem through tax exemptions for nonprofit organizations and favorable tax treatment for donations. Tax exemptions for philanthropic aid already support nonprofit news operations, including ProPublica and other media watchdogs that often engage in reporting that involves expensive big-data analyses. The government should preserve and expand tax deductions for such contributions.[66] The Local News Sustainability Act, which is currently pending in Congress, would go further and allow tax deductions for individuals who take out subscriptions to local media outlets and for businesses that take out ads in local media outlets. It would also exempt local media hires of journalists from payroll taxes.[67] In these ways, government support works through intermediary organizations and individuals, which helps to insulate the editorial judgments from government influence. Similarly, the government can impose requirements on the delivery systems, remote from decisions about what to cover and how. The United States government, for example, has required telecommunications companies to provide universal service, and the government itself has subsidized broadband where individuals and communities cannot afford it.[68]

Strengthening local news through direct government support provides a parallel avenue, although this raises risks of government control and influence. For example, Native Nations have long provided direct aid to their local news outlets.[69] Government licenses for broadcasting are also a form of subsidy, given that the government only charges nominal fees for the rights to use the scarce good of public

committed to a public service as well as profits) and local journalism project, receiving donations, https://www.localjournalismproject.org/give (last visited June 18, 2024).

66 Collaborations through which some news organizations support data analyses through cooperative agreements are the kind of effort that can help and should not be impaired by antitrust or other legal concerns. *See* Ken Doctor, *Newsonomics: The New Knight-Lenfest Initiative Gives a Kick in the Pants to America's Metro Newspapers*, NiemanLab (Feb. 13, 2017), http://www.niemanlab.org/2017/02/newsonomics-the-new-knight-lenfest-initiative-gives-a-kick-in-the-pants-to-americas-metro-newspapers/. Slanted imitators are bound to arise, requiring further watchdogs.

67 Sarah Scire, *Some Questions (and Answers) About the Local News Sustainability Act*, NiemanLab (Sept. 14, 2021), https://www.niemanlab.org/2021/09/some-questions-and-answers-about-the-local-journalism-sustainability-act/.

68 *Universal Service*, FCC, https://www.fcc.gov/general/universal-service (last updated June 13, 2024); *Affordable Connectivity Program*, Internet for All, https://www.internetforall.gov/program/affordable-connectivity-program (last visited June 19, 2024).

69 *See* Sally Smith, *Native Americans in Contemporary News Media*, Am. Archive Pub. Broad, https://americanarchive.org/exhibits/native-narratives/contemporary-news (last visited June 19, 2024) (tracing support back to the Cherokee Nation's support for the Cherokee Phoenix in 1828). For riveting accounts of the ultimately successful effort by journalists in one tribe to secure press independence alongside financial support for news media, *see* Rebecca Landsberry-Baker & Joe Peeler, *Bad Press* (2023), https://badpress.film/ (award-winning documentary film); and Nancy Wetzman, *Documentary Tells Tale of Muskogee Free Press Constitutional Amendment*, State Ct. Report (Nov. 29, 2023), https://statecourtreport.org/our-work/analysis-opinion/documentary-tells-tale-muskogee-nation-free-press-constitutional (reviewing documentary *Bad Press*).

airway frequencies. To strengthen local news coverage, the Federal Communications Commission has proposed a rule that would give priority and expedited license renewals to local stations that provide at a minimum three hours of local programming.[70] (One advocacy organization endorses the proposal but wants the minimum raised to 10 hours.) In the past, licenses predicated on the scarcity of airwaves included conditions that the broadcasters had a duty of public interest coverage. Yet, with the advent of digital delivery systems, that predicate is gone.[71] Instead, the scarcity to justify government regulation today may be the limitations of human attention.

Although it should never entirely crowd out privately funded media, public media created for public purposes helps meet crucial needs for an "information commons" and for competition with private companies, which are incentivized by profit maximization. Surveys have rated public media as the most or among the most trustworthy news organizations for many years.[72] Public media – including websites, podcasts, documentaries, and daily news reports – can make particular differences in addressing holes created by private actors, such as local news deserts.[73] Further bolstering of public media would involve adjustment of rules regarding underwriting by private sources and revision of the Copyright Act's treatment of public media to reflect new distribution platforms.[74]

Growing the public demand for reliable news is also important. Media education can equip people to become informed and aware consumers of media of all sorts, including the risks and practices of digital media.[75] Digital media literacy is associated with greater political engagement and with exposure to diverse viewpoints.[76]

70 Steven Waldman, *How the FCC Could Help Save Local News*, Rebuild Local News (Mar. 15, 2024), https://www.rebuildlocalnews.org/how-the-fcc-could-help-save-local-news/.

71 *See* Josephine Soriano, *The Digital Transition and the First Amendment: Is It Time to Reevaluate Red Lion's Scarcity Rationale?*, 15 B.U. Pub. Int'l L.J. 341 (2006), https://www.bu.edu/pilj/files/2024/04/Soriano.pdf.

72 Linley Sanders, *Trust in Media 2022: Where Americans Get News and Who They Trust for Information*, YouGov (Apr. 5, 2022), https://today.yougov.com/politics/articles/41957-trust-media-2022-where-americans-get-news-poll.

73 Adam Ragusea, *Topple the Towers: Why Public Radio and Television Stations Should Radically Reorient toward Digital-First Local News, and How They Could Do It*, Knight Found. (2017), https://www.knightfoundation.org/public-media-white-paper-2017-ragusea.

74 Blair Levin, *Public Media at 50: What's Next for the Information Commons?*, Knight Found. (2017), https://knightfoundation.org/public-media-white-paper-2017-levin/.

75 *See* Emily Bonilla, *Why Media Literacy Education Matters in the Era of Fake News*, TNTP (Dec. 13, 2016), https://tntp.org/blog/post/why-media-literacy-education-matters-in-the-era-of-fake-news; *What Is Digital Literacy?*, Common Sense Media (June 4, 2020), https://www.commonsensemedia.org/articles/what-is-digital-literacy. A recent study shows that children often feel neglected, misrepresented, or depressed by news they encounter in varied media and also have trouble distinguishing fake news stories from real ones. *News and America's Kids: How Young People Perceive and Are Impacted by the News*, Common Sense Media (Mar. 2017), https://www.commonsensemedia.org/research/news-and-americas-kids.

76 Joseph Kahne et al., *Digital Media Literacy Education and Online Civic and Political Participation*, 6 Int'l J. of Commc'n 1 (2012), http://ijoc.org/index.php/ijoc/article/view/999.

Teaching members of the public how to distinguish user-generated content or stories exchanged by friends from professionally created or vetted material would help users identify and assess the source and reliability of the information they encounter online.[77]

26.3.4 *Problems with Subsidies by the Government and by Philanthropy*

Some federal and state initiatives propose incentivizing financial support for local outlets that hire new journalists, as well as incentives for individuals to subscribe to, and businesses to advertise with, local news entities. For instance, New York State has committed $90 million to support local news.[78] Yet both private philanthropies and governments seeking to boost local news through financial support face two immediate challenges. First, they must determine who or what should be eligible. For example, should a solo blogger qualify? And how can they exclude fake or entirely partisan entities?[79] Second, they must ensure that the news enterprise can maintain its editorial independence and avoid the risks of "capture" or of editorial bias in favor of the funding sources.[80]

These questions expose serious problems with giving the government the power to identify who is and who is not a journalist for purposes of funding; in fact, giving this task to philanthropy is also a problematic grant of power and potential curtailment of free speech.[81] Indeed, the very fact of governmental subsidies can

[77] *See* Katie Benner, *Snapchat Remakes Itself, Splitting the Social from the Media*, N.Y. Times (Nov. 29, 2017), https://www.nytimes.com/2017/11/29/technology/snapchat-redesign-social-media.html.

[78] Cameron Joseph, *New York Just Committed $90 Million to Help Save Local Journalism. Will It Work?*, Colum. Journalism Rev. (May 6, 2024), https://www.cjr.org/the_media_today/new_york_local_journalism_funding.php (noting that "eligible outlets can apply to receive a refundable tax credit of up to $25,000 for the first $50,000 worth of employees' salaries, with a per-company cap of $300,000."). *See* Mike Blinder, *New York State Implements Historic Tax Credits to Support Local Newspaper and Broadcast News Media*, Editor & Publisher (Oct. 20, 2024), https://www.editorandpublisher.com/stories/new-york-state-implements-historic-tax-credits-to-support-local-journalism,249316.

[79] David Martin Davies, *Pink Slime News Is Spreading in News Deserts*, Tex. Pub. Radio (Apr. 13, 2023, 10:06 AM), https://www.tpr.org/podcast/the-source/2023-04-13/pink-slime-news-is-spreading-in-news-deserts; Priyanjana Bengani, *Hundreds of "Pink Slime" Local News Outlets Are Distributing Algorithmic Stories and Conservative Talking Points*, Colum. Journalism Rev. (Dec. 18, 2019), https://www.cjr.org/tow_center_reports/hundreds-of-pink-slime-local-news-outlets-are-distributing-algorithmic-stories-conservative-talking-points.php.

[80] On capture risks, *compare* Kate Wright et al. Capturing News, Capturing Democracy: Trump and the Voice of America (2024) *with* Legal Services Corp. v. Velazquez, 531 U.S. 533 2001) (government cannot deny funding to publicly supported lawyers seeking to sue the government).

[81] *See* George Will, *Local Media Is Struggling. Government Support Would Make It Worse*, Wash. Post (Feb. 21, 2024), https://www.washingtonpost.com/opinions/2024/02/21/government-subsidies-newspapers/.

undermine the perception and reality of press independence and presents a frustrating paradox: With public funding, the perception of independence, and thus the public's trust, in the news would be further ruptured; yet without public funding, the crucial function of the press holding the government accountable is vitiated.

Potentially promising solutions to identifying who should count as a journalist for purposes of eligibility for funding could come from shifting the selection process to peers or independent private entities. Peer-operated accreditation processes already operate in the academic sphere; the European Union hosts a press council to strengthen self-regulation and journalistic ethics; and guidelines can commit to plural and diverse ownership, management, and editorial judgments.[82] These examples suggest that the methods for identifying who should be eligible for public or private support can be separated from the funder while simultaneously strengthening journalistic norms.

To guard against the danger of the government controlling the media it funds, the United States, Great Britain, and other nations have established mechanisms to minimize government influence on public media outlets.[83] A royal charter in Britain established the BBC as an independent entity, making it a quasi-autonomous nongovernmental entity.[84] Criticisms of bias in the BBC's coverage arise but interestingly, the critiques themselves reflect contrasting and conflicting viewpoints. Because its level of financial support was fixed from the start and tied to license fees attached to television and radio sets, the BBC has been spared the difficulties of needing to seek renewed government support through the politicized legislative process. Yet, as new generations rely on digital devices, this insulation is under pressure, and new funding models are under review.[85]

[82] *See Accreditation & Recognition: About Accreditation*, COUNCIL FOR HIGHER EDUC. ACCREDITATION, https://www.chea.org/about-accreditation (last visited June 19, 2024); *Strengthening Journalistic Ethics and Self-Regulation in Europe*, PRESS COUNCILS.EU, https://www.presscouncils.eu/ (last visited June 19, 2024). Commitments to pluralism can be embedded in institutional designs, such as the multiperson selection teams allocating federal arts and humanities funds, or in the parallel work of diverse funders. *See* Heather Templeton Dill et al., *We Disagree on Many Things, but We Speak with One Voice in Support of Philanthropic Pluralism*, CHRON. PHILANTHROPY (Apr. 13, 2023), https://www.philanthropy.com/article/we-disagree-on-many-things-but-we-speak-with-one-voice-in-support-of-philanthropic-pluralism. *See also Merit Review*, U.S. NAT'L SCI. FOUND., https://www.nsf.gov/bfa/dias/policy/merit_review/ (last visited June 19, 2024).

[83] MINOW, SAVING THE NEWS, *supra* note 1, at 138–42 (steady funding in Britain based on tax on hardware insulated revenues for the BBC to some degree from immediate politics). On recent challenges to the historic funding model posed by migration to internet distribution and calls for new forms, *see* HEATHER EVENNETT, FUTURE FUNDING OF THE BBC: LORDS COMMITTEE REPORT (2022), https://lordslibrary.parliament.uk/future-funding-of-the-bbc-lords-committee-report/.

[84] *See* Alan Pifer, *The Quasi-Non-Governmental Organisation*, in PUBLIC POLICY AND PRIVATE INTERESTS: THE INSTITUTIONS OF COMPROMISE 380–90 (D.C. Hague et al. eds., 1975).

[85] HOUSE OF LORDS, FUTURE FUNDING OF THE BBC: LORDS COMMITTEE REPORT (Dec. 7, 2022), https://lordslibrary.parliament.uk/future-funding-of-the-bbc-lords-committee-report/.

To support its public media, the United States created an intermediary entity, the Corporation for Public Broadcasting, which distributes federal dollars to local public media, including more than 1,000 locally managed radio stations and 360 locally managed television broadcasters.[86] Those entities, in turn, seek and receive funding from varied sources, including local donors and philanthropies, state and local governments, and business sponsorships. But technological and economic changes are also threatening this funding model.[87] If this chapter's analysis of the risks from losing journalism is correct, the nation must pursue new funding approaches and creative ways to guard against distortion.[88]

These funding issues affect the supply of public media, but efforts to boost the demand for quality local news are no less important.

26.3.5 *Further Innovations to Address the Local News Crisis*

By definition, local news does not scale large enough to generate national advertising support, so further innovations are needed.[89] Students in colleges and even high schools already provide valuable coverage of local issues and events. Schools could support these efforts through their own resources, philanthropy, and government subsidies to their institutions. For example, Miami University decided to dedicate part of its student newspaper to local news after a local outlet went out of business.[90] Another potential solution is to deploy artificial intelligence tools to issue reports of local government meetings, which would leave more time for the remaining journalists to do investigative work.[91] Such efforts, however, are controversial due to questions about the reliability of the tools and concerns about threatening the employment of human journalists.[92]

86 *About Public Media*, CORP. FOR PUB. BROAD., https://www.cpb.org/aboutpb (last visited June 19, 2024).

87 *Id.*; *see* Howard Husock, *The Truth About NPR Funding and Its Possible Future*, THE HILL (Apr. 17, 2023), https://thehill.com/opinion/campaign/3950550-the-truth-about-nprs-funding-and-its-possible-future/.

88 *See* Heidi Kitrosser, *Distorting the Press*, *in* THE FUTURE OF PRESS FREEDOM, *supra* note 10, at 391.

89 *See* Christina Koningisor & Jacob Noti-Victor, *Innovation Policy and the Press*, *in* THE FUTURE OF PRESS FREEDOM *supra* note 10, at 437.

90 David Brancaccio & Alex Schroeder, *Solutions for Local News Deserts*, MARKETPLACE MORNING REPORT (Apr. 9, 2024), https://www.marketplace.org/2024/04/09/local-news-outlets-business-model-solutions/.

91 Mark Caro, *AI Is Disrupting the Local News Industry. Will It Unlock Growth or Be an Existential Threat?*, POYNTER (May 8, 2024), https://www.poynter.org/business-work/2024/medill-report-impact-ai-local-news-business-models/; Vikram Oberoi, *How Citymeetings.nyc Uses AI to Make It Easy to Navigate City Council Meetings* (Mar. 29, 2024), https://vikramoberoi.com/posts/how-citymeetings-nyc-uses-ai-to-make-it-easy-to-navigate-city-council-meetings/.

92 *Id.*; Will Henshall, *Experts Warn Congress of Dangers AI Poses to Journalism*, TIME (Jan. 10, 2024), https://time.com/6554118/congress-ai-journalism-hearing/.

Some press advocates propose constructing shared infrastructures for civic news functions and shared "back office" operations for diverse local enterprises.[93] Experiments using short message services (SMS) can supply local information based on people's indicated interests.[94] However, several questions remain: What durable sources of funding can we secure, and how can we ensure diverse sources of news? What measures can we implement to guard against floods of disinformation and misinformation or the increasing proliferation of different information worlds? Focusing on the local news problem may offer a more tractable approach and allow us to build on the sources of trust that remain in this era of distrust.

26.4 REFLECTIONS

Alarm about diminishing local news operations has become to stimulate responses. Philanthropies, governments, and innovators in business and technology are taking action, but it is too soon to tell whether the results will sustainably strengthen reliable and abundant sources of local news in the United States. Failure, however, risks democratic governance and trust, increased public and private corruption, and jeopardy to the health of individuals and communities.

Long-standing traditions of governmental and private investments in newsgathering and reporting offer legal and practical foundations for new reforms, but the challenges to local news in an age of large-scale digital communications require innovation, persistence, and care.

[93] Ken Doctor, *Hard Truths About Reviving Local News*, Nieman Reports (Sept. 14, 2023), https://niemanreports.org/articles/9-hard-truths-about-reviving-local-news/; Ethan Zuckerman, *The Case for Digital Public Infrastructure*, Knight First Amendment Institute at Columbia University (Jan. 17, 2020), https://knightcolumbia.org/content/the-case-for-digital-public-infrastructure.

[94] Katie Hawkins-Gaar, *"It Doesn't Look Like Conventional Journalism": Local Newsrooms Using SMS and Messaging to Reach Audiences*, Press Forward (Mar. 14, 2024), https://www.pressforward.news/it-doesnt-look-like-conventional-journalism-press-forward-funders-support-newsrooms-using-sms-and-messaging-to-reach-audiences/.

For EU product safety concerns, contact us at Calle de José Abascal, 56–1°, 28003 Madrid, Spain or eugpsr@cambridge.org.

www.ingramcontent.com/pod-product-compliance
Ingram Content Group UK Ltd.
Pitfield, Milton Keynes, MK11 3LW, UK
UKHW020746160725
460850UK00017B/257
* 9 7 8 1 0 0 9 5 1 5 5 0 4 *